BATMAN
CHRONICLES

VOLUME SEVEN

BATMAN CREATED BY BOB KANE

*ALL STORIES WRITTEN BY BILL FINGER, ALL COVERS BY JERRY ROBINSON AND
ALL STORIES PENCILLED BY BOB KANE AND INKED BY JERRY ROBINSON — UNLESS OTHERWISE NOTED.*

Dan DiDio SENIOR VP-EXECUTIVE EDITOR ☆ Whitney Ellsworth EDITOR-ORIGINAL SERIES ☆ Bob Joy EDITOR-COLLECTED EDITION
Robbin Brosterman SENIOR ART DIRECTOR ☆ Paul Levitz PRESIDENT & PUBLISHER ☆ Georg Brewer VP-DESIGN & DC DIRECT CREATIVE
Richard Bruning SENIOR VP-CREATIVE DIRECTOR ☆ Patrick Caldon EXECUTIVE VP-FINANCE & OPERATIONS ☆ Chris Caramalis VP-FINANCE
John Cunningham VP-MARKETING ☆ Terri Cunningham VP-MANAGING EDITOR ☆ Amy Genkins SENIOR VP-BUSINESS & LEGAL AFFAIRS
Alison Gill VP-MANUFACTURING ☆ David Hyde VP-PUBLICITY ☆ Hank Kanalz VP-GENERAL MANAGER, WILDSTORM ☆
Jim Lee EDITORIAL DIRECTOR-WILDSTORM ☆ Gregory Novak SENIOR VP-CREATIVE AFFAIRS
Sue Pohja VP-BOOK TRADE SALES ☆ Steve Rotterdam SENIOR VP-SALES & MARKETING ☆ Cheryl Rubin SENIOR VP-BRAND MANAGEMENT
Alysse Soll VP-ADVERTISING & CUSTOM PUBLISHING ☆ Jeff Trojan VP-BUSINESS DEVELOPMENT, DC DIRECT ☆ Bob Wayne VP-SALES

DC Comics, 1700 Broadway, New York, NY 10019
A Warner Bros. Entertainment Company
Printed in Canada. First Printing.
ISBN: 978-1-4012-2134-8

Cover art by Jerry Robinson

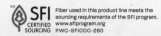

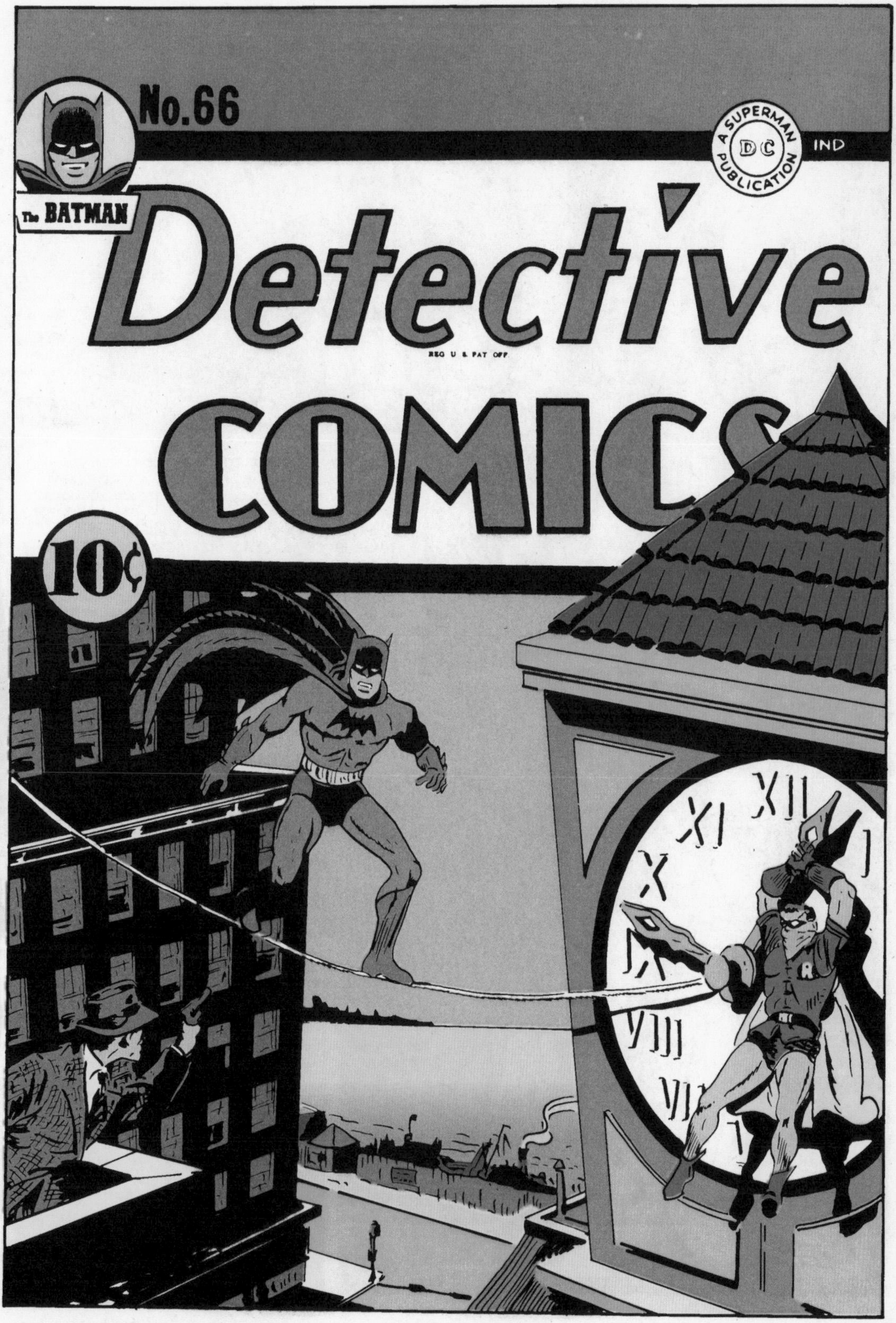
No.66
The BATMAN
A SUPERMAN DC PUBLICATION
IND
Detective
REG U.S. PAT OFF
COMICS
10¢

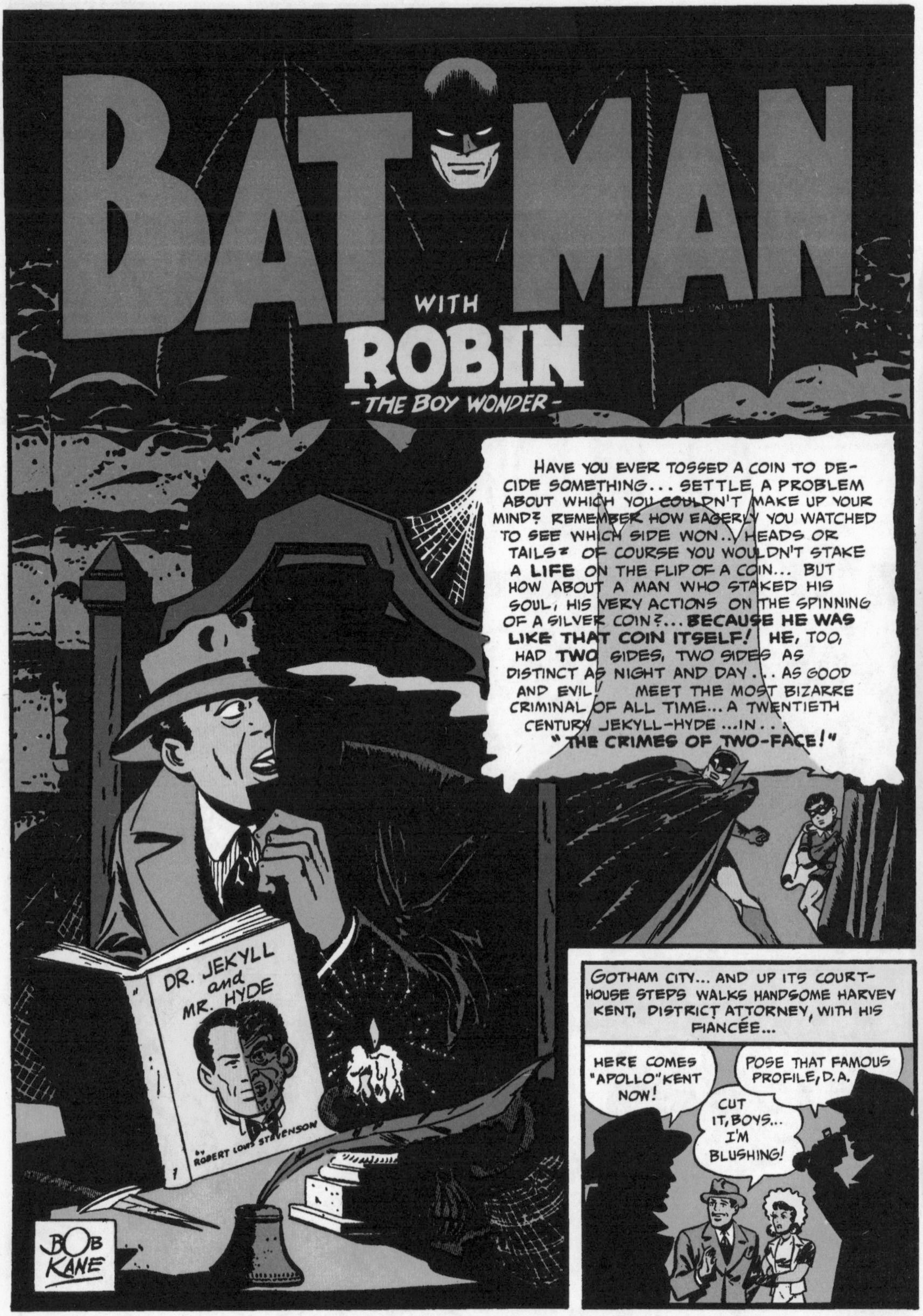
BATMAN
WITH
ROBIN
-THE BOY WONDER-
HAVE YOU EVER TOSSED A COIN TO DECIDE SOMETHING... SETTLE A PROBLEM ABOUT WHICH YOU COULDN'T MAKE UP YOUR MIND? REMEMBER HOW EAGERLY YOU WATCHED TO SEE WHICH SIDE WON... HEADS OR TAILS? OF COURSE YOU WOULDN'T STAKE A LIFE ON THE FLIP OF A COIN... BUT HOW ABOUT A MAN WHO STAKED HIS SOUL, HIS VERY ACTIONS ON THE SPINNING OF A SILVER COIN?... BECAUSE HE WAS LIKE THAT COIN ITSELF! HE, TOO, HAD TWO SIDES, TWO SIDES AS DISTINCT AS NIGHT AND DAY... AS GOOD AND EVIL! MEET THE MOST BIZARRE CRIMINAL OF ALL TIME... A TWENTIETH CENTURY JEKYLL-HYDE ...IN...
"THE CRIMES OF TWO-FACE!"
DR. JEKYLL and MR. HYDE
by ROBERT LOUIS STEVENSON
BOB KANE
GOTHAM CITY... AND UP ITS COURT-HOUSE STEPS WALKS HANDSOME HARVEY KENT, DISTRICT ATTORNEY, WITH HIS FIANCÉE...
HERE COMES "APOLLO" KENT NOW!
POSE THAT FAMOUS PROFILE, D.A.
CUT IT, BOYS... I'M BLUSHING!

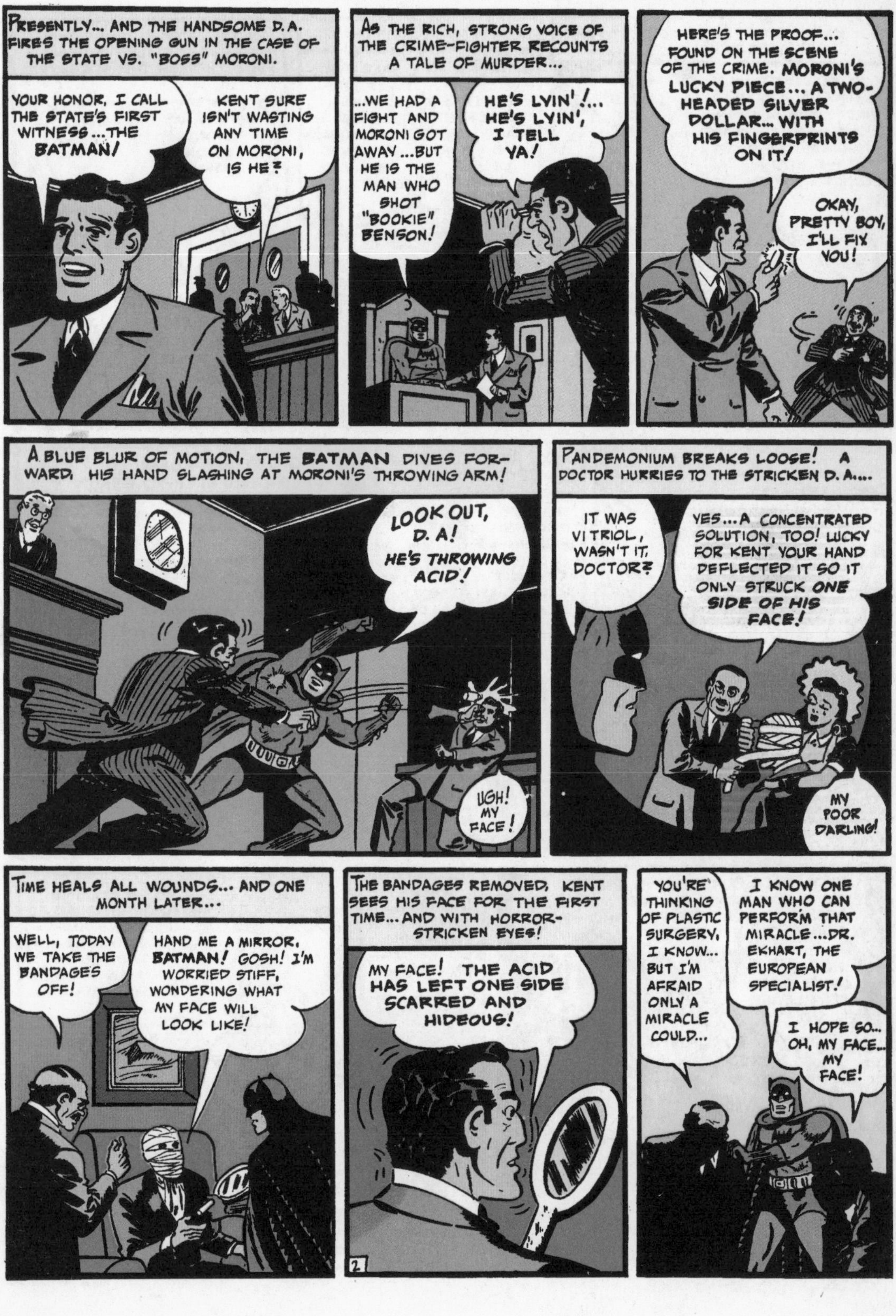
PRESENTLY... AND THE HANDSOME D.A. FIRES THE OPENING GUN IN THE CASE OF THE STATE VS. "BOSS" MORONI.
YOUR HONOR, I CALL THE STATE'S FIRST WITNESS ...THE BATMAN!
KENT SURE ISN'T WASTING ANY TIME ON MORONI, IS HE?
AS THE RICH, STRONG VOICE OF THE CRIME-FIGHTER RECOUNTS A TALE OF MURDER...
...WE HAD A FIGHT AND MORONI GOT AWAY ...BUT HE IS THE MAN WHO SHOT "BOOKIE" BENSON!
HE'S LYIN'!... HE'S LYIN', I TELL YA!
HERE'S THE PROOF... FOUND ON THE SCENE OF THE CRIME. MORONI'S LUCKY PIECE... A TWO-HEADED SILVER DOLLAR... WITH HIS FINGERPRINTS ON IT!
OKAY, PRETTY BOY, I'LL FIX YOU!
A BLUE BLUR OF MOTION, THE BATMAN DIVES FORWARD, HIS HAND SLASHING AT MORONI'S THROWING ARM!
LOOK OUT, D. A! HE'S THROWING ACID!
UGH! MY FACE!
PANDEMONIUM BREAKS LOOSE! A DOCTOR HURRIES TO THE STRICKEN D. A....
IT WAS VITRIOL, WASN'T IT, DOCTOR?
YES...A CONCENTRATED SOLUTION, TOO! LUCKY FOR KENT YOUR HAND DEFLECTED IT SO IT ONLY STRUCK ONE SIDE OF HIS FACE!
MY POOR DARLING!
TIME HEALS ALL WOUNDS... AND ONE MONTH LATER...
WELL, TODAY WE TAKE THE BANDAGES OFF!
HAND ME A MIRROR, BATMAN! GOSH! I'M WORRIED STIFF, WONDERING WHAT MY FACE WILL LOOK LIKE!
THE BANDAGES REMOVED, KENT SEES HIS FACE FOR THE FIRST TIME... AND WITH HORROR-STRICKEN EYES!
MY FACE! THE ACID HAS LEFT ONE SIDE SCARRED AND HIDEOUS!
2
YOU'RE THINKING OF PLASTIC SURGERY, I KNOW... BUT I'M AFRAID ONLY A MIRACLE COULD...
I KNOW ONE MAN WHO CAN PERFORM THAT MIRACLE...DR. EKHART, THE EUROPEAN SPECIALIST!
I HOPE SO... OH, MY FACE... MY FACE!

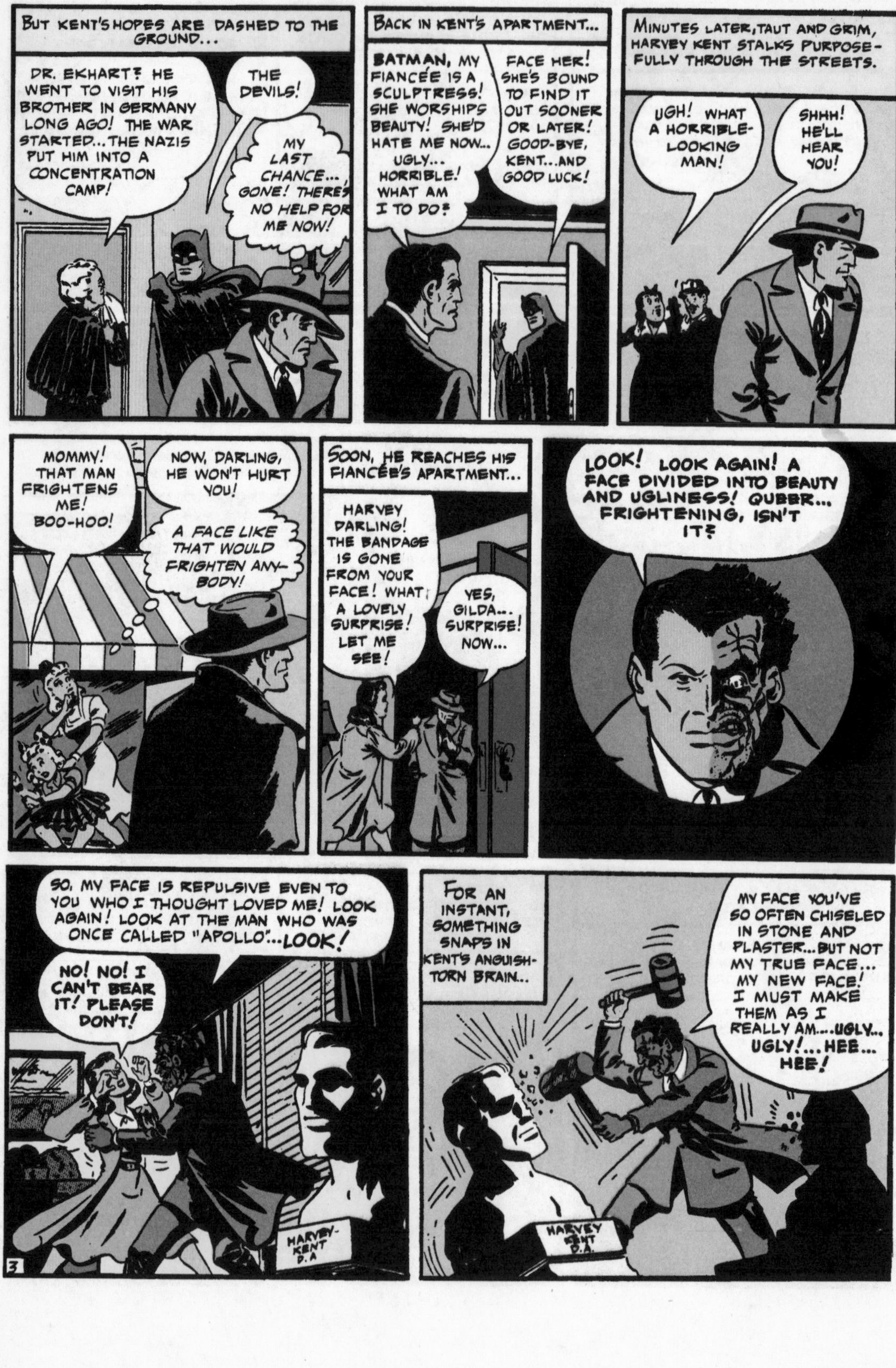

BUT KENT'S HOPES ARE DASHED TO THE GROUND...
DR. EKHART? HE WENT TO VISIT HIS BROTHER IN GERMANY LONG AGO! THE WAR STARTED... THE NAZIS PUT HIM INTO A CONCENTRATION CAMP!
THE DEVILS!
MY LAST CHANCE... GONE! THERE'S NO HELP FOR ME NOW!
BACK IN KENT'S APARTMENT...
BATMAN, MY FIANCÉE IS A SCULPTRESS! SHE WORSHIPS BEAUTY! SHE'D HATE ME NOW... UGLY... HORRIBLE! WHAT AM I TO DO?
FACE HER! SHE'S BOUND TO FIND IT OUT SOONER OR LATER! GOOD-BYE, KENT... AND GOOD LUCK!
MINUTES LATER, TAUT AND GRIM, HARVEY KENT STALKS PURPOSE-FULLY THROUGH THE STREETS.
UGH! WHAT A HORRIBLE-LOOKING MAN!
SHHH! HE'LL HEAR YOU!
MOMMY! THAT MAN FRIGHTENS ME! BOO-HOO!
NOW, DARLING, HE WON'T HURT YOU!
A FACE LIKE THAT WOULD FRIGHTEN ANY-BODY!
SOON, HE REACHES HIS FIANCÉE'S APARTMENT...
HARVEY DARLING! THE BANDAGE IS GONE FROM YOUR FACE! WHAT A LOVELY SURPRISE! LET ME SEE!
YES, GILDA... SURPRISE! NOW...
LOOK! LOOK AGAIN! A FACE DIVIDED INTO BEAUTY AND UGLINESS! QUBBR... FRIGHTENING, ISN'T IT?
SO, MY FACE IS REPULSIVE EVEN TO YOU WHO I THOUGHT LOVED ME! LOOK AGAIN! LOOK AT THE MAN WHO WAS ONCE CALLED "APOLLO"... LOOK!
NO! NO! I CAN'T BEAR IT! PLEASE DON'T!
HARVEY KENT D.A
3
FOR AN INSTANT, SOMETHING SNAPS IN KENT'S ANGUISH-TORN BRAIN...
MY FACE YOU'VE SO OFTEN CHISELED IN STONE AND PLASTER... BUT NOT MY TRUE FACE... MY NEW FACE! I MUST MAKE THEM AS I REALLY AM.... UGLY... UGLY!... HEE... HEE!
HARVEY KENT D.A.

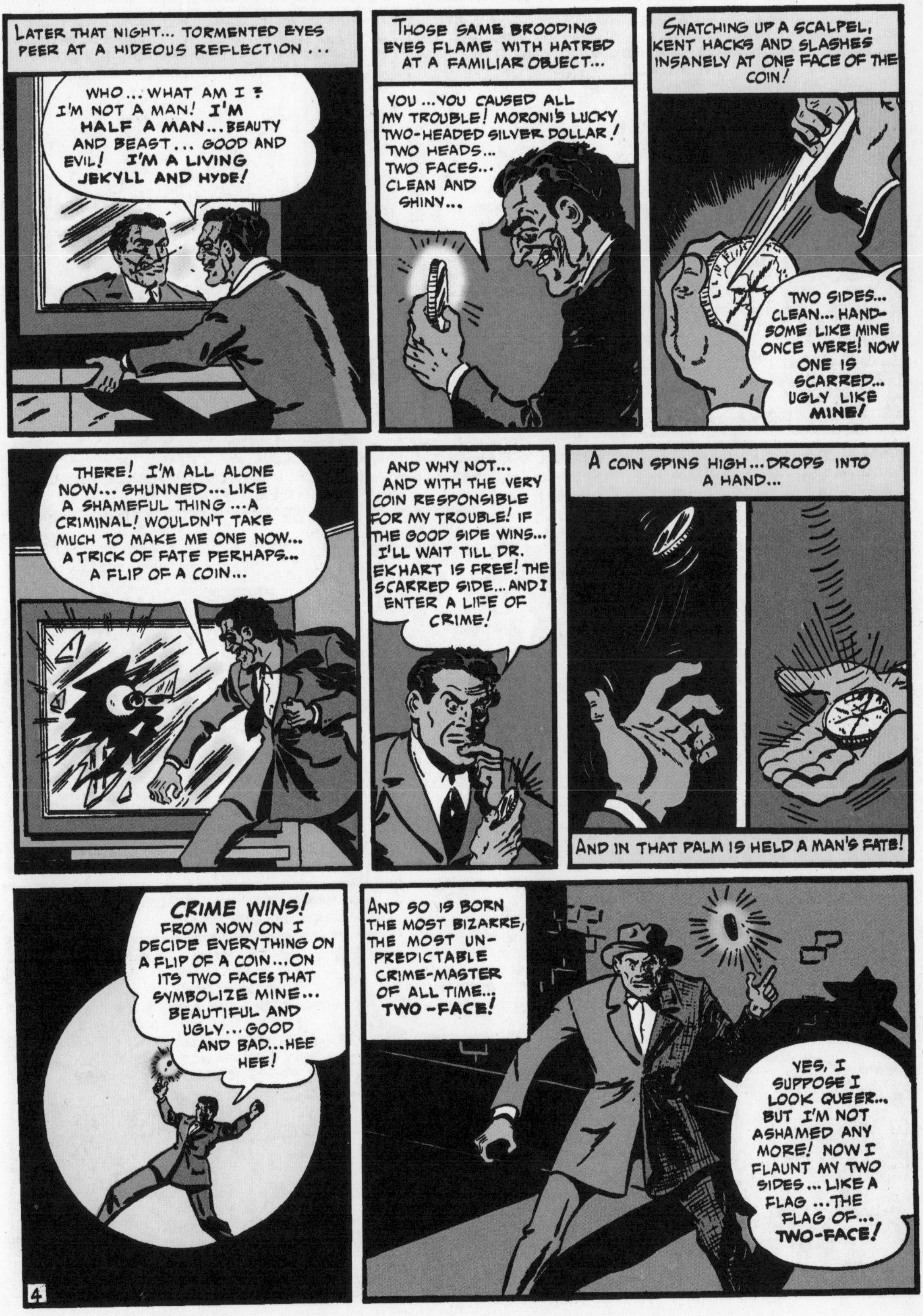
LATER THAT NIGHT... TORMENTED EYES PEER AT A HIDEOUS REFLECTION ...
WHO ... WHAT AM I ? I'M NOT A MAN! I'M HALF A MAN... BEAUTY AND BEAST... GOOD AND EVIL! I'M A LIVING JEKYLL AND HYDE!
THOSE SAME BROODING EYES FLAME WITH HATRED AT A FAMILIAR OBJECT...
YOU ...YOU CAUSED ALL MY TROUBLE! MORONI'S LUCKY TWO-HEADED SILVER DOLLAR! TWO HEADS... TWO FACES... CLEAN AND SHINY...
SNATCHING UP A SCALPEL, KENT HACKS AND SLASHES INSANELY AT ONE FACE OF THE COIN!
TWO SIDES... CLEAN... HAND-SOME LIKE MINE ONCE WERE! NOW ONE IS SCARRED... UGLY LIKE MINE!
THERE! I'M ALL ALONE NOW... SHUNNED... LIKE A SHAMEFUL THING ...A CRIMINAL! WOULDN'T TAKE MUCH TO MAKE ME ONE NOW... A TRICK OF FATE PERHAPS... A FLIP OF A COIN...
AND WHY NOT... AND WITH THE VERY COIN RESPONSIBLE FOR MY TROUBLE! IF THE GOOD SIDE WINS... I'LL WAIT TILL DR. EKHART IS FREE! THE SCARRED SIDE... AND I ENTER A LIFE OF CRIME!
A COIN SPINS HIGH...DROPS INTO A HAND...
AND IN THAT PALM IS HELD A MAN'S FATE!
CRIME WINS! FROM NOW ON I DECIDE EVERYTHING ON A FLIP OF A COIN...ON ITS TWO FACES THAT SYMBOLIZE MINE... BEAUTIFUL AND UGLY... GOOD AND BAD...HEE HEE!
4
AND SO IS BORN THE MOST BIZARRE, THE MOST UN-PREDICTABLE CRIME-MASTER OF ALL TIME... TWO-FACE!
YES, I SUPPOSE I LOOK QUEER... BUT I'M NOT ASHAMED ANY MORE! NOW I FLAUNT MY TWO SIDES ... LIKE A FLAG ...THE FLAG OF... TWO-FACE!

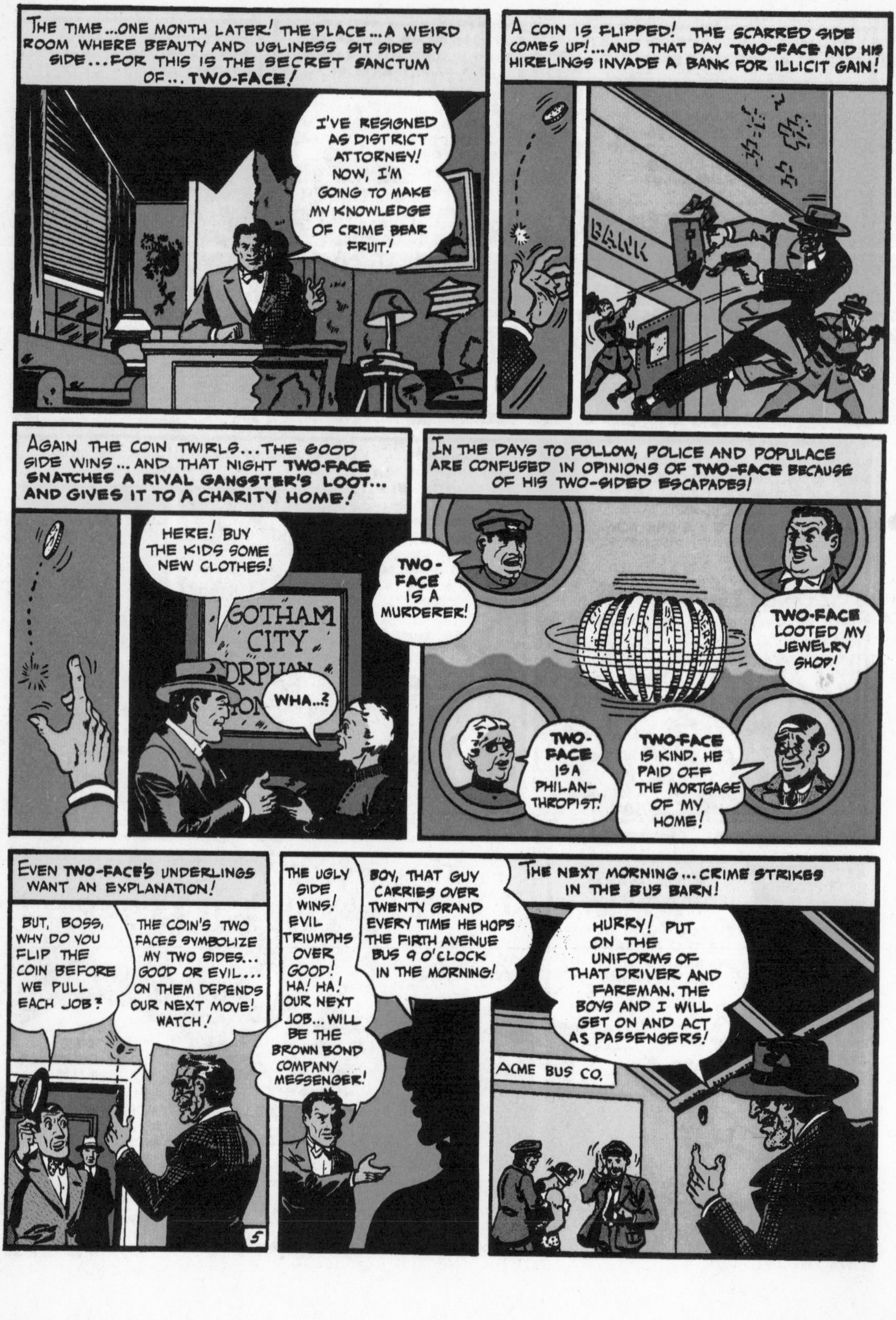

THE TIME...ONE MONTH LATER! THE PLACE...A WEIRD ROOM WHERE BEAUTY AND UGLINESS SIT SIDE BY SIDE...FOR THIS IS THE SECRET SANCTUM OF...TWO-FACE!
I'VE RESIGNED AS DISTRICT ATTORNEY! NOW, I'M GOING TO MAKE MY KNOWLEDGE OF CRIME BEAR FRUIT!
A COIN IS FLIPPED! THE SCARRED SIDE COMES UP!...AND THAT DAY TWO-FACE AND HIS HIRELINGS INVADE A BANK FOR ILLICIT GAIN!
BANK
AGAIN THE COIN TWIRLS...THE GOOD SIDE WINS...AND THAT NIGHT TWO-FACE SNATCHES A RIVAL GANGSTER'S LOOT... AND GIVES IT TO A CHARITY HOME!
HERE! BUY THE KIDS SOME NEW CLOTHES!
GOTHAM CITY
WHA...?
IN THE DAYS TO FOLLOW, POLICE AND POPULACE ARE CONFUSED IN OPINIONS OF TWO-FACE BECAUSE OF HIS TWO-SIDED ESCAPADES!
TWO-FACE IS A MURDERER!
TWO-FACE LOOTED MY JEWELRY SHOP!
TWO-FACE IS A PHILANTHROPIST!
TWO-FACE IS KIND. HE PAID OFF THE MORTGAGE OF MY HOME!
EVEN TWO-FACE'S UNDERLINGS WANT AN EXPLANATION!
BUT, BOSS, WHY DO YOU FLIP THE COIN BEFORE WE PULL EACH JOB?
THE COIN'S TWO FACES SYMBOLIZE MY TWO SIDES...GOOD OR EVIL...ON THEM DEPENDS OUR NEXT MOVE! WATCH!
5
THE UGLY SIDE WINS! EVIL TRIUMPHS OVER GOOD! HA! HA! OUR NEXT JOB...WILL BE THE BROWN BOND COMPANY MESSENGER!
BOY, THAT GUY CARRIES OVER TWENTY GRAND EVERY TIME HE HOPS THE FIRTH AVENUE BUS 9 O'CLOCK IN THE MORNING!
THE NEXT MORNING...CRIME STRIKES IN THE BUS BARN!
HURRY! PUT ON THE UNIFORMS OF THAT DRIVER AND FAREMAN. THE BOYS AND I WILL GET ON AND ACT AS PASSENGERS!
ACME BUS CO.

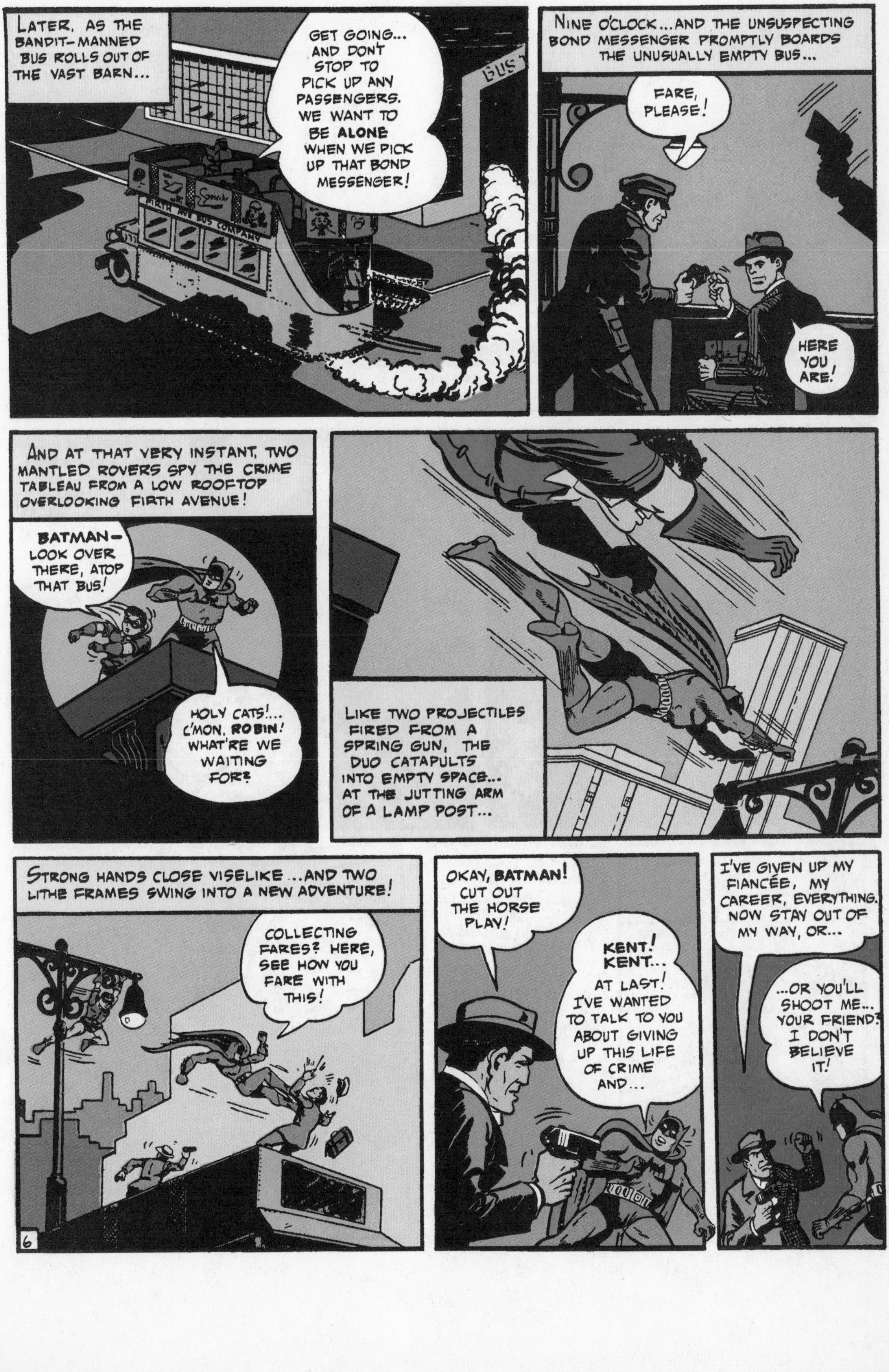
LATER, AS THE BANDIT-MANNED BUS ROLLS OUT OF THE VAST BARN...
GET GOING... AND DON'T STOP TO PICK UP ANY PASSENGERS. WE WANT TO BE ALONE WHEN WE PICK UP THAT BOND MESSENGER!
NINE O'CLOCK...AND THE UNSUSPECTING BOND MESSENGER PROMPTLY BOARDS THE UNUSUALLY EMPTY BUS...
FARE, PLEASE!
HERE YOU ARE!
AND AT THAT VERY INSTANT, TWO MANTLED ROVERS SPY THE CRIME TABLEAU FROM A LOW ROOFTOP OVERLOOKING FIRTH AVENUE!
BATMAN— LOOK OVER THERE, ATOP THAT BUS!
HOLY CATS!... C'MON, ROBIN! WHAT'RE WE WAITING FOR?
LIKE TWO PROJECTILES FIRED FROM A SPRING GUN, THE DUO CATAPULTS INTO EMPTY SPACE... AT THE JUTTING ARM OF A LAMP POST...
STRONG HANDS CLOSE VISELIKE ...AND TWO LITHE FRAMES SWING INTO A NEW ADVENTURE!
COLLECTING FARES? HERE, SEE HOW YOU FARE WITH THIS!
6
OKAY, BATMAN! CUT OUT THE HORSE PLAY!
KENT! KENT... AT LAST! I'VE WANTED TO TALK TO YOU ABOUT GIVING UP THIS LIFE OF CRIME AND...
I'VE GIVEN UP MY FIANCÉE, MY CAREER, EVERYTHING. NOW STAY OUT OF MY WAY, OR...
...OR YOU'LL SHOOT ME... YOUR FRIEND? I DON'T BELIEVE IT!

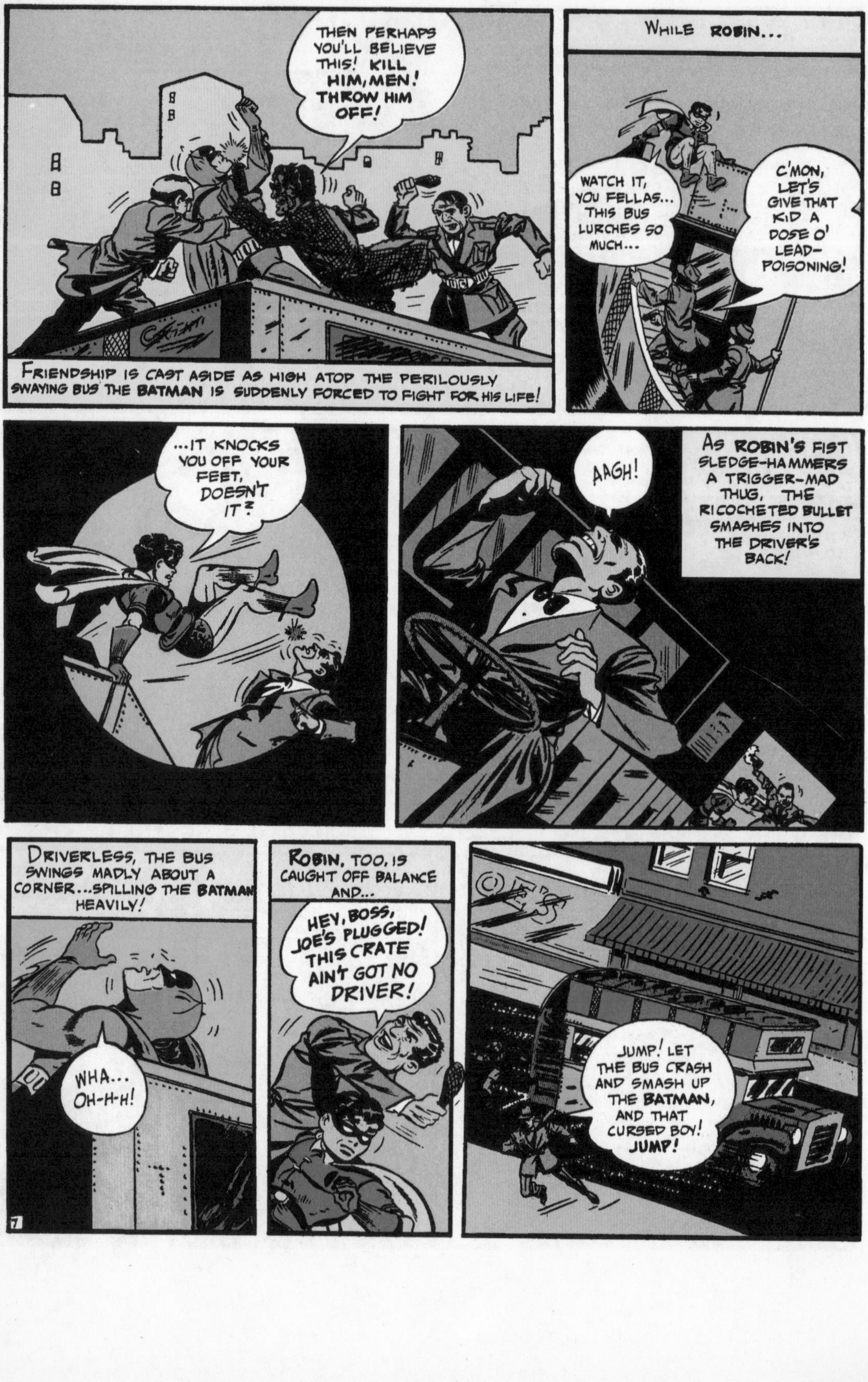
THEN PERHAPS YOU'LL BELIEVE THIS! KILL HIM, MEN! THROW HIM OFF!
FRIENDSHIP IS CAST ASIDE AS HIGH ATOP THE PERILOUSLY SWAYING BUS THE BATMAN IS SUDDENLY FORCED TO FIGHT FOR HIS LIFE!
WHILE ROBIN...
WATCH IT, YOU FELLAS... THIS BUS LURCHES SO MUCH...
C'MON, LET'S GIVE THAT KID A DOSE O' LEAD-POISONING!
...IT KNOCKS YOU OFF YOUR FEET, DOESN'T IT?
AS ROBIN'S FIST SLEDGE-HAMMERS A TRIGGER-MAD THUG, THE RICOCHETED BULLET SMASHES INTO THE DRIVER'S BACK!
AAGH!
DRIVERLESS, THE BUS SWINGS MADLY ABOUT A CORNER...SPILLING THE BATMAN HEAVILY!
WHA... OH-H-H!
ROBIN, TOO, IS CAUGHT OFF BALANCE AND...
HEY, BOSS, JOE'S PLUGGED! THIS CRATE AIN'T GOT NO DRIVER!
JUMP! LET THE BUS CRASH AND SMASH UP THE BATMAN, AND THAT CURSED BOY! JUMP!

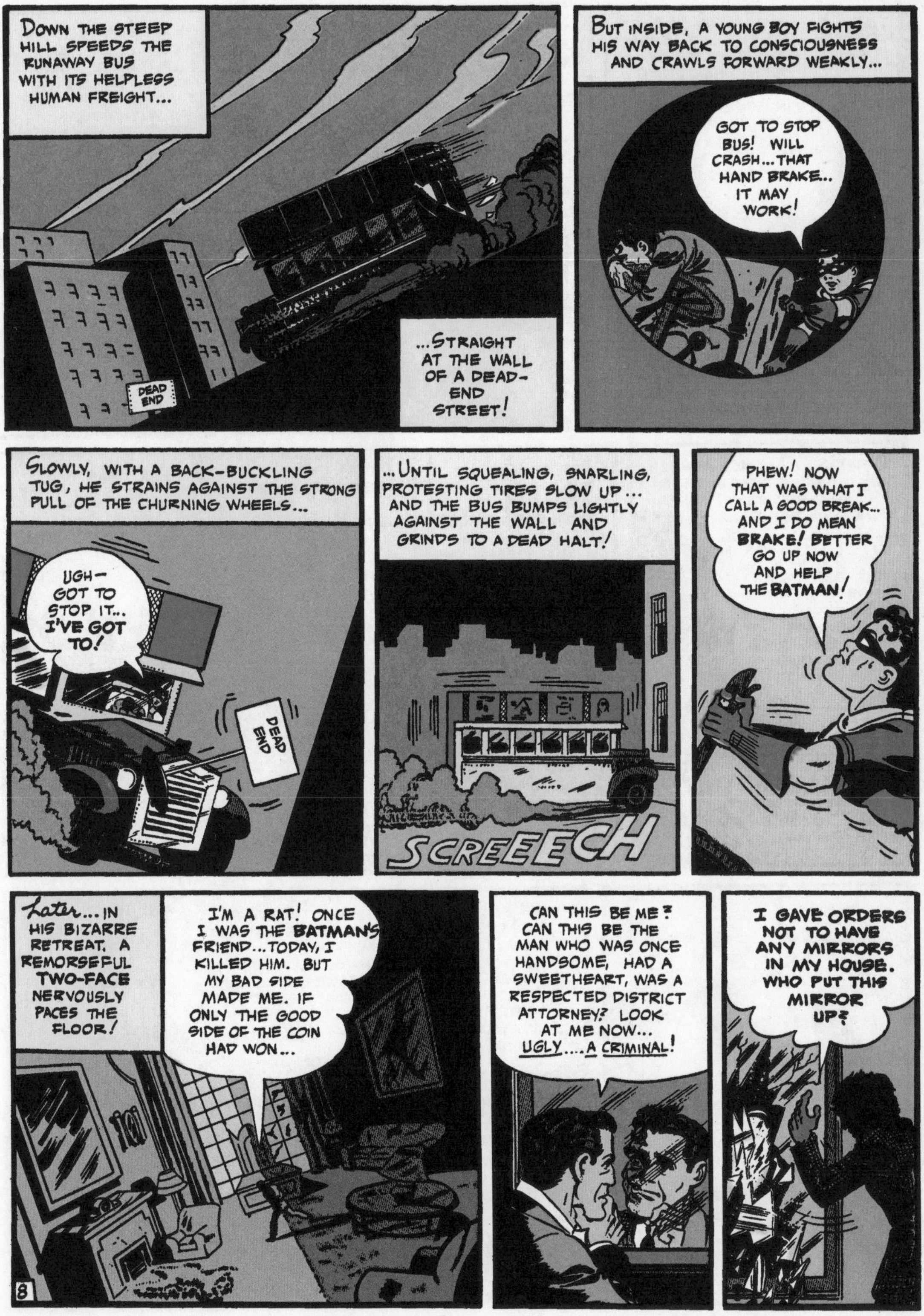

DOWN THE STEEP HILL SPEEDS THE RUNAWAY BUS WITH ITS HELPLESS HUMAN FREIGHT...
DEAD END
...STRAIGHT AT THE WALL OF A DEAD-END STREET!
BUT INSIDE, A YOUNG BOY FIGHTS HIS WAY BACK TO CONSCIOUSNESS AND CRAWLS FORWARD WEAKLY...
GOT TO STOP BUS! WILL CRASH...THAT HAND BRAKE.. IT MAY WORK!
SLOWLY, WITH A BACK-BUCKLING TUG, HE STRAINS AGAINST THE STRONG PULL OF THE CHURNING WHEELS...
UGH- GOT TO STOP IT... I'VE GOT TO!
DEAD END
...UNTIL SQUEALING, SNARLING, PROTESTING TIRES SLOW UP... AND THE BUS BUMPS LIGHTLY AGAINST THE WALL AND GRINDS TO A DEAD HALT!
SCREEECH
PHEW! NOW THAT WAS WHAT I CALL A GOOD BREAK... AND I DO MEAN BRAKE! BETTER GO UP NOW AND HELP THE BATMAN!
Later... IN HIS BIZARRE RETREAT, A REMORSEFUL TWO-FACE NERVOUSLY PACES THE FLOOR!
I'M A RAT! ONCE I WAS THE BATMAN'S FRIEND...TODAY, I KILLED HIM. BUT MY BAD SIDE MADE ME. IF ONLY THE GOOD SIDE OF THE COIN HAD WON...
8
CAN THIS BE ME? CAN THIS BE THE MAN WHO WAS ONCE HANDSOME, HAD A SWEETHEART, WAS A RESPECTED DISTRICT ATTORNEY? LOOK AT ME NOW... UGLY....A CRIMINAL!
I GAVE ORDERS NOT TO HAVE ANY MIRRORS IN MY HOUSE. WHO PUT THIS MIRROR UP?

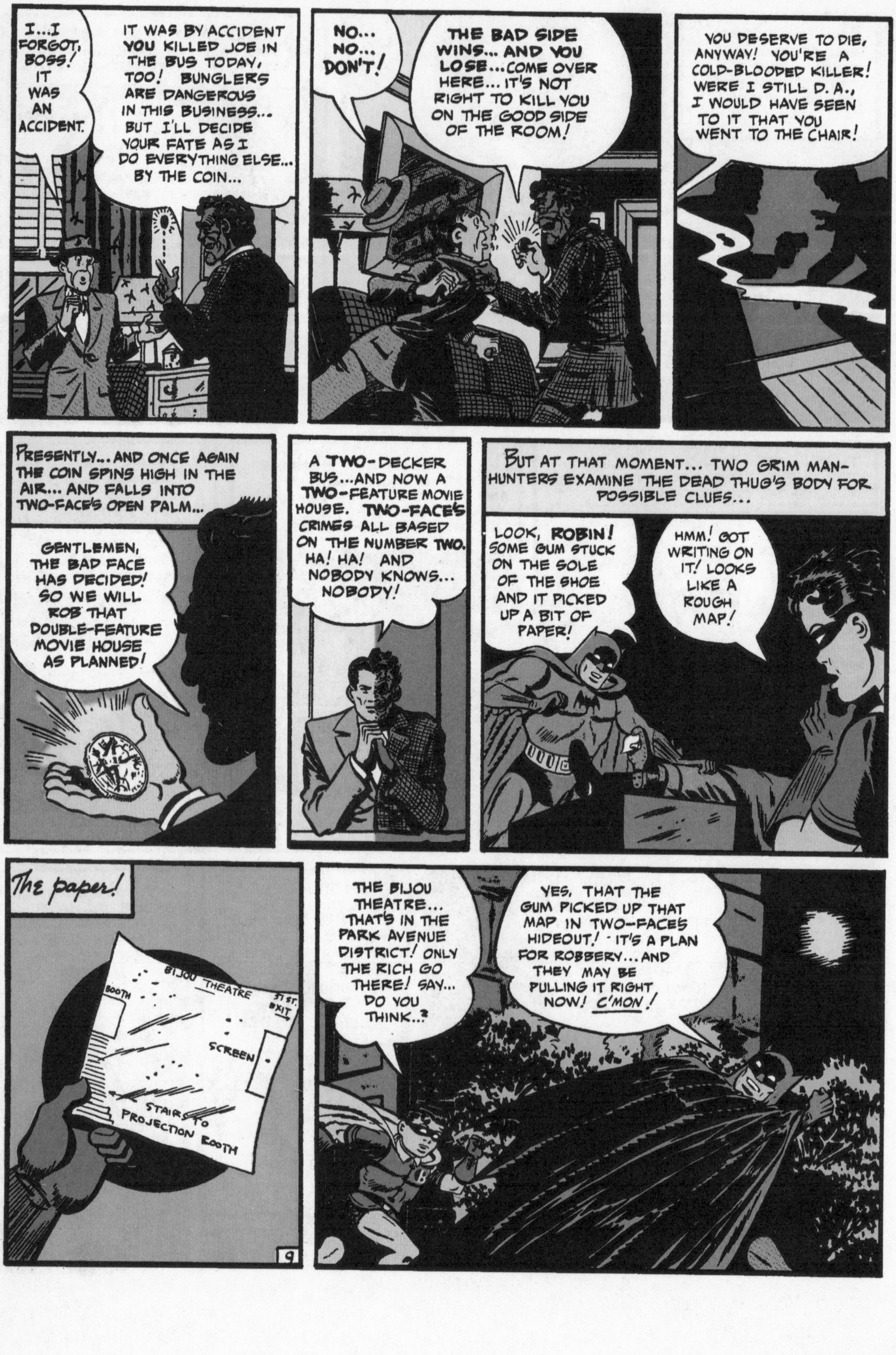

I...I FORGOT, BOSS! IT WAS AN ACCIDENT.
IT WAS BY ACCIDENT YOU KILLED JOE IN THE BUS TODAY, TOO! BUNGLERS ARE DANGEROUS IN THIS BUSINESS... BUT I'LL DECIDE YOUR FATE AS I DO EVERYTHING ELSE... BY THE COIN...
NO... NO... DON'T!
THE BAD SIDE WINS... AND YOU LOSE... COME OVER HERE... IT'S NOT RIGHT TO KILL YOU ON THE GOOD SIDE OF THE ROOM!
YOU DESERVE TO DIE, ANYWAY! YOU'RE A COLD-BLOODED KILLER! WERE I STILL D. A., I WOULD HAVE SEEN TO IT THAT YOU WENT TO THE CHAIR!
PRESENTLY... AND ONCE AGAIN THE COIN SPINS HIGH IN THE AIR... AND FALLS INTO TWO-FACE'S OPEN PALM...
GENTLEMEN, THE BAD FACE HAS DECIDED! SO WE WILL ROB THAT DOUBLE-FEATURE MOVIE HOUSE AS PLANNED!
A TWO-DECKER BUS...AND NOW A TWO-FEATURE MOVIE HOUSE. TWO-FACE'S CRIMES ALL BASED ON THE NUMBER TWO. HA! HA! AND NOBODY KNOWS... NOBODY!
BUT AT THAT MOMENT... TWO GRIM MAN-HUNTERS EXAMINE THE DEAD THUG'S BODY FOR POSSIBLE CLUES...
LOOK, ROBIN! SOME GUM STUCK ON THE SOLE OF THE SHOE AND IT PICKED UP A BIT OF PAPER!
HMM! GOT WRITING ON IT! LOOKS LIKE A ROUGH MAP!
The paper!
BIJOU THEATRE
BOOTH
31 ST. EXIT
SCREEN
STAIRS TO PROJECTION BOOTH
9
THE BIJOU THEATRE... THAT'S IN THE PARK AVENUE DISTRICT! ONLY THE RICH GO THERE! SAY... DO YOU THINK..?
YES, THAT THE GUM PICKED UP THAT MAP IN TWO-FACE'S HIDEOUT! IT'S A PLAN FOR ROBBERY... AND THEY MAY BE PULLING IT RIGHT NOW! C'MON!

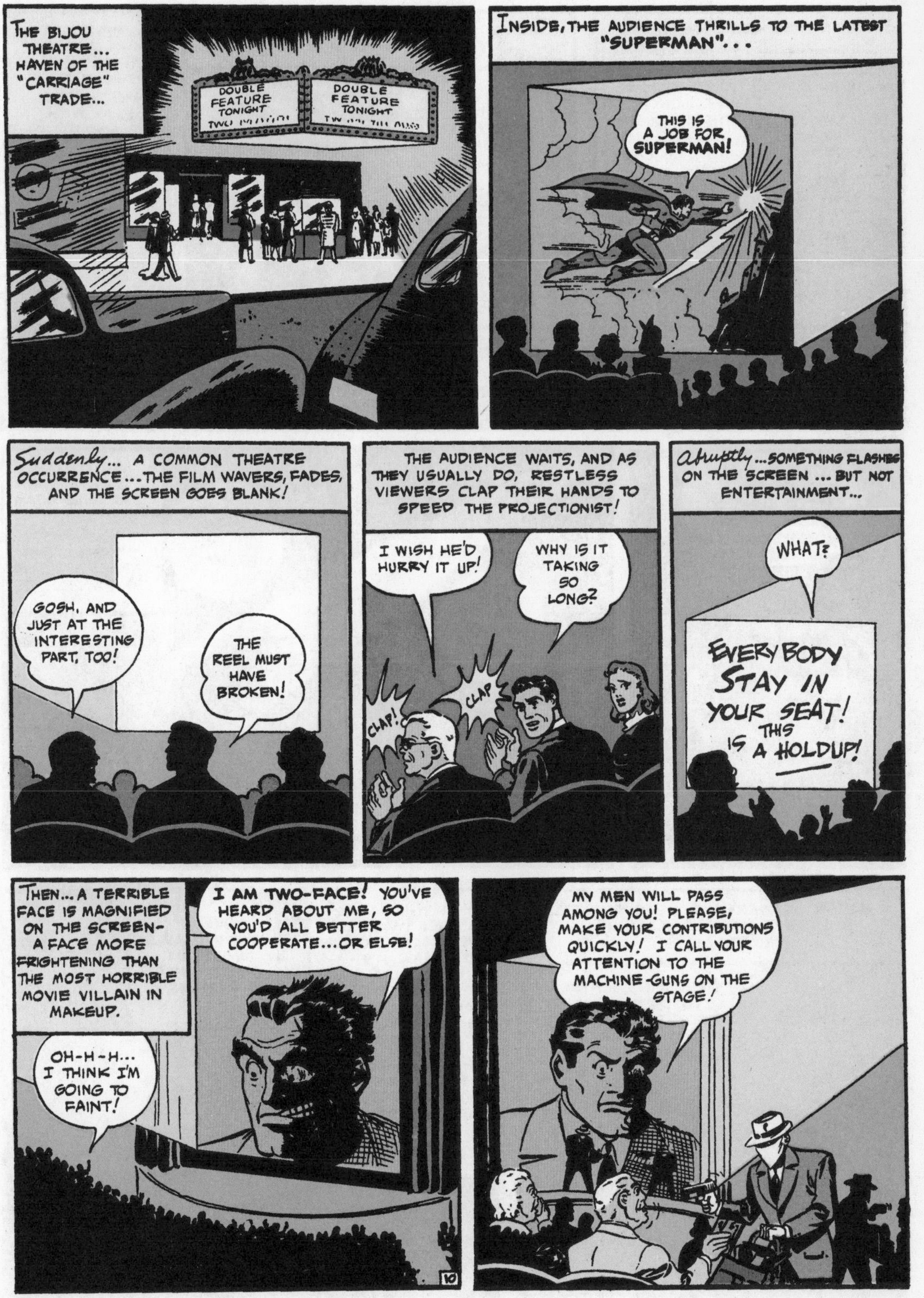
THE BIJOU THEATRE... HAVEN OF THE "CARRIAGE" TRADE...
DOUBLE FEATURE TONIGHT
DOUBLE FEATURE TONIGHT
INSIDE, THE AUDIENCE THRILLS TO THE LATEST "SUPERMAN"...
THIS IS A JOB FOR SUPERMAN!
Suddenly... A COMMON THEATRE OCCURRENCE... THE FILM WAVERS, FADES, AND THE SCREEN GOES BLANK!
GOSH, AND JUST AT THE INTERESTING PART, TOO!
THE REEL MUST HAVE BROKEN!
THE AUDIENCE WAITS, AND AS THEY USUALLY DO, RESTLESS VIEWERS CLAP THEIR HANDS TO SPEED THE PROJECTIONIST!
I WISH HE'D HURRY IT UP!
WHY IS IT TAKING SO LONG?
CLAP!
CLAP
abruptly... SOMETHING FLASHES ON THE SCREEN ... BUT NOT ENTERTAINMENT...
WHAT?
EVERYBODY STAY IN YOUR SEAT! THIS IS A HOLDUP!
THEN... A TERRIBLE FACE IS MAGNIFIED ON THE SCREEN- A FACE MORE FRIGHTENING THAN THE MOST HORRIBLE MOVIE VILLAIN IN MAKEUP.
I AM TWO-FACE! YOU'VE HEARD ABOUT ME, SO YOU'D ALL BETTER COOPERATE... OR ELSE!
OH-H-H... I THINK I'M GOING TO FAINT!
10
MY MEN WILL PASS AMONG YOU! PLEASE, MAKE YOUR CONTRIBUTIONS QUICKLY! I CALL YOUR ATTENTION TO THE MACHINE-GUNS ON THE STAGE!

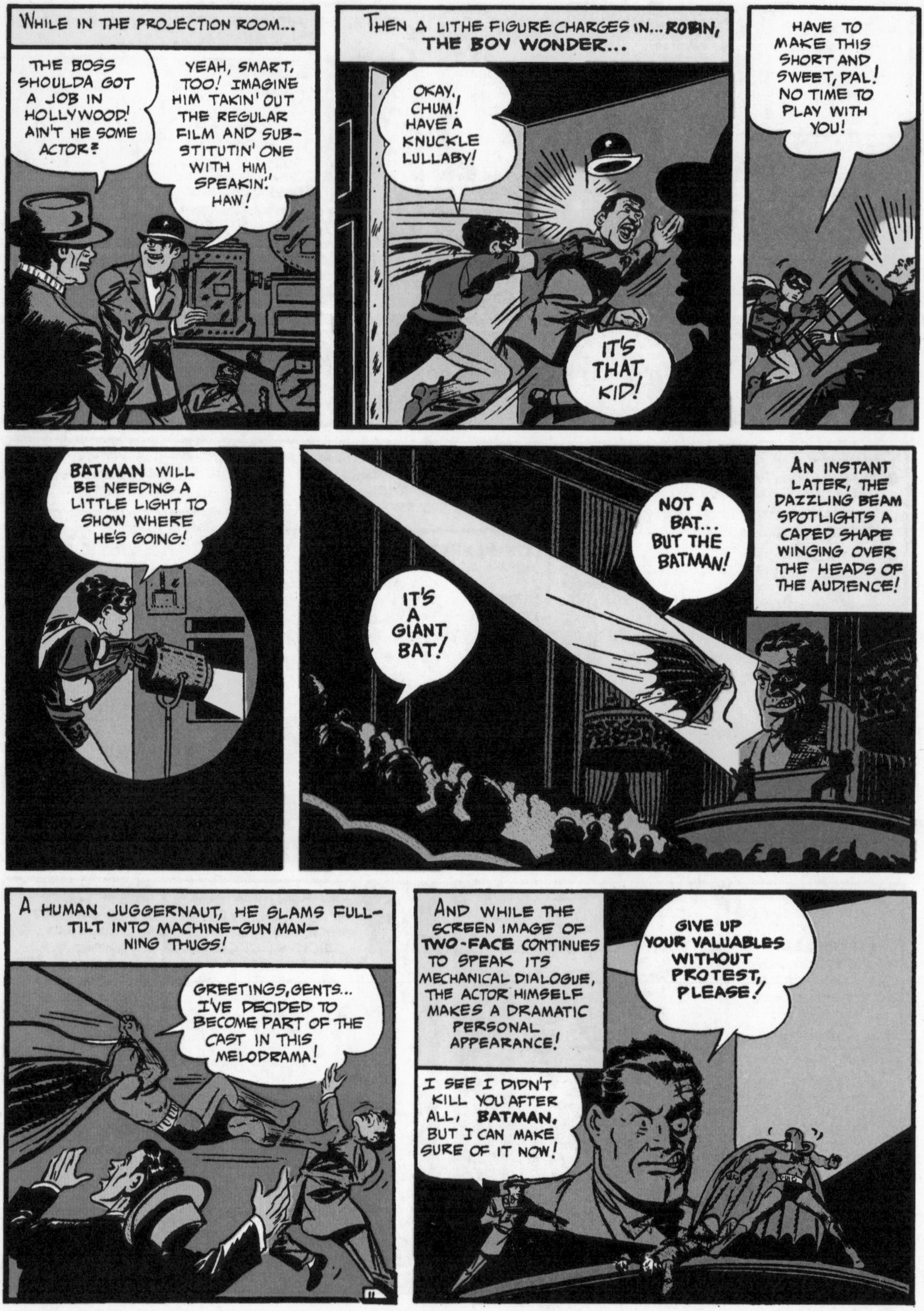

WHILE IN THE PROJECTION ROOM...
THE BOSS SHOULDA GOT A JOB IN HOLLYWOOD! AIN'T HE SOME ACTOR?
YEAH, SMART, TOO! IMAGINE HIM TAKIN' OUT THE REGULAR FILM AND SUB-STITUTIN' ONE WITH HIM SPEAKIN'! HAW!
THEN A LITHE FIGURE CHARGES IN... ROBIN, THE BOY WONDER...
OKAY, CHUM! HAVE A KNUCKLE LULLABY!
IT'S THAT KID!
HAVE TO MAKE THIS SHORT AND SWEET, PAL! NO TIME TO PLAY WITH YOU!
BATMAN WILL BE NEEDING A LITTLE LIGHT TO SHOW WHERE HE'S GOING!
AN INSTANT LATER, THE DAZZLING BEAM SPOTLIGHTS A CAPED SHAPE WINGING OVER THE HEADS OF THE AUDIENCE!
NOT A BAT... BUT THE BATMAN!
IT'S A GIANT BAT!
A HUMAN JUGGERNAUT, HE SLAMS FULL-TILT INTO MACHINE-GUN MAN-NING THUGS!
GREETINGS, GENTS... I'VE DECIDED TO BECOME PART OF THE CAST IN THIS MELODRAMA!
AND WHILE THE SCREEN IMAGE OF TWO-FACE CONTINUES TO SPEAK ITS MECHANICAL DIALOGUE, THE ACTOR HIMSELF MAKES A DRAMATIC PERSONAL APPEARANCE!
GIVE UP YOUR VALUABLES WITHOUT PROTEST, PLEASE!
I SEE I DIDN'T KILL YOU AFTER ALL, BATMAN. BUT I CAN MAKE SURE OF IT NOW!

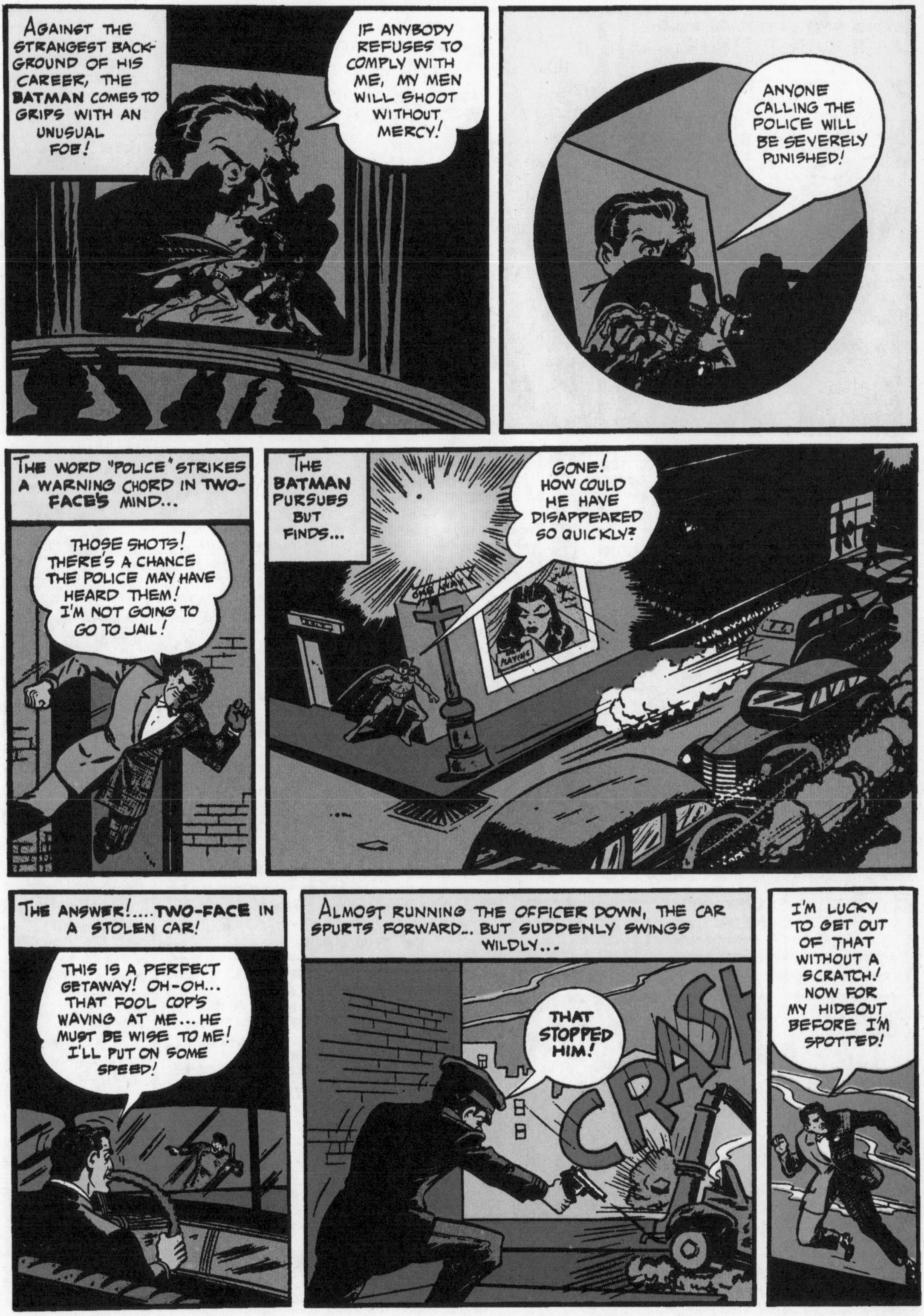
AGAINST THE STRANGEST BACKGROUND OF HIS CAREER, THE BATMAN COMES TO GRIPS WITH AN UNUSUAL FOE!
IF ANYBODY REFUSES TO COMPLY WITH ME, MY MEN WILL SHOOT WITHOUT MERCY!
ANYONE CALLING THE POLICE WILL BE SEVERELY PUNISHED!
THE WORD "POLICE" STRIKES A WARNING CHORD IN TWO-FACE'S MIND...
THOSE SHOTS! THERE'S A CHANCE THE POLICE MAY HAVE HEARD THEM! I'M NOT GOING TO GO TO JAIL!
THE BATMAN PURSUES BUT FINDS...
GONE! HOW COULD HE HAVE DISAPPEARED SO QUICKLY?
THE ANSWER!.....TWO-FACE IN A STOLEN CAR!
THIS IS A PERFECT GETAWAY! OH-OH... THAT FOOL COP'S WAVING AT ME... HE MUST BE WISE TO ME! I'LL PUT ON SOME SPEED!
ALMOST RUNNING THE OFFICER DOWN, THE CAR SPURTS FORWARD.. BUT SUDDENLY SWINGS WILDLY...
THAT STOPPED HIM!
CRASH
I'M LUCKY TO GET OUT OF THAT WITHOUT A SCRATCH! NOW FOR MY HIDEOUT BEFORE I'M SPOTTED!

Panel 1

SOME TIME LATER, AS TWO-FACE STEPS CONFIDENTLY INTO HIS LAIR...

AT LAST! SAFE AT HOME!

NOT QUITE!

Panel 2

BATMAN! HOW...?

VERY SIMPLE! WHEN THE POLICEMAN HIT YOUR TIRE, I WAS ATTRACTED BY THE SHOT...SPOTTED YOU, AND TRAILED YOU HERE!

Panel 3

YOU WOULD HAVE MADE THE PERFECT GETAWAY...IF YOU HADN'T MADE THE MISTAKE OF DRIVING DOWN A ONE-WAY STREET THE WRONG WAY! THAT'S WHY THE COP TRIED TO STOP YOU...NOT BECAUSE HE THOUGHT YOU WERE A CROOK!

HA! HOW IRONICAL THAT I, WHO PLANNED MY CRIME CAREER ON THE NUMBER TWO, SHOULD BE TRIPPED UP BY A ONE WAY STREET!

Panel 4

WAIT! YOU'RE NOT TAKING ME IN! I'LL KILL YOU FIRST!

GO AHEAD! SHOOT...YOU FOOL! KENT, BE SMART! GIVE YOURSELF UP! THE COURT REMEMBERS YOUR FINE RECORD AS A D.A.! THEY'LL KNOW THIS IS ONLY TEMPORARY INSANITY INDUCED BY YOUR TERRIBLE MISFORTUNE!

Panel 5

I'LL EVEN SPEAK FOR YOU! YOU'LL GET A LIGHT SENTENCE! BY THE TIME YOUR TERM IS UP, PERHAPS DR. EKHART WILL BE FREE. YOU'LL GET YOUR FACE FIXED! YOU CAN START YOUR LIFE ALL OVER AGAIN. WHAT DO YOU SAY?

Panel 6

IT'S WHAT THE COIN SAYS! IT DECIDES EVERYTHING FOR ME! IF THE SCARRED SIDE COMES UP...I KILL YOU AND CONTINUE A CAREER OF CRIME, AND IF THE GOOD SIDE COMES...I GO WITH YOU!

Panel 7

A QUICK FLIP... AND THE COIN SPINS HIGH INTO THE AIR!

Panel 8

DOWN IT DROPS LIKE A SHINING SUN... HITS THE FLOOR!...

Panel 9

...ROLLS OVER THE FLOOR-BOARDS... HITS A CRACK, AND...

... AND STANDS ON ITS EDGE!

13

Panel 10

THE BATMAN WAITS ON THE GOOD SIDE OF THE ROOM...TWO-FACE ON THE BAD...

WELL...STANDING UP. LOOKS LIKE YOU'LL HAVE TO FLIP OVER AGAIN!

NO, BATMAN!...I TOSS ONCE AGAINST CHANCE! AND SINCE I CAN'T DECIDE FOR MYSELF, IT'S UP TO FATE TO DECIDE WHAT TO DO WITH MY LIFE NOW!

Panel 11

A MAN'S WHOLE BEING AND FUTURE RESTS IN FATE'S HAND! WHICH WAY WILL SHE TOSS HIM... TO GOOD...OR TO EVIL? THE ANSWER TO THIS AMAZING RIDDLE OF TWO-FACE WILL BE FOUND IN THE OCTOBER ISSUE OF --- DETECTIVE COMICS.

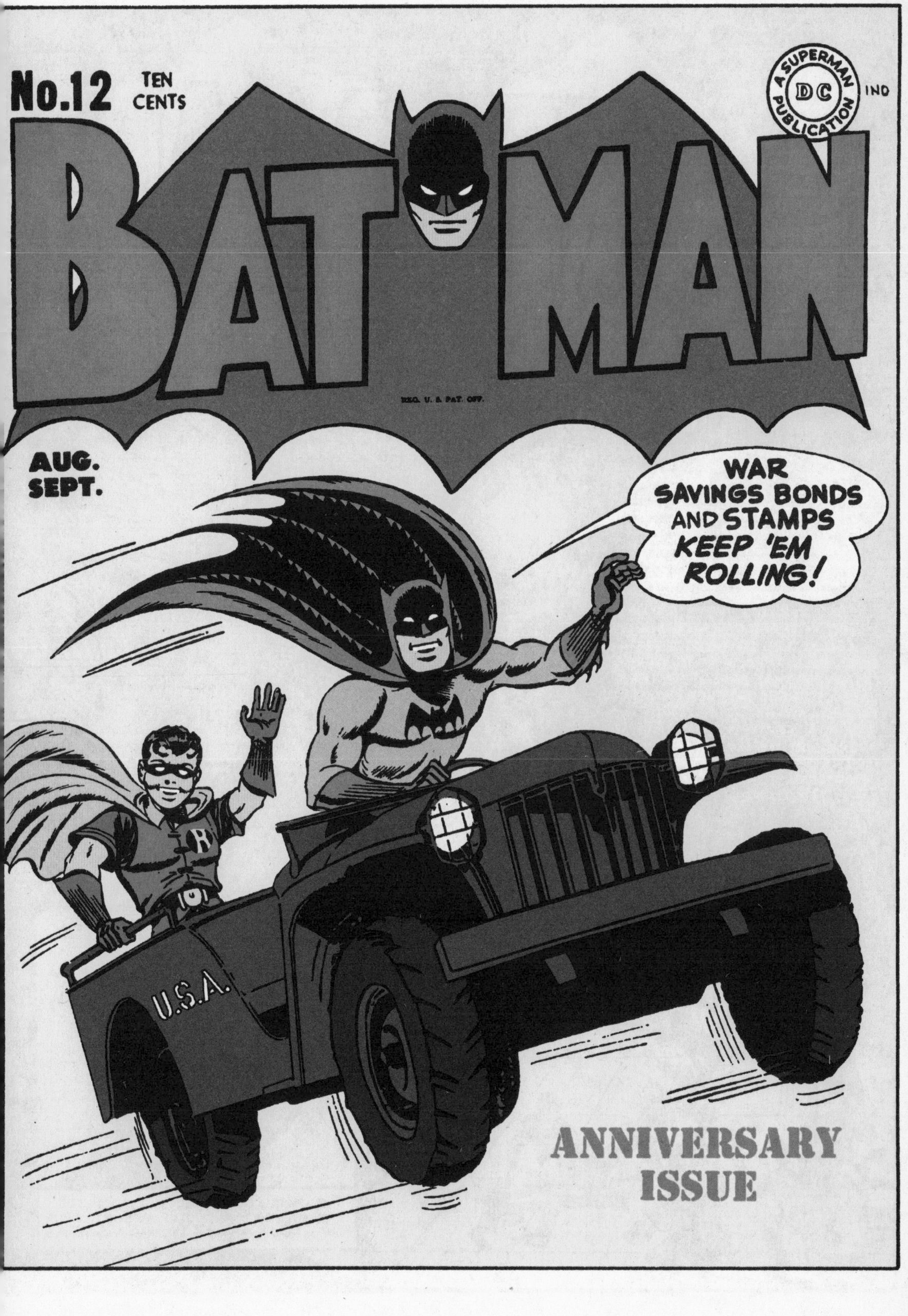
No.12
TEN CENTS
A SUPERMAN DC PUBLICATION
INC
BATMAN
REG. U. S. PAT. OFF.
AUG. SEPT.
WAR SAVINGS BONDS AND STAMPS KEEP 'EM ROLLING!
U.S.A.
ANNIVERSARY ISSUE

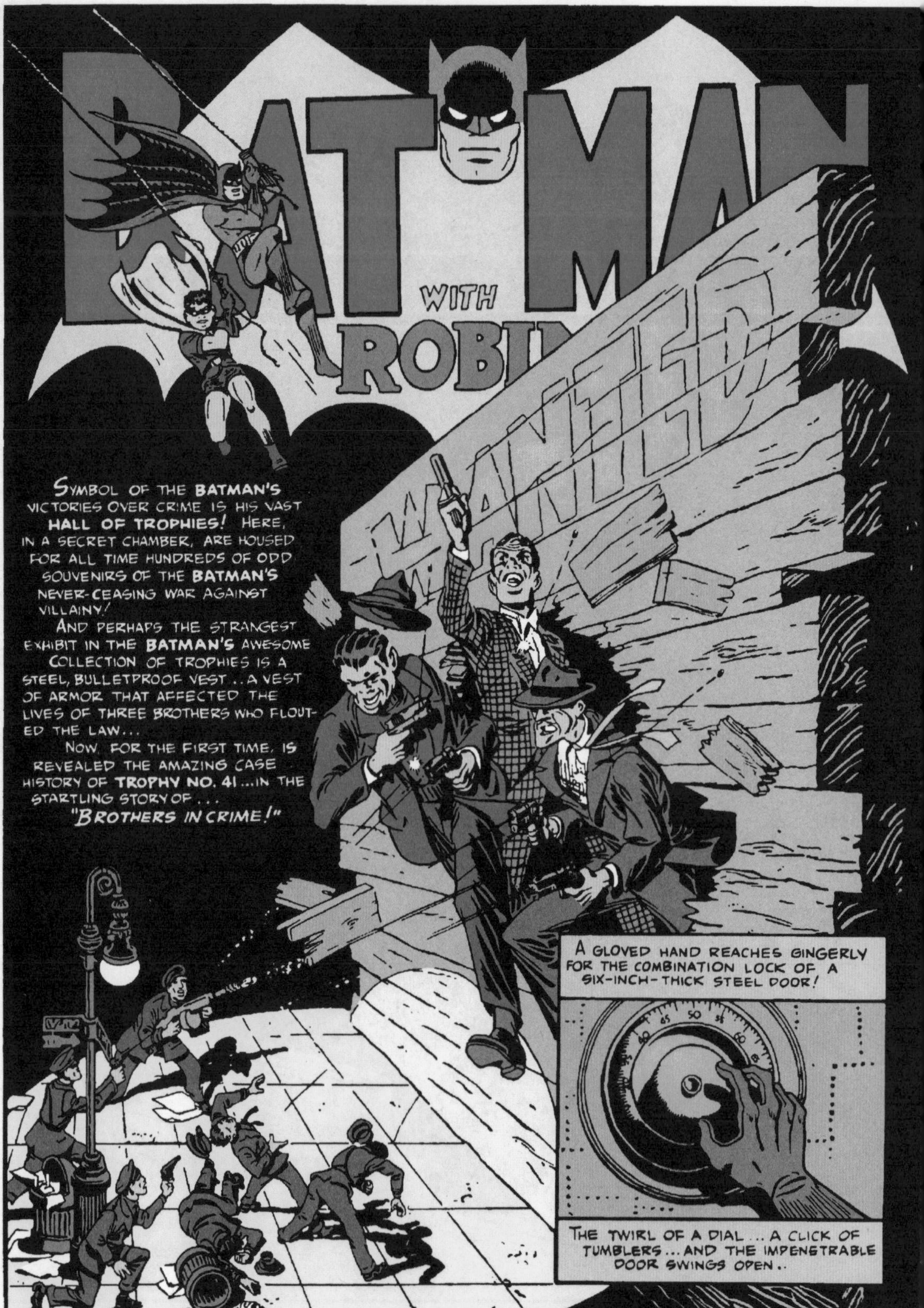
BATMAN
WITH
ROBIN
WANTED
SYMBOL OF THE BATMAN'S VICTORIES OVER CRIME IS HIS VAST HALL OF TROPHIES! HERE, IN A SECRET CHAMBER, ARE HOUSED FOR ALL TIME HUNDREDS OF ODD SOUVENIRS OF THE BATMAN'S NEVER-CEASING WAR AGAINST VILLAINY!
AND PERHAPS THE STRANGEST EXHIBIT IN THE BATMAN'S AWESOME COLLECTION OF TROPHIES IS A STEEL, BULLETPROOF VEST .. A VEST OF ARMOR THAT AFFECTED THE LIVES OF THREE BROTHERS WHO FLOUTED THE LAW...
NOW, FOR THE FIRST TIME, IS REVEALED THE AMAZING CASE HISTORY OF TROPHY NO. 41 ...IN THE STARTLING STORY OF . . .
"BROTHERS IN CRIME!"
A GLOVED HAND REACHES GINGERLY FOR THE COMBINATION LOCK OF A SIX-INCH-THICK STEEL DOOR!
THE TWIRL OF A DIAL ... A CLICK OF TUMBLERS ... AND THE IMPENETRABLE DOOR SWINGS OPEN ..

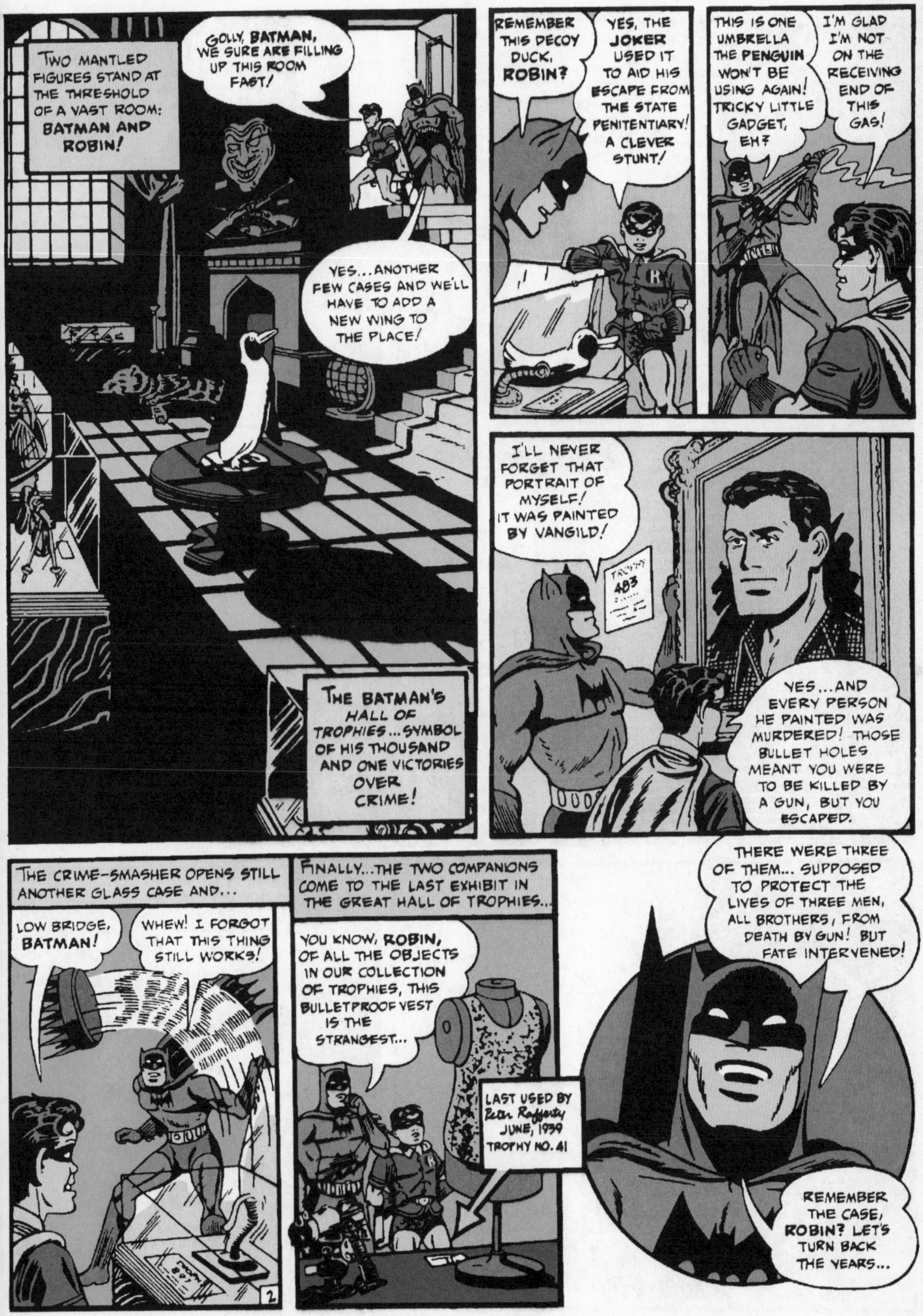
TWO MANTLED FIGURES STAND AT THE THRESHOLD OF A VAST ROOM: BATMAN AND ROBIN!
GOLLY, BATMAN, WE SURE ARE FILLING UP THIS ROOM FAST!
YES... ANOTHER FEW CASES AND WE'LL HAVE TO ADD A NEW WING TO THE PLACE!
THE BATMAN'S HALL OF TROPHIES... SYMBOL OF HIS THOUSAND AND ONE VICTORIES OVER CRIME!
REMEMBER THIS DECOY DUCK, ROBIN?
YES, THE JOKER USED IT TO AID HIS ESCAPE FROM THE STATE PENITENTIARY! A CLEVER STUNT!
THIS IS ONE UMBRELLA THE PENGUIN WON'T BE USING AGAIN! TRICKY LITTLE GADGET, EH?
I'M GLAD I'M NOT ON THE RECEIVING END OF THIS GAS!
I'LL NEVER FORGET THAT PORTRAIT OF MYSELF! IT WAS PAINTED BY VANGILD!
TROPHY 483
YES... AND EVERY PERSON HE PAINTED WAS MURDERED! THOSE BULLET HOLES MEANT YOU WERE TO BE KILLED BY A GUN, BUT YOU ESCAPED.
THE CRIME-SMASHER OPENS STILL ANOTHER GLASS CASE AND...
LOW BRIDGE, BATMAN!
WHEW! I FORGOT THAT THIS THING STILL WORKS!
2
FINALLY... THE TWO COMPANIONS COME TO THE LAST EXHIBIT IN THE GREAT HALL OF TROPHIES...
YOU KNOW, ROBIN, OF ALL THE OBJECTS IN OUR COLLECTION OF TROPHIES, THIS BULLETPROOF VEST IS THE STRANGEST...
LAST USED BY Peter Rafferty JUNE, 1939 TROPHY NO. 41
THERE WERE THREE OF THEM... SUPPOSED TO PROTECT THE LIVES OF THREE MEN, ALL BROTHERS, FROM DEATH BY GUN! BUT FATE INTERVENED!
REMEMBER THE CASE, ROBIN? LET'S TURN BACK THE YEARS...

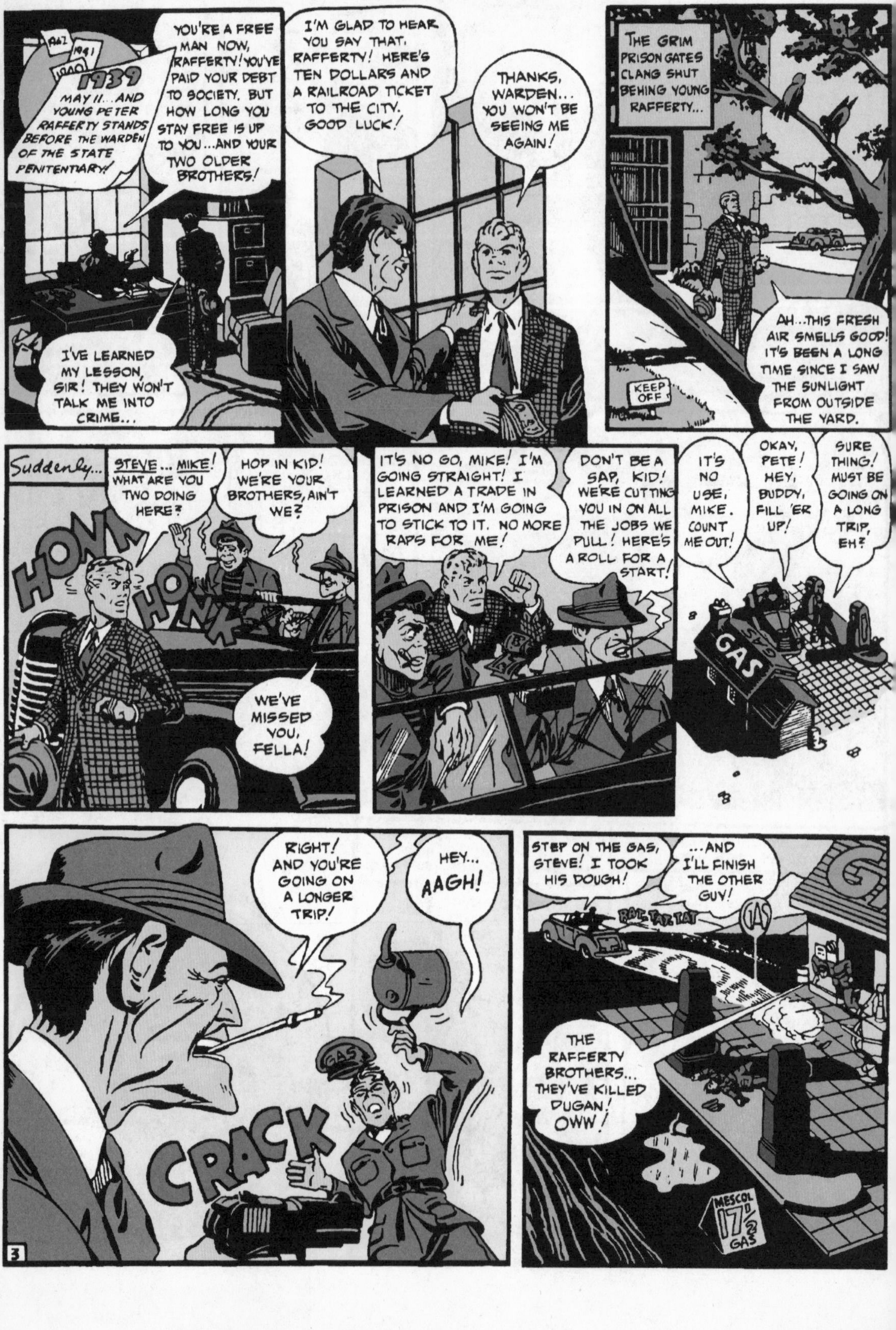
1942
1941
1940
1939
MAY 11... AND YOUNG PETER RAFFERTY STANDS BEFORE THE WARDEN OF THE STATE PENITENTIARY!
YOU'RE A FREE MAN NOW, RAFFERTY! YOU'VE PAID YOUR DEBT TO SOCIETY. BUT HOW LONG YOU STAY FREE IS UP TO YOU... AND YOUR TWO OLDER BROTHERS!
I'VE LEARNED MY LESSON, SIR! THEY WON'T TALK ME INTO CRIME...
I'M GLAD TO HEAR YOU SAY THAT, RAFFERTY! HERE'S TEN DOLLARS AND A RAILROAD TICKET TO THE CITY. GOOD LUCK!
THANKS, WARDEN... YOU WON'T BE SEEING ME AGAIN!
THE GRIM PRISON GATES CLANG SHUT BEHIND YOUNG RAFFERTY...
AH... THIS FRESH AIR SMELLS GOOD! IT'S BEEN A LONG TIME SINCE I SAW THE SUNLIGHT FROM OUTSIDE THE YARD.
KEEP OFF
Suddenly...
STEVE... MIKE! WHAT ARE YOU TWO DOING HERE?
HOP IN KID! WE'RE YOUR BROTHERS, AIN'T WE?
HONK
HONK
WE'VE MISSED YOU, FELLA!
IT'S NO GO, MIKE! I'M GOING STRAIGHT! I LEARNED A TRADE IN PRISON AND I'M GOING TO STICK TO IT. NO MORE RAPS FOR ME!
DON'T BE A SAP, KID! WE'RE CUTTING YOU IN ON ALL THE JOBS WE PULL! HERE'S A ROLL FOR A START!
IT'S NO USE, MIKE. COUNT ME OUT!
OKAY, PETE! HEY, BUDDY, FILL 'ER UP!
SURE THING! MUST BE GOING ON A LONG TRIP, EH?
GAS
RIGHT! AND YOU'RE GOING ON A LONGER TRIP!
HEY... AAGH!
CRACK
GAS
3
STEP ON THE GAS, STEVE! I TOOK HIS DOUGH!
...AND I'LL FINISH THE OTHER GUY!
RAT-TAT-TAT
GAS
THE RAFFERTY BROTHERS... THEY'VE KILLED DUGAN! OWW!
MESCOL 17½ GAS

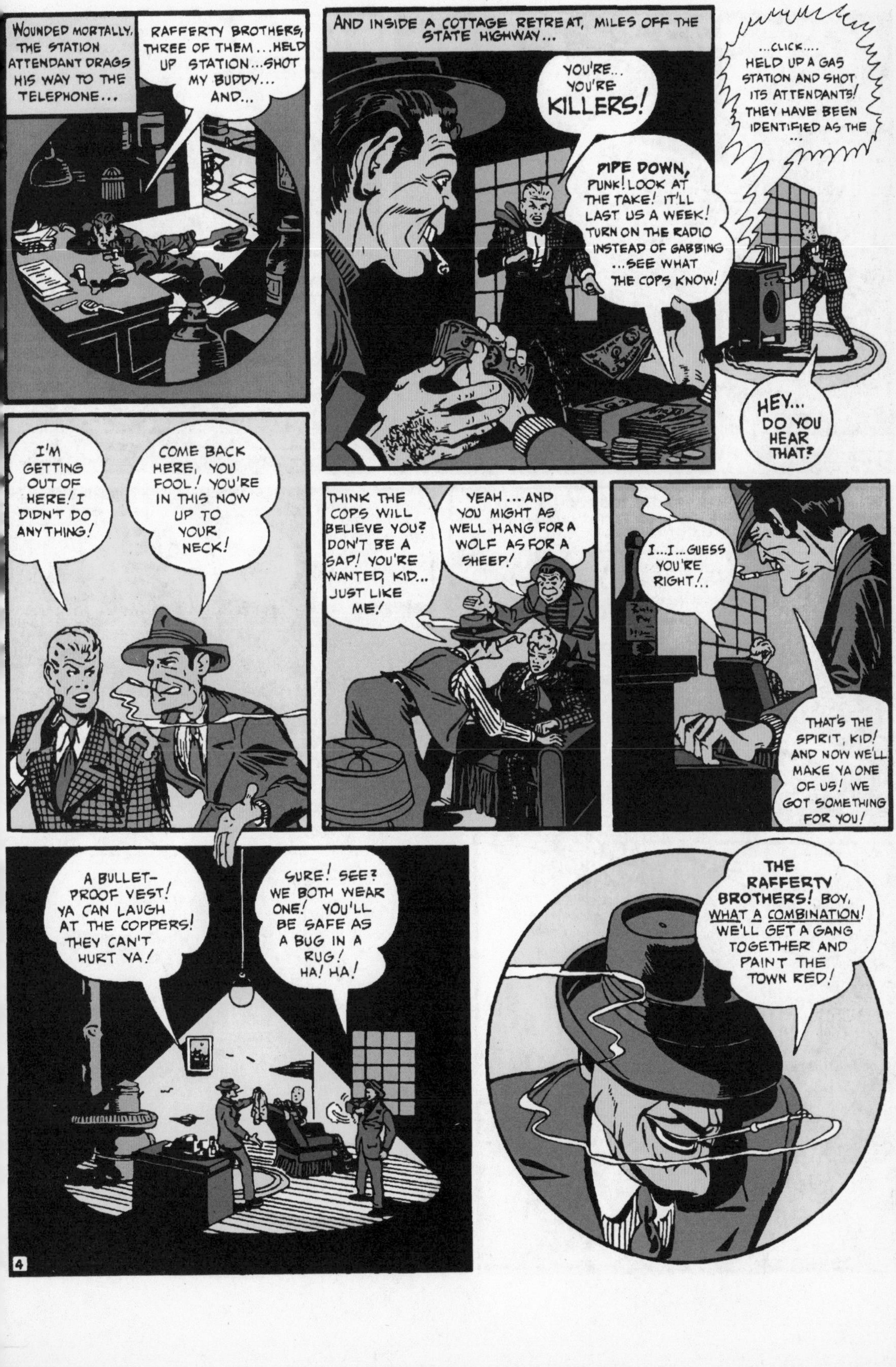
WOUNDED MORTALLY, THE STATION ATTENDANT DRAGS HIS WAY TO THE TELEPHONE...
RAFFERTY BROTHERS, THREE OF THEM... HELD UP STATION... SHOT MY BUDDY... AND...
AND INSIDE A COTTAGE RETREAT, MILES OFF THE STATE HIGHWAY...
YOU'RE... YOU'RE KILLERS!
DIPE DOWN, PUNK! LOOK AT THE TAKE! IT'LL LAST US A WEEK! TURN ON THE RADIO INSTEAD OF GABBING ...SEE WHAT THE COPS KNOW!
...CLICK.... HELD UP A GAS STATION AND SHOT ITS ATTENDANTS! THEY HAVE BEEN IDENTIFIED AS THE ...
HEY... DO YOU HEAR THAT?
I'M GETTING OUT OF HERE! I DIDN'T DO ANYTHING!
COME BACK HERE, YOU FOOL! YOU'RE IN THIS NOW UP TO YOUR NECK!
THINK THE COPS WILL BELIEVE YOU? DON'T BE A SAP! YOU'RE WANTED, KID... JUST LIKE ME!
YEAH ... AND YOU MIGHT AS WELL HANG FOR A WOLF AS FOR A SHEEP!
I...I...GUESS YOU'RE RIGHT!..
THAT'S THE SPIRIT, KID! AND NOW WE'LL MAKE YA ONE OF US! WE GOT SOMETHING FOR YOU!
A BULLET-PROOF VEST! YA CAN LAUGH AT THE COPPERS! THEY CAN'T HURT YA!
SURE! SEE? WE BOTH WEAR ONE! YOU'LL BE SAFE AS A BUG IN A RUG! HA! HA!
THE RAFFERTY BROTHERS! BOY, WHAT A COMBINATION! WE'LL GET A GANG TOGETHER AND PAINT THE TOWN RED!
4

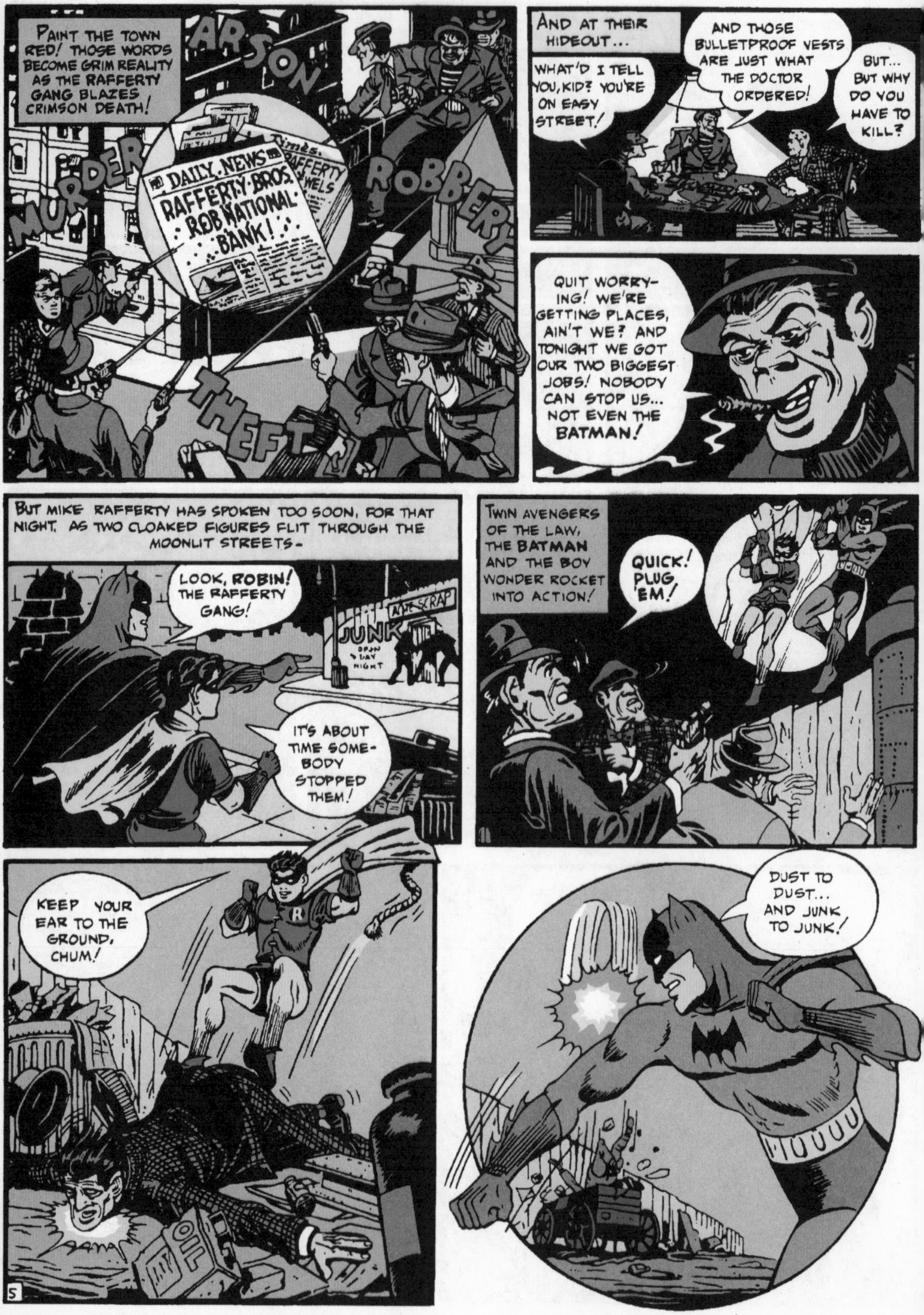
PAINT THE TOWN RED! THOSE WORDS BECOME GRIM REALITY AS THE RAFFERTY GANG BLAZES CRIMSON DEATH!
ARSON
MURDER
DAILY NEWS
RAFFERTY BROS ROB NATIONAL BANK!
ROBBERY
THEFT
AND AT THEIR HIDEOUT...
WHAT'D I TELL YOU, KID? YOU'RE ON EASY STREET!
AND THOSE BULLETPROOF VESTS ARE JUST WHAT THE DOCTOR ORDERED!
BUT... BUT WHY DO YOU HAVE TO KILL?
QUIT WORRYING! WE'RE GETTING PLACES, AIN'T WE? AND TONIGHT WE GOT OUR TWO BIGGEST JOBS! NOBODY CAN STOP US... NOT EVEN THE BATMAN!
BUT MIKE RAFFERTY HAS SPOKEN TOO SOON, FOR THAT NIGHT, AS TWO CLOAKED FIGURES FLIT THROUGH THE MOONLIT STREETS-
LOOK, ROBIN! THE RAFFERTY GANG!
JUNK
OPEN DAY NIGHT
IT'S ABOUT TIME SOMEBODY STOPPED THEM!
TWIN AVENGERS OF THE LAW, THE BATMAN AND THE BOY WONDER ROCKET INTO ACTION!
QUICK! PLUG 'EM!
KEEP YOUR EAR TO THE GROUND, CHUM!
OIL
5
DUST TO DUST... AND JUNK TO JUNK!

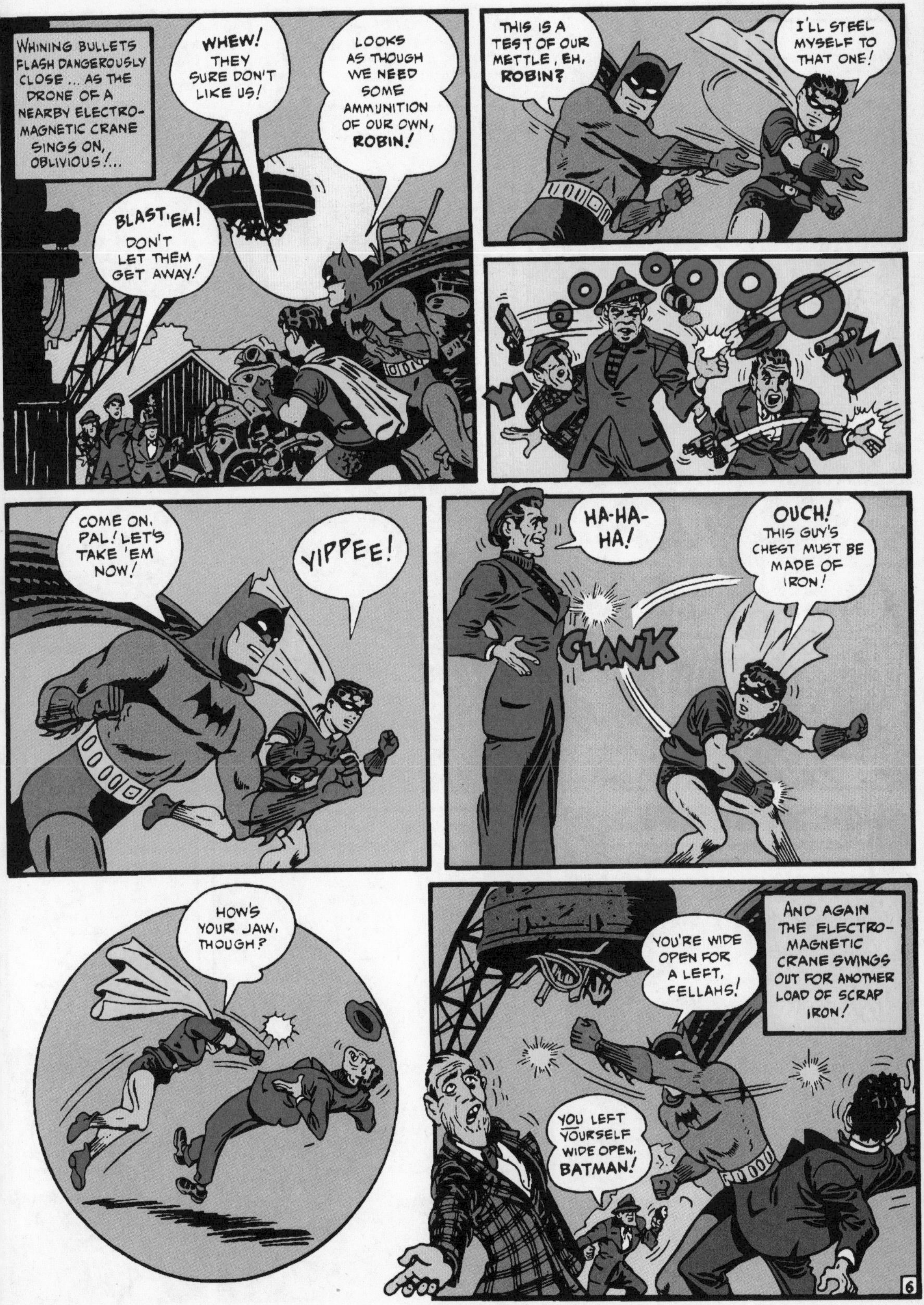

WHINING BULLETS FLASH DANGEROUSLY CLOSE ... AS THE DRONE OF A NEARBY ELECTRO-MAGNETIC CRANE SINGS ON, OBLIVIOUS!...
WHEW! THEY SURE DON'T LIKE US!
LOOKS AS THOUGH WE NEED SOME AMMUNITION OF OUR OWN, ROBIN!
BLAST 'EM! DON'T LET THEM GET AWAY!
THIS IS A TEST OF OUR METTLE, EH, ROBIN?
I'LL STEEL MYSELF TO THAT ONE!
YI
OOOOOOW
COME ON, PAL! LET'S TAKE 'EM NOW!
YIPPEE!
HA-HA-HA!
OUCH! THIS GUY'S CHEST MUST BE MADE OF IRON!
CLANK
HOW'S YOUR JAW, THOUGH?
AND AGAIN THE ELECTRO-MAGNETIC CRANE SWINGS OUT FOR ANOTHER LOAD OF SCRAP IRON!
YOU'RE WIDE OPEN FOR A LEFT, FELLAHS!
YOU LEFT YOURSELF WIDE OPEN, BATMAN!
6

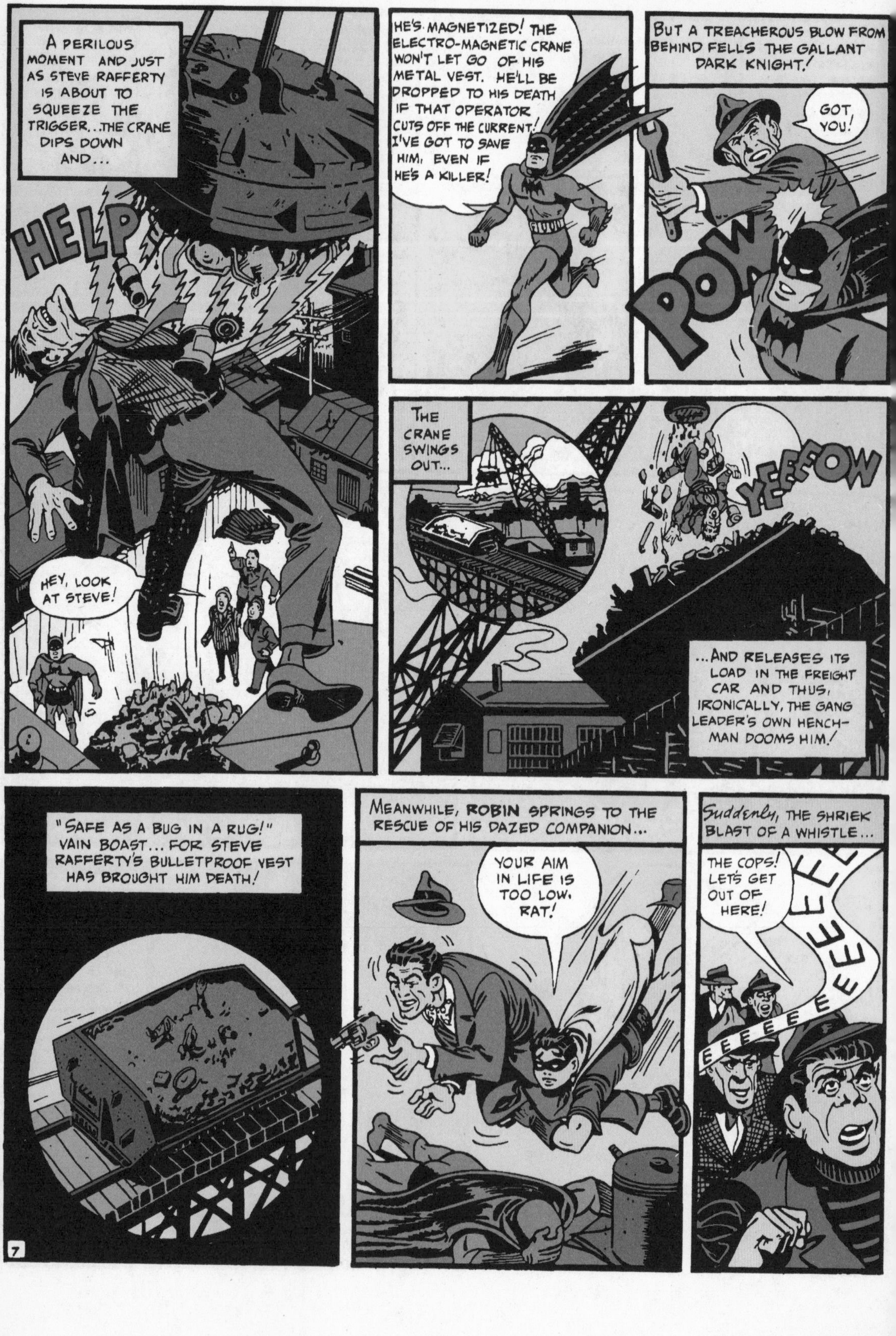
A PERILOUS MOMENT AND JUST AS STEVE RAFFERTY IS ABOUT TO SQUEEZE THE TRIGGER...THE CRANE DIPS DOWN AND...
HELP
HEY, LOOK AT STEVE!
HE'S MAGNETIZED! THE ELECTRO-MAGNETIC CRANE WON'T LET GO OF HIS METAL VEST. HE'LL BE DROPPED TO HIS DEATH IF THAT OPERATOR CUTS OFF THE CURRENT! I'VE GOT TO SAVE HIM, EVEN IF HE'S A KILLER!
BUT A TREACHEROUS BLOW FROM BEHIND FELLS THE GALLANT DARK KNIGHT!
GOT YOU!
POW
THE CRANE SWINGS OUT...
YEEEOW
...AND RELEASES ITS LOAD IN THE FREIGHT CAR AND THUS, IRONICALLY, THE GANG LEADER'S OWN HENCHMAN DOOMS HIM!
"SAFE AS A BUG IN A RUG!" VAIN BOAST... FOR STEVE RAFFERTY'S BULLETPROOF VEST HAS BROUGHT HIM DEATH!
7
MEANWHILE, ROBIN SPRINGS TO THE RESCUE OF HIS DAZED COMPANION...
YOUR AIM IN LIFE IS TOO LOW, RAT!
Suddenly, THE SHRIEK BLAST OF A WHISTLE...
THE COPS! LET'S GET OUT OF HERE!
EEEEEEEEEEEE

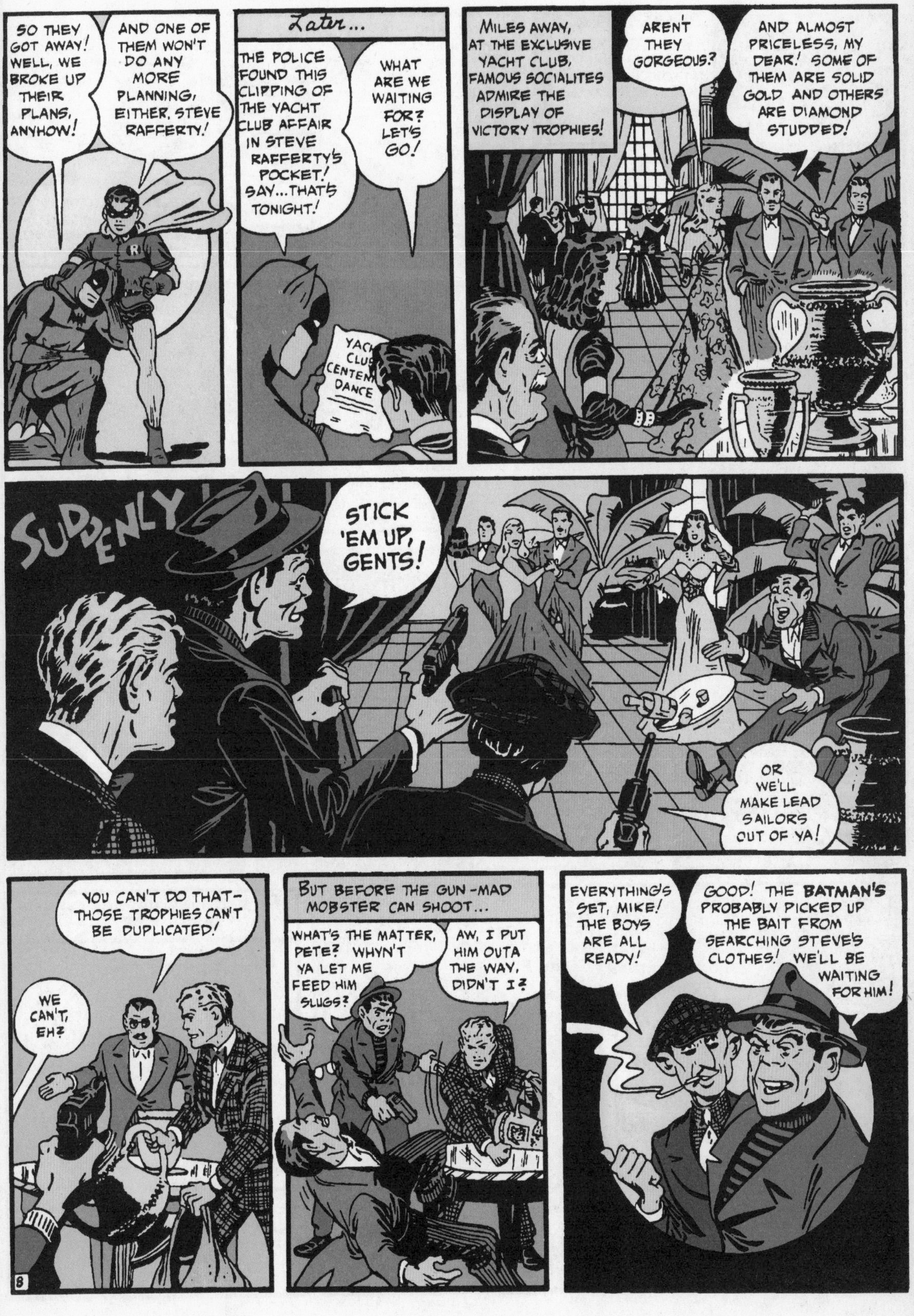
SO THEY GOT AWAY! WELL, WE BROKE UP THEIR PLANS, ANYHOW!
AND ONE OF THEM WON'T DO ANY MORE PLANNING, EITHER, STEVE RAFFERTY!
Later...
THE POLICE FOUND THIS CLIPPING OF THE YACHT CLUB AFFAIR IN STEVE RAFFERTY'S POCKET! SAY...THAT'S TONIGHT!
WHAT ARE WE WAITING FOR? LET'S GO!
MILES AWAY, AT THE EXCLUSIVE YACHT CLUB, FAMOUS SOCIALITES ADMIRE THE DISPLAY OF VICTORY TROPHIES!
AREN'T THEY GORGEOUS?
AND ALMOST PRICELESS, MY DEAR! SOME OF THEM ARE SOLID GOLD AND OTHERS ARE DIAMOND STUDDED!
SUDDENLY
STICK 'EM UP, GENTS!
OR WE'LL MAKE LEAD SAILORS OUT OF YA!
YOU CAN'T DO THAT-THOSE TROPHIES CAN'T BE DUPLICATED!
WE CAN'T, EH?
8
BUT BEFORE THE GUN-MAD MOBSTER CAN SHOOT...
WHAT'S THE MATTER, PETE? WHYN'T YA LET ME FEED HIM SLUGS?
AW, I PUT HIM OUTA THE WAY, DIDN'T I?
EVERYTHING'S SET, MIKE! THE BOYS ARE ALL READY!
GOOD! THE BATMAN'S PROBABLY PICKED UP THE BAIT FROM SEARCHING STEVE'S CLOTHES! WE'LL BE WAITING FOR HIM!

At that moment, the streamlined Batmobile nears the yacht club at a mile-a-minute clip...

YACHT CLUB →

THEY'RE PULLING UP THE DRAW-BRIDGE!

WE CAN'T STOP! WE'LL HAVE TO GO AHEAD! HOLD TIGHT!

WHO SAID YOU SHOULD NEVER CROSS A BRIDGE BEFORE COMING TO IT?

I DUNNO... BUT WE'RE DOING IT!

ZOOM

Accelerating to full speed, the super-charged car shoots forward across empty space.

ZUMP

YEOW! BACK TO THE CLUB HOUSE! WE'LL FIX 'EM!

...And makes a four-wheel landing!

LAST STOP!

ALL OUT— FOR ACTION!

As the power-house pair leaps toward the club veranda, a huge wire mesh-net swoops down from above.

HA! THEY WALKED RIGHT IN-TO IT!

LOOK AT 'EM--THE BATMAN AND ROBIN! SOME CATCH!

HURRY UP! WE'LL TAKE 'EM FOR A NEW KIND OF RIDE!

THEY'LL BE DEAD FISH IN NO TIME!

WELL, I GUESS I'LL MEET THE GANG AT THE HIDEOUT. NO ONE COULD SAVE BATMAN AND ROBIN NOW. NOT EVEN ME!

NOTHING IN MY UTILITY BELT IS SHARP ENOUGH TO CUT THIS WIRE! EXCEPT... MAYBE...

THERE'S NO WAY OF ESCAPE! WE'LL DROWN!

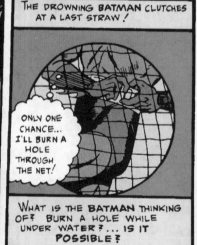

THE DROWNING BATMAN clutches at a last straw!

ONLY ONE CHANCE... I'LL BURN A HOLE THROUGH THE NET!

WHAT IS THE BATMAN THINKING OF? BURN A HOLE WHILE UNDER WATER?... IS IT POSSIBLE?

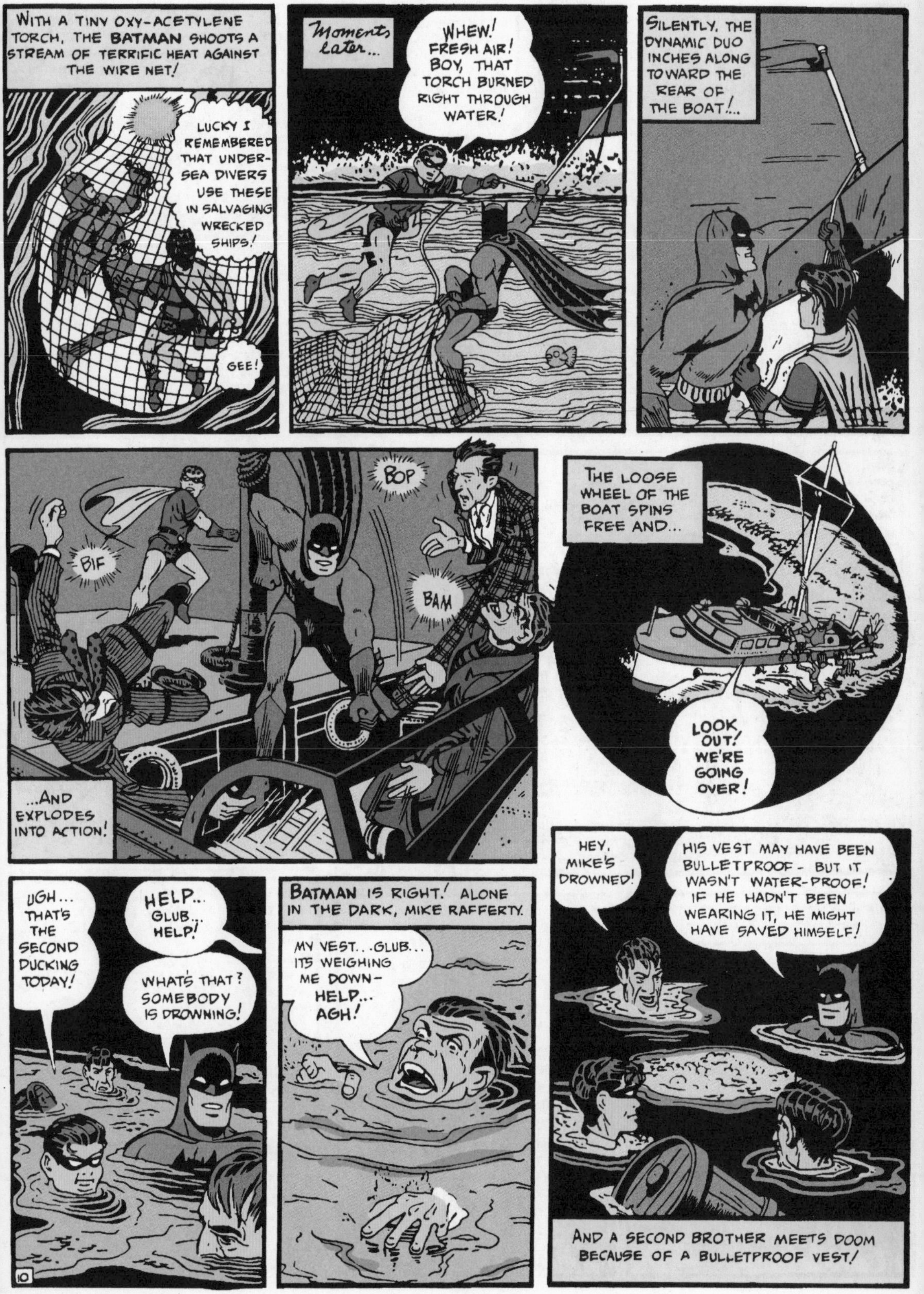

WITH A TINY OXY-ACETYLENE TORCH, THE BATMAN SHOOTS A STREAM OF TERRIFIC HEAT AGAINST THE WIRE NET!
LUCKY I REMEMBERED THAT UNDER-SEA DIVERS USE THESE IN SALVAGING WRECKED SHIPS!
GEE!
Moments later...
WHEW! FRESH AIR! BOY, THAT TORCH BURNED RIGHT THROUGH WATER!
SILENTLY, THE DYNAMIC DUO INCHES ALONG TOWARD THE REAR OF THE BOAT!...
BOP
BIF
BAM
...AND EXPLODES INTO ACTION!
THE LOOSE WHEEL OF THE BOAT SPINS FREE AND...
LOOK OUT! WE'RE GOING OVER!
UGH... THAT'S THE SECOND DUCKING TODAY!
HELP... GLUB... HELP!
WHAT'S THAT? SOMEBODY IS DROWNING!
10
BATMAN IS RIGHT! ALONE IN THE DARK, MIKE RAFFERTY.
MY VEST...GLUB... ITS WEIGHING ME DOWN- HELP... AGH!
HEY, MIKE'S DROWNED!
HIS VEST MAY HAVE BEEN BULLETPROOF - BUT IT WASN'T WATER-PROOF! IF HE HADN'T BEEN WEARING IT, HE MIGHT HAVE SAVED HIMSELF!
AND A SECOND BROTHER MEETS DOOM BECAUSE OF A BULLETPROOF VEST!

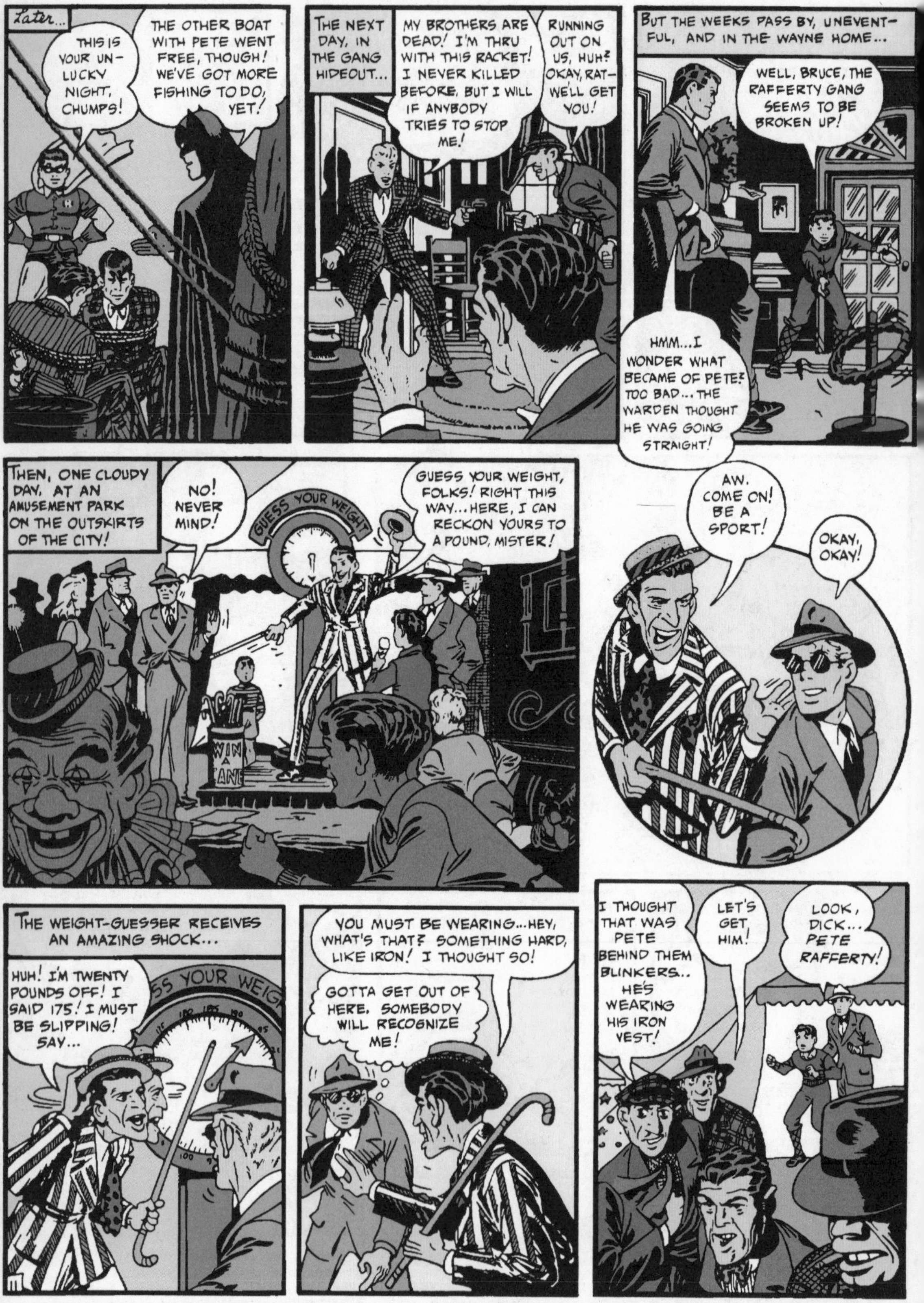
Later...
THIS IS YOUR UNLUCKY NIGHT, CHUMPS!
THE OTHER BOAT WITH PETE WENT FREE, THOUGH! WE'VE GOT MORE FISHING TO DO, YET!
THE NEXT DAY, IN THE GANG HIDEOUT...
MY BROTHERS ARE DEAD! I'M THRU WITH THIS RACKET! I NEVER KILLED BEFORE, BUT I WILL IF ANYBODY TRIES TO STOP ME!
RUNNING OUT ON US, HUH? OKAY, RAT-- WE'LL GET YOU!
BUT THE WEEKS PASS BY, UNEVENTFUL, AND IN THE WAYNE HOME...
WELL, BRUCE, THE RAFFERTY GANG SEEMS TO BE BROKEN UP!
HMM...I WONDER WHAT BECAME OF PETE? TOO BAD... THE WARDEN THOUGHT HE WAS GOING STRAIGHT!
THEN, ONE CLOUDY DAY, AT AN AMUSEMENT PARK ON THE OUTSKIRTS OF THE CITY!
NO! NEVER MIND!
GUESS YOUR WEIGHT
GUESS YOUR WEIGHT, FOLKS! RIGHT THIS WAY... HERE, I CAN RECKON YOURS TO A POUND, MISTER!
WIN A CANE
AW. COME ON! BE A SPORT!
OKAY, OKAY!
THE WEIGHT-GUESSER RECEIVES AN AMAZING SHOCK...
HUH! I'M TWENTY POUNDS OFF! I SAID 175! I MUST BE SLIPPING! SAY...
YOU MUST BE WEARING...HEY, WHAT'S THAT? SOMETHING HARD, LIKE IRON! I THOUGHT SO!
GOTTA GET OUT OF HERE. SOMEBODY WILL RECOGNIZE ME!
I THOUGHT THAT WAS PETE BEHIND THEM BLINKERS.. HE'S WEARING HIS IRON VEST!
LET'S GET HIM!
LOOK, DICK... PETE RAFFERTY!

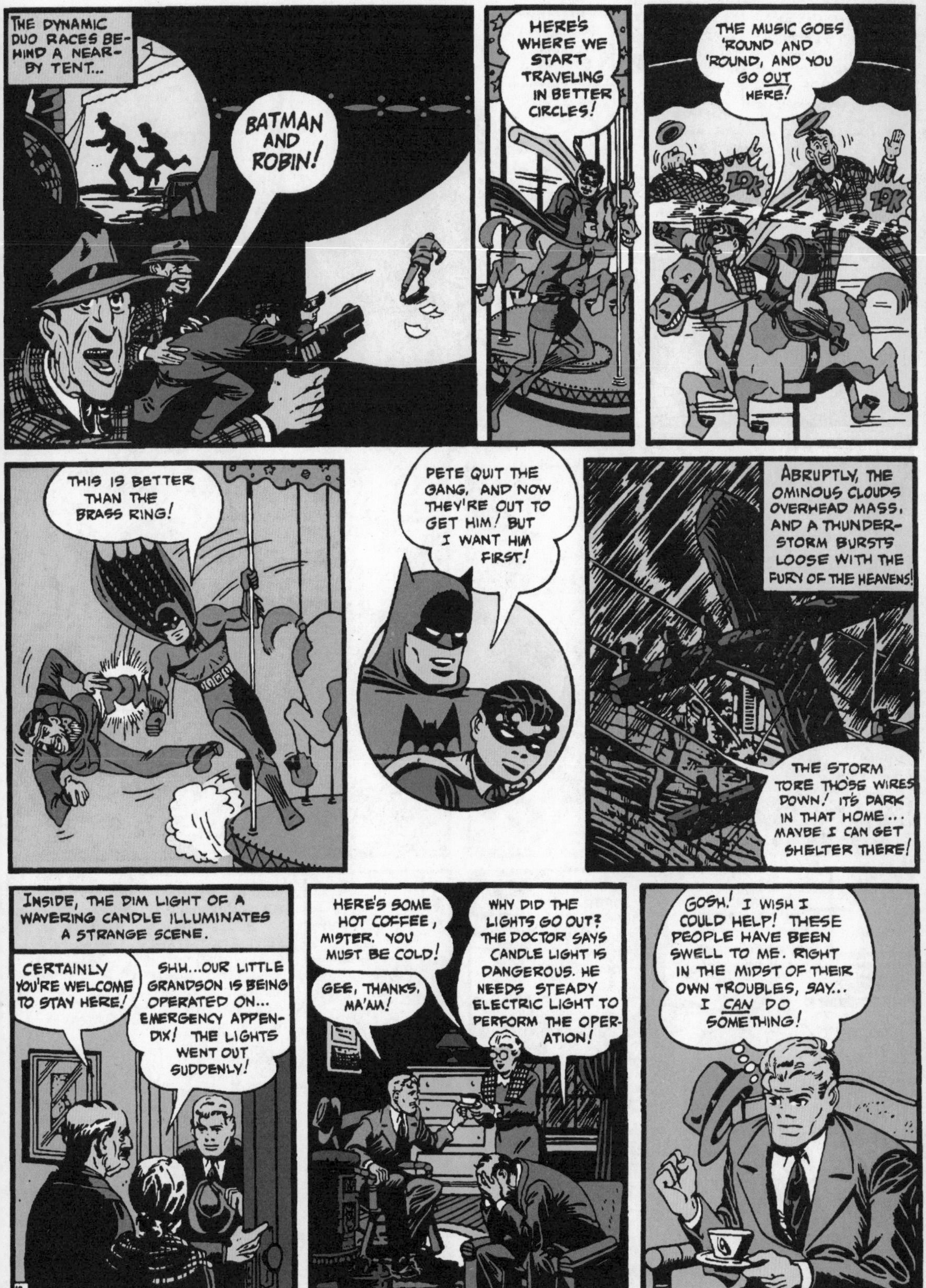
THE DYNAMIC DUO RACES BEHIND A NEAR-BY TENT...
BATMAN AND ROBIN!
HERE'S WHERE WE START TRAVELING IN BETTER CIRCLES!
THE MUSIC GOES 'ROUND AND 'ROUND, AND YOU GO OUT HERE!
ZOK
ZOK
THIS IS BETTER THAN THE BRASS RING!
PETE QUIT THE GANG, AND NOW THEY'RE OUT TO GET HIM! BUT I WANT HIM FIRST!
ABRUPTLY, THE OMINOUS CLOUDS OVERHEAD MASS, AND A THUNDER-STORM BURSTS LOOSE WITH THE FURY OF THE HEAVENS!
THE STORM TORE THOSE WIRES DOWN! IT'S DARK IN THAT HOME... MAYBE I CAN GET SHELTER THERE!
INSIDE, THE DIM LIGHT OF A WAVERING CANDLE ILLUMINATES A STRANGE SCENE.
CERTAINLY YOU'RE WELCOME TO STAY HERE!
SHH...OUR LITTLE GRANDSON IS BEING OPERATED ON... EMERGENCY APPEN-DIX! THE LIGHTS WENT OUT SUDDENLY!
12
HERE'S SOME HOT COFFEE, MISTER. YOU MUST BE COLD!
GEE, THANKS, MA'AM!
WHY DID THE LIGHTS GO OUT? THE DOCTOR SAYS CANDLE LIGHT IS DANGEROUS. HE NEEDS STEADY ELECTRIC LIGHT TO PERFORM THE OPER-ATION!
GOSH! I WISH I COULD HELP! THESE PEOPLE HAVE BEEN SWELL TO ME. RIGHT IN THE MIDST OF THEIR OWN TROUBLES, SAY... I CAN DO SOMETHING!

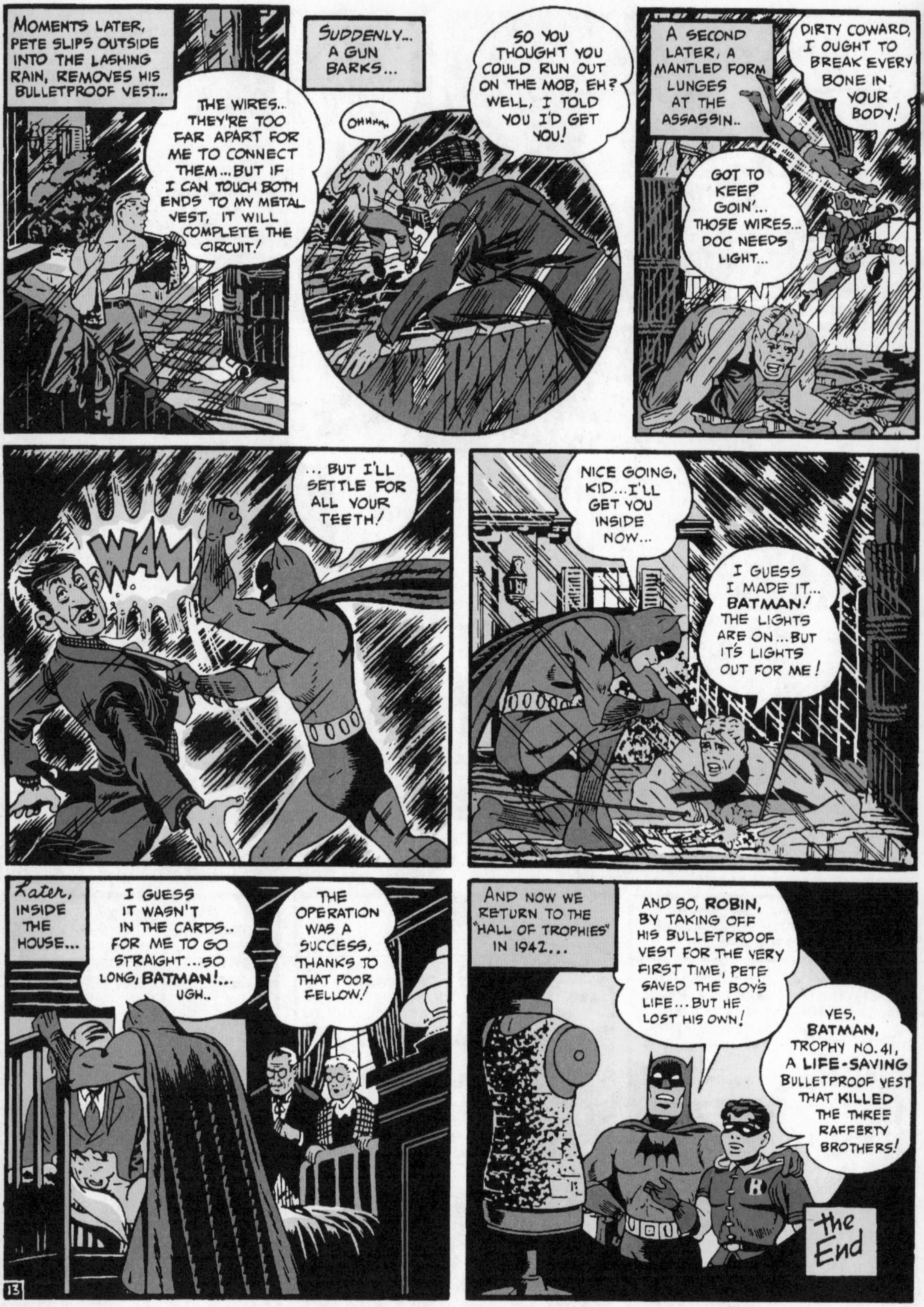

MOMENTS LATER, PETE SLIPS OUTSIDE INTO THE LASHING RAIN, REMOVES HIS BULLETPROOF VEST...
THE WIRES.. THEY'RE TOO FAR APART FOR ME TO CONNECT THEM... BUT IF I CAN TOUCH BOTH ENDS TO MY METAL VEST, IT WILL COMPLETE THE CIRCUIT!
SUDDENLY.. A GUN BARKS...
OHHHHH..
SO YOU THOUGHT YOU COULD RUN OUT ON THE MOB, EH? WELL, I TOLD YOU I'D GET YOU!
A SECOND LATER, A MANTLED FORM LUNGES AT THE ASSASSIN..
DIRTY COWARD, I OUGHT TO BREAK EVERY BONE IN YOUR BODY!
POW
GOT TO KEEP GOIN'... THOSE WIRES... DOC NEEDS LIGHT...
... BUT I'LL SETTLE FOR ALL YOUR TEETH!
WAM
NICE GOING, KID... I'LL GET YOU INSIDE NOW...
I GUESS I MADE IT... BATMAN! THE LIGHTS ARE ON... BUT IT'S LIGHTS OUT FOR ME!
Later, INSIDE THE HOUSE...
I GUESS IT WASN'T IN THE CARDS.. FOR ME TO GO STRAIGHT... SO LONG, BATMAN!... UGH..
THE OPERATION WAS A SUCCESS, THANKS TO THAT POOR FELLOW!
13
AND NOW WE RETURN TO THE "HALL OF TROPHIES" IN 1942...
AND SO, ROBIN, BY TAKING OFF HIS BULLETPROOF VEST FOR THE VERY FIRST TIME, PETE SAVED THE BOY'S LIFE... BUT HE LOST HIS OWN!
YES, BATMAN, TROPHY NO. 41, A LIFE-SAVING BULLETPROOF VEST THAT KILLED THE THREE RAFFERTY BROTHERS!
the End

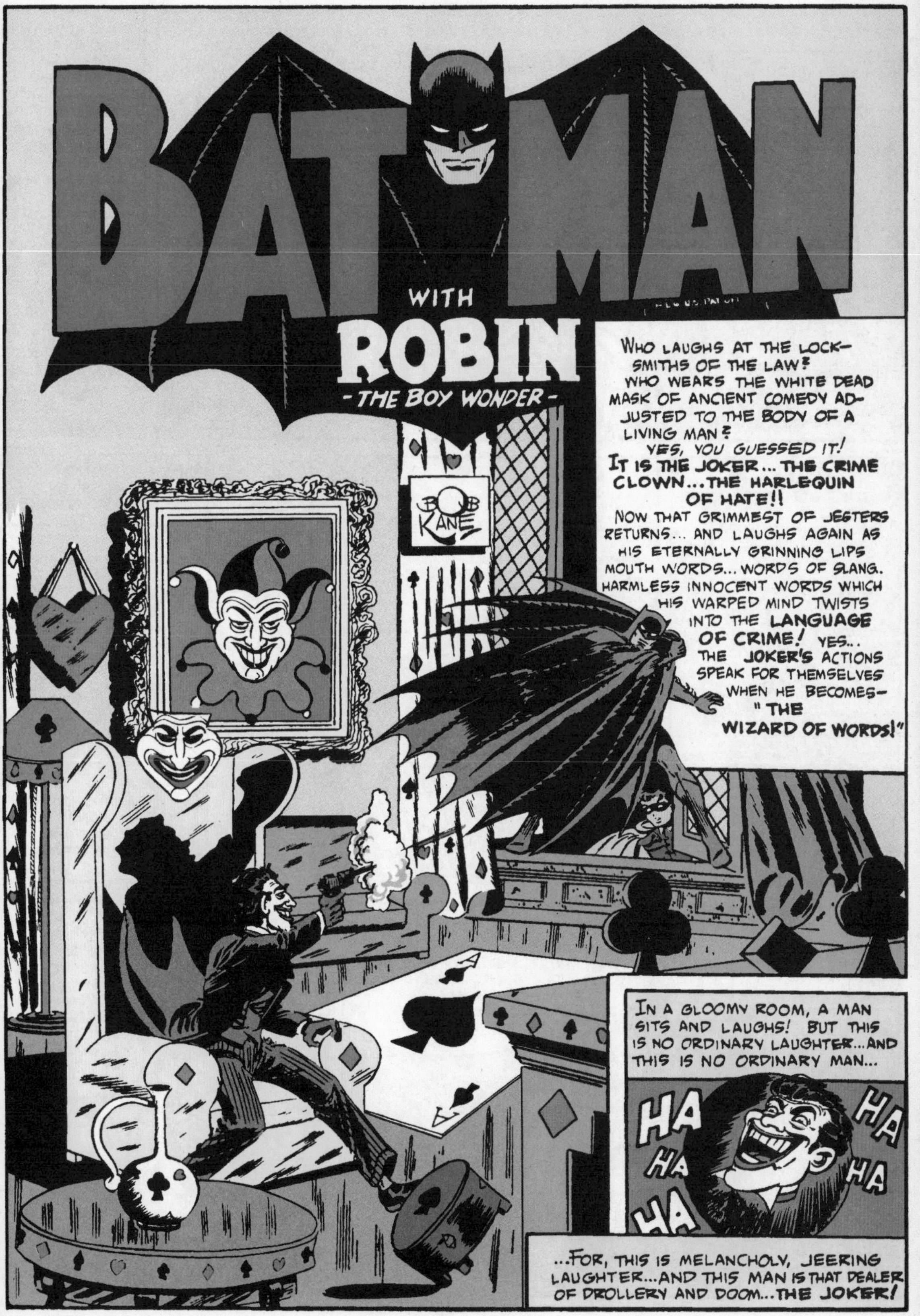

BATMAN
WITH
ROBIN
-THE BOY WONDER-
BOB KANE
WHO LAUGHS AT THE LOCKSMITHS OF THE LAW? WHO WEARS THE WHITE DEAD MASK OF ANCIENT COMEDY ADJUSTED TO THE BODY OF A LIVING MAN? YES, YOU GUESSED IT! IT IS THE JOKER... THE CRIME CLOWN... THE HARLEQUIN OF HATE!! NOW THAT GRIMMEST OF JESTERS RETURNS... AND LAUGHS AGAIN AS HIS ETERNALLY GRINNING LIPS MOUTH WORDS... WORDS OF SLANG. HARMLESS INNOCENT WORDS WHICH HIS WARPED MIND TWISTS INTO THE LANGUAGE OF CRIME! YES.. THE JOKER'S ACTIONS SPEAK FOR THEMSELVES WHEN HE BECOMES- "THE WIZARD OF WORDS!"
IN A GLOOMY ROOM, A MAN SITS AND LAUGHS! BUT THIS IS NO ORDINARY LAUGHTER...AND THIS IS NO ORDINARY MAN...
HA HA HA HA HA HA
...FOR, THIS IS MELANCHOLY, JEERING LAUGHTER...AND THIS MAN IS THAT DEALER OF DROLLERY AND DOOM...THE JOKER!

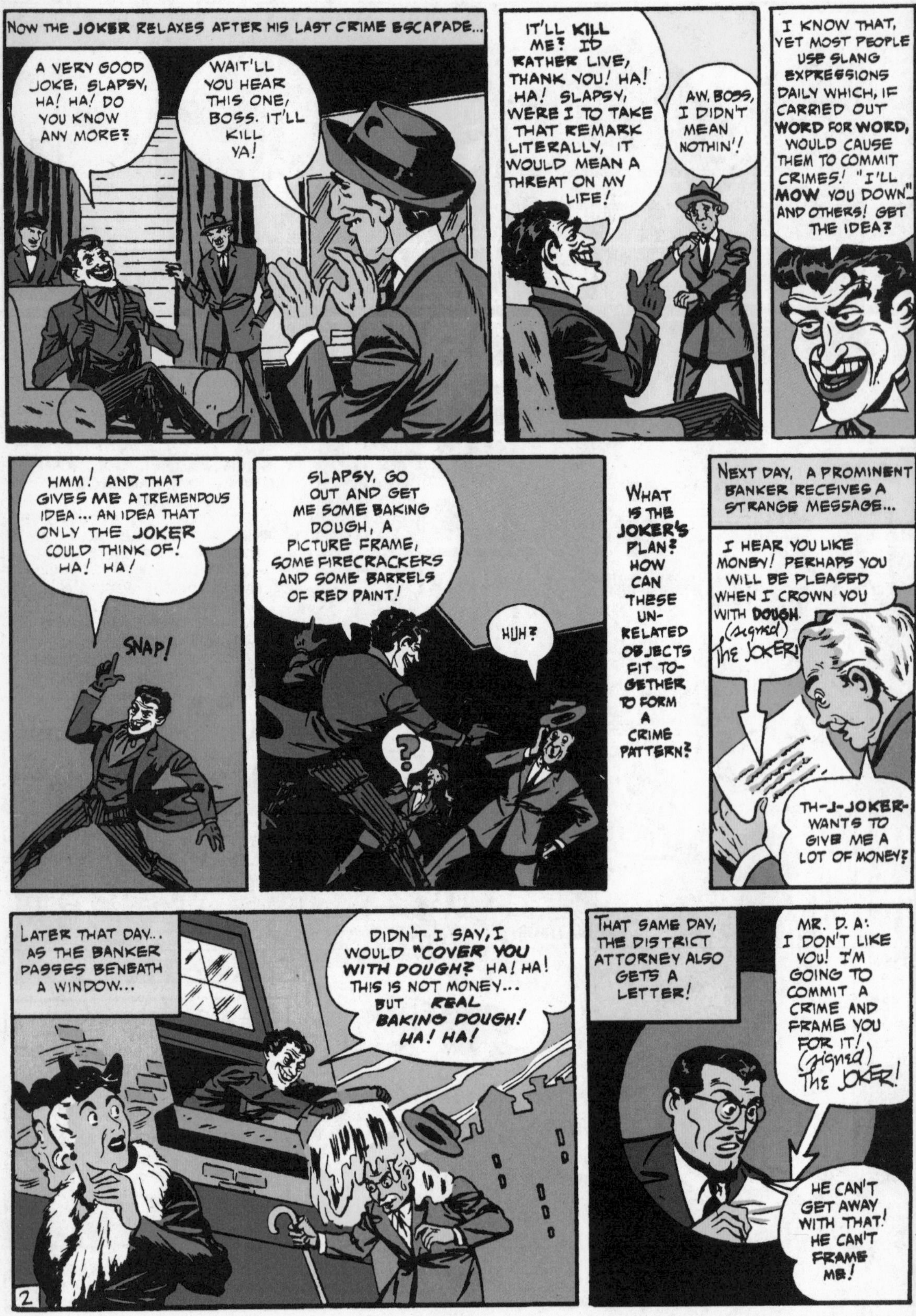
NOW THE JOKER RELAXES AFTER HIS LAST CRIME ESCAPADE...
A VERY GOOD JOKE, SLAPSY, HA! HA! DO YOU KNOW ANY MORE?
WAIT'LL YOU HEAR THIS ONE, BOSS. IT'LL KILL YA!
IT'LL KILL ME? I'D RATHER LIVE, THANK YOU! HA! HA! SLAPSY, WERE I TO TAKE THAT REMARK LITERALLY, IT WOULD MEAN A THREAT ON MY LIFE!
AW, BOSS, I DIDN'T MEAN NOTHIN'!
I KNOW THAT, YET MOST PEOPLE USE SLANG EXPRESSIONS DAILY WHICH, IF CARRIED OUT WORD FOR WORD, WOULD CAUSE THEM TO COMMIT CRIMES! "I'LL MOW YOU DOWN" AND OTHERS! GET THE IDEA?
HMM! AND THAT GIVES ME A TREMENDOUS IDEA... AN IDEA THAT ONLY THE JOKER COULD THINK OF! HA! HA!
SNAP!
SLAPSY, GO OUT AND GET ME SOME BAKING DOUGH, A PICTURE FRAME, SOME FIRECRACKERS AND SOME BARRELS OF RED PAINT!
HUH?
?
WHAT IS THE JOKER'S PLAN? HOW CAN THESE UN-RELATED OBJECTS FIT TO-GETHER TO FORM A CRIME PATTERN?
NEXT DAY, A PROMINENT BANKER RECEIVES A STRANGE MESSAGE...
I HEAR YOU LIKE MONEY! PERHAPS YOU WILL BE PLEASED WHEN I CROWN YOU WITH DOUGH. (signed) THE JOKER!
TH-J-JOKER WANTS TO GIVE ME A LOT OF MONEY?
LATER THAT DAY... AS THE BANKER PASSES BENEATH A WINDOW...
DIDN'T I SAY, I WOULD "COVER YOU WITH DOUGH? HA! HA! THIS IS NOT MONEY... BUT REAL BAKING DOUGH! HA! HA!
2
THAT SAME DAY, THE DISTRICT ATTORNEY ALSO GETS A LETTER!
MR. D. A: I DON'T LIKE YOU! I'M GOING TO COMMIT A CRIME AND FRAME YOU FOR IT! (signed) THE JOKER!
HE CAN'T GET AWAY WITH THAT! HE CAN'T FRAME ME!

BUT THE D.A. IS WRONG... ALL THE WAY! FOR, THE NEXT DAY...

WH... WHAT'S HAPPENED?

THE JOKER FRAMED ME... BUT NOT IN THE WAY I EXPECTED!

THEN, THE MAYOR RECEIVES A MESSAGE!

"You'll see fireworks in your office when I start with you. The JOKER"

OH-H-H... FIREWORKS! THAT MEANS HE'S GOING TO MAKE SOME SORT OF TROUBLE FOR ME!

BUT WHEN THE MAYOR ENTERS HIS OFFICE THE NEXT DAY, HE IS GREETED BY...

FIREWORKS! THE JOKER ACTUALLY DID MAKE FIREWORKS IN MY OFFICE!

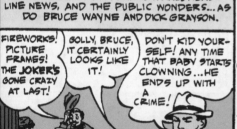

THE PLAGUE OF MAD PRANKS MAKES HEAD-LINE NEWS, AND THE PUBLIC WONDERS... AS DO BRUCE WAYNE AND DICK GRAYSON.

FIREWORKS! PICTURE FRAMES! THE JOKER'S GONE CRAZY AT LAST!

GOLLY, BRUCE, IT CERTAINLY LOOKS LIKE IT!

DON'T KID YOUR-SELF! ANY TIME THAT BABY STARTS CLOWNING... HE ENDS UP WITH A CRIME!

IS BRUCE RIGHT? IS THERE A CALCULATING THREAD OF EVIL WINDING THROUGH THIS PATTERN OF MAD MIRTH? LET'S SEE...

THE NEXT DAY... COMMISSIONER GORDON GETS A NOTE.

SO... HE EXPECTS TO HAVE A RIP-ROARING TIME MAKING WHOOPEE, EH? I'LL HAVE THE BOYS PATROL THE NIGHT CLUB!

Gordon! Your police force had better watch out, for my men and I are going to PAINT THE TOWN RED! Whoopee! The Joker

SOME TIME LATER, A POLICE-MAN STARES IN WIDE-EYED ASTONISHMENT...

WHA... WHAT'S GOING ON AROUND HERE?

NOTHIN' MUCH! I'M JUST PAINTIN' THE SIDEWALK RED! HA!

AND SO IT GOES, AS AT VARIOUS SPOTS IN THE CITY FUGITIVE HOOD-LUMS LEAVE BEHIND A WAKE OF RED PAINT...

HAW! HAW!

HEY, YOU! COME BACK HERE!

WHILE HIGH IN THE SKY, THE JOKER RELEASES A FLOOD OF SCARLET OVER THE ROOF-TOPS...

HA... HA! I WARNED THEM I WOULD PAINT THE TOWN RED... AND I AM! HA... HA!

BANK

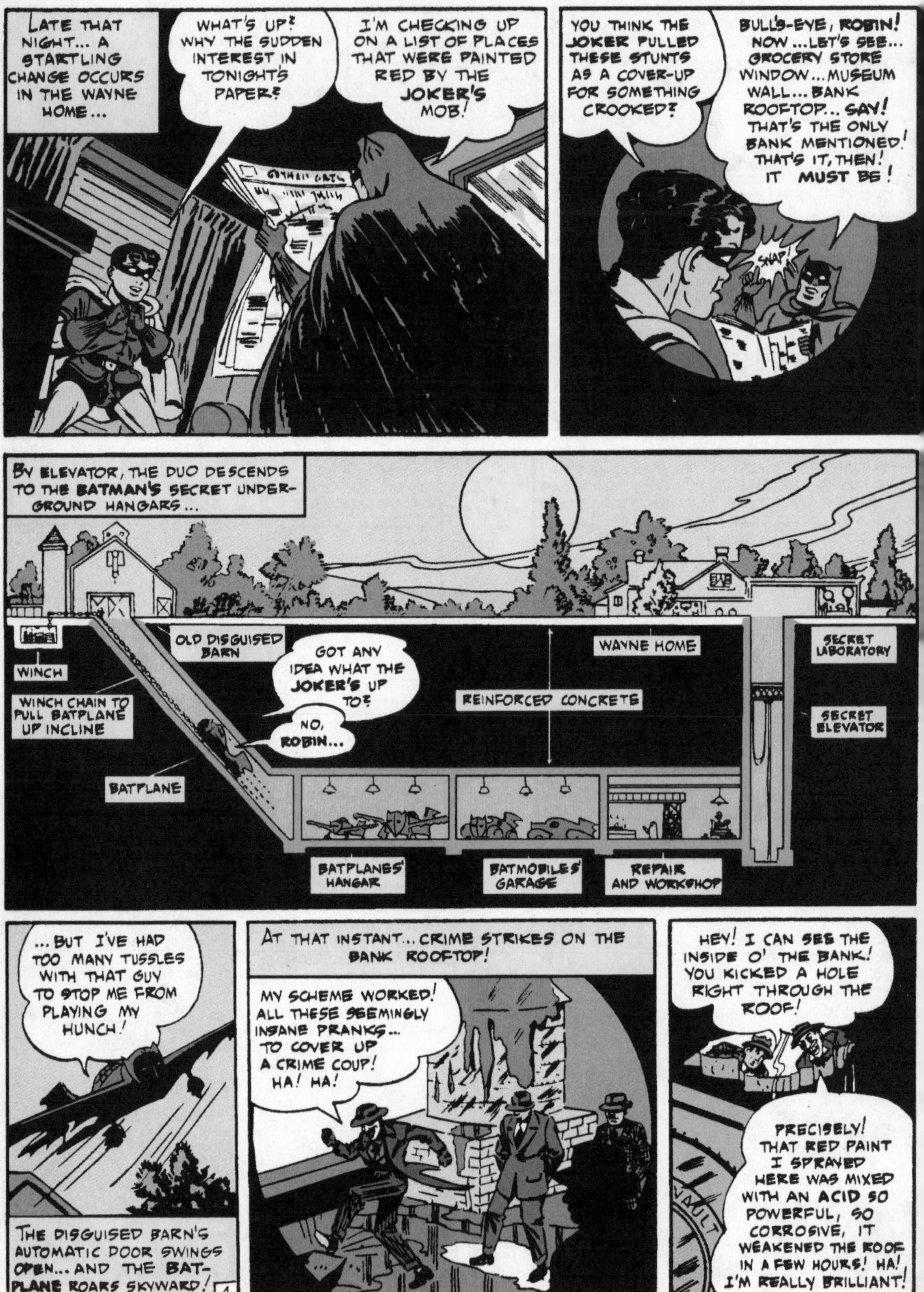
LATE THAT NIGHT... A STARTLING CHANGE OCCURS IN THE WAYNE HOME...
WHAT'S UP? WHY THE SUDDEN INTEREST IN TONIGHT'S PAPER?
I'M CHECKING UP ON A LIST OF PLACES THAT WERE PAINTED RED BY THE JOKER'S MOB!
YOU THINK THE JOKER PULLED THESE STUNTS AS A COVER-UP FOR SOMETHING CROOKED?
BULL'S-EYE, ROBIN! NOW ...LET'S SEE... GROCERY STORE WINDOW...MUSEUM WALL... BANK ROOFTOP... SAY! THAT'S THE ONLY BANK MENTIONED! THAT'S IT, THEN! IT MUST BE!
SNAP!
BY ELEVATOR, THE DUO DESCENDS TO THE BATMAN'S SECRET UNDER-GROUND HANGARS...
OLD DISGUISED BARN
WINCH
WINCH CHAIN TO PULL BATPLANE UP INCLINE
BATPLANE
GOT ANY IDEA WHAT THE JOKER'S UP TO?
NO, ROBIN...
WAYNE HOME
REINFORCED CONCRETE
SECRET LABORATORY
SECRET ELEVATOR
BATPLANES' HANGAR
BATMOBILES' GARAGE
REPAIR AND WORKSHOP
...BUT I'VE HAD TOO MANY TUSSLES WITH THAT GUY TO STOP ME FROM PLAYING MY HUNCH!
THE DISGUISED BARN'S AUTOMATIC DOOR SWINGS OPEN... AND THE BAT-PLANE ROARS SKYWARD!
4
AT THAT INSTANT...CRIME STRIKES ON THE BANK ROOFTOP!
MY SCHEME WORKED! ALL THESE SEEMINGLY INSANE PRANKS... TO COVER UP A CRIME COUP! HA! HA!
HEY! I CAN SEE THE INSIDE O' THE BANK! YOU KICKED A HOLE RIGHT THROUGH THE ROOF!
PRECISELY! THAT RED PAINT I SPRAYED HERE WAS MIXED WITH AN ACID SO POWERFUL, SO CORROSIVE, IT WEAKENED THE ROOF IN A FEW HOURS! HA! I'M REALLY BRILLIANT!
VAULT

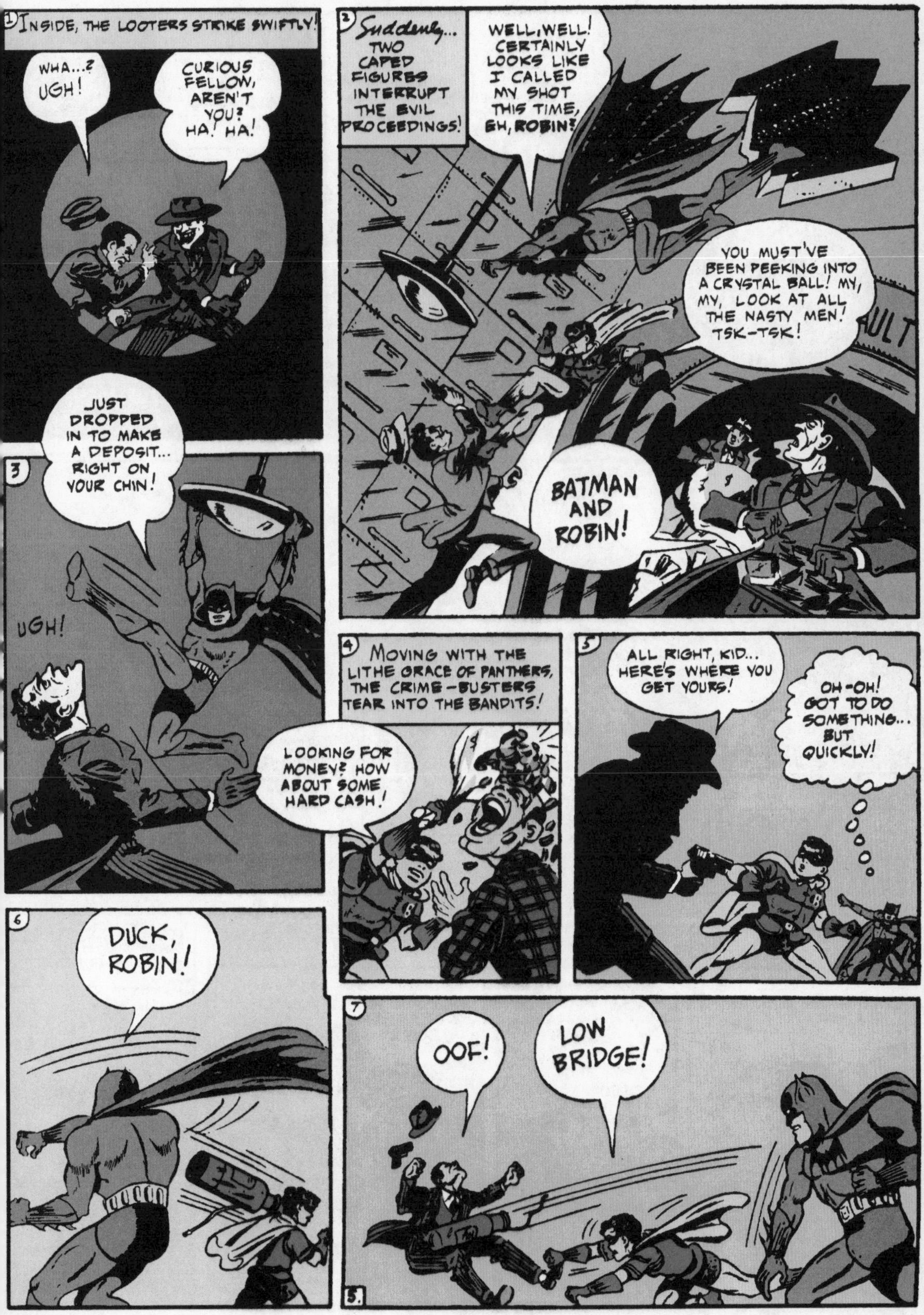
1
INSIDE, THE LOOTERS STRIKE SWIFTLY!
WHA...? UGH!
CURIOUS FELLOW, AREN'T YOU? HA! HA!
2
Suddenly... TWO CAPED FIGURES INTERRUPT THE EVIL PROCEEDINGS!
WELL, WELL! CERTAINLY LOOKS LIKE I CALLED MY SHOT THIS TIME, EH, ROBIN?
YOU MUST'VE BEEN PEEKING INTO A CRYSTAL BALL! MY, MY, LOOK AT ALL THE NASTY MEN! TSK-TSK!
BATMAN AND ROBIN!
3
JUST DROPPED IN TO MAKE A DEPOSIT... RIGHT ON YOUR CHIN!
UGH!
4
MOVING WITH THE LITHE GRACE OF PANTHERS, THE CRIME-BUSTERS TEAR INTO THE BANDITS!
LOOKING FOR MONEY? HOW ABOUT SOME HARD CASH!
5
ALL RIGHT, KID... HERE'S WHERE YOU GET YOURS!
OH-OH! GOT TO DO SOMETHING... BUT QUICKLY!
6
DUCK, ROBIN!
7
OOF!
LOW BRIDGE!
5.

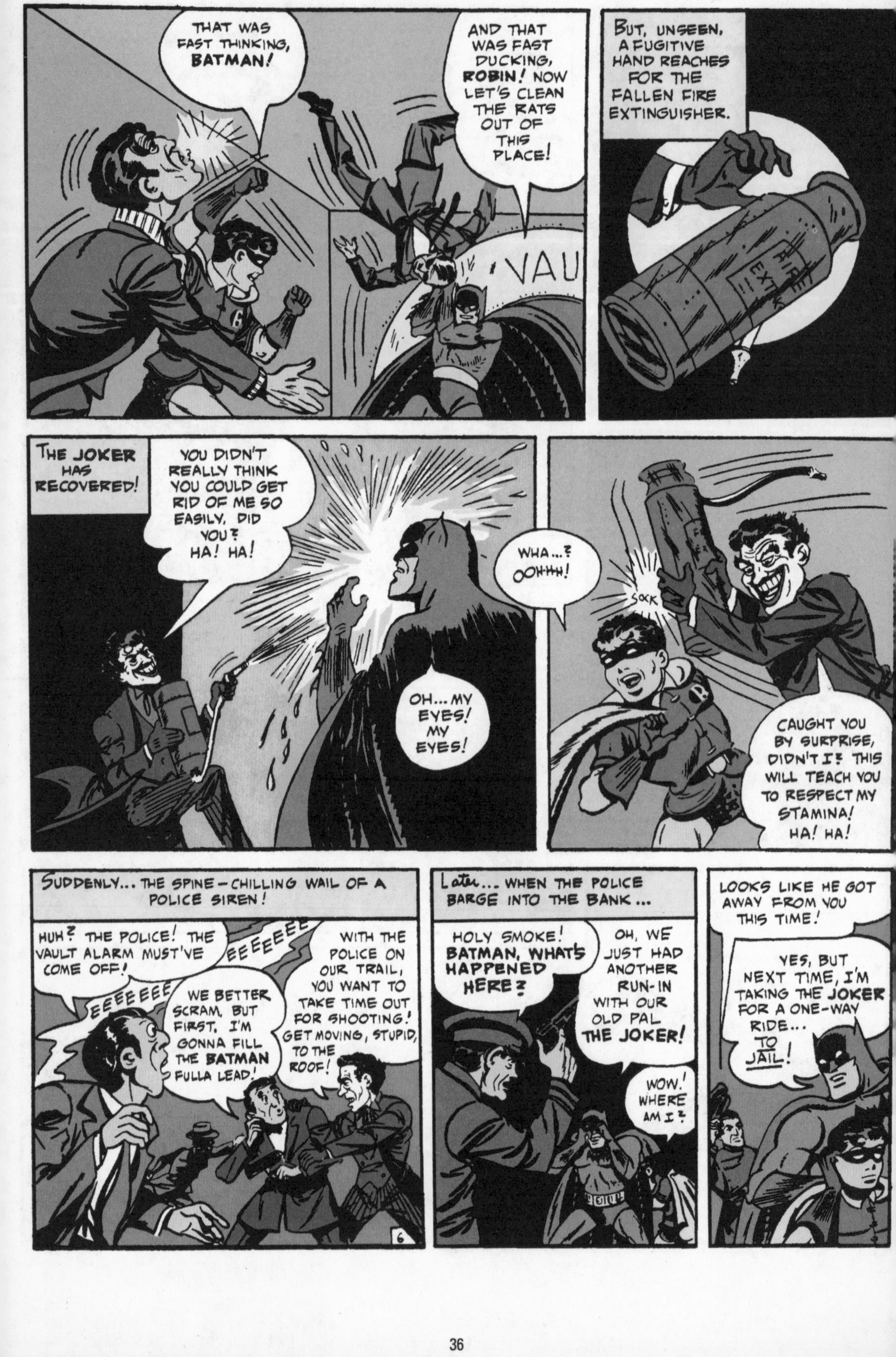

THAT WAS FAST THINKING, BATMAN!
AND THAT WAS FAST DUCKING, ROBIN! NOW LET'S CLEAN THE RATS OUT OF THIS PLACE!
VAU
BUT, UNSEEN, A FUGITIVE HAND REACHES FOR THE FALLEN FIRE EXTINGUISHER.
THE JOKER HAS RECOVERED!
YOU DIDN'T REALLY THINK YOU COULD GET RID OF ME SO EASILY, DID YOU? HA! HA!
OH... MY EYES! MY EYES!
WHA...? OOHHH!
SOCK
CAUGHT YOU BY SURPRISE, DIDN'T I? THIS WILL TEACH YOU TO RESPECT MY STAMINA! HA! HA!
SUDDENLY... THE SPINE-CHILLING WAIL OF A POLICE SIREN!
HUH? THE POLICE! THE VAULT ALARM MUST'VE COME OFF!
EEEEEEEE
EEEEEEE
WE BETTER SCRAM, BUT FIRST, I'M GONNA FILL THE BATMAN FULLA LEAD!
WITH THE POLICE ON OUR TRAIL, YOU WANT TO TAKE TIME OUT FOR SHOOTING! GET MOVING, STUPID, TO THE ROOF!
6
LATER... WHEN THE POLICE BARGE INTO THE BANK...
HOLY SMOKE! BATMAN, WHAT'S HAPPENED HERE?
OH, WE JUST HAD ANOTHER RUN-IN WITH OUR OLD PAL THE JOKER!
WOW! WHERE AM I?
LOOKS LIKE HE GOT AWAY FROM YOU THIS TIME!
YES, BUT NEXT TIME, I'M TAKING THE JOKER FOR A ONE-WAY RIDE... TO JAIL!

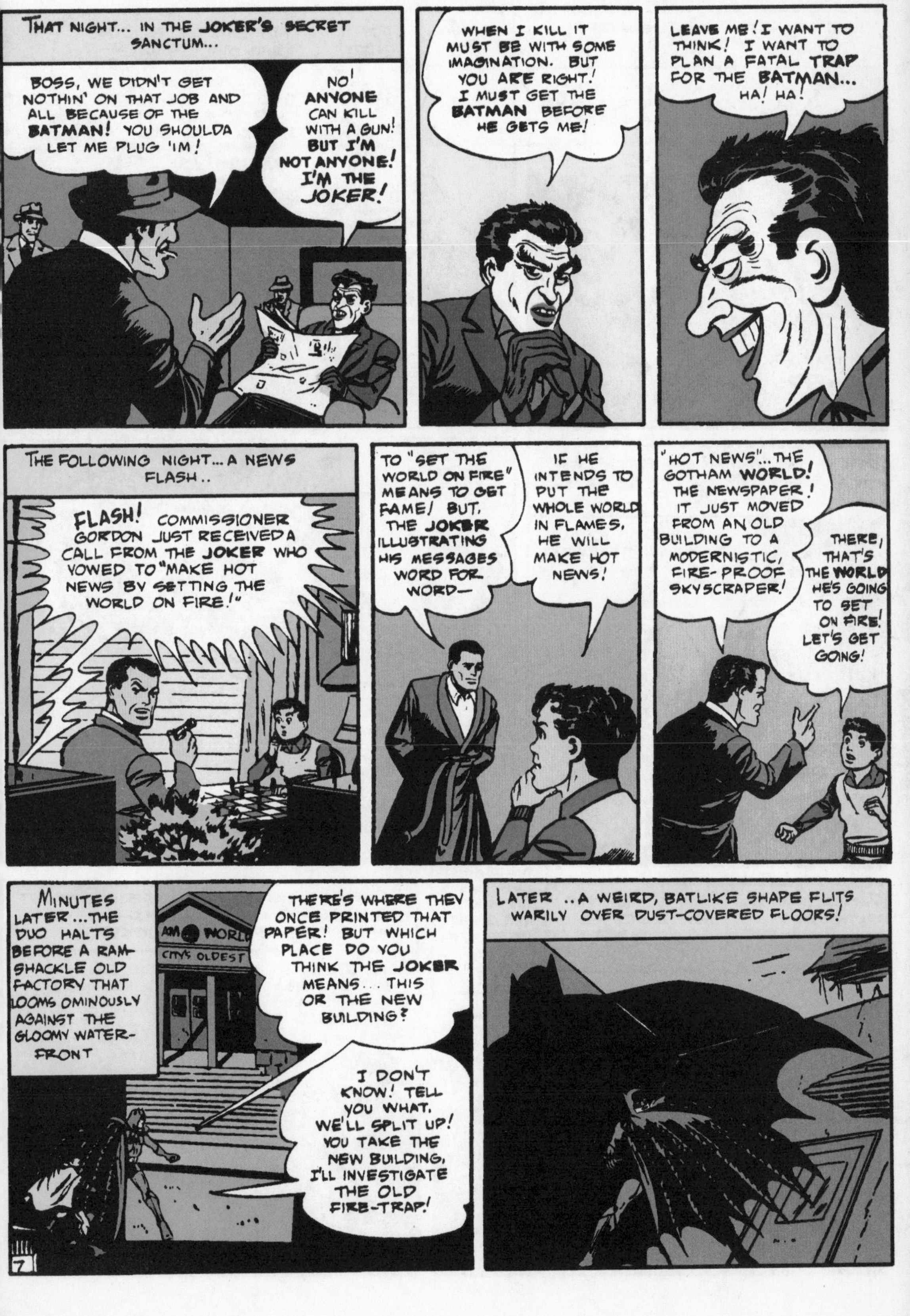

THAT NIGHT... IN THE JOKER'S SECRET SANCTUM...
BOSS, WE DIDN'T GET NOTHIN' ON THAT JOB AND ALL BECAUSE OF THE BATMAN! YOU SHOULDA LET ME PLUG 'IM!
NO! ANYONE CAN KILL WITH A GUN! BUT I'M NOT ANYONE! I'M THE JOKER!
WHEN I KILL IT MUST BE WITH SOME IMAGINATION. BUT YOU ARE RIGHT! I MUST GET THE BATMAN BEFORE HE GETS ME!
LEAVE ME! I WANT TO THINK! I WANT TO PLAN A FATAL TRAP FOR THE BATMAN... HA! HA!
THE FOLLOWING NIGHT... A NEWS FLASH..
FLASH! COMMISSIONER GORDON JUST RECEIVED A CALL FROM THE JOKER WHO VOWED TO "MAKE HOT NEWS BY SETTING THE WORLD ON FIRE!"
TO "SET THE WORLD ON FIRE" MEANS TO GET FAME! BUT, THE JOKER ILLUSTRATING HIS MESSAGES WORD FOR WORD—
IF HE INTENDS TO PUT THE WHOLE WORLD IN FLAMES, HE WILL MAKE HOT NEWS!
"HOT NEWS"... THE GOTHAM WORLD! THE NEWSPAPER! IT JUST MOVED FROM AN OLD BUILDING TO A MODERNISTIC, FIRE-PROOF SKYSCRAPER!
THERE, THAT'S THE WORLD HE'S GOING TO SET ON FIRE! LET'S GET GOING!
MINUTES LATER... THE DUO HALTS BEFORE A RAMSHACKLE OLD FACTORY THAT LOOMS OMINOUSLY AGAINST THE GLOOMY WATER-FRONT
CITY'S OLDEST
THERE'S WHERE THEY ONCE PRINTED THAT PAPER! BUT WHICH PLACE DO YOU THINK THE JOKER MEANS... THIS OR THE NEW BUILDING?
I DON'T KNOW! TELL YOU WHAT. WE'LL SPLIT UP! YOU TAKE THE NEW BUILDING, I'LL INVESTIGATE THE OLD FIRE-TRAP!
7
LATER ..A WEIRD, BATLIKE SHAPE FLITS WARILY OVER DUST-COVERED FLOORS!

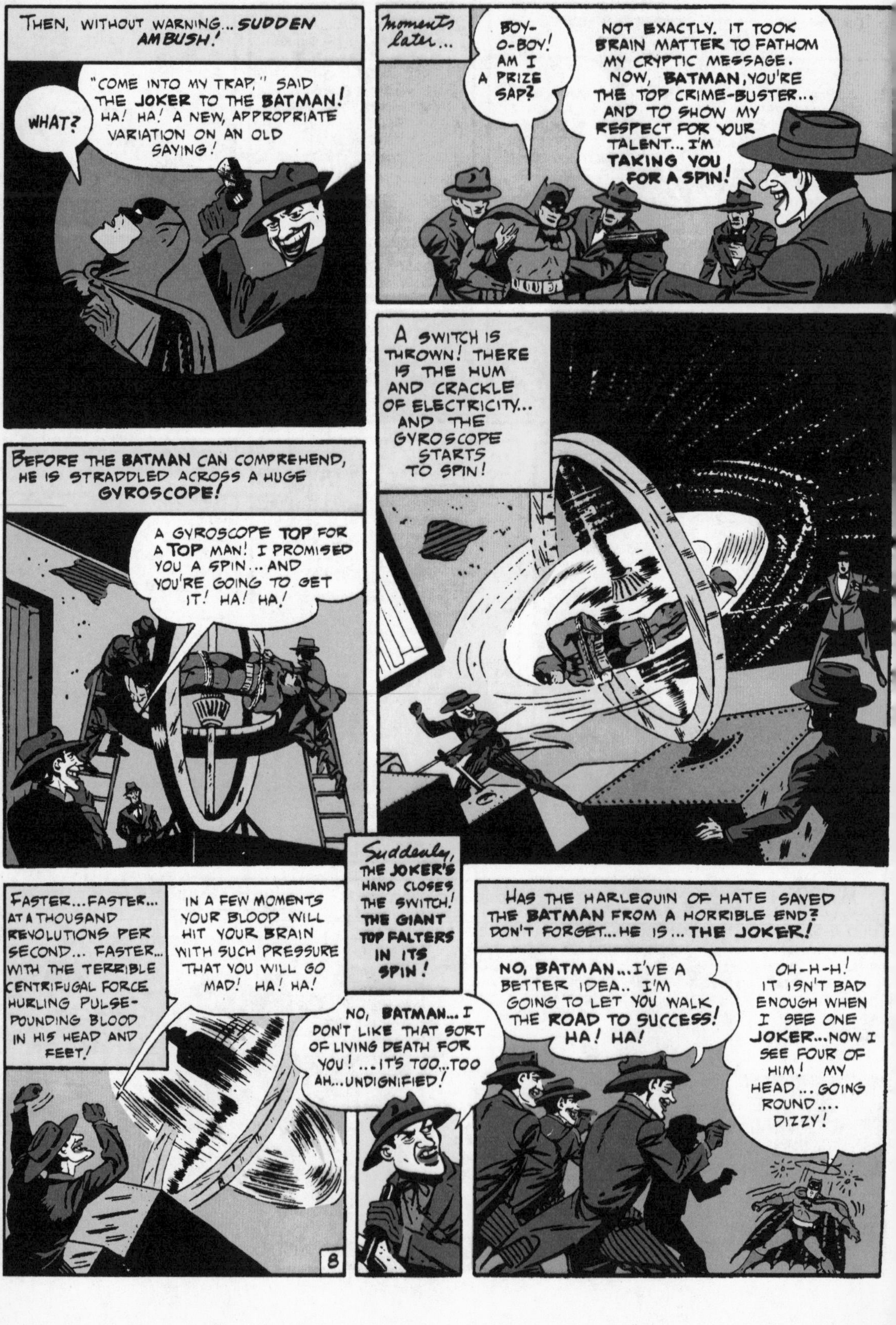

THEN, WITHOUT WARNING... SUDDEN AMBUSH!
WHAT?
"COME INTO MY TRAP," SAID THE JOKER TO THE BATMAN! HA! HA! A NEW, APPROPRIATE VARIATION ON AN OLD SAYING!
Moments later...
BOY-O-BOY! AM I A PRIZE SAP?
NOT EXACTLY. IT TOOK BRAIN MATTER TO FATHOM MY CRYPTIC MESSAGE. NOW, BATMAN, YOU'RE THE TOP CRIME-BUSTER... AND TO SHOW MY RESPECT FOR YOUR TALENT... I'M TAKING YOU FOR A SPIN!
BEFORE THE BATMAN CAN COMPREHEND, HE IS STRADDLED ACROSS A HUGE GYROSCOPE!
A GYROSCOPE TOP FOR A TOP MAN! I PROMISED YOU A SPIN... AND YOU'RE GOING TO GET IT! HA! HA!
A SWITCH IS THROWN! THERE IS THE HUM AND CRACKLE OF ELECTRICITY... AND THE GYROSCOPE STARTS TO SPIN!
FASTER... FASTER... AT A THOUSAND REVOLUTIONS PER SECOND... FASTER... WITH THE TERRIBLE CENTRIFUGAL FORCE HURLING PULSE-POUNDING BLOOD IN HIS HEAD AND FEET!
IN A FEW MOMENTS YOUR BLOOD WILL HIT YOUR BRAIN WITH SUCH PRESSURE THAT YOU WILL GO MAD! HA! HA!
8
Suddenly, THE JOKER'S HAND CLOSES THE SWITCH! THE GIANT TOP FALTERS IN ITS SPIN!
NO, BATMAN... I DON'T LIKE THAT SORT OF LIVING DEATH FOR YOU! ... IT'S TOO...TOO AH...UNDIGNIFIED!
HAS THE HARLEQUIN OF HATE SAVED THE BATMAN FROM A HORRIBLE END? DON'T FORGET... HE IS... THE JOKER!
NO, BATMAN... I'VE A BETTER IDEA.. I'M GOING TO LET YOU WALK THE ROAD TO SUCCESS! HA! HA!
OH-H-H! IT ISN'T BAD ENOUGH WHEN I SEE ONE JOKER... NOW I SEE FOUR OF HIM! MY HEAD... GOING ROUND.... DIZZY!

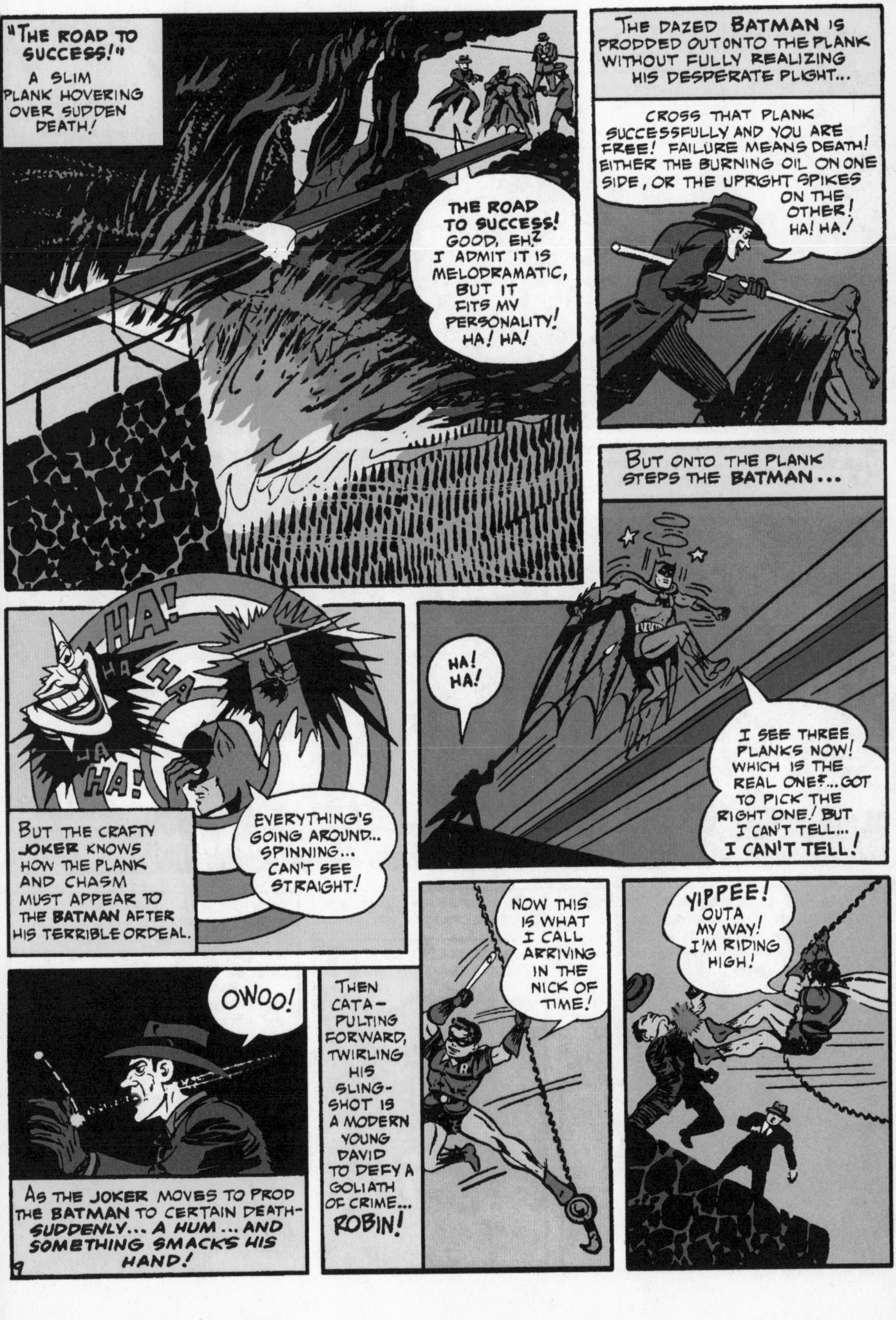
"THE ROAD TO SUCCESS!" A SLIM PLANK HOVERING OVER SUDDEN DEATH!
THE ROAD TO SUCCESS! GOOD, EH? I ADMIT IT IS MELODRAMATIC, BUT IT FITS MY PERSONALITY! HA! HA!
THE DAZED BATMAN IS PRODDED OUT ONTO THE PLANK WITHOUT FULLY REALIZING HIS DESPERATE PLIGHT...
CROSS THAT PLANK SUCCESSFULLY AND YOU ARE FREE! FAILURE MEANS DEATH! EITHER THE BURNING OIL ON ONE SIDE, OR THE UPRIGHT SPIKES ON THE OTHER! HA! HA!
BUT ONTO THE PLANK STEPS THE BATMAN...
HA! HA!
I SEE THREE PLANKS NOW! WHICH IS THE REAL ONE?...GOT TO PICK THE RIGHT ONE! BUT I CAN'T TELL... I CAN'T TELL!
HA! HA HA HA! HA!
EVERYTHING'S GOING AROUND... SPINNING... CAN'T SEE STRAIGHT!
BUT THE CRAFTY JOKER KNOWS HOW THE PLANK AND CHASM MUST APPEAR TO THE BATMAN AFTER HIS TERRIBLE ORDEAL.
OWOO!
AS THE JOKER MOVES TO PROD THE BATMAN TO CERTAIN DEATH-SUDDENLY... A HUM... AND SOMETHING SMACKS HIS HAND!
THEN CATA-PULTING FORWARD, TWIRLING HIS SLING-SHOT IS A MODERN YOUNG DAVID TO DEFY A GOLIATH OF CRIME... ROBIN!
NOW THIS IS WHAT I CALL ARRIVING IN THE NICK OF TIME!
YIPPEE! OUTA MY WAY! I'M RIDING HIGH!

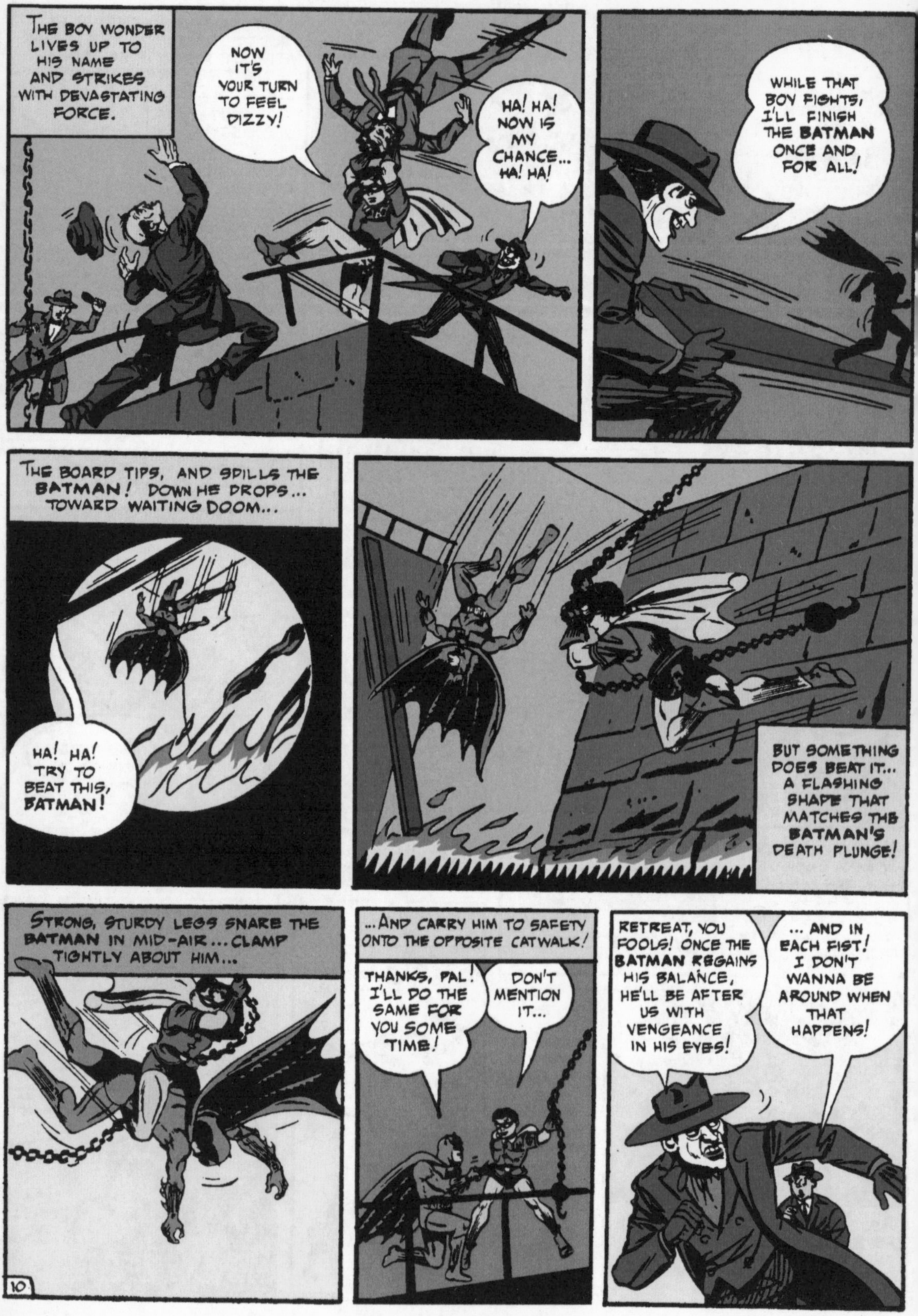

THE BOY WONDER LIVES UP TO HIS NAME AND STRIKES WITH DEVASTATING FORCE.
NOW IT'S YOUR TURN TO FEEL DIZZY!
HA! HA! NOW IS MY CHANCE... HA! HA!
WHILE THAT BOY FIGHTS, I'LL FINISH THE BATMAN ONCE AND FOR ALL!
THE BOARD TIPS, AND SPILLS THE BATMAN! DOWN HE DROPS... TOWARD WAITING DOOM...
HA! HA! TRY TO BEAT THIS, BATMAN!
BUT SOMETHING DOES BEAT IT... A FLASHING SHAPE THAT MATCHES THE BATMAN'S DEATH PLUNGE!
STRONG, STURDY LEGS SNARE THE BATMAN IN MID-AIR... CLAMP TIGHTLY ABOUT HIM...
10
...AND CARRY HIM TO SAFETY ONTO THE OPPOSITE CATWALK!
THANKS, PAL! I'LL DO THE SAME FOR YOU SOME TIME!
DON'T MENTION IT...
RETREAT, YOU FOOLS! ONCE THE BATMAN REGAINS HIS BALANCE, HE'LL BE AFTER US WITH VENGEANCE IN HIS EYES!
... AND IN EACH FIST! I DON'T WANNA BE AROUND WHEN THAT HAPPENS!

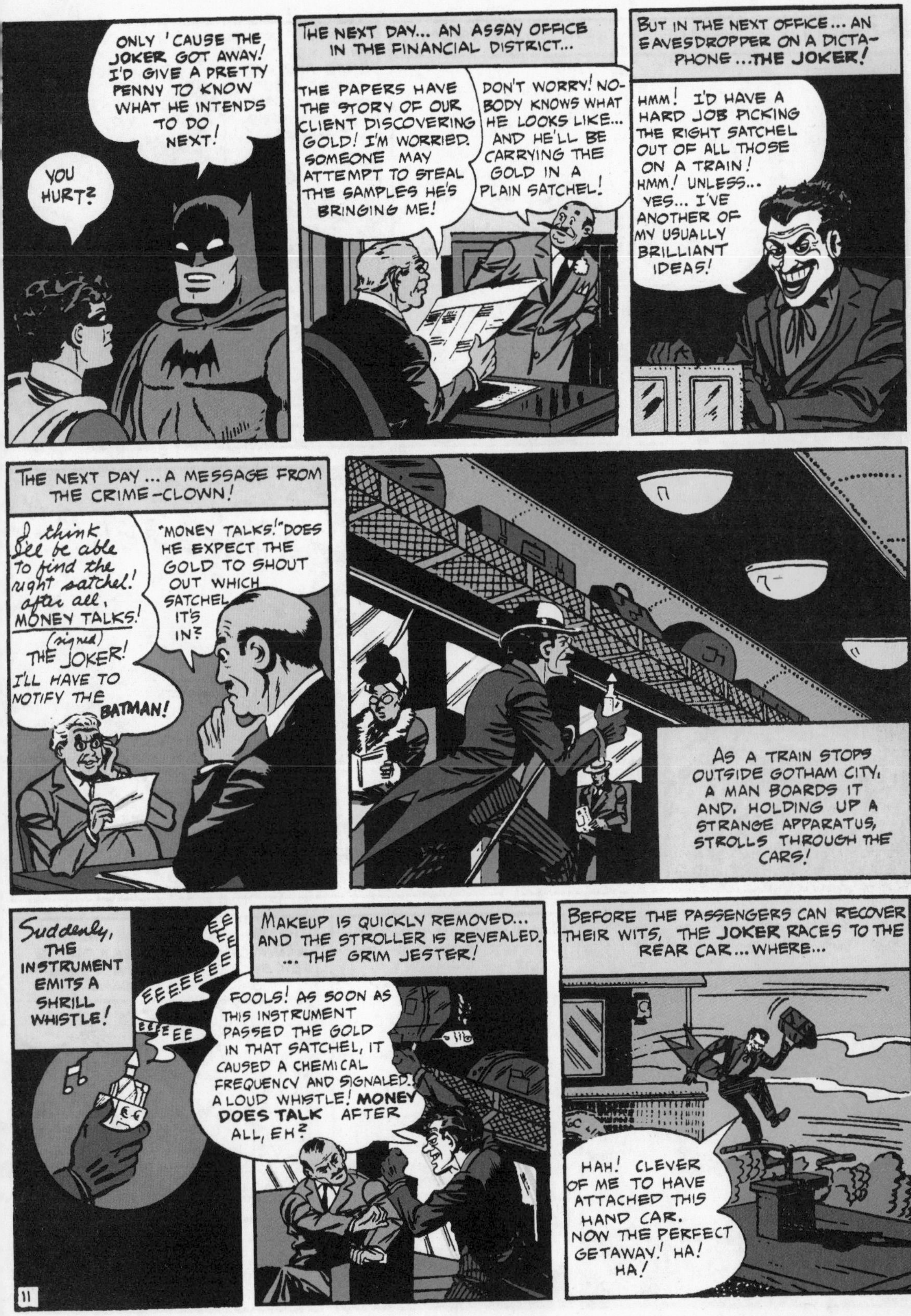

ONLY 'CAUSE THE JOKER GOT AWAY! I'D GIVE A PRETTY PENNY TO KNOW WHAT HE INTENDS TO DO NEXT!
YOU HURT?
THE NEXT DAY... AN ASSAY OFFICE IN THE FINANCIAL DISTRICT...
THE PAPERS HAVE THE STORY OF OUR CLIENT DISCOVERING GOLD! I'M WORRIED. SOMEONE MAY ATTEMPT TO STEAL THE SAMPLES HE'S BRINGING ME!
DON'T WORRY! NOBODY KNOWS WHAT HE LOOKS LIKE... AND HE'LL BE CARRYING THE GOLD IN A PLAIN SATCHEL!
BUT IN THE NEXT OFFICE... AN EAVESDROPPER ON A DICTAPHONE ...THE JOKER!
HMM! I'D HAVE A HARD JOB PICKING THE RIGHT SATCHEL OUT OF ALL THOSE ON A TRAIN! HMM! UNLESS... YES... I'VE ANOTHER OF MY USUALLY BRILLIANT IDEAS!
THE NEXT DAY ... A MESSAGE FROM THE CRIME-CLOWN!
I think I'll be able to find the right satchel! after all, MONEY TALKS! (signed) THE JOKER!
"MONEY TALKS!" DOES HE EXPECT THE GOLD TO SHOUT OUT WHICH SATCHEL IT'S IN?
I'LL HAVE TO NOTIFY THE BATMAN!
AS A TRAIN STOPS OUTSIDE GOTHAM CITY, A MAN BOARDS IT AND, HOLDING UP A STRANGE APPARATUS, STROLLS THROUGH THE CARS!
Suddenly, THE INSTRUMENT EMITS A SHRILL WHISTLE!
EEEEEEEEE
EEEEEEEE
EEEEEE
MAKEUP IS QUICKLY REMOVED... AND THE STROLLER IS REVEALED. ... THE GRIM JESTER!
FOOLS! AS SOON AS THIS INSTRUMENT PASSED THE GOLD IN THAT SATCHEL, IT CAUSED A CHEMICAL FREQUENCY AND SIGNALED A LOUD WHISTLE! MONEY DOES TALK AFTER ALL, EH?
BEFORE THE PASSENGERS CAN RECOVER THEIR WITS, THE JOKER RACES TO THE REAR CAR... WHERE...
HAH! CLEVER OF ME TO HAVE ATTACHED THIS HAND CAR. NOW THE PERFECT GETAWAY! HA! HA!
11

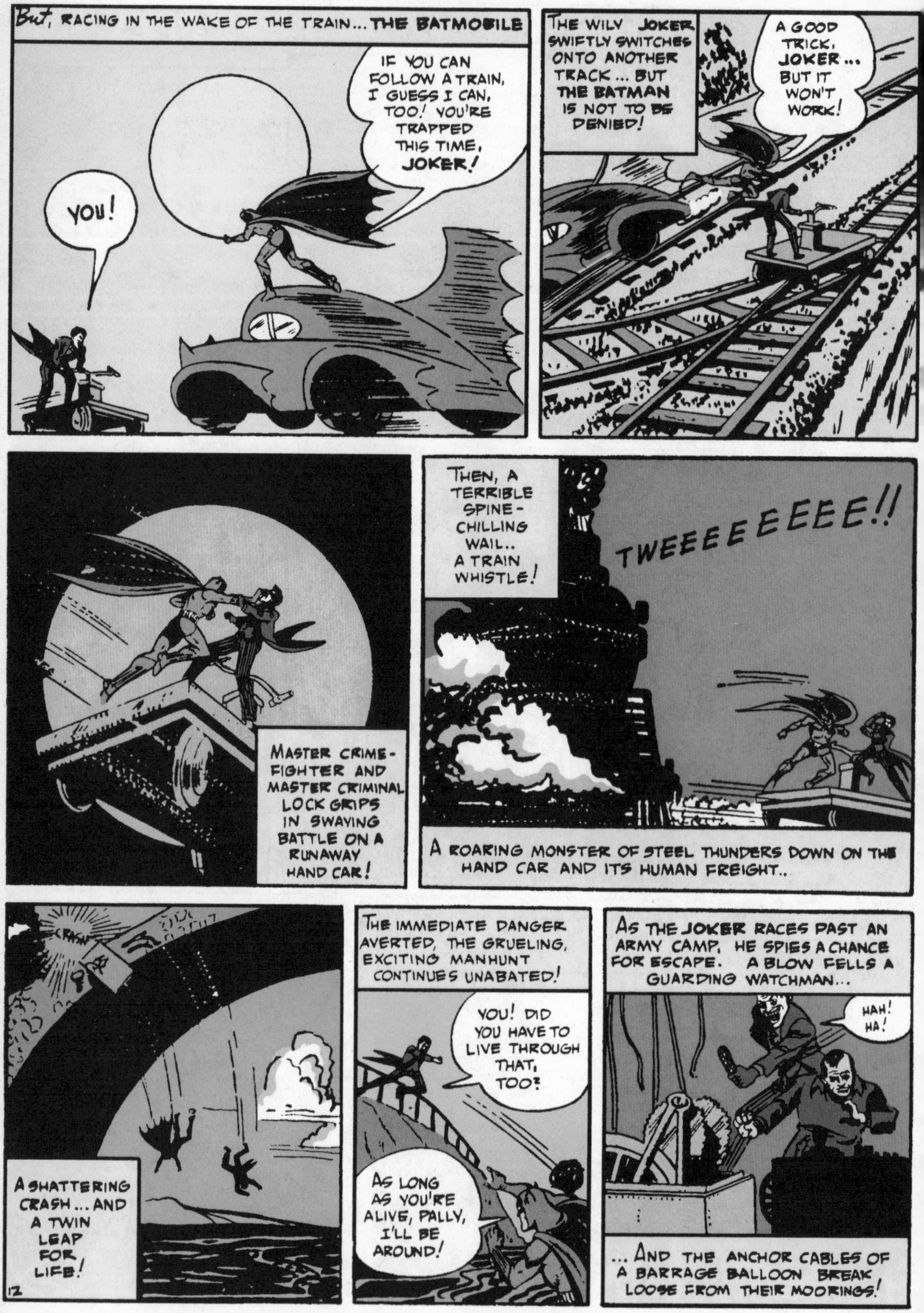

But, racing in the wake of the train... THE BATMOBILE
IF YOU CAN FOLLOW A TRAIN, I GUESS I CAN, TOO! YOU'RE TRAPPED THIS TIME, JOKER!
YOU!
THE WILY JOKER SWIFTLY SWITCHES ONTO ANOTHER TRACK ... BUT THE BATMAN IS NOT TO BE DENIED!
A GOOD TRICK, JOKER ... BUT IT WON'T WORK!
MASTER CRIME-FIGHTER AND MASTER CRIMINAL LOCK GRIPS IN SWAYING BATTLE ON A RUNAWAY HAND CAR!
THEN, A TERRIBLE SPINE-CHILLING WAIL.. A TRAIN WHISTLE!
TWEEEEEEEEE!!
A ROARING MONSTER OF STEEL THUNDERS DOWN ON THE HAND CAR AND ITS HUMAN FREIGHT..
CRASH
A SHATTERING CRASH ... AND A TWIN LEAP FOR LIFE!
12
THE IMMEDIATE DANGER AVERTED, THE GRUELING, EXCITING MANHUNT CONTINUES UNABATED!
YOU! DID YOU HAVE TO LIVE THROUGH THAT, TOO?
AS LONG AS YOU'RE ALIVE, PALLY, I'LL BE AROUND!
AS THE JOKER RACES PAST AN ARMY CAMP, HE SPIES A CHANCE FOR ESCAPE. A BLOW FELLS A GUARDING WATCHMAN...
HAH! HA!
... AND THE ANCHOR CABLES OF A BARRAGE BALLOON BREAK LOOSE FROM THEIR MOORINGS!

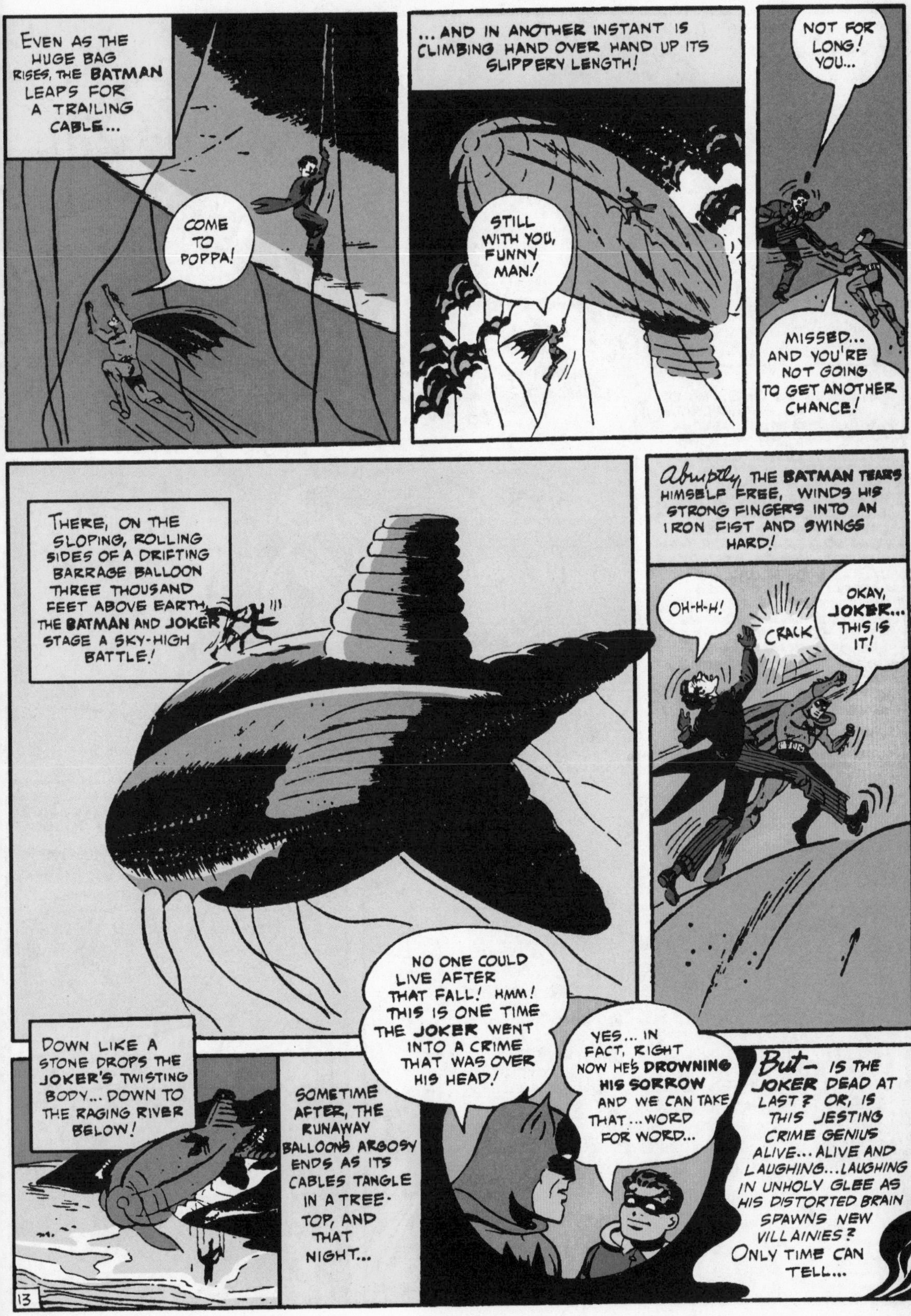
EVEN AS THE HUGE BAG RISES, THE BATMAN LEAPS FOR A TRAILING CABLE...
COME TO POPPA!
...AND IN ANOTHER INSTANT IS CLIMBING HAND OVER HAND UP ITS SLIPPERY LENGTH!
STILL WITH YOU, FUNNY MAN!
NOT FOR LONG! YOU...
MISSED... AND YOU'RE NOT GOING TO GET ANOTHER CHANCE!
THERE, ON THE SLOPING, ROLLING SIDES OF A DRIFTING BARRAGE BALLOON THREE THOUSAND FEET ABOVE EARTH, THE BATMAN AND JOKER STAGE A SKY-HIGH BATTLE!
Abruptly, THE BATMAN TEARS HIMSELF FREE, WINDS HIS STRONG FINGERS INTO AN IRON FIST AND SWINGS HARD!
OH-H-H!
CRACK
OKAY, JOKER... THIS IS IT!
DOWN LIKE A STONE DROPS THE JOKER'S TWISTING BODY... DOWN TO THE RAGING RIVER BELOW!
13
SOMETIME AFTER, THE RUNAWAY BALLOON'S ARGOSY ENDS AS ITS CABLES TANGLE IN A TREE-TOP, AND THAT NIGHT...
NO ONE COULD LIVE AFTER THAT FALL! HMM! THIS IS ONE TIME THE JOKER WENT INTO A CRIME THAT WAS OVER HIS HEAD!
YES... IN FACT, RIGHT NOW HE'S DROWNING HIS SORROW AND WE CAN TAKE THAT... WORD FOR WORD...
But- IS THE JOKER DEAD AT LAST? OR, IS THIS JESTING CRIME GENIUS ALIVE... ALIVE AND LAUGHING... LAUGHING IN UNHOLY GLEE AS HIS DISTORTED BRAIN SPAWNS NEW VILLAINIES? ONLY TIME CAN TELL...

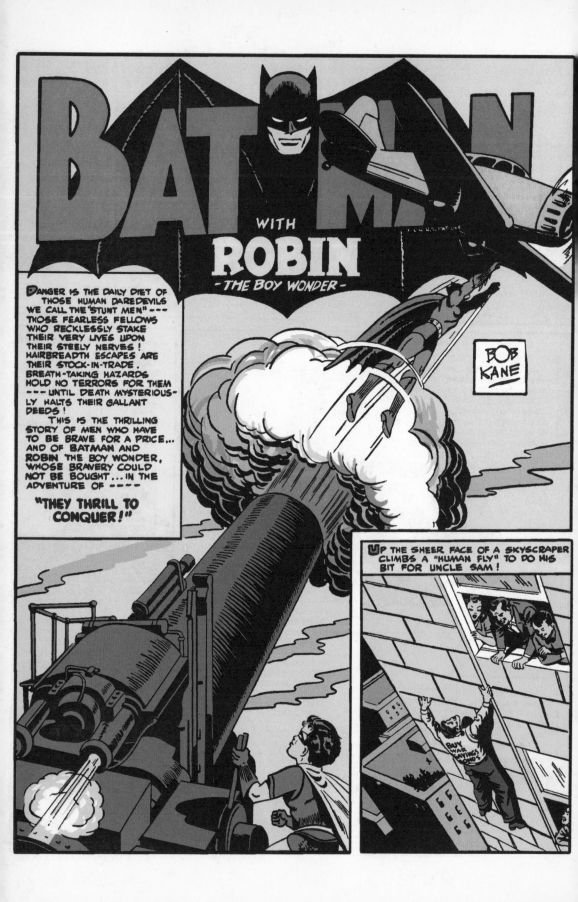

BATMAN

WITH
ROBIN
-THE BOY WONDER-

BOB KANE

DANGER IS THE DAILY DIET OF THOSE HUMAN DAREDEVILS WE CALL THE "STUNT MEN" --- THOSE FEARLESS FELLOWS WHO RECKLESSLY STAKE THEIR VERY LIVES UPON THEIR STEELY NERVES! HAIRBREADTH ESCAPES ARE THEIR STOCK-IN-TRADE. BREATH-TAKING HAZARDS HOLD NO TERRORS FOR THEM --- UNTIL DEATH MYSTERIOUSLY HALTS THEIR GALLANT DEEDS!

THIS IS THE THRILLING STORY OF MEN WHO HAVE TO BE BRAVE FOR A PRICE,... AND OF BATMAN AND ROBIN THE BOY WONDER, WHOSE BRAVERY COULD NOT BE BOUGHT...IN THE ADVENTURE OF ----

"THEY THRILL TO CONQUER!"

UP THE SHEER FACE OF A SKYSCRAPER CLIMBS A "HUMAN FLY" TO DO HIS BIT FOR UNCLE SAM!

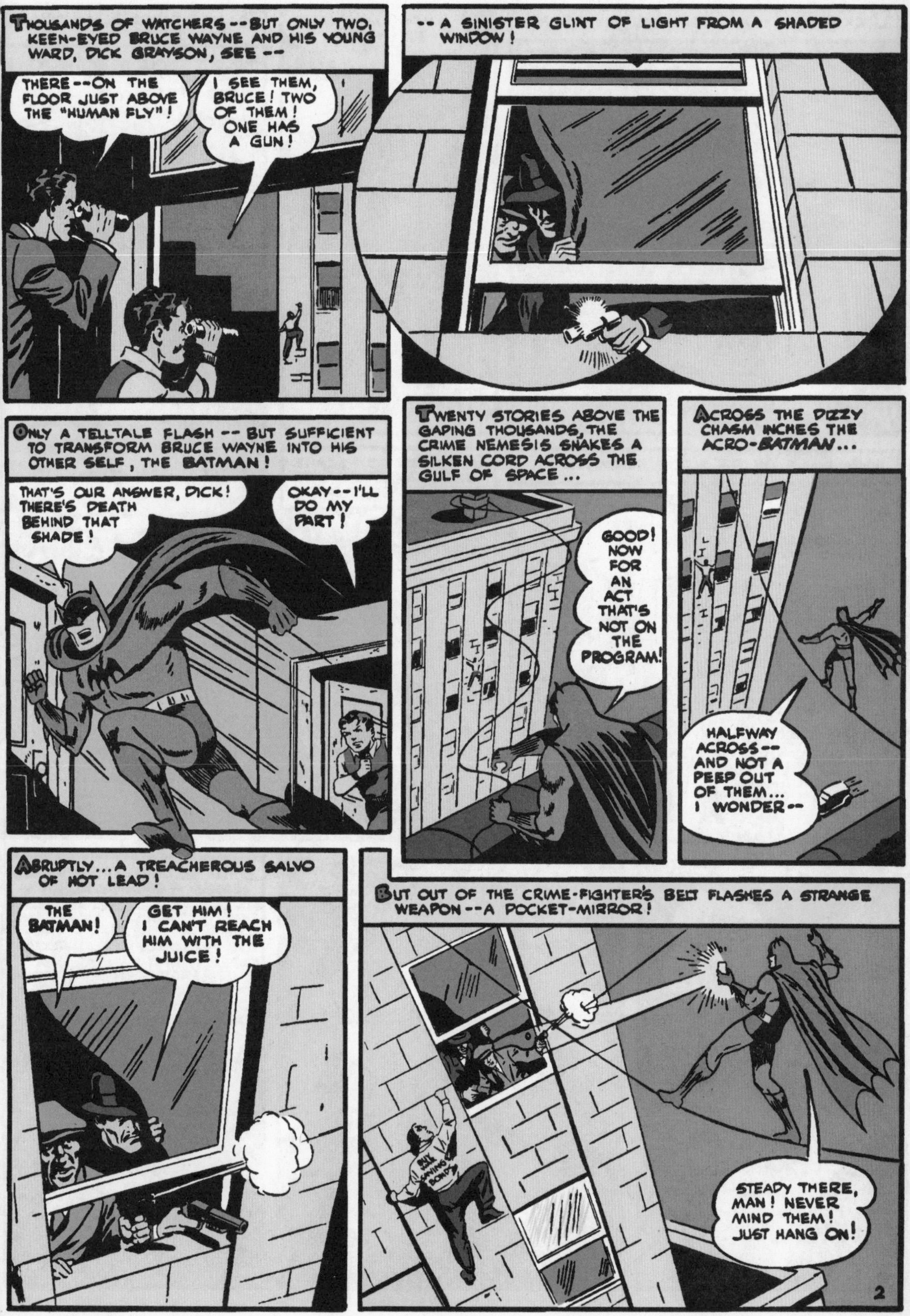
THOUSANDS OF WATCHERS--BUT ONLY TWO, KEEN-EYED BRUCE WAYNE AND HIS YOUNG WARD, DICK GRAYSON, SEE--
THERE--ON THE FLOOR JUST ABOVE THE "HUMAN FLY"!
I SEE THEM, BRUCE! TWO OF THEM! ONE HAS A GUN!
--A SINISTER GLINT OF LIGHT FROM A SHADED WINDOW!
ONLY A TELLTALE FLASH--BUT SUFFICIENT TO TRANSFORM BRUCE WAYNE INTO HIS OTHER SELF, THE BATMAN!
THAT'S OUR ANSWER, DICK! THERE'S DEATH BEHIND THAT SHADE!
OKAY--I'LL DO MY PART!
TWENTY STORIES ABOVE THE GAPING THOUSANDS, THE CRIME NEMESIS SNAKES A SILKEN CORD ACROSS THE GULF OF SPACE...
GOOD! NOW FOR AN ACT THAT'S NOT ON THE PROGRAM!
ACROSS THE DIZZY CHASM INCHES THE ACRO-BATMAN...
HALFWAY ACROSS--AND NOT A PEEP OUT OF THEM... I WONDER--
ABRUPTLY... A TREACHEROUS SALVO OF HOT LEAD!
THE BATMAN!
GET HIM! I CAN'T REACH HIM WITH THE JUICE!
BUT OUT OF THE CRIME-FIGHTER'S BELT FLASHES A STRANGE WEAPON--A POCKET-MIRROR!
STEADY THERE, MAN! NEVER MIND THEM! JUST HANG ON!
2

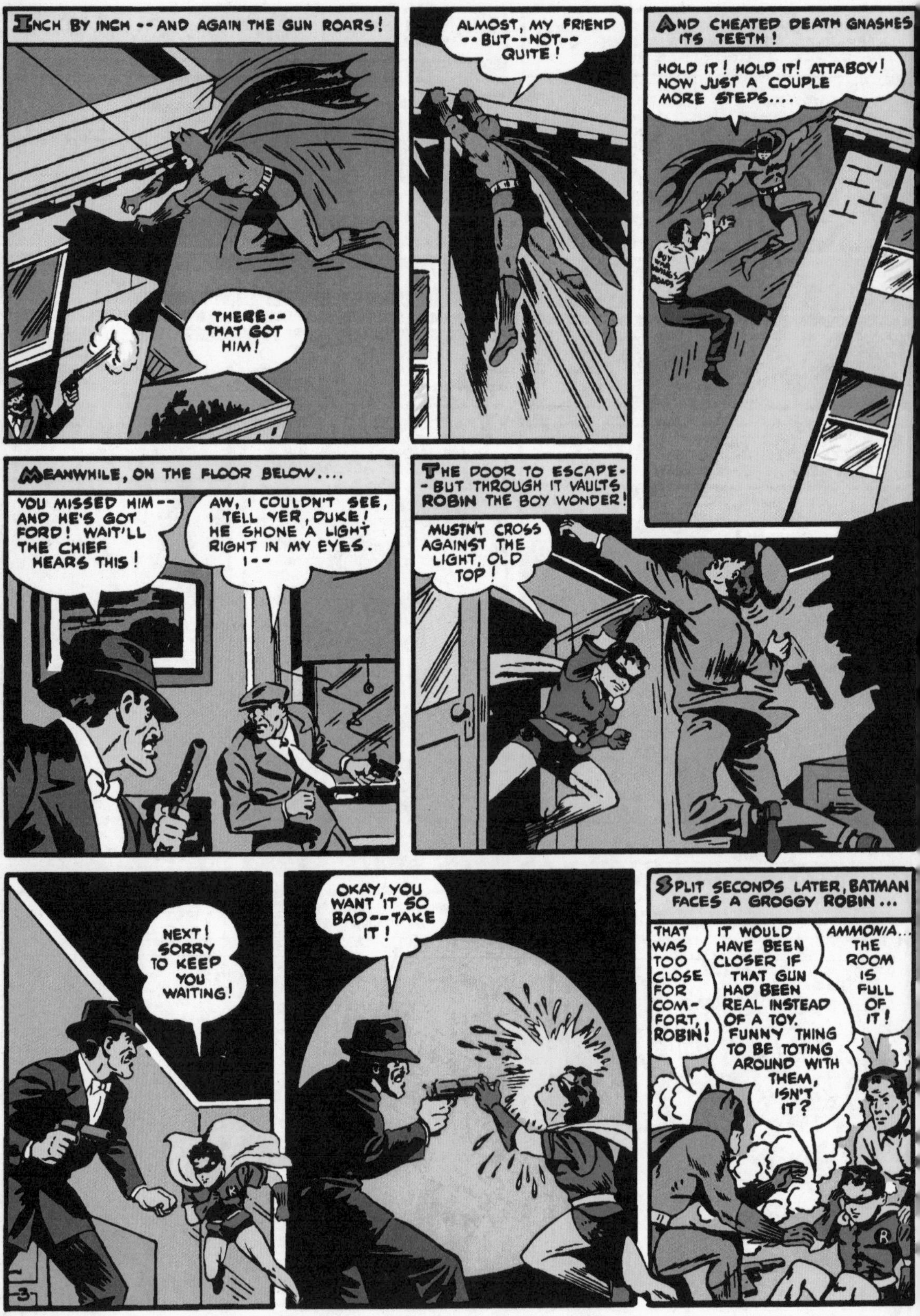
INCH BY INCH -- AND AGAIN THE GUN ROARS!
THERE-- THAT GOT HIM!
ALMOST, MY FRIEND -- BUT-- NOT-- QUITE!
AND CHEATED DEATH GNASHES ITS TEETH!
HOLD IT! HOLD IT! ATTABOY! NOW JUST A COUPLE MORE STEPS....
MEANWHILE, ON THE FLOOR BELOW....
YOU MISSED HIM-- AND HE'S GOT FORD! WAIT'LL THE CHIEF HEARS THIS!
AW, I COULDN'T SEE, I TELL YER, DUKE! HE SHONE A LIGHT RIGHT IN MY EYES. I--
THE DOOR TO ESCAPE- -BUT THROUGH IT VAULTS ROBIN THE BOY WONDER!
MUSTN'T CROSS AGAINST THE LIGHT, OLD TOP!
NEXT! SORRY TO KEEP YOU WAITING!
OKAY, YOU WANT IT SO BAD--TAKE IT!
SPLIT SECONDS LATER, BATMAN FACES A GROGGY ROBIN...
THAT WAS TOO CLOSE FOR COM-FORT, ROBIN!
IT WOULD HAVE BEEN CLOSER IF THAT GUN HAD BEEN REAL INSTEAD OF A TOY. FUNNY THING TO BE TOTING AROUND WITH THEM, ISN'T IT?
AMMONIA... THE ROOM IS FULL OF IT!
3

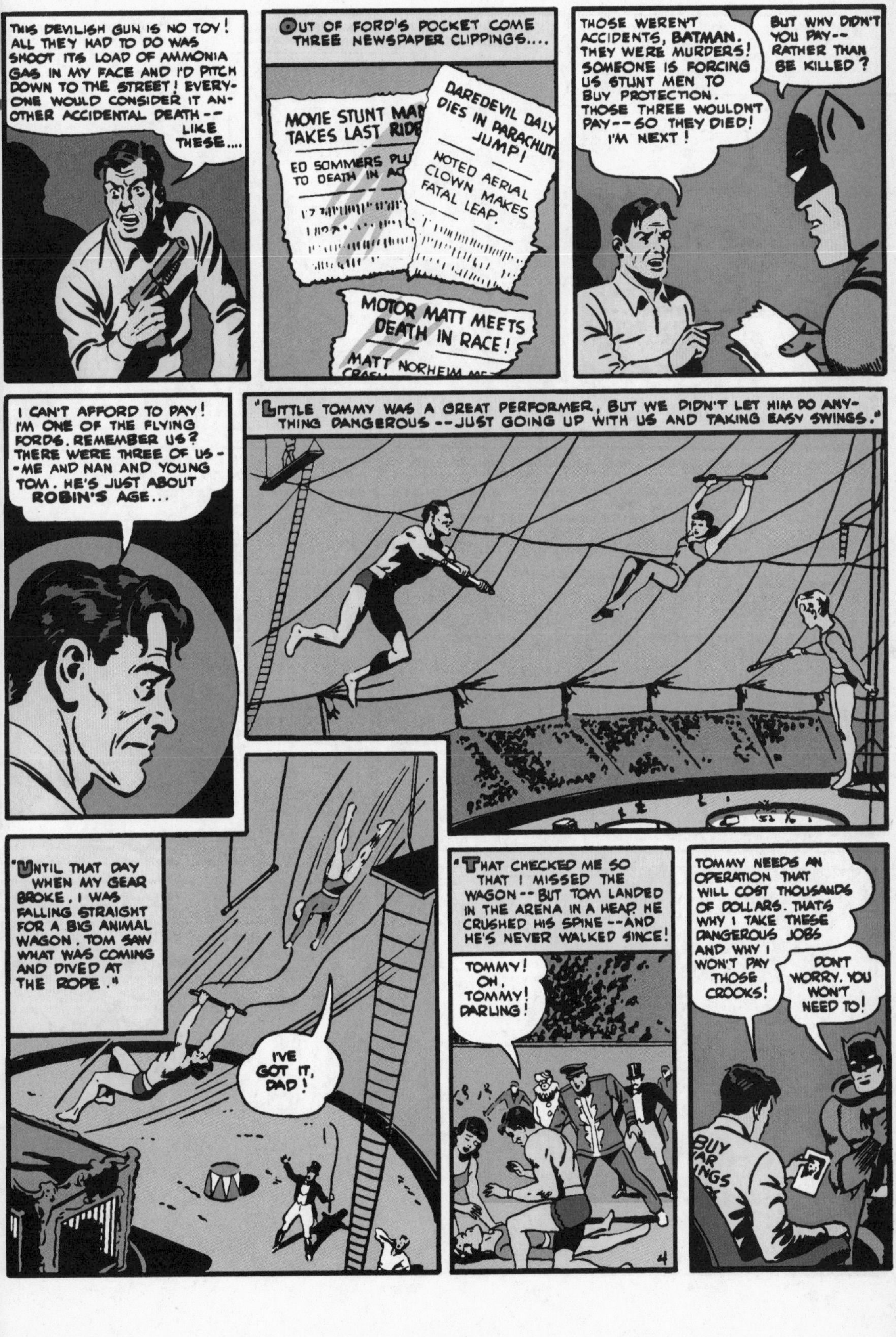

THIS DEVILISH GUN IS NO TOY! ALL THEY HAD TO DO WAS SHOOT ITS LOAD OF AMMONIA GAS IN MY FACE AND I'D PITCH DOWN TO THE STREET! EVERYONE WOULD CONSIDER IT ANOTHER ACCIDENTAL DEATH -- LIKE THESE....
OUT OF FORD'S POCKET COME THREE NEWSPAPER CLIPPINGS....
MOVIE STUNT MAN TAKES LAST RIDE
ED SOMMERS PLU TO DEATH IN AC
DAREDEVIL DALY DIES IN PARACHUTE JUMP!
NOTED AERIAL CLOWN MAKES FATAL LEAP.
MOTOR MATT MEETS DEATH IN RACE!
MATT NORHEIM
THOSE WEREN'T ACCIDENTS, BATMAN. THEY WERE MURDERS! SOMEONE IS FORCING US STUNT MEN TO BUY PROTECTION. THOSE THREE WOULDN'T PAY--SO THEY DIED! I'M NEXT!
BUT WHY DIDN'T YOU PAY--RATHER THAN BE KILLED?
I CAN'T AFFORD TO PAY! I'M ONE OF THE FLYING FORDS. REMEMBER US? THERE WERE THREE OF US--ME AND NAN AND YOUNG TOM. HE'S JUST ABOUT ROBIN'S AGE...
"LITTLE TOMMY WAS A GREAT PERFORMER, BUT WE DIDN'T LET HIM DO ANYTHING DANGEROUS--JUST GOING UP WITH US AND TAKING EASY SWINGS."
"UNTIL THAT DAY WHEN MY GEAR BROKE. I WAS FALLING STRAIGHT FOR A BIG ANIMAL WAGON. TOM SAW WHAT WAS COMING AND DIVED AT THE ROPE."
I'VE GOT IT, DAD!
"THAT CHECKED ME SO THAT I MISSED THE WAGON--BUT TOM LANDED IN THE ARENA IN A HEAP. HE CRUSHED HIS SPINE--AND HE'S NEVER WALKED SINCE!
TOMMY! OH, TOMMY! DARLING!
4
TOMMY NEEDS AN OPERATION THAT WILL COST THOUSANDS OF DOLLARS. THAT'S WHY I TAKE THESE DANGEROUS JOBS AND WHY I WON'T PAY THOSE CROOKS!
DON'T WORRY. YOU WON'T NEED TO!

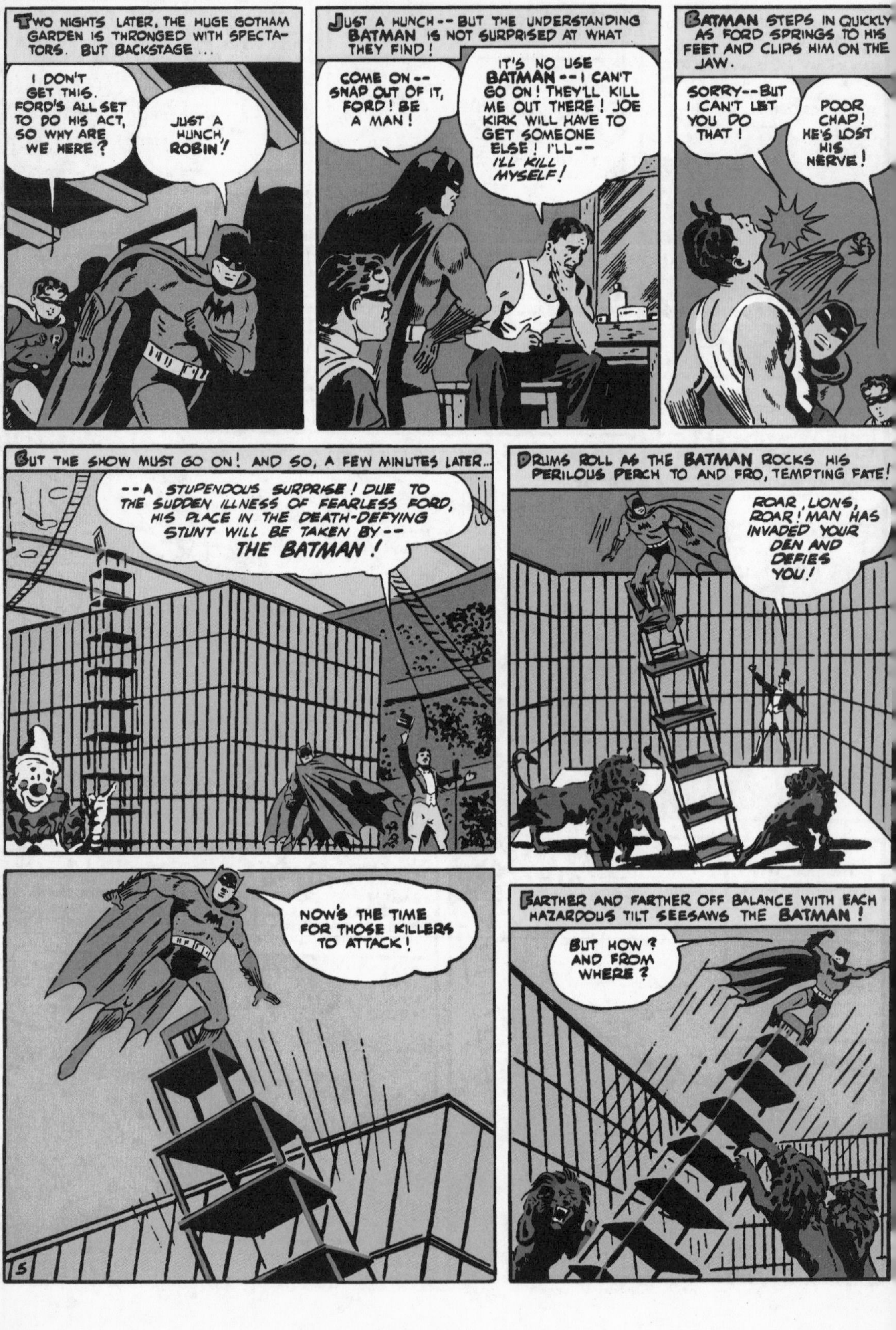
TWO NIGHTS LATER, THE HUGE GOTHAM GARDEN IS THRONGED WITH SPECTATORS. BUT BACKSTAGE ...
I DON'T GET THIS. FORD'S ALL SET TO DO HIS ACT, SO WHY ARE WE HERE?
JUST A HUNCH, ROBIN!
JUST A HUNCH -- BUT THE UNDERSTANDING BATMAN IS NOT SURPRISED AT WHAT THEY FIND!
COME ON -- SNAP OUT OF IT, FORD! BE A MAN!
IT'S NO USE BATMAN -- I CAN'T GO ON! THEY'LL KILL ME OUT THERE! JOE KIRK WILL HAVE TO GET SOMEONE ELSE! I'LL -- I'LL KILL MYSELF!
BATMAN STEPS IN QUICKLY AS FORD SPRINGS TO HIS FEET AND CLIPS HIM ON THE JAW.
SORRY--BUT I CAN'T LET YOU DO THAT!
POOR CHAP! HE'S LOST HIS NERVE!
BUT THE SHOW MUST GO ON! AND SO, A FEW MINUTES LATER...
-- A STUPENDOUS SURPRISE! DUE TO THE SUDDEN ILLNESS OF FEARLESS FORD, HIS PLACE IN THE DEATH-DEFYING STUNT WILL BE TAKEN BY -- THE BATMAN!
DRUMS ROLL AS THE BATMAN ROCKS HIS PERILOUS PERCH TO AND FRO, TEMPTING FATE!
ROAR, LIONS, ROAR! MAN HAS INVADED YOUR DEN AND DEFIES YOU!
NOW'S THE TIME FOR THOSE KILLERS TO ATTACK!
5
FARTHER AND FARTHER OFF BALANCE WITH EACH HAZARDOUS TILT SEESAWS THE BATMAN!
BUT HOW? AND FROM WHERE?

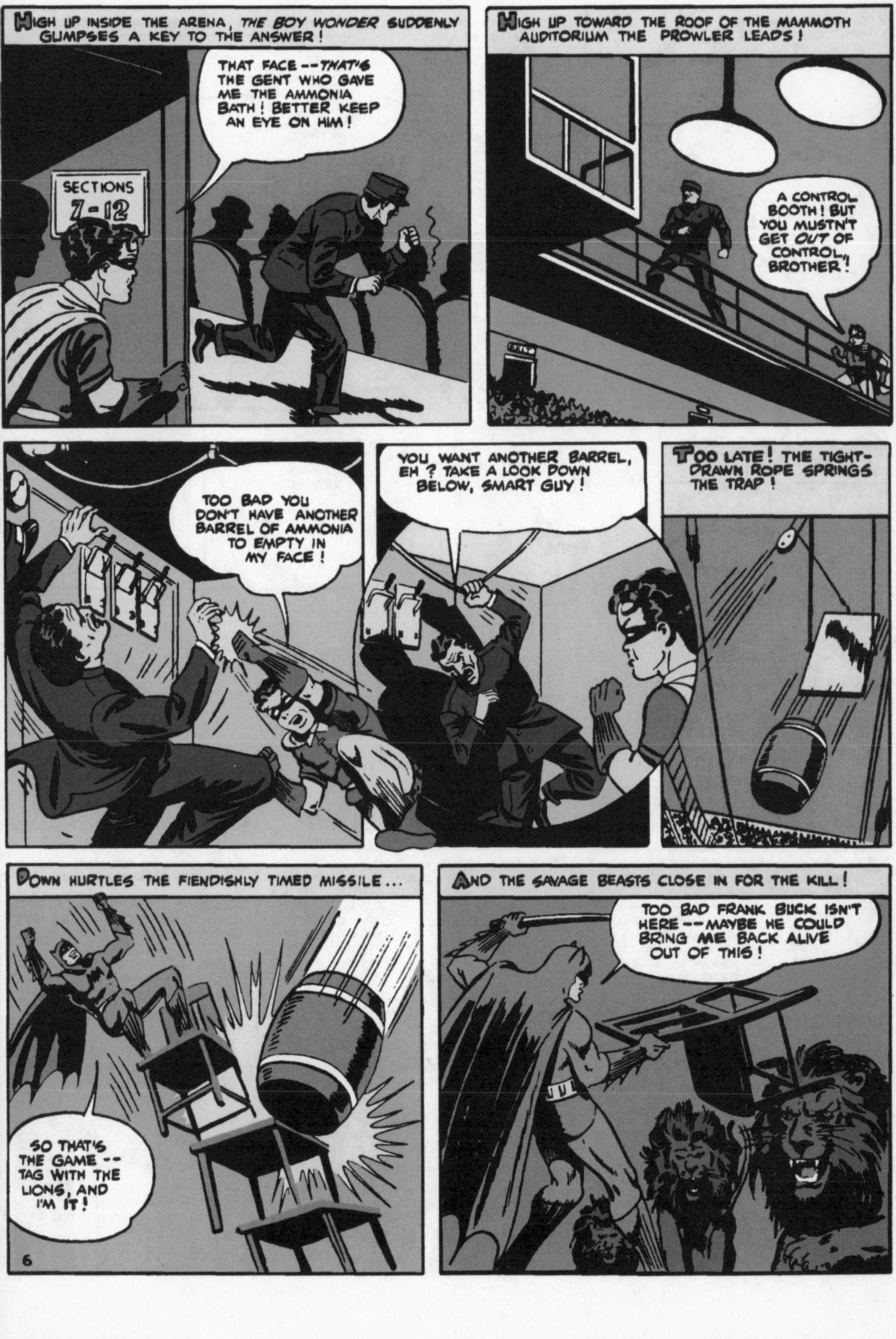
HIGH UP INSIDE THE ARENA, THE BOY WONDER SUDDENLY GLIMPSES A KEY TO THE ANSWER!
THAT FACE--THAT'S THE GENT WHO GAVE ME THE AMMONIA BATH! BETTER KEEP AN EYE ON HIM!
SECTIONS 7-12
HIGH UP TOWARD THE ROOF OF THE MAMMOTH AUDITORIUM THE PROWLER LEADS!
A CONTROL BOOTH! BUT YOU MUSTN'T GET OUT OF CONTROL, BROTHER!
TOO BAD YOU DON'T HAVE ANOTHER BARREL OF AMMONIA TO EMPTY IN MY FACE!
YOU WANT ANOTHER BARREL, EH? TAKE A LOOK DOWN BELOW, SMART GUY!
TOO LATE! THE TIGHT-DRAWN ROPE SPRINGS THE TRAP!
DOWN HURTLES THE FIENDISHLY TIMED MISSILE...
SO THAT'S THE GAME--TAG WITH THE LIONS, AND I'M IT!
6
AND THE SAVAGE BEASTS CLOSE IN FOR THE KILL!
TOO BAD FRANK BUCK ISN'T HERE--MAYBE HE COULD BRING ME BACK ALIVE OUT OF THIS!

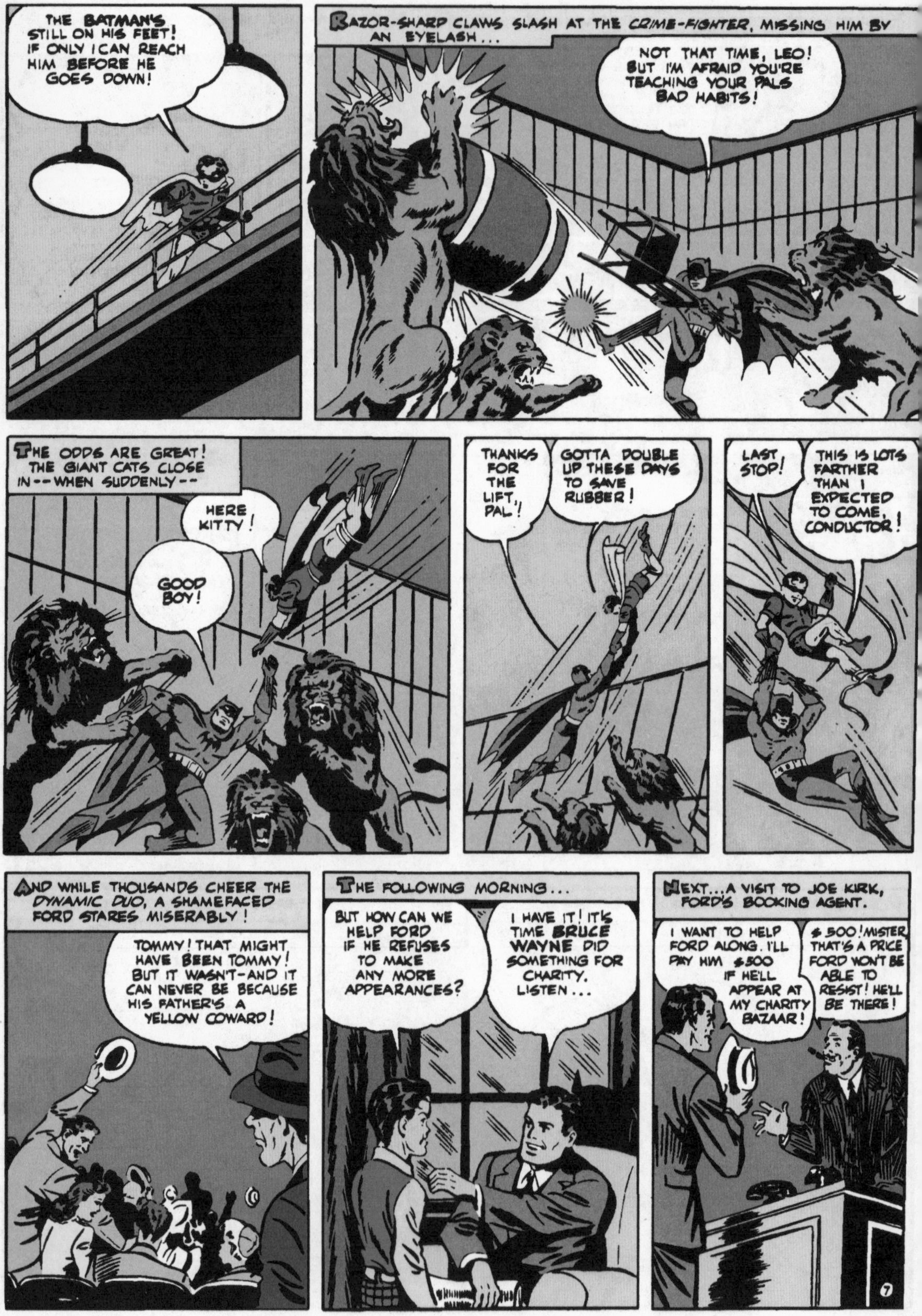
THE BATMAN'S STILL ON HIS FEET! IF ONLY I CAN REACH HIM BEFORE HE GOES DOWN!
RAZOR-SHARP CLAWS SLASH AT THE CRIME-FIGHTER, MISSING HIM BY AN EYELASH...
NOT THAT TIME, LEO! BUT I'M AFRAID YOU'RE TEACHING YOUR PALS BAD HABITS!
THE ODDS ARE GREAT! THE GIANT CATS CLOSE IN--WHEN SUDDENLY--
HERE KITTY!
GOOD BOY!
THANKS FOR THE LIFT, PAL!
GOTTA DOUBLE UP THESE DAYS TO SAVE RUBBER!
LAST STOP!
THIS IS LOTS FARTHER THAN I EXPECTED TO COME, CONDUCTOR!
AND WHILE THOUSANDS CHEER THE DYNAMIC DUO, A SHAMEFACED FORD STARES MISERABLY!
TOMMY! THAT MIGHT HAVE BEEN TOMMY! BUT IT WASN'T--AND IT CAN NEVER BE BECAUSE HIS FATHER'S A YELLOW COWARD!
THE FOLLOWING MORNING...
BUT HOW CAN WE HELP FORD IF HE REFUSES TO MAKE ANY MORE APPEARANCES?
I HAVE IT! IT'S TIME BRUCE WAYNE DID SOMETHING FOR CHARITY. LISTEN...
NEXT...A VISIT TO JOE KIRK, FORD'S BOOKING AGENT.
I WANT TO HELP FORD ALONG. I'LL PAY HIM $500 IF HE'LL APPEAR AT MY CHARITY BAZAAR!
$500! MISTER THAT'S A PRICE FORD WON'T BE ABLE TO RESIST! HE'LL BE THERE!
7

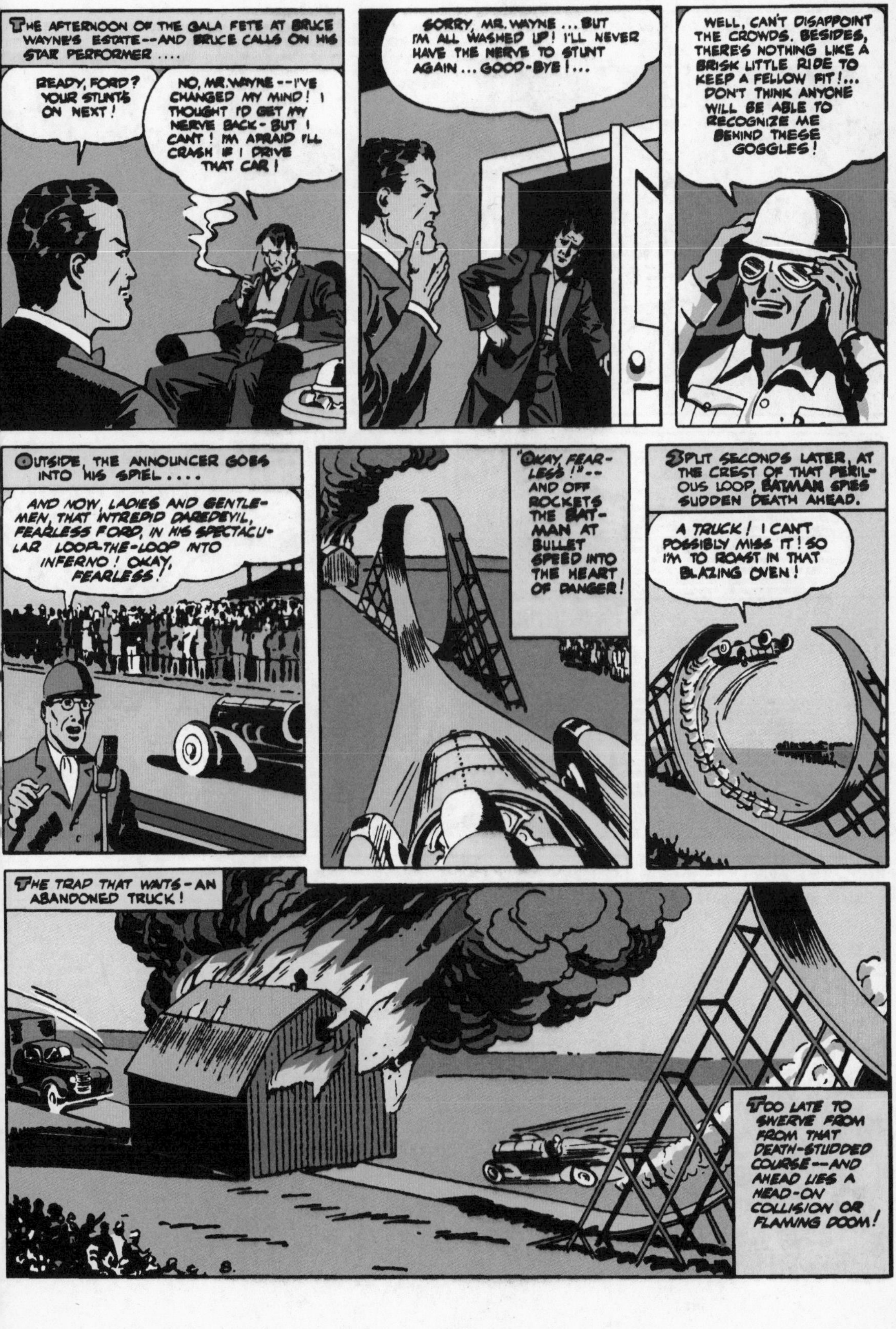
THE AFTERNOON OF THE GALA FETE AT BRUCE WAYNE'S ESTATE--AND BRUCE CALLS ON HIS STAR PERFORMER ....
READY, FORD? YOUR STUNT'S ON NEXT!
NO, MR. WAYNE--I'VE CHANGED MY MIND! I THOUGHT I'D GET MY NERVE BACK-BUT I CANT! I'M AFRAID I'LL CRASH IF I DRIVE THAT CAR!
SORRY, MR. WAYNE ... BUT I'M ALL WASHED UP! I'LL NEVER HAVE THE NERVE TO STUNT AGAIN ... GOOD-BYE!...
WELL, CAN'T DISAPPOINT THE CROWDS. BESIDES, THERE'S NOTHING LIKE A BRISK LITTLE RIDE TO KEEP A FELLOW FIT!... DON'T THINK ANYONE WILL BE ABLE TO RECOGNIZE ME BEHIND THESE GOGGLES!
OUTSIDE, THE ANNOUNCER GOES INTO HIS SPIEL ....
AND NOW, LADIES AND GENTLEMEN, THAT INTREPID DAREDEVIL, FEARLESS FORD, IN HIS SPECTACULAR LOOP-THE-LOOP INTO INFERNO! OKAY, FEARLESS!
"OKAY, FEARLESS!"--AND OFF ROCKETS THE BATMAN AT BULLET SPEED INTO THE HEART OF DANGER!
SPLIT SECONDS LATER, AT THE CREST OF THAT PERILOUS LOOP, BATMAN SPIES SUDDEN DEATH AHEAD.
A TRUCK! I CANT POSSIBLY MISS IT! SO I'M TO ROAST IN THAT BLAZING OVEN!
THE TRAP THAT WAITS-AN ABANDONED TRUCK!
TOO LATE TO SWERVE FROM FROM THAT DEATH-STUDDED COURSE--AND AHEAD LIES A HEAD-ON COLLISION OR FLAMING DOOM!
8.

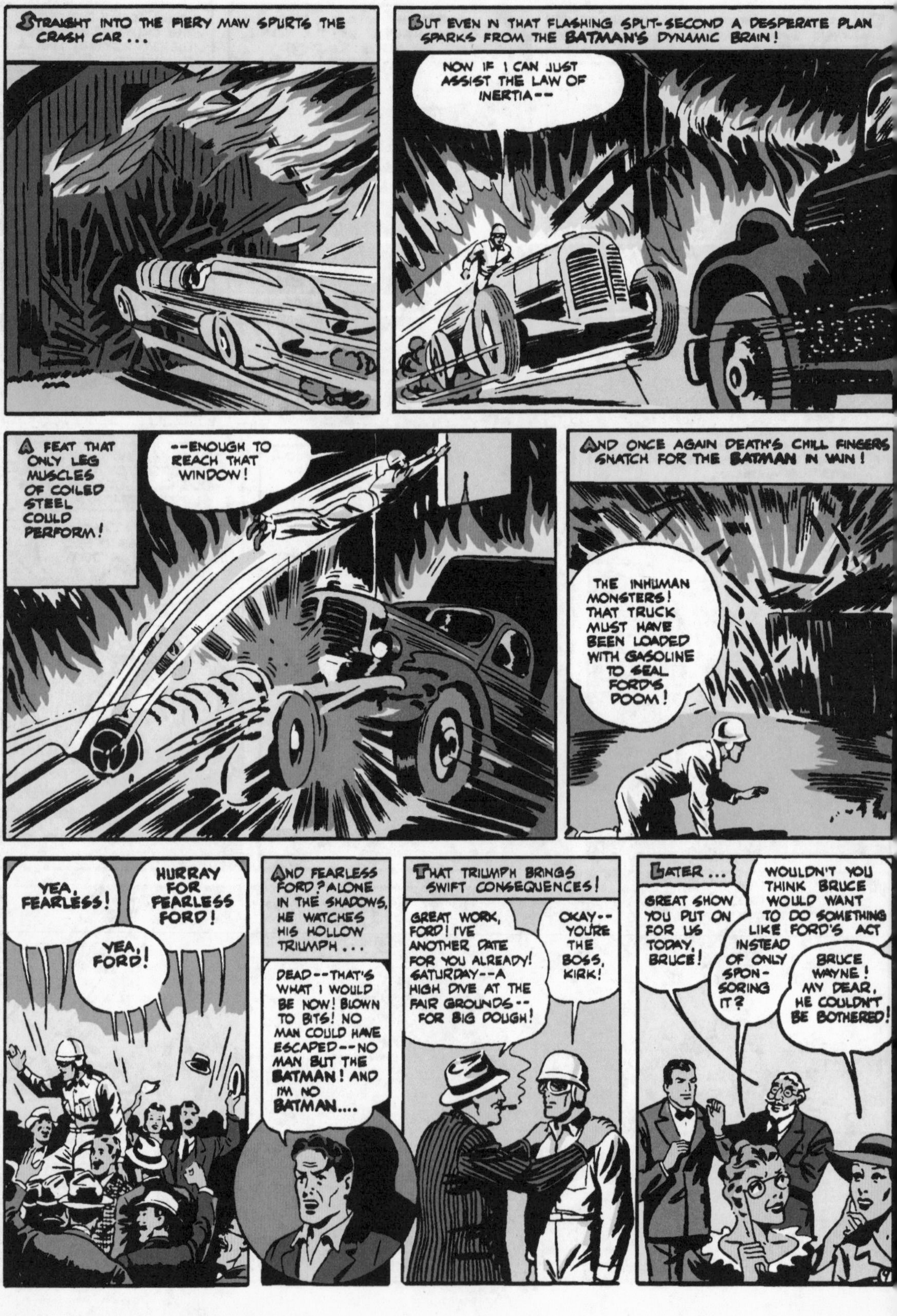
STRAIGHT INTO THE FIERY MAW SPURTS THE CRASH CAR ...
BUT EVEN IN THAT FLASHING SPLIT-SECOND A DESPERATE PLAN SPARKS FROM THE BATMAN'S DYNAMIC BRAIN!
NOW IF I CAN JUST ASSIST THE LAW OF INERTIA--
A FEAT THAT ONLY LEG MUSCLES OF COILED STEEL COULD PERFORM!
--ENOUGH TO REACH THAT WINDOW!
AND ONCE AGAIN DEATH'S CHILL FINGERS SNATCH FOR THE BATMAN IN VAIN!
THE INHUMAN MONSTERS! THAT TRUCK MUST HAVE BEEN LOADED WITH GASOLINE TO SEAL FORD'S DOOM!
YEA, FEARLESS!
HURRAY FOR FEARLESS FORD!
YEA, FORD!
AND FEARLESS FORD? ALONE IN THE SHADOWS, HE WATCHES HIS HOLLOW TRIUMPH ...
DEAD--THAT'S WHAT I WOULD BE NOW! BLOWN TO BITS! NO MAN COULD HAVE ESCAPED--NO MAN BUT THE BATMAN! AND I'M NO BATMAN....
THAT TRIUMPH BRINGS SWIFT CONSEQUENCES!
GREAT WORK, FORD! I'VE ANOTHER DATE FOR YOU ALREADY! SATURDAY--A HIGH DIVE AT THE FAIR GROUNDS-- FOR BIG DOUGH!
OKAY-- YOU'RE THE BOSS, KIRK!
LATER ...
GREAT SHOW YOU PUT ON FOR US TODAY, BRUCE!
WOULDN'T YOU THINK BRUCE WOULD WANT TO DO SOMETHING LIKE FORD'S ACT INSTEAD OF ONLY SPON-SORING IT?
BRUCE WAYNE! MY DEAR, HE COULDN'T BE BOTHERED!

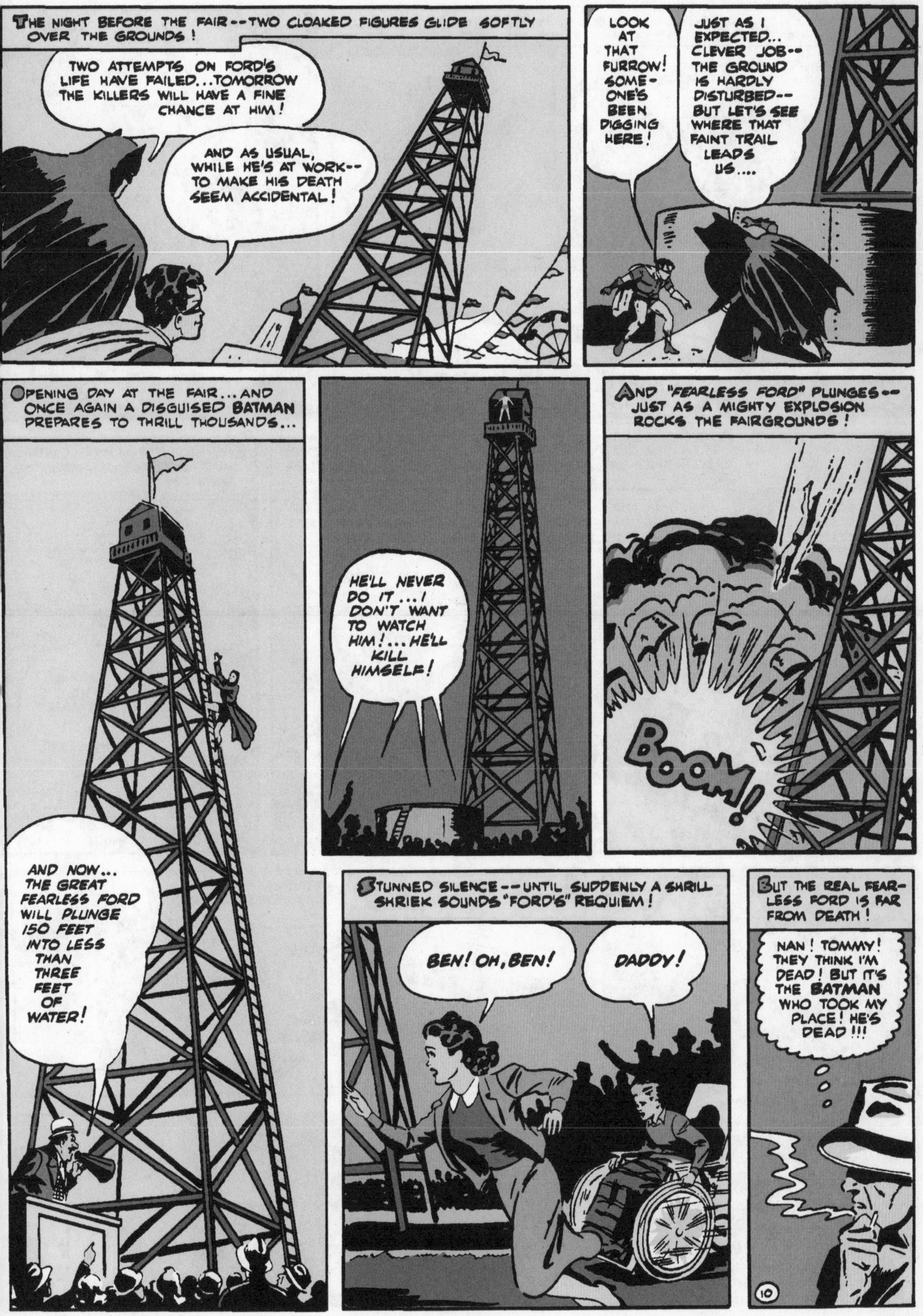
THE NIGHT BEFORE THE FAIR--TWO CLOAKED FIGURES GLIDE SOFTLY OVER THE GROUNDS!
TWO ATTEMPTS ON FORD'S LIFE HAVE FAILED...TOMORROW THE KILLERS WILL HAVE A FINE CHANCE AT HIM!
AND AS USUAL, WHILE HE'S AT WORK--TO MAKE HIS DEATH SEEM ACCIDENTAL!
LOOK AT THAT FURROW! SOME-ONE'S BEEN DIGGING HERE!
JUST AS I EXPECTED... CLEVER JOB--THE GROUND IS HARDLY DISTURBED--BUT LET'S SEE WHERE THAT FAINT TRAIL LEADS US....
OPENING DAY AT THE FAIR...AND ONCE AGAIN A DISGUISED BATMAN PREPARES TO THRILL THOUSANDS...
AND NOW... THE GREAT FEARLESS FORD WILL PLUNGE 150 FEET INTO LESS THAN THREE FEET OF WATER!
HE'LL NEVER DO IT...I DON'T WANT TO WATCH HIM!...HE'LL KILL HIMSELF!
AND "FEARLESS FORD" PLUNGES--JUST AS A MIGHTY EXPLOSION ROCKS THE FAIRGROUNDS!
BOOM!!
STUNNED SILENCE--UNTIL SUDDENLY A SHRILL SHRIEK SOUNDS "FORD'S" REQUIEM!
BEN! OH, BEN!
DADDY!
BUT THE REAL FEAR-LESS FORD IS FAR FROM DEATH!
NAN! TOMMY! THEY THINK I'M DEAD! BUT IT'S THE BATMAN WHO TOOK MY PLACE! HE'S DEAD!!!
10

MEANWHILE, ON THE ALMOST DESERTED MIDWAY, THE ROAR OF THE EXPLOSION CATAPULTS ROBIN INTO STRANGE ACTION...

COME ON, FOLKS-- KNOCK 'EM DOWN!

WIN A PRIZE!

GLAD TO OBLIGE!

TRY YOUR SKILL 5 BALLS 10¢

NO FAIR PRACTICING ON THE CUSTOMERS!

THE CURTAIN AT THE REAR OF THE BOOTH IS ROBIN'S GOAL-THE END OF THE FAINT DIGGING TRAIL FROM THE DIVING TANK!

TWO DOWN-- AND THE PRIZE OUGHT TO BE BACK HERE - KILLER KIRK!

WAITING FOR YOU, YOUNGSTER! GOT YOUR BOTTLES ALL READY!

OUT ON THE FIELD, THE BOMB CRATER YIELDS AN AMAZING SURPRISE!

THAT'S NO-BODY-- IT'S A DUMMY!

JUST A MECHANICAL CONTRAPTION, BUT IT FOOLED ME!

AND FROM THE TOWER OVERHEAD SUDDENLY SPRINGS THE BATMAN!

LOOK OUT!

THAT'S THE BATMAN!

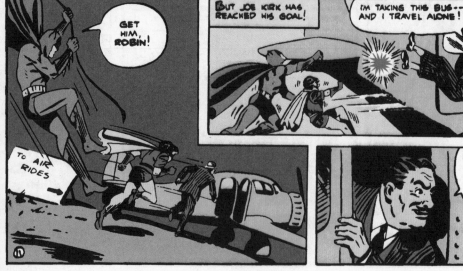

GET HIM, ROBIN!

TO AIR RIDES

BUT JOE KIRK HAS REACHED HIS GOAL!

I'M TAKING THIS BUS-- AND I TRAVEL ALONE!

BETTER TEACH THAT BRAT SOME MANNERS, BATMAN! I AIN'T GOT TIME!

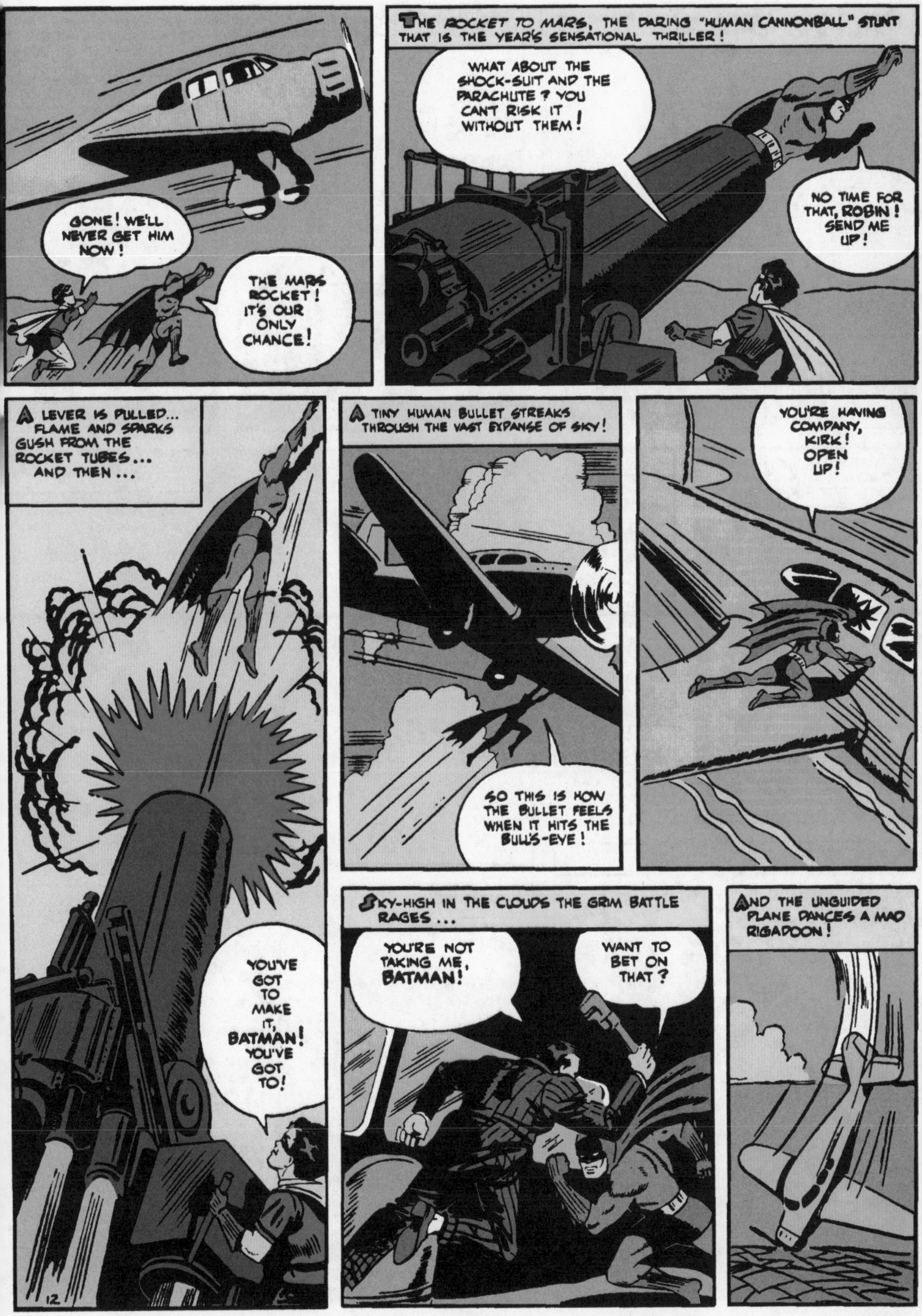
GONE! WE'LL NEVER GET HIM NOW!
THE MARS ROCKET! IT'S OUR ONLY CHANCE!
THE ROCKET TO MARS, THE DARING "HUMAN CANNONBALL" STUNT THAT IS THE YEAR'S SENSATIONAL THRILLER!
WHAT ABOUT THE SHOCK-SUIT AND THE PARACHUTE? YOU CAN'T RISK IT WITHOUT THEM!
NO TIME FOR THAT, ROBIN! SEND ME UP!
A LEVER IS PULLED... FLAME AND SPARKS GUSH FROM THE ROCKET TUBES... AND THEN...
YOU'VE GOT TO MAKE IT, BATMAN! YOU'VE GOT TO!
12
A TINY HUMAN BULLET STREAKS THROUGH THE VAST EXPANSE OF SKY!
SO THIS IS HOW THE BULLET FEELS WHEN IT HITS THE BULL'S-EYE!
YOU'RE HAVING COMPANY, KIRK! OPEN UP!
SKY-HIGH IN THE CLOUDS THE GRIM BATTLE RAGES...
YOU'RE NOT TAKING ME, BATMAN!
WANT TO BET ON THAT?
AND THE UNGUIDED PLANE DANCES A MAD RIGADOON!

PERIL TO ONE HALF OF THE DYNAMIC PARTNERSHIP MEANS ACTION FOR THE OTHER!

THAT'S STRANGE! THOSE DOORS WERE CLOSED--AND NOBODY KNEW WE LEFT THE BATPLANE HERE!

THE MYSTERY SOON CLEARS!

I CAN'T OPERATE THIS THING! SIT DOWN AND GET IT STARTED--OR, SO HELP ME, I'LL PUT A BULLET IN YOU!

RUNNING AWAY, FORD! YOU MISERABLE COWARD!

I'M NOT RUNNING AWAY! I'M AFTER JOE KIRK--THE PROTECTION RACKET BOSS! NOT SATISFIED WITH HIS AGENTS COMMISSION, HE'S BEEN HIJACKING MOST OF EVERY STUNT MAN'S PAY AND KILLING ANYONE WHO WOULDN'T COME ACROSS!

SWIFTLY THE BATPLANE OVERHAULS ITS QUARRY, UNTIL THE BOMBSIGHT MIRRORS KIRK'S SHIP--

AND FEARLESS FORD LIVES UP TO HIS NAME!

BUT DEATH PLAYS ITS LAST CARD--

CAN'T MAKE IT... CAN'T SAVE BATMAN...

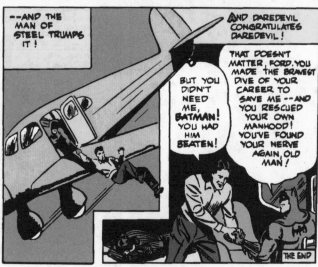

--AND THE MAN OF STEEL TRUMPS IT!

BUT YOU DIDN'T NEED ME, BATMAN! YOU HAD HIM BEATEN!

AND DAREDEVIL CONGRATULATES DAREDEVIL!

THAT DOESN'T MATTER, FORD. YOU MADE THE BRAVEST DIVE OF YOUR CAREER TO SAVE ME --AND YOU RESCUED YOUR OWN MANHOOD! YOU'VE FOUND YOUR NERVE AGAIN, OLD MAN!

THE END

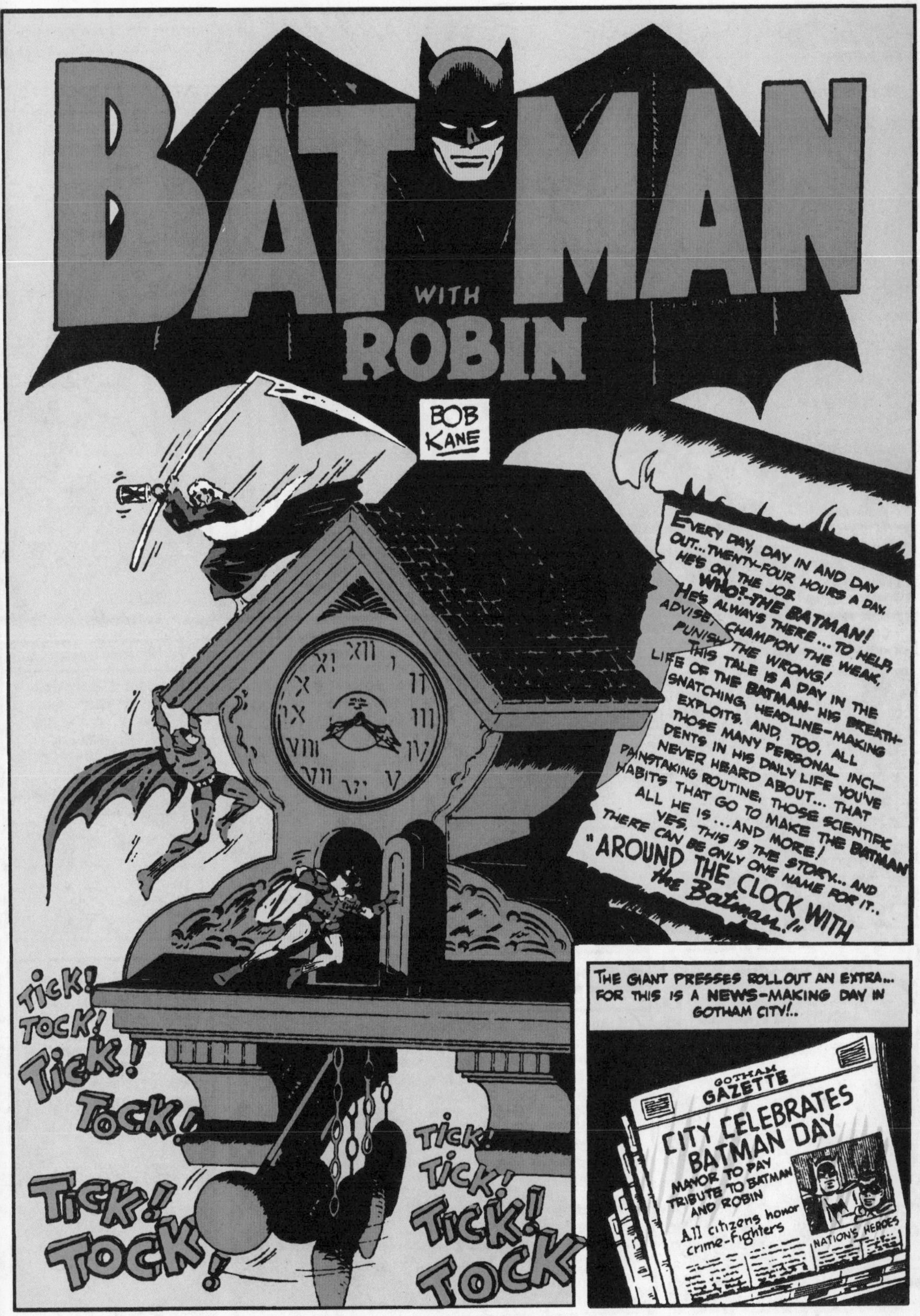

BATMAN
WITH
ROBIN
BOB KANE
EVERY DAY, DAY IN AND DAY OUT...TWENTY-FOUR HOURS A DAY. HE'S ON THE JOB. WHO?--THE BATMAN! HE'S ALWAYS THERE... TO HELP, ADVISE, CHAMPION THE WEAK, PUNISH THE WRONG! THIS TALE IS A DAY IN THE LIFE OF THE BATMAN- HIS BREATH-SNATCHING, HEADLINE-MAKING EXPLOITS, AND, TOO, ALL THOSE MANY PERSONAL INCI-DENTS IN HIS DAILY LIFE YOU'VE NEVER HEARD ABOUT... THAT PAINSTAKING ROUTINE, THOSE SCIENTIFIC HABITS THAT GO TO MAKE THE BATMAN ALL HE IS ... AND MORE! YES, THIS IS THE STORY... AND THERE CAN BE ONLY ONE NAME FOR IT.. "AROUND THE CLOCK WITH the Batman!"
TICK! TOCK! TICK! TOCK!
TICK! TOCK!
TICK! TICK! TICK! TOCK
THE GIANT PRESSES ROLL OUT AN EXTRA... FOR THIS IS A NEWS-MAKING DAY IN GOTHAM CITY!..
GOTHAM GAZETTE
CITY CELEBRATES BATMAN DAY
MAYOR TO PAY TRIBUTE TO BATMAN AND ROBIN
All citizens honor crime-fighters
NATION'S HEROES

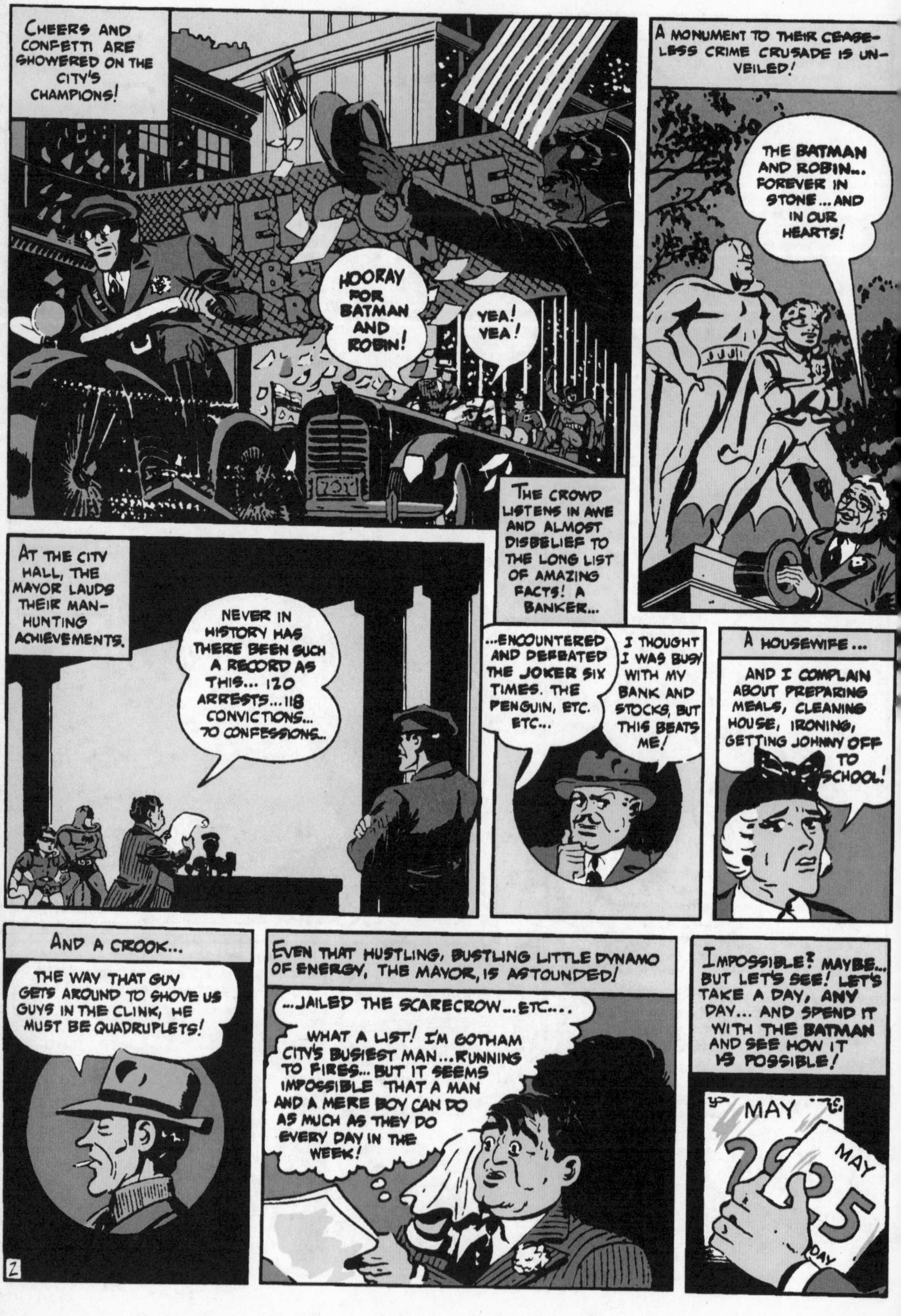
CHEERS AND CONFETTI ARE SHOWERED ON THE CITY'S CHAMPIONS!
WELCOME
HOORAY FOR BATMAN AND ROBIN!
YEA! YEA!
A MONUMENT TO THEIR CEASELESS CRIME CRUSADE IS UNVEILED!
THE BATMAN AND ROBIN... FOREVER IN STONE... AND IN OUR HEARTS!
AT THE CITY HALL, THE MAYOR LAUDS THEIR MAN-HUNTING ACHIEVEMENTS.
NEVER IN HISTORY HAS THERE BEEN SUCH A RECORD AS THIS... 120 ARRESTS... 118 CONVICTIONS... 70 CONFESSIONS...
THE CROWD LISTENS IN AWE AND ALMOST DISBELIEF TO THE LONG LIST OF AMAZING FACTS! A BANKER...
...ENCOUNTERED AND DEFEATED THE JOKER SIX TIMES. THE PENGUIN, ETC. ETC...
I THOUGHT I WAS BUSY WITH MY BANK AND STOCKS, BUT THIS BEATS ME!
A HOUSEWIFE...
AND I COMPLAIN ABOUT PREPARING MEALS, CLEANING HOUSE, IRONING, GETTING JOHNNY OFF TO SCHOOL!
AND A CROOK...
THE WAY THAT GUY GETS AROUND TO SHOVE US GUYS IN THE CLINK, HE MUST BE QUADRUPLETS!
2
EVEN THAT HUSTLING, BUSTLING LITTLE DYNAMO OF ENERGY, THE MAYOR, IS ASTOUNDED!
...JAILED THE SCARECROW... ETC....
WHAT A LIST! I'M GOTHAM CITY'S BUSIEST MAN... RUNNING TO FIRES... BUT IT SEEMS IMPOSSIBLE THAT A MAN AND A MERE BOY CAN DO AS MUCH AS THEY DO EVERY DAY IN THE WEEK!
IMPOSSIBLE? MAYBE... BUT LET'S SEE! LET'S TAKE A DAY, ANY DAY... AND SPEND IT WITH THE BATMAN AND SEE HOW IT IS POSSIBLE!
MAY
MAY
25
DAY

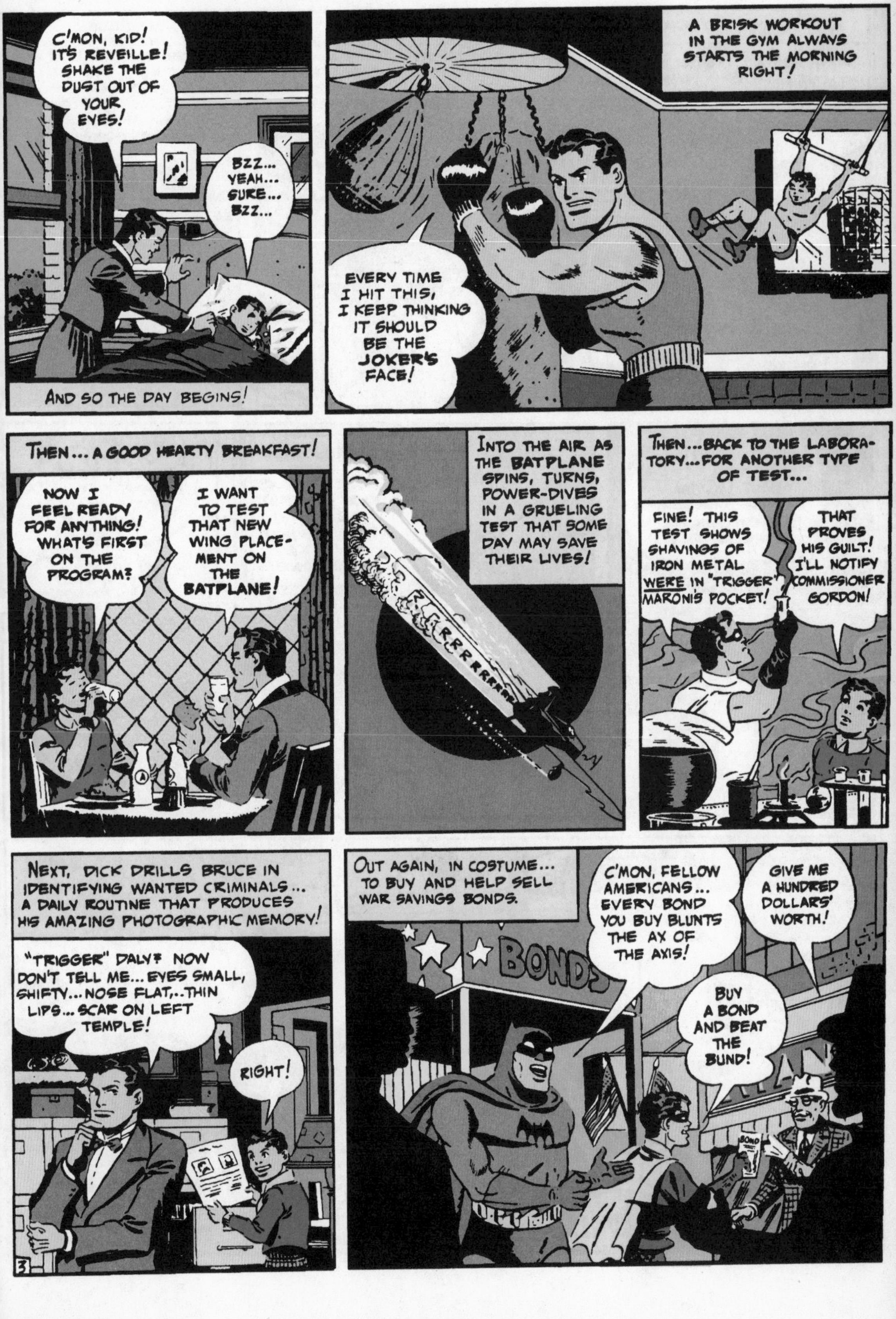
C'MON, KID! IT'S REVEILLE! SHAKE THE DUST OUT OF YOUR EYES!
BZZ... YEAH... SURE... BZZ...
AND SO THE DAY BEGINS!
A BRISK WORKOUT IN THE GYM ALWAYS STARTS THE MORNING RIGHT!
EVERY TIME I HIT THIS, I KEEP THINKING IT SHOULD BE THE JOKER'S FACE!
THEN... A GOOD HEARTY BREAKFAST!
NOW I FEEL READY FOR ANYTHING! WHAT'S FIRST ON THE PROGRAM?
I WANT TO TEST THAT NEW WING PLACEMENT ON THE BATPLANE!
INTO THE AIR AS THE BATPLANE SPINS, TURNS, POWER-DIVES IN A GRUELING TEST THAT SOME DAY MAY SAVE THEIR LIVES!
RRRRRRRRR
THEN...BACK TO THE LABORATORY...FOR ANOTHER TYPE OF TEST...
FINE! THIS TEST SHOWS SHAVINGS OF IRON METAL WERE IN "TRIGGER" MARONI'S POCKET!
THAT PROVES HIS GUILT! I'LL NOTIFY COMMISSIONER GORDON!
NEXT, DICK DRILLS BRUCE IN IDENTIFYING WANTED CRIMINALS... A DAILY ROUTINE THAT PRODUCES HIS AMAZING PHOTOGRAPHIC MEMORY!
"TRIGGER" DALY? NOW DON'T TELL ME... EYES SMALL, SHIFTY... NOSE FLAT,..THIN LIPS... SCAR ON LEFT TEMPLE!
RIGHT!
3
OUT AGAIN, IN COSTUME... TO BUY AND HELP SELL WAR SAVINGS BONDS.
C'MON, FELLOW AMERICANS... EVERY BOND YOU BUY BLUNTS THE AX OF THE AXIS!
GIVE ME A HUNDRED DOLLARS' WORTH!
BUY A BOND AND BEAT THE BUND!
BONDS

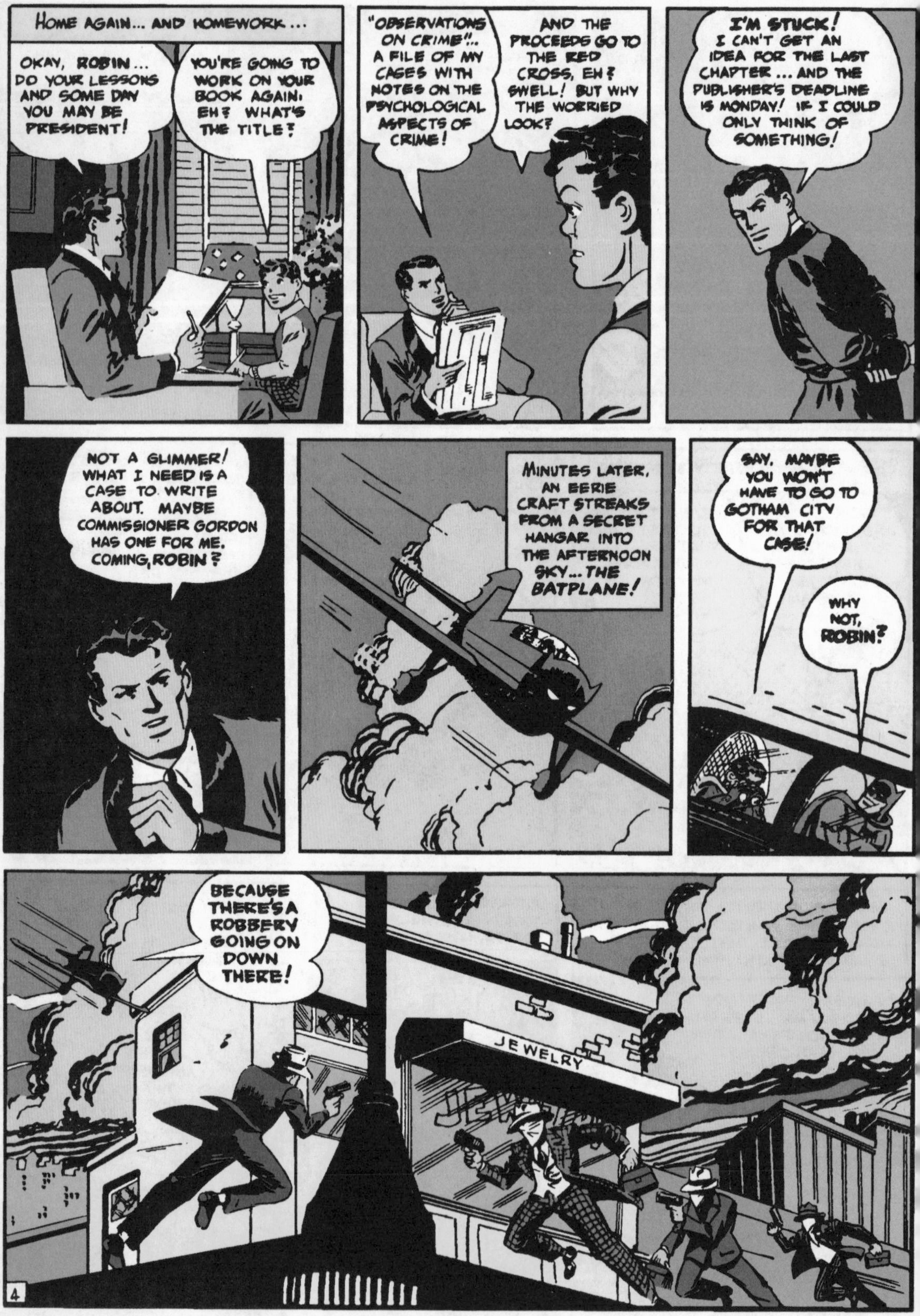

HOME AGAIN... AND HOMEWORK...
OKAY, ROBIN... DO YOUR LESSONS AND SOME DAY YOU MAY BE PRESIDENT!
YOU'RE GOING TO WORK ON YOUR BOOK AGAIN, EH? WHAT'S THE TITLE?
"OBSERVATIONS ON CRIME"... A FILE OF MY CASES WITH NOTES ON THE PSYCHOLOGICAL ASPECTS OF CRIME!
AND THE PROCEEDS GO TO THE RED CROSS, EH? SWELL! BUT WHY THE WORRIED LOOK?
I'M STUCK! I CAN'T GET AN IDEA FOR THE LAST CHAPTER ... AND THE PUBLISHER'S DEADLINE IS MONDAY! IF I COULD ONLY THINK OF SOMETHING!
NOT A GLIMMER! WHAT I NEED IS A CASE TO WRITE ABOUT. MAYBE COMMISSIONER GORDON HAS ONE FOR ME. COMING, ROBIN?
MINUTES LATER, AN EERIE CRAFT STREAKS FROM A SECRET HANGAR INTO THE AFTERNOON SKY... THE BATPLANE!
SAY, MAYBE YOU WON'T HAVE TO GO TO GOTHAM CITY FOR THAT CASE!
WHY NOT, ROBIN?
BECAUSE THERE'S A ROBBERY GOING ON DOWN THERE!
JEWELRY
4

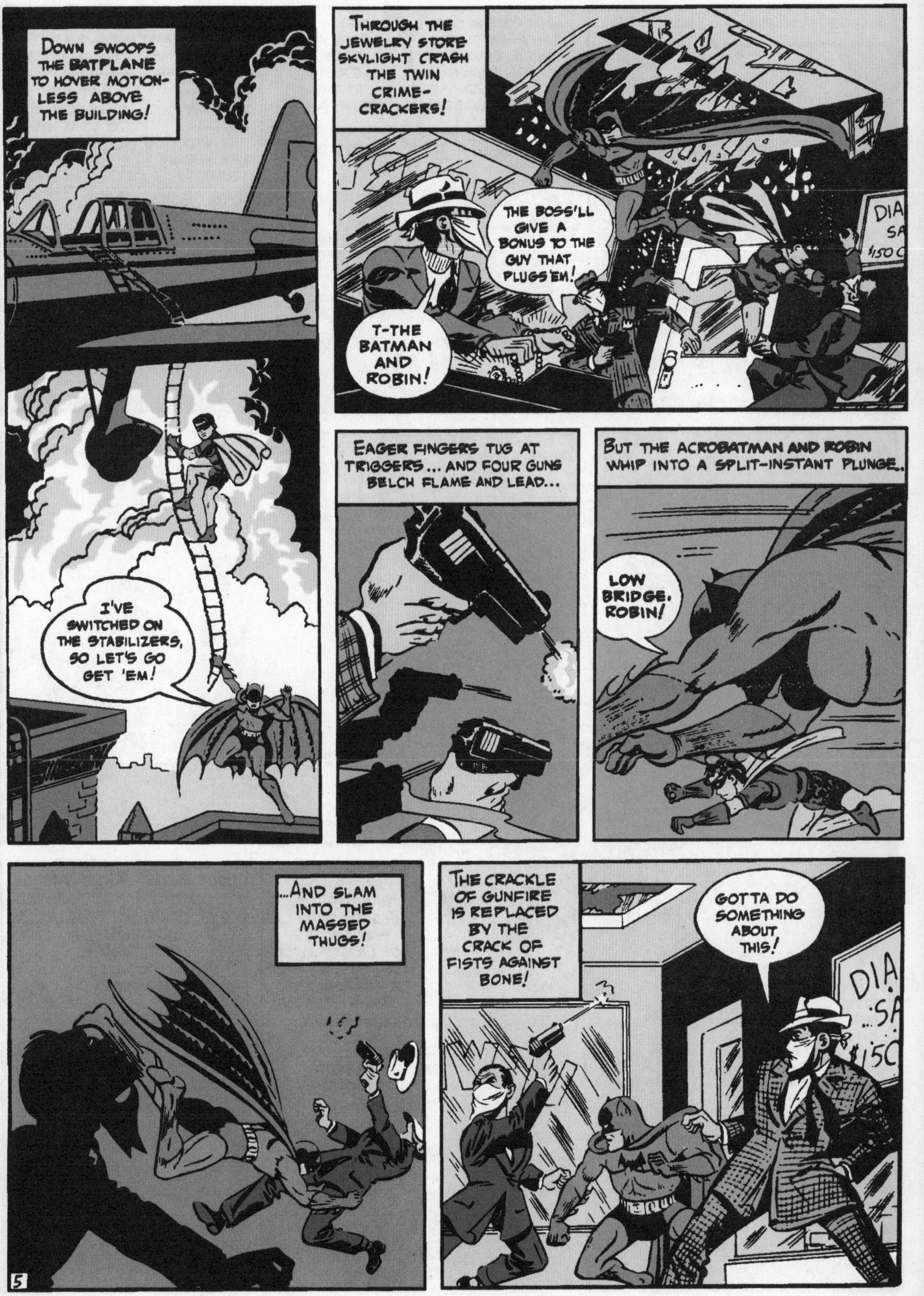
DOWN SWOOPS THE BATPLANE TO HOVER MOTION-LESS ABOVE THE BUILDING!
I'VE SWITCHED ON THE STABILIZERS, SO LET'S GO GET 'EM!
THROUGH THE JEWELRY STORE SKYLIGHT CRASH THE TWIN CRIME-CRACKERS!
T-THE BATMAN AND ROBIN!
THE BOSS'LL GIVE A BONUS TO THE GUY THAT PLUGS 'EM!
EAGER FINGERS TUG AT TRIGGERS... AND FOUR GUNS BELCH FLAME AND LEAD...
BUT THE ACROBATMAN AND ROBIN WHIP INTO A SPLIT-INSTANT PLUNGE..
LOW BRIDGE, ROBIN!
...AND SLAM INTO THE MASSED THUGS!
5
THE CRACKLE OF GUNFIRE IS REPLACED BY THE CRACK OF FISTS AGAINST BONE!
GOTTA DO SOMETHING ABOUT THIS!

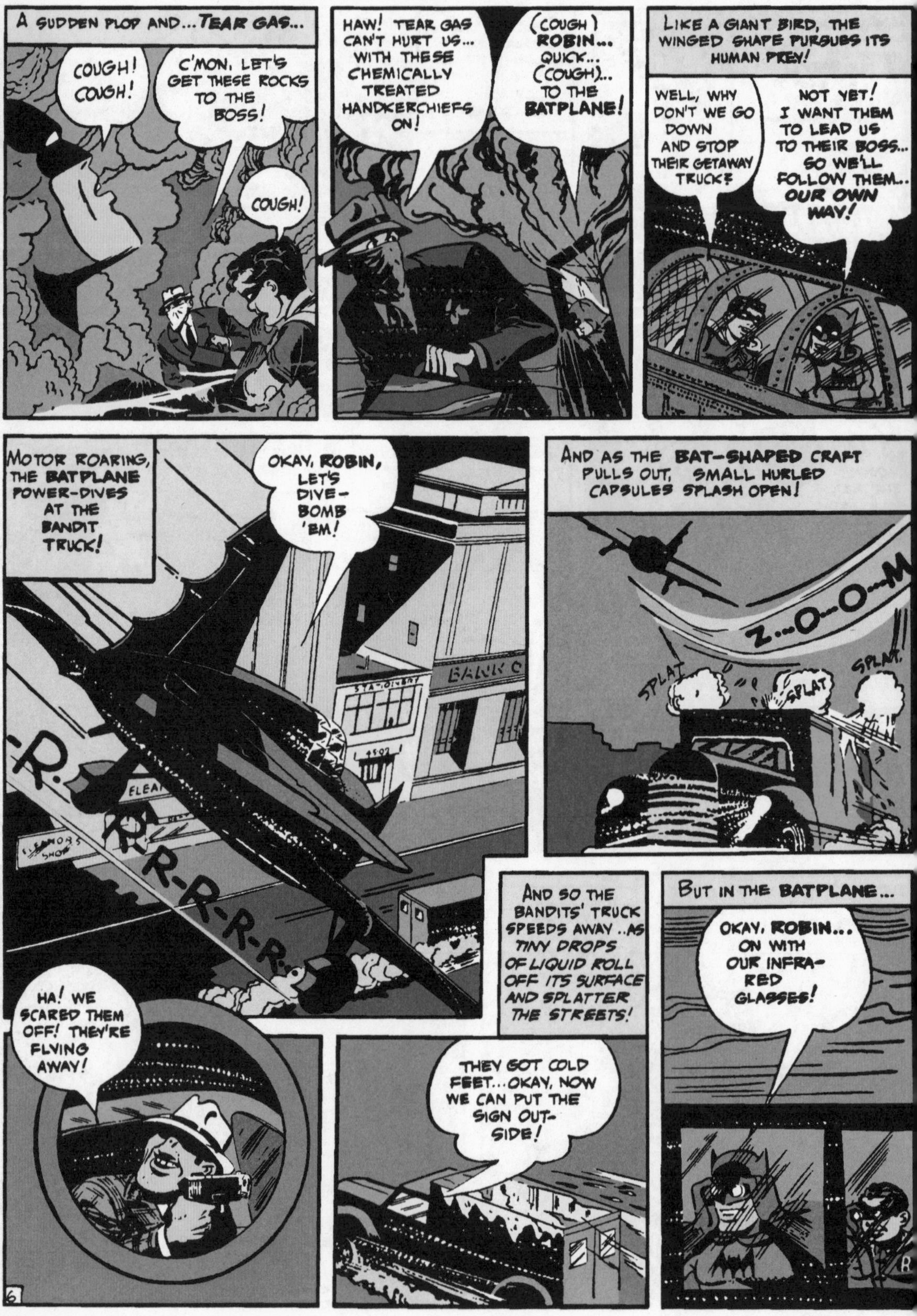
A SUDDEN PLOP AND... TEAR GAS...
COUGH! COUGH!
C'MON, LET'S GET THESE ROCKS TO THE BOSS!
COUGH!
HAW! TEAR GAS CAN'T HURT US... WITH THESE CHEMICALLY TREATED HANDKERCHIEFS ON!
(COUGH) ROBIN... QUICK... (COUGH)... TO THE BATPLANE!
LIKE A GIANT BIRD, THE WINGED SHAPE PURSUES ITS HUMAN PREY!
WELL, WHY DON'T WE GO DOWN AND STOP THEIR GETAWAY TRUCK?
NOT YET! I WANT THEM TO LEAD US TO THEIR BOSS... SO WE'LL FOLLOW THEM... OUR OWN WAY!
MOTOR ROARING, THE BATPLANE POWER-DIVES AT THE BANDIT TRUCK!
OKAY, ROBIN, LET'S DIVE-BOMB 'EM!
R-R-R-R-R-R
AND AS THE BAT-SHAPED CRAFT PULLS OUT, SMALL HURLED CAPSULES SPLASH OPEN!
Z-O-O-M
SPLAT SPLAT SPLAT
AND SO THE BANDITS' TRUCK SPEEDS AWAY..AS TINY DROPS OF LIQUID ROLL OFF ITS SURFACE AND SPLATTER THE STREETS!
BUT IN THE BATPLANE...
OKAY, ROBIN... ON WITH OUR INFRA-RED GLASSES!
HA! WE SCARED THEM OFF! THEY'RE FLYING AWAY!
THEY GOT COLD FEET... OKAY, NOW WE CAN PUT THE SIGN OUT-SIDE!

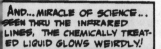

Panel 1: AND... MIRACLE OF SCIENCE... SEEN THRU THE INFRARED LINES, THE CHEMICALLY TREATED LIQUID GLOWS WEIRDLY!

PRETTY EASY TO TRAIL THEM NOW WITHOUT THE BANDITS' KNOWLEDGE!

Panel 2: SOME TIME LATER, THE TRAIL ENDS AT AN OUTDOOR SCULPTURE SHOW!

THAT'S THE TRUCK! THEY PROBABLY STUCK A SIGN ON IT ON THE WAY! CALL THE POLICE ON OUR RADIO, ROBIN!

SCULPTURE EXHIBIT

ART SUPPLIES

Panel 3: FOUR INDIGNANT MEN ARE TAKEN INTO CUSTODY!

NOTHING IN THE TRUCK BUT ART SUPPLIES, SARGE!

SURE! THAT'S OUR BUSINESS... A LEGITIMATE ONE! WE'RE NOT ROBBERS!

Panel 4: THIS IS MR. HODGE, THE ART CONNOISSEUR. HE SAYS THESE MEN ARE OKAY!

YES, WE BUY MATERIALS FROM THEM BECAUSE THEIR PRICES ARE LOW!

IF THE JEWELS AREN'T IN THE TRUCK, THEY MUST BE IN THE SCULPTURE EXHIBIT!

Panel 5: SOME TIME LATER... AN OLD COUPLE JOINS THE SCULPTURE SHOW'S SPECTATORS!

MY, HOW GIGANTIC! TELL ME, SIR, WHY DID YOU MAKE THOSE EYES SO LARGE AND SO DEEP?

THIS PIECE REPRESENTS AN INDIAN HYPNOTIST, AND IT SYMBOLIZES HIS DEEP HYPNOTIC EYES!

Panel 6: EVERYONE HERE SEEMS TO BE A GENUINELY FINE SCULPTOR... TO JUDGE BY THESE PIECES!

NOTHING PHONEY ABOUT THEM! MAYBE THIS ISN'T THE JEWEL CACHE AFTER ALL!

Panel 7: YES... THESE TWO ARE NONE OTHER THAN BATMAN AND ROBIN IN DISGUISE!

WHAT'S UP?

WHEN I STOOD HERE A MINUTE AGO, IT SEEMED AS IF THE EYES IN THAT STATUE LOOKED ALIVE! THERE! SEE IT!

THE BATMAN WATCHES WITH AWE... FOR THE DEEP EYES OF THE TITANIC STATUE BLAZE... WITH AN UNEARTHLY HYPNOTIC LIGHT!

7

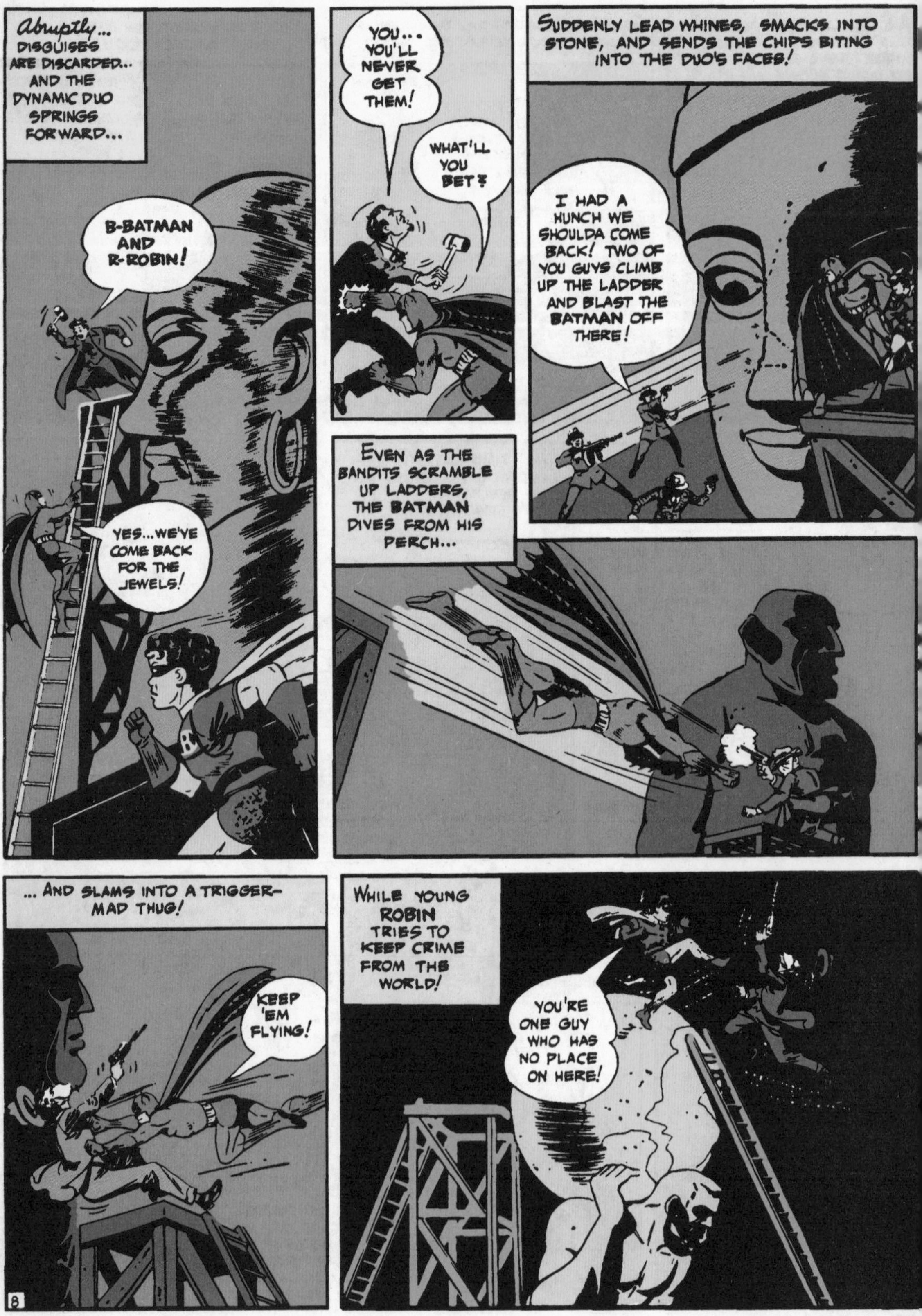
Abruptly... DISGUISES ARE DISCARDED... AND THE DYNAMIC DUO SPRINGS FORWARD...
B-BATMAN AND R-ROBIN!
YES...WE'VE COME BACK FOR THE JEWELS!
YOU... YOU'LL NEVER GET THEM!
WHAT'LL YOU BET?
SUDDENLY LEAD WHINES, SMACKS INTO STONE, AND SENDS THE CHIPS BITING INTO THE DUO'S FACES!
I HAD A HUNCH WE SHOULDA COME BACK! TWO OF YOU GUYS CLIMB UP THE LADDER AND BLAST THE BATMAN OFF THERE!
EVEN AS THE BANDITS SCRAMBLE UP LADDERS, THE BATMAN DIVES FROM HIS PERCH...
... AND SLAMS INTO A TRIGGER-MAD THUG!
KEEP 'EM FLYING!
8
WHILE YOUNG ROBIN TRIES TO KEEP CRIME FROM THE WORLD!
YOU'RE ONE GUY WHO HAS NO PLACE ON HERE!

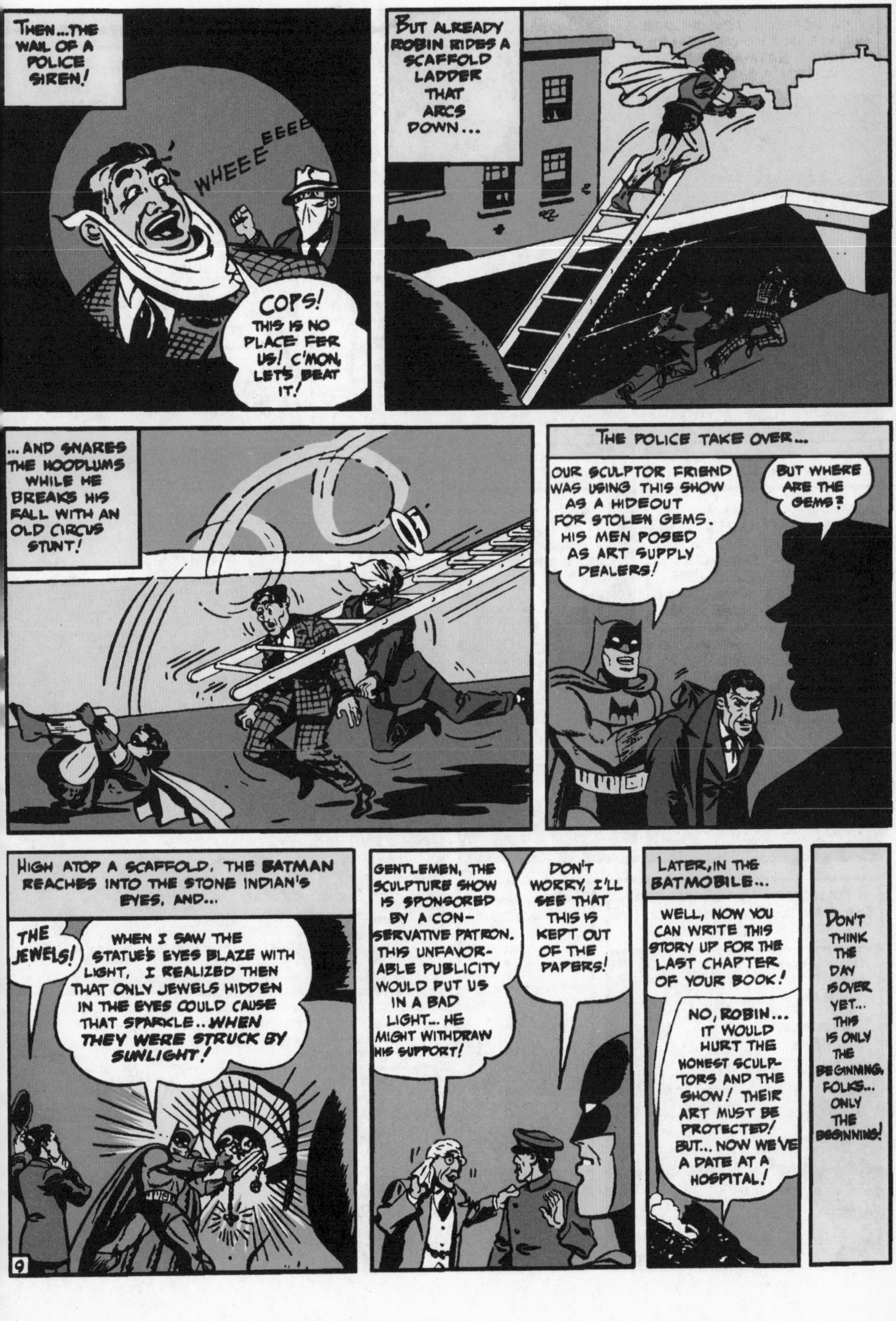
THEN...THE WAIL OF A POLICE SIREN!
WHEEEEEEE
COPS! THIS IS NO PLACE FER US! C'MON, LET'S BEAT IT!
BUT ALREADY ROBIN RIDES A SCAFFOLD LADDER THAT ARCS DOWN...
...AND SNARES THE HOODLUMS WHILE HE BREAKS HIS FALL WITH AN OLD CIRCUS STUNT!
THE POLICE TAKE OVER...
OUR SCULPTOR FRIEND WAS USING THIS SHOW AS A HIDEOUT FOR STOLEN GEMS. HIS MEN POSED AS ART SUPPLY DEALERS!
BUT WHERE ARE THE GEMS?
HIGH ATOP A SCAFFOLD, THE BATMAN REACHES INTO THE STONE INDIAN'S EYES, AND...
THE JEWELS!
WHEN I SAW THE STATUE'S EYES BLAZE WITH LIGHT, I REALIZED THEN THAT ONLY JEWELS HIDDEN IN THE EYES COULD CAUSE THAT SPARKLE...WHEN THEY WERE STRUCK BY SUNLIGHT!
9
GENTLEMEN, THE SCULPTURE SHOW IS SPONSORED BY A CON-SERVATIVE PATRON. THIS UNFAVOR-ABLE PUBLICITY WOULD PUT US IN A BAD LIGHT... HE MIGHT WITHDRAW HIS SUPPORT!
DON'T WORRY, I'LL SEE THAT THIS IS KEPT OUT OF THE PAPERS!
LATER, IN THE BATMOBILE...
WELL, NOW YOU CAN WRITE THIS STORY UP FOR THE LAST CHAPTER OF YOUR BOOK!
NO, ROBIN... IT WOULD HURT THE HONEST SCULP-TORS AND THE SHOW! THEIR ART MUST BE PROTECTED! BUT... NOW WE'VE A DATE AT A HOSPITAL!
DON'T THINK THE DAY IS OVER YET... THIS IS ONLY THE BEGINNING, FOLKS... ONLY THE BEGINNING!

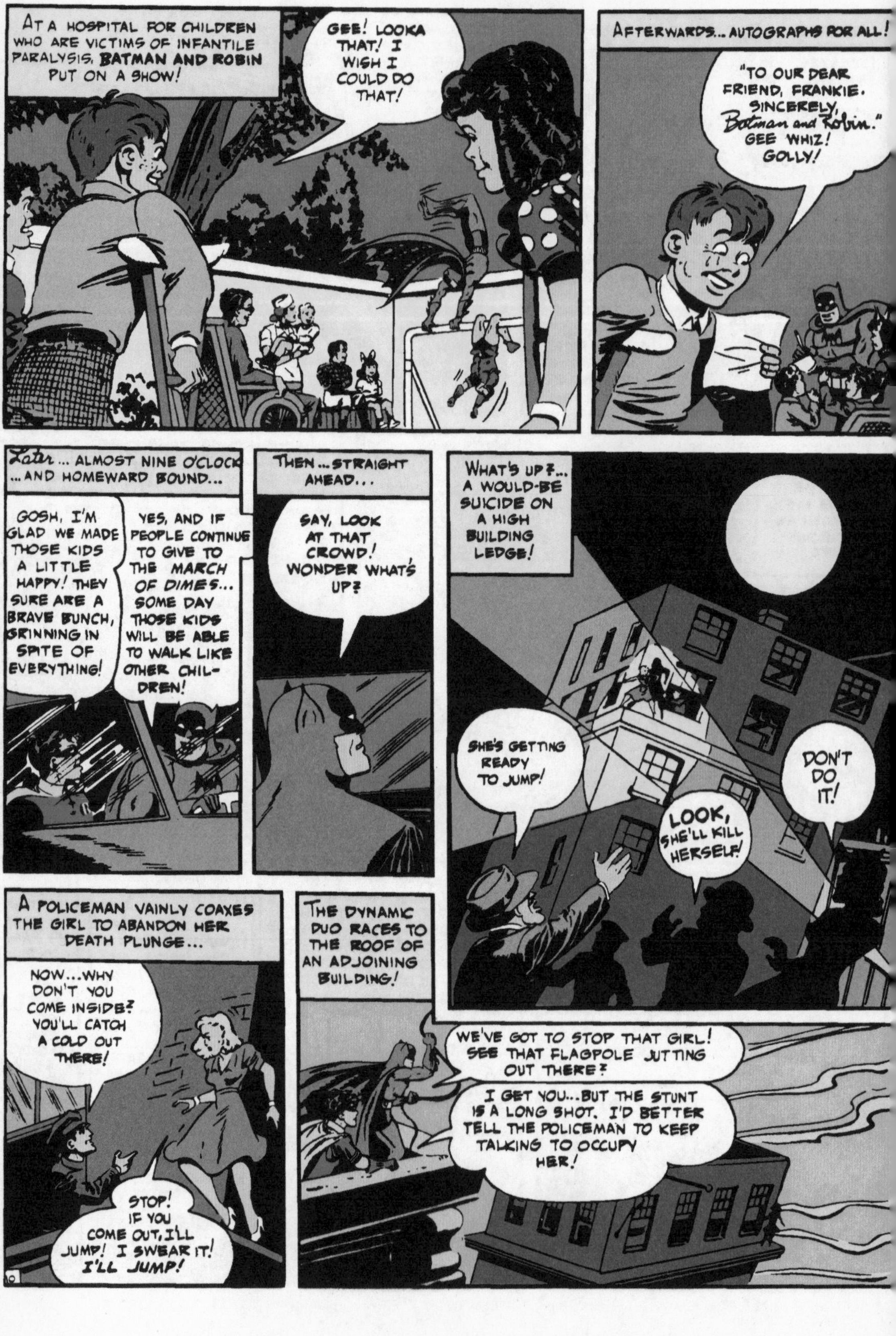
AT A HOSPITAL FOR CHILDREN WHO ARE VICTIMS OF INFANTILE PARALYSIS, BATMAN AND ROBIN PUT ON A SHOW!
GEE! LOOKA THAT! I WISH I COULD DO THAT!
AFTERWARDS... AUTOGRAPHS FOR ALL!
"TO OUR DEAR FRIEND, FRANKIE. SINCERELY, Batman and Robin." GEE WHIZ! GOLLY!
Later... ALMOST NINE O'CLOCK ...AND HOMEWARD BOUND...
GOSH, I'M GLAD WE MADE THOSE KIDS A LITTLE HAPPY! THEY SURE ARE A BRAVE BUNCH, GRINNING IN SPITE OF EVERYTHING!
YES, AND IF PEOPLE CONTINUE TO GIVE TO THE MARCH OF DIMES... SOME DAY THOSE KIDS WILL BE ABLE TO WALK LIKE OTHER CHIL-DREN!
THEN... STRAIGHT AHEAD...
SAY, LOOK AT THAT CROWD! WONDER WHAT'S UP?
WHAT'S UP?... A WOULD-BE SUICIDE ON A HIGH BUILDING LEDGE!
SHE'S GETTING READY TO JUMP!
DON'T DO IT!
LOOK, SHE'LL KILL HERSELF!
A POLICEMAN VAINLY COAXES THE GIRL TO ABANDON HER DEATH PLUNGE...
NOW...WHY DON'T YOU COME INSIDE? YOU'LL CATCH A COLD OUT THERE!
STOP! IF YOU COME OUT, I'LL JUMP! I SWEAR IT! I'LL JUMP!
10
THE DYNAMIC DUO RACES TO THE ROOF OF AN ADJOINING BUILDING!
WE'VE GOT TO STOP THAT GIRL! SEE THAT FLAGPOLE JUTTING OUT THERE?
I GET YOU...BUT THE STUNT IS A LONG SHOT. I'D BETTER TELL THE POLICEMAN TO KEEP TALKING TO OCCUPY HER!

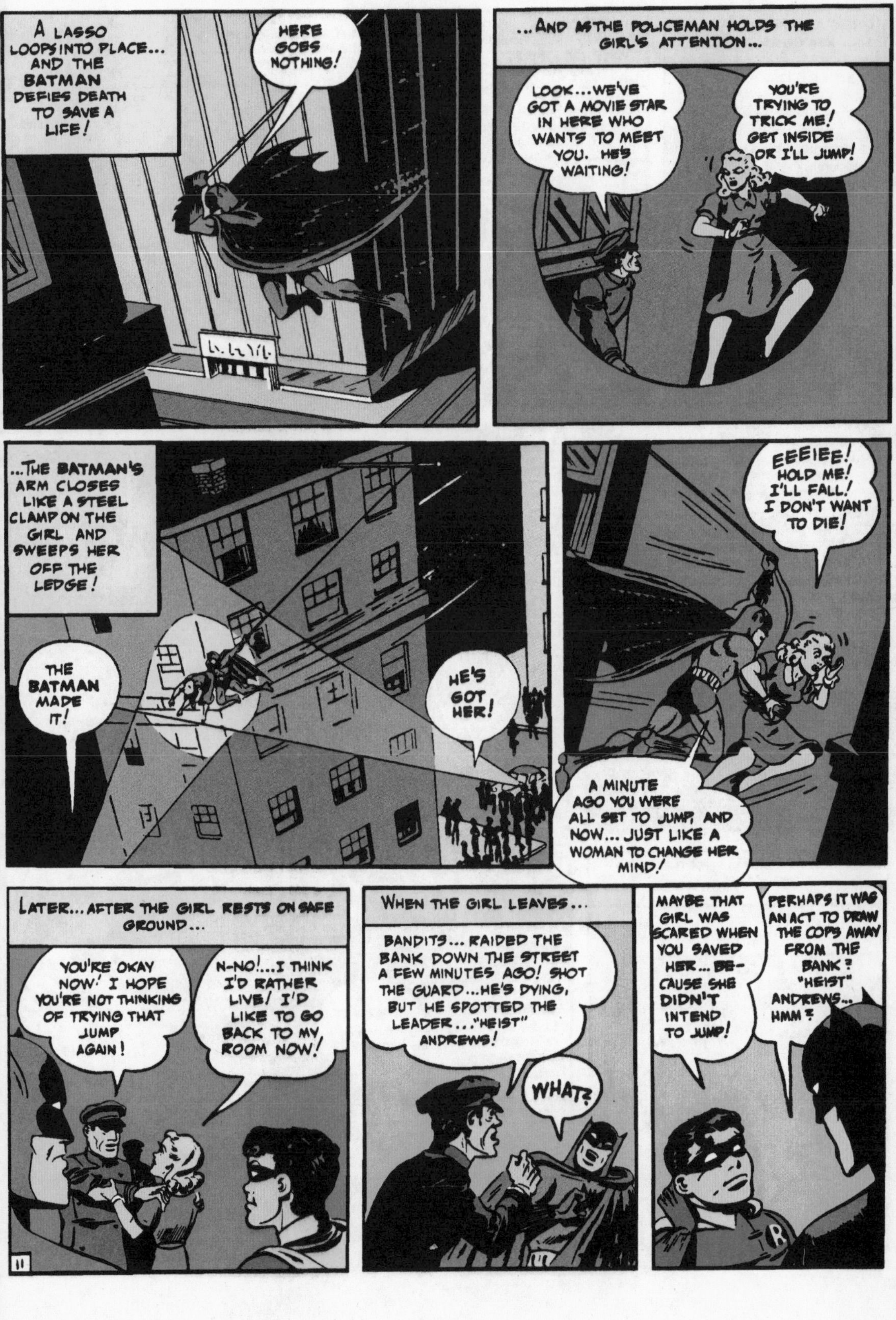

A LASSO LOOPS INTO PLACE... AND THE BATMAN DEFIES DEATH TO SAVE A LIFE!
HERE GOES NOTHING!
...AND AS THE POLICEMAN HOLDS THE GIRL'S ATTENTION...
LOOK...WE'VE GOT A MOVIE STAR IN HERE WHO WANTS TO MEET YOU. HE'S WAITING!
YOU'RE TRYING TO TRICK ME! GET INSIDE OR I'LL JUMP!
...THE BATMAN'S ARM CLOSES LIKE A STEEL CLAMP ON THE GIRL AND SWEEPS HER OFF THE LEDGE!
THE BATMAN MADE IT!
HE'S GOT HER!
EEEIEE! HOLD ME! I'LL FALL! I DON'T WANT TO DIE!
A MINUTE AGO YOU WERE ALL SET TO JUMP, AND NOW... JUST LIKE A WOMAN TO CHANGE HER MIND!
LATER... AFTER THE GIRL RESTS ON SAFE GROUND...
YOU'RE OKAY NOW! I HOPE YOU'RE NOT THINKING OF TRYING THAT JUMP AGAIN!
N-NO!...I THINK I'D RATHER LIVE! I'D LIKE TO GO BACK TO MY ROOM NOW!
11
WHEN THE GIRL LEAVES...
BANDITS... RAIDED THE BANK DOWN THE STREET A FEW MINUTES AGO! SHOT THE GUARD...HE'S DYING, BUT HE SPOTTED THE LEADER..."HEIST" ANDREWS!
WHAT?
MAYBE THAT GIRL WAS SCARED WHEN YOU SAVED HER... BE-CAUSE SHE DIDN'T INTEND TO JUMP!
PERHAPS IT WAS AN ACT TO DRAW THE COPS AWAY FROM THE BANK? "HEIST" ANDREWS... HMM?

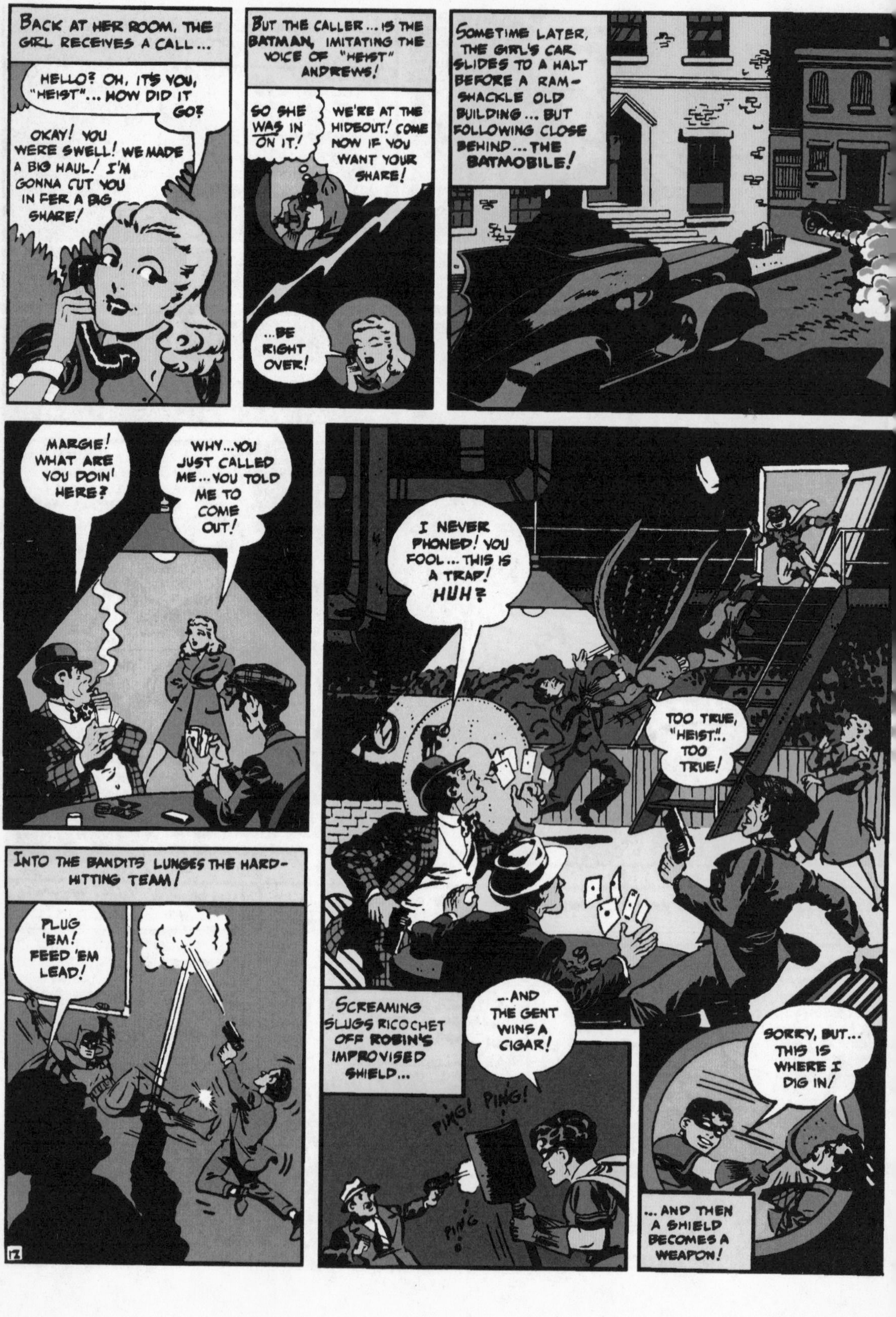

BACK AT HER ROOM, THE GIRL RECEIVES A CALL...
HELLO? OH, IT'S YOU, "HEIST"... HOW DID IT GO?
OKAY! YOU WERE SWELL! WE MADE A BIG HAUL! I'M GONNA CUT YOU IN FER A BIG SHARE!
BUT THE CALLER... IS THE BATMAN, IMITATING THE VOICE OF "HEIST" ANDREWS!
SO SHE WAS IN ON IT!
WE'RE AT THE HIDEOUT! COME NOW IF YOU WANT YOUR SHARE!
...BE RIGHT OVER!
SOMETIME LATER, THE GIRL'S CAR SLIDES TO A HALT BEFORE A RAM-SHACKLE OLD BUILDING... BUT FOLLOWING CLOSE BEHIND... THE BATMOBILE!
MARGIE! WHAT ARE YOU DOIN' HERE?
WHY... YOU JUST CALLED ME... YOU TOLD ME TO COME OUT!
I NEVER PHONED! YOU FOOL... THIS IS A TRAP! HUH?
TOO TRUE, "HEIST"... TOO TRUE!
INTO THE BANDITS LUNGES THE HARD-HITTING TEAM!
PLUG 'EM! FEED 'EM LEAD!
12
SCREAMING SLUGS RICOCHET OFF ROBIN'S IMPROVISED SHIELD...
...AND THE GENT WINS A CIGAR!
PING! PING!
PING
SORRY, BUT... THIS IS WHERE I DIG IN!
...AND THEN A SHIELD BECOMES A WEAPON!

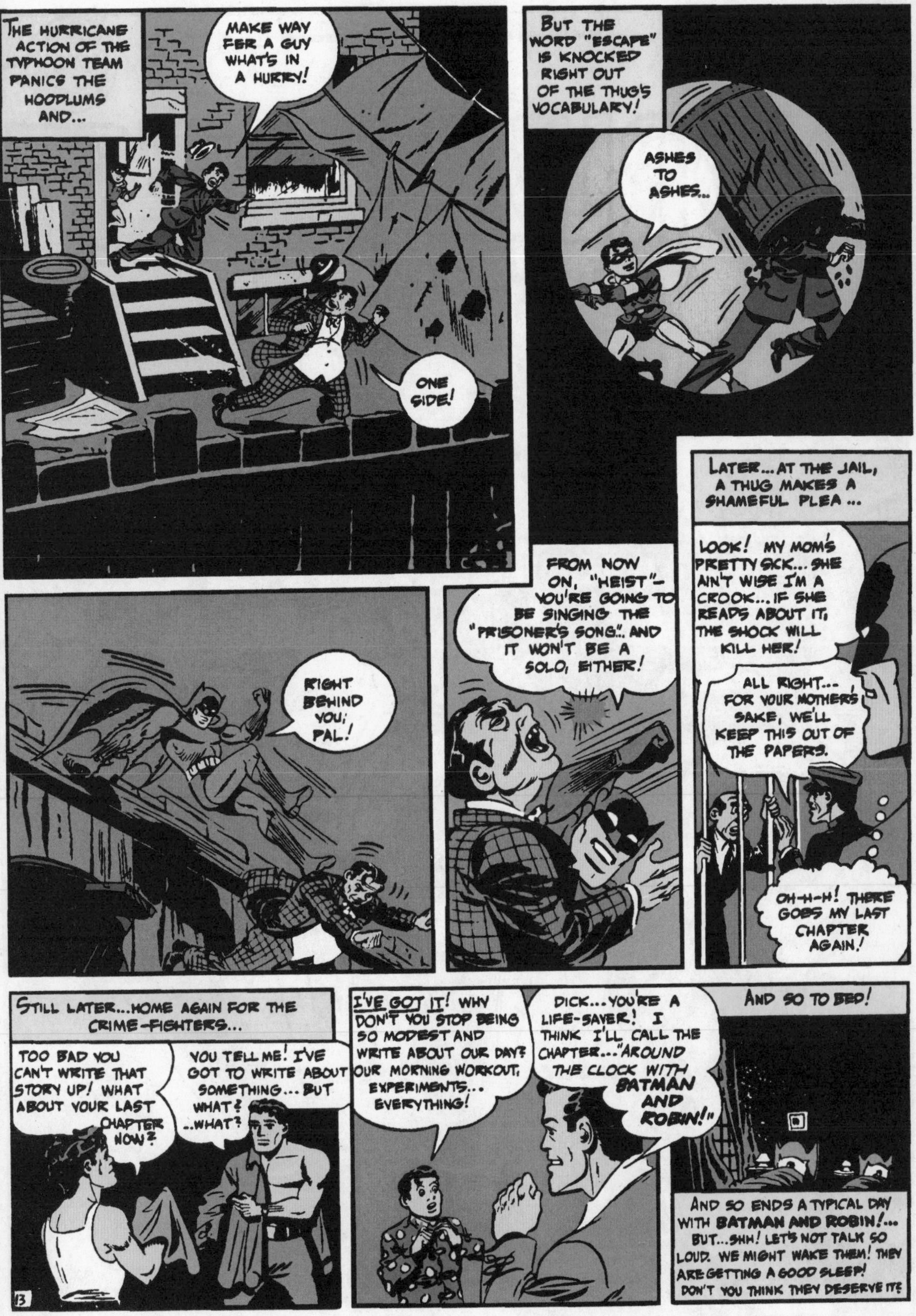
THE HURRICANE ACTION OF THE TYPHOON TEAM PANICS THE HOODLUMS AND...
MAKE WAY FER A GUY WHAT'S IN A HURRY!
ONE SIDE!
BUT THE WORD "ESCAPE" IS KNOCKED RIGHT OUT OF THE THUG'S VOCABULARY!
ASHES TO ASHES...
RIGHT BEHIND YOU, PAL!
FROM NOW ON, "HEIST"— YOU'RE GOING TO BE SINGING THE "PRISONER'S SONG"... AND IT WON'T BE A SOLO, EITHER!
LATER... AT THE JAIL, A THUG MAKES A SHAMEFUL PLEA...
LOOK! MY MOM'S PRETTY SICK... SHE AIN'T WISE I'M A CROOK... IF SHE READS ABOUT IT, THE SHOCK WILL KILL HER!
ALL RIGHT... FOR YOUR MOTHER'S SAKE, WE'LL KEEP THIS OUT OF THE PAPERS.
OH-H-H! THERE GOES MY LAST CHAPTER AGAIN!
STILL LATER... HOME AGAIN FOR THE CRIME-FIGHTERS...
TOO BAD YOU CAN'T WRITE THAT STORY UP! WHAT ABOUT YOUR LAST CHAPTER NOW?
YOU TELL ME! I'VE GOT TO WRITE ABOUT SOMETHING... BUT WHAT? ..WHAT?
13
I'VE GOT IT! WHY DON'T YOU STOP BEING SO MODEST AND WRITE ABOUT OUR DAY? OUR MORNING WORKOUT, EXPERIMENTS... EVERYTHING!
DICK... YOU'RE A LIFE-SAVER! I THINK I'LL CALL THE CHAPTER..."AROUND THE CLOCK WITH BATMAN AND ROBIN!"
AND SO TO BED!
AND SO ENDS A TYPICAL DAY WITH BATMAN AND ROBIN!... BUT...SHH! LET'S NOT TALK SO LOUD. WE MIGHT WAKE THEM! THEY ARE GETTING A GOOD SLEEP! DON'T YOU THINK THEY DESERVE IT?

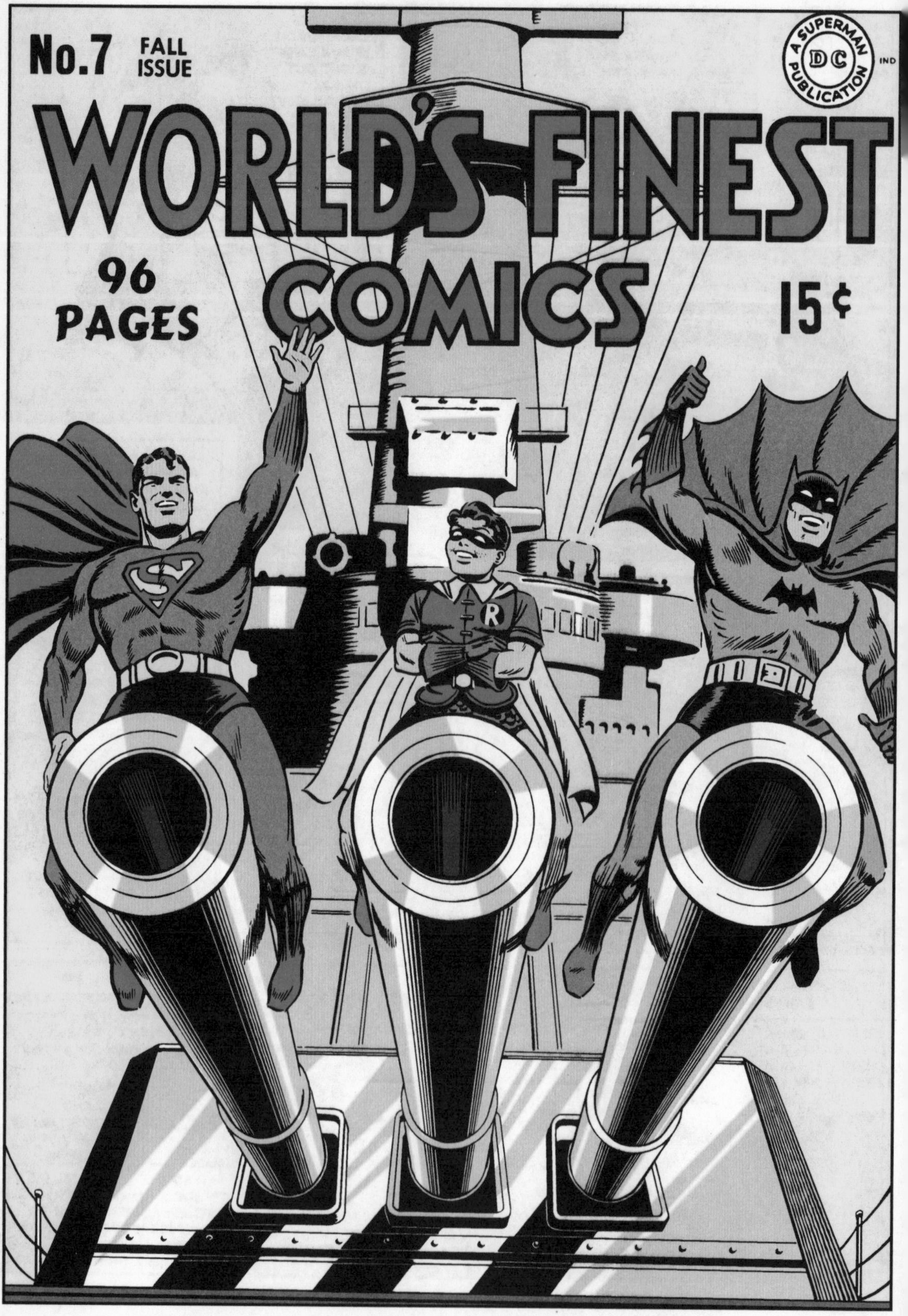

No.7
FALL ISSUE
A SUPERMAN DC PUBLICATION
IND
WORLD'S FINEST COMICS
96 PAGES
15¢

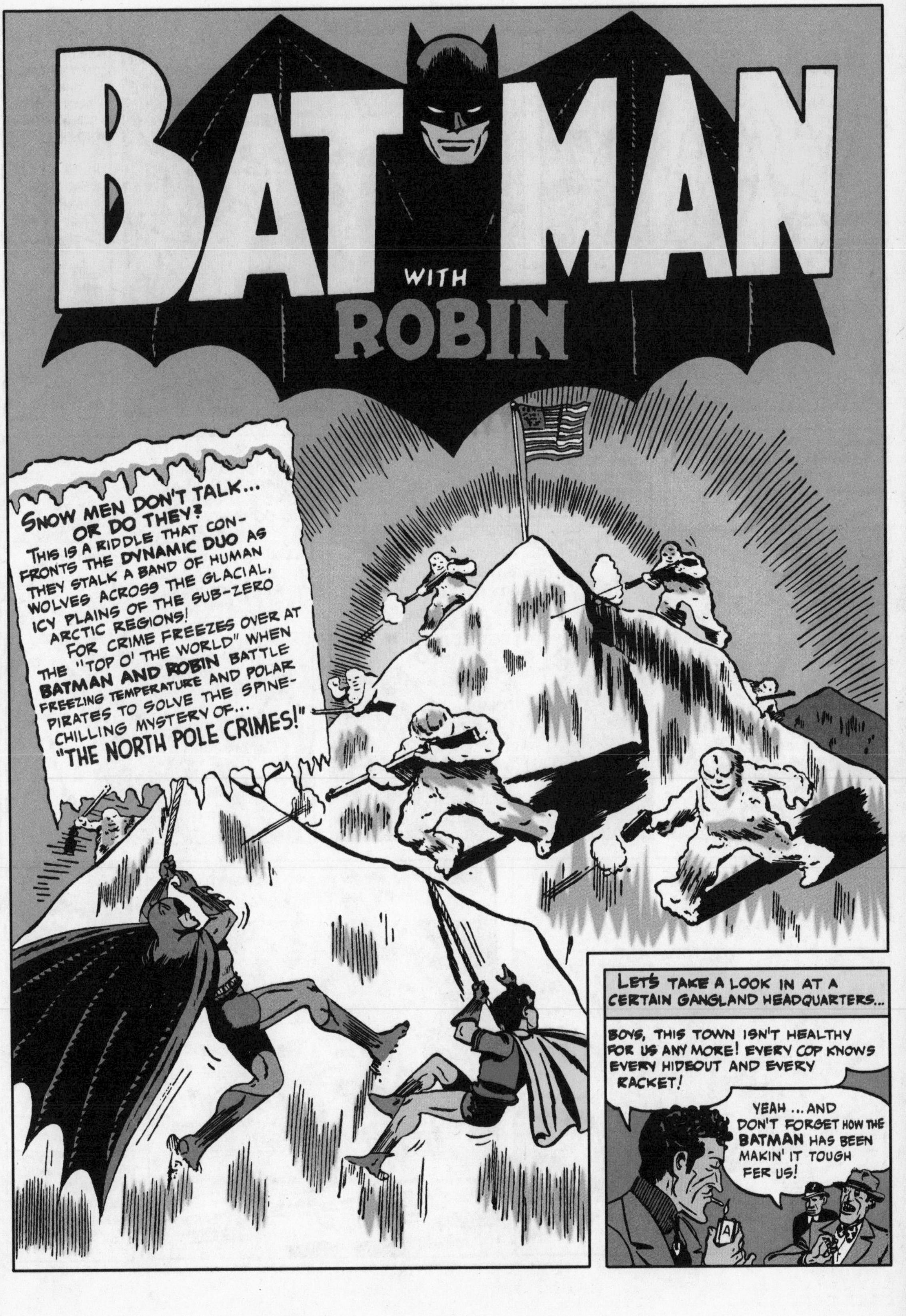
BATMAN
WITH
ROBIN
SNOW MEN DON'T TALK... OR DO THEY?
THIS IS A RIDDLE THAT CONFRONTS THE DYNAMIC DUO AS THEY STALK A BAND OF HUMAN WOLVES ACROSS THE GLACIAL, ICY PLAINS OF THE SUB-ZERO ARCTIC REGIONS!
FOR CRIME FREEZES OVER AT THE "TOP O' THE WORLD" WHEN BATMAN AND ROBIN BATTLE FREEZING TEMPERATURE AND POLAR PIRATES TO SOLVE THE SPINE-CHILLING MYSTERY OF...
"THE NORTH POLE CRIMES!"
LET'S TAKE A LOOK IN AT A CERTAIN GANGLAND HEADQUARTERS...
BOYS, THIS TOWN ISN'T HEALTHY FOR US ANY MORE! EVERY COP KNOWS EVERY HIDEOUT AND EVERY RACKET!
YEAH ... AND DON'T FORGET HOW THE BATMAN HAS BEEN MAKIN' IT TOUGH FER US!

"BOYS, WHILE I'VE BEEN AWAY, I'VE WORKED OUT A SLANT FOR A NEW RACKET... AND A CLEVER HIDEOUT!"

"A NEW ANGLE, EH, BOSS? AIN'T NO WONDER THEY CALL YOU "ANGLES" BIGBEE!"

"BUT, BOSS, WHAT ABOUT THE BATMAN? HE'S SURE TO CATCH WISE!"

"NOT WHERE WE'RE GOING! WE'LL BE THOUSANDS OF MILES AWAY FROM THE BATMAN! FIVE THOUSAND MILES, TO BE EXACT!"

"HUH?"

HIGH UP IN THE FAR-FLUNG NORTH ARE THE COMPANY TRADING POSTS... MAINTAINED TO BARTER AND BUY SEAL SKINS AND FURS FROM ESKIMOS AND TRAPPERS...

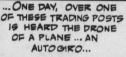

...ONE DAY, OVER ONE OF THESE TRADING POSTS IS HEARD THE DRONE OF A PLANE... AN AUTOGIRO...

FROM IT STEP BANDITS... RUTHLESS AND THOROUGH!

"ONE PEEP OUTA YOU AND YOU'LL BE EATIN' LEAD! OKAY, GUYS, START LOADIN' THE FURS INTO THE PLANE!"

SWIFTLY, THE BANDITS DEPART... PAUSING ONLY LONG ENOUGH TO CONSTRUCT A SNOW MAN!

"THERE THEY GO!"

"HEY! LOOK WHAT THEY LEFT! A SNOW MAN... S' HELP ME!"

"WHAT'S THE IDEA?"

IN THE DAYS TO FOLLOW, IN ALASKA, GREENLAND, BAFFIN ISLAND, AND OTHER NORTHERN POINTS, THE BANDITS STRIKE CLEVERLY AND SWIFTLY...

...SOMETIMES BY PLANE ...SOMETIMES BY SKI PEEPS...

...AND AFTER EACH CRIME, THE BANDITS LEAVE BEHIND A GROTESQUE MEMENTO ...A BLANK-FACED SNOW MAN!

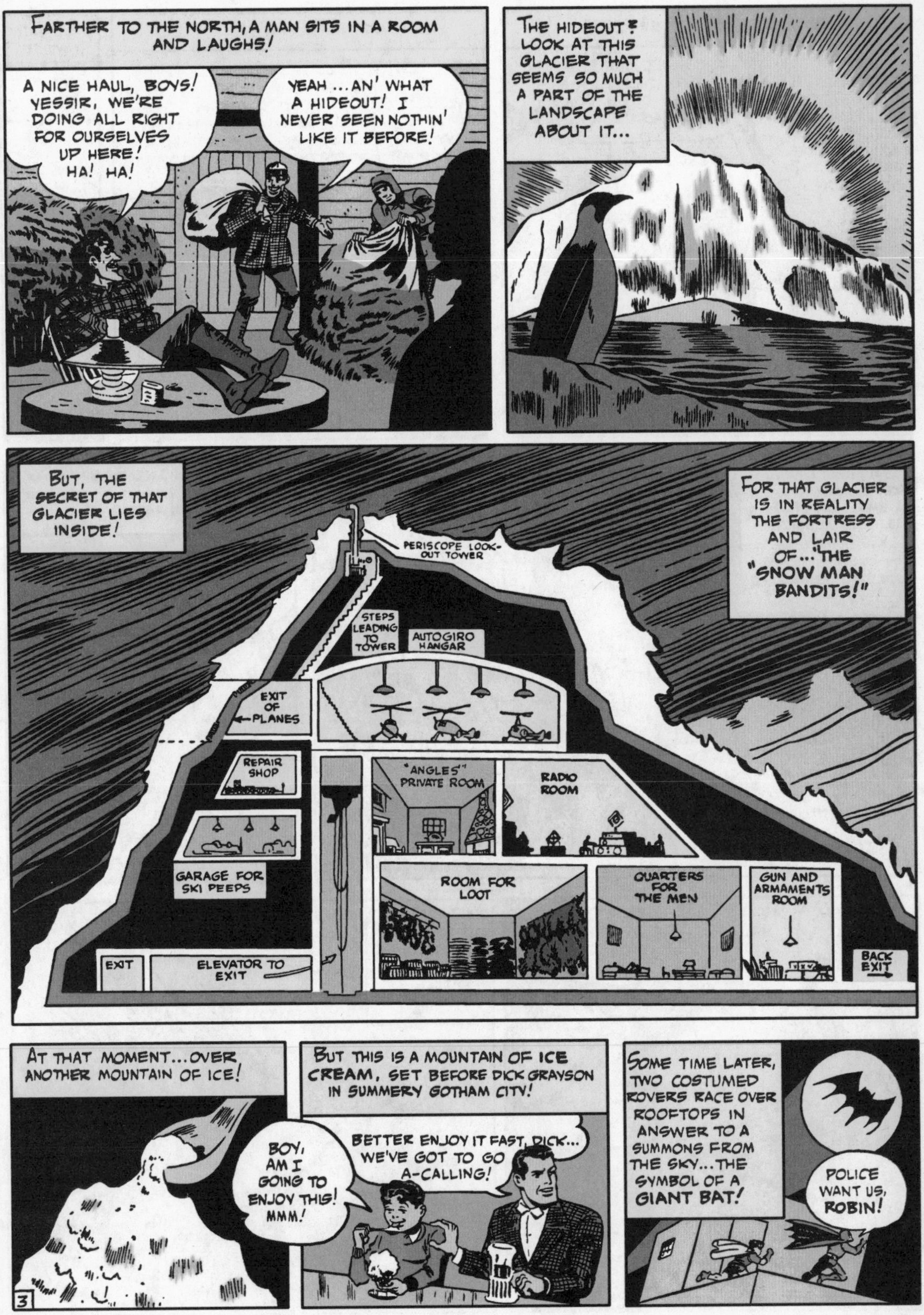

FARTHER TO THE NORTH, A MAN SITS IN A ROOM AND LAUGHS!
A NICE HAUL, BOYS! YESSIR, WE'RE DOING ALL RIGHT FOR OURSELVES UP HERE! HA! HA!
YEAH ... AN' WHAT A HIDEOUT! I NEVER SEEN NOTHIN' LIKE IT BEFORE!
THE HIDEOUT? LOOK AT THIS GLACIER THAT SEEMS SO MUCH A PART OF THE LANDSCAPE ABOUT IT...
BUT, THE SECRET OF THAT GLACIER LIES INSIDE!
FOR THAT GLACIER IS IN REALITY THE FORTRESS AND LAIR OF..."THE "SNOW MAN BANDITS!"
PERISCOPE LOOK-OUT TOWER
STEPS LEADING TO TOWER
AUTOGIRO HANGAR
EXIT OF PLANES
REPAIR SHOP
"ANGLES" PRIVATE ROOM
RADIO ROOM
GARAGE FOR SKI PEEPS
ROOM FOR LOOT
QUARTERS FOR THE MEN
GUN AND ARMAMENTS ROOM
EXIT
ELEVATOR TO EXIT
BACK EXIT
AT THAT MOMENT...OVER ANOTHER MOUNTAIN OF ICE!
3
BUT THIS IS A MOUNTAIN OF ICE CREAM, SET BEFORE DICK GRAYSON IN SUMMERY GOTHAM CITY!
BOY, AM I GOING TO ENJOY THIS! MMM!
BETTER ENJOY IT FAST, DICK... WE'VE GOT TO GO A-CALLING!
SOME TIME LATER, TWO COSTUMED ROVERS RACE OVER ROOFTOPS IN ANSWER TO A SUMMONS FROM THE SKY...THE SYMBOL OF A GIANT BAT!
POLICE WANT US, ROBIN!

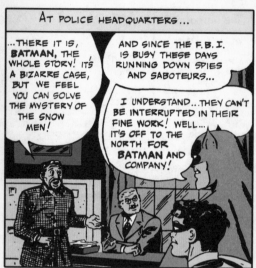

AT POLICE HEADQUARTERS...

...THERE IT IS, BATMAN, THE WHOLE STORY! IT'S A BIZARRE CASE, BUT WE FEEL YOU CAN SOLVE THE MYSTERY OF THE SNOW MEN!

AND SINCE THE F.B.I. IS BUSY THESE DAYS RUNNING DOWN SPIES AND SABOTEURS...

I UNDERSTAND...THEY CAN'T BE INTERRUPTED IN THEIR FINE WORK! WELL... IT'S OFF TO THE NORTH FOR BATMAN AND COMPANY!

LATER AT HOME...

WHEW! HOW CAN WE MOVE IN THESE HEAVY FURS IN CASE WE RUN INTO SOME ACTION?

WE'LL WEAR OUR COSTUMES INTERWOVEN WITH FINE WIRES! ALL WE DO IS CONNECT THEM TO THE SMALL DYNAMOS IN OUR BELTS...AND THE RADIATING HEAT WILL PROTECT US FROM THE COLD!

STILL LATER-A WEIRD CRAFT RISES IN THE NIGHT-SKY!

WELL, ROBIN, HERE WE GO AGAIN...INTO FRESH FIELDS OF CRIME!

THE FIRST LAP... REFUELING AT A SMALL SETTLEMENT IN ALASKA'S KLONDIKE!

IT'S BATMAN AND ROBIN!

HI, MEN... MY GAS TANK'S JUST ABOUT EMPTY! I'D LIKE TO FILL IT UP AND GET GOING AGAIN!

AS BATMAN AND ROBIN STEP INTO THE TRADING STORE FOR GAS...SUDDENLY!

AS SOON AS WE... HEY! WHAT'S THAT?

GUNFIRE! SOMETHING'S HAPPENING!

BANG! BANG!!

IT'S THEM "SNOW MAN" BANDITS!

WHAT A BREAK... RIGHT INTO OUR LAPS! C'MON, ROBIN!

YIPEE! LET'S TAKE 'EM!

FUR TRADING POST

4

AS ONE UNIT, THE TWO-MAN TEAM EXPLODES INTO RAZZLE-DAZZLE ACTION!

MY-MY! THIS IS LIKE OLD TIMES!

YOU SAID IT!

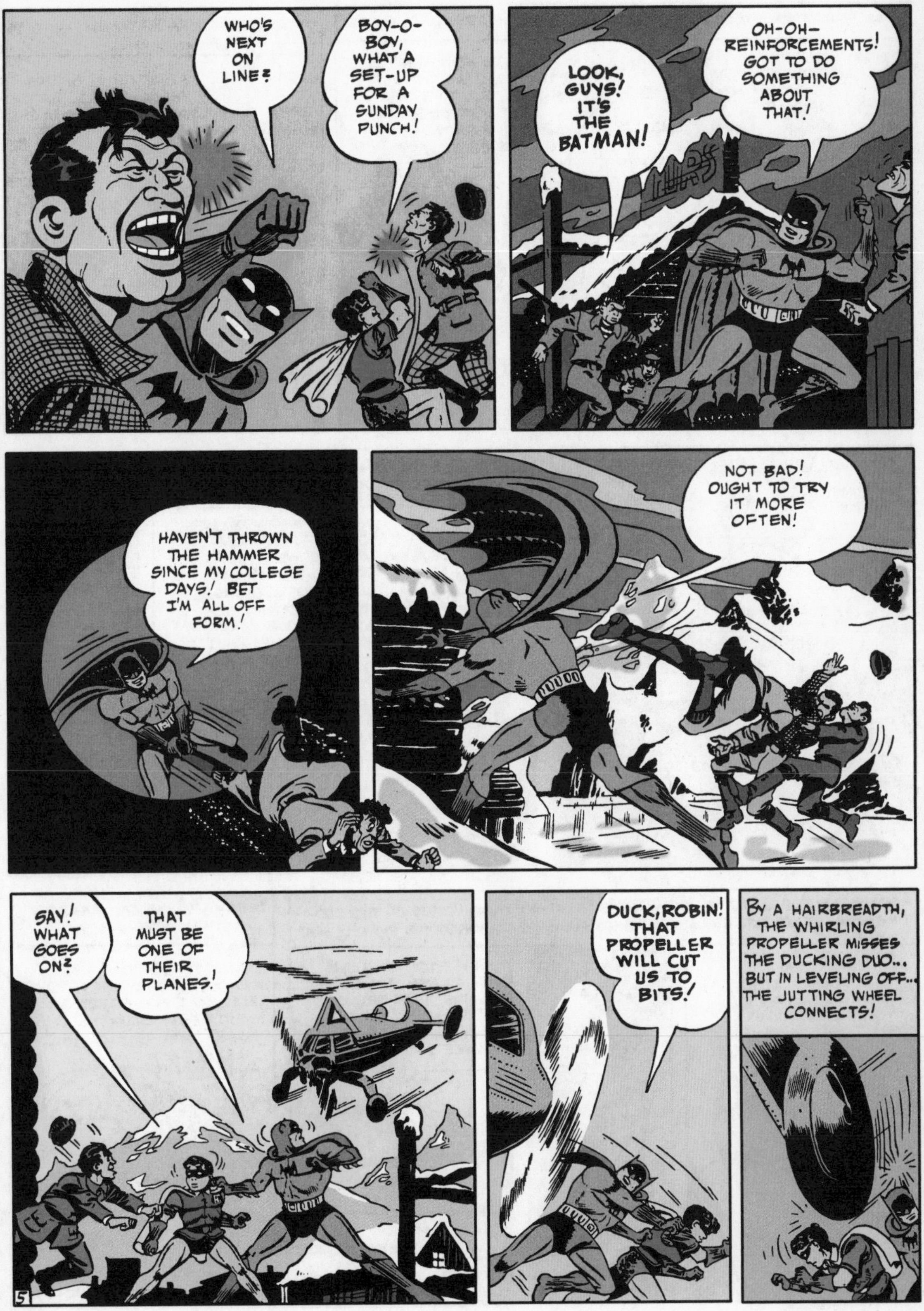
WHO'S NEXT ON LINE?
BOY-O-BOY, WHAT A SET-UP FOR A SUNDAY PUNCH!
LOOK, GUYS! IT'S THE BATMAN!
OH-OH- REINFORCEMENTS! GOT TO DO SOMETHING ABOUT THAT!
HAVEN'T THROWN THE HAMMER SINCE MY COLLEGE DAYS! BET I'M ALL OFF FORM!
NOT BAD! OUGHT TO TRY IT MORE OFTEN!
SAY! WHAT GOES ON?
THAT MUST BE ONE OF THEIR PLANES!
5
DUCK, ROBIN! THAT PROPELLER WILL CUT US TO BITS!
BY A HAIRBREADTH, THE WHIRLING PROPELLER MISSES THE DUCKING DUO... BUT IN LEVELING OFF... THE JUTTING WHEEL CONNECTS!

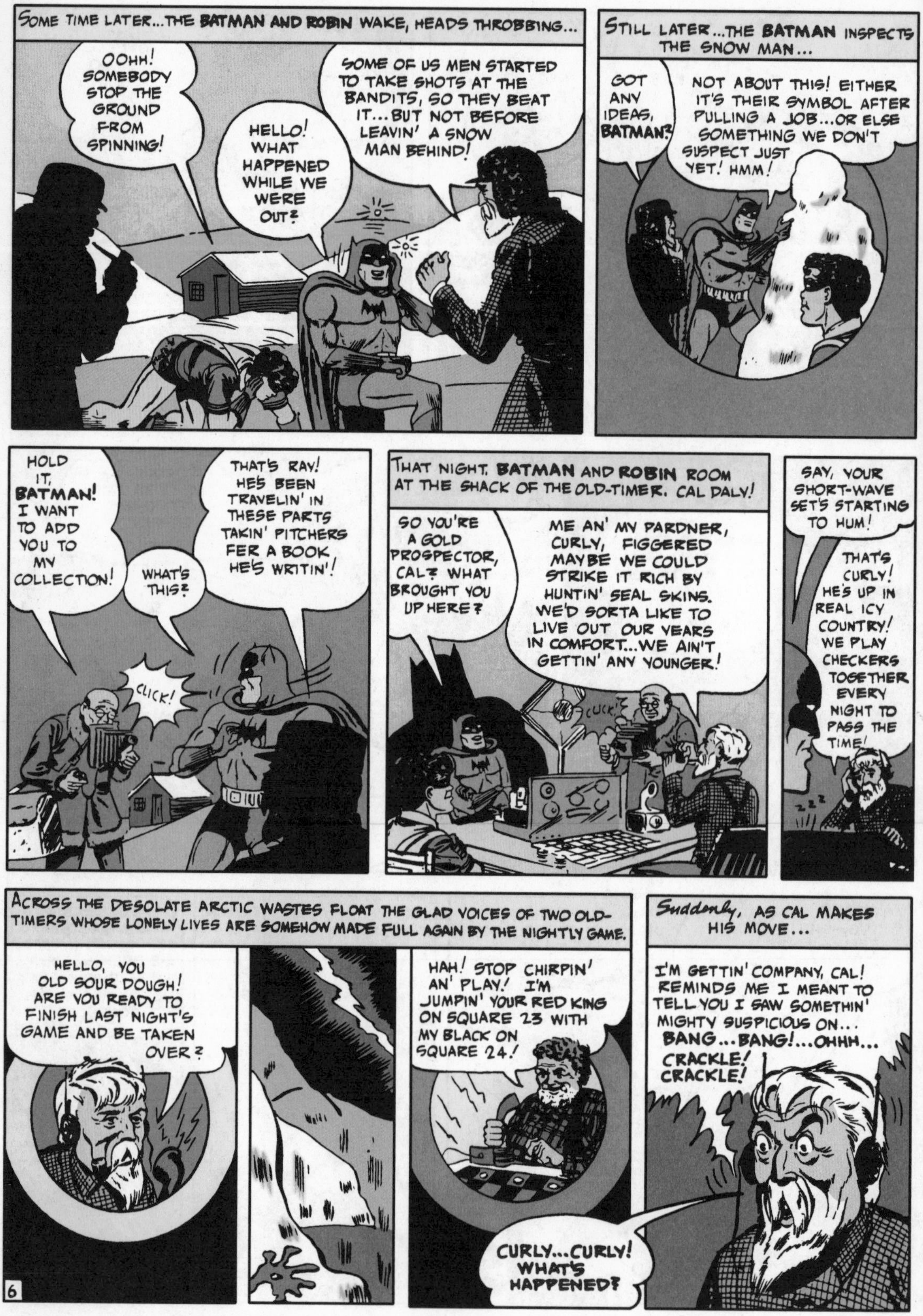
SOME TIME LATER...THE BATMAN AND ROBIN WAKE, HEADS THROBBING...
OOHH! SOMEBODY STOP THE GROUND FROM SPINNING!
HELLO! WHAT HAPPENED WHILE WE WERE OUT?
SOME OF US MEN STARTED TO TAKE SHOTS AT THE BANDITS, SO THEY BEAT IT...BUT NOT BEFORE LEAVIN' A SNOW MAN BEHIND!
STILL LATER...THE BATMAN INSPECTS THE SNOW MAN...
GOT ANY IDEAS, BATMAN?
NOT ABOUT THIS! EITHER IT'S THEIR SYMBOL AFTER PULLING A JOB...OR ELSE SOMETHING WE DON'T SUSPECT JUST YET! HMM!
HOLD IT, BATMAN! I WANT TO ADD YOU TO MY COLLECTION!
WHAT'S THIS?
THAT'S RAY! HE'S BEEN TRAVELIN' IN THESE PARTS TAKIN' PITCHERS FER A BOOK HE'S WRITIN'!
CLICK!
THAT NIGHT, BATMAN AND ROBIN ROOM AT THE SHACK OF THE OLD-TIMER, CAL DALY!
SO YOU'RE A GOLD PROSPECTOR, CAL? WHAT BROUGHT YOU UP HERE?
ME AN' MY PARDNER, CURLY, FIGGERED MAYBE WE COULD STRIKE IT RICH BY HUNTIN' SEAL SKINS. WE'D SORTA LIKE TO LIVE OUT OUR YEARS IN COMFORT...WE AIN'T GETTIN' ANY YOUNGER!
CLICK!
SAY, YOUR SHORT-WAVE SET'S STARTING TO HUM!
THAT'S CURLY! HE'S UP IN REAL ICY COUNTRY! WE PLAY CHECKERS TOGETHER EVERY NIGHT TO PASS THE TIME!
ACROSS THE DESOLATE ARCTIC WASTES FLOAT THE GLAD VOICES OF TWO OLD-TIMERS WHOSE LONELY LIVES ARE SOMEHOW MADE FULL AGAIN BY THE NIGHTLY GAME.
HELLO, YOU OLD SOUR DOUGH! ARE YOU READY TO FINISH LAST NIGHT'S GAME AND BE TAKEN OVER?
HAH! STOP CHIRPIN' AN' PLAY! I'M JUMPIN' YOUR RED KING ON SQUARE 23 WITH MY BLACK ON SQUARE 24!
Suddenly, AS CAL MAKES HIS MOVE...
I'M GETTIN' COMPANY, CAL! REMINDS ME I MEANT TO TELL YOU I SAW SOMETHIN' MIGHTY SUSPICIOUS ON... BANG...BANG!...OHHH... CRACKLE! CRACKLE!
CURLY...CURLY! WHAT'S HAPPENED?
6

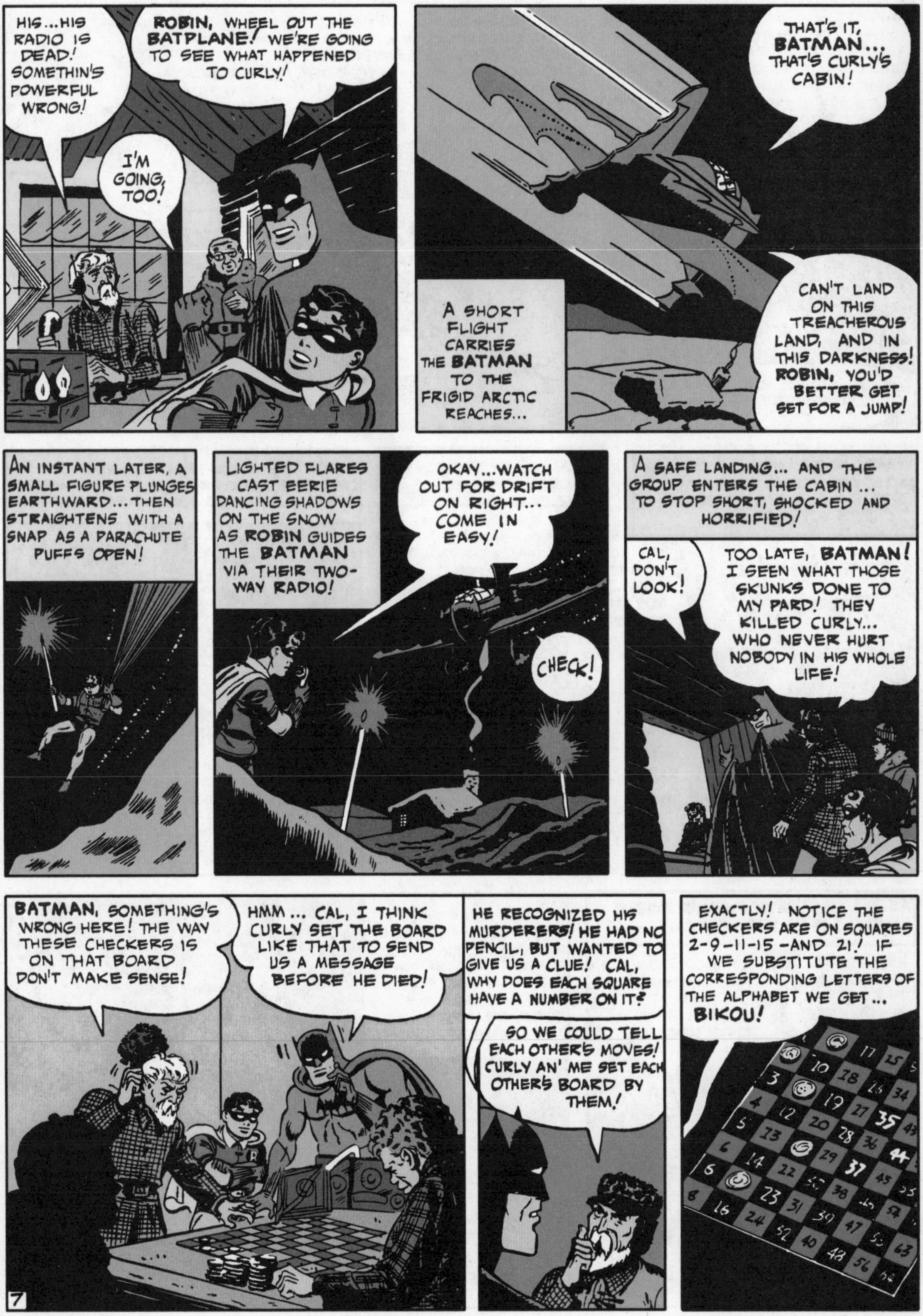
HIS...HIS RADIO IS DEAD! SOMETHIN'S POWERFUL WRONG!
ROBIN, WHEEL OUT THE BATPLANE! WE'RE GOING TO SEE WHAT HAPPENED TO CURLY!
I'M GOING, TOO!
THAT'S IT, BATMAN... THAT'S CURLY'S CABIN!
A SHORT FLIGHT CARRIES THE BATMAN TO THE FRIGID ARCTIC REACHES...
CAN'T LAND ON THIS TREACHEROUS LAND, AND IN THIS DARKNESS! ROBIN, YOU'D BETTER GET SET FOR A JUMP!
AN INSTANT LATER, A SMALL FIGURE PLUNGES EARTHWARD... THEN STRAIGHTENS WITH A SNAP AS A PARACHUTE PUFFS OPEN!
LIGHTED FLARES CAST EERIE DANCING SHADOWS ON THE SNOW AS ROBIN GUIDES THE BATMAN VIA THEIR TWO-WAY RADIO!
OKAY...WATCH OUT FOR DRIFT ON RIGHT... COME IN EASY!
CHECK!
A SAFE LANDING... AND THE GROUP ENTERS THE CABIN ... TO STOP SHORT, SHOCKED AND HORRIFIED!
CAL, DON'T LOOK!
TOO LATE, BATMAN! I SEEN WHAT THOSE SKUNKS DONE TO MY PARD! THEY KILLED CURLY... WHO NEVER HURT NOBODY IN HIS WHOLE LIFE!
BATMAN, SOMETHING'S WRONG HERE! THE WAY THESE CHECKERS IS ON THAT BOARD DON'T MAKE SENSE!
HMM ... CAL, I THINK CURLY SET THE BOARD LIKE THAT TO SEND US A MESSAGE BEFORE HE DIED!
HE RECOGNIZED HIS MURDERERS! HE HAD NO PENCIL, BUT WANTED TO GIVE US A CLUE! CAL, WHY DOES EACH SQUARE HAVE A NUMBER ON IT?
SO WE COULD TELL EACH OTHER'S MOVES! CURLY AN' ME SET EACH OTHER'S BOARD BY THEM!
EXACTLY! NOTICE THE CHECKERS ARE ON SQUARES 2-9-11-15-AND 21! IF WE SUBSTITUTE THE CORRESPONDING LETTERS OF THE ALPHABET WE GET... BIKOU!
7

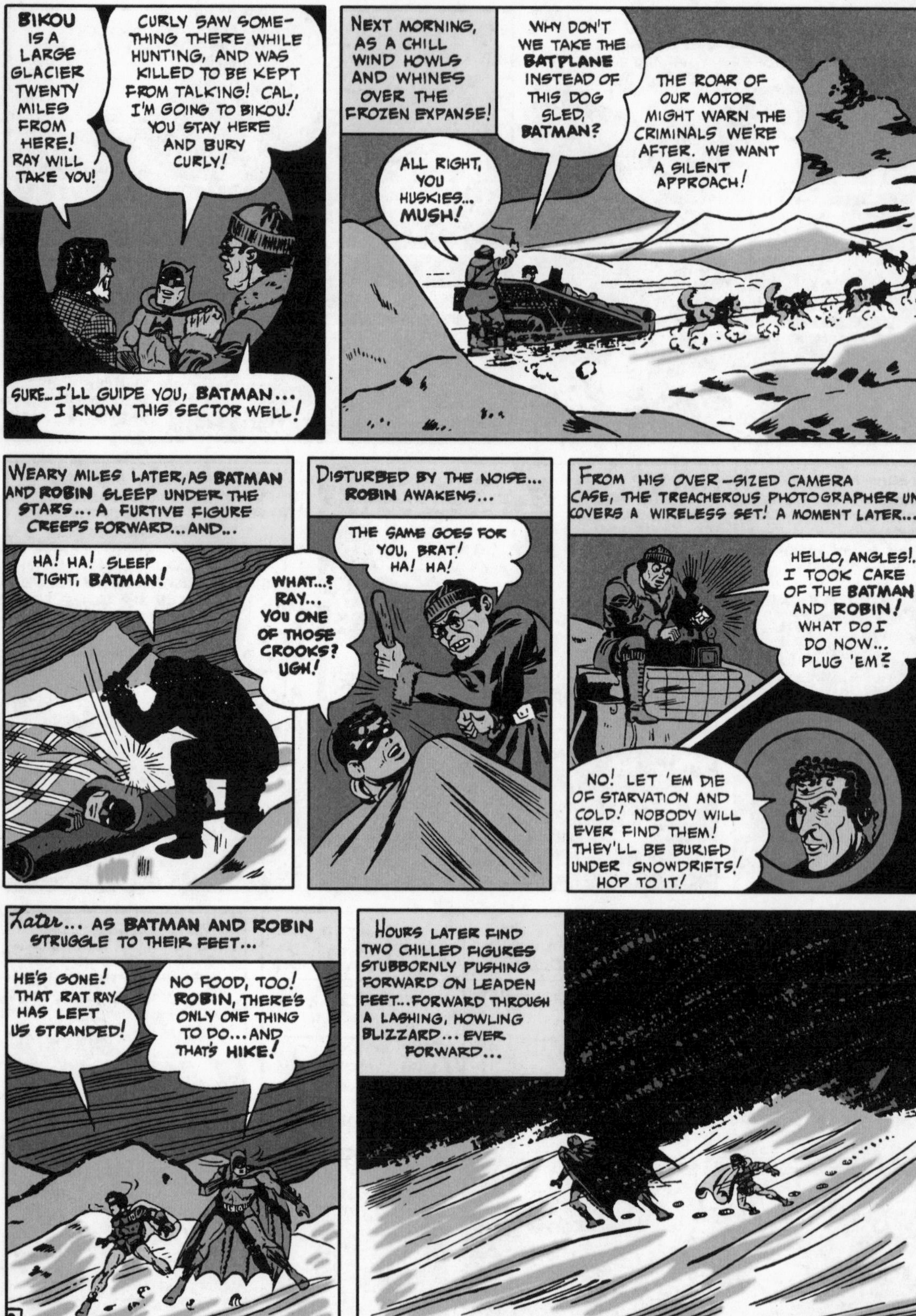
BIKOU IS A LARGE GLACIER TWENTY MILES FROM HERE! RAY WILL TAKE YOU!
CURLY SAW SOMETHING THERE WHILE HUNTING, AND WAS KILLED TO BE KEPT FROM TALKING! CAL, I'M GOING TO BIKOU! YOU STAY HERE AND BURY CURLY!
SURE.. I'LL GUIDE YOU, BATMAN... I KNOW THIS SECTOR WELL!
NEXT MORNING, AS A CHILL WIND HOWLS AND WHINES OVER THE FROZEN EXPANSE!
WHY DON'T WE TAKE THE BATPLANE INSTEAD OF THIS DOG SLED, BATMAN?
THE ROAR OF OUR MOTOR MIGHT WARN THE CRIMINALS WE'RE AFTER. WE WANT A SILENT APPROACH!
ALL RIGHT, YOU HUSKIES... MUSH!
WEARY MILES LATER, AS BATMAN AND ROBIN SLEEP UNDER THE STARS... A FURTIVE FIGURE CREEPS FORWARD... AND...
HA! HA! SLEEP TIGHT, BATMAN!
DISTURBED BY THE NOISE... ROBIN AWAKENS...
THE SAME GOES FOR YOU, BRAT! HA! HA!
WHAT...? RAY... YOU ONE OF THOSE CROOKS? UGH!
FROM HIS OVER-SIZED CAMERA CASE, THE TREACHEROUS PHOTOGRAPHER UNCOVERS A WIRELESS SET! A MOMENT LATER...
HELLO, ANGLES!... I TOOK CARE OF THE BATMAN AND ROBIN! WHAT DO I DO NOW... PLUG 'EM?
NO! LET 'EM DIE OF STARVATION AND COLD! NOBODY WILL EVER FIND THEM! THEY'LL BE BURIED UNDER SNOWDRIFTS! HOP TO IT!
Later... AS BATMAN AND ROBIN STRUGGLE TO THEIR FEET...
HE'S GONE! THAT RAT RAY HAS LEFT US STRANDED!
NO FOOD, TOO! ROBIN, THERE'S ONLY ONE THING TO DO... AND THAT'S HIKE!
8
HOURS LATER FIND TWO CHILLED FIGURES STUBBORNLY PUSHING FORWARD ON LEADEN FEET... FORWARD THROUGH A LASHING, HOWLING BLIZZARD... EVER FORWARD...

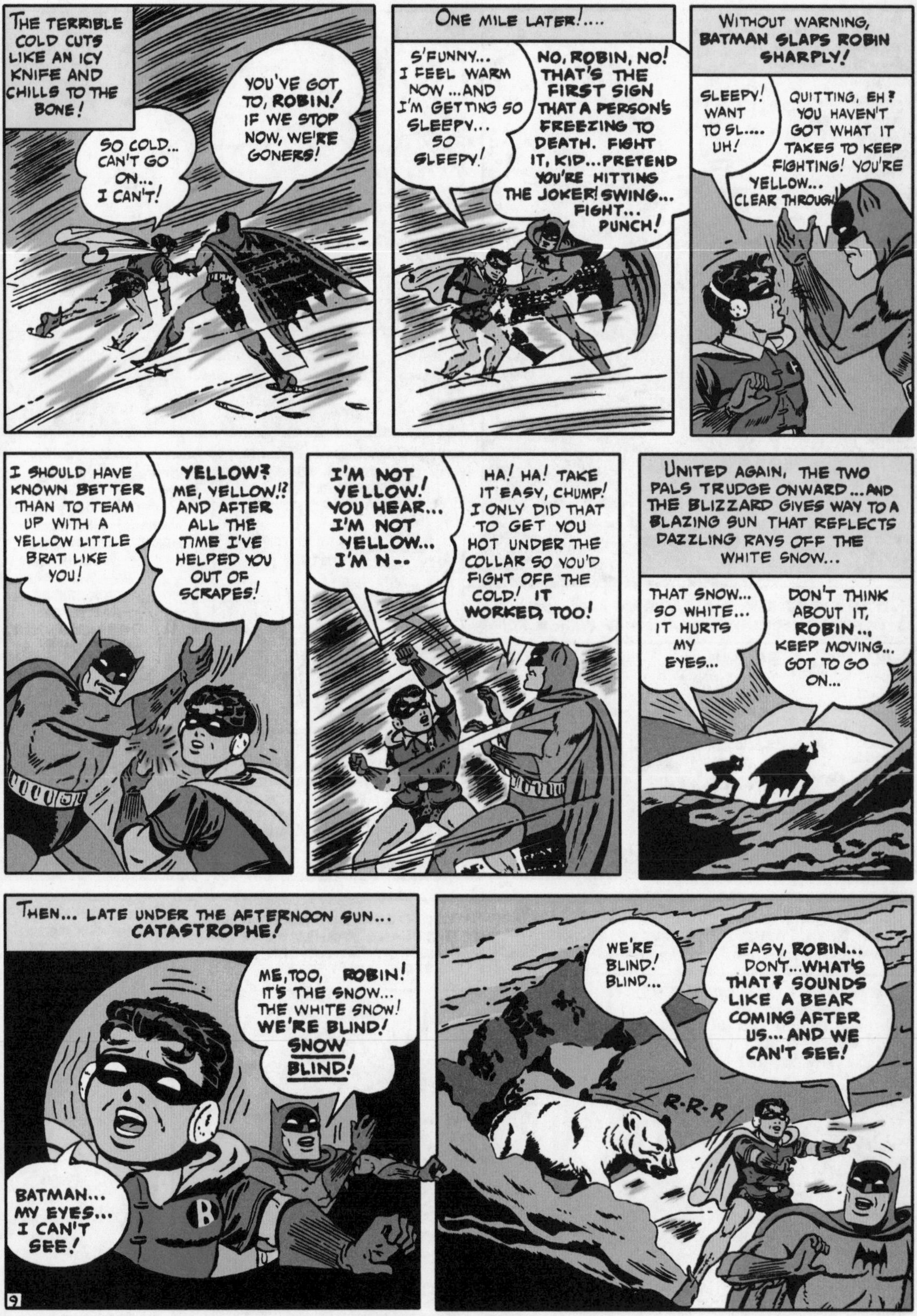

THE TERRIBLE COLD CUTS LIKE AN ICY KNIFE AND CHILLS TO THE BONE!
SO COLD... CAN'T GO ON... I CAN'T!
YOU'VE GOT TO, ROBIN! IF WE STOP NOW, WE'RE GONERS!
ONE MILE LATER!....
S'FUNNY... I FEEL WARM NOW ...AND I'M GETTING SO SLEEPY... SO SLEEPY!
NO, ROBIN, NO! THAT'S THE FIRST SIGN THAT A PERSON'S FREEZING TO DEATH. FIGHT IT, KID...PRETEND YOU'RE HITTING THE JOKER! SWING... FIGHT... PUNCH!
WITHOUT WARNING, BATMAN SLAPS ROBIN SHARPLY!
SLEEPY! WANT TO SL.... UH!
QUITTING, EH? YOU HAVEN'T GOT WHAT IT TAKES TO KEEP FIGHTING! YOU'RE YELLOW... CLEAR THROUGH!
I SHOULD HAVE KNOWN BETTER THAN TO TEAM UP WITH A YELLOW LITTLE BRAT LIKE YOU!
YELLOW? ME, YELLOW!? AND AFTER ALL THE TIME I'VE HELPED YOU OUT OF SCRAPES!
I'M NOT YELLOW! YOU HEAR... I'M NOT YELLOW... I'M N--
HA! HA! TAKE IT EASY, CHUMP! I ONLY DID THAT TO GET YOU HOT UNDER THE COLLAR SO YOU'D FIGHT OFF THE COLD! IT WORKED, TOO!
UNITED AGAIN, THE TWO PALS TRUDGE ONWARD...AND THE BLIZZARD GIVES WAY TO A BLAZING SUN THAT REFLECTS DAZZLING RAYS OFF THE WHITE SNOW...
THAT SNOW... SO WHITE... IT HURTS MY EYES...
DON'T THINK ABOUT IT, ROBIN.., KEEP MOVING... GOT TO GO ON...
THEN... LATE UNDER THE AFTERNOON SUN... CATASTROPHE!
BATMAN... MY EYES... I CAN'T SEE!
ME, TOO, ROBIN! IT'S THE SNOW... THE WHITE SNOW! WE'RE BLIND! SNOW BLIND!
B
9
WE'RE BLIND! BLIND...
EASY, ROBIN... DON'T...WHAT'S THAT? SOUNDS LIKE A BEAR COMING AFTER US... AND WE CAN'T SEE!
R-R-R

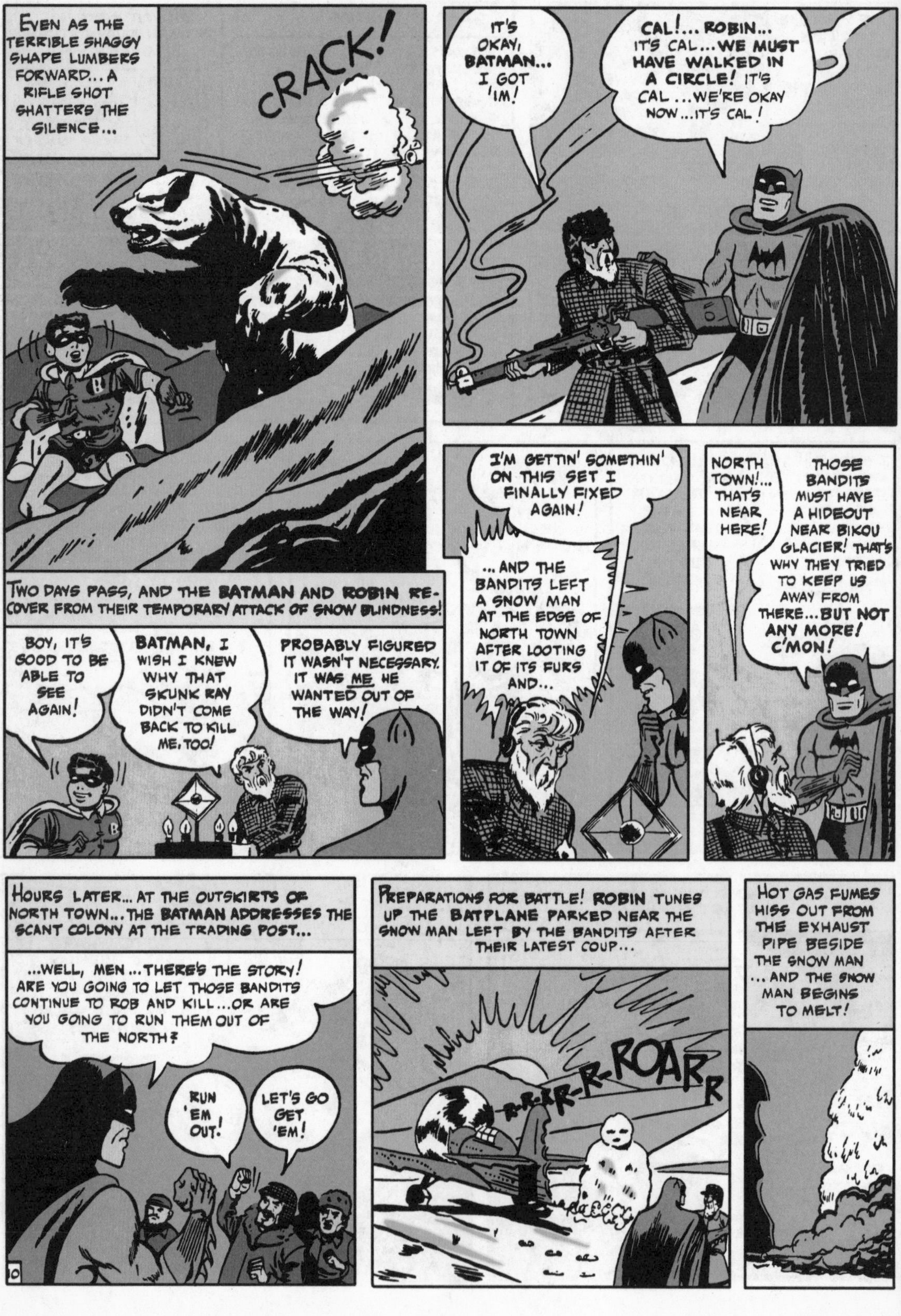

EVEN AS THE TERRIBLE SHAGGY SHAPE LUMBERS FORWARD... A RIFLE SHOT SHATTERS THE SILENCE...
CRACK!
IT'S OKAY, BATMAN... I GOT 'IM!
CAL!... ROBIN... IT'S CAL... WE MUST HAVE WALKED IN A CIRCLE! IT'S CAL... WE'RE OKAY NOW... IT'S CAL!
TWO DAYS PASS, AND THE BATMAN AND ROBIN RECOVER FROM THEIR TEMPORARY ATTACK OF SNOW BLINDNESS!
BOY, IT'S GOOD TO BE ABLE TO SEE AGAIN!
BATMAN, I WISH I KNEW WHY THAT SKUNK RAY DIDN'T COME BACK TO KILL ME, TOO!
PROBABLY FIGURED IT WASN'T NECESSARY. IT WAS ME HE WANTED OUT OF THE WAY!
I'M GETTIN' SOMETHIN' ON THIS SET I FINALLY FIXED AGAIN!
... AND THE BANDITS LEFT A SNOW MAN AT THE EDGE OF NORTH TOWN AFTER LOOTING IT OF ITS FURS AND...
NORTH TOWN!... THAT'S NEAR HERE!
THOSE BANDITS MUST HAVE A HIDEOUT NEAR BIKOU GLACIER! THAT'S WHY THEY TRIED TO KEEP US AWAY FROM THERE... BUT NOT ANY MORE! C'MON!
HOURS LATER... AT THE OUTSKIRTS OF NORTH TOWN... THE BATMAN ADDRESSES THE SCANT COLONY AT THE TRADING POST...
...WELL, MEN... THERE'S THE STORY! ARE YOU GOING TO LET THOSE BANDITS CONTINUE TO ROB AND KILL... OR ARE YOU GOING TO RUN THEM OUT OF THE NORTH?
RUN 'EM OUT!
LET'S GO GET 'EM!
10
PREPARATIONS FOR BATTLE! ROBIN TUNES UP THE BATPLANE PARKED NEAR THE SNOW MAN LEFT BY THE BANDITS AFTER THEIR LATEST COUP...
R-R-R-R-R-ROARR
HOT GAS FUMES HISS OUT FROM THE EXHAUST PIPE BESIDE THE SNOW MAN ... AND THE SNOW MAN BEGINS TO MELT!

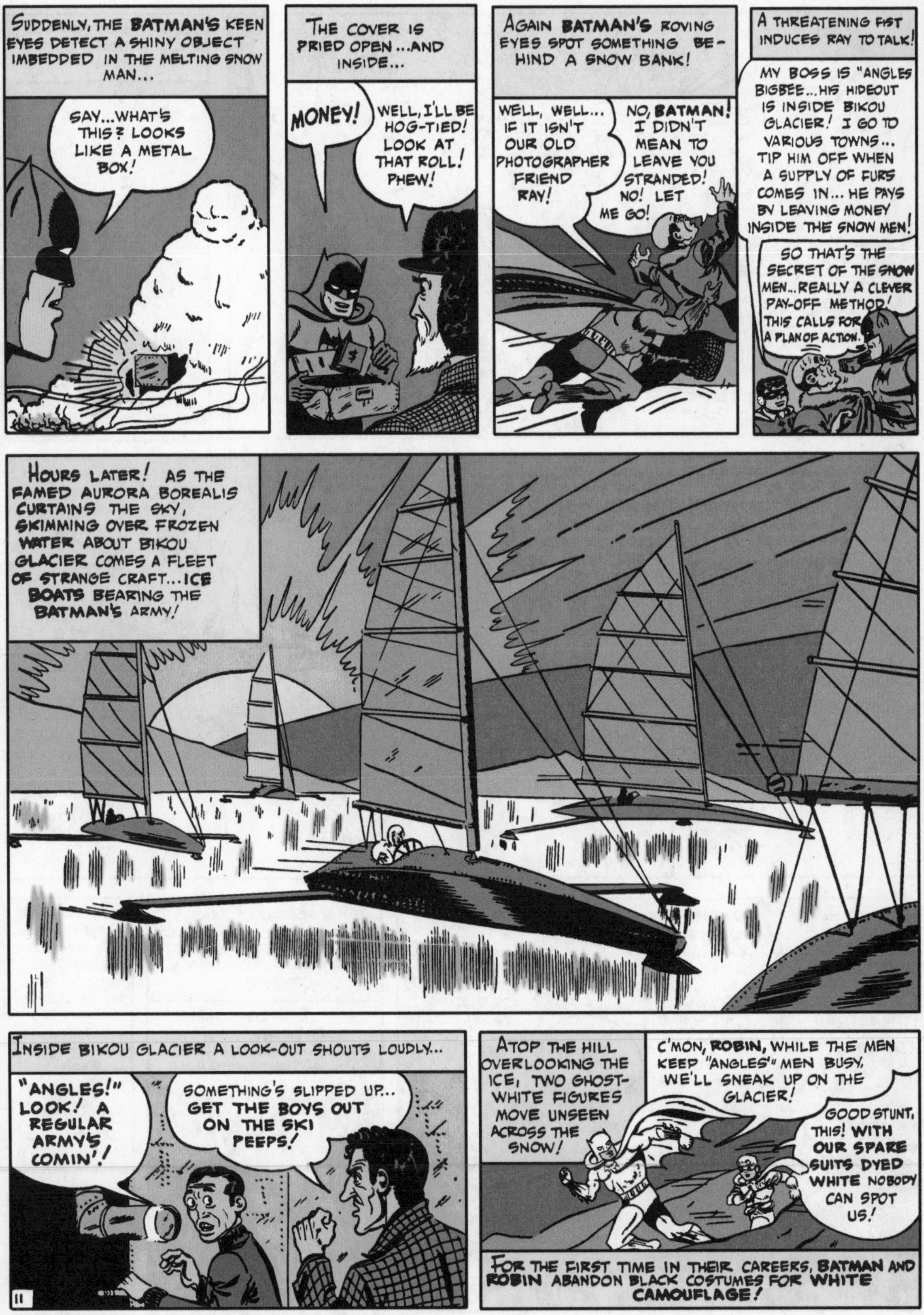
SUDDENLY, THE BATMAN'S KEEN EYES DETECT A SHINY OBJECT IMBEDDED IN THE MELTING SNOW MAN...
SAY...WHAT'S THIS? LOOKS LIKE A METAL BOX!
THE COVER IS PRIED OPEN...AND INSIDE...
MONEY!
WELL, I'LL BE HOG-TIED! LOOK AT THAT ROLL! PHEW!
AGAIN BATMAN'S ROVING EYES SPOT SOMETHING BEHIND A SNOW BANK!
WELL, WELL... IF IT ISN'T OUR OLD PHOTOGRAPHER FRIEND RAY!
NO, BATMAN! I DIDN'T MEAN TO LEAVE YOU STRANDED! NO! LET ME GO!
A THREATENING FIST INDUCES RAY TO TALK!
MY BOSS IS "ANGLES BIGBEE...HIS HIDEOUT IS INSIDE BIKOU GLACIER! I GO TO VARIOUS TOWNS... TIP HIM OFF WHEN A SUPPLY OF FURS COMES IN... HE PAYS BY LEAVING MONEY INSIDE THE SNOW MEN!
SO THAT'S THE SECRET OF THE SNOW MEN...REALLY A CLEVER PAY-OFF METHOD! THIS CALLS FOR A PLAN OF ACTION.
HOURS LATER! AS THE FAMED AURORA BOREALIS CURTAINS THE SKY, SKIMMING OVER FROZEN WATER ABOUT BIKOU GLACIER COMES A FLEET OF STRANGE CRAFT...ICE BOATS BEARING THE BATMAN'S ARMY!
INSIDE BIKOU GLACIER A LOOK-OUT SHOUTS LOUDLY...
"ANGLES!" LOOK! A REGULAR ARMY'S COMIN'!
SOMETHING'S SLIPPED UP... GET THE BOYS OUT ON THE SKI PEEPS!
11
ATOP THE HILL OVERLOOKING THE ICE, TWO GHOST-WHITE FIGURES MOVE UNSEEN ACROSS THE SNOW!
C'MON, ROBIN, WHILE THE MEN KEEP "ANGLES" MEN BUSY, WE'LL SNEAK UP ON THE GLACIER!
GOOD STUNT, THIS! WITH OUR SPARE SUITS DYED WHITE NOBODY CAN SPOT US!
FOR THE FIRST TIME IN THEIR CAREERS, BATMAN AND ROBIN ABANDON BLACK COSTUMES FOR WHITE CAMOUFLAGE!

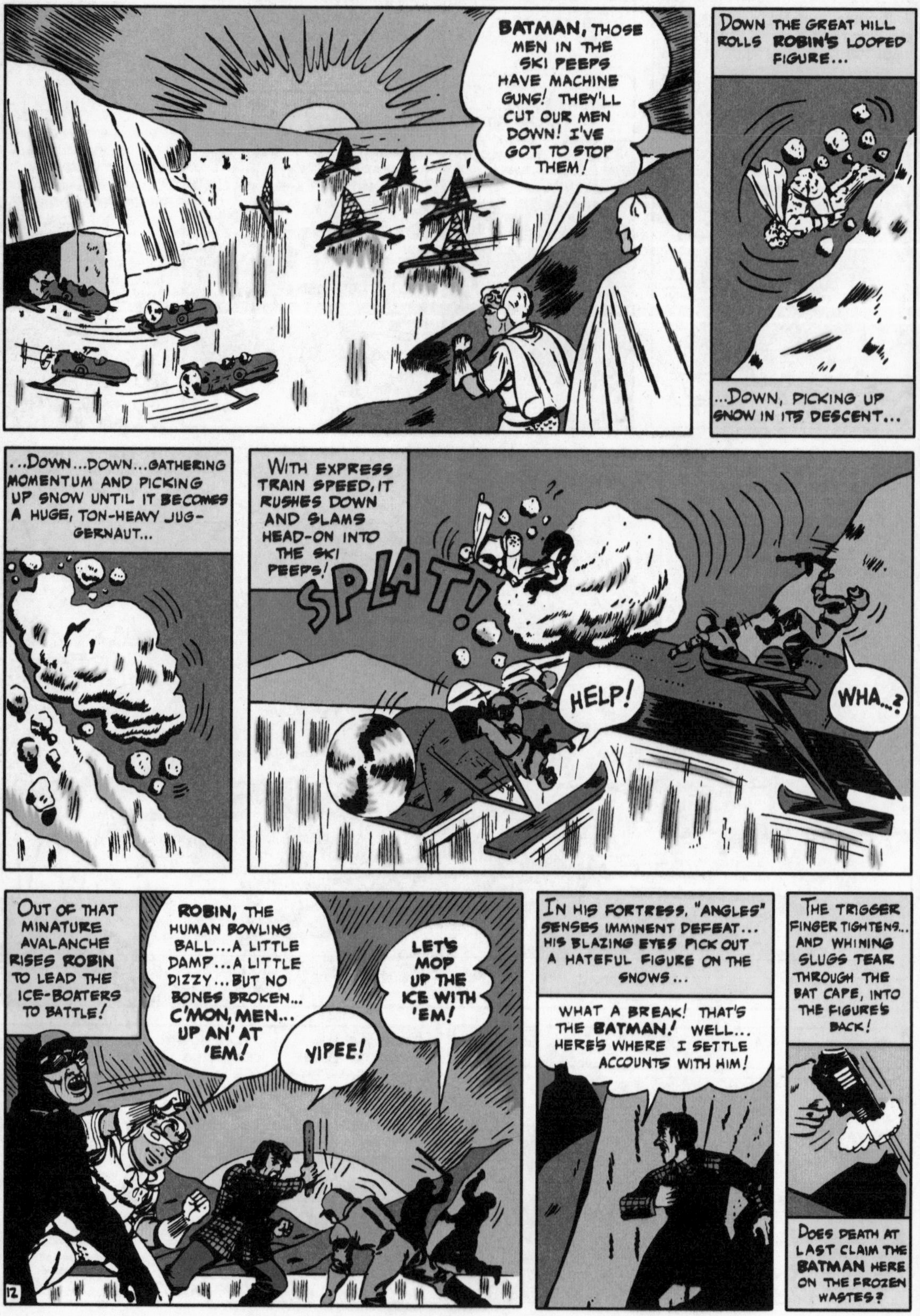
BATMAN, THOSE MEN IN THE SKI PEEPS HAVE MACHINE GUNS! THEY'LL CUT OUR MEN DOWN! I'VE GOT TO STOP THEM!
DOWN THE GREAT HILL ROLLS ROBIN'S LOOPED FIGURE...
...DOWN, PICKING UP SNOW IN ITS DESCENT...
...DOWN...DOWN...GATHERING MOMENTUM AND PICKING UP SNOW UNTIL IT BECOMES A HUGE, TON-HEAVY JUG-GERNAUT...
WITH EXPRESS TRAIN SPEED, IT RUSHES DOWN AND SLAMS HEAD-ON INTO THE SKI PEEPS!
SPLAT!
HELP!
WHA..?
OUT OF THAT MINATURE AVALANCHE RISES ROBIN TO LEAD THE ICE-BOATERS TO BATTLE!
ROBIN, THE HUMAN BOWLING BALL...A LITTLE DAMP...A LITTLE DIZZY...BUT NO BONES BROKEN... C'MON, MEN... UP AN' AT 'EM!
YIPEE!
LET'S MOP UP THE ICE WITH 'EM!
12
IN HIS FORTRESS, "ANGLES" SENSES IMMINENT DEFEAT... HIS BLAZING EYES PICK OUT A HATEFUL FIGURE ON THE SNOWS...
WHAT A BREAK! THAT'S THE BATMAN! WELL... HERE'S WHERE I SETTLE ACCOUNTS WITH HIM!
THE TRIGGER FINGER TIGHTENS... AND WHINING SLUGS TEAR THROUGH THE BAT CAPE, INTO THE FIGURE'S BACK!
DOES DEATH AT LAST CLAIM THE BATMAN HERE ON THE FROZEN WASTES?

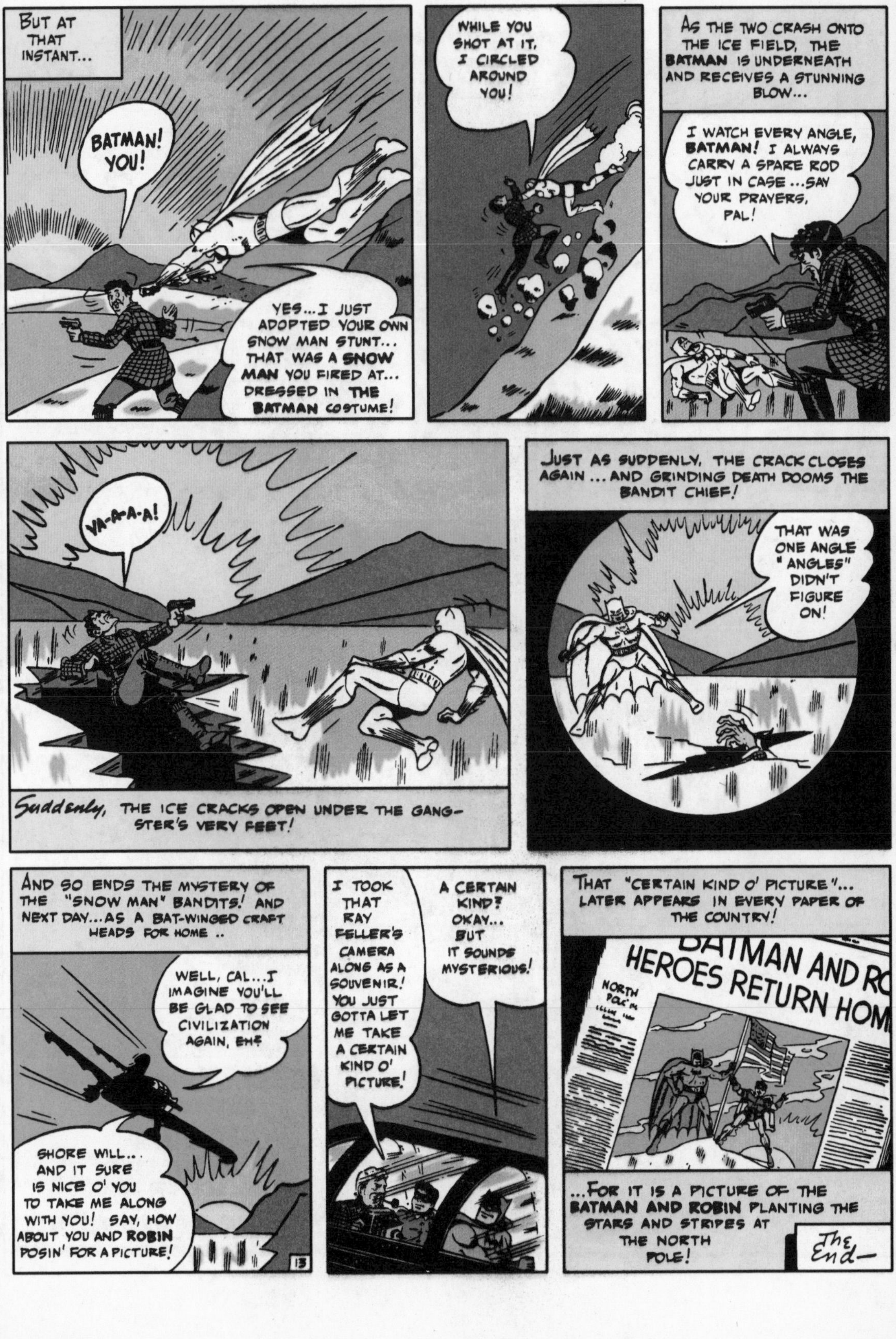
BUT AT THAT INSTANT...
BATMAN! YOU!
YES...I JUST ADOPTED YOUR OWN SNOW MAN STUNT... THAT WAS A SNOW MAN YOU FIRED AT... DRESSED IN THE BATMAN COSTUME!
WHILE YOU SHOT AT IT, I CIRCLED AROUND YOU!
AS THE TWO CRASH ONTO THE ICE FIELD, THE BATMAN IS UNDERNEATH AND RECEIVES A STUNNING BLOW...
I WATCH EVERY ANGLE, BATMAN! I ALWAYS CARRY A SPARE ROD JUST IN CASE ...SAY YOUR PRAYERS, PAL!
YA-A-A-A!
Suddenly, THE ICE CRACKS OPEN UNDER THE GANG-STER'S VERY FEET!
JUST AS SUDDENLY, THE CRACK CLOSES AGAIN ... AND GRINDING DEATH DOOMS THE BANDIT CHIEF!
THAT WAS ONE ANGLE "ANGLES" DIDN'T FIGURE ON!
AND SO ENDS THE MYSTERY OF THE "SNOW MAN" BANDITS! AND NEXT DAY...AS A BAT-WINGED CRAFT HEADS FOR HOME ..
WELL, CAL...I IMAGINE YOU'LL BE GLAD TO SEE CIVILIZATION AGAIN, EH?
SHORE WILL... AND IT SURE IS NICE O' YOU TO TAKE ME ALONG WITH YOU! SAY, HOW ABOUT YOU AND ROBIN POSIN' FOR A PICTURE!
13
I TOOK THAT RAY FELLER'S CAMERA ALONG AS A SOUVENIR! YOU JUST GOTTA LET ME TAKE A CERTAIN KIND O' PICTURE!
A CERTAIN KIND? OKAY... BUT IT SOUNDS MYSTERIOUS!
THAT "CERTAIN KIND O' PICTURE"... LATER APPEARS IN EVERY PAPER OF THE COUNTRY!
BATMAN AND RO
HEROES RETURN HOM
NORTH POLE
...FOR IT IS A PICTURE OF THE BATMAN AND ROBIN PLANTING THE STARS AND STRIPES AT THE NORTH POLE!
The End—

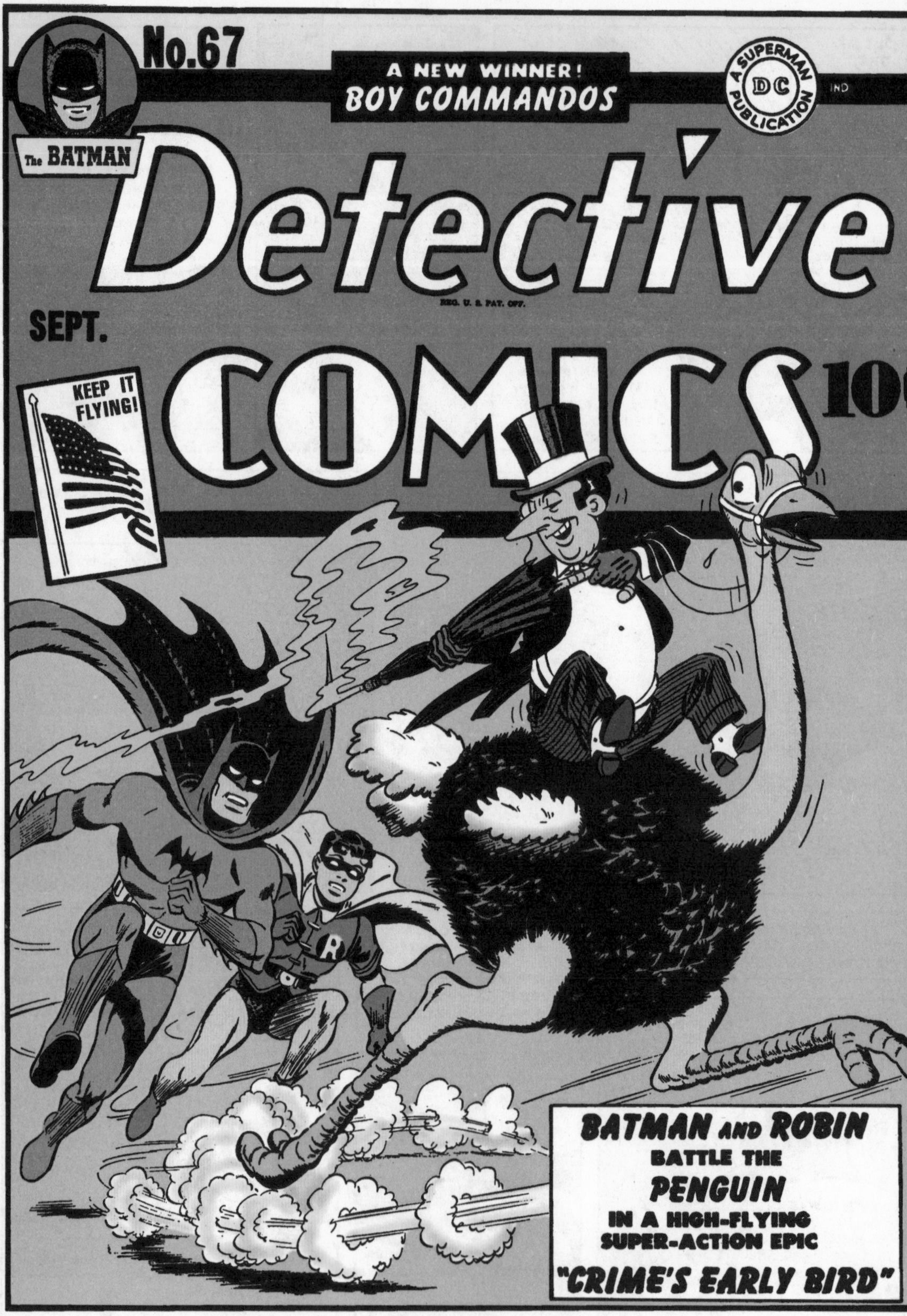
No.67
A NEW WINNER!
BOY COMMANDOS
A SUPERMAN DC PUBLICATION
The BATMAN
Detective
SEPT.
COMICS
10¢
KEEP IT FLYING!
BATMAN AND ROBIN
BATTLE THE
PENGUIN
IN A HIGH-FLYING
SUPER-ACTION EPIC
"CRIME'S EARLY BIRD"

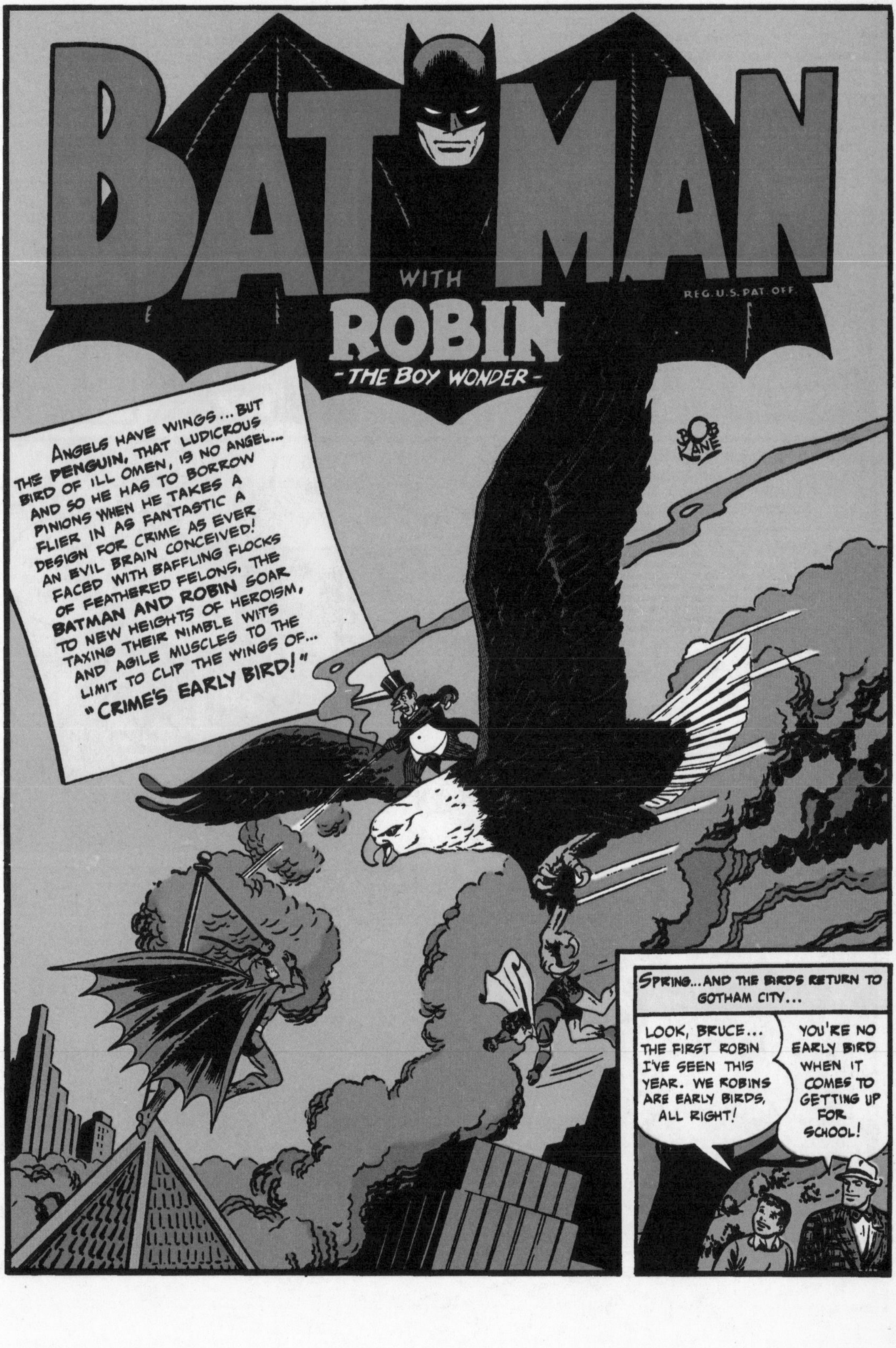
BATMAN
WITH
ROBIN
-THE BOY WONDER-
REG. U.S. PAT. OFF.
BOB KANE
ANGELS HAVE WINGS... BUT THE PENGUIN, THAT LUDICROUS BIRD OF ILL OMEN, IS NO ANGEL... AND SO HE HAS TO BORROW PINIONS WHEN HE TAKES A FLIER IN AS FANTASTIC A DESIGN FOR CRIME AS EVER AN EVIL BRAIN CONCEIVED! FACED WITH BAFFLING FLOCKS OF FEATHERED FELONS, THE BATMAN AND ROBIN SOAR TO NEW HEIGHTS OF HEROISM, TAXING THEIR NIMBLE WITS AND AGILE MUSCLES TO THE LIMIT TO CLIP THE WINGS OF... "CRIME'S EARLY BIRD!"
SPRING... AND THE BIRDS RETURN TO GOTHAM CITY...
LOOK, BRUCE... THE FIRST ROBIN I'VE SEEN THIS YEAR. WE ROBINS ARE EARLY BIRDS, ALL RIGHT!
YOU'RE NO EARLY BIRD WHEN IT COMES TO GETTING UP FOR SCHOOL!

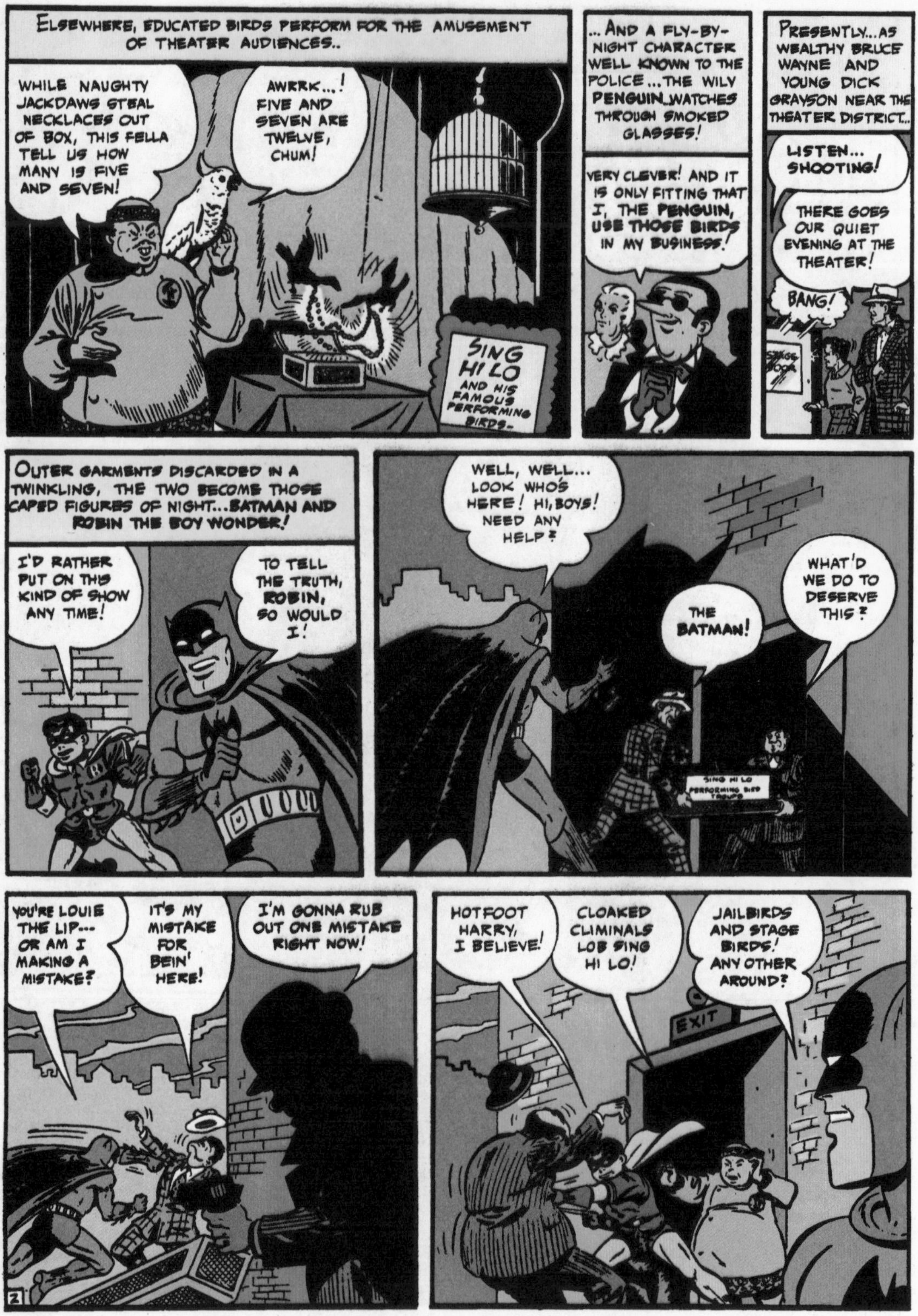
ELSEWHERE, EDUCATED BIRDS PERFORM FOR THE AMUSEMENT OF THEATER AUDIENCES..
WHILE NAUGHTY JACKDAWS STEAL NECKLACES OUT OF BOX, THIS FELLA TELL US HOW MANY IS FIVE AND SEVEN!
AWRRK...! FIVE AND SEVEN ARE TWELVE, CHUM!
SING HI LO AND HIS FAMOUS PERFORMING BIRDS-
... AND A FLY-BY-NIGHT CHARACTER WELL KNOWN TO THE POLICE ... THE WILY PENGUIN WATCHES THROUGH SMOKED GLASSES!
VERY CLEVER! AND IT IS ONLY FITTING THAT I, THE PENGUIN, USE THOSE BIRDS IN MY BUSINESS!
PRESENTLY...AS WEALTHY BRUCE WAYNE AND YOUNG DICK GRAYSON NEAR THE THEATER DISTRICT..
LISTEN... SHOOTING!
THERE GOES OUR QUIET EVENING AT THE THEATER!
BANG!
OUTER GARMENTS DISCARDED IN A TWINKLING, THE TWO BECOME THOSE CAPED FIGURES OF NIGHT...BATMAN AND ROBIN THE BOY WONDER!
I'D RATHER PUT ON THIS KIND OF SHOW ANY TIME!
TO TELL THE TRUTH, ROBIN, SO WOULD I!
WELL, WELL... LOOK WHO'S HERE! HI, BOYS! NEED ANY HELP?
THE BATMAN!
WHAT'D WE DO TO DESERVE THIS?
SING HI LO PERFORMING BIRD TROUPE
YOU'RE LOUIE THE LIP--- OR AM I MAKING A MISTAKE?
IT'S MY MISTAKE FOR BEIN' HERE!
I'M GONNA RUB OUT ONE MISTAKE RIGHT NOW!
HOTFOOT HARRY, I BELIEVE!
CLOAKED CLIMINALS LOB SING HI LO!
JAILBIRDS AND STAGE BIRDS! ANY OTHER AROUND?
EXIT

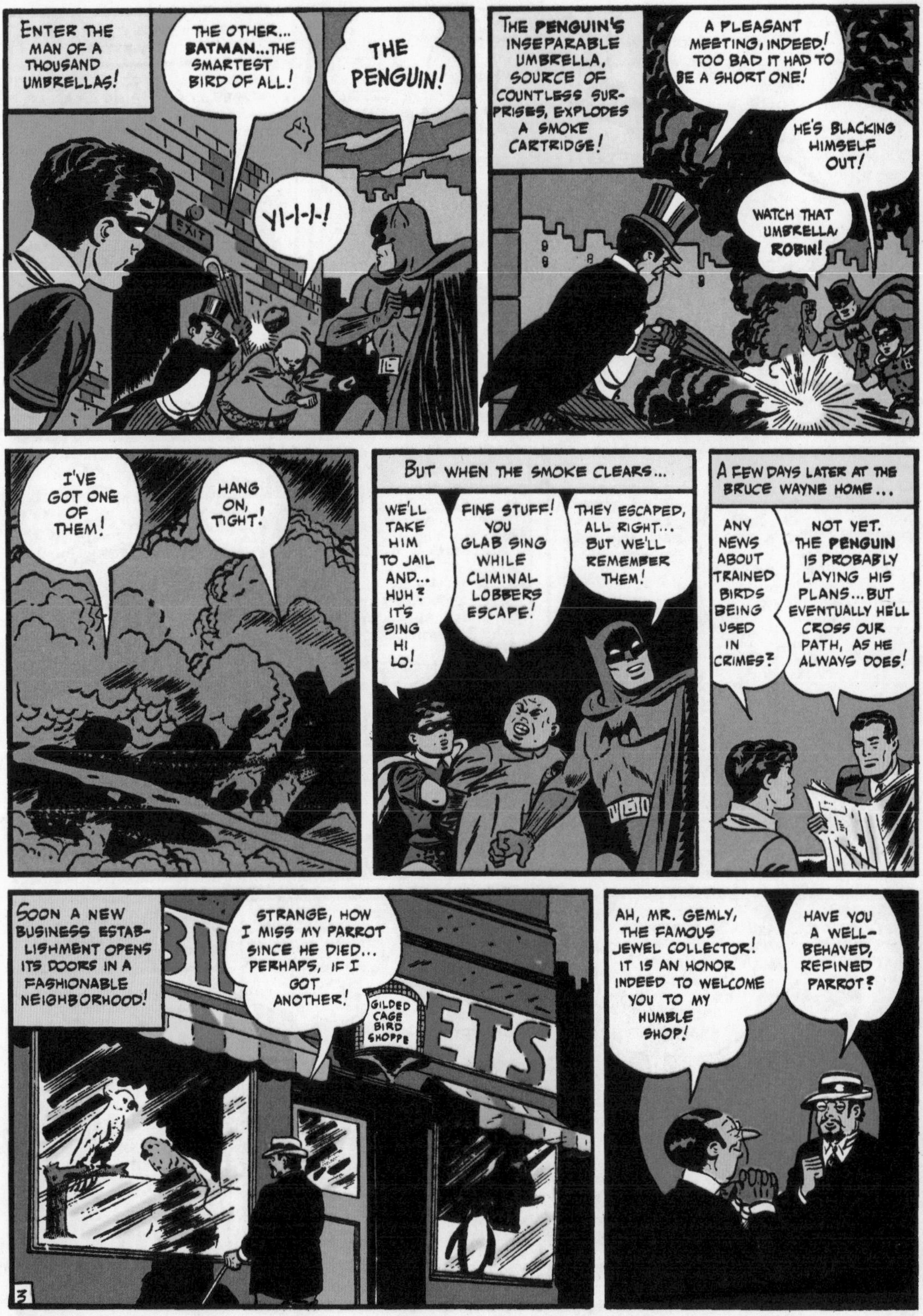

ENTER THE MAN OF A THOUSAND UMBRELLAS!
THE OTHER... BATMAN...THE SMARTEST BIRD OF ALL!
THE PENGUIN!
EXIT
YI-I-I-!
THE PENGUIN'S INSEPARABLE UMBRELLA, SOURCE OF COUNTLESS SURPRISES, EXPLODES A SMOKE CARTRIDGE!
A PLEASANT MEETING, INDEED! TOO BAD IT HAD TO BE A SHORT ONE!
HE'S BLACKING HIMSELF OUT!
WATCH THAT UMBRELLA, ROBIN!
I'VE GOT ONE OF THEM!
HANG ON, TIGHT!
BUT WHEN THE SMOKE CLEARS...
WE'LL TAKE HIM TO JAIL AND... HUH? IT'S SING HI LO!
FINE STUFF! YOU GLAB SING WHILE CLIMINAL LOBBERS ESCAPE!
THEY ESCAPED, ALL RIGHT... BUT WE'LL REMEMBER THEM!
A FEW DAYS LATER AT THE BRUCE WAYNE HOME...
ANY NEWS ABOUT TRAINED BIRDS BEING USED IN CRIMES?
NOT YET. THE PENGUIN IS PROBABLY LAYING HIS PLANS...BUT EVENTUALLY HE'LL CROSS OUR PATH, AS HE ALWAYS DOES!
SOON A NEW BUSINESS ESTABLISHMENT OPENS ITS DOORS IN A FASHIONABLE NEIGHBORHOOD!
STRANGE, HOW I MISS MY PARROT SINCE HE DIED... PERHAPS, IF I GOT ANOTHER!
GILDED CAGE BIRD SHOPPE
ETS
3
AH, MR. GEMLY, THE FAMOUS JEWEL COLLECTOR! IT IS AN HONOR INDEED TO WELCOME YOU TO MY HUMBLE SHOP!
HAVE YOU A WELL-BEHAVED, REFINED PARROT?

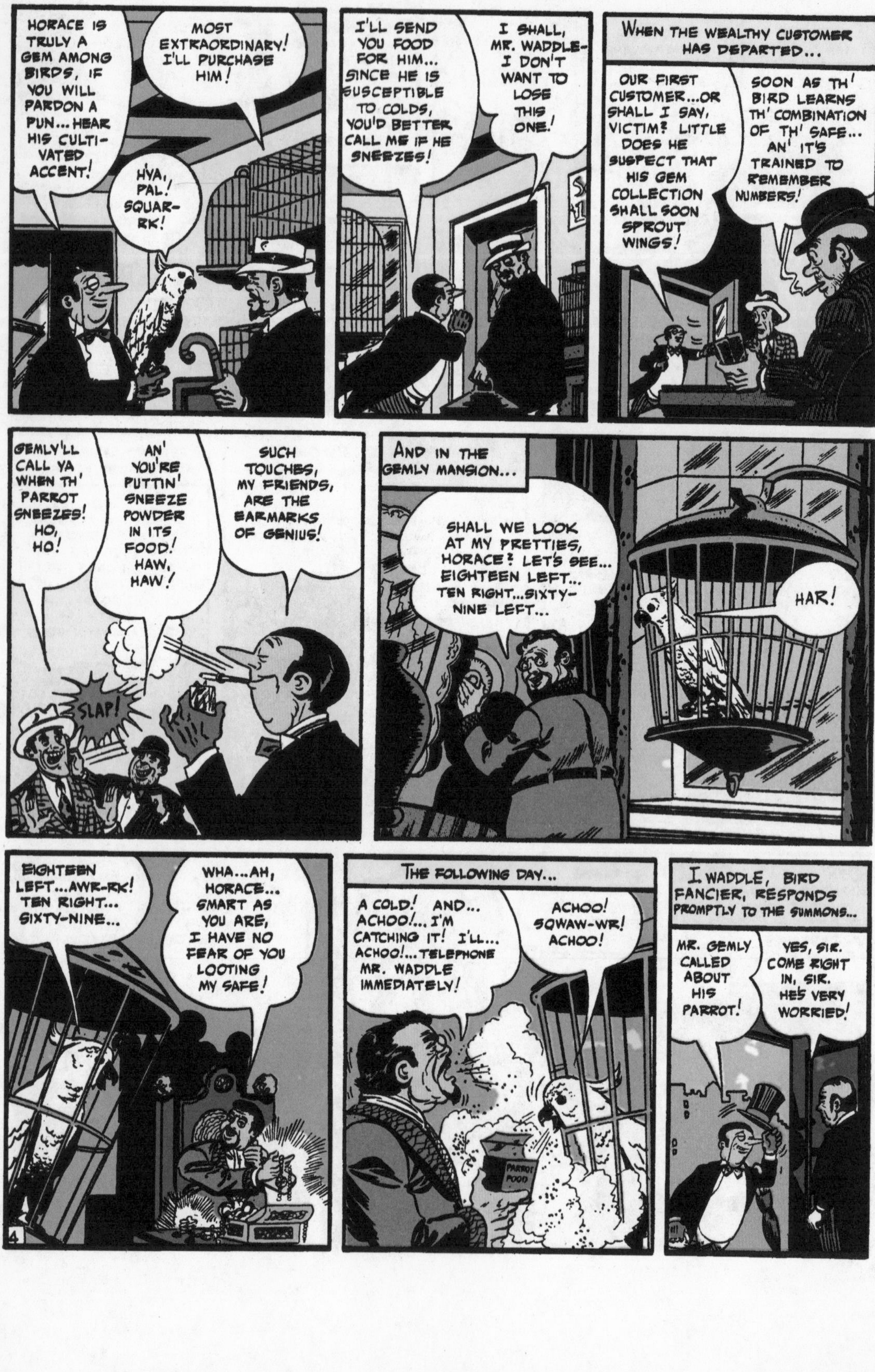
HORACE IS TRULY A GEM AMONG BIRDS, IF YOU WILL PARDON A PUN... HEAR HIS CULTIVATED ACCENT!
MOST EXTRAORDINARY! I'LL PURCHASE HIM!
HYA, PAL! SQUARRK!
I'LL SEND YOU FOOD FOR HIM... SINCE HE IS SUSCEPTIBLE TO COLDS, YOU'D BETTER CALL ME IF HE SNEEZES!
I SHALL, MR. WADDLE-- I DON'T WANT TO LOSE THIS ONE!
WHEN THE WEALTHY CUSTOMER HAS DEPARTED...
OUR FIRST CUSTOMER...OR SHALL I SAY, VICTIM? LITTLE DOES HE SUSPECT THAT HIS GEM COLLECTION SHALL SOON SPROUT WINGS!
SOON AS TH' BIRD LEARNS TH' COMBINATION OF TH' SAFE... AN' IT'S TRAINED TO REMEMBER NUMBERS!
GEMLY'LL CALL YA WHEN TH' PARROT SNEEZES! HO, HO!
AN' YOU'RE PUTTIN' SNEEZE POWDER IN ITS FOOD! HAW, HAW!
SUCH TOUCHES, MY FRIENDS, ARE THE EARMARKS OF GENIUS!
SLAP!
AND IN THE GEMLY MANSION...
SHALL WE LOOK AT MY PRETTIES, HORACE? LET'S SEE... EIGHTEEN LEFT... TEN RIGHT...SIXTY-NINE LEFT...
HAR!
EIGHTEEN LEFT...AWR-RK! TEN RIGHT... SIXTY-NINE...
WHA...AH, HORACE... SMART AS YOU ARE, I HAVE NO FEAR OF YOU LOOTING MY SAFE!
4
THE FOLLOWING DAY...
A COLD! AND... ACHOO!... I'M CATCHING IT! I'LL... ACHOO!...TELEPHONE MR. WADDLE IMMEDIATELY!
ACHOO! SQWAW-WR! ACHOO!
PARROT FOOD
I. WADDLE, BIRD FANCIER, RESPONDS PROMPTLY TO THE SUMMONS...
MR. GEMLY CALLED ABOUT HIS PARROT!
YES, SIR. COME RIGHT IN, SIR. HE'S VERY WORRIED!

IT CAME ON QUITE SUDDENLY. I HOPE IT ISN'T SERIOUS!

MMM...WE SHALL SEE... HOW DO YOU FEEL, HORACE?

AWRK! EIGHTEEN LEFT...TEN RIGHT... SIXTY-NINE LEFT...

DO YOU KNOW WHAT HE'S TALKING ABOUT, MR. GEMLY?

ER—NO, I DON'T... HE MUST BE DELIRIOUS! HA! HA!

THE PUDGY ARCH-CROOK PRESSES A BUTTON IN THE HANDLE OF HIS AMAZING UMBRELLA, AND...

A COLORLESS, ODORLESS GAS FILLS THE AIR... BUT DOES NOT AFFECT THE PENGUIN, WHO HAS THOUGHTFULLY THRUST COTTON WADS SOAKED WITH CHEMICALS INTO HIS NOSTRILS...

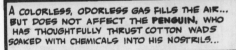

I MUST HAVE CAUGHT WHATEVER AILS HORACE... I FEEL DIZZY...

SIT DOWN. THE FEELING WILL PASS IN A MOMENT!

ALL FEELING HAS LEFT THE OLD FOOL FOREVER... AND THE JEWELS ARE ABOUT TO LEAVE HIM, TOO... TOO BAD I HAD TO SACRIFICE HORACE...

FLY AWAY HOME, LITTLE HOMING PIGEON, WITH THE SACKS OF SWAG! THIS IS BETTER THAN RISKING GETTING CAUGHT WITH THE LOOT!

A PERFECT CRIME IS A WORK OF ART! THE GAS CONTAINED THE GERM OF PSITTACOSIS... PARROT FEVER... WHICH IS FATAL TO HUMANS AS WELL AS BIRDS. NO ONE CAN POSSIBLY SUSPECT ME!

Later...

IT WAS PARROT FEVER, ALL RIGHT... NOTHING SUSPICIOUS...

THANKS, DOC... YOU CAN GO, MR. WADDLE...AND I'M SORRY WE HAD TO SEARCH YOU!

QUITE ALL RIGHT, SIR!

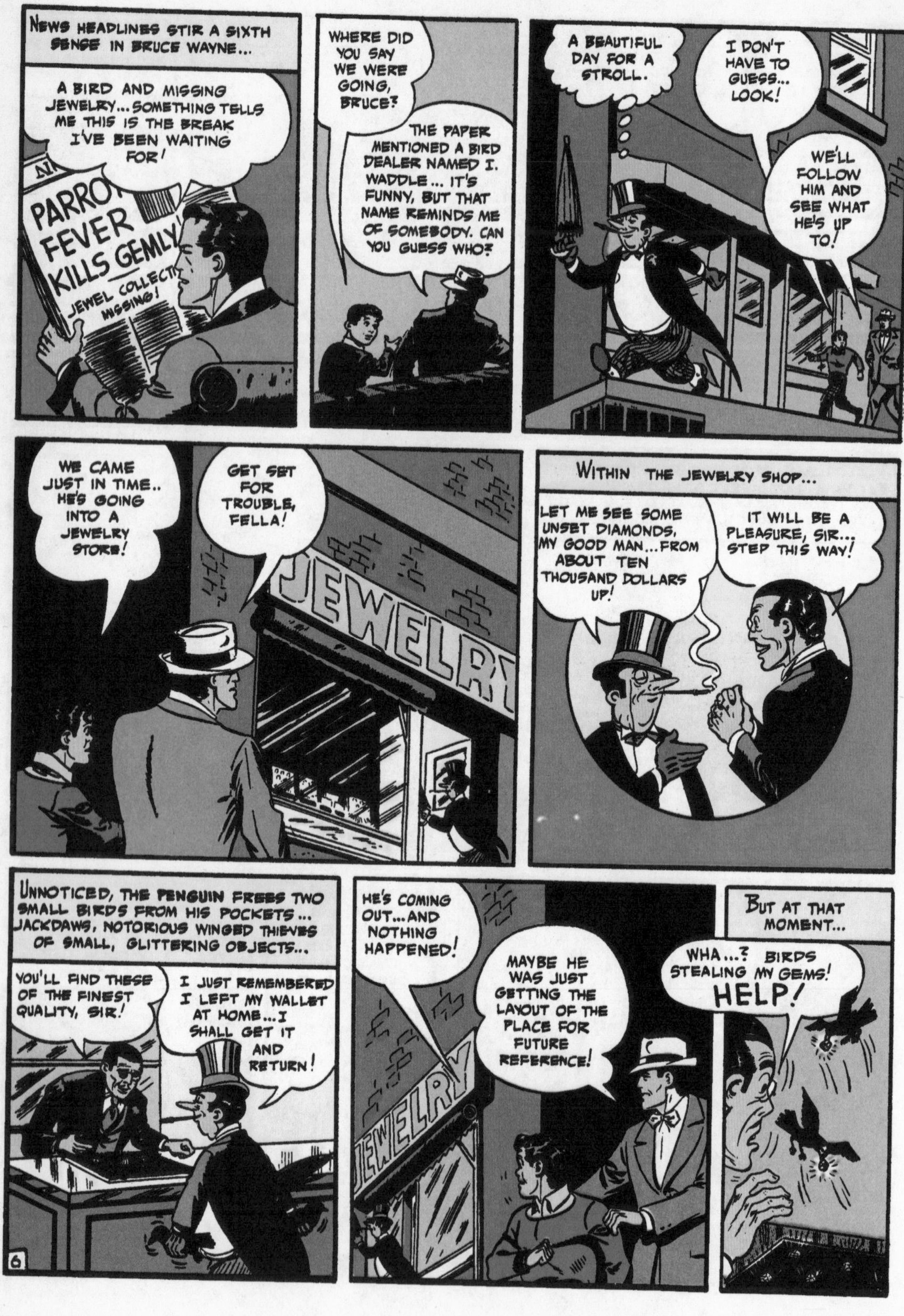
NEWS HEADLINES STIR A SIXTH SENSE IN BRUCE WAYNE...
A BIRD AND MISSING JEWELRY... SOMETHING TELLS ME THIS IS THE BREAK I'VE BEEN WAITING FOR!
PARROT FEVER KILLS GEMLY
JEWEL COLLECT MISSING!
WHERE DID YOU SAY WE WERE GOING, BRUCE?
THE PAPER MENTIONED A BIRD DEALER NAMED I. WADDLE... IT'S FUNNY, BUT THAT NAME REMINDS ME OF SOMEBODY. CAN YOU GUESS WHO?
A BEAUTIFUL DAY FOR A STROLL.
I DON'T HAVE TO GUESS... LOOK!
WE'LL FOLLOW HIM AND SEE WHAT HE'S UP TO!
WE CAME JUST IN TIME.. HE'S GOING INTO A JEWELRY STORE!
GET SET FOR TROUBLE, FELLA!
JEWELRY
WITHIN THE JEWELRY SHOP...
LET ME SEE SOME UNSET DIAMONDS, MY GOOD MAN... FROM ABOUT TEN THOUSAND DOLLARS UP!
IT WILL BE A PLEASURE, SIR... STEP THIS WAY!
UNNOTICED, THE PENGUIN FREES TWO SMALL BIRDS FROM HIS POCKETS... JACKDAWS, NOTORIOUS WINGED THIEVES OF SMALL, GLITTERING OBJECTS...
YOU'LL FIND THESE OF THE FINEST QUALITY, SIR!
I JUST REMEMBERED I LEFT MY WALLET AT HOME... I SHALL GET IT AND RETURN!
6
HE'S COMING OUT... AND NOTHING HAPPENED!
MAYBE HE WAS JUST GETTING THE LAYOUT OF THE PLACE FOR FUTURE REFERENCE!
JEWELRY
BUT AT THAT MOMENT...
WHA...? BIRDS STEALING MY GEMS! HELP!

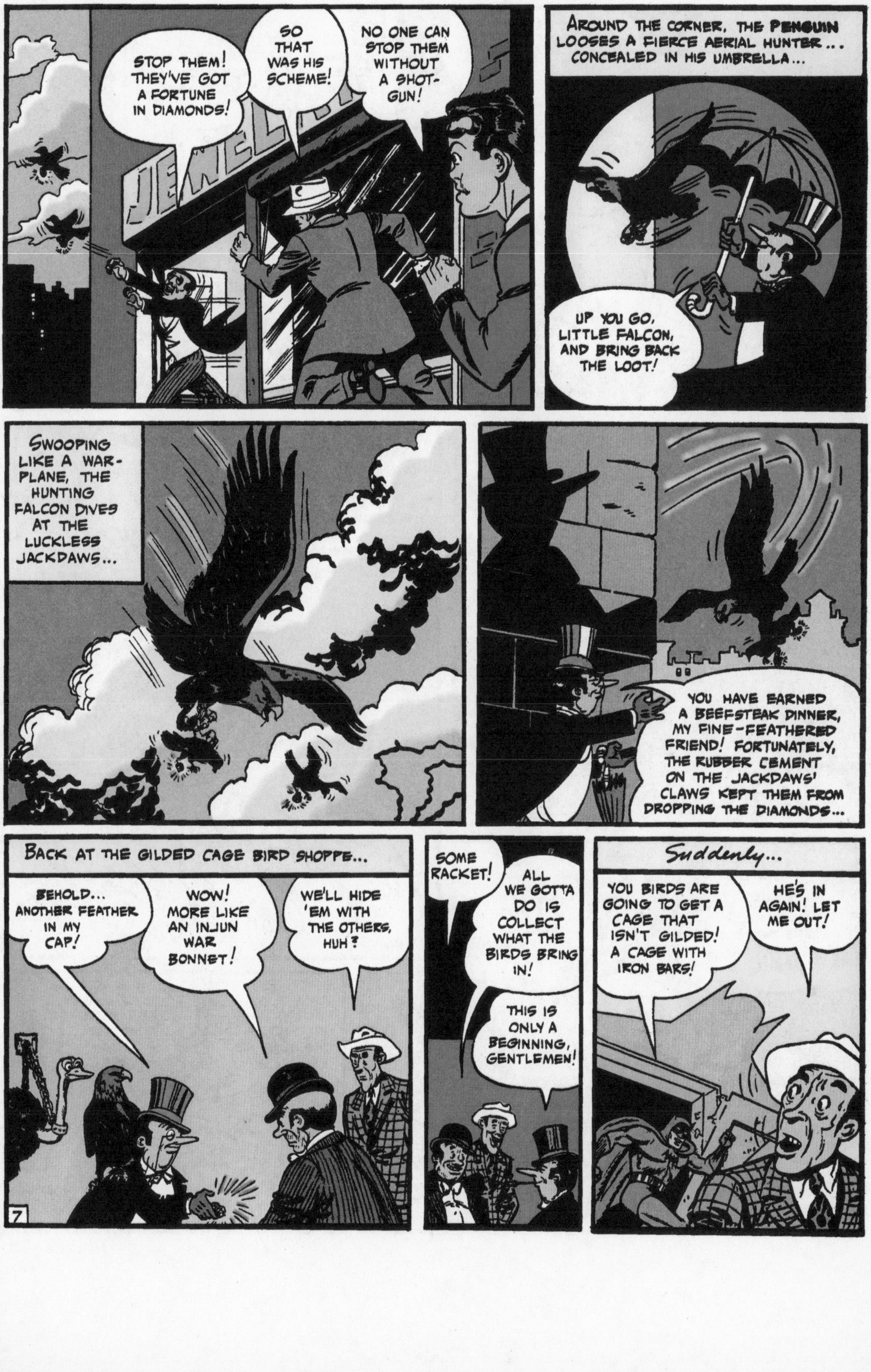
STOP THEM! THEY'VE GOT A FORTUNE IN DIAMONDS!
SO THAT WAS HIS SCHEME!
NO ONE CAN STOP THEM WITHOUT A SHOT-GUN!
AROUND THE CORNER, THE PENGUIN LOOSES A FIERCE AERIAL HUNTER... CONCEALED IN HIS UMBRELLA...
UP YOU GO, LITTLE FALCON, AND BRING BACK THE LOOT!
SWOOPING LIKE A WAR-PLANE, THE HUNTING FALCON DIVES AT THE LUCKLESS JACKDAWS...
YOU HAVE EARNED A BEEFSTEAK DINNER, MY FINE-FEATHERED FRIEND! FORTUNATELY, THE RUBBER CEMENT ON THE JACKDAWS' CLAWS KEPT THEM FROM DROPPING THE DIAMONDS...
BACK AT THE GILDED CAGE BIRD SHOPPE...
BEHOLD... ANOTHER FEATHER IN MY CAP!
WOW! MORE LIKE AN INJUN WAR BONNET!
WE'LL HIDE 'EM WITH THE OTHERS, HUH?
7
SOME RACKET!
ALL WE GOTTA DO IS COLLECT WHAT THE BIRDS BRING IN!
THIS IS ONLY A BEGINNING, GENTLEMEN!
Suddenly...
YOU BIRDS ARE GOING TO GET A CAGE THAT ISN'T GILDED! A CAGE WITH IRON BARS!
HE'S IN AGAIN! LET ME OUT!

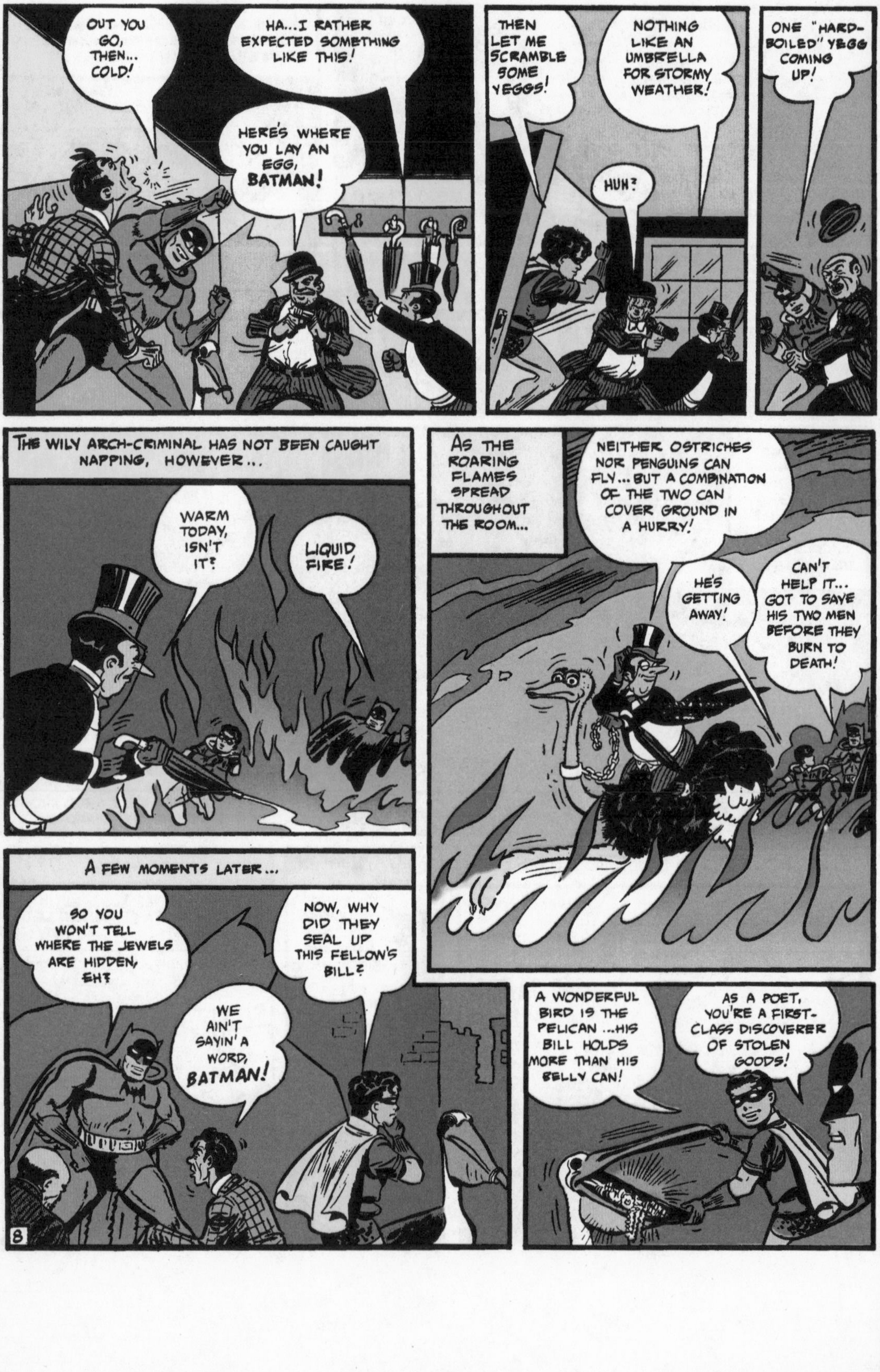
OUT YOU GO, THEN... COLD!
HA...I RATHER EXPECTED SOMETHING LIKE THIS!
HERE'S WHERE YOU LAY AN EGG, BATMAN!
THEN LET ME SCRAMBLE SOME YEGGS!
NOTHING LIKE AN UMBRELLA FOR STORMY WEATHER!
HUH?
ONE "HARD-BOILED" YEGG COMING UP!
THE WILY ARCH-CRIMINAL HAS NOT BEEN CAUGHT NAPPING, HOWEVER...
WARM TODAY, ISN'T IT?
LIQUID FIRE!
AS THE ROARING FLAMES SPREAD THROUGHOUT THE ROOM...
NEITHER OSTRICHES NOR PENGUINS CAN FLY... BUT A COMBINATION OF THE TWO CAN COVER GROUND IN A HURRY!
HE'S GETTING AWAY!
CAN'T HELP IT... GOT TO SAVE HIS TWO MEN BEFORE THEY BURN TO DEATH!
A FEW MOMENTS LATER...
SO YOU WON'T TELL WHERE THE JEWELS ARE HIDDEN, EH?
NOW, WHY DID THEY SEAL UP THIS FELLOW'S BILL?
WE AIN'T SAYIN' A WORD, BATMAN!
8
A WONDERFUL BIRD IS THE PELICAN ...HIS BILL HOLDS MORE THAN HIS BELLY CAN!
AS A POET, YOU'RE A FIRST-CLASS DISCOVERER OF STOLEN GOODS!

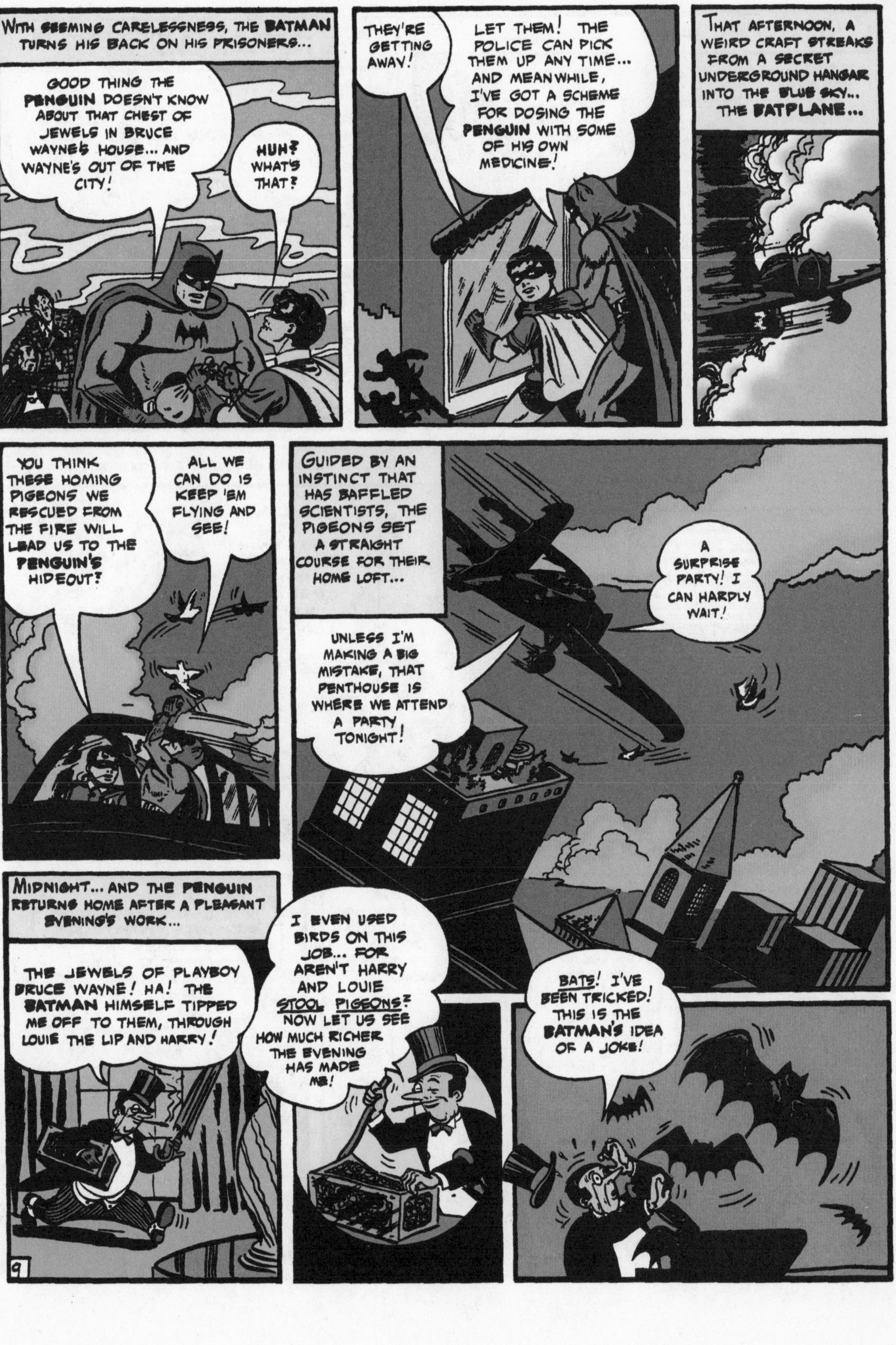

WITH SEEMING CARELESSNESS, THE BATMAN TURNS HIS BACK ON HIS PRISONERS...
GOOD THING THE PENGUIN DOESN'T KNOW ABOUT THAT CHEST OF JEWELS IN BRUCE WAYNE'S HOUSE... AND WAYNE'S OUT OF THE CITY!
HUH? WHAT'S THAT?
THEY'RE GETTING AWAY!
LET THEM! THE POLICE CAN PICK THEM UP ANY TIME... AND MEANWHILE, I'VE GOT A SCHEME FOR DOSING THE PENGUIN WITH SOME OF HIS OWN MEDICINE!
THAT AFTERNOON, A WEIRD CRAFT STREAKS FROM A SECRET UNDERGROUND HANGAR INTO THE BLUE SKY... THE BATPLANE...
YOU THINK THESE HOMING PIGEONS WE RESCUED FROM THE FIRE WILL LEAD US TO THE PENGUIN'S HIDEOUT?
ALL WE CAN DO IS KEEP 'EM FLYING AND SEE!
GUIDED BY AN INSTINCT THAT HAS BAFFLED SCIENTISTS, THE PIGEONS SET A STRAIGHT COURSE FOR THEIR HOME LOFT...
A SURPRISE PARTY! I CAN HARDLY WAIT!
UNLESS I'M MAKING A BIG MISTAKE, THAT PENTHOUSE IS WHERE WE ATTEND A PARTY TONIGHT!
MIDNIGHT... AND THE PENGUIN RETURNS HOME AFTER A PLEASANT EVENING'S WORK...
THE JEWELS OF PLAYBOY BRUCE WAYNE! HA! THE BATMAN HIMSELF TIPPED ME OFF TO THEM, THROUGH LOUIE THE LIP AND HARRY!
I EVEN USED BIRDS ON THIS JOB... FOR AREN'T HARRY AND LOUIE STOOL PIGEONS? NOW LET US SEE HOW MUCH RICHER THE EVENING HAS MADE ME!
BATS! I'VE BEEN TRICKED! THIS IS THE BATMAN'S IDEA OF A JOKE!
9

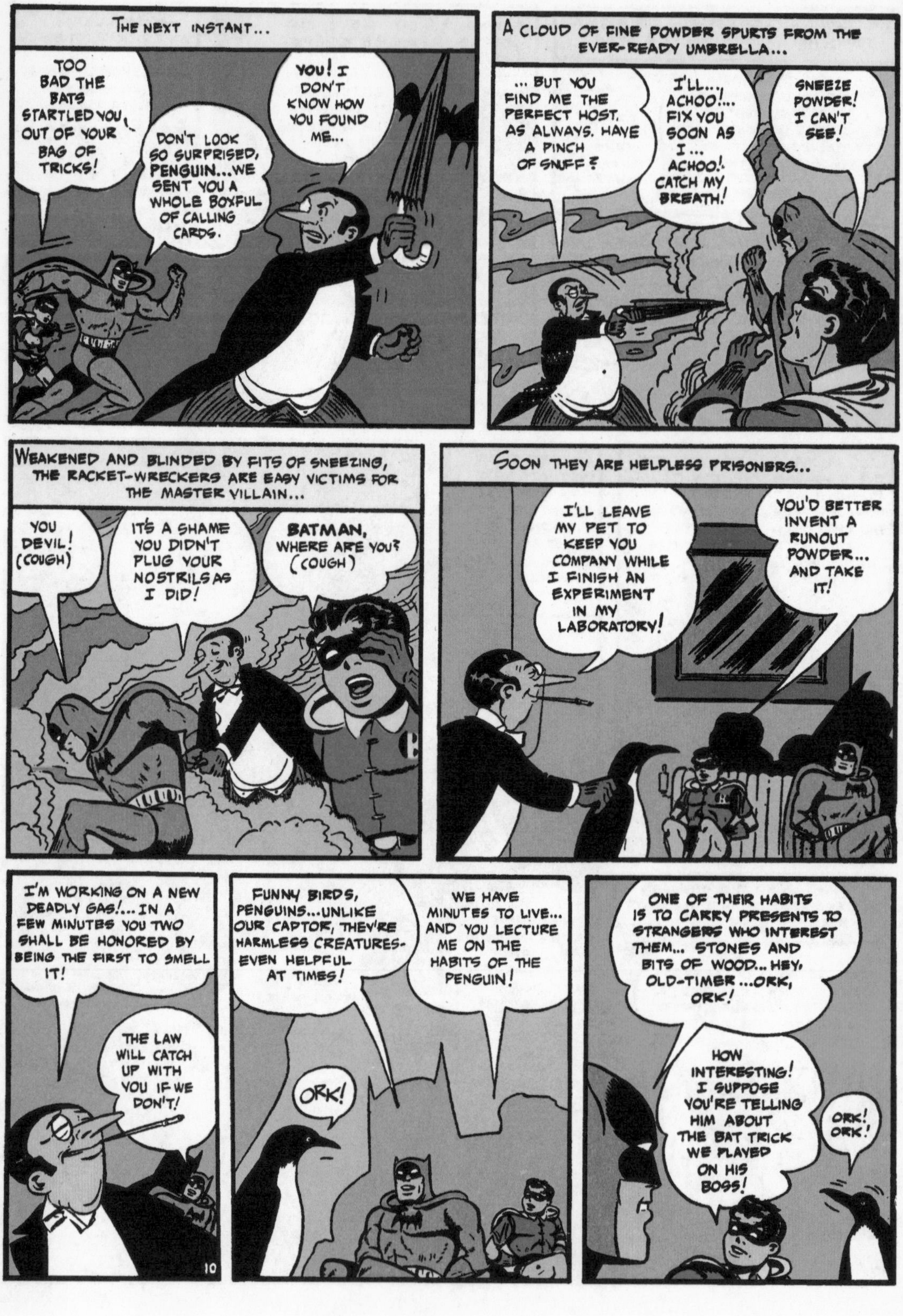
THE NEXT INSTANT...
TOO BAD THE BATS STARTLED YOU OUT OF YOUR BAG OF TRICKS!
DON'T LOOK SO SURPRISED, PENGUIN...WE SENT YOU A WHOLE BOXFUL OF CALLING CARDS.
YOU! I DON'T KNOW HOW YOU FOUND ME...
A CLOUD OF FINE POWDER SPURTS FROM THE EVER-READY UMBRELLA...
... BUT YOU FIND ME THE PERFECT HOST, AS ALWAYS. HAVE A PINCH OF SNUFF?
I'LL... ACHOO!... FIX YOU SOON AS I... ACHOO!. CATCH MY BREATH!
SNEEZE POWDER! I CAN'T SEE!
WEAKENED AND BLINDED BY FITS OF SNEEZING, THE RACKET-WRECKERS ARE EASY VICTIMS FOR THE MASTER VILLAIN...
YOU DEVIL! (COUGH)
IT'S A SHAME YOU DIDN'T PLUG YOUR NOSTRILS AS I DID!
BATMAN, WHERE ARE YOU? (COUGH)
SOON THEY ARE HELPLESS PRISONERS...
I'LL LEAVE MY PET TO KEEP YOU COMPANY WHILE I FINISH AN EXPERIMENT IN MY LABORATORY!
YOU'D BETTER INVENT A RUNOUT POWDER... AND TAKE IT!
I'M WORKING ON A NEW DEADLY GAS!... IN A FEW MINUTES YOU TWO SHALL BE HONORED BY BEING THE FIRST TO SMELL IT!
THE LAW WILL CATCH UP WITH YOU IF WE DON'T!
10
FUNNY BIRDS, PENGUINS...UNLIKE OUR CAPTOR, THEY'RE HARMLESS CREATURES- EVEN HELPFUL AT TIMES!
WE HAVE MINUTES TO LIVE... AND YOU LECTURE ME ON THE HABITS OF THE PENGUIN!
ORK!
ONE OF THEIR HABITS IS TO CARRY PRESENTS TO STRANGERS WHO INTEREST THEM... STONES AND BITS OF WOOD... HEY, OLD-TIMER ...ORK, ORK!
HOW INTERESTING! I SUPPOSE YOU'RE TELLING HIM ABOUT THE BAT TRICK WE PLAYED ON HIS BOSS!
ORK! ORK!

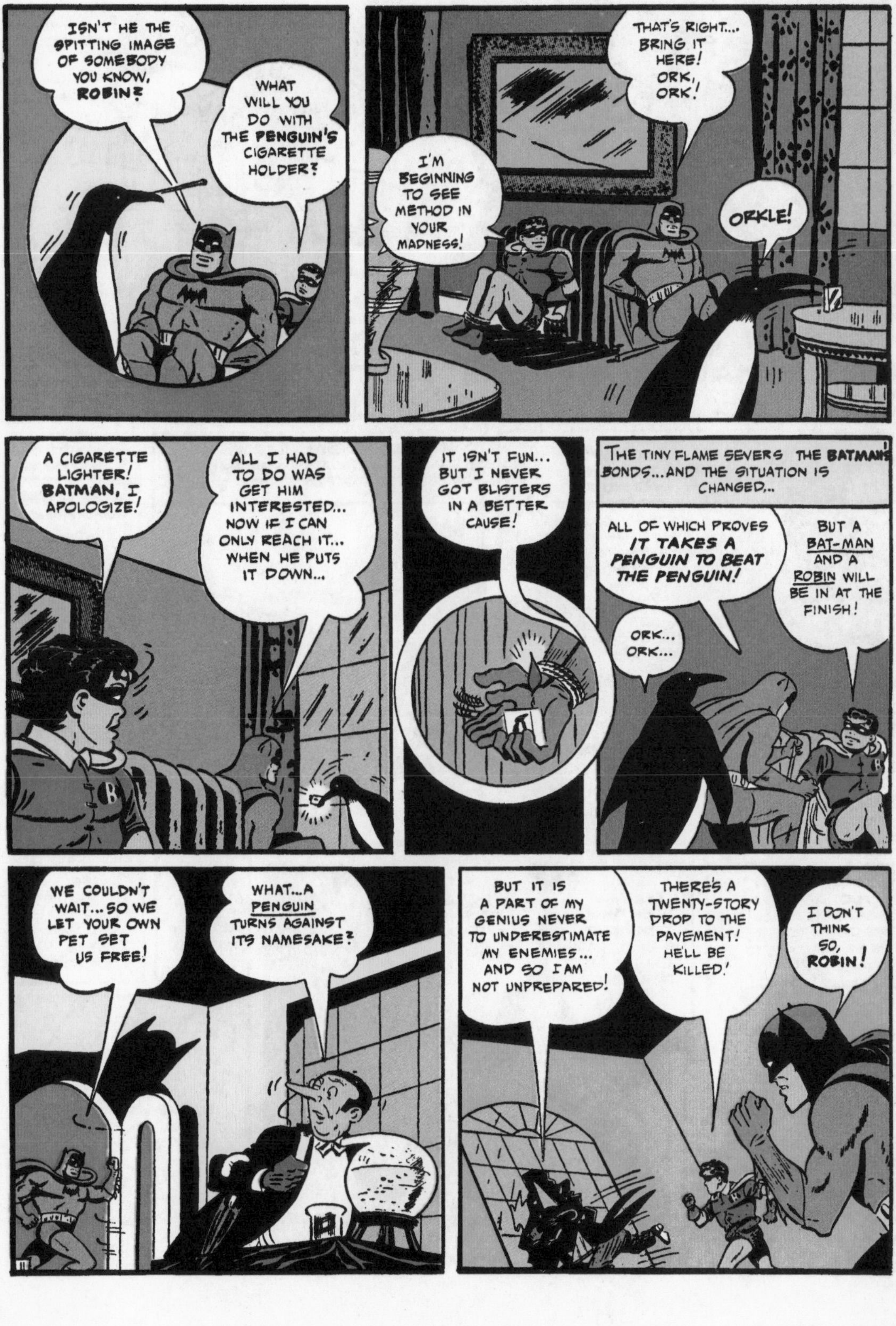
ISN'T HE THE SPITTING IMAGE OF SOMEBODY YOU KNOW, ROBIN?
WHAT WILL YOU DO WITH THE PENGUIN'S CIGARETTE HOLDER?
THAT'S RIGHT... BRING IT HERE! ORK, ORK!
I'M BEGINNING TO SEE METHOD IN YOUR MADNESS!
ORKLE!
A CIGARETTE LIGHTER! BATMAN, I APOLOGIZE!
ALL I HAD TO DO WAS GET HIM INTERESTED... NOW IF I CAN ONLY REACH IT... WHEN HE PUTS IT DOWN...
IT ISN'T FUN... BUT I NEVER GOT BLISTERS IN A BETTER CAUSE!
THE TINY FLAME SEVERS THE BATMAN'S BONDS...AND THE SITUATION IS CHANGED...
ALL OF WHICH PROVES IT TAKES A PENGUIN TO BEAT THE PENGUIN!
BUT A BAT-MAN AND A ROBIN WILL BE IN AT THE FINISH!
ORK... ORK...
WE COULDN'T WAIT... SO WE LET YOUR OWN PET SET US FREE!
WHAT...A PENGUIN TURNS AGAINST ITS NAMESAKE?
BUT IT IS A PART OF MY GENIUS NEVER TO UNDERESTIMATE MY ENEMIES... AND SO I AM NOT UNPREPARED!
THERE'S A TWENTY-STORY DROP TO THE PAVEMENT! HE'LL BE KILLED!
I DON'T THINK SO, ROBIN!

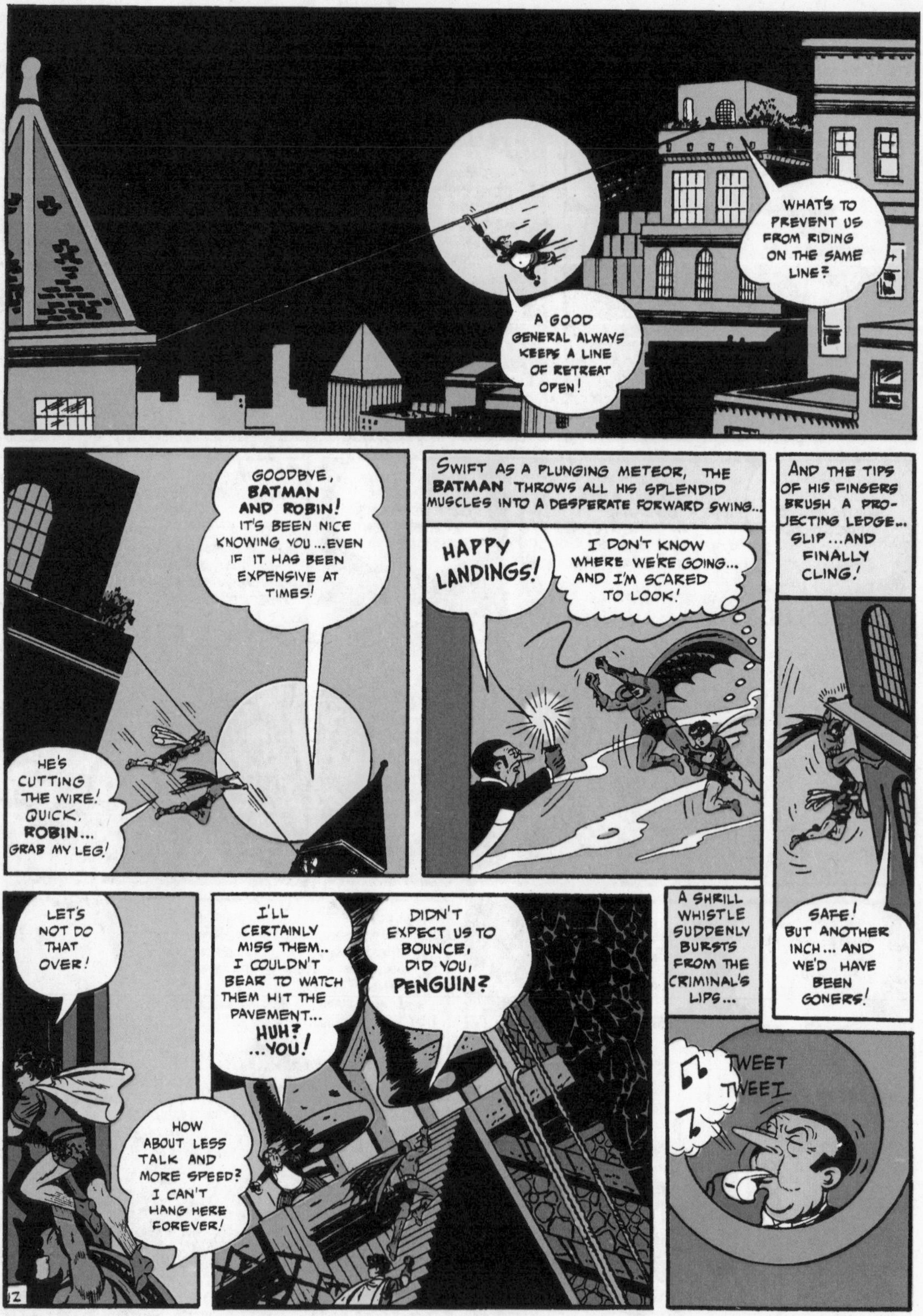
WHAT'S TO PREVENT US FROM RIDING ON THE SAME LINE?
A GOOD GENERAL ALWAYS KEEPS A LINE OF RETREAT OPEN!
GOODBYE, BATMAN AND ROBIN! IT'S BEEN NICE KNOWING YOU ...EVEN IF IT HAS BEEN EXPENSIVE AT TIMES!
HE'S CUTTING THE WIRE! QUICK, ROBIN... GRAB MY LEG!
SWIFT AS A PLUNGING METEOR, THE BATMAN THROWS ALL HIS SPLENDID MUSCLES INTO A DESPERATE FORWARD SWING...
HAPPY LANDINGS!
I DON'T KNOW WHERE WE'RE GOING... AND I'M SCARED TO LOOK!
AND THE TIPS OF HIS FINGERS BRUSH A PROJECTING LEDGE... SLIP... AND FINALLY CLING!
SAFE! BUT ANOTHER INCH... AND WE'D HAVE BEEN GONERS!
LET'S NOT DO THAT OVER!
HOW ABOUT LESS TALK AND MORE SPEED? I CAN'T HANG HERE FOREVER!
12
I'LL CERTAINLY MISS THEM.. I COULDN'T BEAR TO WATCH THEM HIT THE PAVEMENT... HUH? ...YOU!
DIDN'T EXPECT US TO BOUNCE, DID YOU, PENGUIN?
A SHRILL WHISTLE SUDDENLY BURSTS FROM THE CRIMINAL'S LIPS...
TWEET TWEET

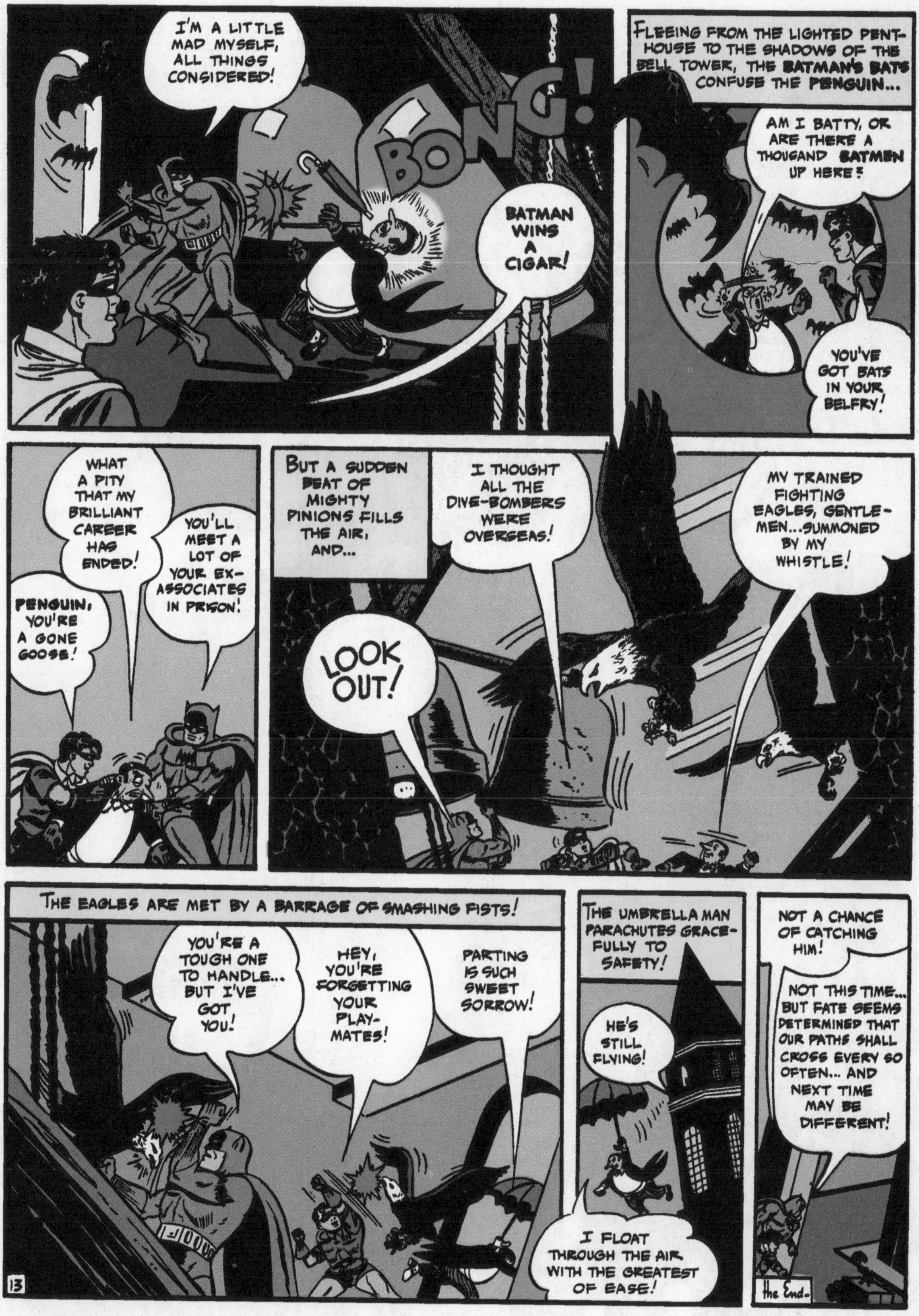
I'M A LITTLE MAD MYSELF, ALL THINGS CONSIDERED!
BONG!
BATMAN WINS A CIGAR!
FLEEING FROM THE LIGHTED PENT-HOUSE TO THE SHADOWS OF THE BELL TOWER, THE BATMAN'S BATS CONFUSE THE PENGUIN...
AM I BATTY, OR ARE THERE A THOUSAND BATMEN UP HERE?
YOU'VE GOT BATS IN YOUR BELFRY!
WHAT A PITY THAT MY BRILLIANT CAREER HAS ENDED!
YOU'LL MEET A LOT OF YOUR EX-ASSOCIATES IN PRISON!
PENGUIN, YOU'RE A GONE GOOSE!
BUT A SUDDEN BEAT OF MIGHTY PINIONS FILLS THE AIR, AND...
I THOUGHT ALL THE DIVE-BOMBERS WERE OVERSEAS!
MY TRAINED FIGHTING EAGLES, GENTLE-MEN...SUMMONED BY MY WHISTLE!
LOOK OUT!
THE EAGLES ARE MET BY A BARRAGE OF SMASHING FISTS!
YOU'RE A TOUGH ONE TO HANDLE... BUT I'VE GOT YOU!
HEY, YOU'RE FORGETTING YOUR PLAY-MATES!
PARTING IS SUCH SWEET SORROW!
13
THE UMBRELLA MAN PARACHUTES GRACE-FULLY TO SAFETY!
HE'S STILL FLYING!
I FLOAT THROUGH THE AIR WITH THE GREATEST OF EASE!
NOT A CHANCE OF CATCHING HIM!
NOT THIS TIME... BUT FATE SEEMS DETERMINED THAT OUR PATHS SHALL CROSS EVERY SO OFTEN... AND NEXT TIME MAY BE DIFFERENT!
The End.

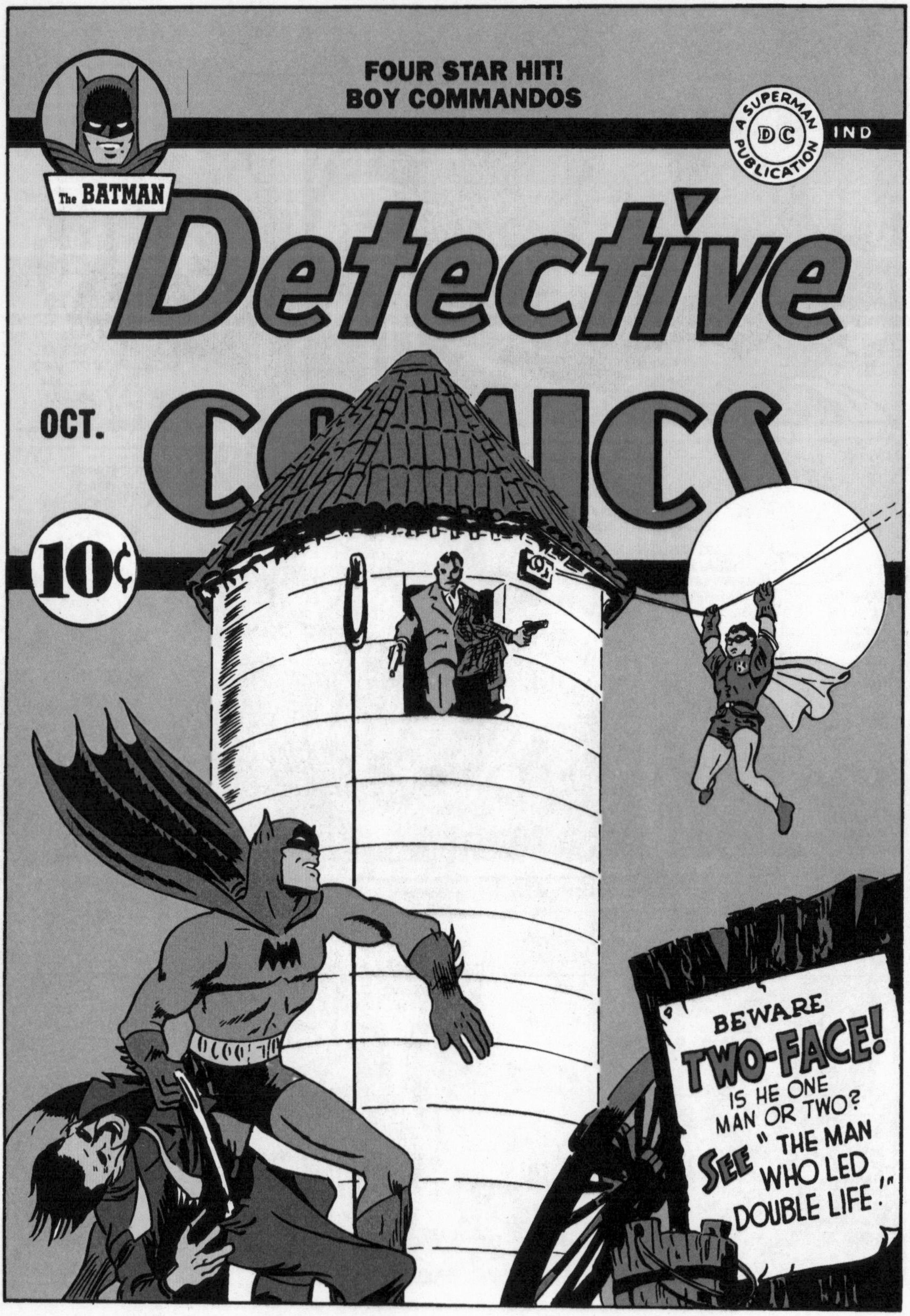
FOUR STAR HIT!
BOY COMMANDOS
The BATMAN
A SUPERMAN DC PUBLICATION
IND
Detective
OCT.
COMICS
10¢
BEWARE
TWO-FACE!
IS HE ONE
MAN OR TWO?
SEE "THE MAN
WHO LED
DOUBLE LIFE!"

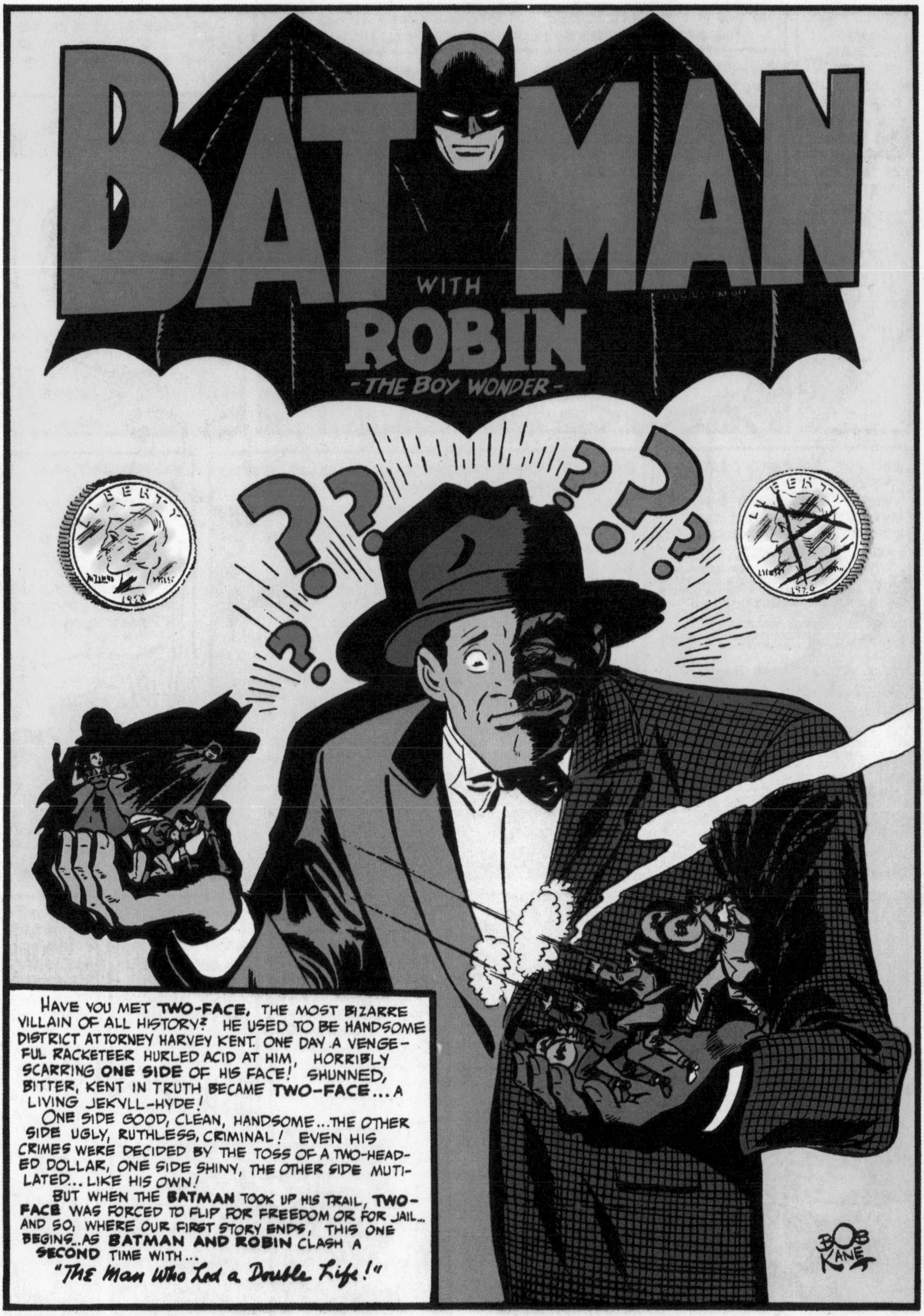
BATMAN
WITH
ROBIN
-THE BOY WONDER-
HAVE YOU MET TWO-FACE, THE MOST BIZARRE VILLAIN OF ALL HISTORY? HE USED TO BE HANDSOME DISTRICT ATTORNEY HARVEY KENT. ONE DAY A VENGE-FUL RACKETEER HURLED ACID AT HIM, HORRIBLY SCARRING ONE SIDE OF HIS FACE! SHUNNED, BITTER, KENT IN TRUTH BECAME TWO-FACE... A LIVING JEKYLL-HYDE!
ONE SIDE GOOD, CLEAN, HANDSOME... THE OTHER SIDE UGLY, RUTHLESS, CRIMINAL! EVEN HIS CRIMES WERE DECIDED BY THE TOSS OF A TWO-HEAD-ED DOLLAR, ONE SIDE SHINY, THE OTHER SIDE MUTI-LATED... LIKE HIS OWN!
BUT WHEN THE BATMAN TOOK UP HIS TRAIL, TWO-FACE WAS FORCED TO FLIP FOR FREEDOM OR FOR JAIL... AND SO, WHERE OUR FIRST STORY ENDS, THIS ONE BEGINS... AS BATMAN AND ROBIN CLASH A SECOND TIME WITH...
"THE Man Who Led a Double Life!"
BOB KANE

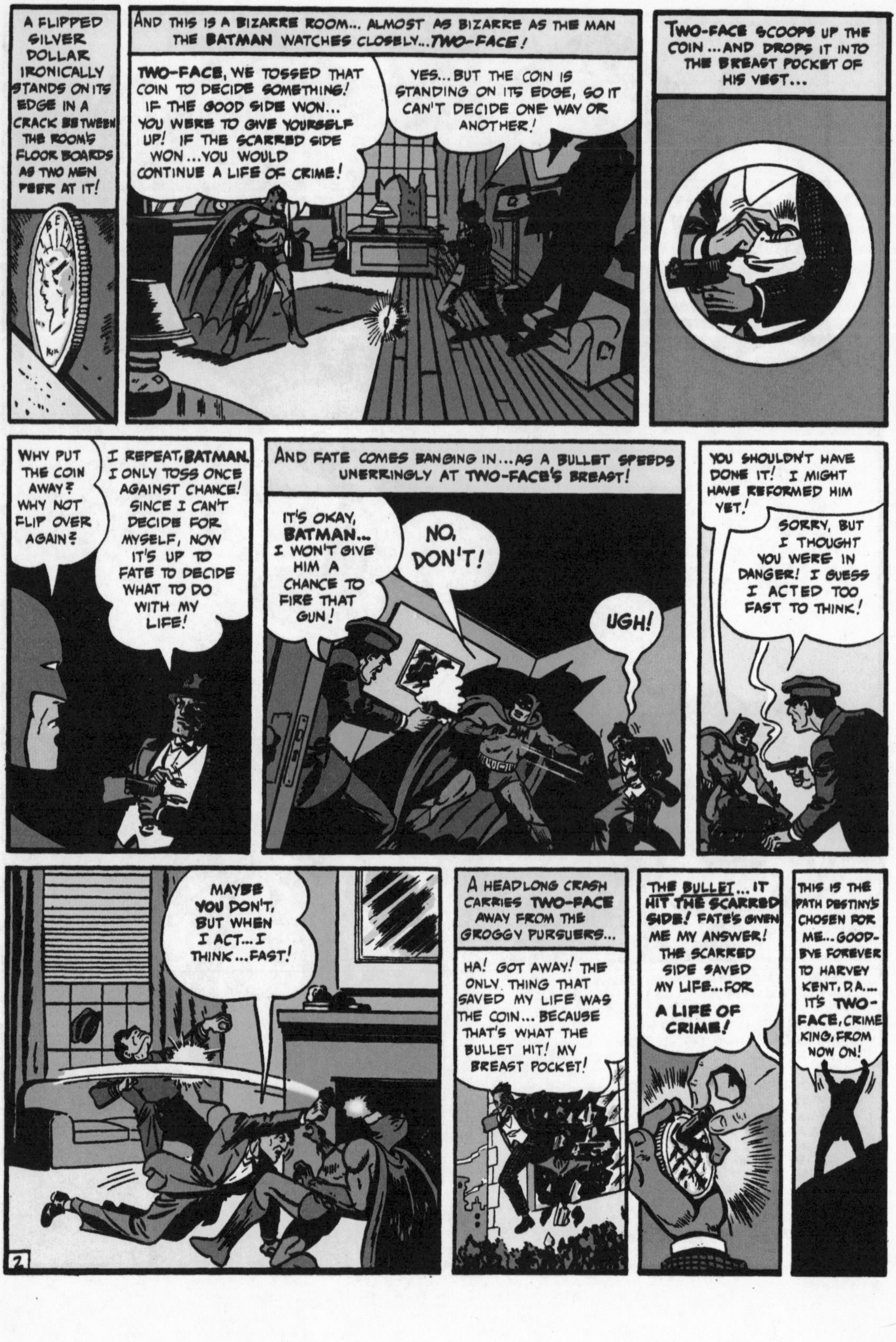
A FLIPPED SILVER DOLLAR IRONICALLY STANDS ON ITS EDGE IN A CRACK BETWEEN THE ROOM'S FLOOR BOARDS AS TWO MEN PEER AT IT!
AND THIS IS A BIZARRE ROOM... ALMOST AS BIZARRE AS THE MAN THE BATMAN WATCHES CLOSELY...TWO-FACE!
TWO-FACE, WE TOSSED THAT COIN TO DECIDE SOMETHING! IF THE GOOD SIDE WON... YOU WERE TO GIVE YOURSELF UP! IF THE SCARRED SIDE WON...YOU WOULD CONTINUE A LIFE OF CRIME!
YES... BUT THE COIN IS STANDING ON ITS EDGE, SO IT CAN'T DECIDE ONE WAY OR ANOTHER!
TWO-FACE SCOOPS UP THE COIN ...AND DROPS IT INTO THE BREAST POCKET OF HIS VEST...
WHY PUT THE COIN AWAY? WHY NOT FLIP OVER AGAIN?
I REPEAT, BATMAN, I ONLY TOSS ONCE AGAINST CHANCE! SINCE I CAN'T DECIDE FOR MYSELF, NOW IT'S UP TO FATE TO DECIDE WHAT TO DO WITH MY LIFE!
AND FATE COMES BANGING IN...AS A BULLET SPEEDS UNERRINGLY AT TWO-FACE'S BREAST!
IT'S OKAY, BATMAN... I WON'T GIVE HIM A CHANCE TO FIRE THAT GUN!
NO, DON'T!
UGH!
YOU SHOULDN'T HAVE DONE IT! I MIGHT HAVE REFORMED HIM YET!
SORRY, BUT I THOUGHT YOU WERE IN DANGER! I GUESS I ACTED TOO FAST TO THINK!
MAYBE YOU DON'T, BUT WHEN I ACT...I THINK...FAST!
A HEADLONG CRASH CARRIES TWO-FACE AWAY FROM THE GROGGY PURSUERS...
HA! GOT AWAY! THE ONLY THING THAT SAVED MY LIFE WAS THE COIN... BECAUSE THAT'S WHAT THE BULLET HIT! MY BREAST POCKET!
THE BULLET... IT HIT THE SCARRED SIDE! FATE'S GIVEN ME MY ANSWER! THE SCARRED SIDE SAVED MY LIFE...FOR A LIFE OF CRIME!
THIS IS THE PATH DESTINY'S CHOSEN FOR ME...GOOD-BYE FOREVER TO HARVEY KENT, D.A.... IT'S TWO-FACE, CRIME KING, FROM NOW ON!

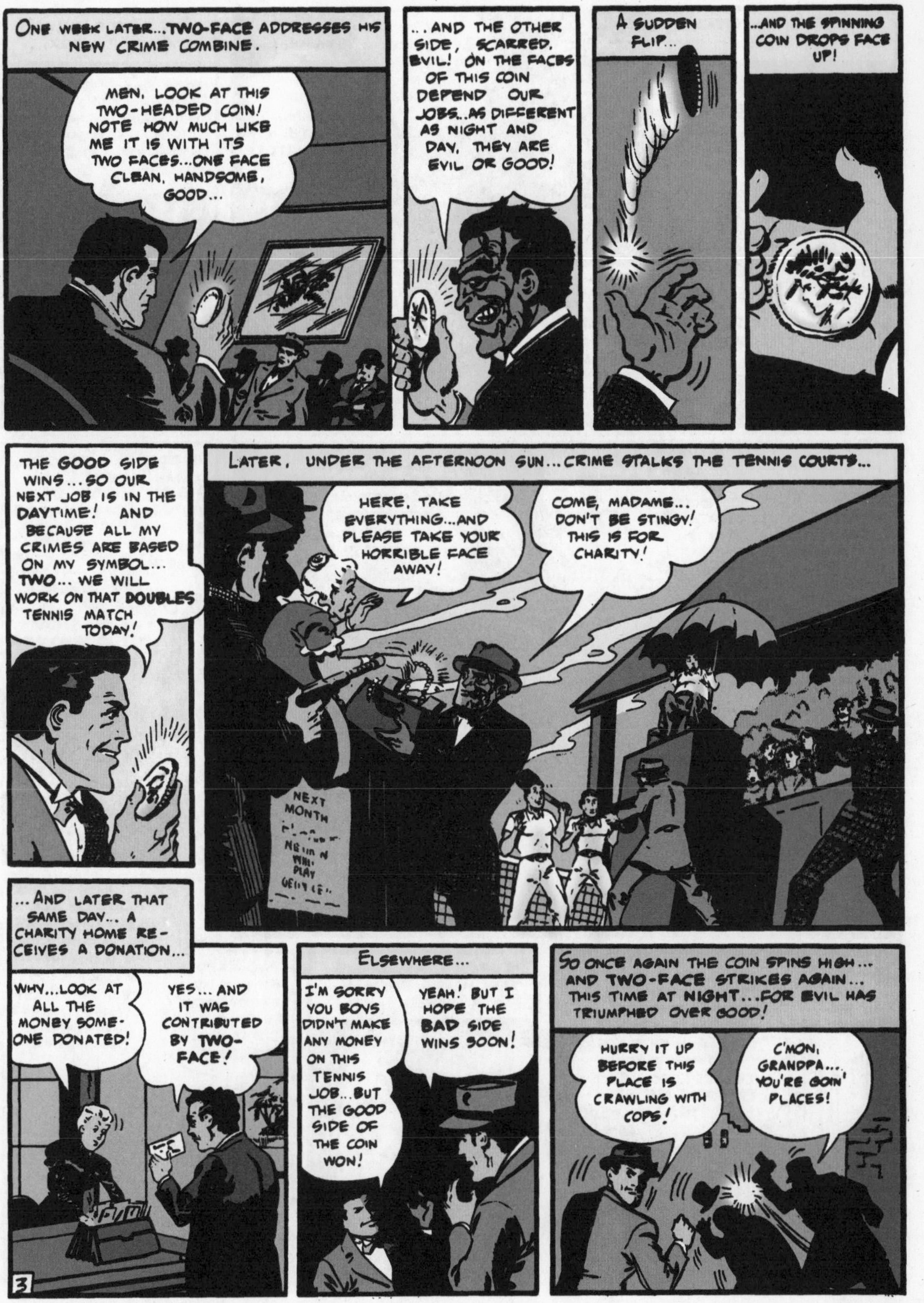

ONE WEEK LATER... TWO-FACE ADDRESSES HIS NEW CRIME COMBINE.
MEN, LOOK AT THIS TWO-HEADED COIN! NOTE HOW MUCH LIKE ME IT IS WITH ITS TWO FACES...ONE FACE CLEAN, HANDSOME, GOOD...
...AND THE OTHER SIDE, SCARRED, EVIL! ON THE FACES OF THIS COIN DEPEND OUR JOBS...AS DIFFERENT AS NIGHT AND DAY, THEY ARE EVIL OR GOOD!
A SUDDEN FLIP...
...AND THE SPINNING COIN DROPS FACE UP!
THE GOOD SIDE WINS...SO OUR NEXT JOB IS IN THE DAYTIME! AND BECAUSE ALL MY CRIMES ARE BASED ON MY SYMBOL... TWO... WE WILL WORK ON THAT DOUBLES TENNIS MATCH TODAY!
LATER, UNDER THE AFTERNOON SUN... CRIME STALKS THE TENNIS COURTS...
HERE, TAKE EVERYTHING...AND PLEASE TAKE YOUR HORRIBLE FACE AWAY!
COME, MADAME... DON'T BE STINGY! THIS IS FOR CHARITY!
NEXT MONTH
...AND LATER THAT SAME DAY... A CHARITY HOME RE-CEIVES A DONATION...
WHY...LOOK AT ALL THE MONEY SOME-ONE DONATED!
YES... AND IT WAS CONTRIBUTED BY TWO-FACE!
ELSEWHERE...
I'M SORRY YOU BOYS DIDN'T MAKE ANY MONEY ON THIS TENNIS JOB...BUT THE GOOD SIDE OF THE COIN WON!
YEAH! BUT I HOPE THE BAD SIDE WINS SOON!
SO ONCE AGAIN THE COIN SPINS HIGH... AND TWO-FACE STRIKES AGAIN... THIS TIME AT NIGHT...FOR EVIL HAS TRIUMPHED OVER GOOD!
HURRY IT UP BEFORE THIS PLACE IS CRAWLING WITH COPS!
C'MON, GRANDPA... YOU'RE GOIN' PLACES!

HEADLINE NEWS HITS THE FRONT PAGES!

EXTRA DAILY GLOBE

HENRY LOGAN KIDNAPPED

MATCH KING SNATCHED BEFORE ADVERTISING CLUB.

HENRY LOGAN

I'LL BET WE'RE PUT ON THAT LOGAN SNATCH!

SNAP IT UP, ROBIN... THAT'S HEADQUARTERS CALLING US!

AT THAT VERY INSTANT... TWO LYNX-LITHE FIGURES FLASH LIKE TWIN COMETS OVER THE ROOFTOPS!

... AND SURE ENOUGH... SOME TIME LATER...

WHY THIS MYSTERIOUS RIDE, COMMISSIONER GORDON?

TO THE HENRY LOGAN HOME!

SEE? I GUESSED RIGHT!

LATER...THE CAR HALTS... AND THE TRIO STEPS INTO A HUGE BARN-LIKE STRUCTURE...

OOPS! SLIPPED... ON A MATCH STICK!

GREAT SCOTT! ALL OF THE THINGS HERE ARE MADE OF MATCHSTICKS! WHAT IS THIS PLACE, ANYWAY?

MY HOBBY HOUSE. I COME HERE WHEN I DON'T WANT TO BE DISTURBED!

HENRY LOGAN! B-BUT YOU'VE BEEN KIDNAPPED!

USE YOUR EYES... I'M HERE! COULDN'T BE KIDNAPPED IF I'M HERE, BAH!

THEN WHO _WAS_ KIDNAPPED?

IT WAS HIS DOUBLE!

YES... MY DOUBLE! I HATE GOING TO STUFFY DINNERS, CLUBS!...I SEND MY DOUBLE IN MY PLACE!...HE'S PERFECTLY TRAINED!...FOOLS MY BEST FRIENDS. HEE! HEE!

4

THE GROUCHY MILLIONAIRE THEN HANDS BATMAN A PAPER...

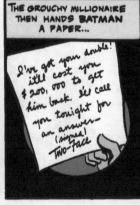

I've got your double! It'll cost you $200,000 to get him back. I'll call you tonight for an answer—
(signed)
TWO-FACE

TWO-FACE! BUT HOW DID HE KNOW ABOUT THE DOUBLE IF IT WAS SUCH A SECRET?

WHEN HE WAS HARVEY KENT, D.A., I CONFIDED IN HIM...HE PROMISED TO KEEP MY SECRET... NOW HE'S TAKING ADVANTAGE OF IT. HMPH!

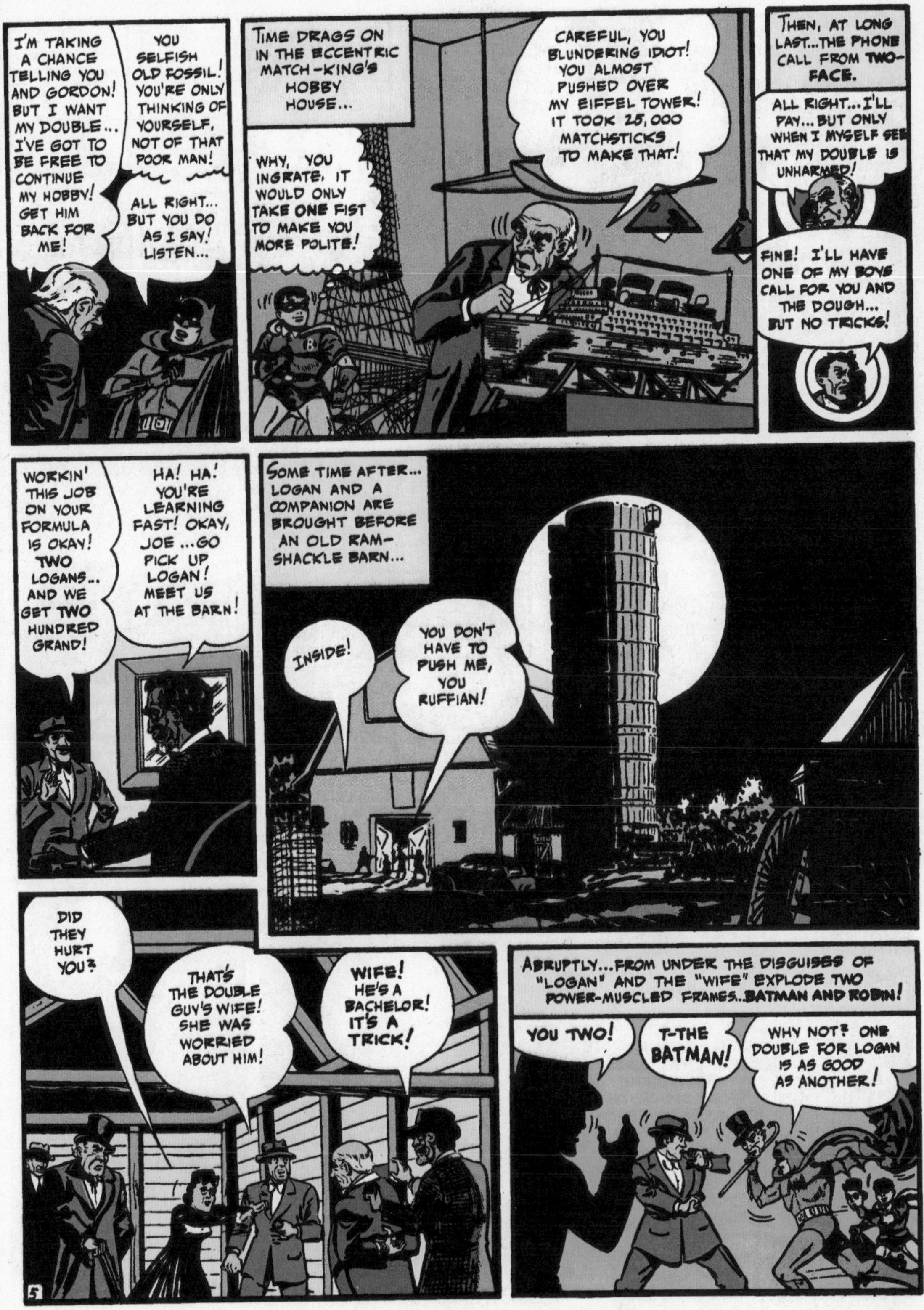
I'M TAKING A CHANCE TELLING YOU AND GORDON! BUT I WANT MY DOUBLE... I'VE GOT TO BE FREE TO CONTINUE MY HOBBY! GET HIM BACK FOR ME!
YOU SELFISH OLD FOSSIL! YOU'RE ONLY THINKING OF YOURSELF, NOT OF THAT POOR MAN!
ALL RIGHT... BUT YOU DO AS I SAY! LISTEN...
TIME DRAGS ON IN THE ECCENTRIC MATCH-KING'S HOBBY HOUSE...
CAREFUL, YOU BLUNDERING IDIOT! YOU ALMOST PUSHED OVER MY EIFFEL TOWER! IT TOOK 25,000 MATCHSTICKS TO MAKE THAT!
WHY, YOU INGRATE, IT WOULD ONLY TAKE ONE FIST TO MAKE YOU MORE POLITE!
THEN, AT LONG LAST... THE PHONE CALL FROM TWO-FACE.
ALL RIGHT... I'LL PAY... BUT ONLY WHEN I MYSELF SEE THAT MY DOUBLE IS UNHARMED!
FINE! I'LL HAVE ONE OF MY BOYS CALL FOR YOU AND THE DOUGH... BUT NO TRICKS!
WORKIN' THIS JOB ON YOUR FORMULA IS OKAY! TWO LOGANS... AND WE GET TWO HUNDRED GRAND!
HA! HA! YOU'RE LEARNING FAST! OKAY, JOE ...GO PICK UP LOGAN! MEET US AT THE BARN!
SOME TIME AFTER... LOGAN AND A COMPANION ARE BROUGHT BEFORE AN OLD RAM-SHACKLE BARN...
INSIDE!
YOU DON'T HAVE TO PUSH ME, YOU RUFFIAN!
DID THEY HURT YOU?
THAT'S THE DOUBLE GUY'S WIFE! SHE WAS WORRIED ABOUT HIM!
WIFE! HE'S A BACHELOR! IT'S A TRICK!
5
ABRUPTLY... FROM UNDER THE DISGUISES OF "LOGAN" AND THE "WIFE" EXPLODE TWO POWER-MUSCLED FRAMES..BATMAN AND ROBIN!
YOU TWO!
T-THE BATMAN!
WHY NOT? ONE DOUBLE FOR LOGAN IS AS GOOD AS ANOTHER!

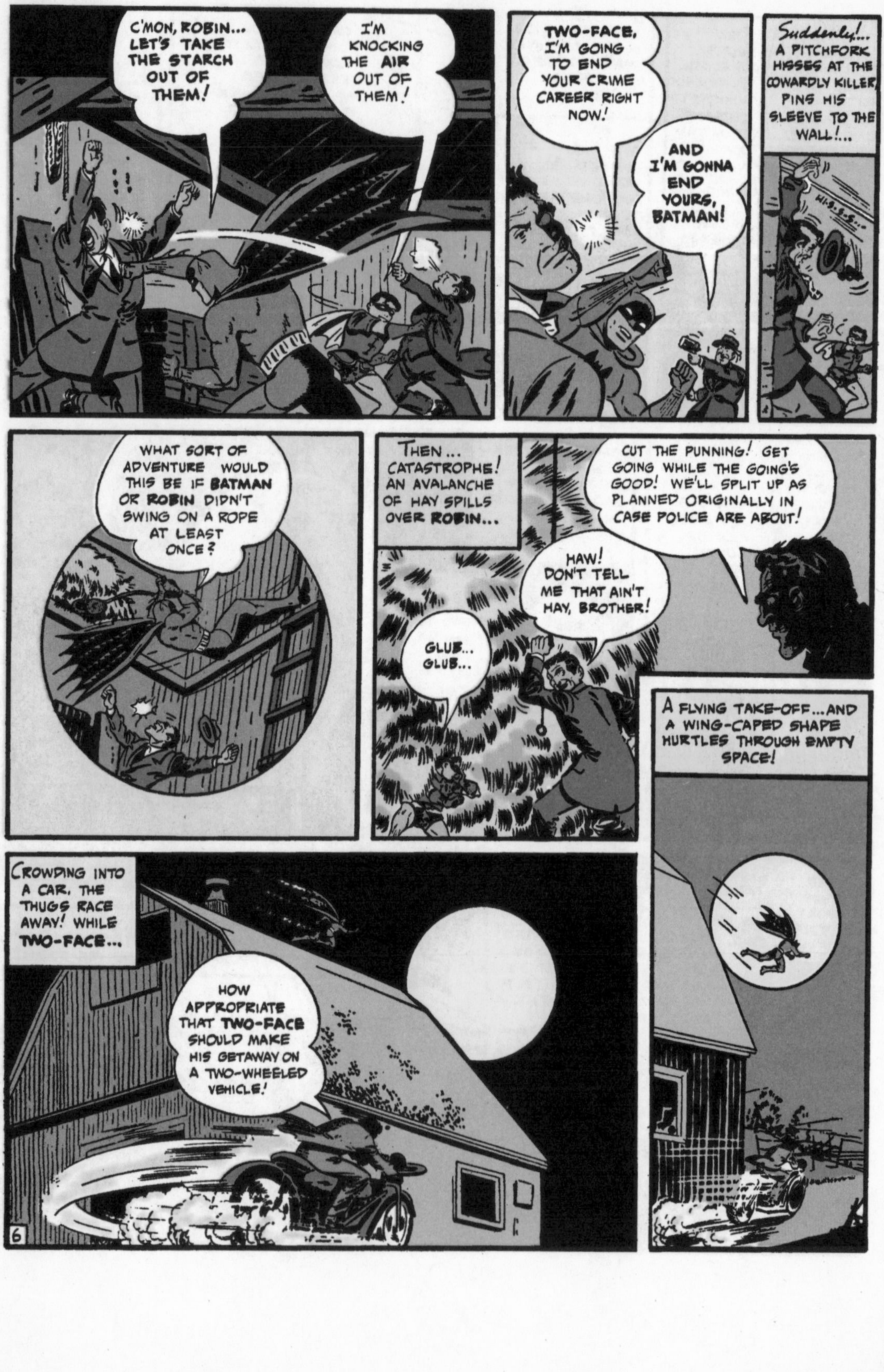
C'MON, ROBIN... LET'S TAKE THE STARCH OUT OF THEM!
I'M KNOCKING THE AIR OUT OF THEM!
TWO-FACE, I'M GOING TO END YOUR CRIME CAREER RIGHT NOW!
AND I'M GONNA END YOURS, BATMAN!
Suddenly!... A PITCHFORK HISSES AT THE COWARDLY KILLER, PINS HIS SLEEVE TO THE WALL!...
H-I-S-S-S...
WHAT SORT OF ADVENTURE WOULD THIS BE IF BATMAN OR ROBIN DIDN'T SWING ON A ROPE AT LEAST ONCE?
THEN... CATASTROPHE! AN AVALANCHE OF HAY SPILLS OVER ROBIN...
CUT THE PUNNING! GET GOING WHILE THE GOING'S GOOD! WE'LL SPLIT UP AS PLANNED ORIGINALLY IN CASE POLICE ARE ABOUT!
HAW! DON'T TELL ME THAT AIN'T HAY, BROTHER!
GLUB... GLUB...
A FLYING TAKE-OFF...AND A WING-CAPED SHAPE HURTLES THROUGH EMPTY SPACE!
CROWDING INTO A CAR, THE THUGS RACE AWAY! WHILE TWO-FACE...
HOW APPROPRIATE THAT TWO-FACE SHOULD MAKE HIS GETAWAY ON A TWO-WHEELED VEHICLE!
6

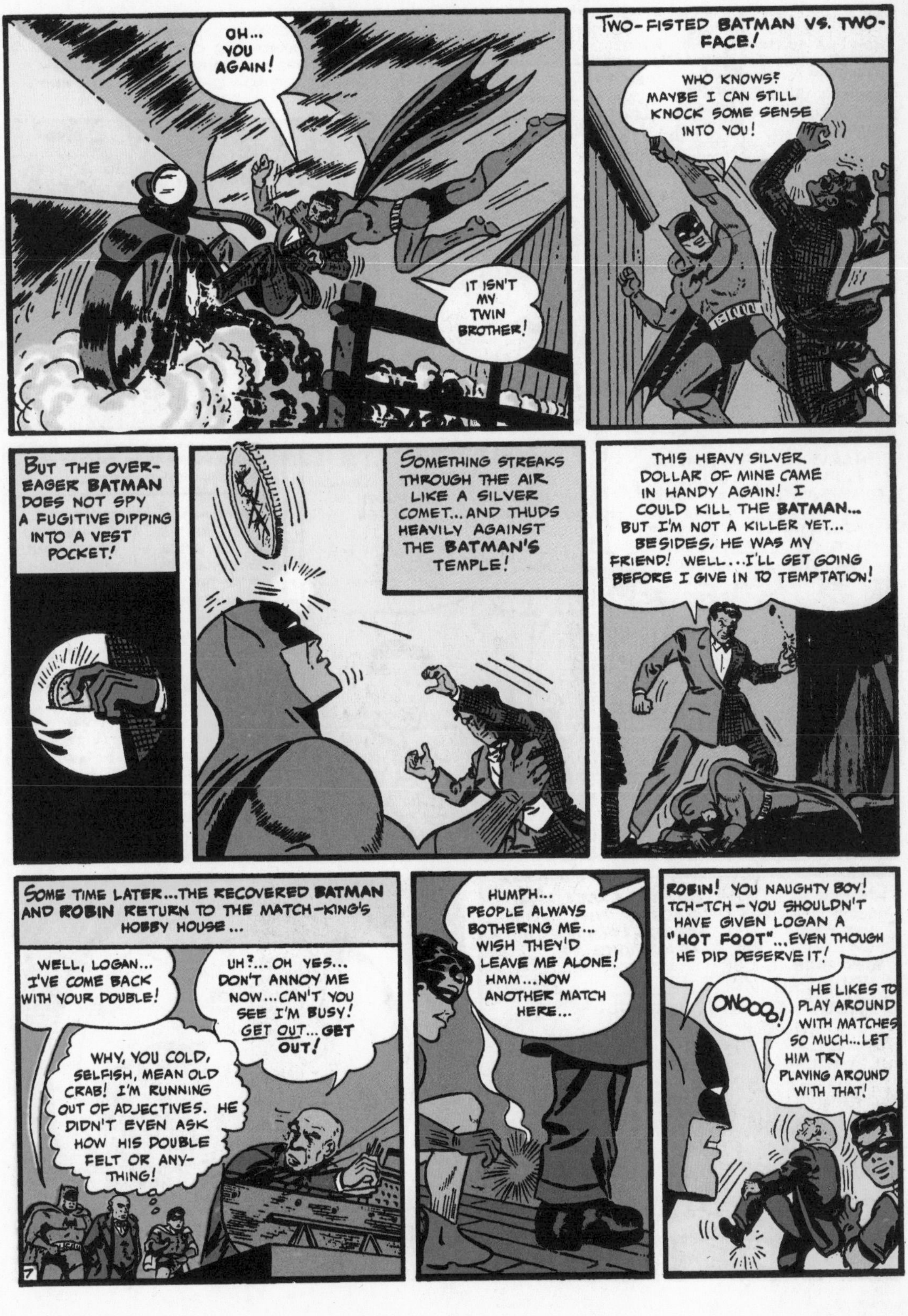
OH... YOU AGAIN!
IT ISN'T MY TWIN BROTHER!
TWO-FISTED BATMAN VS. TWO-FACE!
WHO KNOWS? MAYBE I CAN STILL KNOCK SOME SENSE INTO YOU!
BUT THE OVER-EAGER BATMAN DOES NOT SPY A FUGITIVE DIPPING INTO A VEST POCKET!
SOMETHING STREAKS THROUGH THE AIR LIKE A SILVER COMET... AND THUDS HEAVILY AGAINST THE BATMAN'S TEMPLE!
THIS HEAVY SILVER DOLLAR OF MINE CAME IN HANDY AGAIN! I COULD KILL THE BATMAN... BUT I'M NOT A KILLER YET... BESIDES, HE WAS MY FRIEND! WELL... I'LL GET GOING BEFORE I GIVE IN TO TEMPTATION!
SOME TIME LATER... THE RECOVERED BATMAN AND ROBIN RETURN TO THE MATCH-KING'S HOBBY HOUSE...
WELL, LOGAN... I'VE COME BACK WITH YOUR DOUBLE!
UH?... OH YES... DON'T ANNOY ME NOW... CAN'T YOU SEE I'M BUSY! GET OUT... GET OUT!
WHY, YOU COLD, SELFISH, MEAN OLD CRAB! I'M RUNNING OUT OF ADJECTIVES. HE DIDN'T EVEN ASK HOW HIS DOUBLE FELT OR ANY-THING!
7
HUMPH... PEOPLE ALWAYS BOTHERING ME... WISH THEY'D LEAVE ME ALONE! HMM... NOW ANOTHER MATCH HERE...
ROBIN! YOU NAUGHTY BOY! TCH-TCH - YOU SHOULDN'T HAVE GIVEN LOGAN A "HOT FOOT"... EVEN THOUGH HE DID DESERVE IT!
OWOOOO!
HE LIKES TO PLAY AROUND WITH MATCHES SO MUCH... LET HIM TRY PLAYING AROUND WITH THAT!

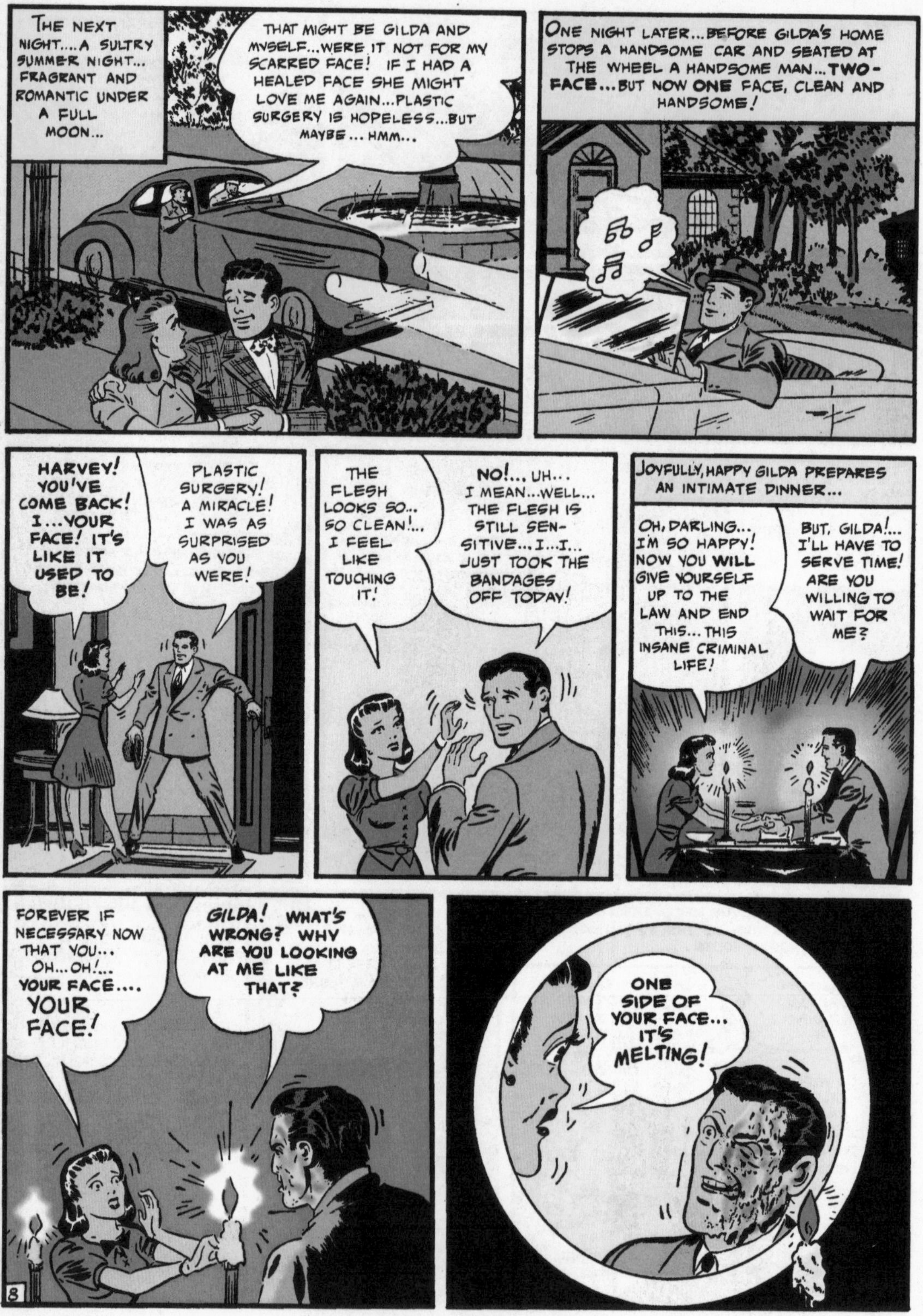

THE NEXT NIGHT....A SULTRY SUMMER NIGHT... FRAGRANT AND ROMANTIC UNDER A FULL MOON...
THAT MIGHT BE GILDA AND MYSELF...WERE IT NOT FOR MY SCARRED FACE! IF I HAD A HEALED FACE SHE MIGHT LOVE ME AGAIN...PLASTIC SURGERY IS HOPELESS...BUT MAYBE... HMM...
ONE NIGHT LATER...BEFORE GILDA'S HOME STOPS A HANDSOME CAR AND SEATED AT THE WHEEL A HANDSOME MAN...TWO-FACE...BUT NOW ONE FACE, CLEAN AND HANDSOME!
HARVEY! YOU'VE COME BACK! I...YOUR FACE! IT'S LIKE IT USED TO BE!
PLASTIC SURGERY! A MIRACLE! I WAS AS SURPRISED AS YOU WERE!
THE FLESH LOOKS SO... SO CLEAN!... I FEEL LIKE TOUCHING IT!
NO!... UH... I MEAN...WELL... THE FLESH IS STILL SENSITIVE... I...I... JUST TOOK THE BANDAGES OFF TODAY!
JOYFULLY, HAPPY GILDA PREPARES AN INTIMATE DINNER...
OH, DARLING... I'M SO HAPPY! NOW YOU WILL GIVE YOURSELF UP TO THE LAW AND END THIS... THIS INSANE CRIMINAL LIFE!
BUT, GILDA!... I'LL HAVE TO SERVE TIME! ARE YOU WILLING TO WAIT FOR ME?
FOREVER IF NECESSARY NOW THAT YOU... OH...OH!... YOUR FACE.... YOUR FACE!
GILDA! WHAT'S WRONG? WHY ARE YOU LOOKING AT ME LIKE THAT?
8
ONE SIDE OF YOUR FACE... IT'S MELTING!

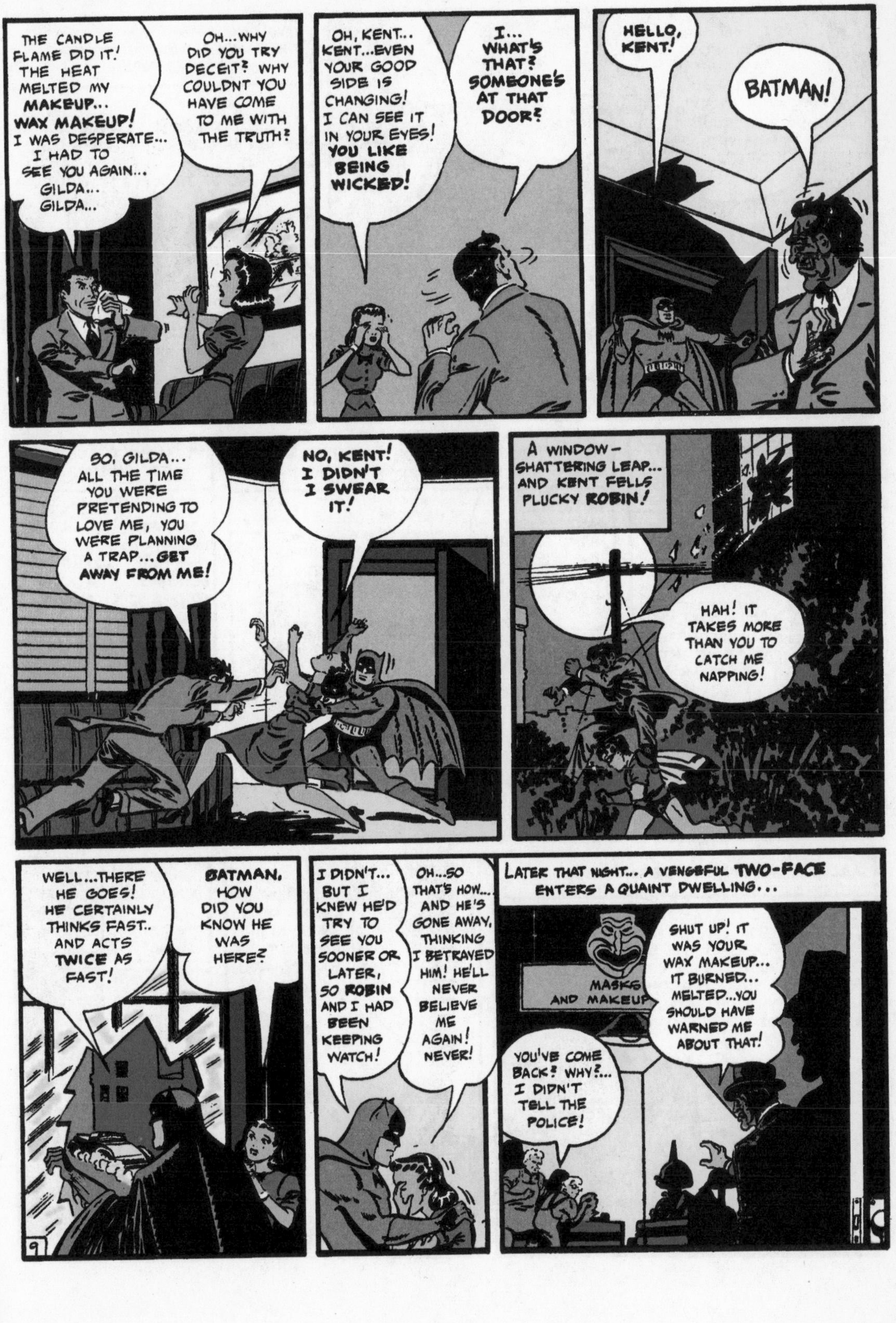
THE CANDLE FLAME DID IT! THE HEAT MELTED MY MAKEUP... WAX MAKEUP! I WAS DESPERATE... I HAD TO SEE YOU AGAIN... GILDA... GILDA...
OH... WHY DID YOU TRY DECEIT? WHY COULDNT YOU HAVE COME TO ME WITH THE TRUTH?
OH, KENT... KENT... EVEN YOUR GOOD SIDE IS CHANGING! I CAN SEE IT IN YOUR EYES! YOU LIKE BEING WICKED!
I... WHAT'S THAT? SOMEONE'S AT THAT DOOR?
HELLO, KENT!
BATMAN!
SO, GILDA... ALL THE TIME YOU WERE PRETENDING TO LOVE ME, YOU WERE PLANNING A TRAP... GET AWAY FROM ME!
NO, KENT! I DIDN'T I SWEAR IT!
A WINDOW-SHATTERING LEAP... AND KENT FELLS PLUCKY ROBIN!
HAH! IT TAKES MORE THAN YOU TO CATCH ME NAPPING!
WELL... THERE HE GOES! HE CERTAINLY THINKS FAST.. AND ACTS TWICE AS FAST!
BATMAN, HOW DID YOU KNOW HE WAS HERE?
9
I DIDN'T... BUT I KNEW HE'D TRY TO SEE YOU SOONER OR LATER, SO ROBIN AND I HAD BEEN KEEPING WATCH!
OH... SO THAT'S HOW... AND HE'S GONE AWAY, THINKING I BETRAYED HIM! HE'LL NEVER BELIEVE ME AGAIN! NEVER!
LATER THAT NIGHT... A VENGEFUL TWO-FACE ENTERS A QUAINT DWELLING...
MASKS AND MAKEUP
SHUT UP! IT WAS YOUR WAX MAKEUP... IT BURNED... MELTED... YOU SHOULD HAVE WARNED ME ABOUT THAT!
YOU'VE COME BACK? WHY?... I DIDN'T TELL THE POLICE!

SET THIS PLACE ON FIRE, BOYS! IT WAS FIRE THAT RUINED ME WITH MY GIRL... SO I'LL RUIN HIM WITH FIRE!

NO! NO!

YOU CAN'T... UGH!

SOME TIME AFTER...WITH HIS FAMILY... THE MASK-MAKER WATCHES SMOLDERING RUINS...

ALL I'VE WORKED FOR, GONE! WE'RE PENNILESS... HOMELESS...ALL BECAUSE OF TWO-FACE!

FATHER, SOME DAY... SOMEHOW... I'LL MAKE HIM PAY FOR THIS! I SWEAR IT!

LATER THAT NIGHT, BRUCE WAYNE, THE BATMAN, PONDERS...

ROBIN! I'VE GOT TO STOP TWO-FACE! I'VE GOT TO HAVE A PLAN OF ACTION! I CAN'T USE MAKEUP AGAIN ...OR CAN I...?

I DON'T KNOW! SOUNDS RISKY TO ME! BETTER THINK OF SOMETHING ELSE...

THE NEXT NIGHT AS ONE OF TWO-FACE'S THUGS ENTERS A NOTORIOUS CRIMINAL HAUNT...

SAY, AL, I WANT YOU TO MEET "GETAWAY" GEORGE! HE JUST BLEW IN FROM CHI!

"GETAWAY" GEORGE?... SAY... YOU'RE THE GUY WHO MADE A REP BY MAKIN' FAST GETAWAYS FROM JOBS! GLAD TO MEETCHA!

SOON THE TWO BECOME GOOD FRIENDS...

SO YOU WORK FOR TWO-FACE, EH? HE'S BIG-TIME! I'D LIKE TO WORK FOR A BIG SHOT LIKE HIM!

WELL, MAYBE I CAN FIX IT! WE COULD USE A GOOD DRIVER!

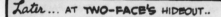

Later... AT TWO-FACE'S HIDEOUT..

"GETAWAY".. I COULD USE YOU BUT I'M CAUTIOUS ABOUT NEW MEN! WHO KNOWS? YOU MIGHT BE THE BATMAN IN MAKEUP!

BOSS, I KNOW YOU'RE LEERY 'CAUSE THE BATMAN FOOLED US WITH MAKEUP BEFORE... BUT THIS GUY IS OKAY!

LISTEN, TWO-FACE, I DON'T WANTA WORK FOR YOU IF YOU FEEL THAT WAY ABOUT ME!

HMM! YOU HAVE A WELL-KNOWN REP... AND I NEED A GOOD DRIVER! YOU'RE HIRED!

THE NEXT MORNING... A COIN TWIRLS HIGH..

...AND DROPS INTO AN OPEN PALM!

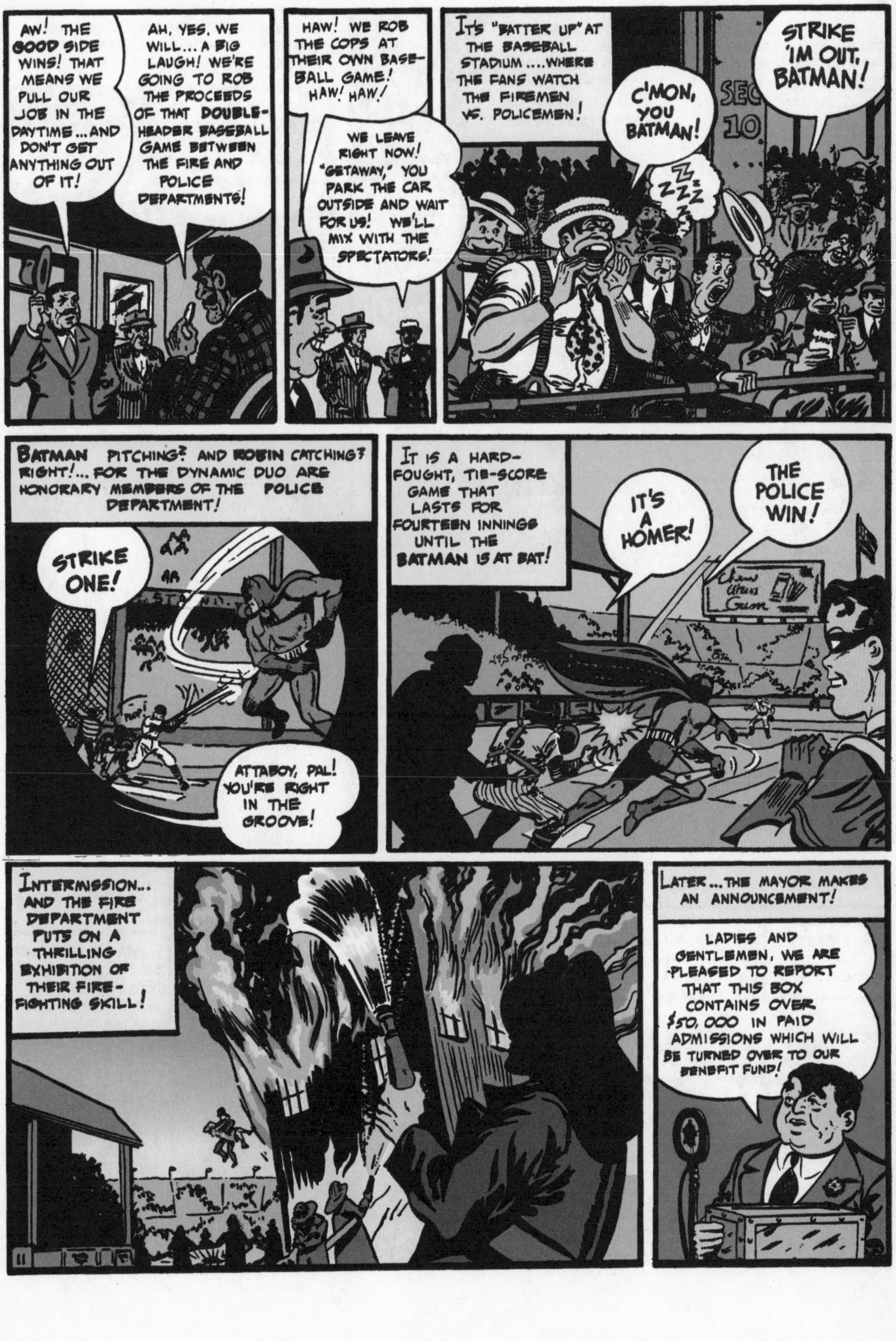
AW! THE GOOD SIDE WINS! THAT MEANS WE PULL OUR JOB IN THE DAYTIME ...AND DON'T GET ANYTHING OUT OF IT!
AH, YES, WE WILL... A BIG LAUGH! WE'RE GOING TO ROB THE PROCEEDS OF THAT DOUBLE-HEADER BASEBALL GAME BETWEEN THE FIRE AND POLICE DEPARTMENTS!
HAW! WE ROB THE COPS AT THEIR OWN BASE-BALL GAME! HAW! HAW!
WE LEAVE RIGHT NOW! "GETAWAY," YOU PARK THE CAR OUTSIDE AND WAIT FOR US! WE'LL MIX WITH THE SPECTATORS!
IT'S "BATTER UP" AT THE BASEBALL STADIUM .... WHERE THE FANS WATCH THE FIREMEN VS. POLICEMEN!
C'MON, YOU BATMAN!
ZZZZ
STRIKE 'IM OUT, BATMAN!
SEC 10
BATMAN PITCHING? AND ROBIN CATCHING? RIGHT!... FOR THE DYNAMIC DUO ARE HONORARY MEMBERS OF THE POLICE DEPARTMENT!
STRIKE ONE!
ATTABOY, PAL! YOU'RE RIGHT IN THE GROOVE!
IT IS A HARD-FOUGHT, TIE-SCORE GAME THAT LASTS FOR FOURTEEN INNINGS UNTIL THE BATMAN IS AT BAT!
IT'S A HOMER!
THE POLICE WIN!
INTERMISSION... AND THE FIRE DEPARTMENT PUTS ON A THRILLING EXHIBITION OF THEIR FIRE-FIGHTING SKILL!
LATER ... THE MAYOR MAKES AN ANNOUNCEMENT!
LADIES AND GENTLEMEN, WE ARE PLEASED TO REPORT THAT THIS BOX CONTAINS OVER $50,000 IN PAID ADMISSIONS WHICH WILL BE TURNED OVER TO OUR BENEFIT FUND!

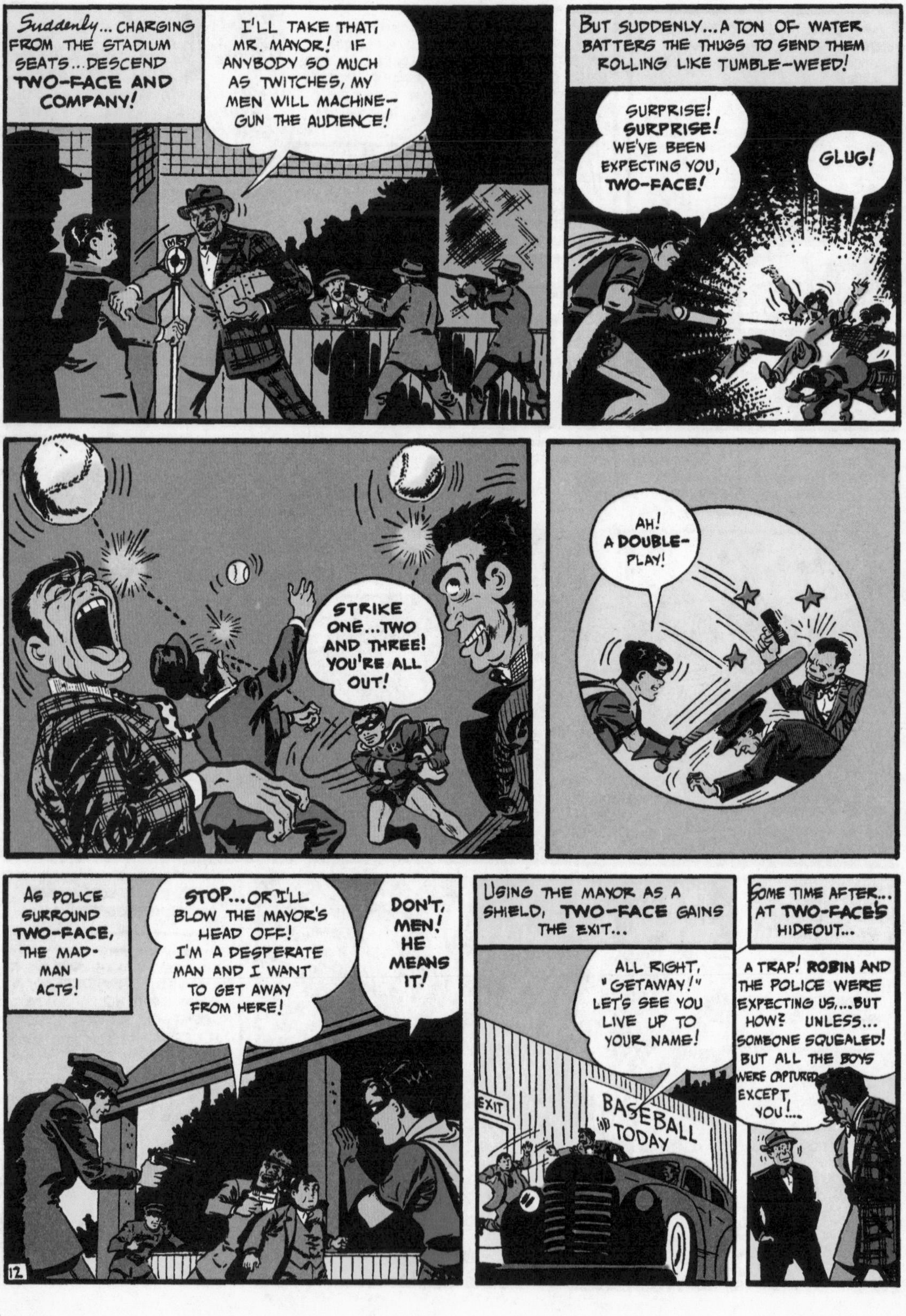

Suddenly... CHARGING FROM THE STADIUM SEATS...DESCEND TWO-FACE AND COMPANY!
I'LL TAKE THAT, MR. MAYOR! IF ANYBODY SO MUCH AS TWITCHES, MY MEN WILL MACHINE-GUN THE AUDIENCE!
BUT SUDDENLY...A TON OF WATER BATTERS THE THUGS TO SEND THEM ROLLING LIKE TUMBLE-WEED!
SURPRISE! SURPRISE! WE'VE BEEN EXPECTING YOU, TWO-FACE!
GLUG!
STRIKE ONE...TWO AND THREE! YOU'RE ALL OUT!
AH! A DOUBLE-PLAY!
AS POLICE SURROUND TWO-FACE, THE MAD-MAN ACTS!
STOP...OR I'LL BLOW THE MAYOR'S HEAD OFF! I'M A DESPERATE MAN AND I WANT TO GET AWAY FROM HERE!
DON'T, MEN! HE MEANS IT!
12
USING THE MAYOR AS A SHIELD, TWO-FACE GAINS THE EXIT...
ALL RIGHT, "GETAWAY!" LET'S SEE YOU LIVE UP TO YOUR NAME!
EXIT
BASEBALL AND TODAY
SOME TIME AFTER... AT TWO-FACE'S HIDEOUT...
A TRAP! ROBIN AND THE POLICE WERE EXPECTING US,...BUT HOW? UNLESS... SOMEONE SQUEALED! BUT ALL THE BOYS WERE CAPTURED EXCEPT YOU!...

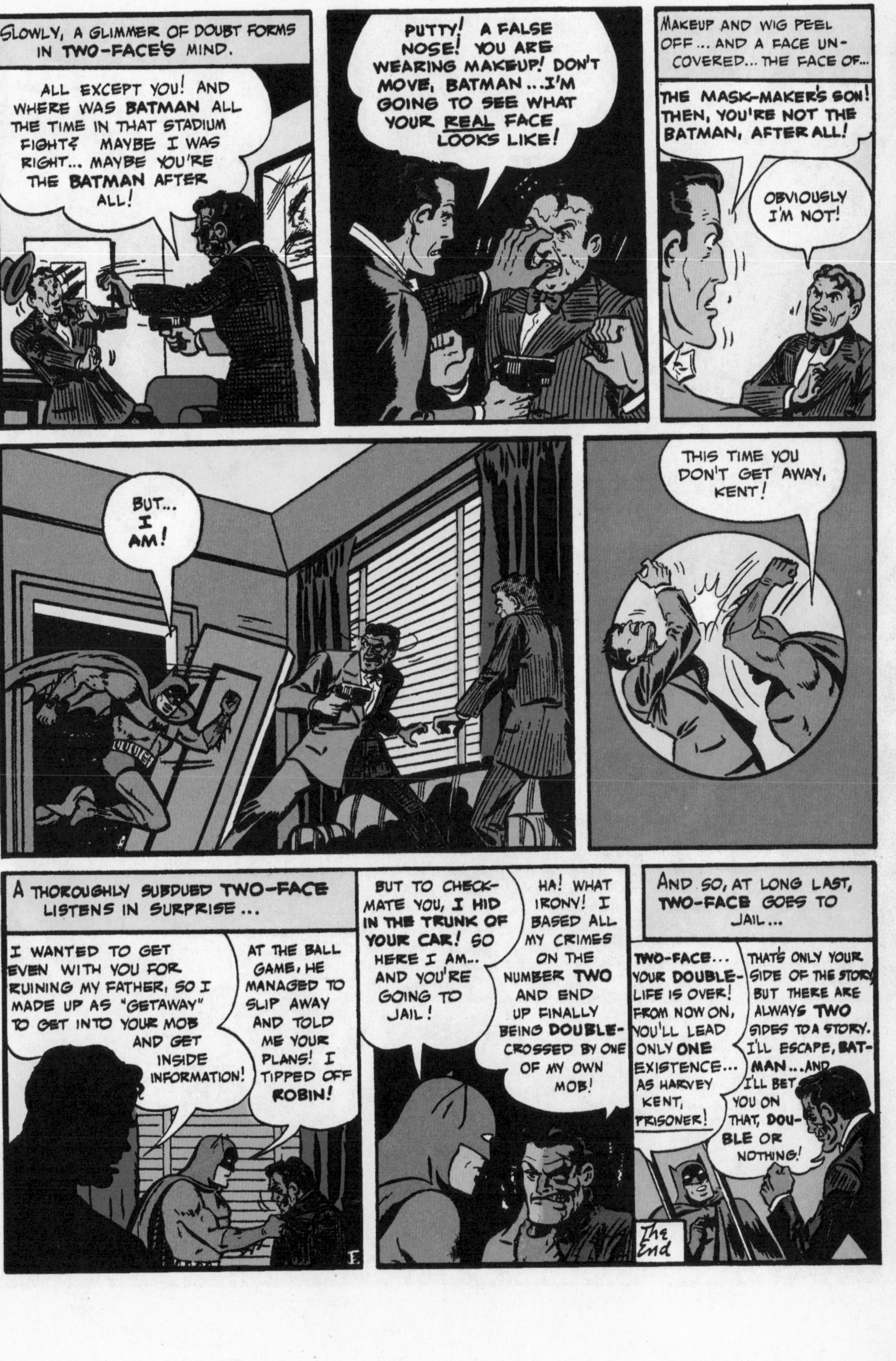

SLOWLY, A GLIMMER OF DOUBT FORMS IN TWO-FACE'S MIND.
ALL EXCEPT YOU! AND WHERE WAS BATMAN ALL THE TIME IN THAT STADIUM FIGHT? MAYBE I WAS RIGHT... MAYBE YOU'RE THE BATMAN AFTER ALL!
PUTTY! A FALSE NOSE! YOU ARE WEARING MAKEUP! DON'T MOVE, BATMAN ...I'M GOING TO SEE WHAT YOUR REAL FACE LOOKS LIKE!
MAKEUP AND WIG PEEL OFF ... AND A FACE UNCOVERED... THE FACE OF...
THE MASK-MAKER'S SON! THEN, YOU'RE NOT THE BATMAN, AFTER ALL!
OBVIOUSLY I'M NOT!
BUT... I AM!
THIS TIME YOU DON'T GET AWAY, KENT!
A THOROUGHLY SUBDUED TWO-FACE LISTENS IN SURPRISE ...
I WANTED TO GET EVEN WITH YOU FOR RUINING MY FATHER, SO I MADE UP AS "GETAWAY" TO GET INTO YOUR MOB AND GET INSIDE INFORMATION!
AT THE BALL GAME, HE MANAGED TO SLIP AWAY AND TOLD ME YOUR PLANS! I TIPPED OFF ROBIN!
BUT TO CHECKMATE YOU, I HID IN THE TRUNK OF YOUR CAR! SO HERE I AM... AND YOU'RE GOING TO JAIL!
HA! WHAT IRONY! I BASED ALL MY CRIMES ON THE NUMBER TWO AND END UP FINALLY BEING DOUBLE-CROSSED BY ONE OF MY OWN MOB!
AND SO, AT LONG LAST, TWO-FACE GOES TO JAIL...
TWO-FACE... YOUR DOUBLE-LIFE IS OVER! FROM NOW ON, YOU'LL LEAD ONLY ONE EXISTENCE... AS HARVEY KENT, PRISONER!
THAT'S ONLY YOUR SIDE OF THE STORY BUT THERE ARE ALWAYS TWO SIDES TO A STORY. I'LL ESCAPE, BATMAN...AND I'LL BET YOU ON THAT, DOUBLE OR NOTHING!
The End

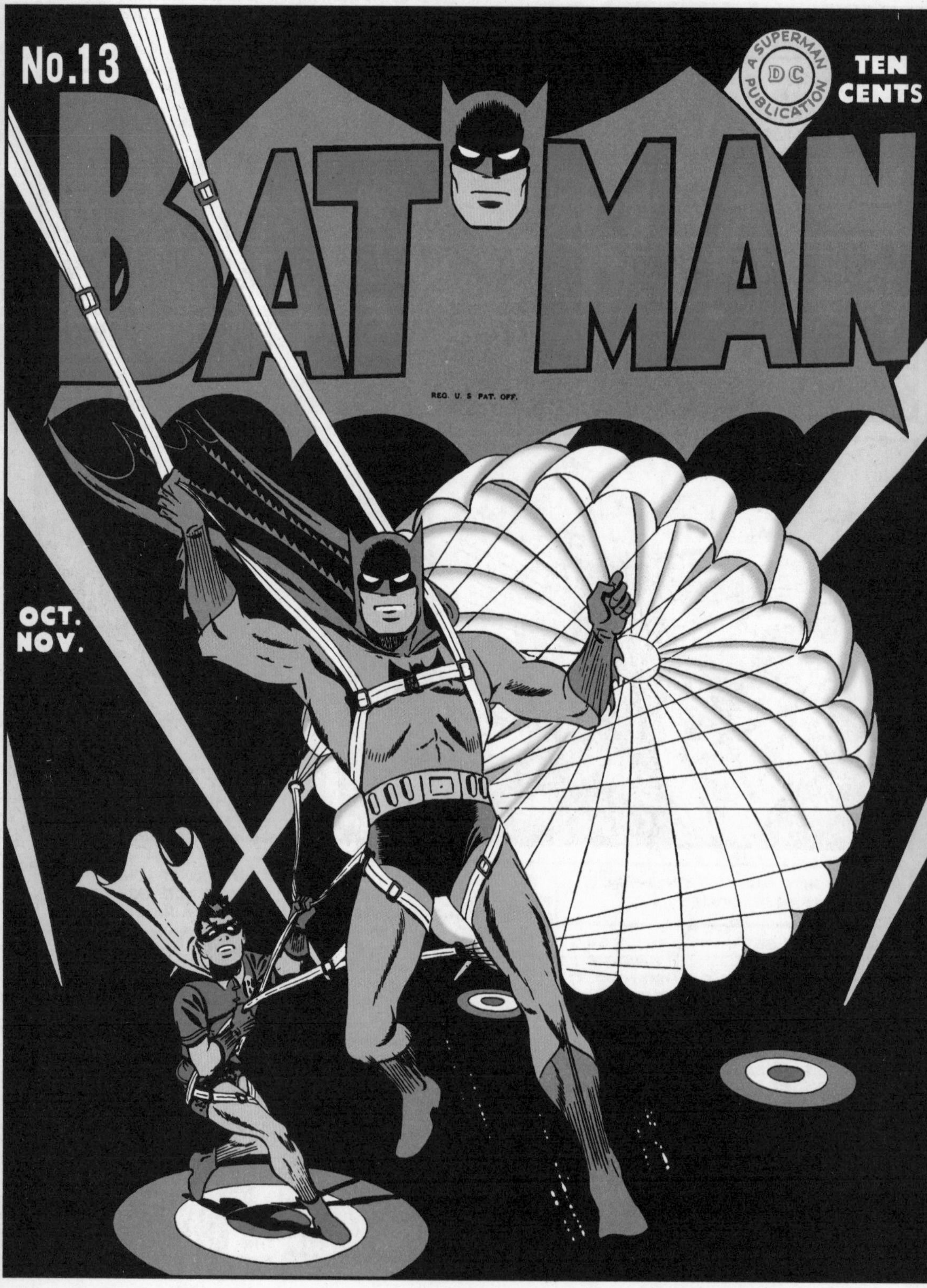
No.13
A SUPERMAN DC PUBLICATION
TEN CENTS
BATMAN
REG. U. S. PAT. OFF.
OCT. NOV.

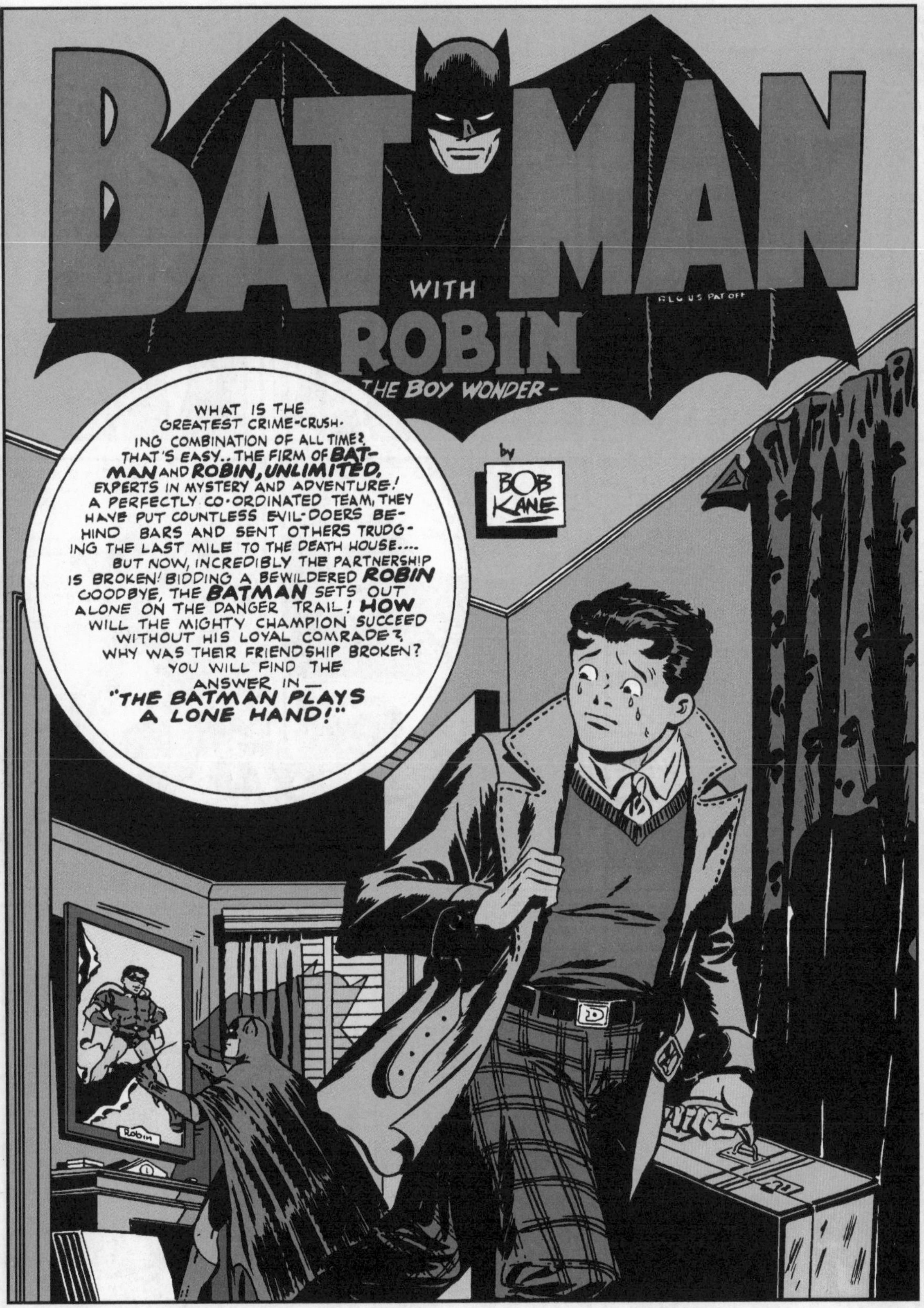

BATMAN
WITH
REG. U.S. PAT. OFF.
ROBIN
-THE BOY WONDER-
WHAT IS THE GREATEST CRIME-CRUSHING COMBINATION OF ALL TIME? THAT'S EASY.. THE FIRM OF BATMAN AND ROBIN, UNLIMITED, EXPERTS IN MYSTERY AND ADVENTURE! A PERFECTLY CO-ORDINATED TEAM, THEY HAVE PUT COUNTLESS EVIL-DOERS BEHIND BARS AND SENT OTHERS TRUDGING THE LAST MILE TO THE DEATH HOUSE.... BUT NOW, INCREDIBLY THE PARTNERSHIP IS BROKEN! BIDDING A BEWILDERED ROBIN GOODBYE, THE BATMAN SETS OUT ALONE ON THE DANGER TRAIL! HOW WILL THE MIGHTY CHAMPION SUCCEED WITHOUT HIS LOYAL COMRADE? WHY WAS THEIR FRIENDSHIP BROKEN? YOU WILL FIND THE ANSWER IN— "THE BATMAN PLAYS A LONE HAND!"
by BOB KANE
Robin

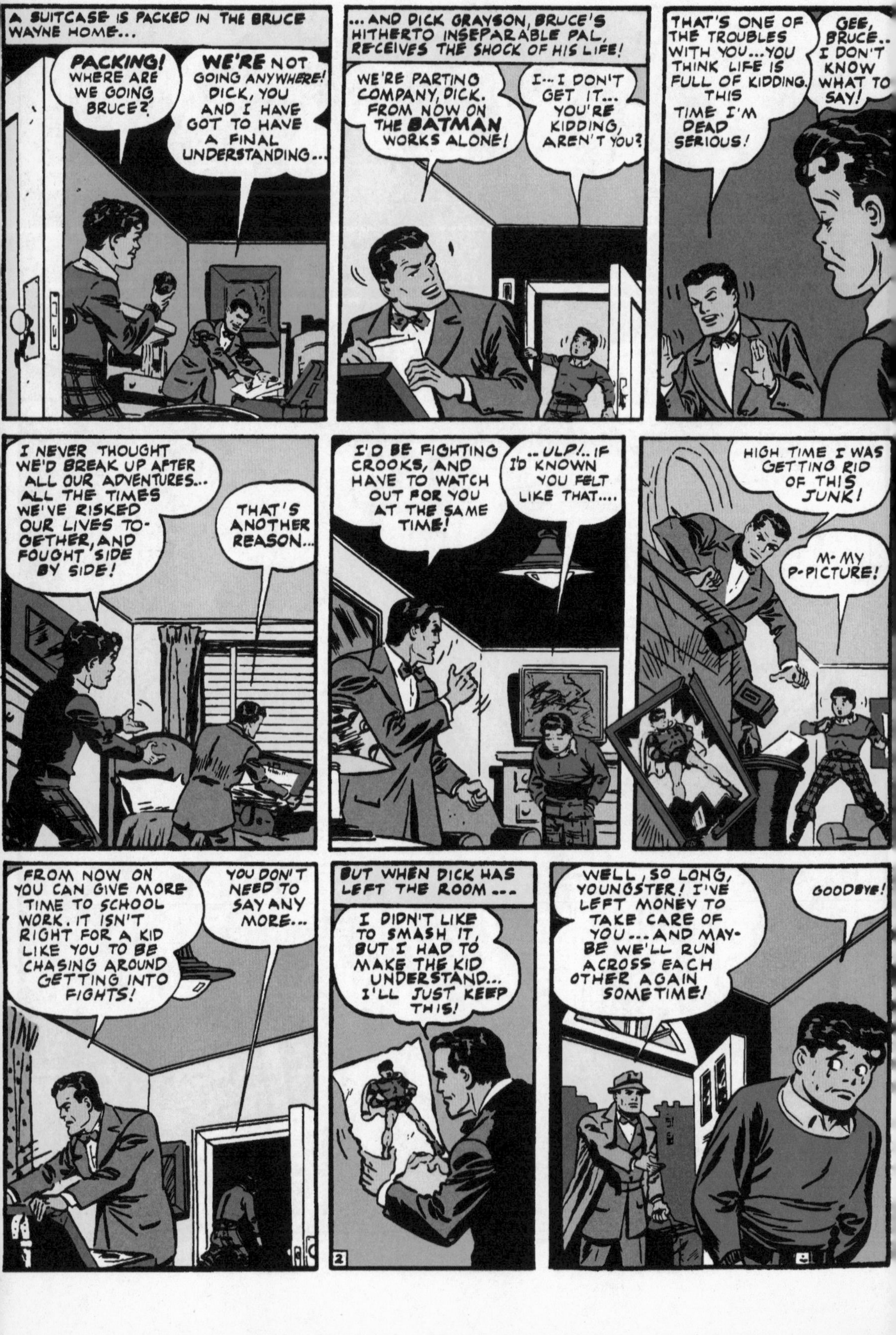
A SUITCASE IS PACKED IN THE BRUCE WAYNE HOME...
PACKING! WHERE ARE WE GOING, BRUCE?
WE'RE NOT GOING ANYWHERE! DICK, YOU AND I HAVE GOT TO HAVE A FINAL UNDERSTANDING...
...AND DICK GRAYSON, BRUCE'S HITHERTO INSEPARABLE PAL, RECEIVES THE SHOCK OF HIS LIFE!
WE'RE PARTING COMPANY, DICK. FROM NOW ON THE BATMAN WORKS ALONE!
I--I DON'T GET IT... YOU'RE KIDDING, AREN'T YOU?
THAT'S ONE OF THE TROUBLES WITH YOU...YOU THINK LIFE IS FULL OF KIDDING. THIS TIME I'M DEAD SERIOUS!
GEE, BRUCE.. I DON'T KNOW WHAT TO SAY!
I NEVER THOUGHT WE'D BREAK UP AFTER ALL OUR ADVENTURES... ALL THE TIMES WE'VE RISKED OUR LIVES TO-GETHER, AND FOUGHT SIDE BY SIDE!
THAT'S ANOTHER REASON...
I'D BE FIGHTING CROOKS, AND HAVE TO WATCH OUT FOR YOU AT THE SAME TIME!
..ULP!.. IF I'D KNOWN YOU FELT LIKE THAT....
HIGH TIME I WAS GETTING RID OF THIS JUNK!
M-MY P-PICTURE!
FROM NOW ON YOU CAN GIVE MORE TIME TO SCHOOL WORK. IT ISN'T RIGHT FOR A KID LIKE YOU TO BE CHASING AROUND GETTING INTO FIGHTS!
YOU DON'T NEED TO SAY ANY MORE...
BUT WHEN DICK HAS LEFT THE ROOM ---
I DIDN'T LIKE TO SMASH IT, BUT I HAD TO MAKE THE KID UNDERSTAND... I'LL JUST KEEP THIS!
2
WELL, SO LONG, YOUNGSTER! I'VE LEFT MONEY TO TAKE CARE OF YOU... AND MAY-BE WE'LL RUN ACROSS EACH OTHER AGAIN SOMETIME!
GOODBYE!

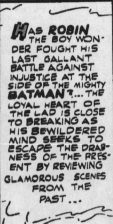 HAS ROBIN THE BOY WONDER FOUGHT HIS LAST GALLANT BATTLE AGAINST INJUSTICE AT THE SIDE OF THE MIGHTY BATMAN?... THE LOYAL HEART OF THE LAD IS CLOSE TO BREAKING AS HIS BEWILDERED MIND SEEKS TO ESCAPE THE DRABNESS OF THE PRESENT BY REVIEWING GLAMOROUS SCENES FROM THE PAST...

 HE CALLED ME A NUISANCE, AFTER ALL THE TIMES I'VE STOOD BY HIM WHEN THINGS LOOKED HOPELESS...

 ...WHEN THE JOKER THOUGHT HE HAD US TRAPPED AND WAS GOING TO GET RID OF US FOR GOOD...

 ...WHEN THE PENGUIN PULLED SURPRISES OUT OF THAT DEADLY UMBRELLA OF HIS...

 ...AND MORE TIMES THAN I CAN COUNT, IF IT HADN'T BEEN FOR ME, THERE WOULDN'T HAVE BEEN ANY MORE BATMAN!

 IT ISN'T TRUE (SOB) I WASN'T EVER IN HIS WAY! HE JUST (SOB) HE JUST DOESN'T LIKE ME ANY MORE!

 SUSPICION REARS ITS UGLY HEAD AS THE BOY'S GRIEF WEARS ITSELF OUT...

OR MAYBE HE WANTS ALL THE GLORY FOR HIMSELF! MAYBE HE THOUGHT ROBIN WAS GETTING TOO POPULAR!

 AND INEVITABLY COMES BLIND, UNREASONING ANGER...

I DON'T WANT HIS MONEY AND I WON'T LIVE IN HIS HOUSE! I'LL RUN AWAY AND SHOW HIM I CAN TAKE CARE OF MYSELF!

SLAM!

3

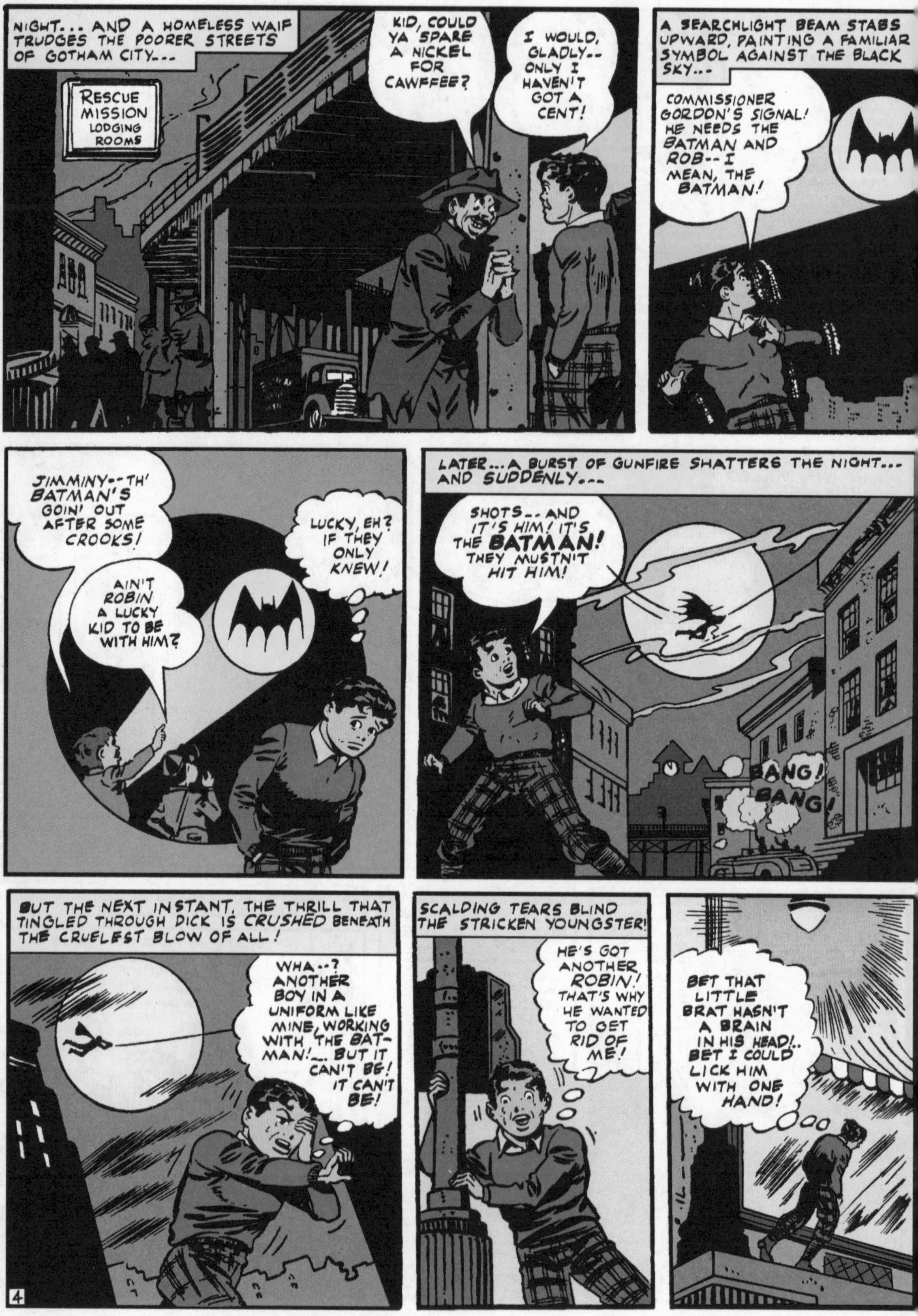
NIGHT... AND A HOMELESS WAIF TRUDGES THE POORER STREETS OF GOTHAM CITY...
RESCUE MISSION LODGING ROOMS
KID, COULD YA SPARE A NICKEL FOR CAWFFEE?
I WOULD, GLADLY-- ONLY I HAVEN'T GOT A CENT!
A SEARCHLIGHT BEAM STABS UPWARD, PAINTING A FAMILIAR SYMBOL AGAINST THE BLACK SKY...
COMMISSIONER GORDON'S SIGNAL! HE NEEDS THE BATMAN AND ROB-- I MEAN, THE BATMAN!
JIMMINY--TH' BATMAN'S GOIN' OUT AFTER SOME CROOKS!
AIN'T ROBIN A LUCKY KID TO BE WITH HIM?
LUCKY, EH? IF THEY ONLY KNEW!
LATER... A BURST OF GUNFIRE SHATTERS THE NIGHT... AND SUDDENLY...
SHOTS-- AND IT'S HIM! IT'S THE BATMAN! THEY MUSTN'T HIT HIM!
BANG! BANG!
BUT THE NEXT INSTANT, THE THRILL THAT TINGLED THROUGH DICK IS CRUSHED BENEATH THE CRUELEST BLOW OF ALL!
WHA--? ANOTHER BOY IN A UNIFORM LIKE MINE, WORKING WITH THE BAT-MAN!-- BUT IT CAN'T BE! IT CAN'T BE!
SCALDING TEARS BLIND THE STRICKEN YOUNGSTER!
HE'S GOT ANOTHER ROBIN! THAT'S WHY HE WANTED TO GET RID OF ME!
BET THAT LITTLE BRAT HASN'T A BRAIN IN HIS HEAD!.. BET I COULD LICK HIM WITH ONE HAND!
4

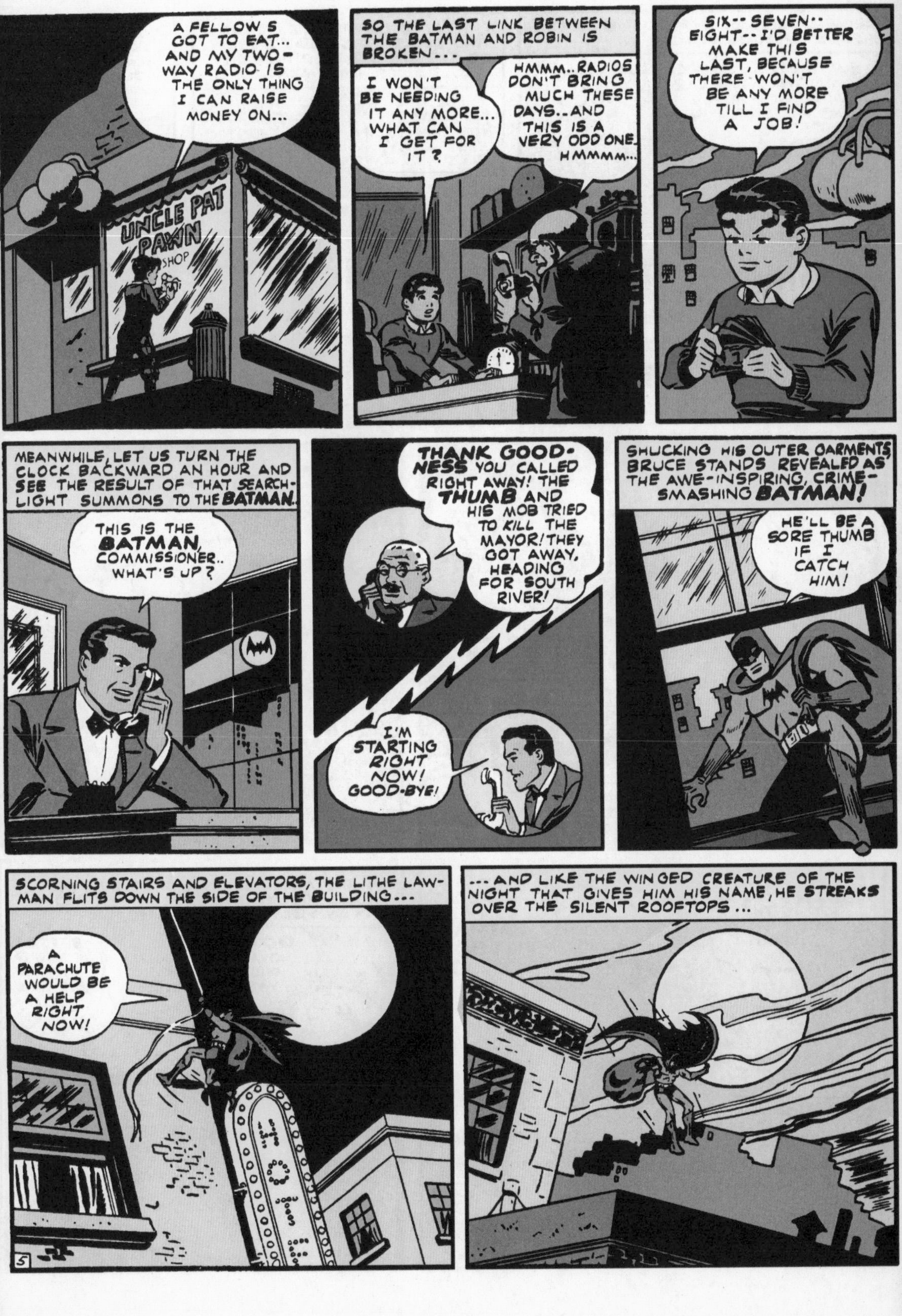
A FELLOW'S GOT TO EAT... AND MY TWO-WAY RADIO IS THE ONLY THING I CAN RAISE MONEY ON...
UNCLE PAT PAWN SHOP
SO THE LAST LINK BETWEEN THE BATMAN AND ROBIN IS BROKEN...
I WON'T BE NEEDING IT ANY MORE... WHAT CAN I GET FOR IT?
HMMM.. RADIOS DON'T BRING MUCH THESE DAYS.. AND THIS IS A VERY ODD ONE. HMMMM...
SIX-- SEVEN-- EIGHT-- I'D BETTER MAKE THIS LAST, BECAUSE THERE WON'T BE ANY MORE TILL I FIND A JOB!
MEANWHILE, LET US TURN THE CLOCK BACKWARD AN HOUR AND SEE THE RESULT OF THAT SEARCH-LIGHT SUMMONS TO THE BATMAN.
THIS IS THE BATMAN, COMMISSIONER.. WHAT'S UP?
THANK GOODNESS YOU CALLED RIGHT AWAY! THE THUMB AND HIS MOB TRIED TO KILL THE MAYOR! THEY GOT AWAY, HEADING FOR SOUTH RIVER!
I'M STARTING RIGHT NOW! GOOD-BYE!
SHUCKING HIS OUTER GARMENTS, BRUCE STANDS REVEALED AS THE AWE-INSPIRING, CRIME-SMASHING BATMAN!
HE'LL BE A SORE THUMB IF I CATCH HIM!
SCORNING STAIRS AND ELEVATORS, THE LITHE LAW-MAN FLITS DOWN THE SIDE OF THE BUILDING...
A PARACHUTE WOULD BE A HELP RIGHT NOW!
5
...AND LIKE THE WINGED CREATURE OF THE NIGHT THAT GIVES HIM HIS NAME, HE STREAKS OVER THE SILENT ROOFTOPS...

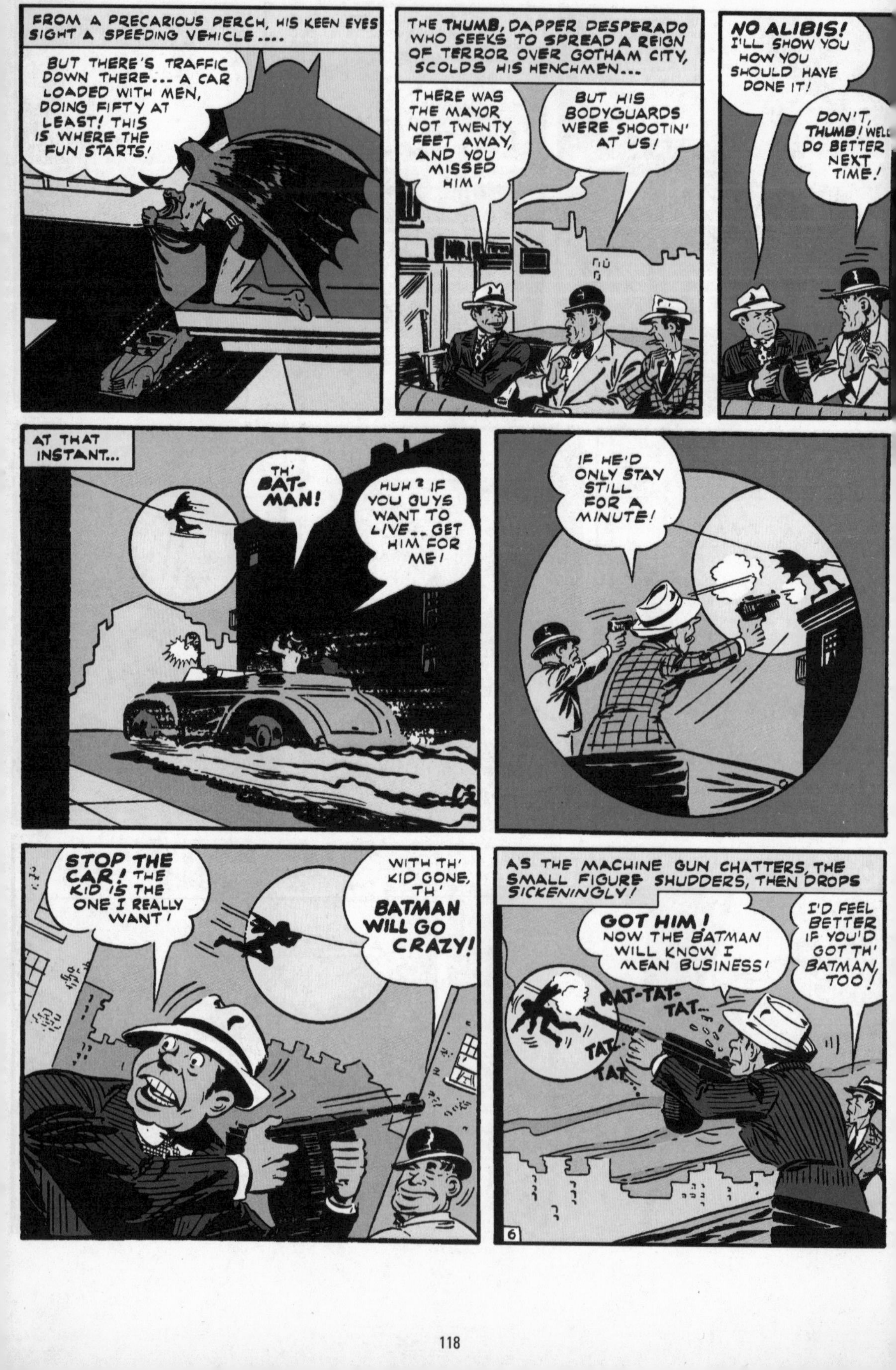

FROM A PRECARIOUS PERCH, HIS KEEN EYES SIGHT A SPEEDING VEHICLE....
BUT THERE'S TRAFFIC DOWN THERE... A CAR LOADED WITH MEN, DOING FIFTY AT LEAST! THIS IS WHERE THE FUN STARTS!
THE THUMB, DAPPER DESPERADO WHO SEEKS TO SPREAD A REIGN OF TERROR OVER GOTHAM CITY, SCOLDS HIS HENCHMEN...
THERE WAS THE MAYOR NOT TWENTY FEET AWAY, AND YOU MISSED HIM!
BUT HIS BODYGUARDS WERE SHOOTIN' AT US!
NO ALIBIS! I'LL SHOW YOU HOW YOU SHOULD HAVE DONE IT!
DON'T, THUMB! WE'LL DO BETTER NEXT TIME!
AT THAT INSTANT...
TH' BAT-MAN!
HUH? IF YOU GUYS WANT TO LIVE.. GET HIM FOR ME!
IF HE'D ONLY STAY STILL FOR A MINUTE!
STOP THE CAR! THE KID IS THE ONE I REALLY WANT!
WITH TH' KID GONE, TH' BATMAN WILL GO CRAZY!
AS THE MACHINE GUN CHATTERS, THE SMALL FIGURE SHUDDERS, THEN DROPS SICKENINGLY!
GOT HIM! NOW THE BATMAN WILL KNOW I MEAN BUSINESS!
I'D FEEL BETTER IF YOU'D GOT TH' BATMAN, TOO!
RAT-TAT-TAT-TAT...
TAT-TAT...
6

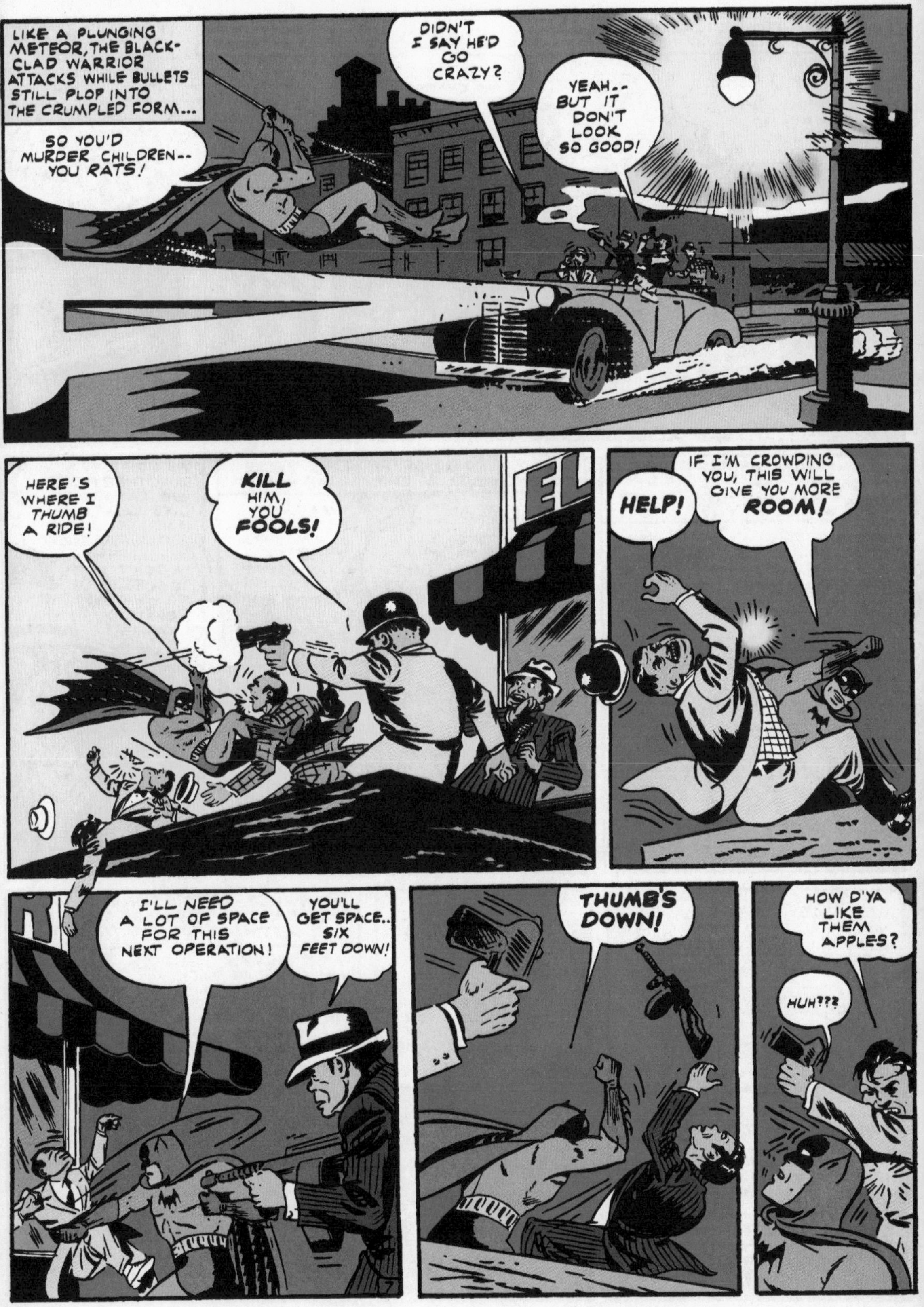
LIKE A PLUNGING METEOR, THE BLACK-CLAD WARRIOR ATTACKS WHILE BULLETS STILL PLOP INTO THE CRUMPLED FORM...
SO YOU'D MURDER CHILDREN-- YOU RATS!
DIDN'T I SAY HE'D GO CRAZY?
YEAH.. BUT IT DON'T LOOK SO GOOD!
HERE'S WHERE I THUMB A RIDE!
KILL HIM, YOU FOOLS!
HELP!
IF I'M CROWDING YOU, THIS WILL GIVE YOU MORE ROOM!
I'LL NEED A LOT OF SPACE FOR THIS NEXT OPERATION!
YOU'LL GET SPACE.. SIX FEET DOWN!
THUMB'S DOWN!
HOW D'YA LIKE THEM APPLES?
HUH???

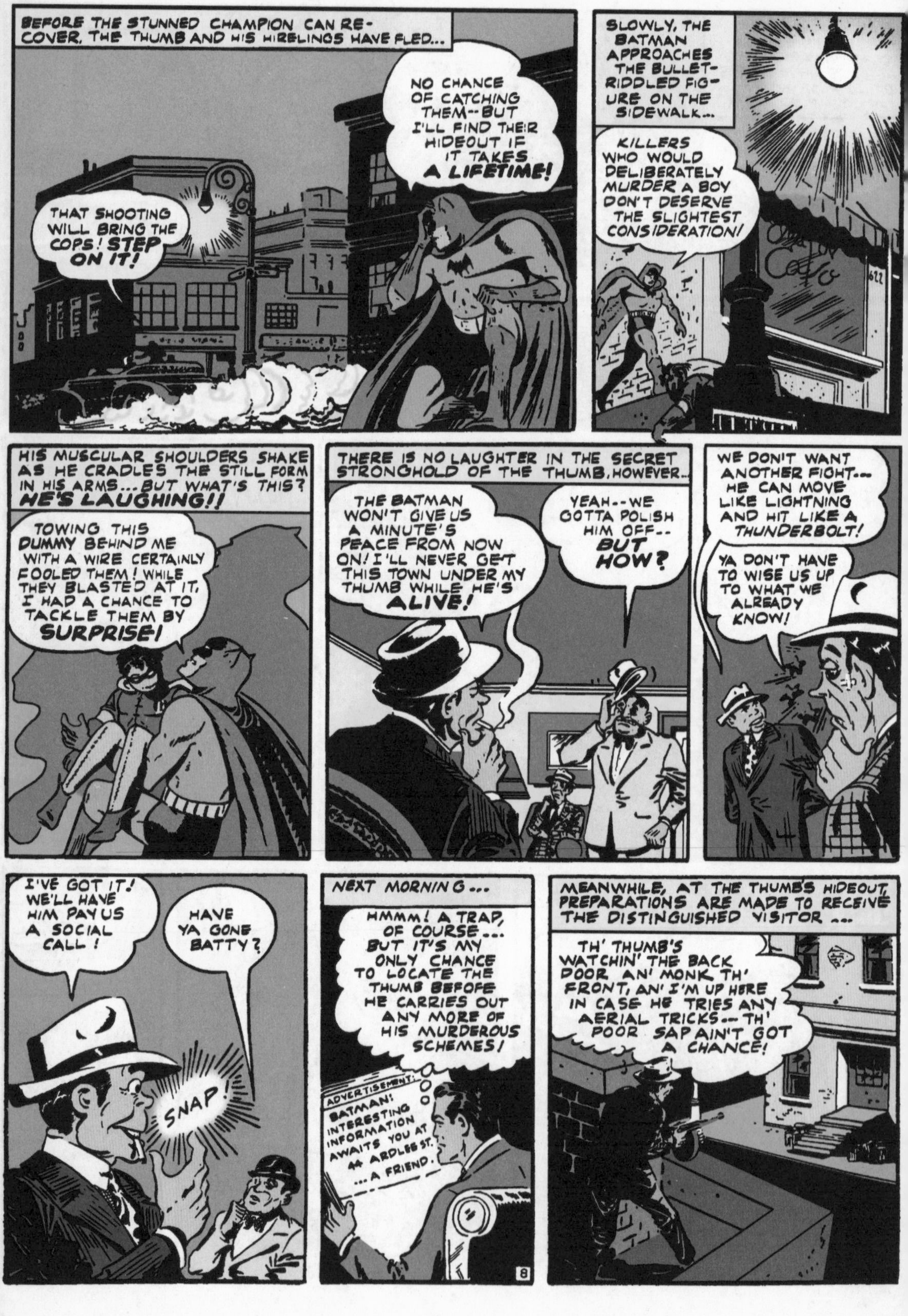
BEFORE THE STUNNED CHAMPION CAN RE-COVER, THE THUMB AND HIS HIRELINGS HAVE FLED...
NO CHANCE OF CATCHING THEM--BUT I'LL FIND THEIR HIDEOUT IF IT TAKES A LIFETIME!
THAT SHOOTING WILL BRING THE COPS! STEP ON IT!
SLOWLY, THE BATMAN APPROACHES THE BULLET-RIDDLED FIG-URE ON THE SIDEWALK...
KILLERS WHO WOULD DELIBERATELY MURDER A BOY DON'T DESERVE THE SLIGHTEST CONSIDERATION!
622
HIS MUSCULAR SHOULDERS SHAKE AS HE CRADLES THE STILL FORM IN HIS ARMS... BUT WHAT'S THIS? HE'S LAUGHING!!
TOWING THIS DUMMY BEHIND ME WITH A WIRE CERTAINLY FOOLED THEM! WHILE THEY BLASTED AT IT, I HAD A CHANCE TO TACKLE THEM BY SURPRISE!
THERE IS NO LAUGHTER IN THE SECRET STRONGHOLD OF THE THUMB, HOWEVER...
THE BATMAN WON'T GIVE US A MINUTE'S PEACE FROM NOW ON! I'LL NEVER GET THIS TOWN UNDER MY THUMB WHILE HE'S ALIVE!
YEAH--WE GOTTA POLISH HIM OFF--BUT HOW?
WE DON'T WANT ANOTHER FIGHT--HE CAN MOVE LIKE LIGHTNING AND HIT LIKE A THUNDERBOLT!
YA DON'T HAVE TO WISE US UP TO WHAT WE ALREADY KNOW!
I'VE GOT IT! WE'LL HAVE HIM PAY US A SOCIAL CALL!
HAVE YA GONE BATTY?
SNAP!
NEXT MORNING...
HMMM! A TRAP, OF COURSE... BUT IT'S MY ONLY CHANCE TO LOCATE THE THUMB BEFORE HE CARRIES OUT ANY MORE OF HIS MURDEROUS SCHEMES!
ADVERTISEMENT: BATMAN: INTERESTING INFORMATION AWAITS YOU AT 44 ARDLEE ST. ...A FRIEND.
8
MEANWHILE, AT THE THUMB'S HIDEOUT, PREPARATIONS ARE MADE TO RECEIVE THE DISTINGUISHED VISITOR...
TH' THUMB'S WATCHIN' THE BACK DOOR AN' MONK TH' FRONT, AN' I'M UP HERE IN CASE HE TRIES ANY AERIAL TRICKS-- TH' POOR SAP AIN'T GOT A CHANCE!

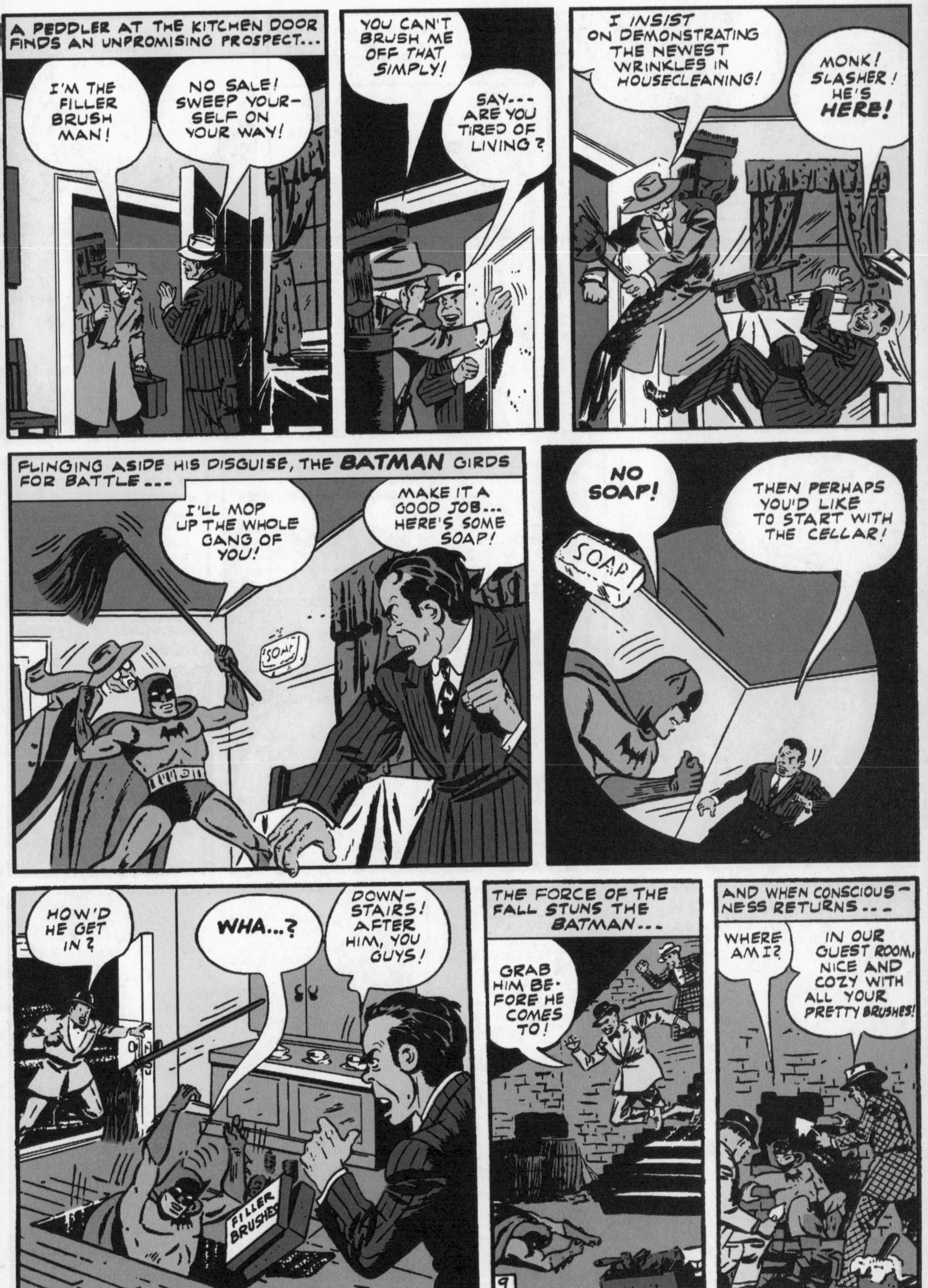

A PEDDLER AT THE KITCHEN DOOR FINDS AN UNPROMISING PROSPECT...
I'M THE FILLER BRUSH MAN!
NO SALE! SWEEP YOURSELF ON YOUR WAY!
YOU CAN'T BRUSH ME OFF THAT SIMPLY!
SAY... ARE YOU TIRED OF LIVING?
I INSIST ON DEMONSTRATING THE NEWEST WRINKLES IN HOUSECLEANING!
MONK! SLASHER! HE'S HERE!
FLINGING ASIDE HIS DISGUISE, THE BATMAN GIRDS FOR BATTLE...
I'LL MOP UP THE WHOLE GANG OF YOU!
MAKE IT A GOOD JOB... HERE'S SOME SOAP!
SOAP
NO SOAP!
SOAP
THEN PERHAPS YOU'D LIKE TO START WITH THE CELLAR!
HOW'D HE GET IN?
WHA...?
DOWN-STAIRS! AFTER HIM, YOU GUYS!
FILLER BRUSHES
THE FORCE OF THE FALL STUNS THE BATMAN...
GRAB HIM BEFORE HE COMES TO!
9
AND WHEN CONSCIOUSNESS RETURNS...
WHERE AM I?
IN OUR GUEST ROOM, NICE AND COZY WITH ALL YOUR PRETTY BRUSHES!

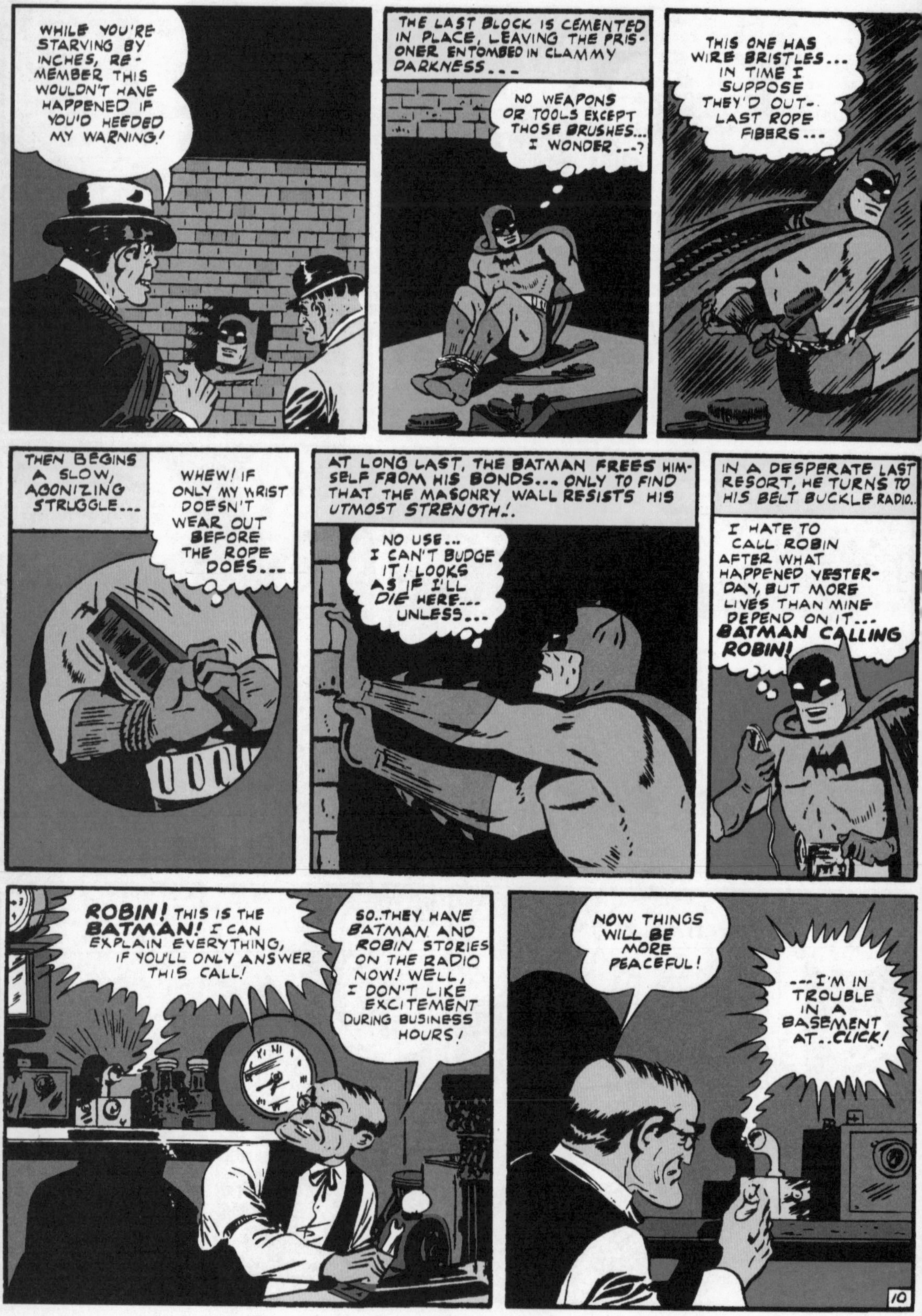
WHILE YOU'RE STARVING BY INCHES, RE-MEMBER THIS WOULDN'T HAVE HAPPENED IF YOU'D HEEDED MY WARNING!
THE LAST BLOCK IS CEMENTED IN PLACE, LEAVING THE PRIS-ONER ENTOMBED IN CLAMMY DARKNESS...
NO WEAPONS OR TOOLS EXCEPT THOSE BRUSHES... I WONDER --?
THIS ONE HAS WIRE BRISTLES... IN TIME I SUPPOSE THEY'D OUT-LAST ROPE FIBERS...
THEN BEGINS A SLOW, AGONIZING STRUGGLE...
WHEW! IF ONLY MY WRIST DOESN'T WEAR OUT BEFORE THE ROPE DOES...
AT LONG LAST, THE BATMAN FREES HIM-SELF FROM HIS BONDS... ONLY TO FIND THAT THE MASONRY WALL RESISTS HIS UTMOST STRENGTH!.
NO USE... I CAN'T BUDGE IT! LOOKS AS IF I'LL DIE HERE... UNLESS...
IN A DESPERATE LAST RESORT, HE TURNS TO HIS BELT BUCKLE RADIO..
I HATE TO CALL ROBIN AFTER WHAT HAPPENED YESTER-DAY, BUT MORE LIVES THAN MINE DEPEND ON IT... BATMAN CALLING ROBIN!
ROBIN! THIS IS THE BATMAN! I CAN EXPLAIN EVERYTHING, IF YOU'LL ONLY ANSWER THIS CALL!
SO..THEY HAVE BATMAN AND ROBIN STORIES ON THE RADIO NOW! WELL, I DON'T LIKE EXCITEMENT DURING BUSINESS HOURS!
NOW THINGS WILL BE MORE PEACEFUL!
---I'M IN TROUBLE IN A BASEMENT AT..CLICK!
10

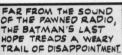

FAR FROM THE SOUND OF THE PAWNED RADIO, THE BATMAN'S LAST HOPE TREADS A WEARY TRAIL OF DISAPPOINTMENT.

NOBODY'LL HIRE ME! IF I HAD THE BATMAN'S RECOMMENDATION... BUT HE DOESN'T GIVE A HOOT ABOUT ME!

LUNCH ROOM

DISHWASHER WANTED

DISILLUSIONED AS THE BOY IS, HIS PULSE LEAPS AS HE OVERHEARS A FAMILIAR NAME.

HUH? THEY'RE TALKING ABOUT HIM!

HAW, HAW! I GET A KICK WHEN I THINK HOW TH' THUMB FIXED TH' BATMAN!

HE WON'T MAKE NO MORE TROUBLE, BURIED IN THAT CELLAR!

DISHWASHER WANTED

OKAY.. START WORKIN'... THE KITCHEN'S THIS WAY!-??

WITH HIM DEAD, WE'LL SQUEEZE MILLIONS OUTA THIS TOWN!

THE BATMAN... DEAD...

OH... NEVER MIND!

GRIEF AND SEARING ANGER BOIL WITHIN DICK'S BREAST AS HE TRAILS THE THUGS, A SMALL BUT DAUNTLESS AVENGER ---

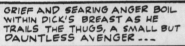

HIS FIRST CASE WITHOUT ME TO HELP-- AND HE FAILED! I'LL BET THAT OTHER KID LET HIM DOWN!

I'M GLAD I KEPT MY UNIFORM WITH ME... NOW THEY'LL KNOW WHO'S GETTING EVEN WITH THEM!

NO THOUGHT OF PERSONAL DANGER ENTERS THE LOYAL MIND OF ROBIN AS HE ENTERS UPON HIS HAZARDOUS ROLE ---

THREE OF THEM-- ALL ARMED! BUT IT DOESN'T MATTER MUCH IF THEY DO KILL ME, NOW THAT HE'S GONE...

THREE "WISE GUYS" GET THE SCARE OF THEIR CROOKED LIVES ---

I'M HERE TO EVEN THINGS UP FOR THE BATMAN!

HEY-- I KILLED YOU MYSELF!

IT'S A GHOST!

BUT BOYISH FURY IS HELPLESS AGAINST THE OVERWHELMING STRENGTH OF GROWN MEN-- AND THE BATTLE LASTS ONLY SECONDS ---

YOU LITTLE WILDCAT-- YOU'VE FOUGHT YOUR LAST FIGHT!

WHY DON'T YOU FIGHT FAIR?

HE'S GOT A PUNCH LIKE A PILE-DRIVER!

11

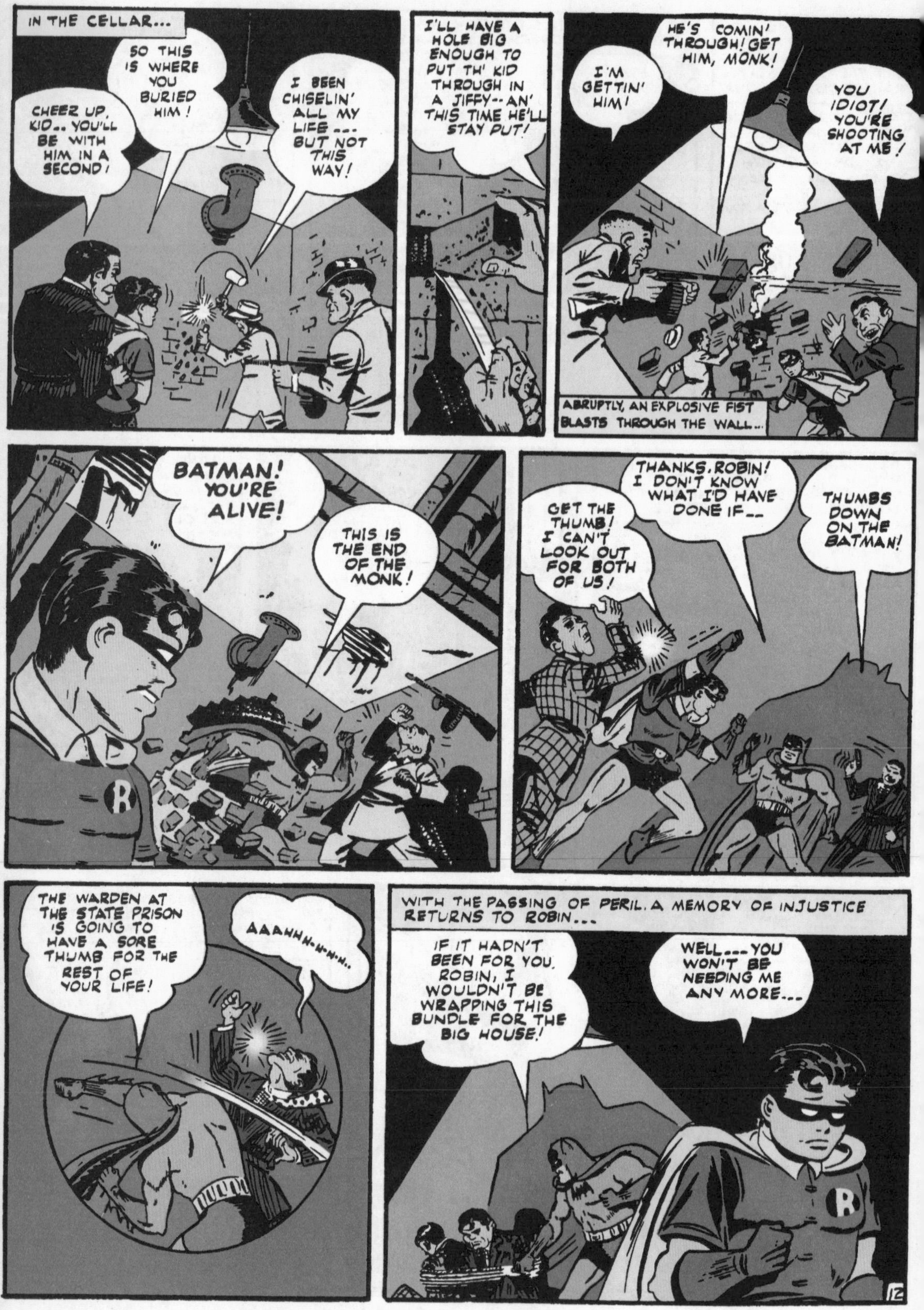

IN THE CELLAR...
SO THIS IS WHERE YOU BURIED HIM!
CHEEZ UP, KID.. YOU'LL BE WITH HIM IN A SECOND!
I BEEN CHISELIN' ALL MY LIFE... BUT NOT THIS WAY!
I'LL HAVE A HOLE BIG ENOUGH TO PUT TH' KID THROUGH IN A JIFFY--AN' THIS TIME HE'LL STAY PUT!
HE'S COMIN' THROUGH! GET HIM, MONK!
I'M GETTIN' HIM!
YOU IDIOT! YOU'RE SHOOTING AT ME!
ABRUPTLY, AN EXPLOSIVE FIST BLASTS THROUGH THE WALL...
BATMAN! YOU'RE ALIVE!
THIS IS THE END OF THE MONK!
THANKS, ROBIN! I DON'T KNOW WHAT I'D HAVE DONE IF--
GET THE THUMB! I CAN'T LOOK OUT FOR BOTH OF US!
THUMBS DOWN ON THE BATMAN!
THE WARDEN AT THE STATE PRISON IS GOING TO HAVE A SORE THUMB FOR THE REST OF YOUR LIFE!
AAAHHH-H-H-H..
WITH THE PASSING OF PERIL, A MEMORY OF INJUSTICE RETURNS TO ROBIN...
IF IT HADN'T BEEN FOR YOU, ROBIN, I WOULDN'T BE WRAPPING THIS BUNDLE FOR THE BIG HOUSE!
WELL... YOU WON'T BE NEEDING ME ANY MORE...
12

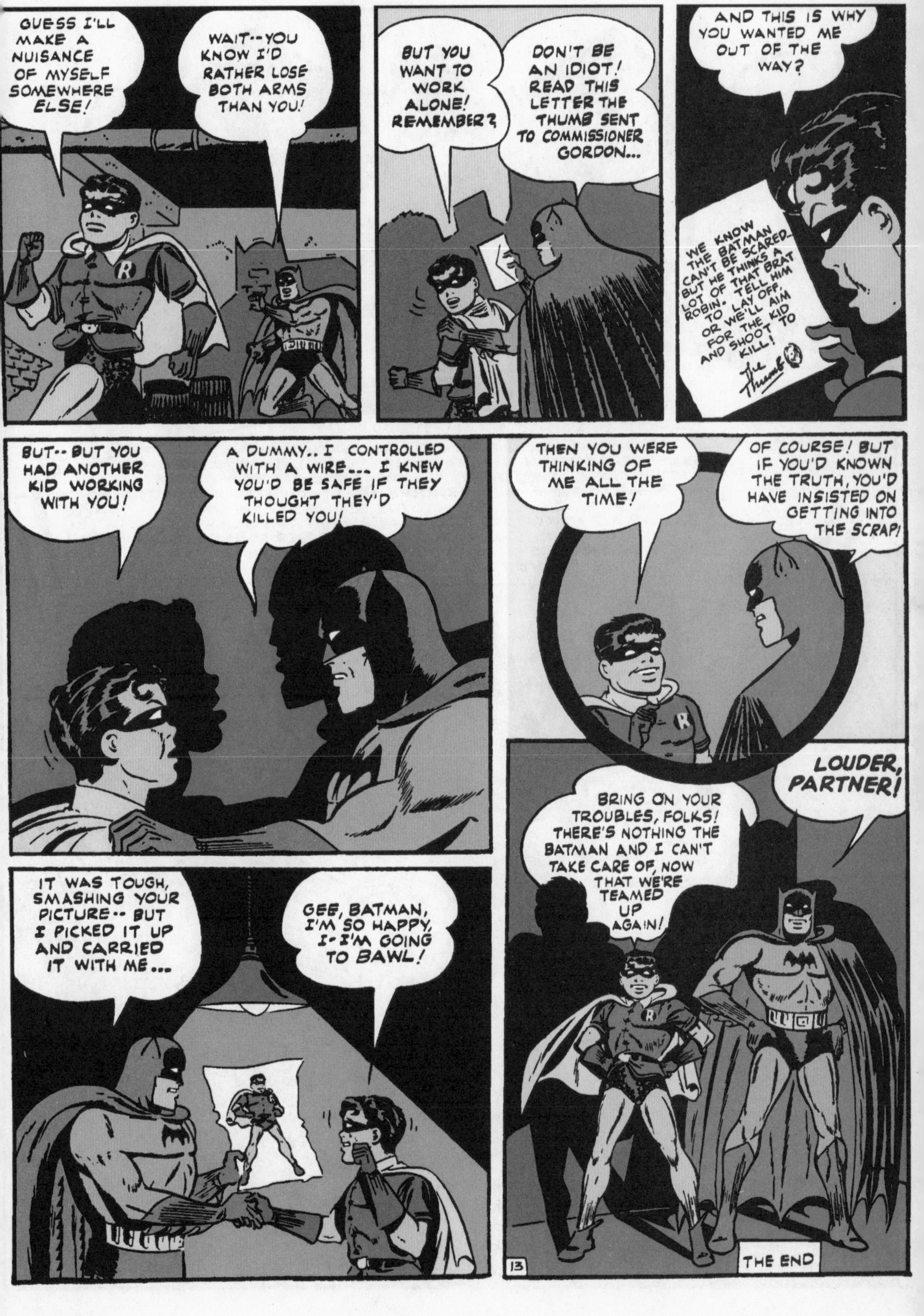
GUESS I'LL MAKE A NUISANCE OF MYSELF SOMEWHERE ELSE!
WAIT--YOU KNOW I'D RATHER LOSE BOTH ARMS THAN YOU!
BUT YOU WANT TO WORK ALONE! REMEMBER?
DON'T BE AN IDIOT! READ THIS LETTER THE THUMB SENT TO COMMISSIONER GORDON...
AND THIS IS WHY YOU WANTED ME OUT OF THE WAY?
WE KNOW THE BATMAN CAN'T BE SCARED-- BUT HE THINKS A LOT OF THAT BRAT ROBIN. TELL HIM TO LAY OFF, OR WE'LL AIM FOR THE KID AND SHOOT TO KILL!
BUT--BUT YOU HAD ANOTHER KID WORKING WITH YOU!
A DUMMY.. I CONTROLLED WITH A WIRE... I KNEW YOU'D BE SAFE IF THEY THOUGHT THEY'D KILLED YOU!
THEN YOU WERE THINKING OF ME ALL THE TIME!
OF COURSE! BUT IF YOU'D KNOWN THE TRUTH, YOU'D HAVE INSISTED ON GETTING INTO THE SCRAP!
IT WAS TOUGH, SMASHING YOUR PICTURE-- BUT I PICKED IT UP AND CARRIED IT WITH ME...
GEE, BATMAN, I'M SO HAPPY, I-I'M GOING TO BAWL!
BRING ON YOUR TROUBLES, FOLKS! THERE'S NOTHING THE BATMAN AND I CAN'T TAKE CARE OF, NOW THAT WE'RE TEAMED UP AGAIN!
LOUDER, PARTNER!
13
THE END

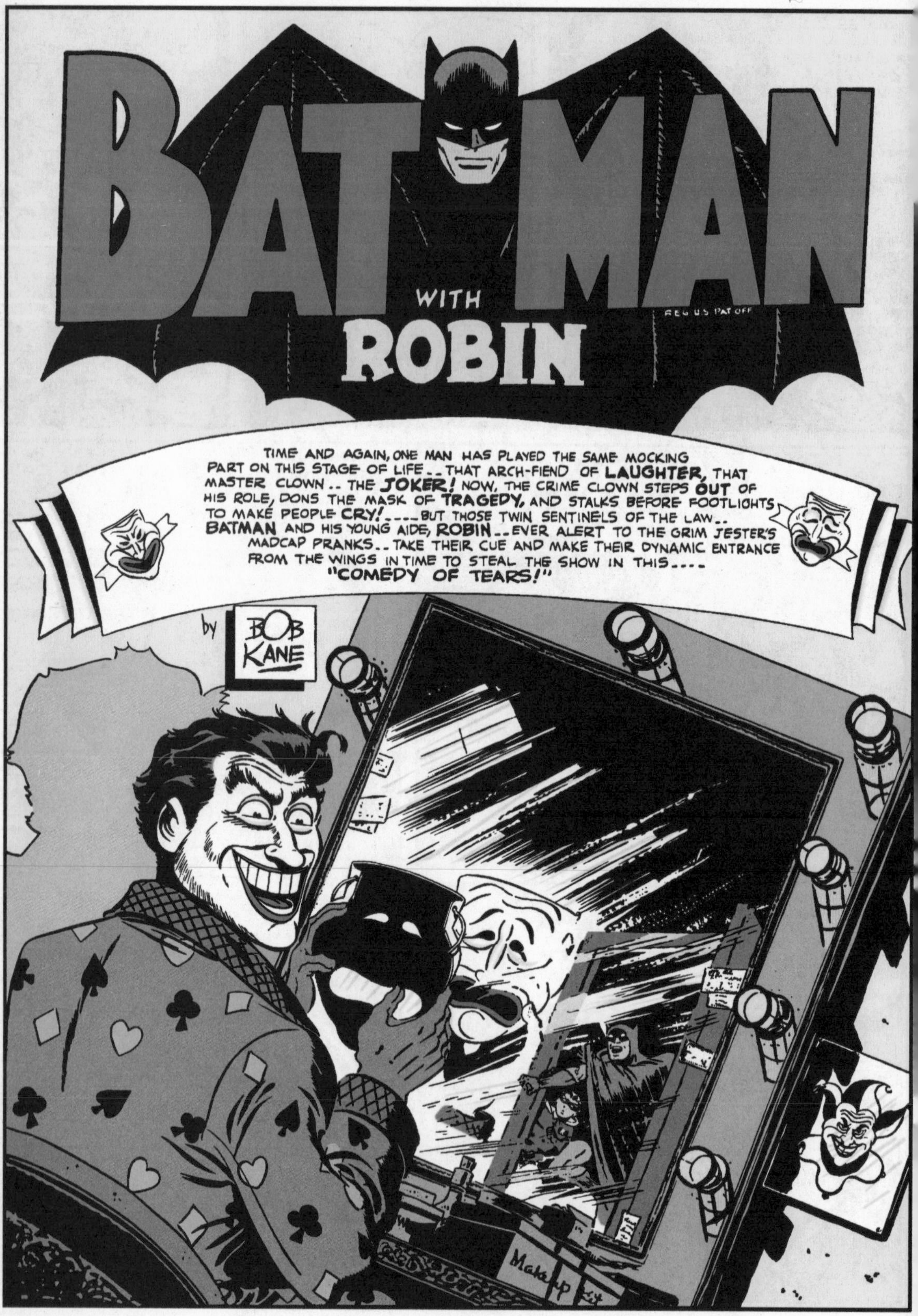
BATMAN
WITH
ROBIN
REG. U.S. PAT. OFF.
TIME AND AGAIN, ONE MAN HAS PLAYED THE SAME MOCKING PART ON THIS STAGE OF LIFE.. THAT ARCH-FIEND OF **LAUGHTER,** THAT MASTER CLOWN.. THE **JOKER!** NOW, THE CRIME CLOWN STEPS **OUT** OF HIS ROLE, DONS THE MASK OF **TRAGEDY,** AND STALKS BEFORE FOOTLIGHTS TO MAKE PEOPLE **CRY!**.... BUT THOSE TWIN SENTINELS OF THE LAW.. **BATMAN** AND HIS YOUNG AIDE, **ROBIN**.. EVER ALERT TO THE GRIM JESTER'S MADCAP PRANKS.. TAKE THEIR CUE AND MAKE THEIR DYNAMIC ENTRANCE FROM THE WINGS IN TIME TO STEAL THE SHOW IN THIS....
"COMEDY OF TEARS!"
by BOB KANE

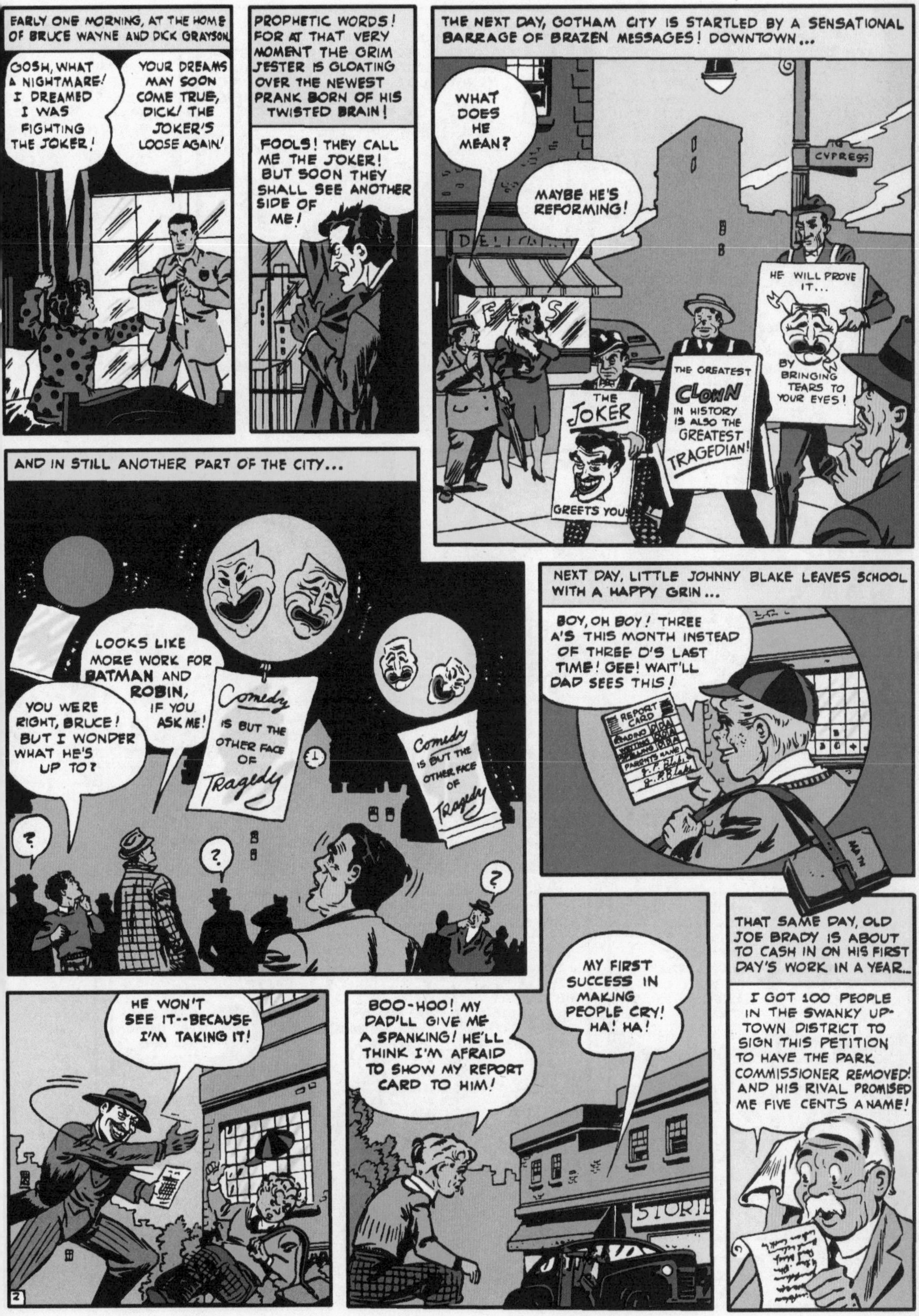

EARLY ONE MORNING, AT THE HOME OF BRUCE WAYNE AND DICK GRAYSON
GOSH, WHAT A NIGHTMARE! I DREAMED I WAS FIGHTING THE JOKER!
YOUR DREAMS MAY SOON COME TRUE, DICK! THE JOKER'S LOOSE AGAIN!
PROPHETIC WORDS! FOR AT THAT VERY MOMENT THE GRIM JESTER IS GLOATING OVER THE NEWEST PRANK BORN OF HIS TWISTED BRAIN!
FOOLS! THEY CALL ME THE JOKER! BUT SOON THEY SHALL SEE ANOTHER SIDE OF ME!
THE NEXT DAY, GOTHAM CITY IS STARTLED BY A SENSATIONAL BARRAGE OF BRAZEN MESSAGES! DOWNTOWN...
WHAT DOES HE MEAN?
MAYBE HE'S REFORMING!
CYPRESS
THE JOKER GREETS YOU!
THE GREATEST CLOWN IN HISTORY IS ALSO THE GREATEST TRAGEDIAN!
HE WILL PROVE IT... BY BRINGING TEARS TO YOUR EYES!
AND IN STILL ANOTHER PART OF THE CITY...
LOOKS LIKE MORE WORK FOR BATMAN AND ROBIN, IF YOU ASK ME!
YOU WERE RIGHT, BRUCE! BUT I WONDER WHAT HE'S UP TO?
Comedy IS BUT THE OTHER FACE OF TRAGEDY
Comedy IS BUT THE OTHER FACE OF Tragedy
?
?
?
NEXT DAY, LITTLE JOHNNY BLAKE LEAVES SCHOOL WITH A HAPPY GRIN...
BOY, OH BOY! THREE A'S THIS MONTH INSTEAD OF THREE D'S LAST TIME! GEE! WAIT'LL DAD SEES THIS!
REPORT CARD
HE WON'T SEE IT--BECAUSE I'M TAKING IT!
BOO-HOO! MY DAD'LL GIVE ME A SPANKING! HE'LL THINK I'M AFRAID TO SHOW MY REPORT CARD TO HIM!
MY FIRST SUCCESS IN MAKING PEOPLE CRY! HA! HA!
STORIE
THAT SAME DAY, OLD JOE BRADY IS ABOUT TO CASH IN ON HIS FIRST DAY'S WORK IN A YEAR...
I GOT 100 PEOPLE IN THE SWANKY UP-TOWN DISTRICT TO SIGN THIS PETITION TO HAVE THE PARK COMMISSIONER REMOVED! AND HIS RIVAL PROMISED ME FIVE CENTS A NAME!

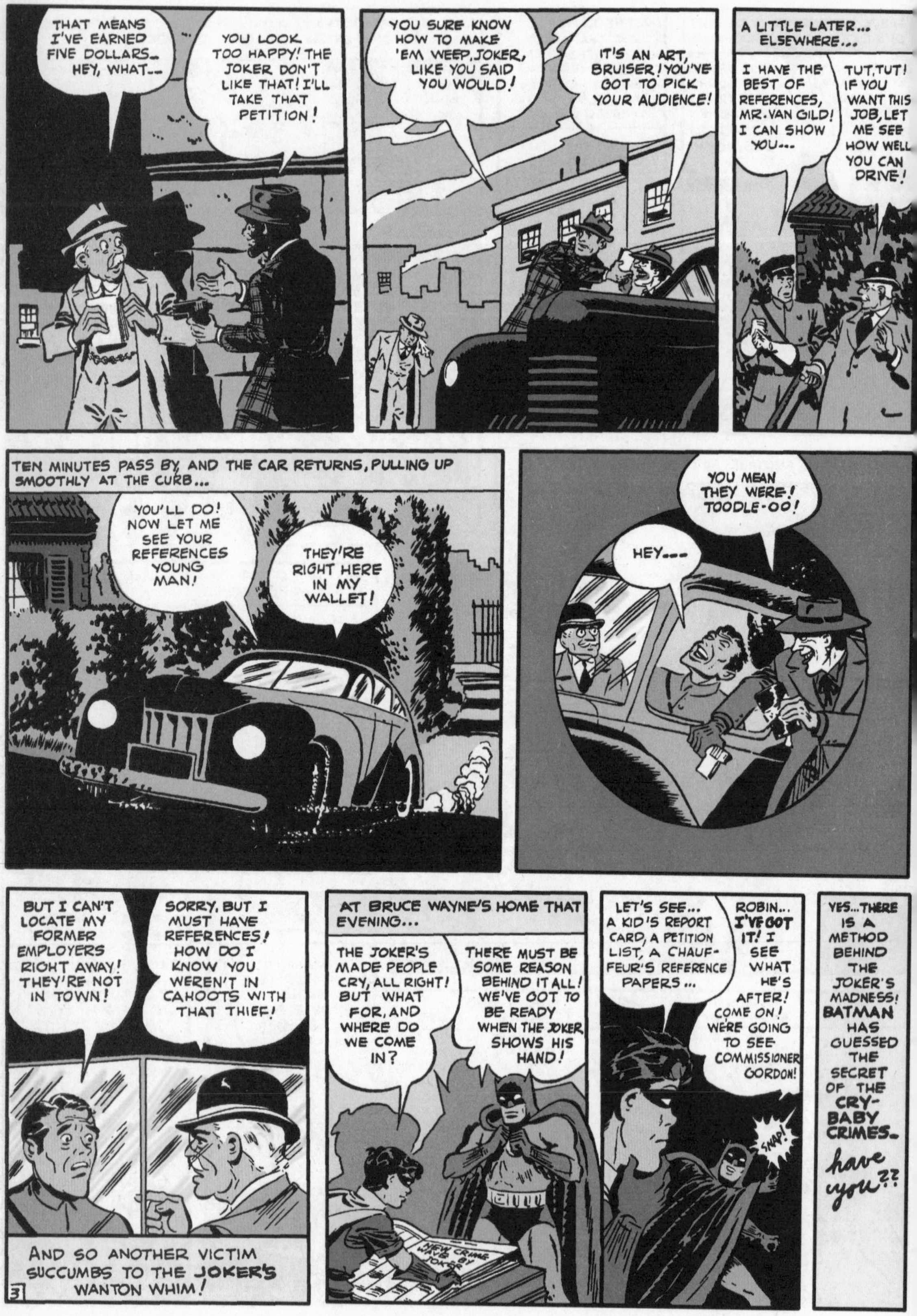

THAT MEANS I'VE EARNED FIVE DOLLARS-- HEY, WHAT--
YOU LOOK TOO HAPPY! THE JOKER DON'T LIKE THAT! I'LL TAKE THAT PETITION!
YOU SURE KNOW HOW TO MAKE 'EM WEEP, JOKER, LIKE YOU SAID YOU WOULD!
IT'S AN ART, BRUISER! YOU'VE GOT TO PICK YOUR AUDIENCE!
A LITTLE LATER... ELSEWHERE...
I HAVE THE BEST OF REFERENCES, MR. VAN GILD! I CAN SHOW YOU...
TUT, TUT! IF YOU WANT THIS JOB, LET ME SEE HOW WELL YOU CAN DRIVE!
TEN MINUTES PASS BY, AND THE CAR RETURNS, PULLING UP SMOOTHLY AT THE CURB...
YOU'LL DO! NOW LET ME SEE YOUR REFERENCES YOUNG MAN!
THEY'RE RIGHT HERE IN MY WALLET!
HEY---
YOU MEAN THEY WERE! TOODLE-OO!
BUT I CAN'T LOCATE MY FORMER EMPLOYERS RIGHT AWAY! THEY'RE NOT IN TOWN!
SORRY, BUT I MUST HAVE REFERENCES! HOW DO I KNOW YOU WEREN'T IN CAHOOTS WITH THAT THIEF!
AND SO ANOTHER VICTIM SUCCUMBS TO THE JOKER'S WANTON WHIM!
3
AT BRUCE WAYNE'S HOME THAT EVENING...
THE JOKER'S MADE PEOPLE CRY, ALL RIGHT! BUT WHAT FOR, AND WHERE DO WE COME IN?
THERE MUST BE SOME REASON BEHIND IT ALL! WE'VE GOT TO BE READY WHEN THE JOKER SHOWS HIS HAND!
NEW CRIME WAVE BY JOKER
LET'S SEE... A KID'S REPORT CARD, A PETITION LIST, A CHAUFFEUR'S REFERENCE PAPERS...
ROBIN... I'VE GOT IT! I SEE WHAT HE'S AFTER! COME ON! WE'RE GOING TO SEE COMMISSIONER GORDON!
SNAP!
YES... THERE IS A METHOD BEHIND THE JOKER'S MADNESS! BATMAN HAS GUESSED THE SECRET OF THE CRY-BABY CRIMES-- have you??

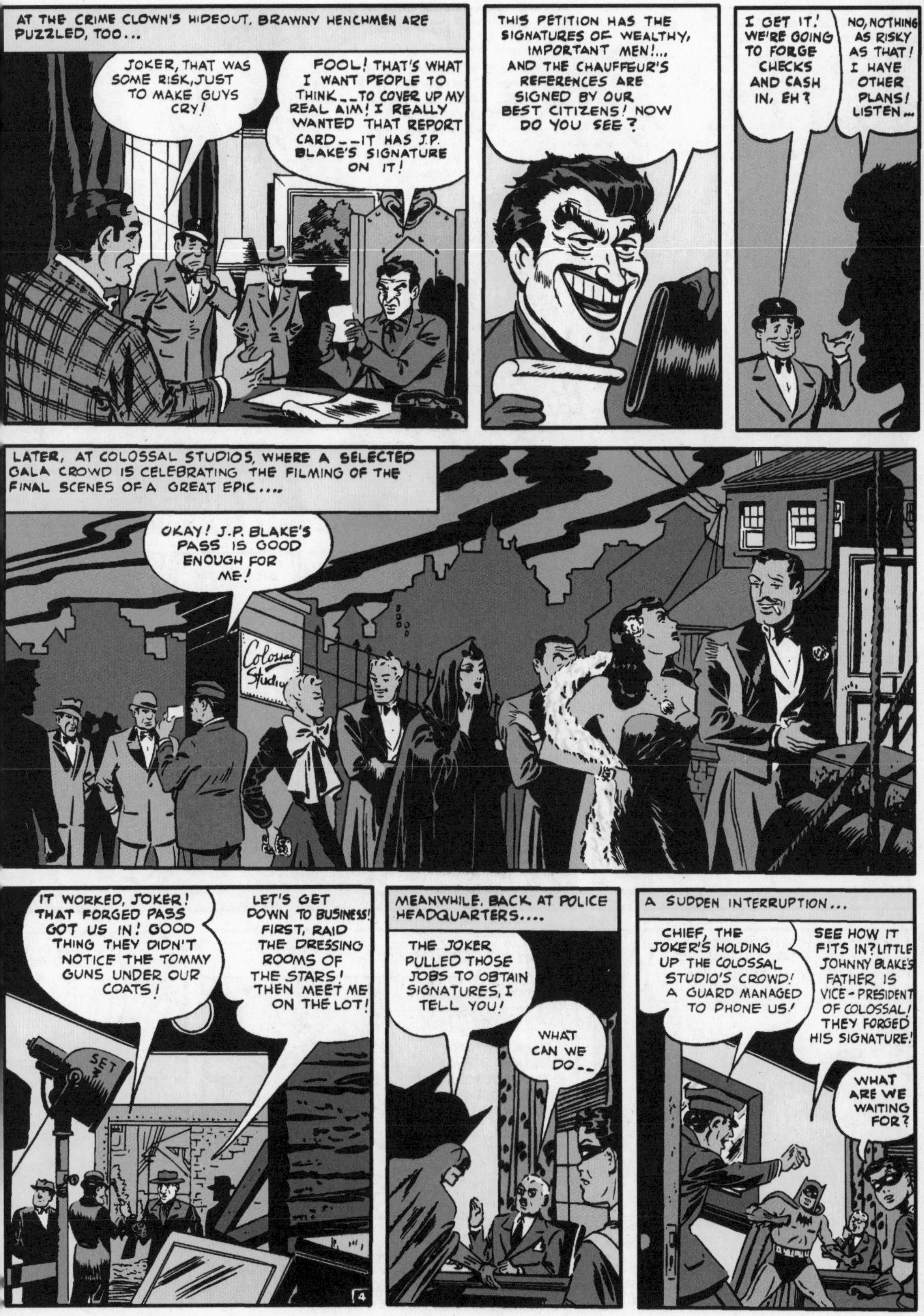
AT THE CRIME CLOWN'S HIDEOUT, BRAWNY HENCHMEN ARE PUZZLED, TOO...
JOKER, THAT WAS SOME RISK, JUST TO MAKE GUYS CRY!
FOOL! THAT'S WHAT I WANT PEOPLE TO THINK--TO COVER UP MY REAL AIM! I REALLY WANTED THAT REPORT CARD--IT HAS J.P. BLAKE'S SIGNATURE ON IT!
THIS PETITION HAS THE SIGNATURES OF WEALTHY, IMPORTANT MEN!... AND THE CHAUFFEUR'S REFERENCES ARE SIGNED BY OUR BEST CITIZENS! NOW DO YOU SEE?
I GET IT! WE'RE GOING TO FORGE CHECKS AND CASH IN, EH?
NO, NOTHING AS RISKY AS THAT! I HAVE OTHER PLANS! LISTEN...
LATER, AT COLOSSAL STUDIOS, WHERE A SELECTED GALA CROWD IS CELEBRATING THE FILMING OF THE FINAL SCENES OF A GREAT EPIC....
OKAY! J.P. BLAKE'S PASS IS GOOD ENOUGH FOR ME!
Colossal Studio
IT WORKED, JOKER! THAT FORGED PASS GOT US IN! GOOD THING THEY DIDN'T NOTICE THE TOMMY GUNS UNDER OUR COATS!
LET'S GET DOWN TO BUSINESS! FIRST, RAID THE DRESSING ROOMS OF THE STARS! THEN MEET ME ON THE LOT!
SET 3
4
MEANWHILE, BACK AT POLICE HEADQUARTERS....
THE JOKER PULLED THOSE JOBS TO OBTAIN SIGNATURES, I TELL YOU!
WHAT CAN WE DO--
A SUDDEN INTERRUPTION...
CHIEF, THE JOKER'S HOLDING UP THE COLOSSAL STUDIO'S CROWD! A GUARD MANAGED TO PHONE US!
SEE HOW IT FITS IN? LITTLE JOHNNY BLAKE'S FATHER IS VICE-PRESIDENT OF COLOSSAL! THEY FORGED HIS SIGNATURE!
WHAT ARE WE WAITING FOR?

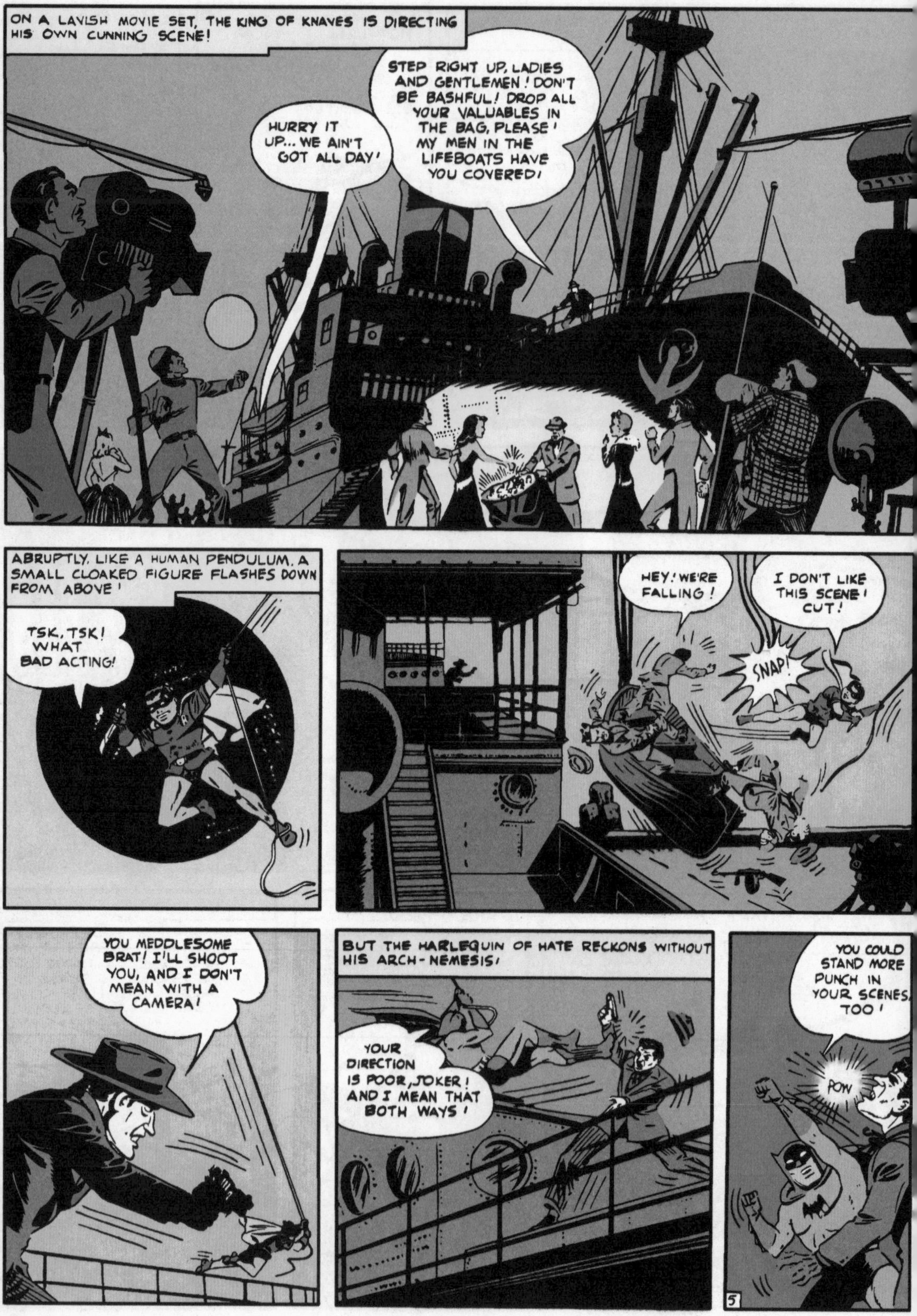
ON A LAVISH MOVIE SET, THE KING OF KNAVES IS DIRECTING HIS OWN CUNNING SCENE!
HURRY IT UP... WE AIN'T GOT ALL DAY!
STEP RIGHT UP, LADIES AND GENTLEMEN! DON'T BE BASHFUL! DROP ALL YOUR VALUABLES IN THE BAG, PLEASE! MY MEN IN THE LIFEBOATS HAVE YOU COVERED!
ABRUPTLY, LIKE A HUMAN PENDULUM, A SMALL CLOAKED FIGURE FLASHES DOWN FROM ABOVE!
TSK, TSK! WHAT BAD ACTING!
HEY! WE'RE FALLING!
I DON'T LIKE THIS SCENE! CUT!
SNAP!
YOU MEDDLESOME BRAT! I'LL SHOOT YOU, AND I DON'T MEAN WITH A CAMERA!
BUT THE HARLEQUIN OF HATE RECKONS WITHOUT HIS ARCH-NEMESIS!
YOUR DIRECTION IS POOR, JOKER! AND I MEAN THAT BOTH WAYS!
YOU COULD STAND MORE PUNCH IN YOUR SCENES, TOO!
POW
5

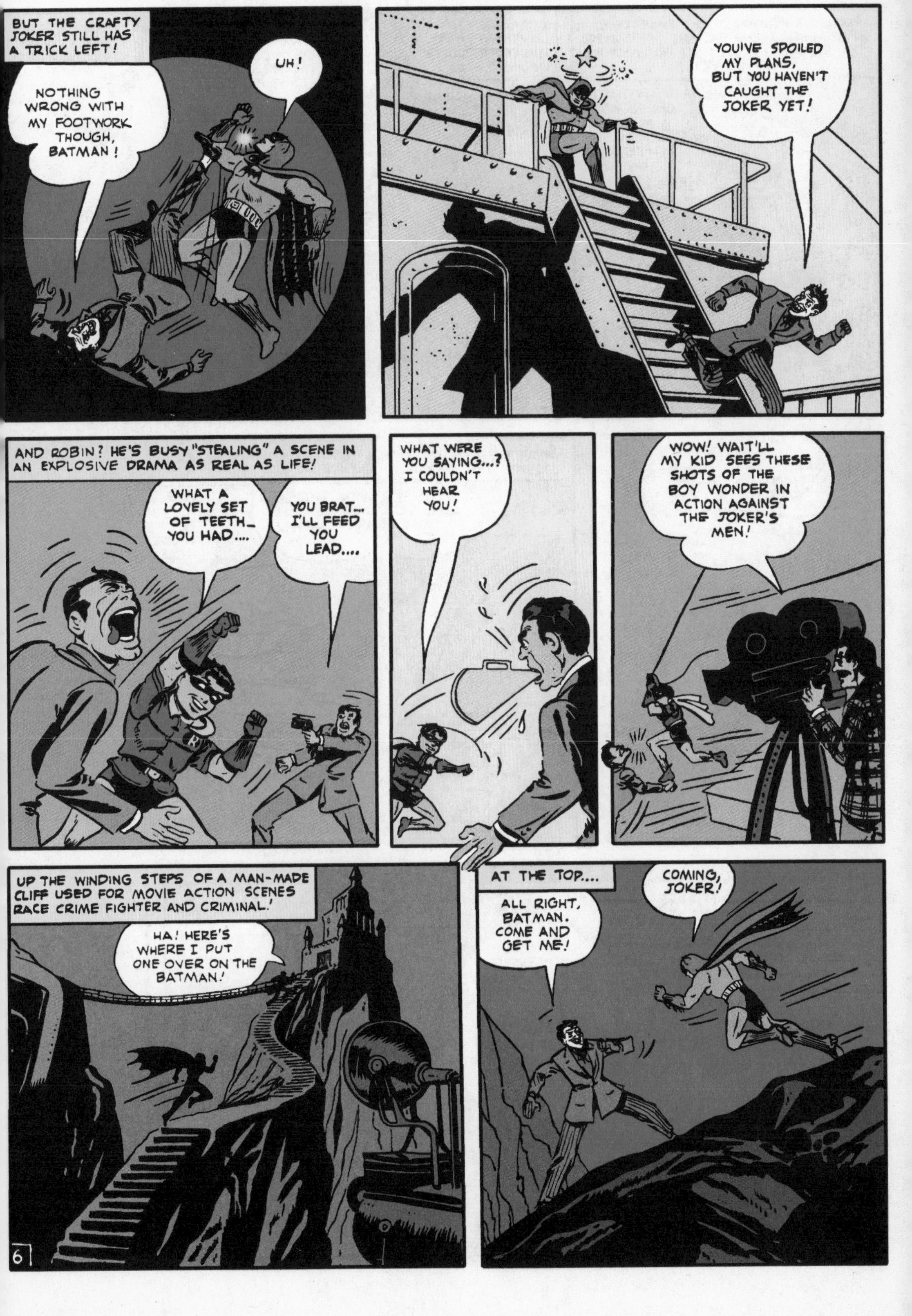

BUT THE CRAFTY JOKER STILL HAS A TRICK LEFT!
NOTHING WRONG WITH MY FOOTWORK THOUGH, BATMAN!
UH!
YOU'VE SPOILED MY PLANS, BUT YOU HAVEN'T CAUGHT THE JOKER YET!
AND ROBIN? HE'S BUSY "STEALING" A SCENE IN AN EXPLOSIVE DRAMA AS REAL AS LIFE!
WHAT A LOVELY SET OF TEETH_ YOU HAD....
YOU BRAT... I'LL FEED YOU LEAD....
WHAT WERE YOU SAYING...? I COULDN'T HEAR YOU!
WOW! WAIT'LL MY KID SEES THESE SHOTS OF THE BOY WONDER IN ACTION AGAINST THE JOKER'S MEN!
UP THE WINDING STEPS OF A MAN-MADE CLIFF USED FOR MOVIE ACTION SCENES RACE CRIME FIGHTER AND CRIMINAL.'
HA! HERE'S WHERE I PUT ONE OVER ON THE BATMAN.'
6
AT THE TOP....
ALL RIGHT, BATMAN. COME AND GET ME!
COMING, JOKER!

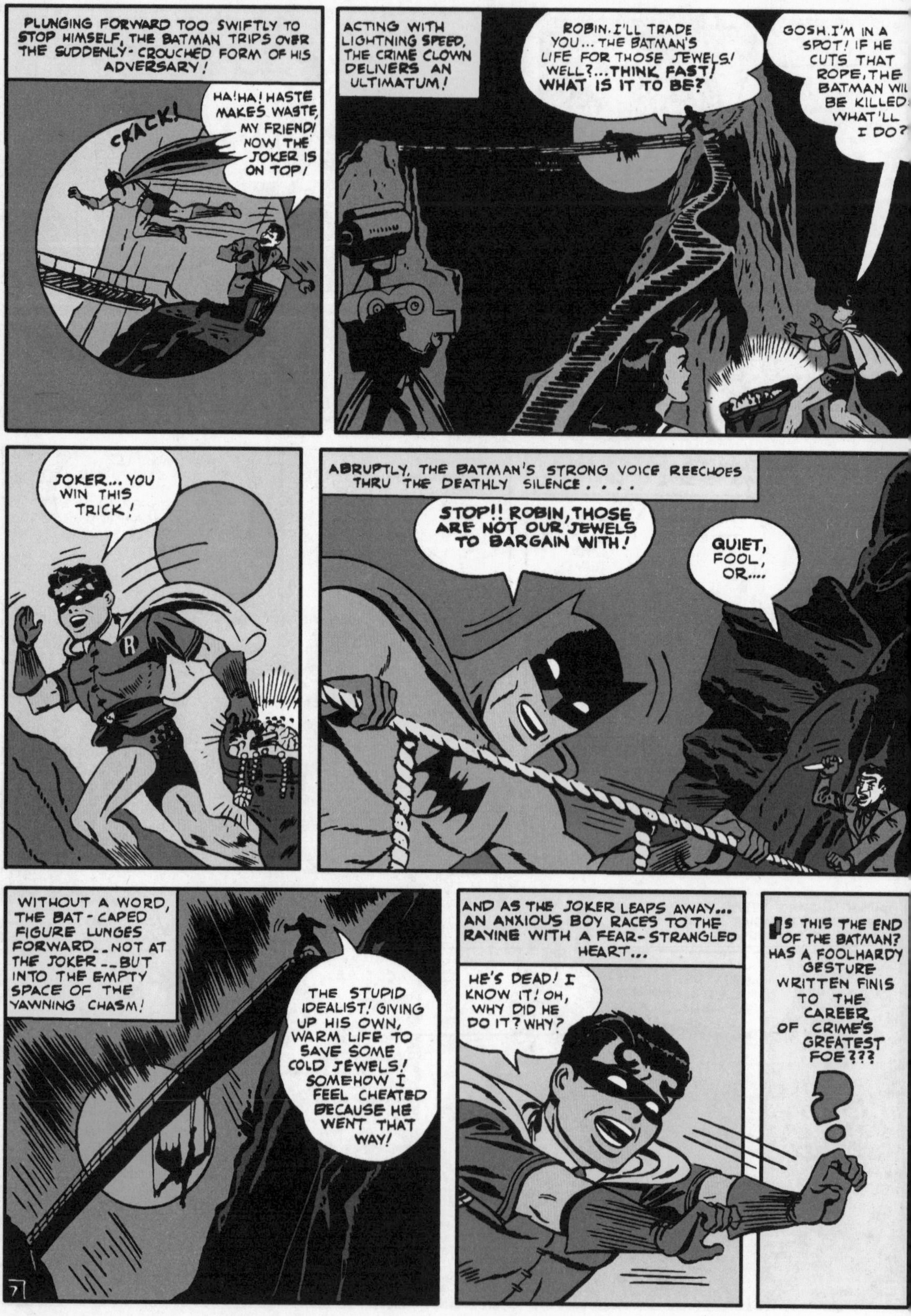

PLUNGING FORWARD TOO SWIFTLY TO STOP HIMSELF, THE BATMAN TRIPS OVER THE SUDDENLY-CROUCHED FORM OF HIS ADVERSARY!
CRACK!
HA! HA! HASTE MAKES WASTE, MY FRIEND! NOW THE JOKER IS ON TOP!
ACTING WITH LIGHTNING SPEED, THE CRIME CLOWN DELIVERS AN ULTIMATUM!
ROBIN, I'LL TRADE YOU... THE BATMAN'S LIFE FOR THOSE JEWELS! WELL?...THINK FAST! WHAT IS IT TO BE?
GOSH, I'M IN A SPOT! IF HE CUTS THAT ROPE, THE BATMAN WIL BE KILLED! WHAT'LL I DO?
JOKER... YOU WIN THIS TRICK!
ABRUPTLY, THE BATMAN'S STRONG VOICE REECHOES THRU THE DEATHLY SILENCE . . . .
STOP!! ROBIN, THOSE ARE NOT OUR JEWELS TO BARGAIN WITH!
QUIET, FOOL, OR....
WITHOUT A WORD, THE BAT-CAPED FIGURE LUNGES FORWARD--NOT AT THE JOKER--BUT INTO THE EMPTY SPACE OF THE YAWNING CHASM!
THE STUPID IDEALIST! GIVING UP HIS OWN, WARM LIFE TO SAVE SOME COLD JEWELS! SOMEHOW I FEEL CHEATED BECAUSE HE WENT THAT WAY!
7
AND AS THE JOKER LEAPS AWAY... AN ANXIOUS BOY RACES TO THE RAVINE WITH A FEAR-STRANGLED HEART...
HE'S DEAD! I KNOW IT! OH, WHY DID HE DO IT? WHY?
IS THIS THE END OF THE BATMAN? HAS A FOOLHARDY GESTURE WRITTEN FINIS TO THE CAREER OF CRIME'S GREATEST FOE???
?

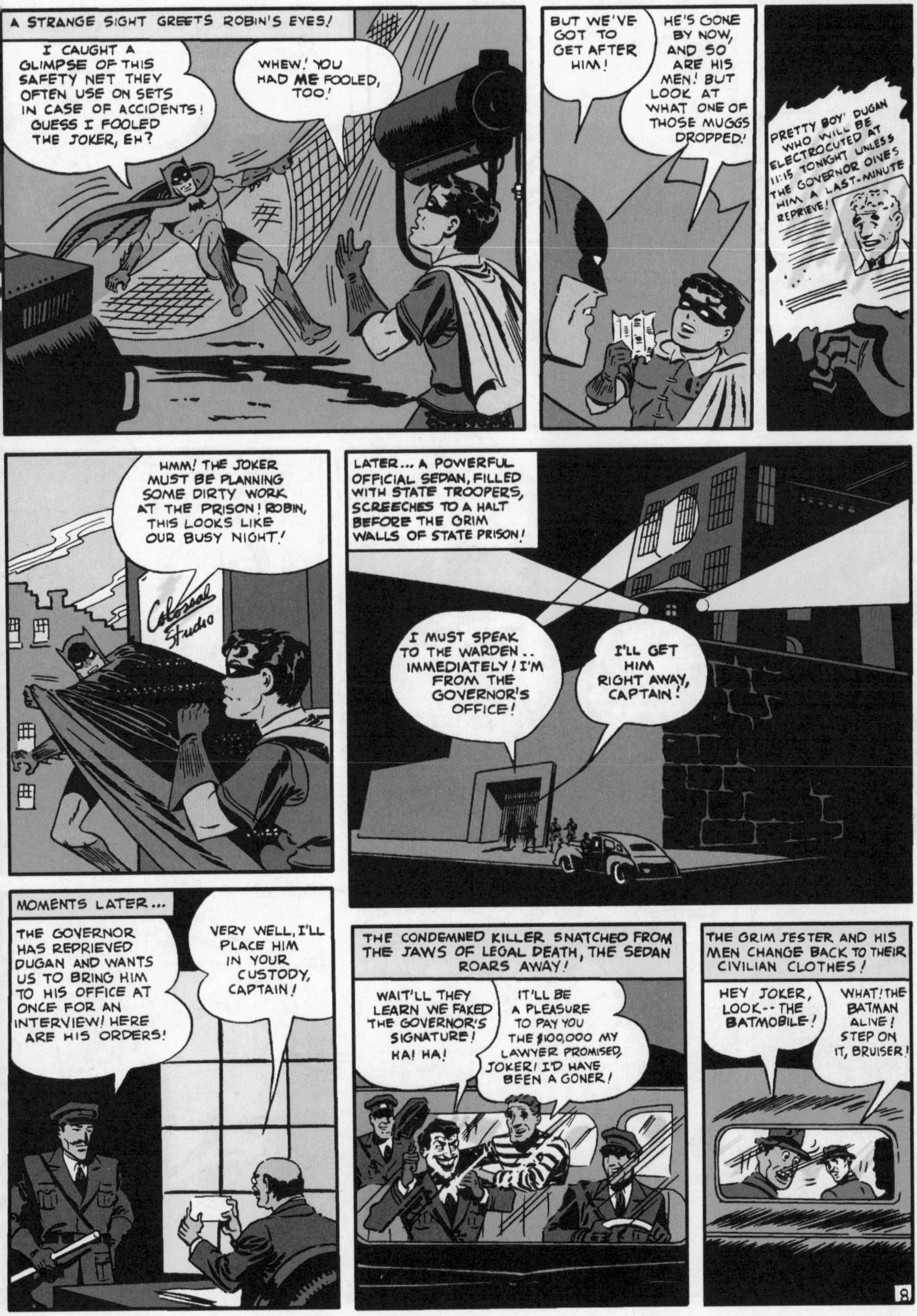
A STRANGE SIGHT GREETS ROBIN'S EYES!
I CAUGHT A GLIMPSE OF THIS SAFETY NET THEY OFTEN USE ON SETS IN CASE OF ACCIDENTS! GUESS I FOOLED THE JOKER, EH?
WHEW! YOU HAD ME FOOLED, TOO!
BUT WE'VE GOT TO GET AFTER HIM!
HE'S GONE BY NOW, AND SO ARE HIS MEN! BUT LOOK AT WHAT ONE OF THOSE MUGGS DROPPED!
PRETTY BOY' DUGAN WHO WILL BE ELECTROCUTED AT 11:15 TONIGHT UNLESS THE GOVERNOR GIVES HIM A LAST-MINUTE REPRIEVE!
HMM! THE JOKER MUST BE PLANNING SOME DIRTY WORK AT THE PRISON! ROBIN, THIS LOOKS LIKE OUR BUSY NIGHT!
Colossal Studio
LATER... A POWERFUL OFFICIAL SEDAN, FILLED WITH STATE TROOPERS, SCREECHES TO A HALT BEFORE THE GRIM WALLS OF STATE PRISON!
I MUST SPEAK TO THE WARDEN.. IMMEDIATELY! I'M FROM THE GOVERNOR'S OFFICE!
I'LL GET HIM RIGHT AWAY, CAPTAIN!
MOMENTS LATER...
THE GOVERNOR HAS REPRIEVED DUGAN AND WANTS US TO BRING HIM TO HIS OFFICE AT ONCE FOR AN INTERVIEW! HERE ARE HIS ORDERS!
VERY WELL, I'LL PLACE HIM IN YOUR CUSTODY, CAPTAIN!
THE CONDEMNED KILLER SNATCHED FROM THE JAWS OF LEGAL DEATH, THE SEDAN ROARS AWAY!
WAIT'LL THEY LEARN WE FAKED THE GOVERNOR'S SIGNATURE! HA! HA!
IT'LL BE A PLEASURE TO PAY YOU THE $100,000 MY LAWYER PROMISED, JOKER! I'D HAVE BEEN A GONER!
THE GRIM JESTER AND HIS MEN CHANGE BACK TO THEIR CIVILIAN CLOTHES!
HEY JOKER, LOOK-- THE BATMOBILE!
WHAT! THE BATMAN ALIVE! STEP ON IT, BRUISER!
8

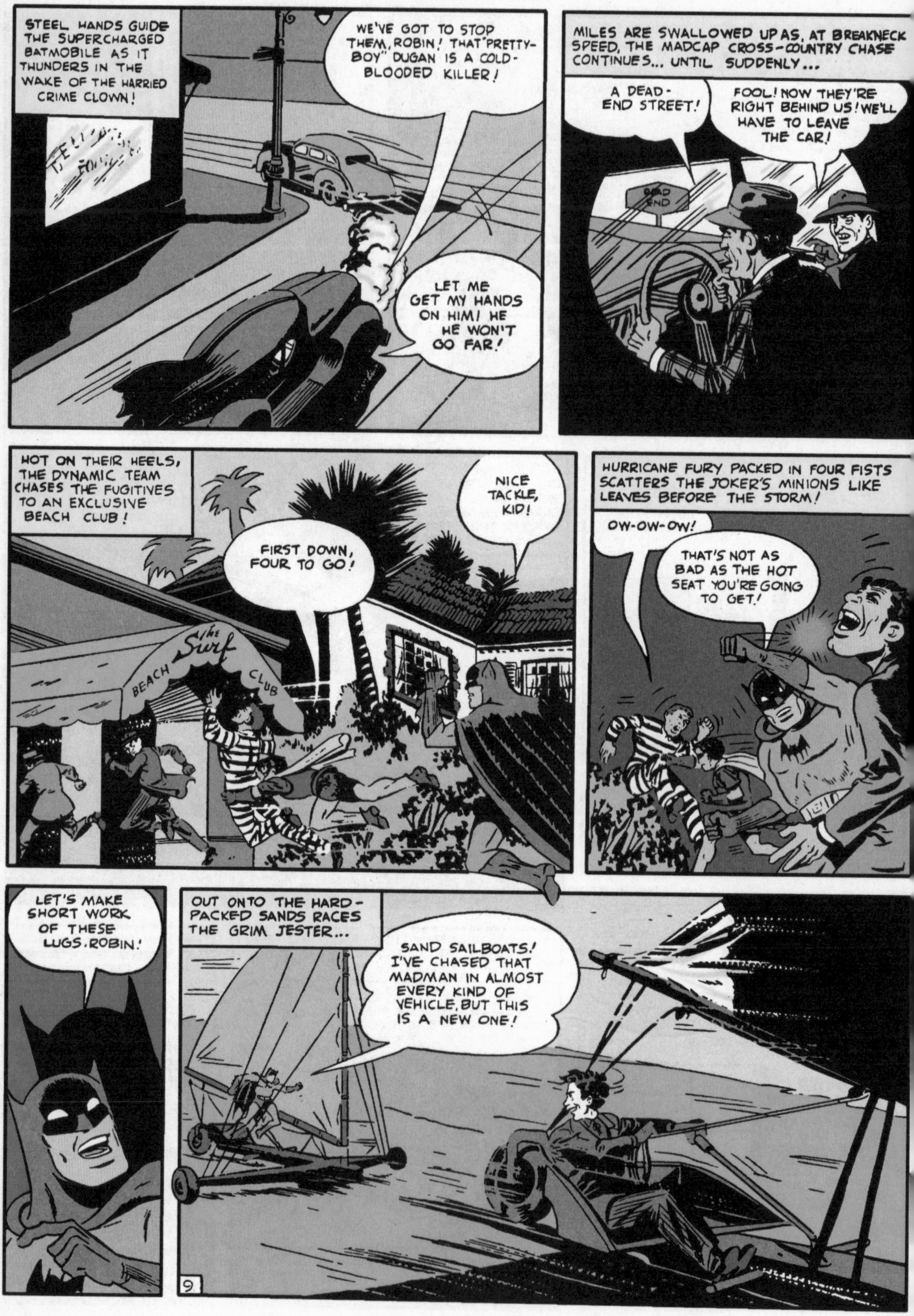
STEEL HANDS GUIDE THE SUPERCHARGED BATMOBILE AS IT THUNDERS IN THE WAKE OF THE HARRIED CRIME CLOWN!
WE'VE GOT TO STOP THEM, ROBIN! THAT "PRETTY-BOY" DUGAN IS A COLD-BLOODED KILLER!
LET ME GET MY HANDS ON HIM! HE HE WON'T GO FAR!
MILES ARE SWALLOWED UP AS, AT BREAKNECK SPEED, THE MADCAP CROSS-COUNTRY CHASE CONTINUES... UNTIL SUDDENLY...
A DEAD-END STREET!
FOOL! NOW THEY'RE RIGHT BEHIND US! WE'LL HAVE TO LEAVE THE CAR!
DEAD END
HOT ON THEIR HEELS, THE DYNAMIC TEAM CHASES THE FUGITIVES TO AN EXCLUSIVE BEACH CLUB!
FIRST DOWN, FOUR TO GO!
NICE TACKLE, KID!
The Surf BEACH CLUB
HURRICANE FURY PACKED IN FOUR FISTS SCATTERS THE JOKER'S MINIONS LIKE LEAVES BEFORE THE STORM!
OW-OW-OW!
THAT'S NOT AS BAD AS THE HOT SEAT YOU'RE GOING TO GET!
LET'S MAKE SHORT WORK OF THESE LUGS, ROBIN!
OUT ONTO THE HARD-PACKED SANDS RACES THE GRIM JESTER...
SAND SAILBOATS! I'VE CHASED THAT MADMAN IN ALMOST EVERY KIND OF VEHICLE, BUT THIS IS A NEW ONE!
9.

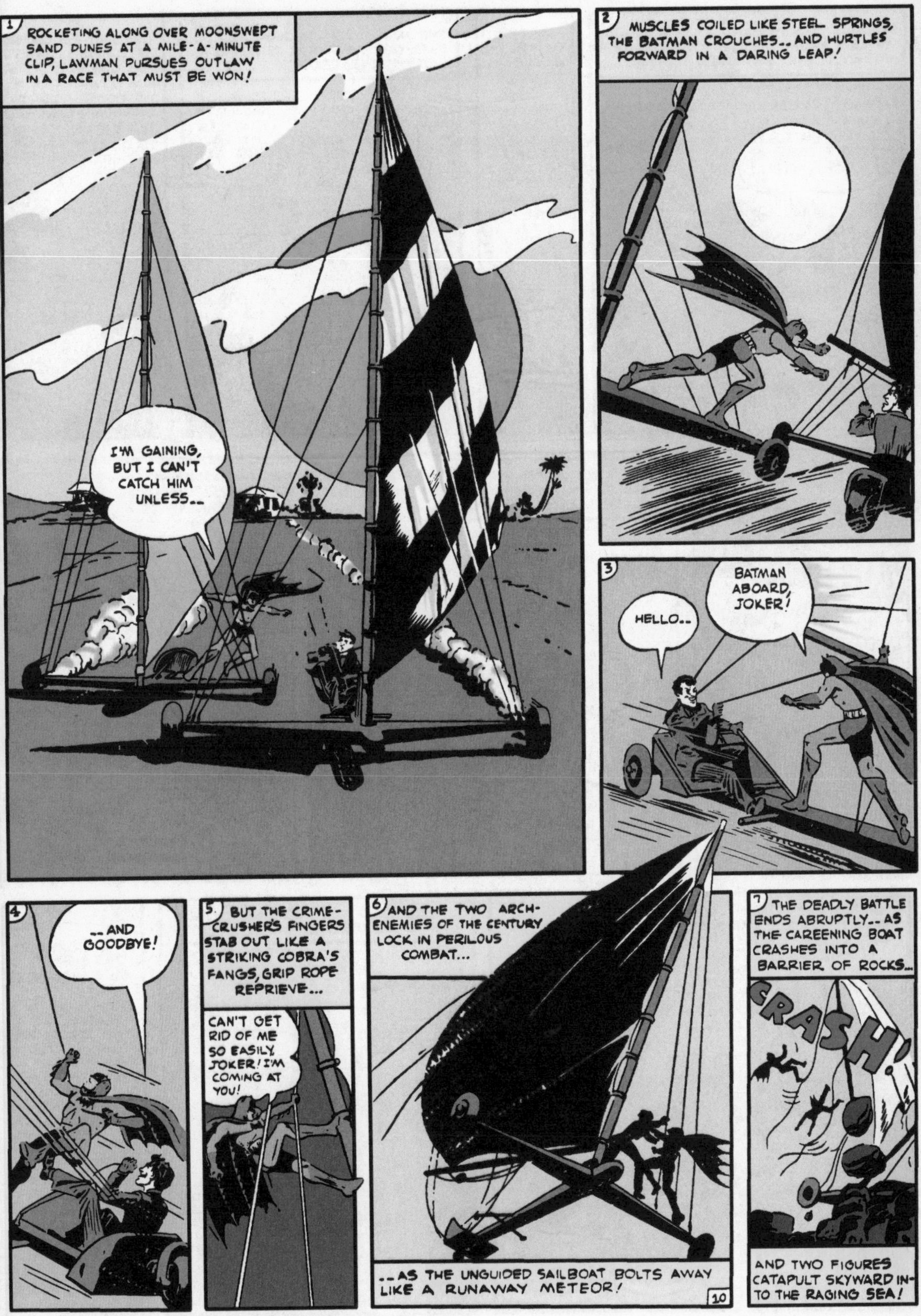
ROCKETING ALONG OVER MOONSWEPT SAND DUNES AT A MILE-A-MINUTE CLIP, LAWMAN PURSUES OUTLAW IN A RACE THAT MUST BE WON!
I'M GAINING, BUT I CAN'T CATCH HIM UNLESS..
MUSCLES COILED LIKE STEEL SPRINGS, THE BATMAN CROUCHES.. AND HURTLES FORWARD IN A DARING LEAP!
HELLO..
BATMAN ABOARD, JOKER!
..AND GOODBYE!
BUT THE CRIME-CRUSHER'S FINGERS STAB OUT LIKE A STRIKING COBRA'S FANGS, GRIP ROPE REPRIEVE...
CAN'T GET RID OF ME SO EASILY, JOKER! I'M COMING AT YOU!
AND THE TWO ARCH-ENEMIES OF THE CENTURY LOCK IN PERILOUS COMBAT...
..AS THE UNGUIDED SAILBOAT BOLTS AWAY LIKE A RUNAWAY METEOR!
10
THE DEADLY BATTLE ENDS ABRUPTLY.. AS THE CAREENING BOAT CRASHES INTO A BARRIER OF ROCKS..
CRASH!
AND TWO FIGURES CATAPULT SKYWARD INTO THE RAGING SEA!

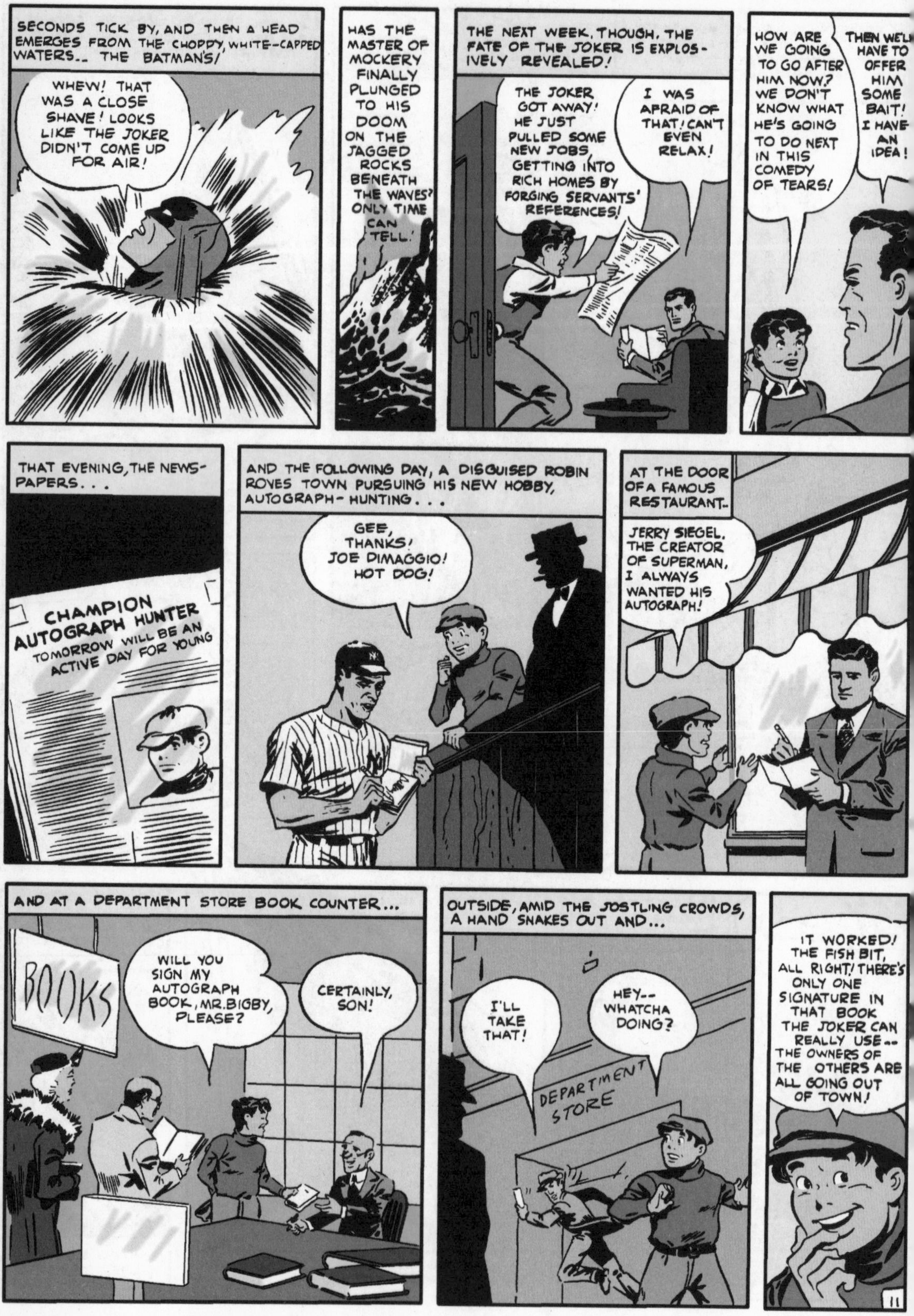
SECONDS TICK BY, AND THEN A HEAD EMERGES FROM THE CHOPPY, WHITE-CAPPED WATERS.. THE BATMAN'S!
WHEW! THAT WAS A CLOSE SHAVE! LOOKS LIKE THE JOKER DIDN'T COME UP FOR AIR!
HAS THE MASTER OF MOCKERY FINALLY PLUNGED TO HIS DOOM ON THE JAGGED ROCKS BENEATH THE WAVES? ONLY TIME CAN TELL.
THE NEXT WEEK, THOUGH, THE FATE OF THE JOKER IS EXPLOSIVELY REVEALED!
THE JOKER GOT AWAY! HE JUST PULLED SOME NEW JOBS, GETTING INTO RICH HOMES BY FORGING SERVANTS' REFERENCES!
I WAS AFRAID OF THAT! CAN'T EVEN RELAX!
HOW ARE WE GOING TO GO AFTER HIM NOW? WE DON'T KNOW WHAT HE'S GOING TO DO NEXT IN THIS COMEDY OF TEARS!
THEN WE'LL HAVE TO OFFER HIM SOME BAIT! I HAVE AN IDEA!
THAT EVENING, THE NEWSPAPERS...
CHAMPION AUTOGRAPH HUNTER
TOMORROW WILL BE AN ACTIVE DAY FOR YOUNG
AND THE FOLLOWING DAY, A DISGUISED ROBIN ROVES TOWN PURSUING HIS NEW HOBBY, AUTOGRAPH-HUNTING...
GEE, THANKS! JOE DIMAGGIO! HOT DOG!
AT THE DOOR OF A FAMOUS RESTAURANT..
JERRY SIEGEL, THE CREATOR OF SUPERMAN, I ALWAYS WANTED HIS AUTOGRAPH!
AND AT A DEPARTMENT STORE BOOK COUNTER...
BOOKS
WILL YOU SIGN MY AUTOGRAPH BOOK, MR. BIGBY, PLEASE?
CERTAINLY, SON!
OUTSIDE, AMID THE JOSTLING CROWDS, A HAND SNAKES OUT AND...
I'LL TAKE THAT!
HEY-- WHATCHA DOING?
DEPARTMENT STORE
IT WORKED! THE FISH BIT, ALL RIGHT! THERE'S ONLY ONE SIGNATURE IN THAT BOOK THE JOKER CAN REALLY USE-- THE OWNERS OF THE OTHERS ARE ALL GOING OUT OF TOWN!
11

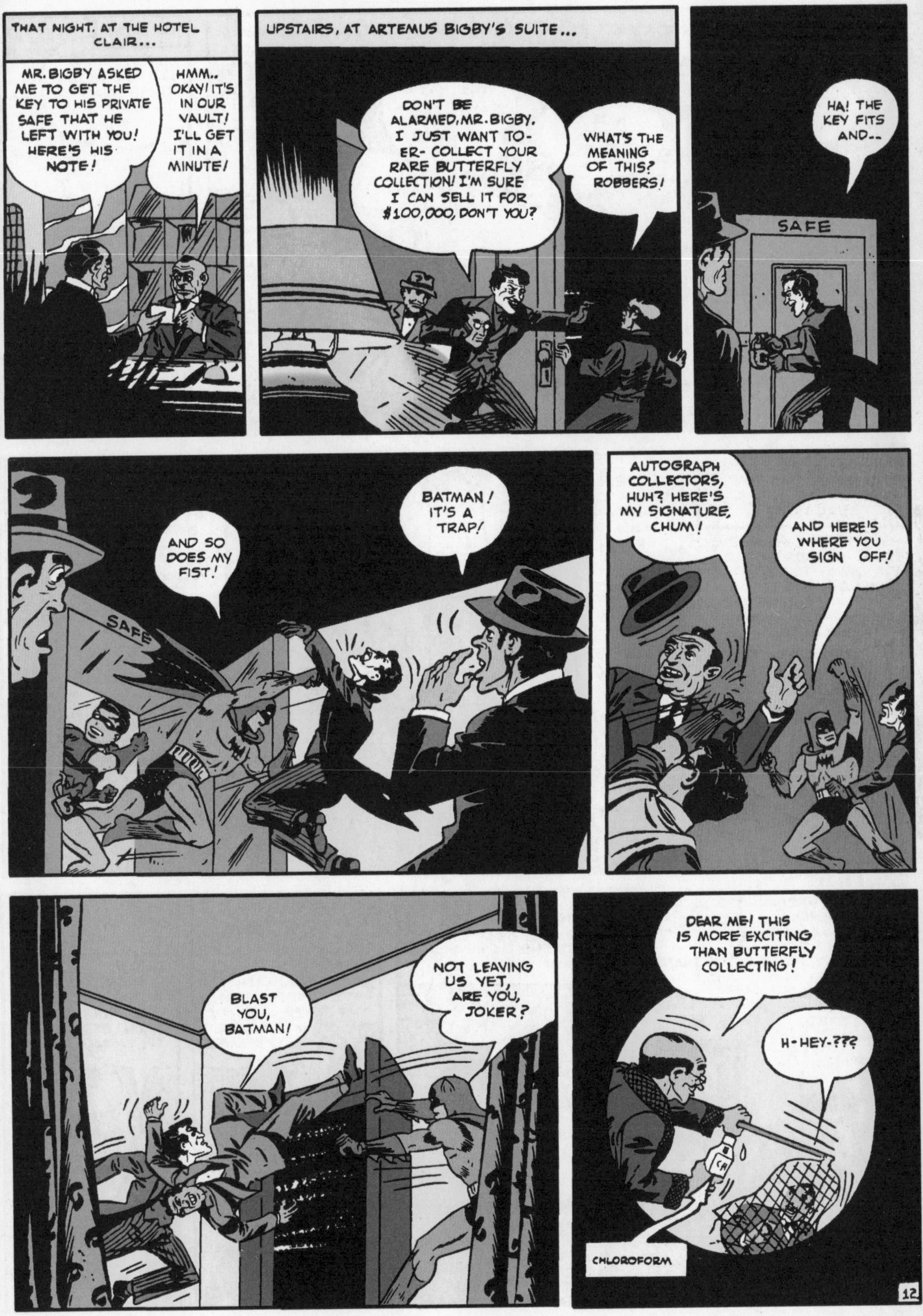
THAT NIGHT. AT THE HOTEL CLAIR...
MR. BIGBY ASKED ME TO GET THE KEY TO HIS PRIVATE SAFE THAT HE LEFT WITH YOU! HERE'S HIS NOTE!
HMM.. OKAY! IT'S IN OUR VAULT! I'LL GET IT IN A MINUTE!
UPSTAIRS, AT ARTEMUS BIGBY'S SUITE...
DON'T BE ALARMED, MR. BIGBY. I JUST WANT TO- ER- COLLECT YOUR RARE BUTTERFLY COLLECTION! I'M SURE I CAN SELL IT FOR $100,000, DON'T YOU?
WHAT'S THE MEANING OF THIS? ROBBERS!
HA! THE KEY FITS AND--
SAFE
AND SO DOES MY FIST!
BATMAN! IT'S A TRAP!
SAFE
AUTOGRAPH COLLECTORS, HUH? HERE'S MY SIGNATURE, CHUM!
AND HERE'S WHERE YOU SIGN OFF!
BLAST YOU, BATMAN!
NOT LEAVING US YET, ARE YOU, JOKER?
DEAR ME! THIS IS MORE EXCITING THAN BUTTERFLY COLLECTING!
H-HEY-???
CHLOROFORM
12

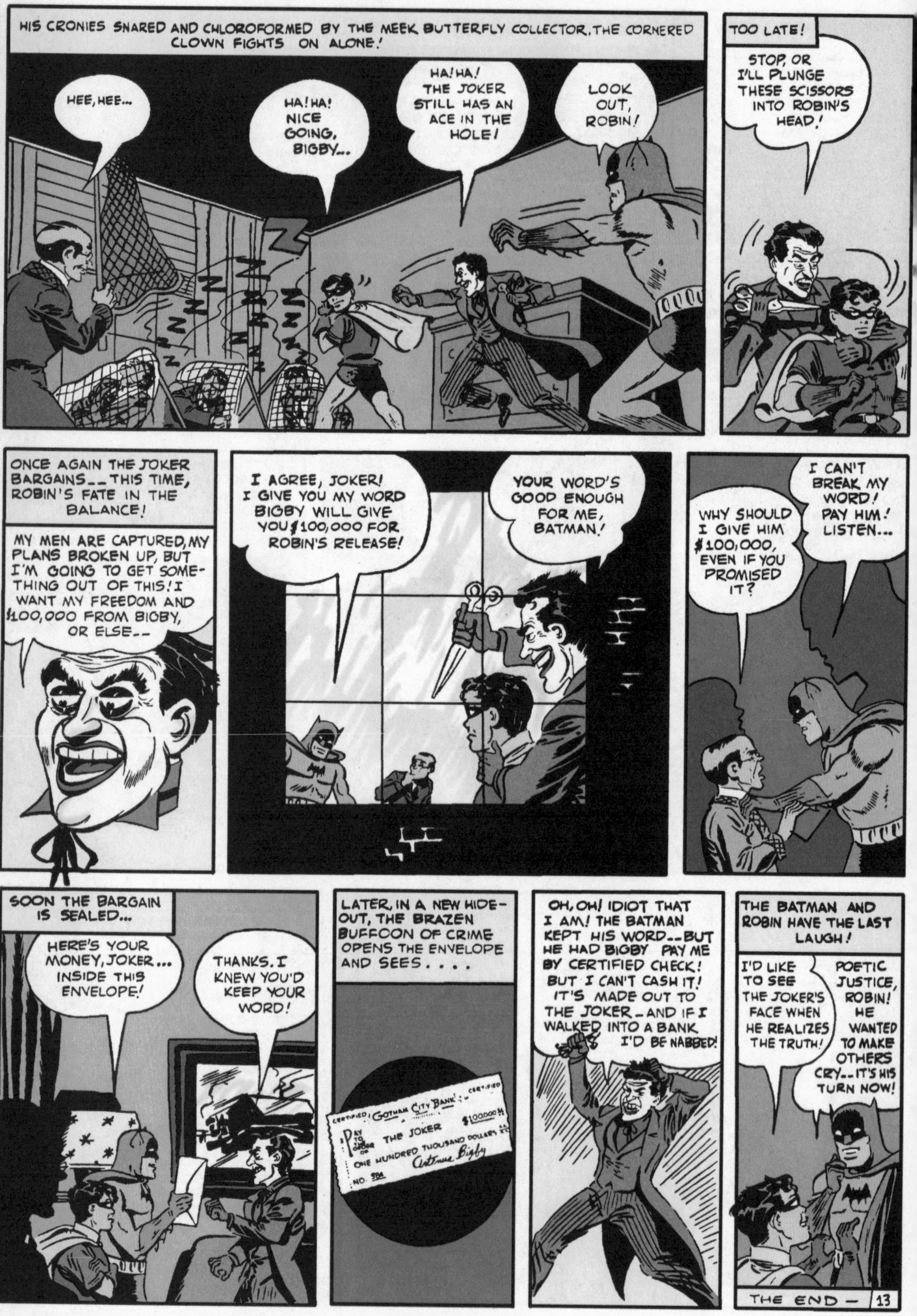
HIS CRONIES SNARED AND CHLOROFORMED BY THE MEEK BUTTERFLY COLLECTOR, THE CORNERED CLOWN FIGHTS ON ALONE!
HEE, HEE...
HA! HA! NICE GOING, BIGBY...
HA! HA! THE JOKER STILL HAS AN ACE IN THE HOLE!
LOOK OUT, ROBIN!
TOO LATE!
STOP, OR I'LL PLUNGE THESE SCISSORS INTO ROBIN'S HEAD!
ONCE AGAIN THE JOKER BARGAINS-- THIS TIME, ROBIN'S FATE IN THE BALANCE!
MY MEN ARE CAPTURED, MY PLANS BROKEN UP, BUT I'M GOING TO GET SOMETHING OUT OF THIS! I WANT MY FREEDOM AND $100,000 FROM BIGBY, OR ELSE--
I AGREE, JOKER! I GIVE YOU MY WORD BIGBY WILL GIVE YOU $100,000 FOR ROBIN'S RELEASE!
YOUR WORD'S GOOD ENOUGH FOR ME, BATMAN!
WHY SHOULD I GIVE HIM $100,000, EVEN IF YOU PROMISED IT?
I CAN'T BREAK MY WORD! PAY HIM! LISTEN...
SOON THE BARGAIN IS SEALED...
HERE'S YOUR MONEY, JOKER... INSIDE THIS ENVELOPE!
THANKS. I KNEW YOU'D KEEP YOUR WORD!
LATER, IN A NEW HIDE-OUT, THE BRAZEN BUFFOON OF CRIME OPENS THE ENVELOPE AND SEES . . . .
CERTIFIED GOTHAM CITY BANK CERTIFIED
PAY TO THE ORDER OF THE JOKER $100,000
ONE HUNDRED THOUSAND DOLLARS
NO. 304
OH, OH! IDIOT THAT I AM! THE BATMAN KEPT HIS WORD--BUT HE HAD BIGBY PAY ME BY CERTIFIED CHECK! BUT I CAN'T CASH IT! IT'S MADE OUT TO THE JOKER - AND IF I WALKED INTO A BANK I'D BE NABBED!
THE BATMAN AND ROBIN HAVE THE LAST LAUGH!
I'D LIKE TO SEE THE JOKER'S FACE WHEN HE REALIZES THE TRUTH!
POETIC JUSTICE, ROBIN! HE WANTED TO MAKE OTHERS CRY--IT'S HIS TURN NOW!
THE END - 13

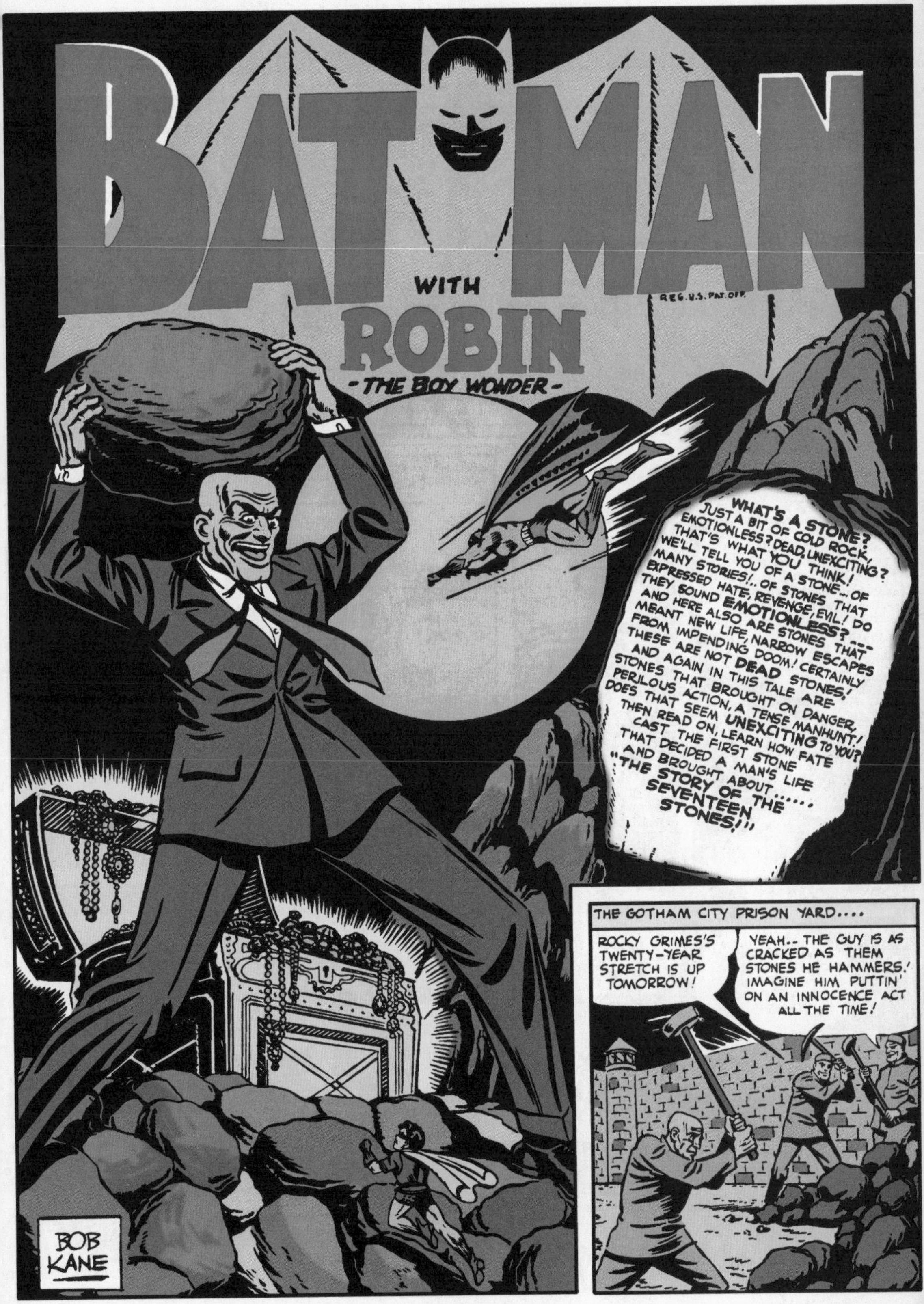
BATMAN
WITH
ROBIN
-THE BOY WONDER-
REG. U.S. PAT. OFF.
WHAT'S A STONE? JUST A BIT OF COLD ROCK, EMOTIONLESS? DEAD, UNEXCITING? THAT'S WHAT YOU THINK! WE'LL TELL YOU OF A STONE... OF MANY STORIES!.. OF STONES THAT EXPRESSED HATE, REVENGE, EVIL! DO THEY SOUND EMOTIONLESS? --- AND HERE ALSO ARE STONES THAT MEANT NEW LIFE, NARROW ESCAPES FROM IMPENDING DOOM! CERTAINLY THESE ARE NOT DEAD STONES! AND AGAIN IN THIS TALE ARE STONES THAT BROUGHT ON DANGER, PERILOUS ACTION, A TENSE MANHUNT! DOES THAT SEEM UNEXCITING TO YOU? THEN READ ON, LEARN HOW FATE CAST THE FIRST STONE THAT DECIDED A MAN'S LIFE AND BROUGHT ABOUT..... "THE STORY OF THE SEVENTEEN STONES!"
BOB KANE
THE GOTHAM CITY PRISON YARD....
ROCKY GRIMES'S TWENTY-YEAR STRETCH IS UP TOMORROW!
YEAH.. THE GUY IS AS CRACKED AS THEM STONES HE HAMMERS! IMAGINE HIM PUTTIN' ON AN INNOCENCE ACT ALL THE TIME!

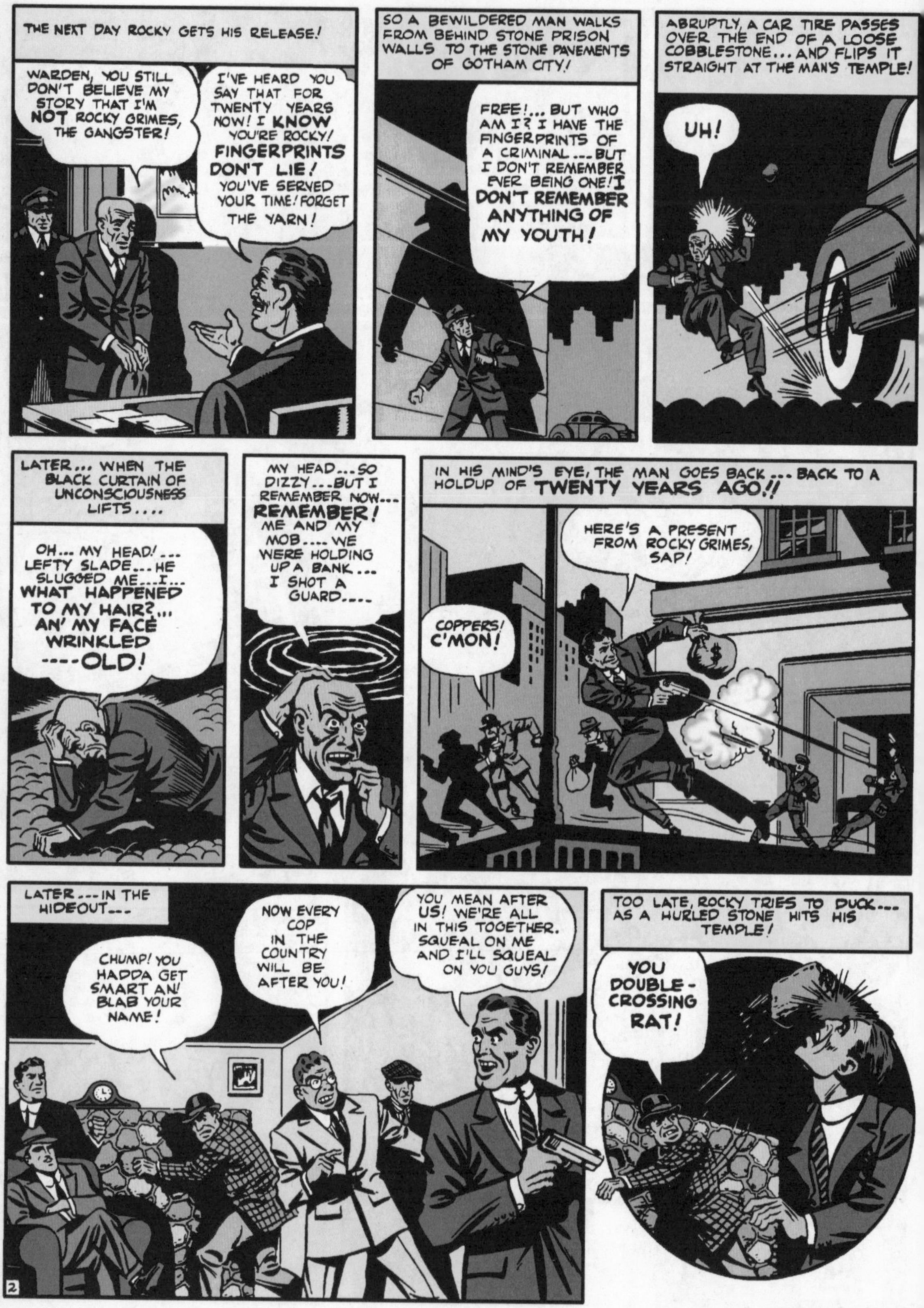

THE NEXT DAY ROCKY GETS HIS RELEASE!
WARDEN, YOU STILL DON'T BELIEVE MY STORY THAT I'M NOT ROCKY GRIMES, THE GANGSTER!
I'VE HEARD YOU SAY THAT FOR TWENTY YEARS NOW! I KNOW YOU'RE ROCKY! FINGERPRINTS DON'T LIE! YOU'VE SERVED YOUR TIME! FORGET THE YARN!
SO A BEWILDERED MAN WALKS FROM BEHIND STONE PRISON WALLS TO THE STONE PAVEMENTS OF GOTHAM CITY!
FREE!... BUT WHO AM I? I HAVE THE FINGERPRINTS OF A CRIMINAL... BUT I DON'T REMEMBER EVER BEING ONE! I DON'T REMEMBER ANYTHING OF MY YOUTH!
ABRUPTLY, A CAR TIRE PASSES OVER THE END OF A LOOSE COBBLESTONE... AND FLIPS IT STRAIGHT AT THE MAN'S TEMPLE!
UH!
LATER... WHEN THE BLACK CURTAIN OF UNCONSCIOUSNESS LIFTS....
OH... MY HEAD!... LEFTY SLADE... HE SLUGGED ME... I... WHAT HAPPENED TO MY HAIR?... AN' MY FACE WRINKLED ----OLD!
MY HEAD... SO DIZZY... BUT I REMEMBER NOW... REMEMBER! ME AND MY MOB.... WE WERE HOLDING UP A BANK... I SHOT A GUARD....
IN HIS MIND'S EYE, THE MAN GOES BACK... BACK TO A HOLDUP OF TWENTY YEARS AGO!!
HERE'S A PRESENT FROM ROCKY GRIMES, SAP!
COPPERS! C'MON!
LATER... IN THE HIDEOUT...
CHUMP! YOU HADDA GET SMART AN' BLAB YOUR NAME!
NOW EVERY COP IN THE COUNTRY WILL BE AFTER YOU!
YOU MEAN AFTER US! WE'RE ALL IN THIS TOGETHER. SQUEAL ON ME AND I'LL SQUEAL ON YOU GUYS!
TOO LATE, ROCKY TRIES TO DUCK... AS A HURLED STONE HITS HIS TEMPLE!
YOU DOUBLE-CROSSING RAT!
2

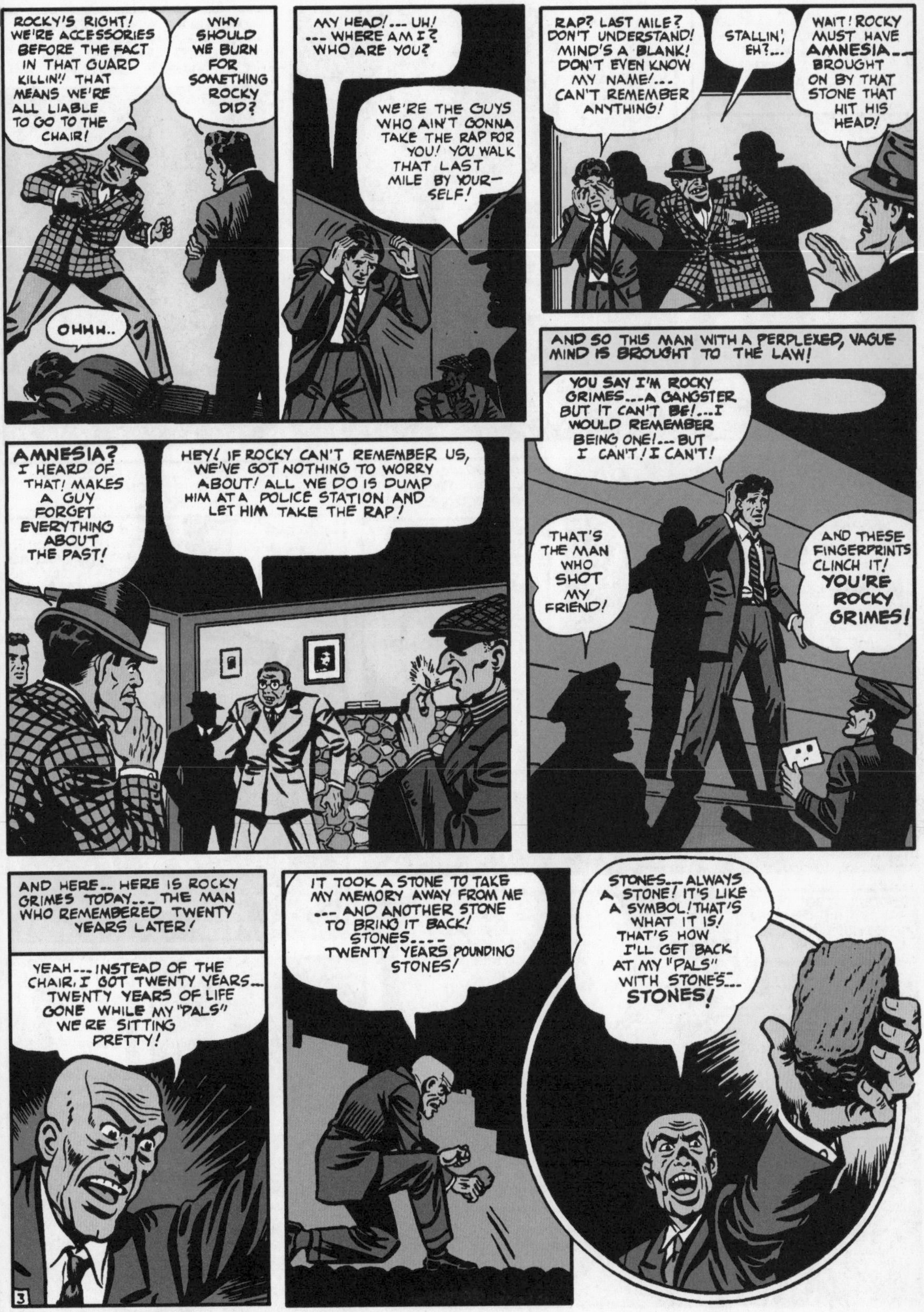
ROCKY'S RIGHT! WE'RE ACCESSORIES BEFORE THE FACT IN THAT GUARD KILLIN'! THAT MEANS WE'RE ALL LIABLE TO GO TO THE CHAIR!
WHY SHOULD WE BURN FOR SOMETHING ROCKY DID?
OHHH..
MY HEAD!--- UH! --- WHERE AM I? WHO ARE YOU?
WE'RE THE GUYS WHO AIN'T GONNA TAKE THE RAP FOR YOU! YOU WALK THAT LAST MILE BY YOURSELF!
RAP? LAST MILE? DON'T UNDERSTAND! MIND'S A BLANK! DON'T EVEN KNOW MY NAME!--- CAN'T REMEMBER ANYTHING!
STALLIN', EH?...
WAIT! ROCKY MUST HAVE AMNESIA-- BROUGHT ON BY THAT STONE THAT HIT HIS HEAD!
AMNESIA? I HEARD OF THAT! MAKES A GUY FORGET EVERYTHING ABOUT THE PAST!
HEY! IF ROCKY CAN'T REMEMBER US, WE'VE GOT NOTHING TO WORRY ABOUT! ALL WE DO IS DUMP HIM AT A POLICE STATION AND LET HIM TAKE THE RAP!
AND SO THIS MAN WITH A PERPLEXED, VAGUE MIND IS BROUGHT TO THE LAW!
YOU SAY I'M ROCKY GRIMES...A GANGSTER BUT IT CAN'T BE!...I WOULD REMEMBER BEING ONE!... BUT I CAN'T! I CAN'T!
THAT'S THE MAN WHO SHOT MY FRIEND!
AND THESE FINGERPRINTS CLINCH IT! YOU'RE ROCKY GRIMES!
AND HERE.. HERE IS ROCKY GRIMES TODAY... THE MAN WHO REMEMBERED TWENTY YEARS LATER!
YEAH --- INSTEAD OF THE CHAIR, I GOT TWENTY YEARS... TWENTY YEARS OF LIFE GONE WHILE MY "PALS" WERE SITTING PRETTY!
3
IT TOOK A STONE TO TAKE MY MEMORY AWAY FROM ME --- AND ANOTHER STONE TO BRING IT BACK! STONES.... TWENTY YEARS POUNDING STONES!
STONES--- ALWAYS A STONE! IT'S LIKE A SYMBOL! THAT'S WHAT IT IS! THAT'S HOW I'LL GET BACK AT MY "PALS" WITH STONES... STONES!

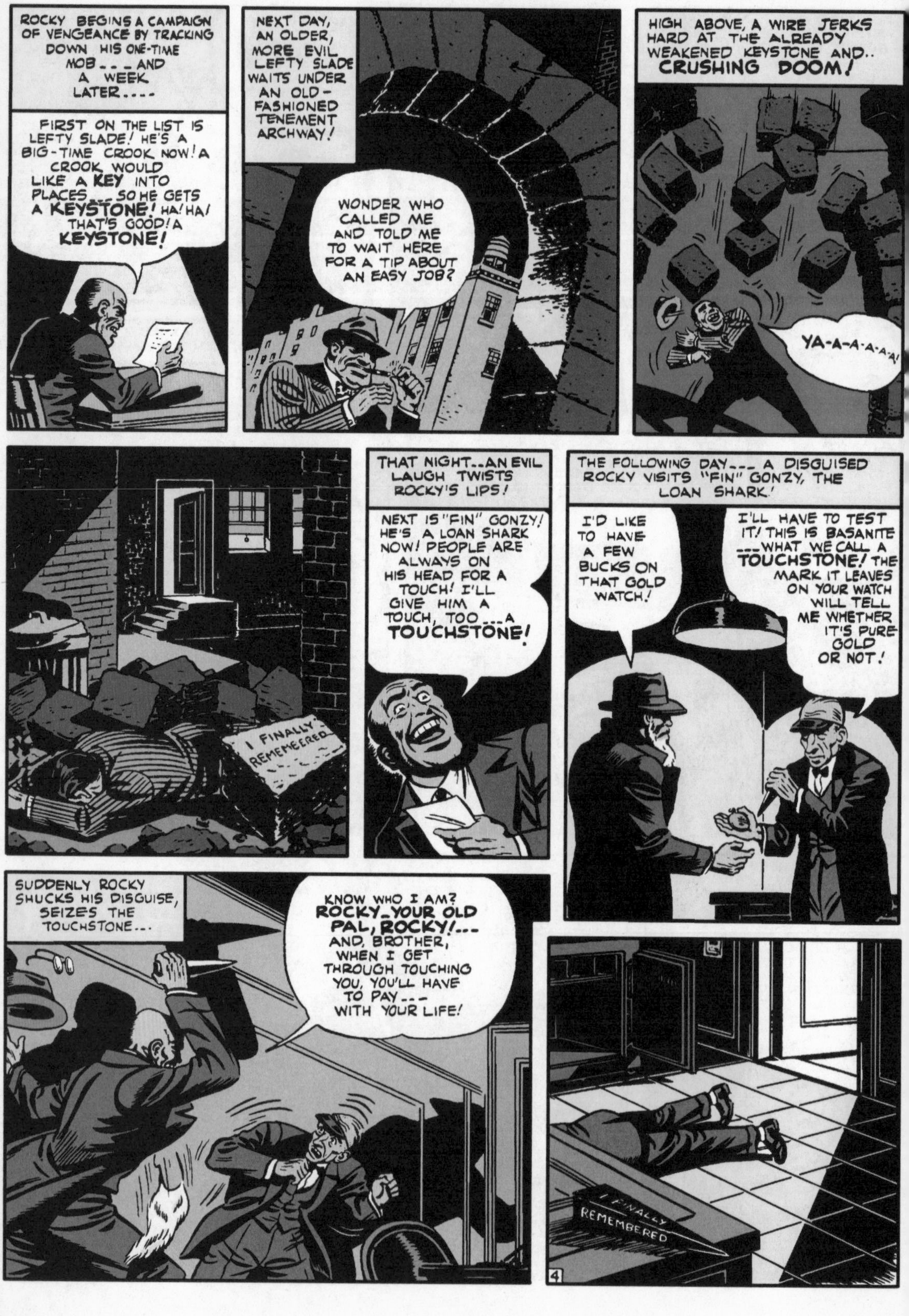
ROCKY BEGINS A CAMPAIGN OF VENGEANCE BY TRACKING DOWN HIS ONE-TIME MOB - - - AND A WEEK LATER - - -
FIRST ON THE LIST IS LEFTY SLADE! HE'S A BIG-TIME CROOK NOW! A CROOK WOULD LIKE A KEY INTO PLACES... SO HE GETS A KEYSTONE! HA! HA! THAT'S GOOD! A KEYSTONE!
NEXT DAY, AN OLDER, MORE EVIL LEFTY SLADE WAITS UNDER AN OLD-FASHIONED TENEMENT ARCHWAY!
WONDER WHO CALLED ME AND TOLD ME TO WAIT HERE FOR A TIP ABOUT AN EASY JOB?
HIGH ABOVE, A WIRE JERKS HARD AT THE ALREADY WEAKENED KEYSTONE AND.. CRUSHING DOOM!
YA-A-A-A-A-A-A!
I FINALLY REMEMBERED
THAT NIGHT..AN EVIL LAUGH TWISTS ROCKY'S LIPS!
NEXT IS "FIN" GONZY! HE'S A LOAN SHARK NOW! PEOPLE ARE ALWAYS ON HIS HEAD FOR A TOUCH! I'LL GIVE HIM A TOUCH, TOO... A TOUCHSTONE!
THE FOLLOWING DAY--- A DISGUISED ROCKY VISITS "FIN" GONZY, THE LOAN SHARK!
I'D LIKE TO HAVE A FEW BUCKS ON THAT GOLD WATCH!
I'LL HAVE TO TEST IT! THIS IS BASANITE ---WHAT WE CALL A TOUCHSTONE! THE MARK IT LEAVES ON YOUR WATCH WILL TELL ME WHETHER IT'S PURE GOLD OR NOT!
SUDDENLY ROCKY SHUCKS HIS DISGUISE, SEIZES THE TOUCHSTONE...
KNOW WHO I AM? ROCKY-YOUR OLD PAL, ROCKY!... AND, BROTHER, WHEN I GET THROUGH TOUCHING YOU, YOU'LL HAVE TO PAY... WITH YOUR LIFE!
I FINALLY REMEMBERED
4

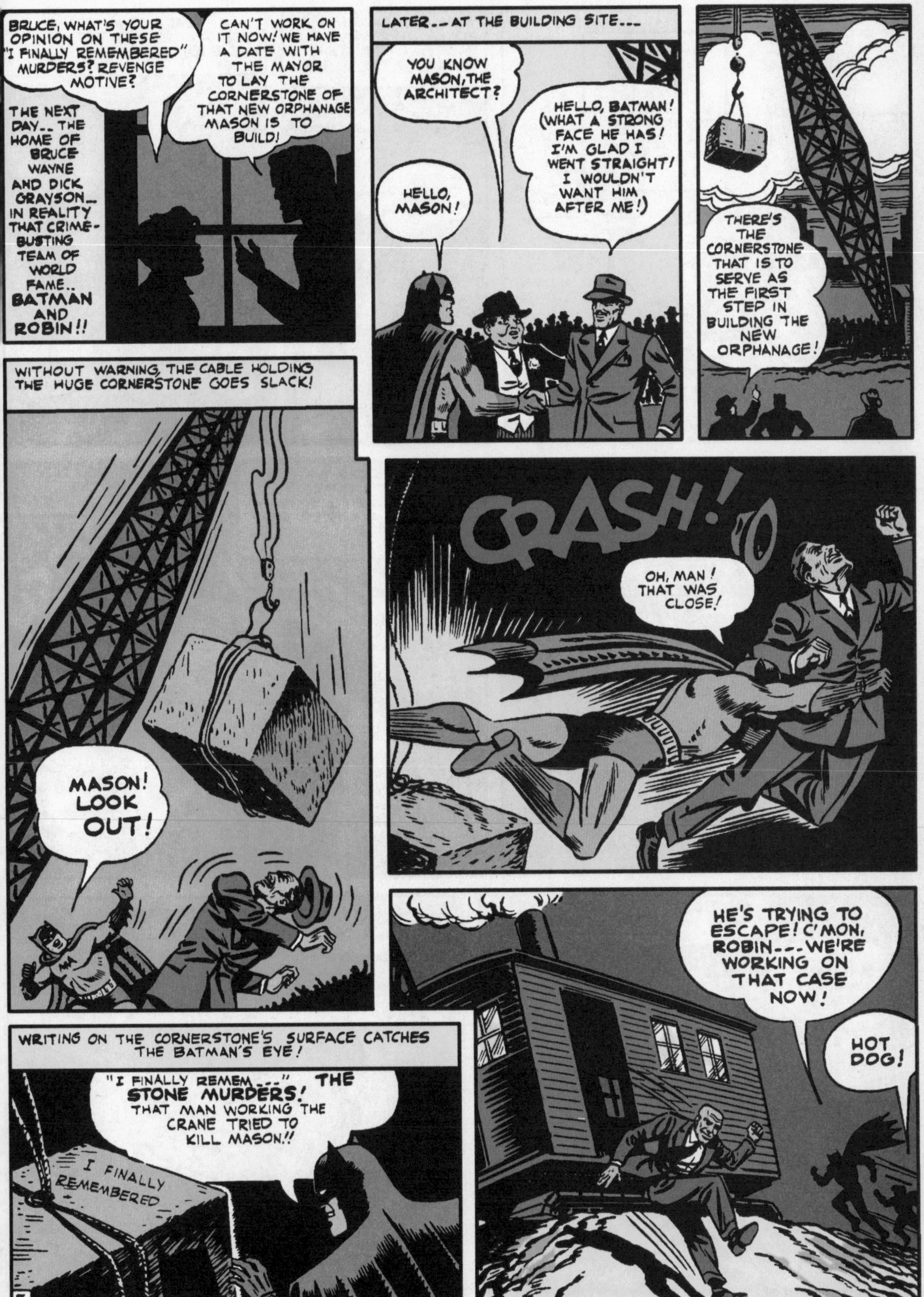

BRUCE, WHAT'S YOUR OPINION ON THESE "I FINALLY REMEMBERED" MURDERS? REVENGE MOTIVE?
CAN'T WORK ON IT NOW! WE HAVE A DATE WITH THE MAYOR TO LAY THE CORNERSTONE OF THAT NEW ORPHANAGE MASON IS TO BUILD!
THE NEXT DAY.. THE HOME OF BRUCE WAYNE AND DICK GRAYSON.. IN REALITY THAT CRIME-BUSTING TEAM OF WORLD FAME.. BATMAN AND ROBIN!!
LATER..-AT THE BUILDING SITE...
YOU KNOW MASON, THE ARCHITECT?
HELLO, MASON!
HELLO, BATMAN! (WHAT A STRONG FACE HE HAS! I'M GLAD I WENT STRAIGHT! I WOULDN'T WANT HIM AFTER ME!)
THERE'S THE CORNERSTONE THAT IS TO SERVE AS THE FIRST STEP IN BUILDING THE NEW ORPHANAGE!
WITHOUT WARNING, THE CABLE HOLDING THE HUGE CORNERSTONE GOES SLACK!
MASON! LOOK OUT!
CRASH!
OH, MAN! THAT WAS CLOSE!
WRITING ON THE CORNERSTONE'S SURFACE CATCHES THE BATMAN'S EYE!
"I FINALLY REMEM..." THE STONE MURDERS! THAT MAN WORKING THE CRANE TRIED TO KILL MASON!!
I FINALLY REMEMBERED
5
HE'S TRYING TO ESCAPE! C'MON, ROBIN...WE'RE WORKING ON THAT CASE NOW!
HOT DOG!

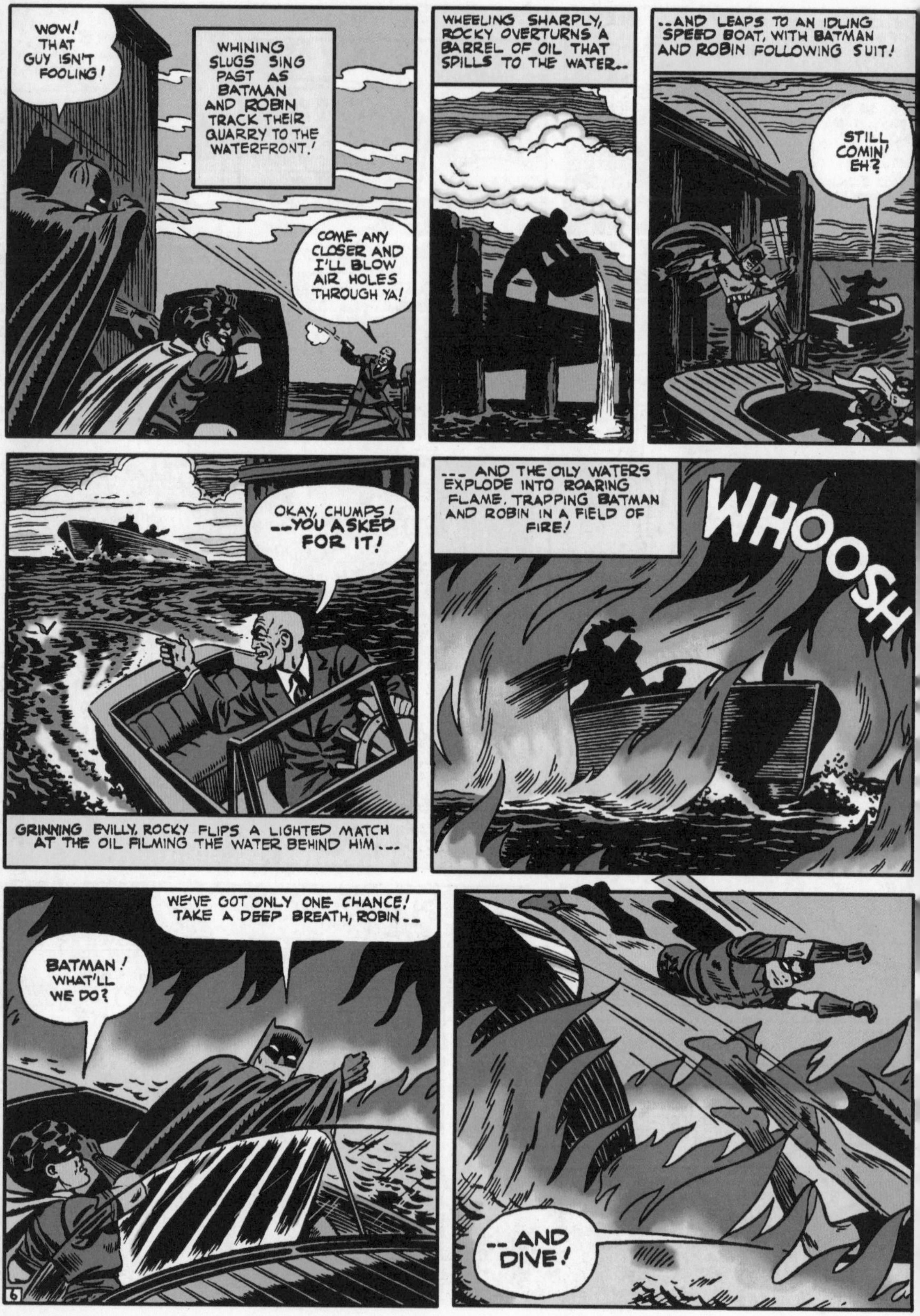
WOW! THAT GUY ISN'T FOOLING!
WHINING SLUGS SING PAST AS BATMAN AND ROBIN TRACK THEIR QUARRY TO THE WATERFRONT!
COME ANY CLOSER AND I'LL BLOW AIR HOLES THROUGH YA!
WHEELING SHARPLY, ROCKY OVERTURNS A BARREL OF OIL THAT SPILLS TO THE WATER..
..AND LEAPS TO AN IDLING SPEED BOAT, WITH BATMAN AND ROBIN FOLLOWING SUIT!
STILL COMIN' EH?
OKAY, CHUMPS! --YOU ASKED FOR IT!
GRINNING EVILLY, ROCKY FLIPS A LIGHTED MATCH AT THE OIL FILMING THE WATER BEHIND HIM...
... AND THE OILY WATERS EXPLODE INTO ROARING FLAME, TRAPPING BATMAN AND ROBIN IN A FIELD OF FIRE!
WHOOSH
BATMAN! WHAT'LL WE DO?
WE'VE GOT ONLY ONE CHANCE! TAKE A DEEP BREATH, ROBIN--
--AND DIVE!

SWIMMING DEEP UNDER THE WATERY INFERNO, BATMAN AND ROBIN SEARCH FOR THE END OF THE DANGER ZONE!

HOPE THE BREAK ISN'T TOO FAR...

I CAN'T HOLD MY BREATH MUCH LONGER...

PRESENTLY TWO HEADS POKE UP INTO FRESH AIR...BEYOND THE BLAZING OIL!

AH!...FRESH AIR!..UH...UH-- SEE ANYTHING OF THE BABY WE WERE CHASING?

NOT A SIGN! HE SURE PULLED A FAST ONE ON US!

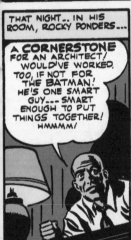

THAT NIGHT.. IN HIS ROOM, ROCKY PONDERS...

A CORNERSTONE FOR AN ARCHITECT! WOULD'VE WORKED, TOO, IF NOT FOR THE BATMAN! HE'S ONE SMART GUY---SMART ENOUGH TO PUT THINGS TOGETHER! HMMMM!

AND AT THAT MOMENT, BATMAN BEARS OUT ROCKY'S THOUGHTS!

ROBIN, THERE'S ONE LINK THAT TIES THIS CASE TOGETHER! STONES! STONES NEARLY KILLED ONE MAN-- CAUSED THE DEATH OF TWO OTHER CRIMINALS!

THEN LET'S LOOK UP THE RECORDS OF THOSE CRIMINALS, FIND OUT WHAT THESE MEN HAD IN COMMON --- AND PRESTO! WE'LL HAVE OUR MURDERER!

LATER ... POLICE HEADQUARTERS ---

HELLO, GORDON! SAY, IS SOMETHING WRONG?

PLENTY! SOME MASKED MAN WALKED IN HERE, THREATENED US WITH A TOMMY GUN, TOOK SOME CARDS FROM THE CRIMINAL FILE AND BURNED THEM!

THERE'S THE REMAINS OF THE CARDS!

GODON, I'VE A HUNCH ABOUT THAT MASKED MAN! I'M GOING TO USE YOUR LABORATORY AND FIND OUT WHAT WAS ON THOSE CARDS!

BUT-- BUT THOSE CARDS ARE BURNED...CHARRED! IT'S IMPOSSIBLE TO READ WHAT WAS ON THEM!

THAT'S WHAT YOU THINK! STICK AROUND AND KEEP YOUR EYES OPEN! YOU'RE GOING TO LEARN SOMETHING!

FIRST WE PLACE THE CHARRED CARDS ON A FLAT PLATE OF GLASS... AND OVER THIS WE PLACE A GLASS DOME WITH A SMALL OPENING AT THE TOP..

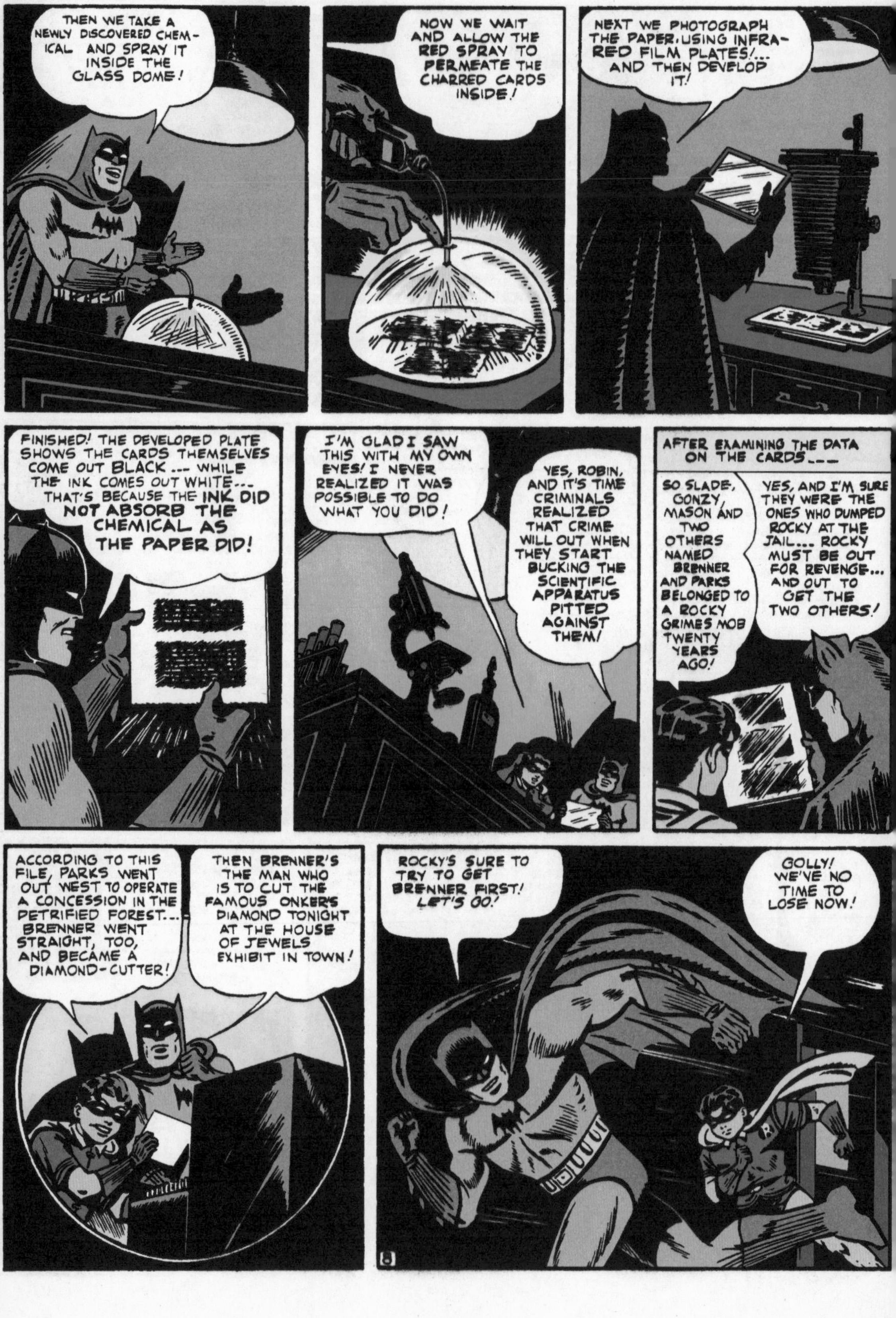

THEN WE TAKE A NEWLY DISCOVERED CHEMICAL AND SPRAY IT INSIDE THE GLASS DOME!
NOW WE WAIT AND ALLOW THE RED SPRAY TO PERMEATE THE CHARRED CARDS INSIDE!
NEXT WE PHOTOGRAPH THE PAPER, USING INFRA-RED FILM PLATES!... AND THEN DEVELOP IT!
FINISHED! THE DEVELOPED PLATE SHOWS THE CARDS THEMSELVES COME OUT BLACK --- WHILE THE INK COMES OUT WHITE--- THAT'S BECAUSE THE INK DID NOT ABSORB THE CHEMICAL AS THE PAPER DID!
I'M GLAD I SAW THIS WITH MY OWN EYES! I NEVER REALIZED IT WAS POSSIBLE TO DO WHAT YOU DID!
YES, ROBIN, AND IT'S TIME CRIMINALS REALIZED THAT CRIME WILL OUT WHEN THEY START BUCKING THE SCIENTIFIC APPARATUS PITTED AGAINST THEM!
AFTER EXAMINING THE DATA ON THE CARDS---
SO SLADE, GONZY, MASON AND TWO OTHERS NAMED BRENNER AND PARKS BELONGED TO A ROCKY GRIMES MOB TWENTY YEARS AGO!
YES, AND I'M SURE THEY WERE THE ONES WHO DUMPED ROCKY AT THE JAIL... ROCKY MUST BE OUT FOR REVENGE... AND OUT TO GET THE TWO OTHERS!
ACCORDING TO THIS FILE, PARKS WENT OUT WEST TO OPERATE A CONCESSION IN THE PETRIFIED FOREST... BRENNER WENT STRAIGHT, TOO, AND BECAME A DIAMOND-CUTTER!
THEN BRENNER'S THE MAN WHO IS TO CUT THE FAMOUS ONKER'S DIAMOND TONIGHT AT THE HOUSE OF JEWELS EXHIBIT IN TOWN!
ROCKY'S SURE TO TRY TO GET BRENNER FIRST! LET'S GO!
GOLLY! WE'VE NO TIME TO LOSE NOW!
8

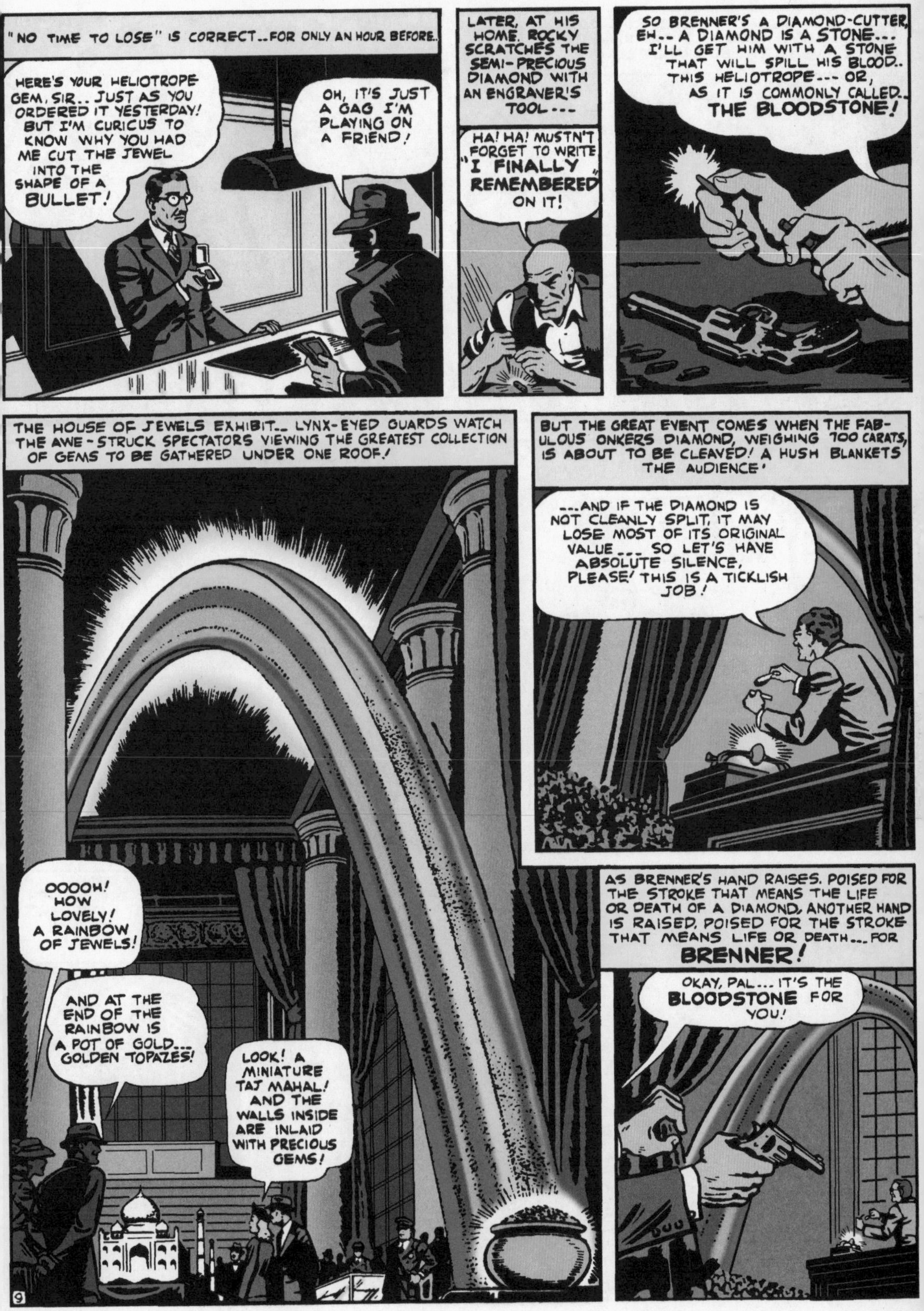

"NO TIME TO LOSE" IS CORRECT..FOR ONLY AN HOUR BEFORE..
HERE'S YOUR HELIOTROPE GEM, SIR.. JUST AS YOU ORDERED IT YESTERDAY! BUT I'M CURICUS TO KNOW WHY YOU HAD ME CUT THE JEWEL INTO THE SHAPE OF A BULLET!
OH, IT'S JUST A GAG I'M PLAYING ON A FRIEND!
LATER, AT HIS HOME, ROCKY SCRATCHES THE SEMI-PRECIOUS DIAMOND WITH AN ENGRAVER'S TOOL---
HA! HA! MUSTN'T FORGET TO WRITE "I FINALLY REMEMBERED" ON IT!
SO BRENNER'S A DIAMOND-CUTTER, EH.. A DIAMOND IS A STONE... I'LL GET HIM WITH A STONE THAT WILL SPILL HIS BLOOD.. THIS HELIOTROPE--- OR, AS IT IS COMMONLY CALLED.. THE BLOODSTONE!
THE HOUSE OF JEWELS EXHIBIT.. LYNX-EYED GUARDS WATCH THE AWE-STRUCK SPECTATORS VIEWING THE GREATEST COLLECTION OF GEMS TO BE GATHERED UNDER ONE ROOF!
OOOOH! HOW LOVELY! A RAINBOW OF JEWELS!
AND AT THE END OF THE RAINBOW IS A POT OF GOLD... GOLDEN TOPAZES!
LOOK! A MINIATURE TAJ MAHAL! AND THE WALLS INSIDE ARE INLAID WITH PRECIOUS GEMS!
9
BUT THE GREAT EVENT COMES WHEN THE FABULOUS ONKERS DIAMOND, WEIGHING 700 CARATS, IS ABOUT TO BE CLEAVED! A HUSH BLANKETS THE AUDIENCE!
---AND IF THE DIAMOND IS NOT CLEANLY SPLIT, IT MAY LOSE MOST OF ITS ORIGINAL VALUE--- SO LET'S HAVE ABSOLUTE SILENCE, PLEASE! THIS IS A TICKLISH JOB!
AS BRENNER'S HAND RAISES, POISED FOR THE STROKE THAT MEANS THE LIFE OR DEATH OF A DIAMOND, ANOTHER HAND IS RAISED, POISED FOR THE STROKE THAT MEANS LIFE OR DEATH... FOR BRENNER!
OKAY, PAL... IT'S THE BLOODSTONE FOR YOU!

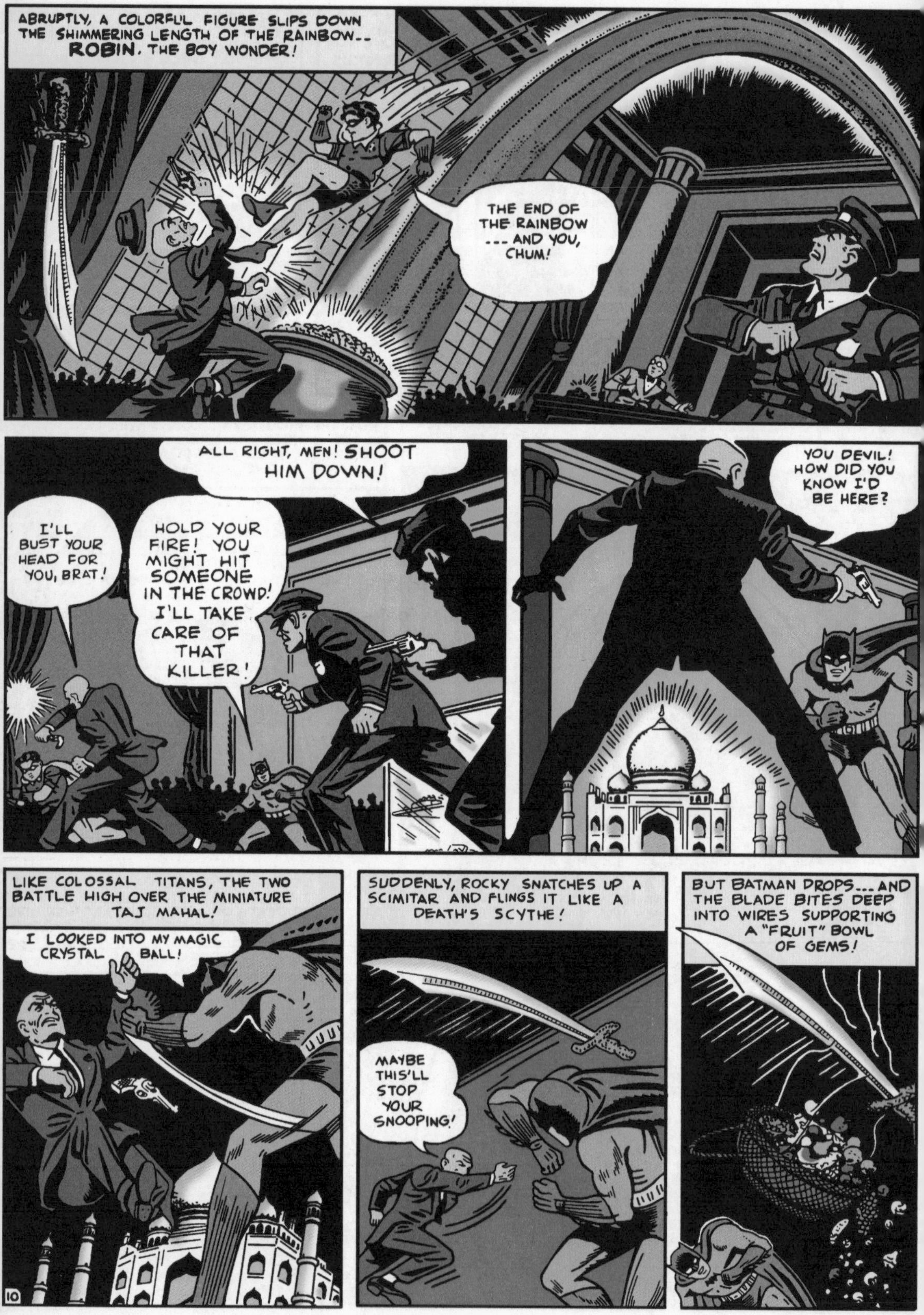

ABRUPTLY, A COLORFUL FIGURE SLIPS DOWN THE SHIMMERING LENGTH OF THE RAINBOW-- ROBIN, THE BOY WONDER!
THE END OF THE RAINBOW --- AND YOU, CHUM!
ALL RIGHT, MEN! SHOOT HIM DOWN!
I'LL BUST YOUR HEAD FOR YOU, BRAT!
HOLD YOUR FIRE! YOU MIGHT HIT SOMEONE IN THE CROWD! I'LL TAKE CARE OF THAT KILLER!
YOU DEVIL! HOW DID YOU KNOW I'D BE HERE?
LIKE COLOSSAL TITANS, THE TWO BATTLE HIGH OVER THE MINIATURE TAJ MAHAL!
I LOOKED INTO MY MAGIC CRYSTAL BALL!
10
SUDDENLY, ROCKY SNATCHES UP A SCIMITAR AND FLINGS IT LIKE A DEATH'S SCYTHE!
MAYBE THIS'LL STOP YOUR SNOOPING!
BUT BATMAN DROPS--- AND THE BLADE BITES DEEP INTO WIRES SUPPORTING A "FRUIT" BOWL OF GEMS!

A WATERFALL OF PRECIOUS STONES CASCADES DOWN ON THE STAMPEDING AUDIENCE!

OH, BOY! SOUVENIRS!

NEVER MIND GRIMES! STOP THOSE PEOPLE! THERE'S A FORTUNE IN GEMS ON THE FLOOR!

WHEE!

HA! HA! PRECIOUS STONES...THEY'RE HELPING ME MAKE A GETAWAY!

BUT.. HOT ON ROCKY'S TWISTING TRAIL ARE TWO HUMAN BLOODHOUNDS...

THERE HE GOES!

AND SOON THE CHASE ENDS.. AT AN ABANDONED OLD STONE QUARRY!

HE RAN INSIDE THAT SHACK! HE'S LOCKING THE DOOR!

THEN WE'LL SMASH THE DOOR IN! C'MON!

CLICK

TWO SLAMMING BODIES TEAR THROUGH THE DOOR... TO CRASH HEAVILY AGAINST A CLEVERLY PLACED UPRIGHT SLAB OF STONE!

OH!

HA! HA! I PLANTED THAT STONE SO SOME DAY IT WOULD STOP SOMEBODY IN A HURRY TO GET AT ME!

UH!

WORKING SWIFTLY, ROCKY BINDS ROBIN, LEAVING HIS FEET FREE!

NOW THAT I'VE LASHED THIS STONE TO YOUR WAIST, YOU'RE ALL SET! HA! HA!

THEN-- DOWN INTO THE WATER-FLOODED QUARRY, ROCKY HURLS ROBIN'S STONE-WEIGHTED BODY!

THAT STONE WON'T CARRY YOU TO THE BOTTOM.....SO YOU'LL TRY TO KEEP ALIVE BY TREADING WATER... BUT SOMETIME SOON YOU'RE GOING TO GET TIRED! HA! HA! GET THE IDEA? HA! HA!

11

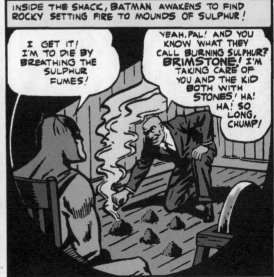

INSIDE THE SHACK, BATMAN AWAKENS TO FIND ROCKY SETTING FIRE TO MOUNDS OF SULPHUR!

I GET IT! I'M TO DIE BY BREATHING THE SULPHUR FUMES!

YEAH, PAL! AND YOU KNOW WHAT THEY CALL BURNING SULPHUR? BRIMSTONE! I'M TAKING CARE OF YOU AND THE KID BOTH WITH STONES! HA! HA! SO LONG, CHUMP!

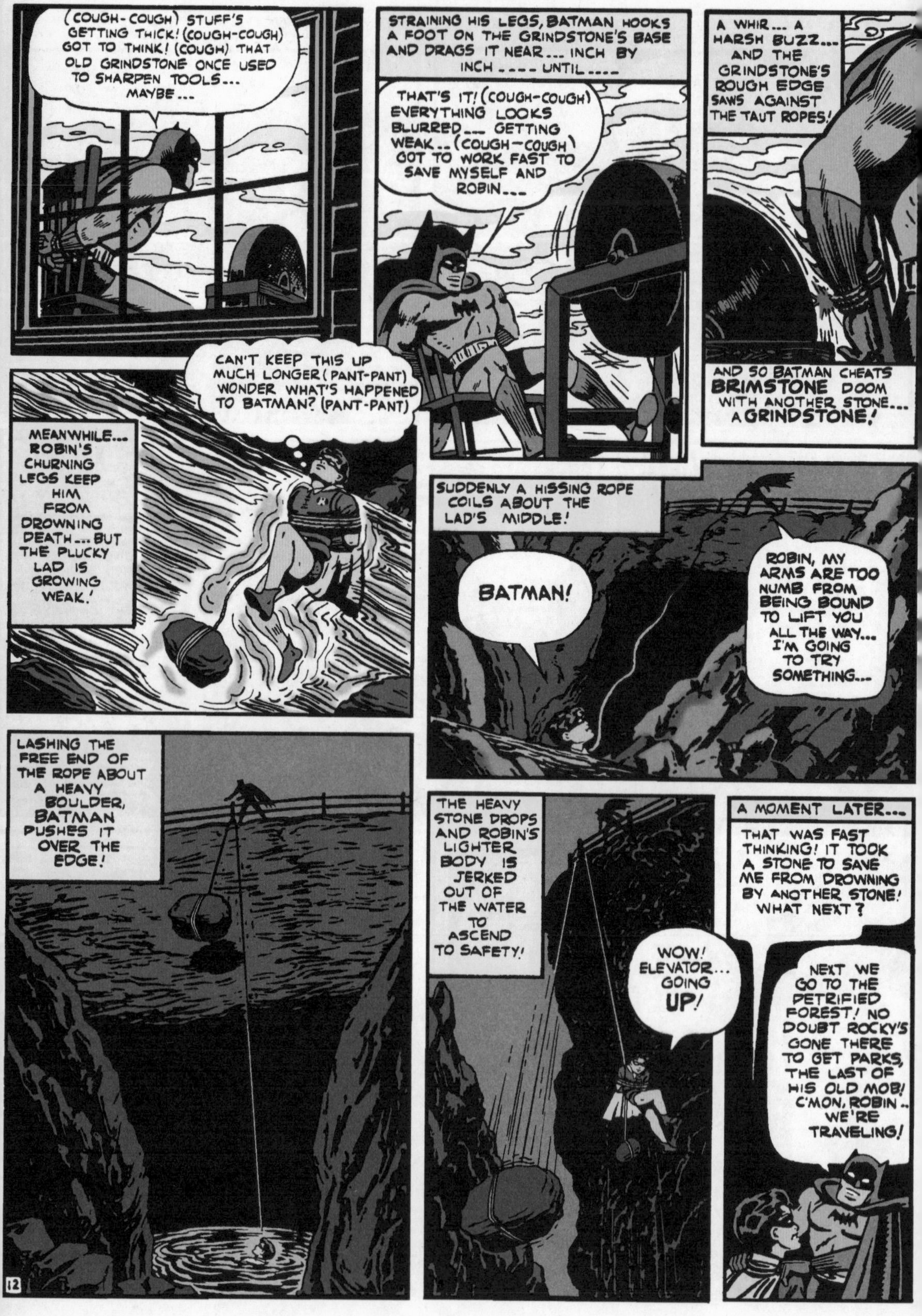
(COUGH-COUGH) STUFF'S GETTING THICK! (COUGH-COUGH) GOT TO THINK! (COUGH) THAT OLD GRINDSTONE ONCE USED TO SHARPEN TOOLS... MAYBE...
STRAINING HIS LEGS, BATMAN HOOKS A FOOT ON THE GRINDSTONE'S BASE AND DRAGS IT NEAR... INCH BY INCH .... UNTIL ....
THAT'S IT! (COUGH-COUGH) EVERYTHING LOOKS BLURRED... GETTING WEAK... (COUGH-COUGH) GOT TO WORK FAST TO SAVE MYSELF AND ROBIN...
A WHIR... A HARSH BUZZ... AND THE GRINDSTONE'S ROUGH EDGE SAWS AGAINST THE TAUT ROPES!
AND SO BATMAN CHEATS BRIMSTONE DOOM WITH ANOTHER STONE... A GRINDSTONE!
CAN'T KEEP THIS UP MUCH LONGER (PANT-PANT) WONDER WHAT'S HAPPENED TO BATMAN? (PANT-PANT)
MEANWHILE... ROBIN'S CHURNING LEGS KEEP HIM FROM DROWNING DEATH... BUT THE PLUCKY LAD IS GROWING WEAK!
SUDDENLY A HISSING ROPE COILS ABOUT THE LAD'S MIDDLE!
BATMAN!
ROBIN, MY ARMS ARE TOO NUMB FROM BEING BOUND TO LIFT YOU ALL THE WAY... I'M GOING TO TRY SOMETHING...
LASHING THE FREE END OF THE ROPE ABOUT A HEAVY BOULDER, BATMAN PUSHES IT OVER THE EDGE!
12
THE HEAVY STONE DROPS AND ROBIN'S LIGHTER BODY IS JERKED OUT OF THE WATER TO ASCEND TO SAFETY!
WOW! ELEVATOR... GOING UP!
A MOMENT LATER...
THAT WAS FAST THINKING! IT TOOK A STONE TO SAVE ME FROM DROWNING BY ANOTHER STONE! WHAT NEXT?
NEXT WE GO TO THE PETRIFIED FOREST! NO DOUBT ROCKY'S GONE THERE TO GET PARKS, THE LAST OF HIS OLD MOB! C'MON, ROBIN... WE'RE TRAVELING!

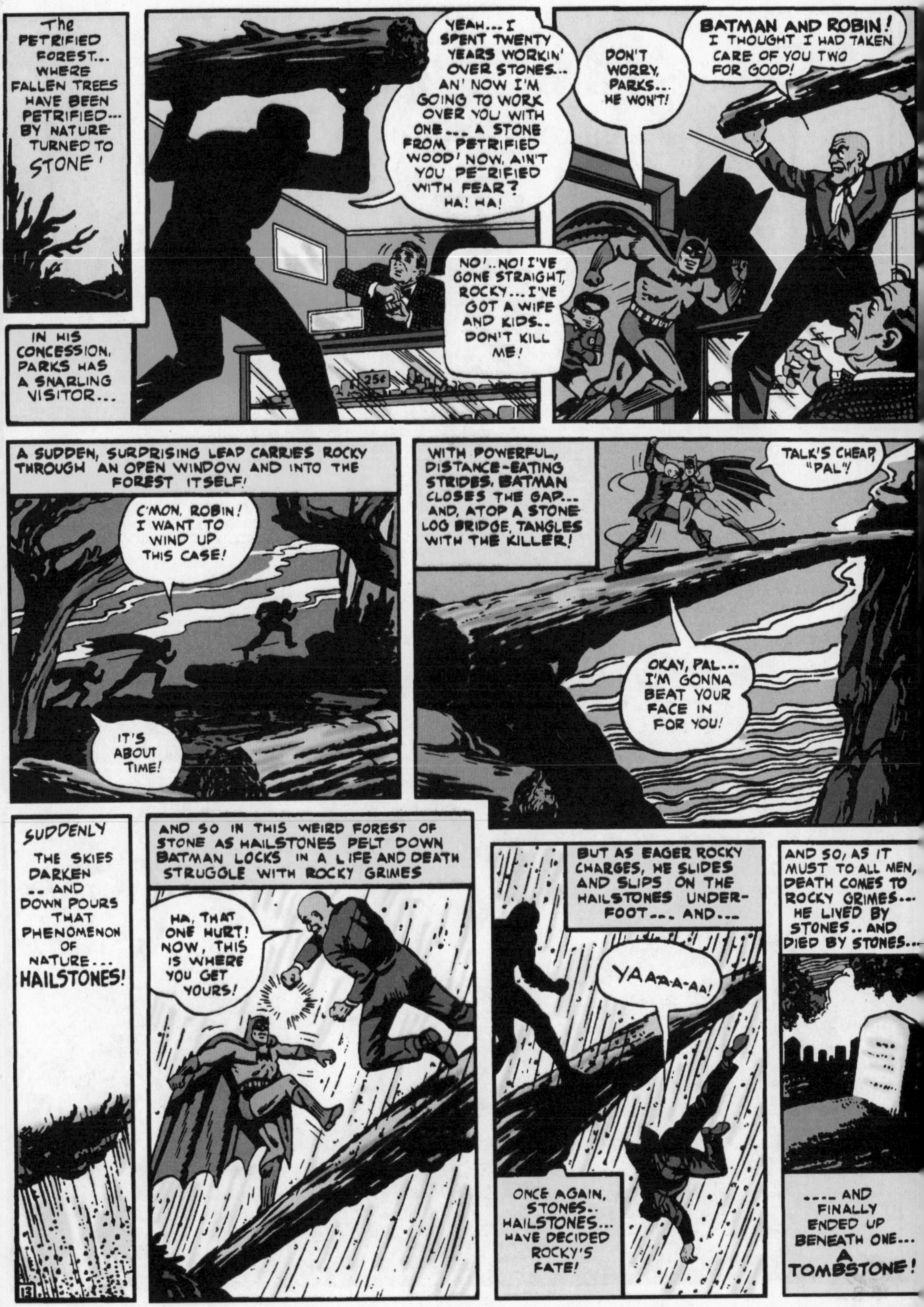

The PETRIFIED FOREST... WHERE FALLEN TREES HAVE BEEN PETRIFIED... BY NATURE TURNED TO STONE!
IN HIS CONCESSION, PARKS HAS A SNARLING VISITOR...
YEAH... I SPENT TWENTY YEARS WORKIN' OVER STONES... AN' NOW I'M GOING TO WORK OVER YOU WITH ONE... A STONE FROM PETRIFIED WOOD! NOW, AIN'T YOU PETRIFIED WITH FEAR? HA! HA!
NO!..NO! I'VE GONE STRAIGHT, ROCKY... I'VE GOT A WIFE AND KIDS.. DON'T KILL ME!
25¢
BATMAN AND ROBIN! I THOUGHT I HAD TAKEN CARE OF YOU TWO FOR GOOD!
DON'T WORRY, PARKS... HE WON'T!
A SUDDEN, SURPRISING LEAP CARRIES ROCKY THROUGH AN OPEN WINDOW AND INTO THE FOREST ITSELF!
C'MON, ROBIN! I WANT TO WIND UP THIS CASE!
IT'S ABOUT TIME!
WITH POWERFUL, DISTANCE-EATING STRIDES, BATMAN CLOSES THE GAP... AND, ATOP A STONE LOG BRIDGE, TANGLES WITH THE KILLER!
TALK'S CHEAP, "PAL"!
OKAY, PAL... I'M GONNA BEAT YOUR FACE IN FOR YOU!
SUDDENLY THE SKIES DARKEN .. AND DOWN POURS THAT PHENOMENON OF NATURE... HAILSTONES!
13
AND SO IN THIS WEIRD FOREST OF STONE AS HAILSTONES PELT DOWN BATMAN LOCKS IN A LIFE AND DEATH STRUGGLE WITH ROCKY GRIMES
HA, THAT ONE HURT! NOW, THIS IS WHERE YOU GET YOURS!
BUT AS EAGER ROCKY CHARGES, HE SLIDES AND SLIPS ON THE HAILSTONES UNDERFOOT... AND...
YAAA-A-AA!
ONCE AGAIN, STONES.. HAILSTONES... HAVE DECIDED ROCKY'S FATE!
AND SO, AS IT MUST TO ALL MEN, DEATH COMES TO ROCKY GRIMES... HE LIVED BY STONES.. AND DIED BY STONES...
.... AND FINALLY ENDED UP BENEATH ONE... A TOMBSTONE!

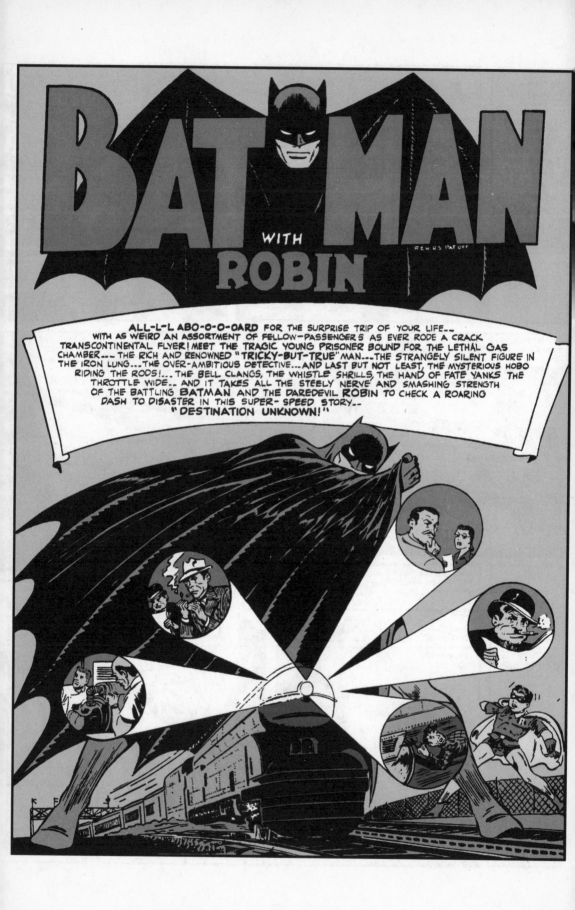

BAT MAN

WITH ROBIN

ALL-L-L ABO-O-OARD for the surprise trip of your life... WITH AS WEIRD AN ASSORTMENT OF FELLOW-PASSENGERS AS EVER RODE A CRACK TRANSCONTINENTAL FLYER! MEET THE TRAGIC YOUNG PRISONER BOUND FOR THE LETHAL GAS CHAMBER... THE RICH AND RENOWNED "TRICKY-BUT-TRUE" MAN... THE STRANGELY SILENT FIGURE IN THE IRON LUNG... THE OVER-AMBITIOUS DETECTIVE... AND LAST BUT NOT LEAST, THE MYSTERIOUS HOBO RIDING THE RODS!... THE BELL CLANGS, THE WHISTLE SHRILLS, THE HAND OF FATE YANKS THE THROTTLE WIDE... AND IT TAKES ALL THE STEELY NERVE AND SMASHING STRENGTH OF THE BATTLING BATMAN AND THE DAREDEVIL ROBIN TO CHECK A ROARING DASH TO DISASTER IN THIS SUPER-SPEED STORY... "DESTINATION UNKNOWN!"

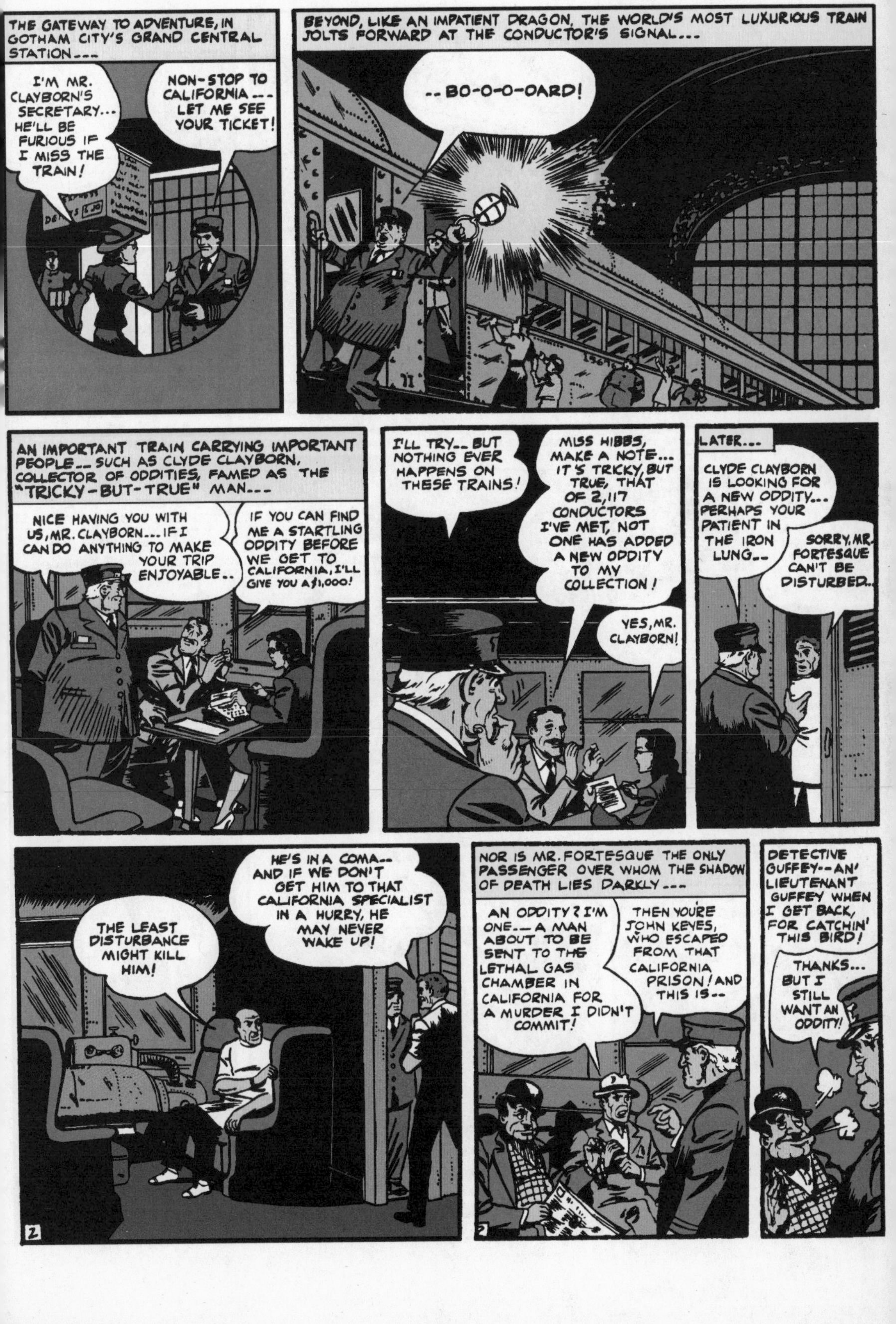
THE GATEWAY TO ADVENTURE, IN GOTHAM CITY'S GRAND CENTRAL STATION---
I'M MR. CLAYBORN'S SECRETARY... HE'LL BE FURIOUS IF I MISS THE TRAIN!
NON-STOP TO CALIFORNIA --- LET ME SEE YOUR TICKET!
BEYOND, LIKE AN IMPATIENT DRAGON, THE WORLD'S MOST LUXURIOUS TRAIN JOLTS FORWARD AT THE CONDUCTOR'S SIGNAL...
--BO-O-O-OARD!
AN IMPORTANT TRAIN CARRYING IMPORTANT PEOPLE-- SUCH AS CLYDE CLAYBORN, COLLECTOR OF ODDITIES, FAMED AS THE "TRICKY-BUT-TRUE" MAN---
NICE HAVING YOU WITH US, MR. CLAYBORN--- IF I CAN DO ANYTHING TO MAKE YOUR TRIP ENJOYABLE--
IF YOU CAN FIND ME A STARTLING ODDITY BEFORE WE GET TO CALIFORNIA, I'LL GIVE YOU A $1,000!
I'LL TRY-- BUT NOTHING EVER HAPPENS ON THESE TRAINS!
MISS HIBBS, MAKE A NOTE... IT'S TRICKY, BUT TRUE, THAT OF 2,117 CONDUCTORS I'VE MET, NOT ONE HAS ADDED A NEW ODDITY TO MY COLLECTION!
YES, MR. CLAYBORN!
LATER...
CLYDE CLAYBORN IS LOOKING FOR A NEW ODDITY... PERHAPS YOUR PATIENT IN THE IRON LUNG--
SORRY, MR. FORTESQUE CAN'T BE DISTURBED..
THE LEAST DISTURBANCE MIGHT KILL HIM!
HE'S IN A COMA-- AND IF WE DON'T GET HIM TO THAT CALIFORNIA SPECIALIST IN A HURRY, HE MAY NEVER WAKE UP!
NOR IS MR. FORTESQUE THE ONLY PASSENGER OVER WHOM THE SHADOW OF DEATH LIES DARKLY ---
AN ODDITY? I'M ONE-- A MAN ABOUT TO BE SENT TO THE LETHAL GAS CHAMBER IN CALIFORNIA FOR A MURDER I DIDN'T COMMIT!
THEN YOU'RE JOHN KEYES, WHO ESCAPED FROM THAT CALIFORNIA PRISON! AND THIS IS--
DETECTIVE GUFFEY--AN' LIEUTENANT GUFFEY WHEN I GET BACK, FOR CATCHIN' THIS BIRD!
THANKS... BUT I STILL WANT AN ODDITY!

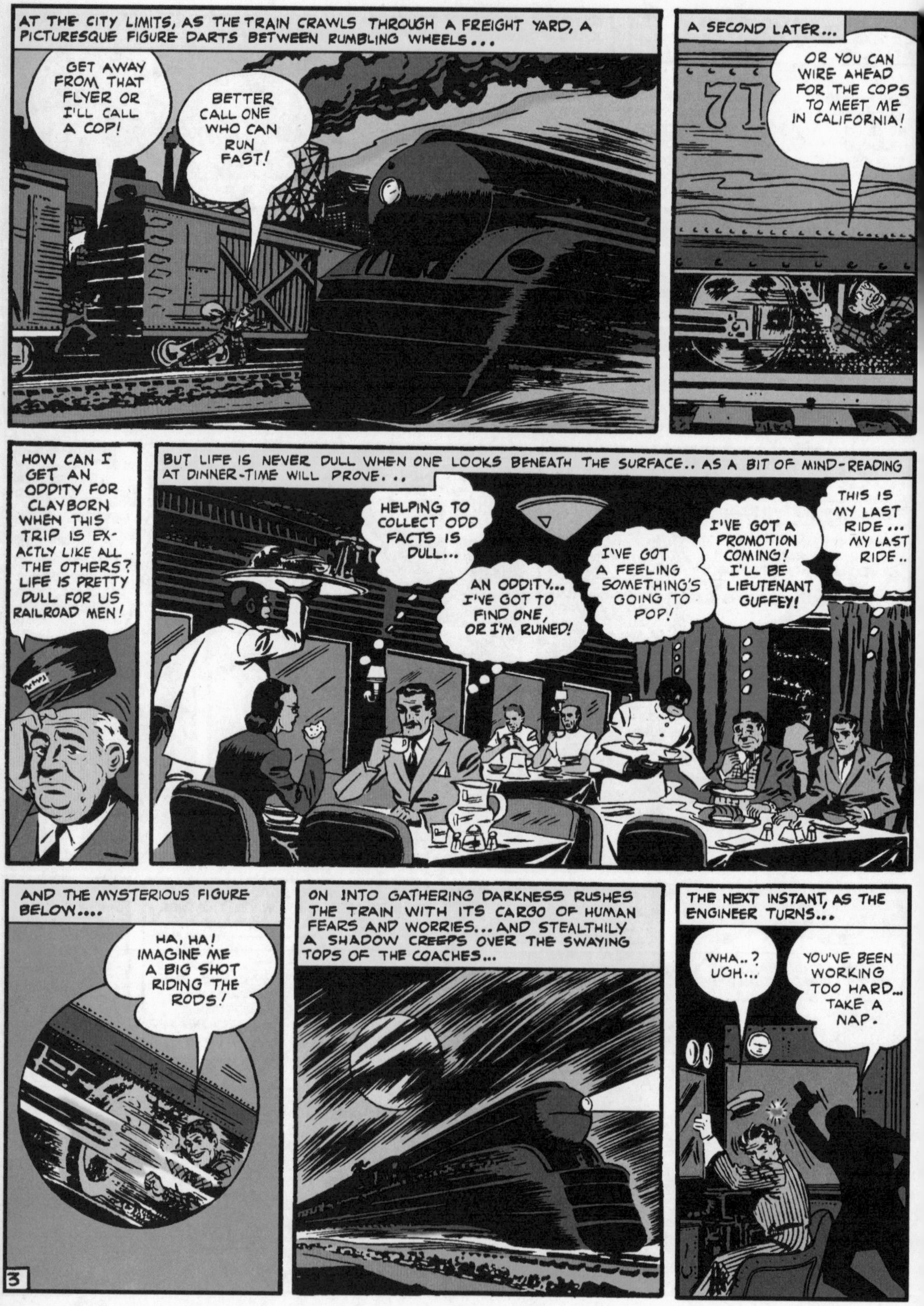
AT THE CITY LIMITS, AS THE TRAIN CRAWLS THROUGH A FREIGHT YARD, A PICTURESQUE FIGURE DARTS BETWEEN RUMBLING WHEELS...
GET AWAY FROM THAT FLYER OR I'LL CALL A COP!
BETTER CALL ONE WHO CAN RUN FAST!
A SECOND LATER...
OR YOU CAN WIRE AHEAD FOR THE COPS TO MEET ME IN CALIFORNIA!
71
HOW CAN I GET AN ODDITY FOR CLAYBORN WHEN THIS TRIP IS EXACTLY LIKE ALL THE OTHERS? LIFE IS PRETTY DULL FOR US RAILROAD MEN!
BUT LIFE IS NEVER DULL WHEN ONE LOOKS BENEATH THE SURFACE.. AS A BIT OF MIND-READING AT DINNER-TIME WILL PROVE..
HELPING TO COLLECT ODD FACTS IS DULL...
AN ODDITY... I'VE GOT TO FIND ONE, OR I'M RUINED!
I'VE GOT A FEELING SOMETHING'S GOING TO POP!
I'VE GOT A PROMOTION COMING! I'LL BE LIEUTENANT GUFFEY!
THIS IS MY LAST RIDE... MY LAST RIDE..
AND THE MYSTERIOUS FIGURE BELOW....
HA, HA! IMAGINE ME A BIG SHOT RIDING THE RODS!
3
ON INTO GATHERING DARKNESS RUSHES THE TRAIN WITH ITS CARGO OF HUMAN FEARS AND WORRIES... AND STEALTHILY A SHADOW CREEPS OVER THE SWAYING TOPS OF THE COACHES...
THE NEXT INSTANT, AS THE ENGINEER TURNS...
WHA..? UGH...
YOU'VE BEEN WORKING TOO HARD... TAKE A NAP.

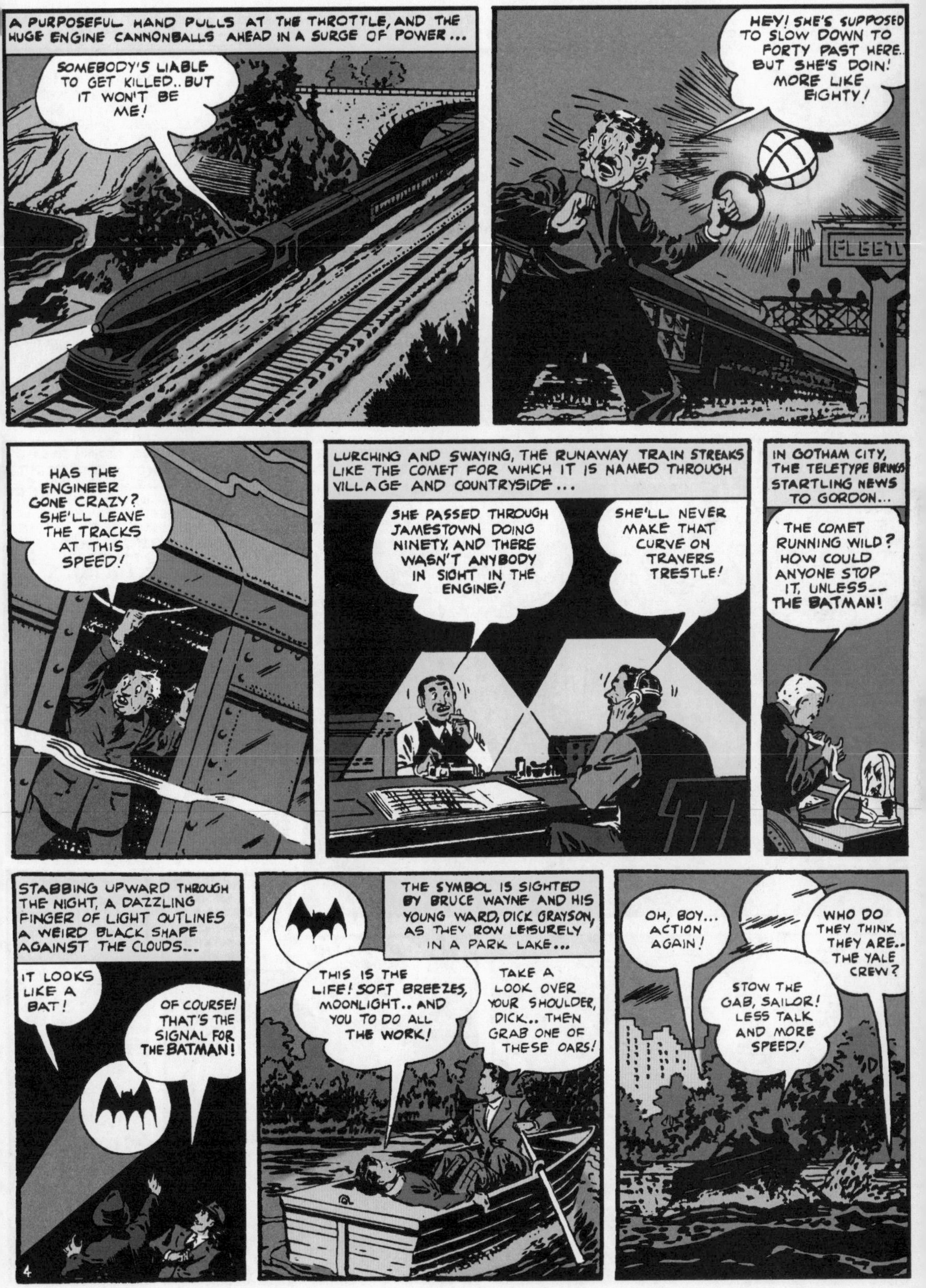
A PURPOSEFUL HAND PULLS AT THE THROTTLE, AND THE HUGE ENGINE CANNONBALLS AHEAD IN A SURGE OF POWER...
SOMEBODY'S LIABLE TO GET KILLED.. BUT IT WON'T BE ME!
HEY! SHE'S SUPPOSED TO SLOW DOWN TO FORTY PAST HERE.. BUT SHE'S DOIN' MORE LIKE EIGHTY!
FLEET
HAS THE ENGINEER GONE CRAZY? SHE'LL LEAVE THE TRACKS AT THIS SPEED!
LURCHING AND SWAYING, THE RUNAWAY TRAIN STREAKS LIKE THE COMET FOR WHICH IT IS NAMED THROUGH VILLAGE AND COUNTRYSIDE...
SHE PASSED THROUGH JAMESTOWN DOING NINETY, AND THERE WASN'T ANYBODY IN SIGHT IN THE ENGINE!
SHE'LL NEVER MAKE THAT CURVE ON TRAVERS TRESTLE!
IN GOTHAM CITY, THE TELETYPE BRINGS STARTLING NEWS TO GORDON...
THE COMET RUNNING WILD? HOW COULD ANYONE STOP IT, UNLESS-- THE BATMAN!
STABBING UPWARD THROUGH THE NIGHT, A DAZZLING FINGER OF LIGHT OUTLINES A WEIRD BLACK SHAPE AGAINST THE CLOUDS...
IT LOOKS LIKE A BAT!
OF COURSE! THAT'S THE SIGNAL FOR THE BATMAN!
4
THE SYMBOL IS SIGHTED BY BRUCE WAYNE AND HIS YOUNG WARD, DICK GRAYSON, AS THEY ROW LEISURELY IN A PARK LAKE...
THIS IS THE LIFE! SOFT BREEZES, MOONLIGHT.. AND YOU TO DO ALL THE WORK!
TAKE A LOOK OVER YOUR SHOULDER, DICK.. THEN GRAB ONE OF THESE OARS!
OH, BOY... ACTION AGAIN!
WHO DO THEY THINK THEY ARE.. THE YALE CREW?
STOW THE GAB, SAILOR! LESS TALK AND MORE SPEED!

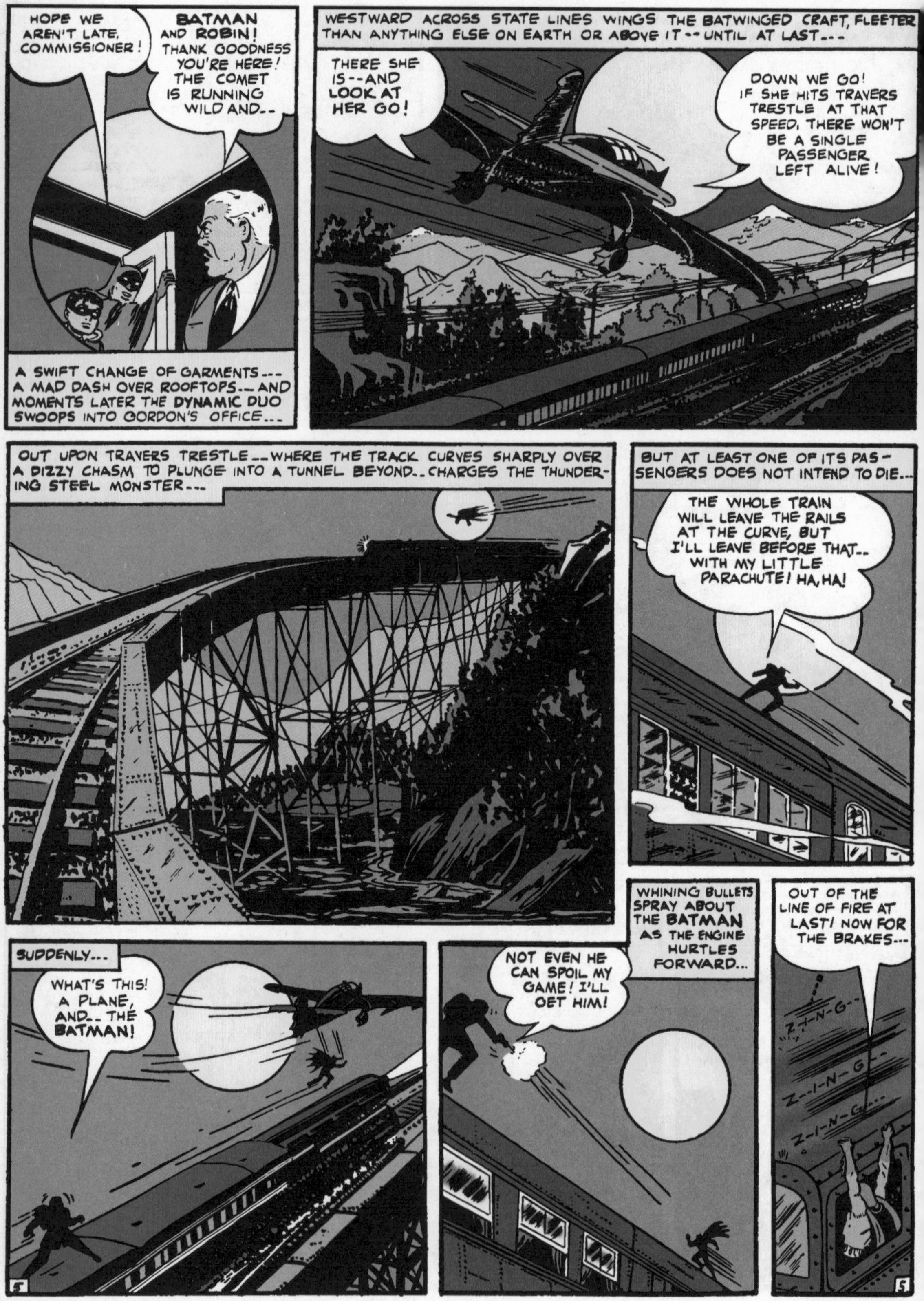

HOPE WE AREN'T LATE, COMMISSIONER!
BATMAN AND ROBIN! THANK GOODNESS YOU'RE HERE! THE COMET IS RUNNING WILD AND--
A SWIFT CHANGE OF GARMENTS--- A MAD DASH OVER ROOFTOPS-- AND MOMENTS LATER THE DYNAMIC DUO SWOOPS INTO GORDON'S OFFICE...
WESTWARD ACROSS STATE LINES WINGS THE BATWINGED CRAFT, FLEETER THAN ANYTHING ELSE ON EARTH OR ABOVE IT -- UNTIL AT LAST---
THERE SHE IS--AND LOOK AT HER GO!
DOWN WE GO! IF SHE HITS TRAVERS TRESTLE AT THAT SPEED, THERE WON'T BE A SINGLE PASSENGER LEFT ALIVE!
OUT UPON TRAVERS TRESTLE -- WHERE THE TRACK CURVES SHARPLY OVER A DIZZY CHASM TO PLUNGE INTO A TUNNEL BEYOND.. CHARGES THE THUNDERING STEEL MONSTER---
BUT AT LEAST ONE OF ITS PASSENGERS DOES NOT INTEND TO DIE...
THE WHOLE TRAIN WILL LEAVE THE RAILS AT THE CURVE, BUT I'LL LEAVE BEFORE THAT.. WITH MY LITTLE PARACHUTE! HA, HA!
SUDDENLY...
WHAT'S THIS! A PLANE, AND.. THE BATMAN!
5
WHINING BULLETS SPRAY ABOUT THE BATMAN AS THE ENGINE HURTLES FORWARD...
NOT EVEN HE CAN SPOIL MY GAME! I'LL GET HIM!
OUT OF THE LINE OF FIRE AT LAST! NOW FOR THE BRAKES---
Z-I-N-G--
Z--I-N-G--
Z-I-N-G---
5

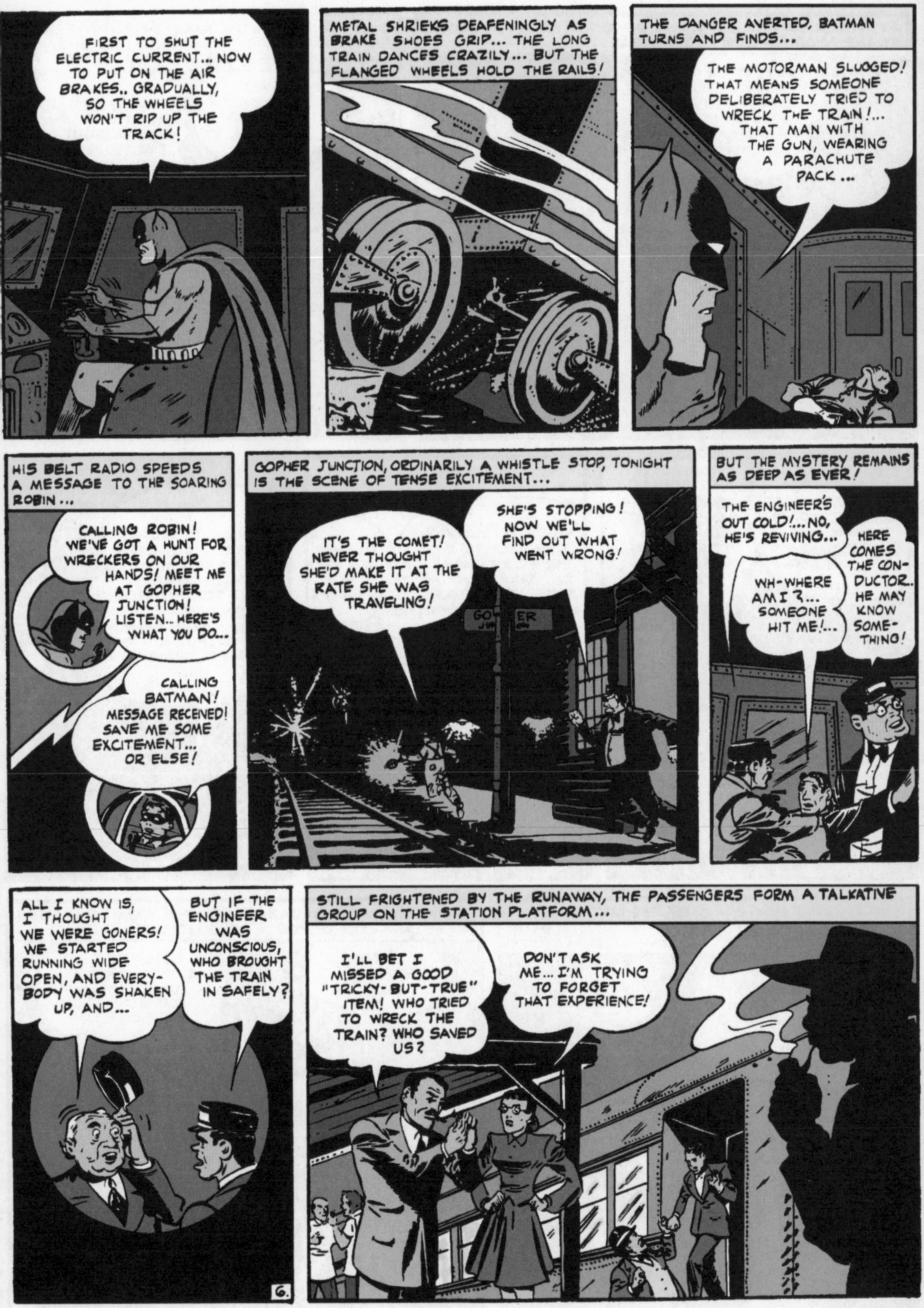
FIRST TO SHUT THE ELECTRIC CURRENT... NOW TO PUT ON THE AIR BRAKES.. GRADUALLY, SO THE WHEELS WON'T RIP UP THE TRACK!
METAL SHRIEKS DEAFENINGLY AS BRAKE SHOES GRIP... THE LONG TRAIN DANCES CRAZILY... BUT THE FLANGED WHEELS HOLD THE RAILS!
THE DANGER AVERTED, BATMAN TURNS AND FINDS...
THE MOTORMAN SLUGGED! THAT MEANS SOMEONE DELIBERATELY TRIED TO WRECK THE TRAIN!... THAT MAN WITH THE GUN, WEARING A PARACHUTE PACK...
HIS BELT RADIO SPEEDS A MESSAGE TO THE SOARING ROBIN...
CALLING ROBIN! WE'VE GOT A HUNT FOR WRECKERS ON OUR HANDS! MEET ME AT GOPHER JUNCTION! LISTEN.. HERE'S WHAT YOU DO...
CALLING BATMAN! MESSAGE RECEIVED! SAVE ME SOME EXCITEMENT... OR ELSE!
GOPHER JUNCTION, ORDINARILY A WHISTLE STOP, TONIGHT IS THE SCENE OF TENSE EXCITEMENT...
IT'S THE COMET! NEVER THOUGHT SHE'D MAKE IT AT THE RATE SHE WAS TRAVELING!
SHE'S STOPPING! NOW WE'LL FIND OUT WHAT WENT WRONG!
BUT THE MYSTERY REMAINS AS DEEP AS EVER!
THE ENGINEER'S OUT COLD!... NO, HE'S REVIVING...
WH-WHERE AM I?... SOMEONE HIT ME!...
HERE COMES THE CONDUCTOR. HE MAY KNOW SOMETHING!
ALL I KNOW IS, I THOUGHT WE WERE GONERS! WE STARTED RUNNING WIDE OPEN, AND EVERYBODY WAS SHAKEN UP, AND...
BUT IF THE ENGINEER WAS UNCONSCIOUS, WHO BROUGHT THE TRAIN IN SAFELY?
6.
STILL FRIGHTENED BY THE RUNAWAY, THE PASSENGERS FORM A TALKATIVE GROUP ON THE STATION PLATFORM...
I'LL BET I MISSED A GOOD "TRICKY-BUT-TRUE" ITEM! WHO TRIED TO WRECK THE TRAIN? WHO SAVED US?
DON'T ASK ME... I'M TRYING TO FORGET THAT EXPERIENCE!

BUT ONE PASSENGER FLITS LIKE A FUGITIVE THROUGH SHADOWS AT THE FARTHER SIDE OF THE TRAIN...

CAN'T TAKE A CHANCE ON BEING SEEN.. THINK I'LL HIDE BEHIND THESE OLD FREIGHTS...

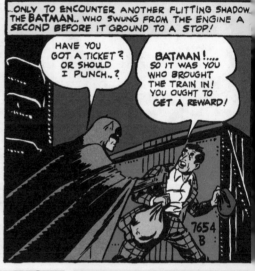

..ONLY TO ENCOUNTER ANOTHER FLITTING SHADOW.. THE BATMAN.. WHO SWUNG FROM THE ENGINE A SECOND BEFORE IT GROUND TO A STOP!

HAVE YOU GOT A TICKET? OR SHOULD I PUNCH..?

BATMAN!.... SO IT WAS YOU WHO BROUGHT THE TRAIN IN! YOU OUGHT TO GET A REWARD!

I DON'T TAKE REWARDS... BUT IF I DID, I MIGHT COLLECT ONE FOR TURNING YOU OVER TO THE AUTHORITIES!

NOT GUILTY, BATMAN! I WAS HANGING ONTO THE RODS, SCARED TO DEATH, WHEN WE HIT THE TRESTLE!

I HOPE HE BELIEVES ME!

WHEN A FELLOW'S DOWN AND OUT, I NEVER KICK HIM! I'LL TAKE YOUR WORD.. TILL I DO A LITTLE INVESTIGATING!

THEN WHY ARE YOU TYING ME UP?

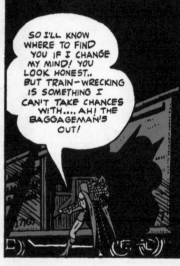

SO I'LL KNOW WHERE TO FIND YOU IF I CHANGE MY MIND! YOU LOOK HONEST.. BUT TRAIN-WRECKING IS SOMETHING I CAN'T TAKE CHANCES WITH.... AH! THE BAGGAGEMAN'S OUT!

SHUCKING HIS FIGHTING GARB, THE BATMAN DISAPPEARS.. AND A MOMENT LATER BRUCE WAYNE STANDS AT THE TICKET WINDOW AT THE STATION...

LUCKY FOR ME THIS TRAIN STOPPED HERE... I'LL TAKE A TICKET THROUGH TO THE END OF THE RUN!

HERE Y'ARE!

MEANWHILE, AT A MAGAZINE STAND, A YOUNG MAN SEEMS TO BE STOCKING UP FOR A LONG LITERARY SESSION...

I'LL TAKE THESE COMIC BOOKS!

GOLLY, KID.. AREN'T YOU GOIN' TO DO NOTHIN' BUT READ FROM HERE ON?

7

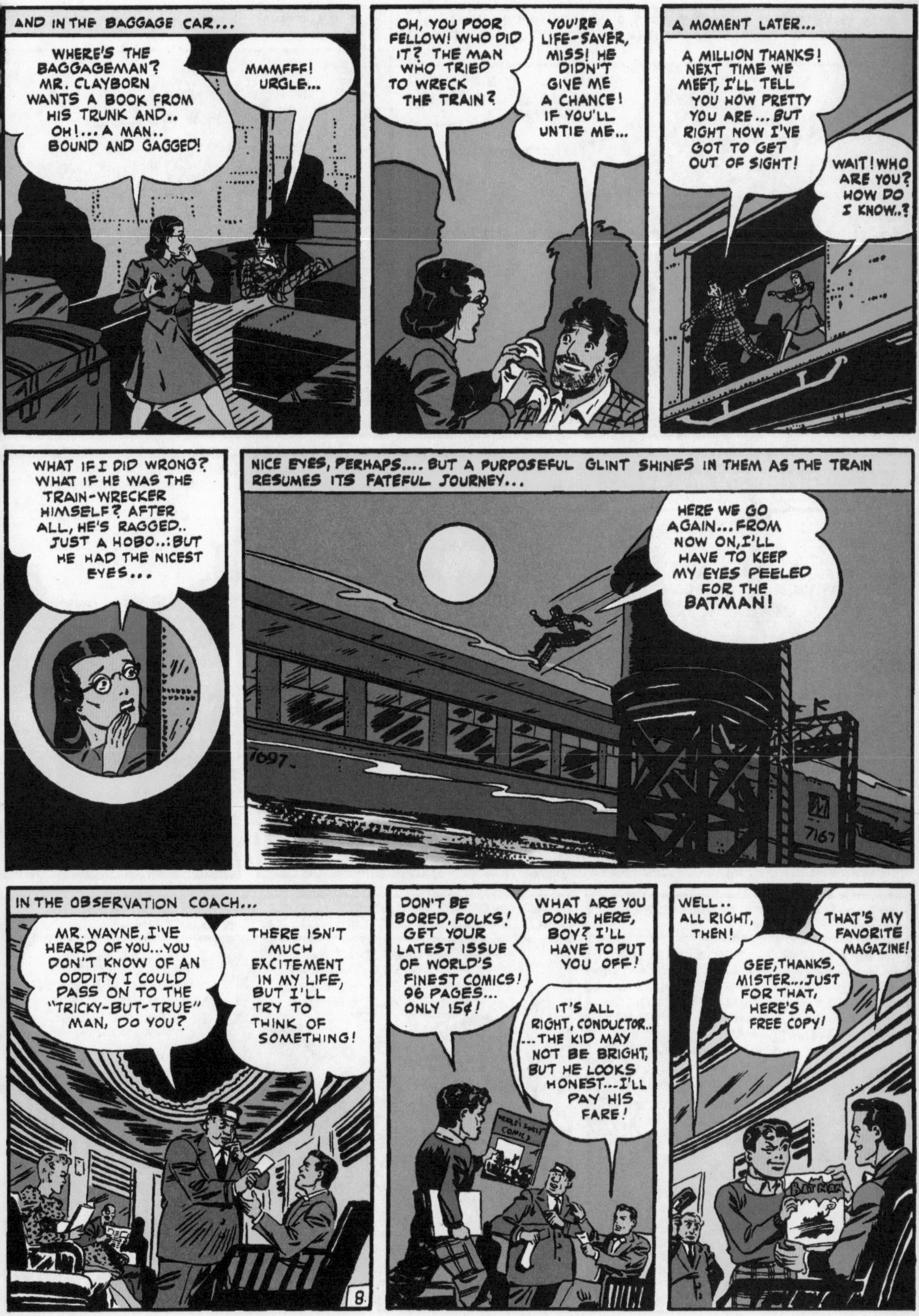
AND IN THE BAGGAGE CAR...
WHERE'S THE BAGGAGEMAN? MR. CLAYBORN WANTS A BOOK FROM HIS TRUNK AND.. OH!... A MAN.. BOUND AND GAGGED!
MMMFFF! URGLE...
OH, YOU POOR FELLOW! WHO DID IT? THE MAN WHO TRIED TO WRECK THE TRAIN?
YOU'RE A LIFE-SAVER, MISS! HE DIDN'T GIVE ME A CHANCE! IF YOU'LL UNTIE ME...
A MOMENT LATER...
A MILLION THANKS! NEXT TIME WE MEET, I'LL TELL YOU HOW PRETTY YOU ARE... BUT RIGHT NOW I'VE GOT TO GET OUT OF SIGHT!
WAIT! WHO ARE YOU? HOW DO I KNOW..?
WHAT IF I DID WRONG? WHAT IF HE WAS THE TRAIN-WRECKER HIMSELF? AFTER ALL, HE'S RAGGED.. JUST A HOBO..: BUT HE HAD THE NICEST EYES...
NICE EYES, PERHAPS.... BUT A PURPOSEFUL GLINT SHINES IN THEM AS THE TRAIN RESUMES ITS FATEFUL JOURNEY...
HERE WE GO AGAIN... FROM NOW ON, I'LL HAVE TO KEEP MY EYES PEELED FOR THE BATMAN!
7097
7167
IN THE OBSERVATION COACH...
MR. WAYNE, I'VE HEARD OF YOU... YOU DON'T KNOW OF AN ODDITY I COULD PASS ON TO THE "TRICKY-BUT-TRUE" MAN, DO YOU?
THERE ISN'T MUCH EXCITEMENT IN MY LIFE, BUT I'LL TRY TO THINK OF SOMETHING!
8.
DON'T BE BORED, FOLKS! GET YOUR LATEST ISSUE OF WORLD'S FINEST COMICS! 96 PAGES... ONLY 15¢!
WHAT ARE YOU DOING HERE, BOY? I'LL HAVE TO PUT YOU OFF!
IT'S ALL RIGHT, CONDUCTOR.. ...THE KID MAY NOT BE BRIGHT, BUT HE LOOKS HONEST... I'LL PAY HIS FARE!
WELL.. ALL RIGHT, THEN!
THAT'S MY FAVORITE MAGAZINE!
GEE, THANKS, MISTER... JUST FOR THAT, HERE'S A FREE COPY!
BATMAN

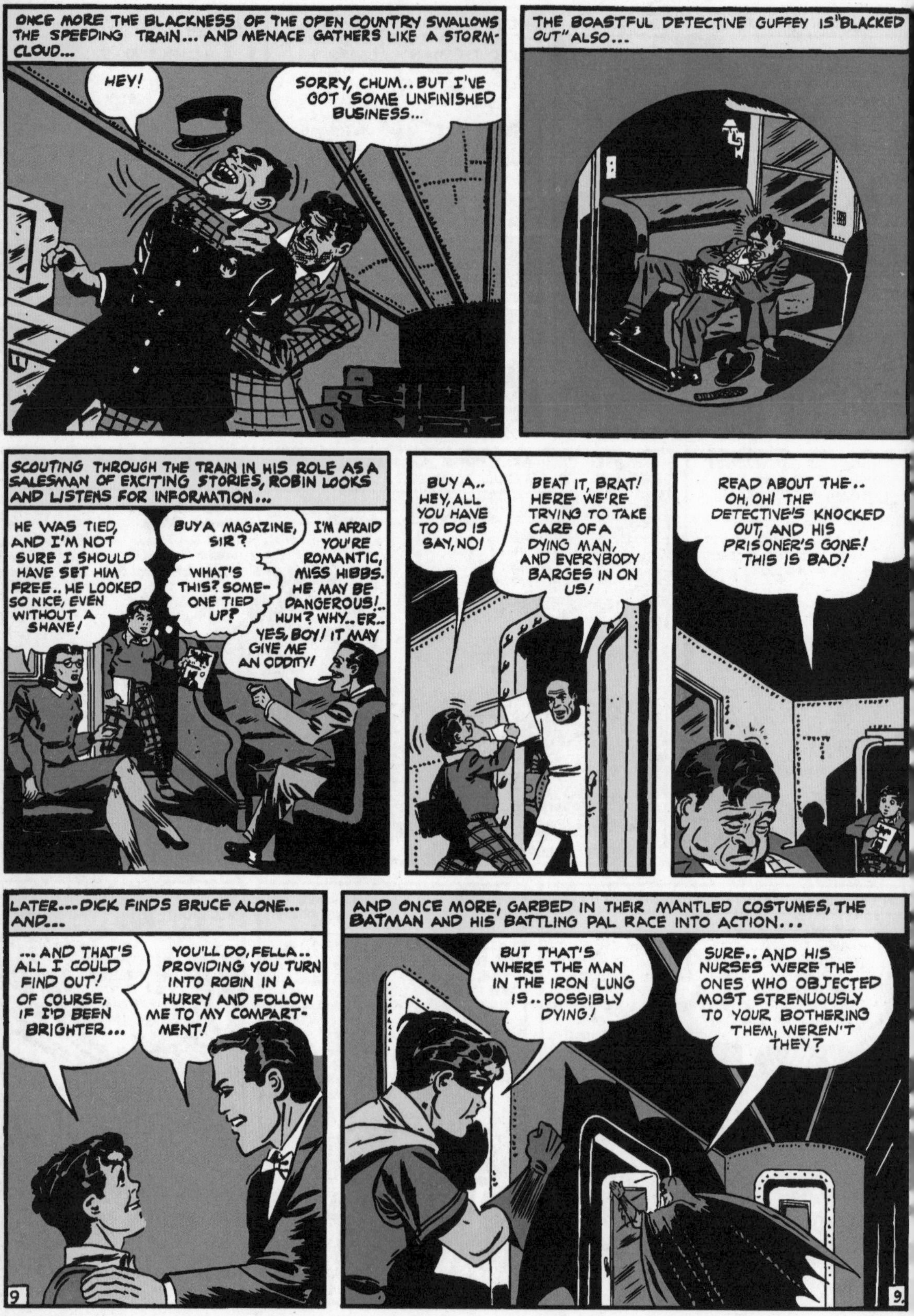

ONCE MORE THE BLACKNESS OF THE OPEN COUNTRY SWALLOWS THE SPEEDING TRAIN... AND MENACE GATHERS LIKE A STORM-CLOUD...
HEY!
SORRY, CHUM.. BUT I'VE GOT SOME UNFINISHED BUSINESS...
THE BOASTFUL DETECTIVE GUFFEY IS "BLACKED OUT" ALSO...
SCOUTING THROUGH THE TRAIN IN HIS ROLE AS A SALESMAN OF EXCITING STORIES, ROBIN LOOKS AND LISTENS FOR INFORMATION...
HE WAS TIED, AND I'M NOT SURE I SHOULD HAVE SET HIM FREE.. HE LOOKED SO NICE, EVEN WITHOUT A SHAVE!
BUY A MAGAZINE, SIR?
I'M AFRAID YOU'RE ROMANTIC, MISS HIBBS. HE MAY BE DANGEROUS!.. HUH? WHY.. ER..
WHAT'S THIS? SOME-ONE TIED UP?
YES, BOY! IT MAY GIVE ME AN ODDITY!
BUY A.. HEY, ALL YOU HAVE TO DO IS SAY, NO!
BEAT IT, BRAT! HERE WE'RE TRYING TO TAKE CARE OF A DYING MAN, AND EVERYBODY BARGES IN ON US!
READ ABOUT THE.. OH, OH! THE DETECTIVE'S KNOCKED OUT, AND HIS PRISONER'S GONE! THIS IS BAD!
LATER... DICK FINDS BRUCE ALONE... AND...
... AND THAT'S ALL I COULD FIND OUT! OF COURSE, IF I'D BEEN BRIGHTER...
YOU'LL DO, FELLA.. PROVIDING YOU TURN INTO ROBIN IN A HURRY AND FOLLOW ME TO MY COMPART-MENT!
9
AND ONCE MORE, GARBED IN THEIR MANTLED COSTUMES, THE BATMAN AND HIS BATTLING PAL RACE INTO ACTION...
BUT THAT'S WHERE THE MAN IN THE IRON LUNG IS.. POSSIBLY DYING!
SURE.. AND HIS NURSES WERE THE ONES WHO OBJECTED MOST STRENUOUSLY TO YOUR BOTHERING THEM, WEREN'T THEY?
9

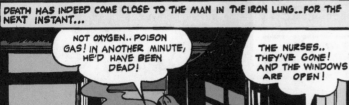

DEATH HAS INDEED COME CLOSE TO THE MAN IN THE IRON LUNG..FOR THE NEXT INSTANT...

NOT OXYGEN.. POISON GAS! IN ANOTHER MINUTE, HE'D HAVE BEEN DEAD!

THE NURSES.. THEY'VE GONE! AND THE WINDOWS ARE OPEN!

THAT FELLOW WILL LIVE, AND THE NURSES COULDN'T HAVE JUMPED OFF AT THIS SPEED! I'M GOING UP ON TOP! YOU GO FORWARD AND SEE WHAT YOU CAN DO!

RIGHT!

CLAMBERING PRECARIOUSLY OVER THE SWAYING TOP OF THE COACH, THE BATMAN SIGHTS.. AND IS SIGHTED BY.. HIS QUARRY!

THE BATMAN AGAIN! I MISSED HIM BEFORE.. BUT THIS TIME I WON'T!

BETTER SHOOT FAST, THEN, RAT!

A PANTHER-SWIFT LUNGE OF A TRAINED, POWERFUL FRAME, AND...

HANG ON WHEN YOU'RE HIT, OR THE JAIL AT THE END OF THE LINE WILL BE OUT A CUSTOMER!

SHUT YOUR EYES, BATMAN...

I'D RATHER FALL OFF THAN GET HIT AGAIN!

BUT NOT EVEN THE BATMAN'S LIGHTNING SPEED CAN OUTMATCH BLASTING LEAD.. AND THE CRIMINAL'S BULLET STRIKES WITH PILE-DRIVER FORCE!

...I GOT A SURPRISE FOR YOU!

CRACK!

OOHHH-W-H.. HE'S GOT ME...

FAR TOWARD THE FRONT OF THE TRAIN, ROBIN HEARS THE BARK OF THE SHOT...

A SHOT! AND THE BATMAN'S HIT! I.. I'VE GOT TO DO SOMETHING!

5213 77067

10

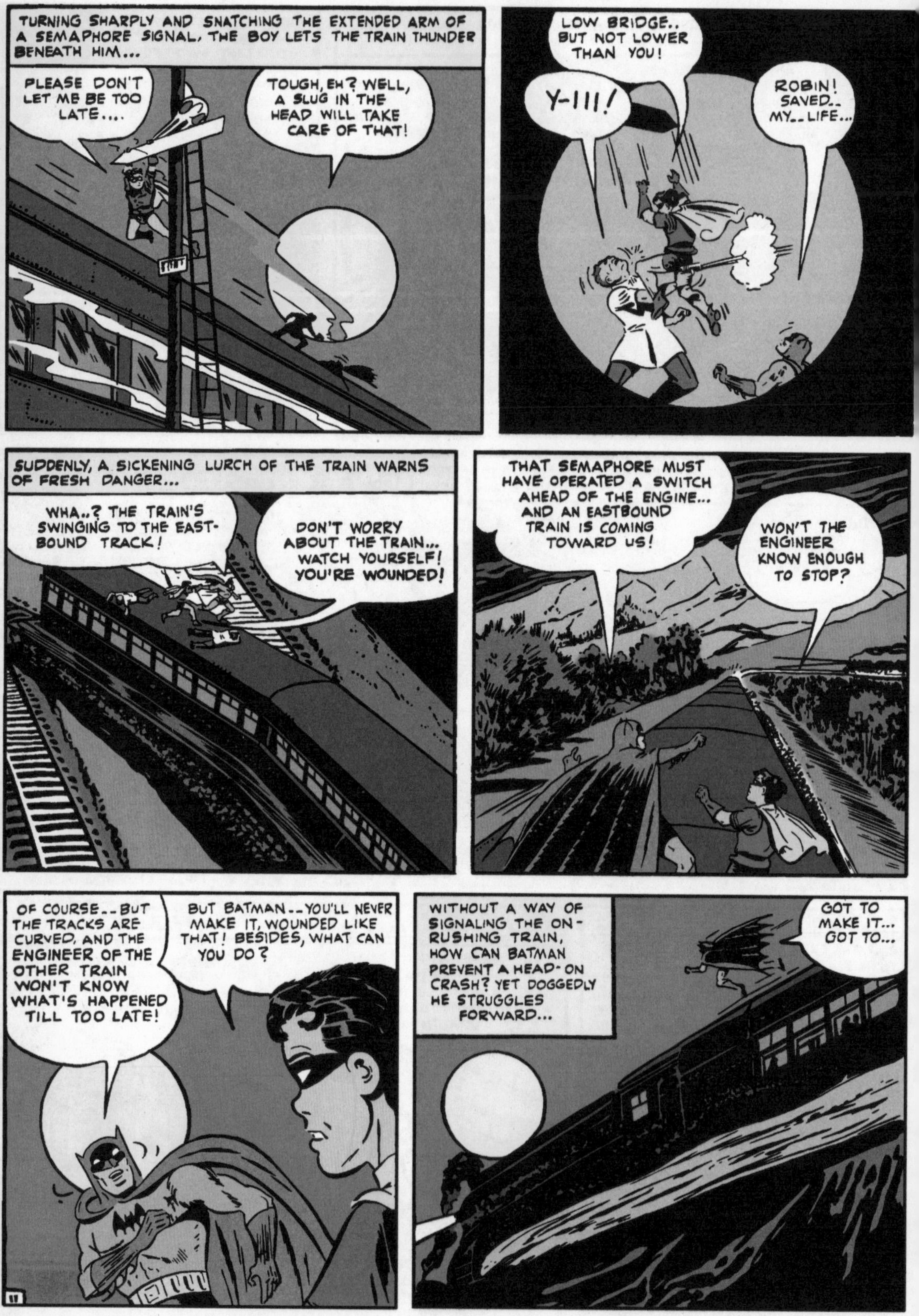
TURNING SHARPLY AND SNATCHING THE EXTENDED ARM OF A SEMAPHORE SIGNAL, THE BOY LETS THE TRAIN THUNDER BENEATH HIM...
PLEASE DON'T LET ME BE TOO LATE....
TOUGH, EH? WELL, A SLUG IN THE HEAD WILL TAKE CARE OF THAT!
LOW BRIDGE.. BUT NOT LOWER THAN YOU!
Y-III!
ROBIN! SAVED.. MY..LIFE...
SUDDENLY, A SICKENING LURCH OF THE TRAIN WARNS OF FRESH DANGER...
WHA..? THE TRAIN'S SWINGING TO THE EAST-BOUND TRACK!
DON'T WORRY ABOUT THE TRAIN... WATCH YOURSELF! YOU'RE WOUNDED!
THAT SEMAPHORE MUST HAVE OPERATED A SWITCH AHEAD OF THE ENGINE... AND AN EASTBOUND TRAIN IS COMING TOWARD US!
WON'T THE ENGINEER KNOW ENOUGH TO STOP?
OF COURSE..BUT THE TRACKS ARE CURVED, AND THE ENGINEER OF THE OTHER TRAIN WON'T KNOW WHAT'S HAPPENED TILL TOO LATE!
BUT BATMAN..YOU'LL NEVER MAKE IT, WOUNDED LIKE THAT! BESIDES, WHAT CAN YOU DO?
WITHOUT A WAY OF SIGNALING THE ON-RUSHING TRAIN, HOW CAN BATMAN PREVENT A HEAD-ON CRASH? YET DOGGEDLY HE STRUGGLES FORWARD...
GOT TO MAKE IT... GOT TO...

THE ENGINEER, HELPLESSLY AWARE OF THE PERIL, KNOWS NOTHING OF THE WOUNDED MAN FIGHTING A VALIANT BATTLE OVERHEAD...

GOT TO.. KEEP GOING...

I'VE CUT THE ELECTRIC AND SET THE BRAKES... WHAT ELSE CAN I DO?

7165

NOW HE LOWERS HIMSELF TO THE COWCATCHER!... BUT WHAT DOES THAT MEAN, EXCEPT THAT BATMAN WILL BE THE FIRST TO DIE WHEN STEEL MEETS STEEL IN THUNDERING CHAOS?...

AT LAST... IF ONLY I'M IN TIME...

ABOARD THE EASTBOUND EXPRESS, THE ENGINEER BLINKS AT A STRANGE SIGHT...

SOMETHING FUNNY... COME HERE, JOE, AND TELL ME WHAT YOU SEE AHEAD OF THAT WESTBOUND ENGINE!

WHAT'S UP?

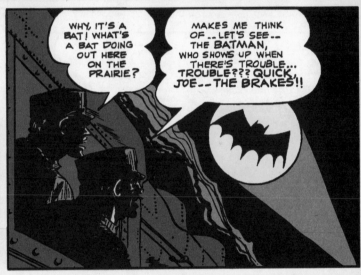

WHY, IT'S A BAT! WHAT'S A BAT DOING OUT HERE ON THE PRAIRIE?

MAKES ME THINK OF.. LET'S SEE.. THE BATMAN, WHO SHOWS UP WHEN THERE'S TROUBLE... TROUBLE??? QUICK, JOE-- THE BRAKES!!

A BAT!....BUT BENEATH THE WEIRD SYMBOL, A MAN'S GRIM DETERMINATION KEEPS IT FLYING!

THE BAT EMBLEM... RIPPED FROM THE FRONT OF MY UNIFORM ...MAYBE IT WILL WARN THEM!

TWO THUNDERING DRAGONS SHUDDER AND SCREECH UNDER THE SQUEEZE OF AIR BRAKES... SHUDDER AND SLACKEN THEIR TERRIFIC SPEED...

BATMAN! YOU -- YOU SAVED US!

EXCUSE ME-- TIRED-- GOT TO SIT DOWN SOMEWHERE..

ANOTHER SECOND WOULD HAVE SEEN THE WORST WRECK IN TEN YEARS!

12

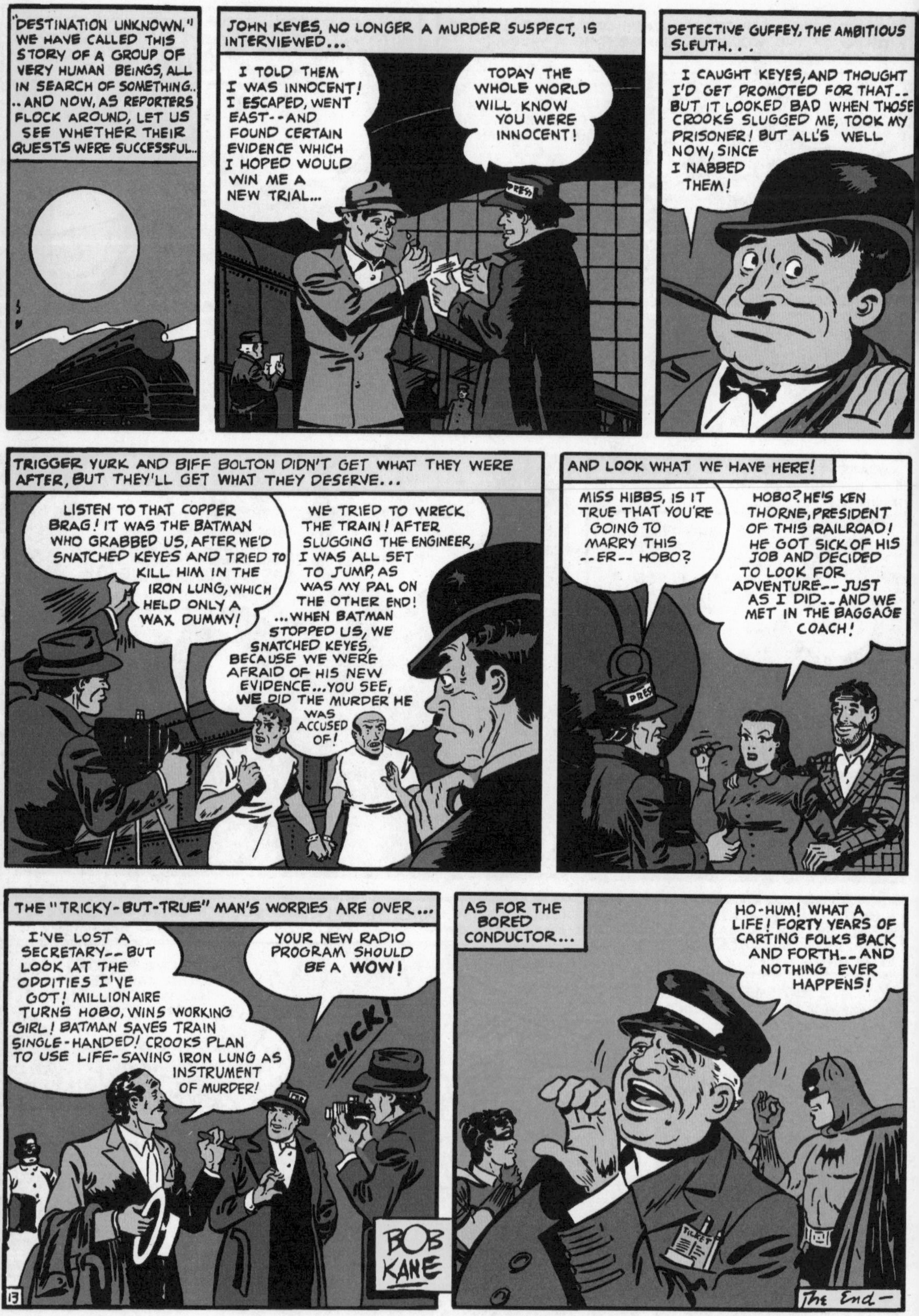
"DESTINATION UNKNOWN," WE HAVE CALLED THIS STORY OF A GROUP OF VERY HUMAN BEINGS, ALL IN SEARCH OF SOMETHING.. ..AND NOW, AS REPORTERS FLOCK AROUND, LET US SEE WHETHER THEIR QUESTS WERE SUCCESSFUL..
JOHN KEYES, NO LONGER A MURDER SUSPECT, IS INTERVIEWED...
I TOLD THEM I WAS INNOCENT! I ESCAPED, WENT EAST--AND FOUND CERTAIN EVIDENCE WHICH I HOPED WOULD WIN ME A NEW TRIAL...
TODAY THE WHOLE WORLD WILL KNOW YOU WERE INNOCENT!
DETECTIVE GUFFEY, THE AMBITIOUS SLEUTH. . .
I CAUGHT KEYES, AND THOUGHT I'D GET PROMOTED FOR THAT-- BUT IT LOOKED BAD WHEN THOSE CROOKS SLUGGED ME, TOOK MY PRISONER! BUT ALL'S WELL NOW, SINCE I NABBED THEM!
TRIGGER YURK AND BIFF BOLTON DIDN'T GET WHAT THEY WERE AFTER, BUT THEY'LL GET WHAT THEY DESERVE...
LISTEN TO THAT COPPER BRAG! IT WAS THE BATMAN WHO GRABBED US, AFTER WE'D SNATCHED KEYES AND TRIED TO KILL HIM IN THE IRON LUNG, WHICH HELD ONLY A WAX DUMMY!
WE TRIED TO WRECK THE TRAIN! AFTER SLUGGING THE ENGINEER, I WAS ALL SET TO JUMP, AS WAS MY PAL ON THE OTHER END! ...WHEN BATMAN STOPPED US, WE SNATCHED KEYES, BECAUSE WE WERE AFRAID OF HIS NEW EVIDENCE...YOU SEE, WE DID THE MURDER HE WAS ACCUSED OF!
AND LOOK WHAT WE HAVE HERE!
MISS HIBBS, IS IT TRUE THAT YOU'RE GOING TO MARRY THIS --ER-- HOBO?
HOBO? HE'S KEN THORNE, PRESIDENT OF THIS RAILROAD! HE GOT SICK OF HIS JOB AND DECIDED TO LOOK FOR ADVENTURE-- JUST AS I DID-- AND WE MET IN THE BAGGAGE COACH!
THE "TRICKY-BUT-TRUE" MAN'S WORRIES ARE OVER...
I'VE LOST A SECRETARY-- BUT LOOK AT THE ODDITIES I'VE GOT! MILLIONAIRE TURNS HOBO, WINS WORKING GIRL! BATMAN SAVES TRAIN SINGLE-HANDED! CROOKS PLAN TO USE LIFE-SAVING IRON LUNG AS INSTRUMENT OF MURDER!
YOUR NEW RADIO PROGRAM SHOULD BE A WOW!
CLICK!
BOB KANE
13
AS FOR THE BORED CONDUCTOR...
HO-HUM! WHAT A LIFE! FORTY YEARS OF CARTING FOLKS BACK AND FORTH-- AND NOTHING EVER HAPPENS!
The End—

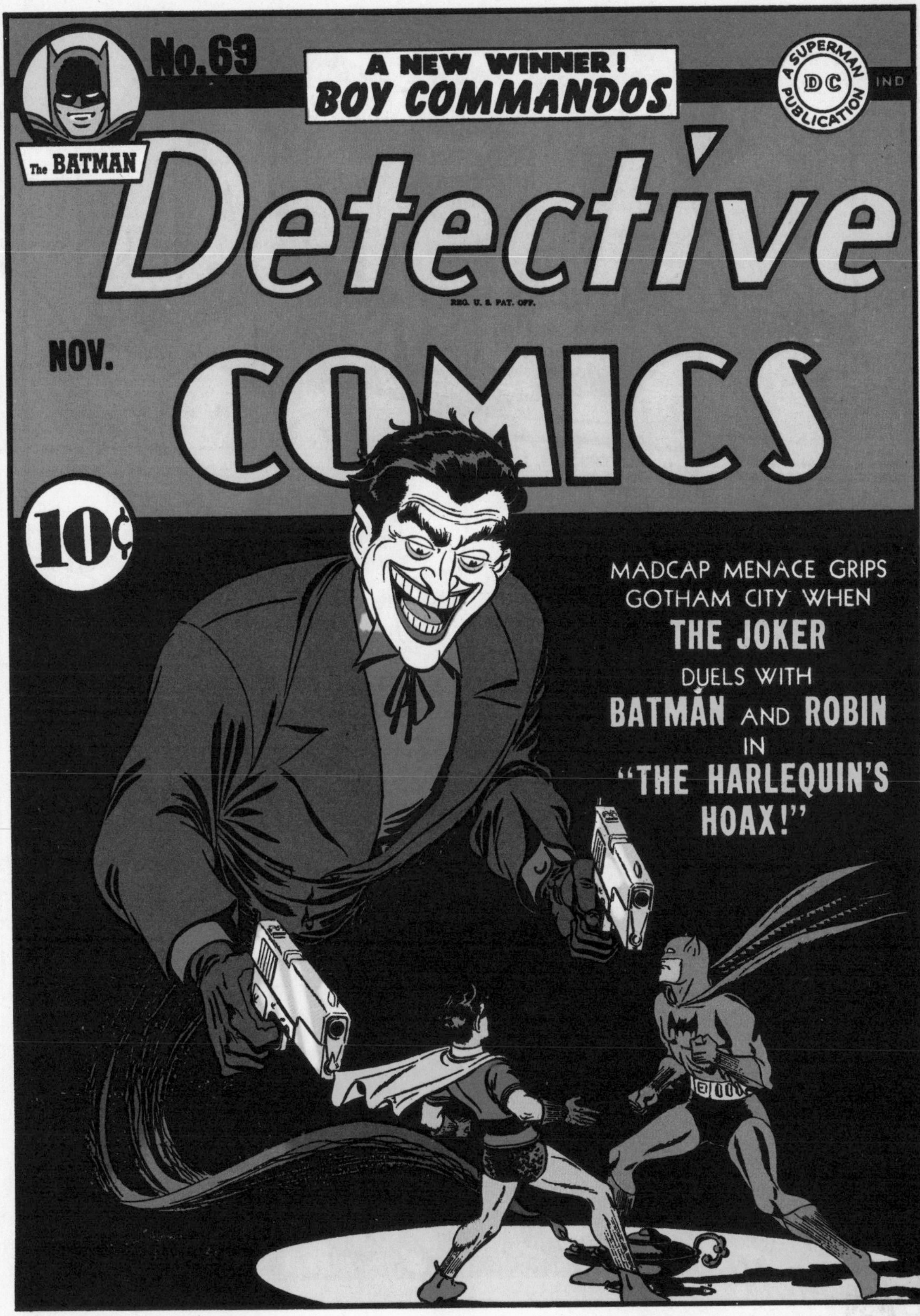

No. 69
A NEW WINNER! BOY COMMANDOS
A SUPERMAN DC PUBLICATION
IND
The BATMAN
Detective
REG. U. S. PAT. OFF.
NOV.
COMICS
10¢
MADCAP MENACE GRIPS GOTHAM CITY WHEN THE JOKER DUELS WITH BATMAN AND ROBIN IN "THE HARLEQUIN'S HOAX!"

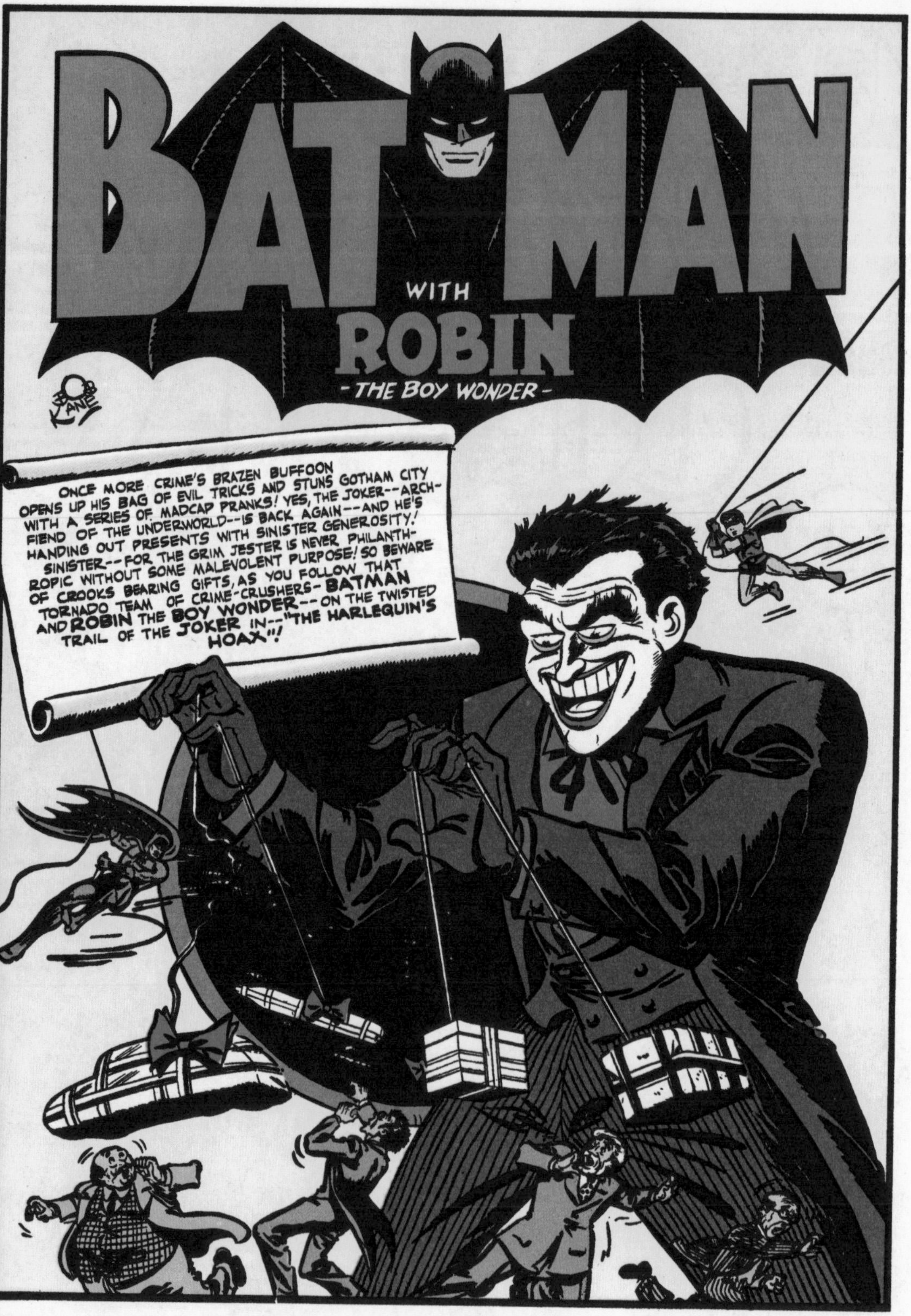
BATMAN
WITH
ROBIN
-THE BOY WONDER-
BOB KANE
ONCE MORE CRIME'S BRAZEN BUFFOON OPENS UP HIS BAG OF EVIL TRICKS AND STUNS GOTHAM CITY WITH A SERIES OF MADCAP PRANKS! YES, THE JOKER--ARCH-FIEND OF THE UNDERWORLD--IS BACK AGAIN--AND HE'S HANDING OUT PRESENTS WITH SINISTER GENEROSITY! SINISTER--FOR THE GRIM JESTER IS NEVER PHILANTHROPIC WITHOUT SOME MALEVOLENT PURPOSE! SO BEWARE OF CROOKS BEARING GIFTS, AS YOU FOLLOW THAT TORNADO TEAM OF CRIME-CRUSHERS- BATMAN AND ROBIN THE BOY WONDER--ON THE TWISTED TRAIL OF THE JOKER IN--"THE HARLEQUIN'S HOAX"!

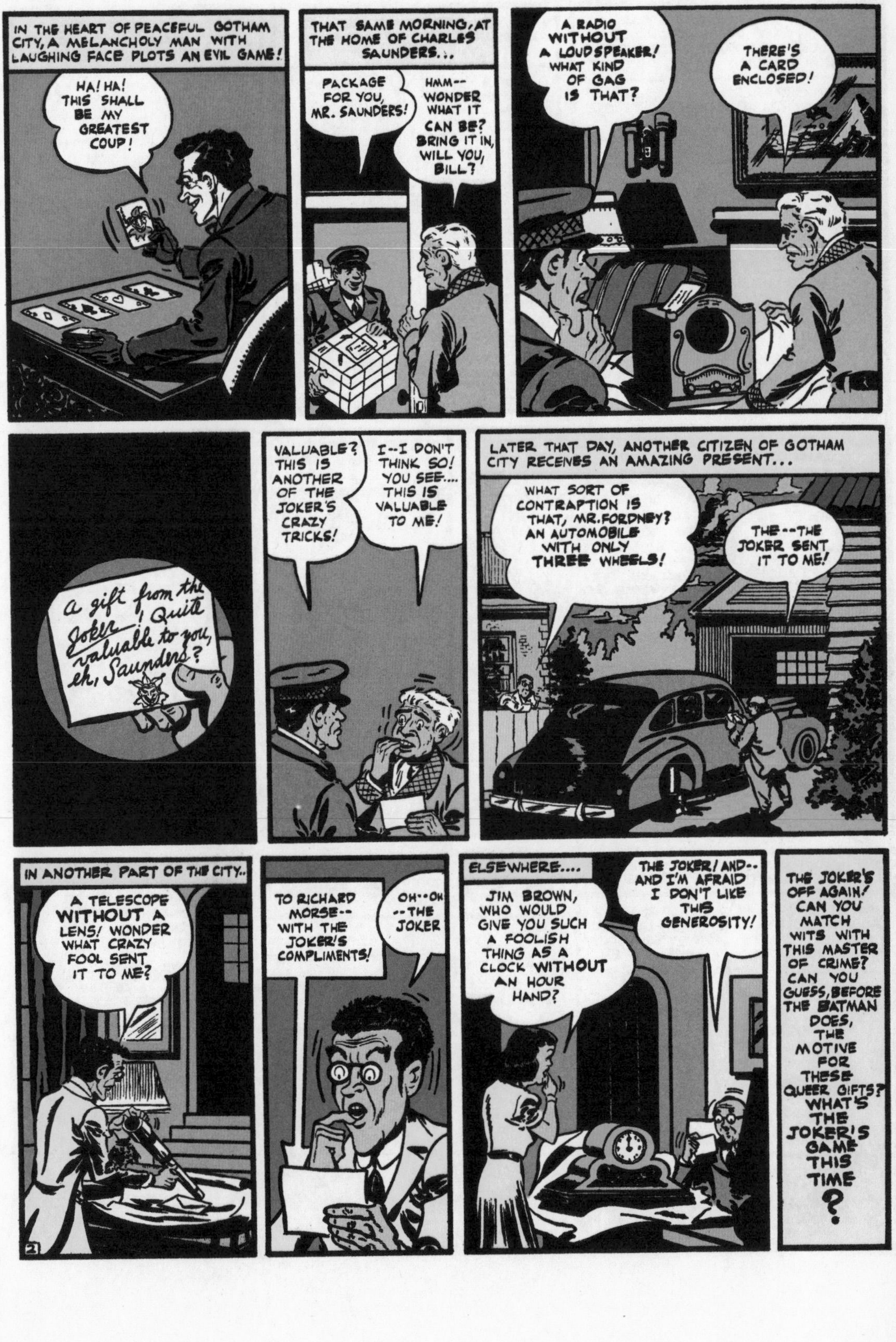
IN THE HEART OF PEACEFUL GOTHAM CITY, A MELANCHOLY MAN WITH LAUGHING FACE PLOTS AN EVIL GAME!
HA! HA! THIS SHALL BE MY GREATEST COUP!
THAT SAME MORNING, AT THE HOME OF CHARLES SAUNDERS...
PACKAGE FOR YOU, MR. SAUNDERS!
HMM-- WONDER WHAT IT CAN BE? BRING IT IN, WILL YOU, BILL?
A RADIO WITHOUT A LOUDSPEAKER! WHAT KIND OF GAG IS THAT?
THERE'S A CARD ENCLOSED!
a gift from the Joker! Quite valuable to you, eh, Saunders?
VALUABLE? THIS IS ANOTHER OF THE JOKER'S CRAZY TRICKS!
I--I DON'T THINK SO! YOU SEE.... THIS IS VALUABLE TO ME!
LATER THAT DAY, ANOTHER CITIZEN OF GOTHAM CITY RECEIVES AN AMAZING PRESENT...
WHAT SORT OF CONTRAPTION IS THAT, MR. FORDNEY? AN AUTOMOBILE WITH ONLY THREE WHEELS!
THE--THE JOKER SENT IT TO ME!
IN ANOTHER PART OF THE CITY..
A TELESCOPE WITHOUT A LENS! WONDER WHAT CRAZY FOOL SENT IT TO ME?
TO RICHARD MORSE-- WITH THE JOKER'S COMPLIMENTS!
OH--OH --THE JOKER
ELSEWHERE....
JIM BROWN, WHO WOULD GIVE YOU SUCH A FOOLISH THING AS A CLOCK WITHOUT AN HOUR HAND?
THE JOKER! AND-- AND I'M AFRAID I DON'T LIKE THIS GENEROSITY!
THE JOKER'S OFF AGAIN! CAN YOU MATCH WITS WITH THIS MASTER OF CRIME? CAN YOU GUESS, BEFORE THE BATMAN DOES, THE MOTIVE FOR THESE QUEER GIFTS? WHAT'S THE JOKER'S GAME THIS TIME ?
2

MEANWHILE OTHER PERSONS PLAY A GAME-- A GAME OF CHANCE! BRUCE WAYNE AND LINDA PAGE MAKE MERRY AT THE FUN PARK!

MISSED AGAIN, BUD! HOW ABOUT TRYIN' SOME MORE?

OH, BRUCE, COME ON! I WANT TO GO ON THE PARACHUTE JUMP!

MINUTES LATER... BRUCE AND LINDA ARE BEING PULLED UP 200 FEET INTO THE SKY!

SAY, I HADN'T REALIZED THESE THINGS GO UP SO HIGH!

SISSY! DON'T TELL ME YOU'RE SCARED, BRUCE?

THE 'CHUTE REACHES THE TOP! CONTACT--AND THE DUO BEGINS A THRILLING PLUNGE THRU SPACE!

WHEEEE!

BETTER HOLD TIGHT, LINDA!

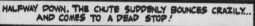

HALFWAY DOWN, THE CHUTE SUDDENLY BOUNCES CRAZILY... AND COMES TO A DEAD STOP!

BRUCE! WHAT'S HAPPENED? WHY AREN'T WE MOVING?

SOMETHING'S GONE WRONG! I'M AFRAID WE'RE STUCK UP HERE TILL THEY LOCATE THE TROUBLE!!

THE NEWS SPREADS LIKE WILDFIRE! SHOUTING, EXCITED HUMANS PUSH FORWARD, EYES TURNED UP TO THE HELPLESS COUPLE!

THAT'S THEM! THEY'RE HANGING 100 FEET UP!

THAT'S LINDA PAGE AND PLAYBOY BRUCE WAYNE! WOW! I'VE GOT A STORY!

ONE INSANE HOUR LATER! SANDWICHES AND A MIKE ARE HAULED UP TO THE PAIR ...

IF ANY OF MY FAMILY ARE LISTENING IN, I DON'T WANT THEM TO WORRY IF I'M LATE FOR SUPPER!

AND IF MY WARD, DICK, IS LISTENING TO MY VOICE, DON'T WORRY IF I'M LATE FOR SUPPER!

ANOTHER HOUR PASSES... SLOWLY! THEN A MILE-LONG FLOOD OF LIGHT BLAZONS A WEIRD SYMBOL AGAINST THE SKY!

LOOK! A BAT!

THAT'S FROM POLICE HEADQUARTERS! THEY'RE CALLING M...THE BATMAN!

JUST THINK, BRUCE! SOMEWHERE THE BATMAN IS GOING INTO ACTION NOW!

LIKE FUN! HE'S STUCK HERE IN A PARACHUTE!

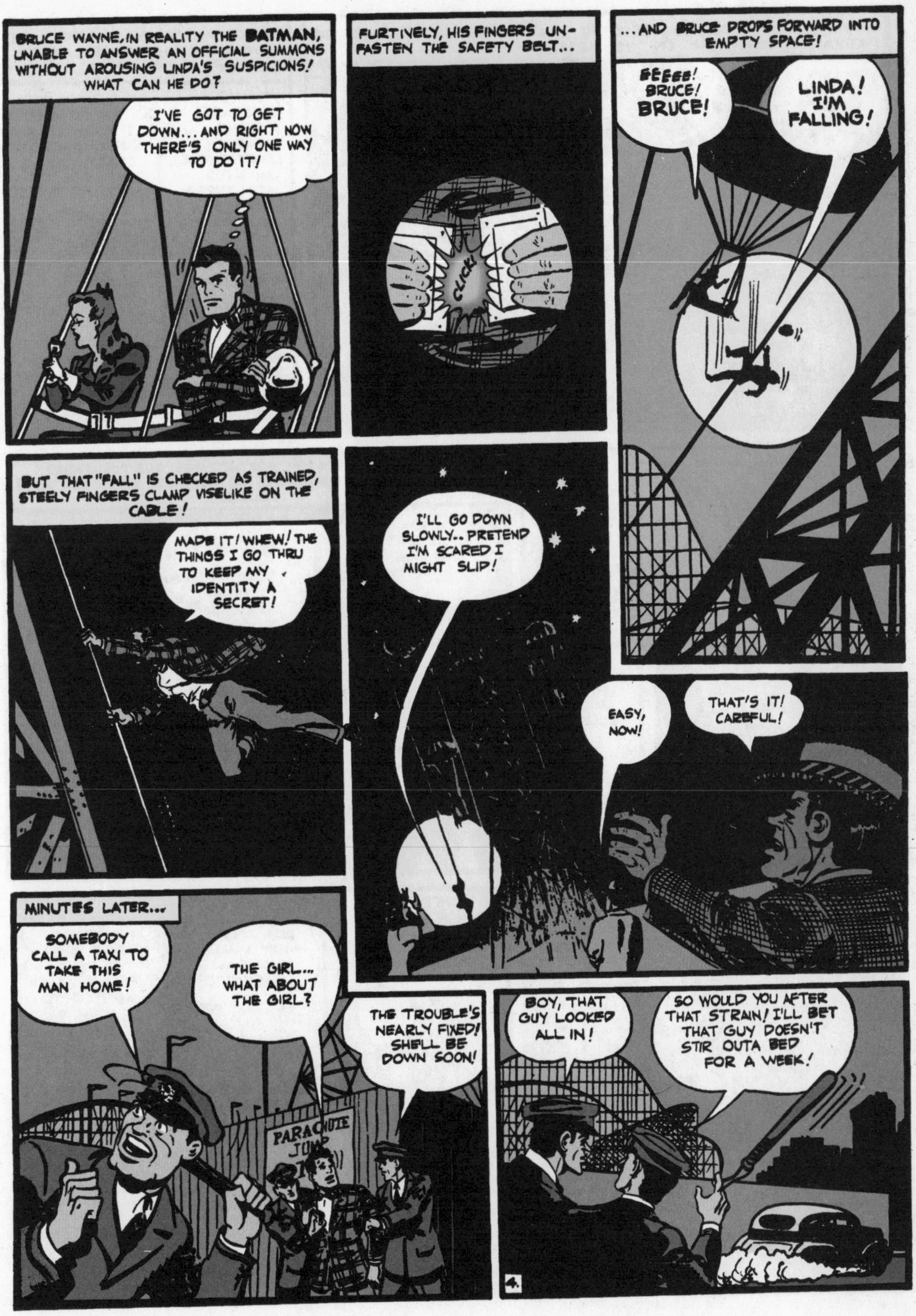

BRUCE WAYNE, IN REALITY THE BATMAN, UNABLE TO ANSWER AN OFFICIAL SUMMONS WITHOUT AROUSING LINDA'S SUSPICIONS! WHAT CAN HE DO?
I'VE GOT TO GET DOWN... AND RIGHT NOW THERE'S ONLY ONE WAY TO DO IT!
FURTIVELY, HIS FINGERS UN-FASTEN THE SAFETY BELT...
CLICK!
...AND BRUCE DROPS FORWARD INTO EMPTY SPACE!
EEEEE! BRUCE! BRUCE!
LINDA! I'M FALLING!
BUT THAT "FALL" IS CHECKED AS TRAINED, STEELY FINGERS CLAMP VISELIKE ON THE CABLE!
MADE IT! WHEW! THE THINGS I GO THRU TO KEEP MY IDENTITY A SECRET!
I'LL GO DOWN SLOWLY.. PRETEND I'M SCARED I MIGHT SLIP!
EASY, NOW!
THAT'S IT! CAREFUL!
MINUTES LATER...
SOMEBODY CALL A TAXI TO TAKE THIS MAN HOME!
THE GIRL... WHAT ABOUT THE GIRL?
THE TROUBLE'S NEARLY FIXED! SHE'LL BE DOWN SOON!
PARACHUTE JUMP
BOY, THAT GUY LOOKED ALL IN!
SO WOULD YOU AFTER THAT STRAIN! I'LL BET THAT GUY DOESN'T STIR OUTA BED FOR A WEEK!
4.

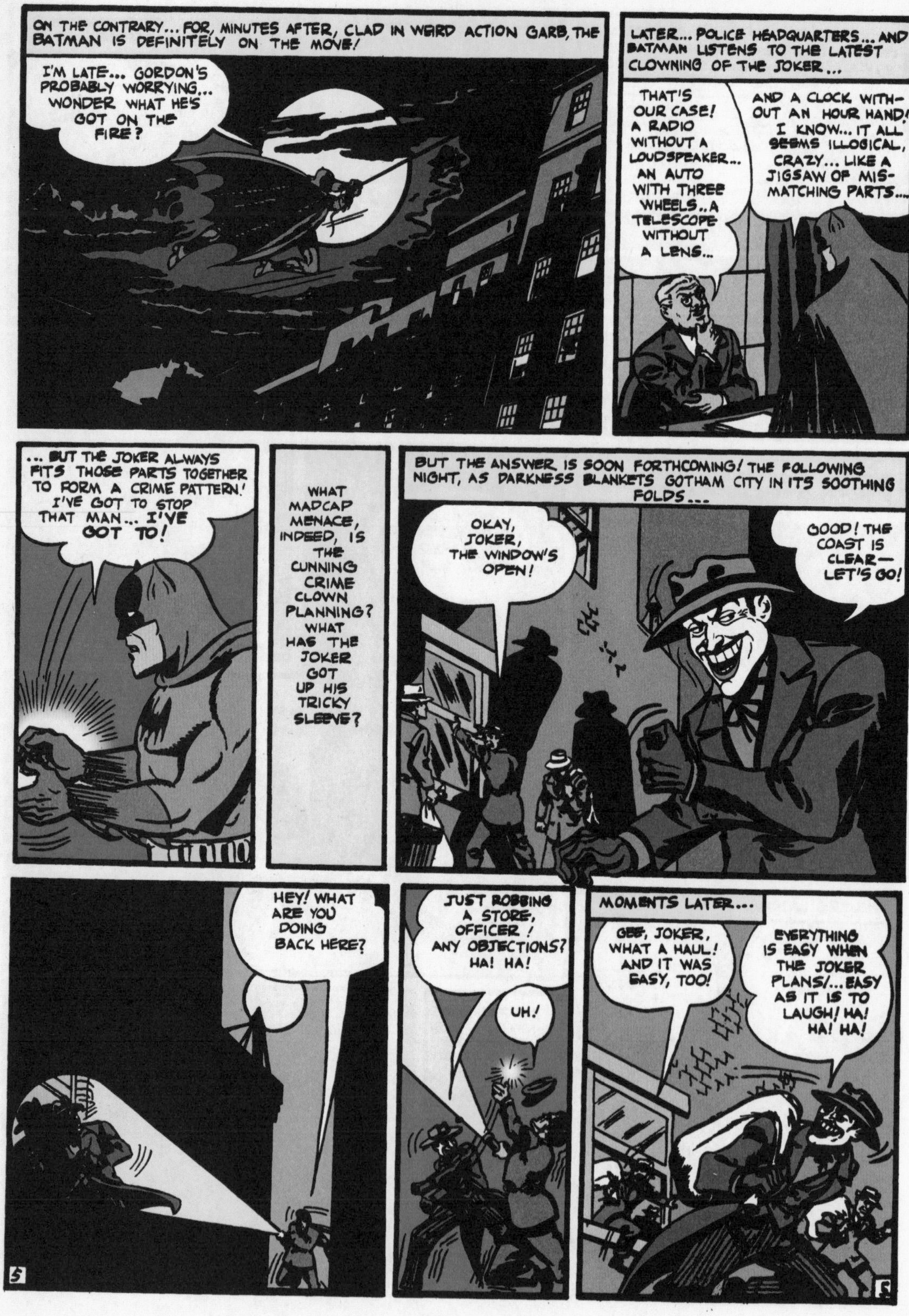

ON THE CONTRARY... FOR, MINUTES AFTER, CLAD IN WEIRD ACTION GARB, THE BATMAN IS DEFINITELY ON THE MOVE!
I'M LATE... GORDON'S PROBABLY WORRYING... WONDER WHAT HE'S GOT ON THE FIRE?
LATER... POLICE HEADQUARTERS... AND BATMAN LISTENS TO THE LATEST CLOWNING OF THE JOKER...
THAT'S OUR CASE! A RADIO WITHOUT A LOUDSPEAKER... AN AUTO WITH THREE WHEELS.. A TELESCOPE WITHOUT A LENS...
AND A CLOCK WITHOUT AN HOUR HAND! I KNOW... IT ALL SEEMS ILLOGICAL, CRAZY... LIKE A JIGSAW OF MIS-MATCHING PARTS...
... BUT THE JOKER ALWAYS FITS THOSE PARTS TOGETHER TO FORM A CRIME PATTERN! I'VE GOT TO STOP THAT MAN... I'VE GOT TO!
WHAT MADCAP MENACE, INDEED, IS THE CUNNING CRIME CLOWN PLANNING? WHAT HAS THE JOKER GOT UP HIS TRICKY SLEEVE?
BUT THE ANSWER IS SOON FORTHCOMING! THE FOLLOWING NIGHT, AS DARKNESS BLANKETS GOTHAM CITY IN ITS SOOTHING FOLDS...
OKAY, JOKER, THE WINDOW'S OPEN!
GOOD! THE COAST IS CLEAR— LET'S GO!
HEY! WHAT ARE YOU DOING BACK HERE?
JUST ROBBING A STORE, OFFICER! ANY OBJECTIONS? HA! HA!
UH!
MOMENTS LATER...
GEE, JOKER, WHAT A HAUL! AND IT WAS EASY, TOO!
EVERYTHING IS EASY WHEN THE JOKER PLANS!... EASY AS IT IS TO LAUGH! HA! HA! HA!

MORNING... AND NEWSPAPER HEADLINES SCREAM CRIME AT CITIZENS OF GOTHAM CITY!

WUXTRY! JOKER ROBS DEPARTMENT STORE! WUXTRY!

...AND POLICE FOUND THE BURGLAR ALARMS OFF, BRUCE! THAT'S HOW THE JOKER PULLED THE JOB SO EASILY!

YES... AND NOTICE THE NAME OF THE MANAGER OF THAT STORE... CHARLES SAUNDERS!

WHY... HE'S THE FELLOW WHO RECEIVED THAT RADIO WITHOUT A LOUDSPEAKER FROM THE JOKER! SAY, THINK IT WAS AN INSIDE JOB?

MIGHTY QUEER, DICK! BATMAN AND ROBIN ARE GOING TO DO SOME DETECTIVE WORK TONIGHT!

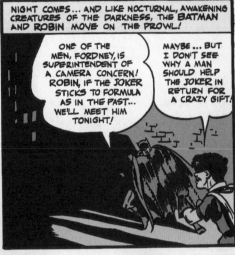

NIGHT COMES... AND LIKE NOCTURNAL, AWAKENING CREATURES OF THE DARKNESS, THE BATMAN AND ROBIN MOVE ON THE PROWL!

ONE OF THE MEN, FORDNEY, IS SUPERINTENDENT OF A CAMERA CONCERN! ROBIN, IF THE JOKER STICKS TO FORMULA AS IN THE PAST... WE'LL MEET HIM TONIGHT!

MAYBE... BUT I DON'T SEE WHY A MAN SHOULD HELP THE JOKER IN RETURN FOR A CRAZY GIFT!

THE STORAGE WAREHOUSE OF THE SHUTTER CAMERA CO...

THESE BARRELS WERE STORED HERE TONIGHT, AND FORDNEY SAID NOT TO TOUCH 'EM! WONDER WHAT'S IN 'EM?

YOU WON'T HAVE TO WONDER LONG! HA! HA!

OWH-HH-HH...

HAW! HAW! THAT WAS A SWELL STUNT, JOKER, SNEAKING US IN INSIDE THE BARRELS!

YES.. FORDNEY WAS VERY OBLIGING, WASN'T HE? NOW LET'S GET AT THOSE EXPENSIVE CAMERAS STORED IN HERE!

BUT, ALSO STORED IN THE WAREHOUSE IS DYNAMITE... DYNAMITE IN THE PERSONS OF BATMAN AND ROBIN THE BOY WONDER!

YOU!!

RIGHT, ROBIN... AND NOW THIS CALLS FOR SOME FISTICUFFS!

LOOKS LIKE YOU CALLED YOUR SHOT, BATMAN!

SHUTTER CAMERA

HANDLE WITH CARE

CAUTION!

6

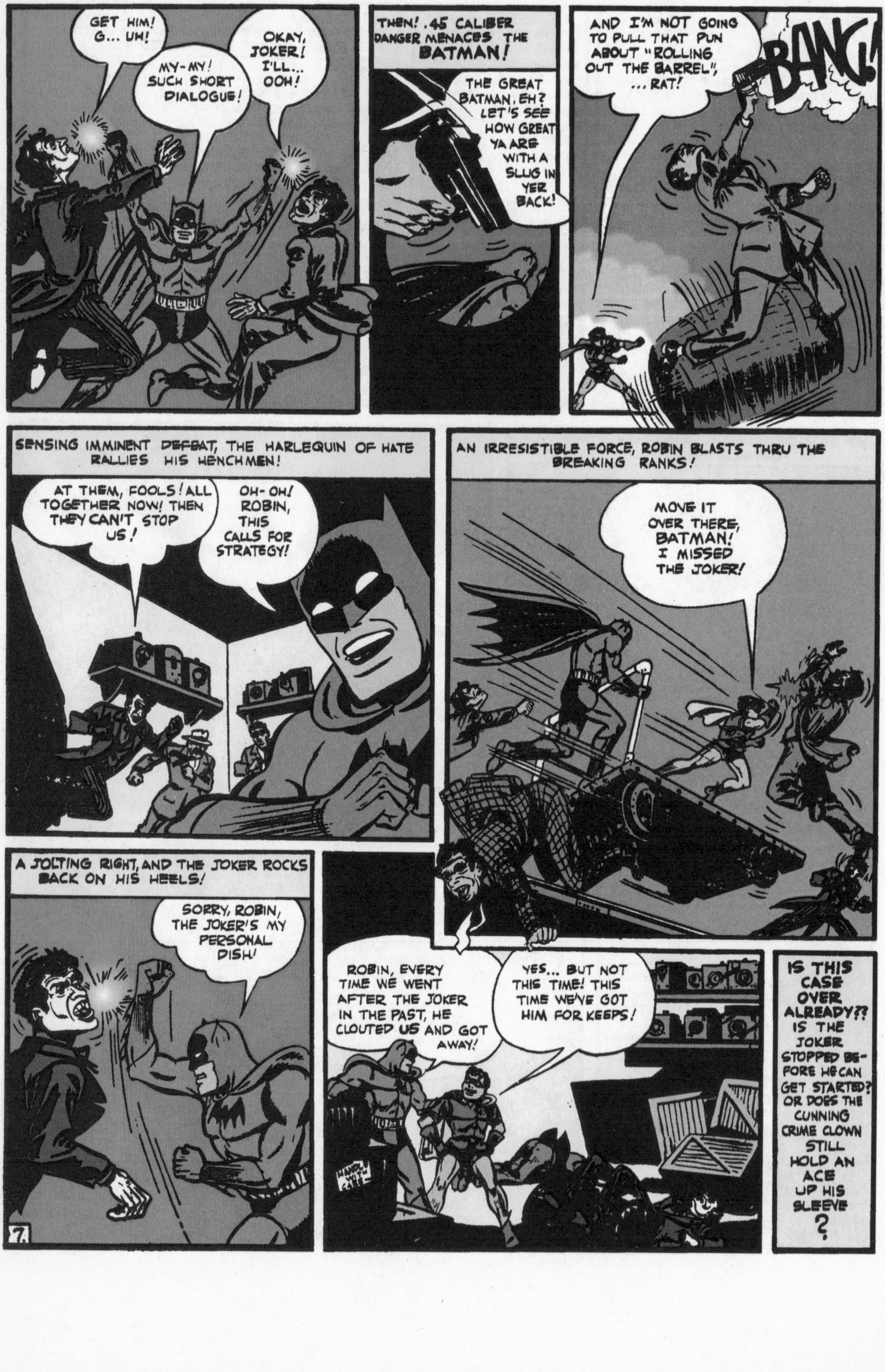
GET HIM! G... UH!
MY-MY! SUCH SHORT DIALOGUE!
OKAY, JOKER! I'LL... OOH!
THEN! .45 CALIBER DANGER MENACES THE BATMAN!
THE GREAT BATMAN, EH? LET'S SEE HOW GREAT YA ARE WITH A SLUG IN YER BACK!
AND I'M NOT GOING TO PULL THAT PUN ABOUT "ROLLING OUT THE BARREL", ... RAT!
BANG!
SENSING IMMINENT DEFEAT, THE HARLEQUIN OF HATE RALLIES HIS HENCHMEN!
AT THEM, FOOLS! ALL TOGETHER NOW! THEN THEY CAN'T STOP US!
OH-OH! ROBIN, THIS CALLS FOR STRATEGY!
AN IRRESISTIBLE FORCE, ROBIN BLASTS THRU THE BREAKING RANKS!
MOVE IT OVER THERE, BATMAN! I MISSED THE JOKER!
A JOLTING RIGHT, AND THE JOKER ROCKS BACK ON HIS HEELS!
SORRY, ROBIN, THE JOKER'S MY PERSONAL DISH!
7
ROBIN, EVERY TIME WE WENT AFTER THE JOKER IN THE PAST, HE CLOUTED US AND GOT AWAY!
YES... BUT NOT THIS TIME! THIS TIME WE'VE GOT HIM FOR KEEPS!
HANDLE WITH CARE
IS THIS CASE OVER ALREADY?? IS THE JOKER STOPPED BEFORE HE CAN GET STARTED? OR DOES THE CUNNING CRIME CLOWN STILL HOLD AN ACE UP HIS SLEEVE ?

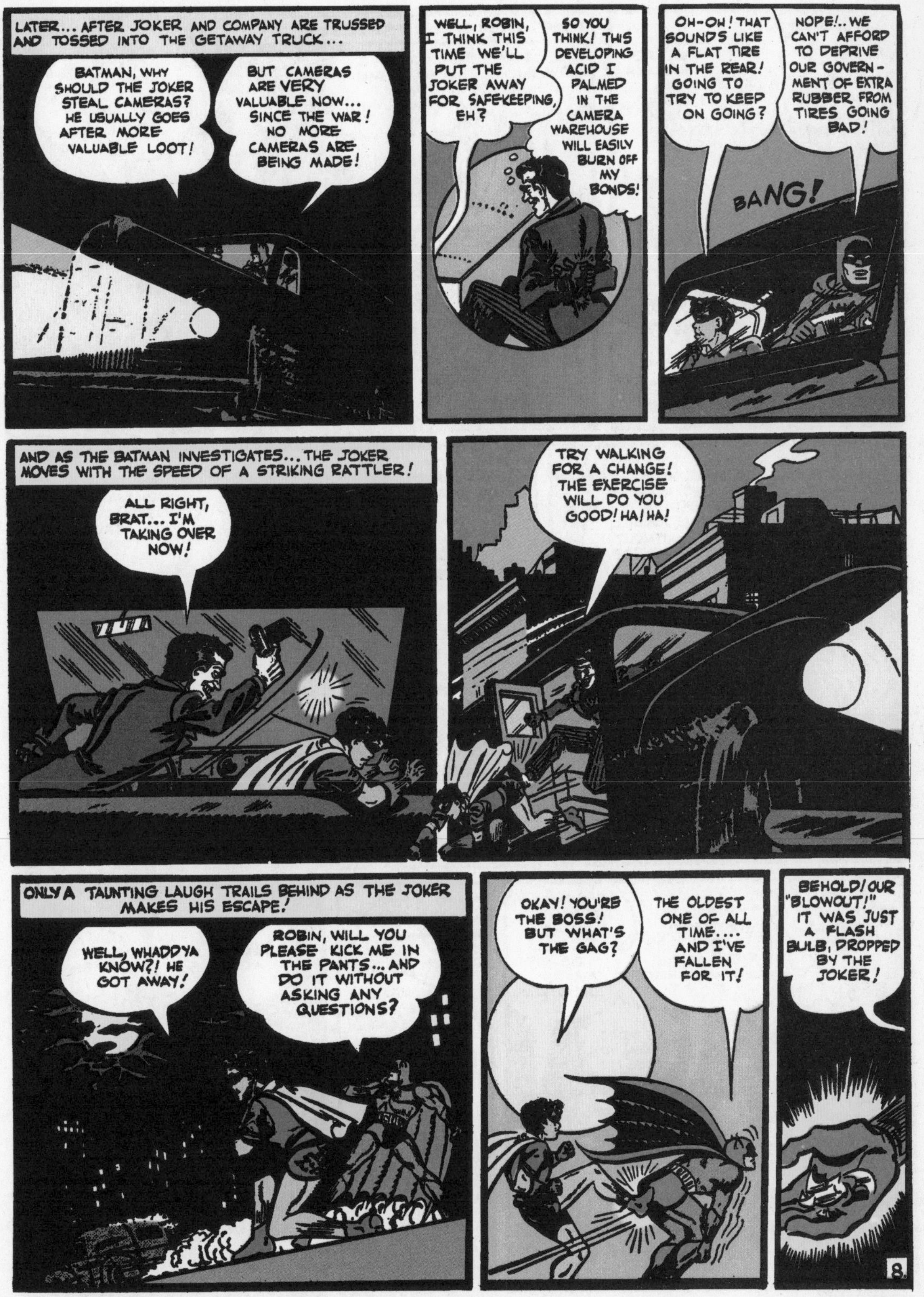
LATER... AFTER JOKER AND COMPANY ARE TRUSSED AND TOSSED INTO THE GETAWAY TRUCK...
BATMAN, WHY SHOULD THE JOKER STEAL CAMERAS? HE USUALLY GOES AFTER MORE VALUABLE LOOT!
BUT CAMERAS ARE VERY VALUABLE NOW... SINCE THE WAR! NO MORE CAMERAS ARE BEING MADE!
WELL, ROBIN, I THINK THIS TIME WE'LL PUT THE JOKER AWAY FOR SAFEKEEPING, EH?
SO YOU THINK! THIS DEVELOPING ACID I PALMED IN THE CAMERA WAREHOUSE WILL EASILY BURN OFF MY BONDS!
OH-OH! THAT SOUNDS LIKE A FLAT TIRE IN THE REAR! GOING TO TRY TO KEEP ON GOING?
NOPE!.. WE CAN'T AFFORD TO DEPRIVE OUR GOVERNMENT OF EXTRA RUBBER FROM TIRES GOING BAD!
BANG!
AND AS THE BATMAN INVESTIGATES... THE JOKER MOVES WITH THE SPEED OF A STRIKING RATTLER!
ALL RIGHT, BRAT... I'M TAKING OVER NOW!
TRY WALKING FOR A CHANGE! THE EXERCISE WILL DO YOU GOOD! HA! HA!
ONLY A TAUNTING LAUGH TRAILS BEHIND AS THE JOKER MAKES HIS ESCAPE!
WELL, WHADDYA KNOW?! HE GOT AWAY!
ROBIN, WILL YOU PLEASE KICK ME IN THE PANTS... AND DO IT WITHOUT ASKING ANY QUESTIONS?
OKAY! YOU'RE THE BOSS! BUT WHAT'S THE GAG?
THE OLDEST ONE OF ALL TIME.... AND I'VE FALLEN FOR IT!
BEHOLD! OUR "BLOWOUT!" IT WAS JUST A FLASH BULB, DROPPED BY THE JOKER!
8

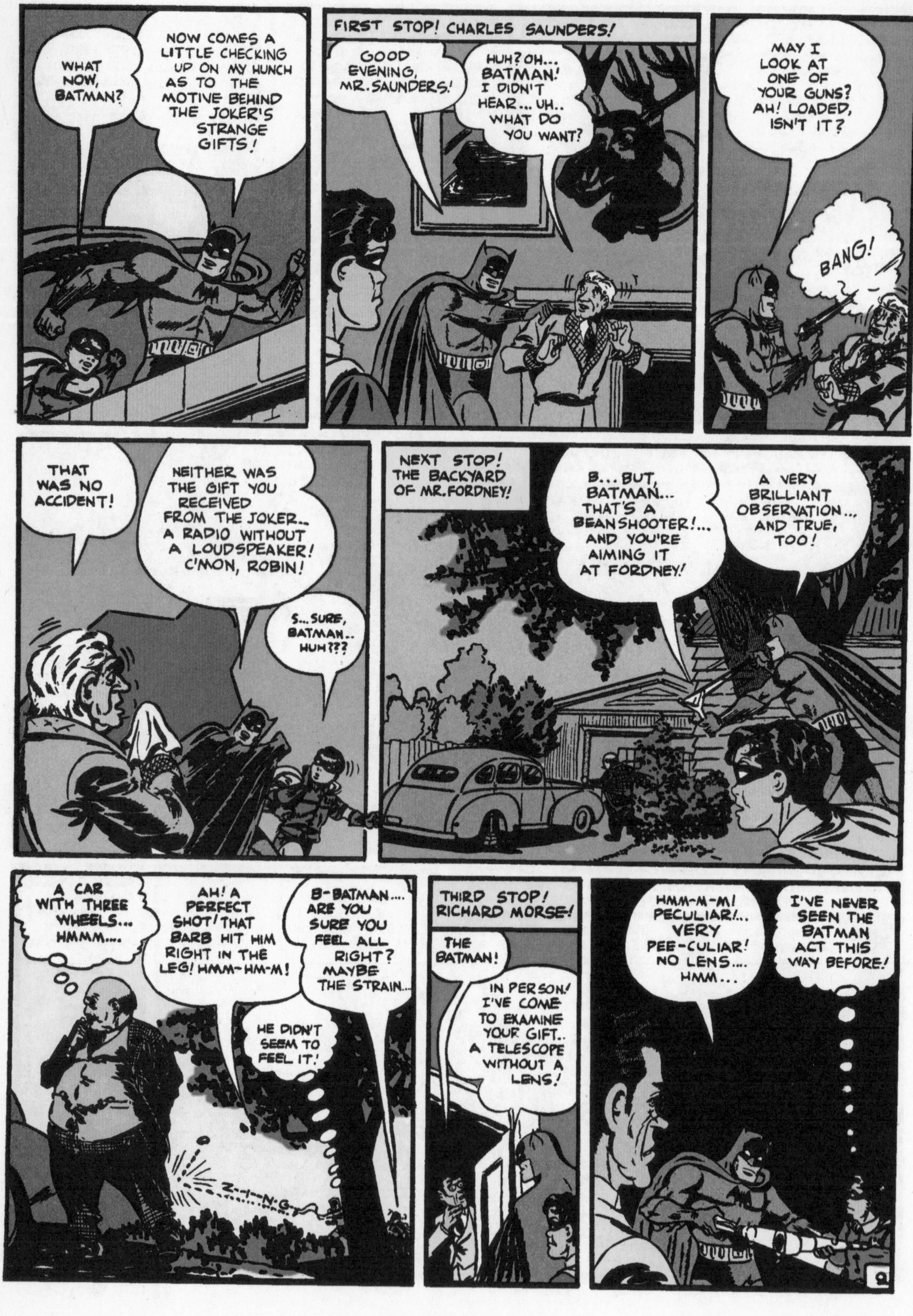
WHAT NOW, BATMAN?
NOW COMES A LITTLE CHECKING UP ON MY HUNCH AS TO THE MOTIVE BEHIND THE JOKER'S STRANGE GIFTS!
FIRST STOP! CHARLES SAUNDERS!
GOOD EVENING, MR. SAUNDERS!
HUH? OH... BATMAN! I DIDN'T HEAR... UH.. WHAT DO YOU WANT?
MAY I LOOK AT ONE OF YOUR GUNS? AH! LOADED, ISN'T IT?
BANG!
THAT WAS NO ACCIDENT!
NEITHER WAS THE GIFT YOU RECEIVED FROM THE JOKER.. A RADIO WITHOUT A LOUDSPEAKER! C'MON, ROBIN!
S...SURE, BATMAN.. HUH???
NEXT STOP! THE BACKYARD OF MR. FORDNEY!
B... BUT, BATMAN... THAT'S A BEANSHOOTER!... AND YOU'RE AIMING IT AT FORDNEY!
A VERY BRILLIANT OBSERVATION... AND TRUE, TOO!
A CAR WITH THREE WHEELS... HMMM....
AH! A PERFECT SHOT! THAT BARB HIT HIM RIGHT IN THE LEG! HMM-HM-M!
B-BATMAN.... ARE YOU SURE YOU FEEL ALL RIGHT? MAYBE THE STRAIN...
HE DIDN'T SEEM TO FEEL IT!
Z-I-N-G
THIRD STOP! RICHARD MORSE!
THE BATMAN!
IN PERSON! I'VE COME TO EXAMINE YOUR GIFT.. A TELESCOPE WITHOUT A LENS!
HMM-M-M! PECULIAR!... VERY PEE-CULIAR! NO LENS.... HMM...
I'VE NEVER SEEN THE BATMAN ACT THIS WAY BEFORE!
9

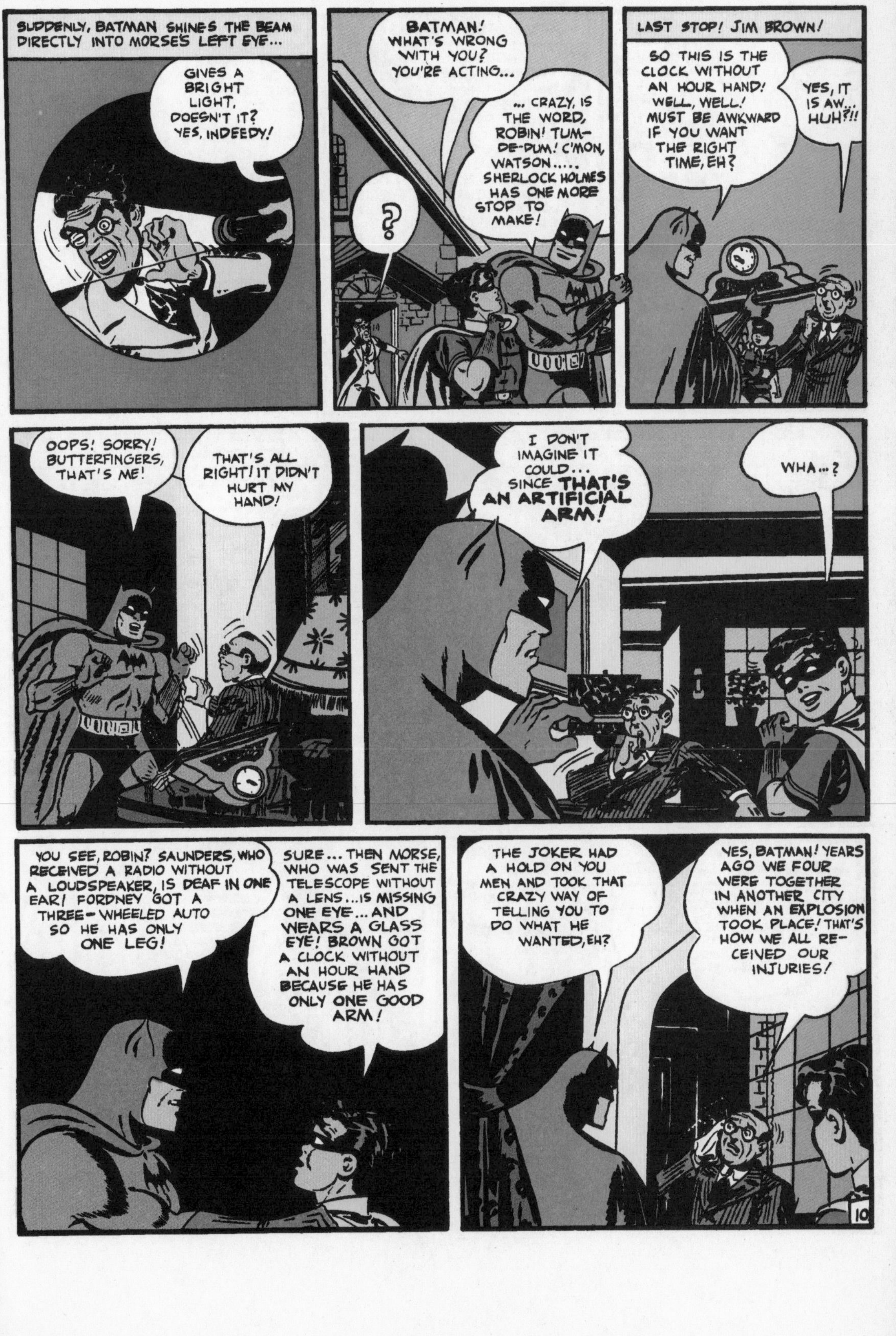
SUDDENLY, BATMAN SHINES THE BEAM DIRECTLY INTO MORSE'S LEFT EYE...
GIVES A BRIGHT LIGHT, DOESN'T IT? YES, INDEEDY!
BATMAN! WHAT'S WRONG WITH YOU? YOU'RE ACTING...
... CRAZY, IS THE WORD, ROBIN! TUM-DE-DUM! C'MON, WATSON..... SHERLOCK HOLMES HAS ONE MORE STOP TO MAKE!
?
LAST STOP! JIM BROWN!
SO THIS IS THE CLOCK WITHOUT AN HOUR HAND! WELL, WELL! MUST BE AWKWARD IF YOU WANT THE RIGHT TIME, EH?
YES, IT IS AW... HUH?!!
OOPS! SORRY! BUTTERFINGERS, THAT'S ME!
THAT'S ALL RIGHT! IT DIDN'T HURT MY HAND!
I DON'T IMAGINE IT COULD... SINCE THAT'S AN ARTIFICIAL ARM!
WHA...?
YOU SEE, ROBIN? SAUNDERS, WHO RECEIVED A RADIO WITHOUT A LOUDSPEAKER, IS DEAF IN ONE EAR! FORDNEY GOT A THREE-WHEELED AUTO SO HE HAS ONLY ONE LEG!
SURE... THEN MORSE, WHO WAS SENT THE TELESCOPE WITHOUT A LENS... IS MISSING ONE EYE... AND WEARS A GLASS EYE! BROWN GOT A CLOCK WITHOUT AN HOUR HAND BECAUSE HE HAS ONLY ONE GOOD ARM!
THE JOKER HAD A HOLD ON YOU MEN AND TOOK THAT CRAZY WAY OF TELLING YOU TO DO WHAT HE WANTED, EH?
YES, BATMAN! YEARS AGO WE FOUR WERE TOGETHER IN ANOTHER CITY WHEN AN EXPLOSION TOOK PLACE! THAT'S HOW WE ALL RECEIVED OUR INJURIES!
10

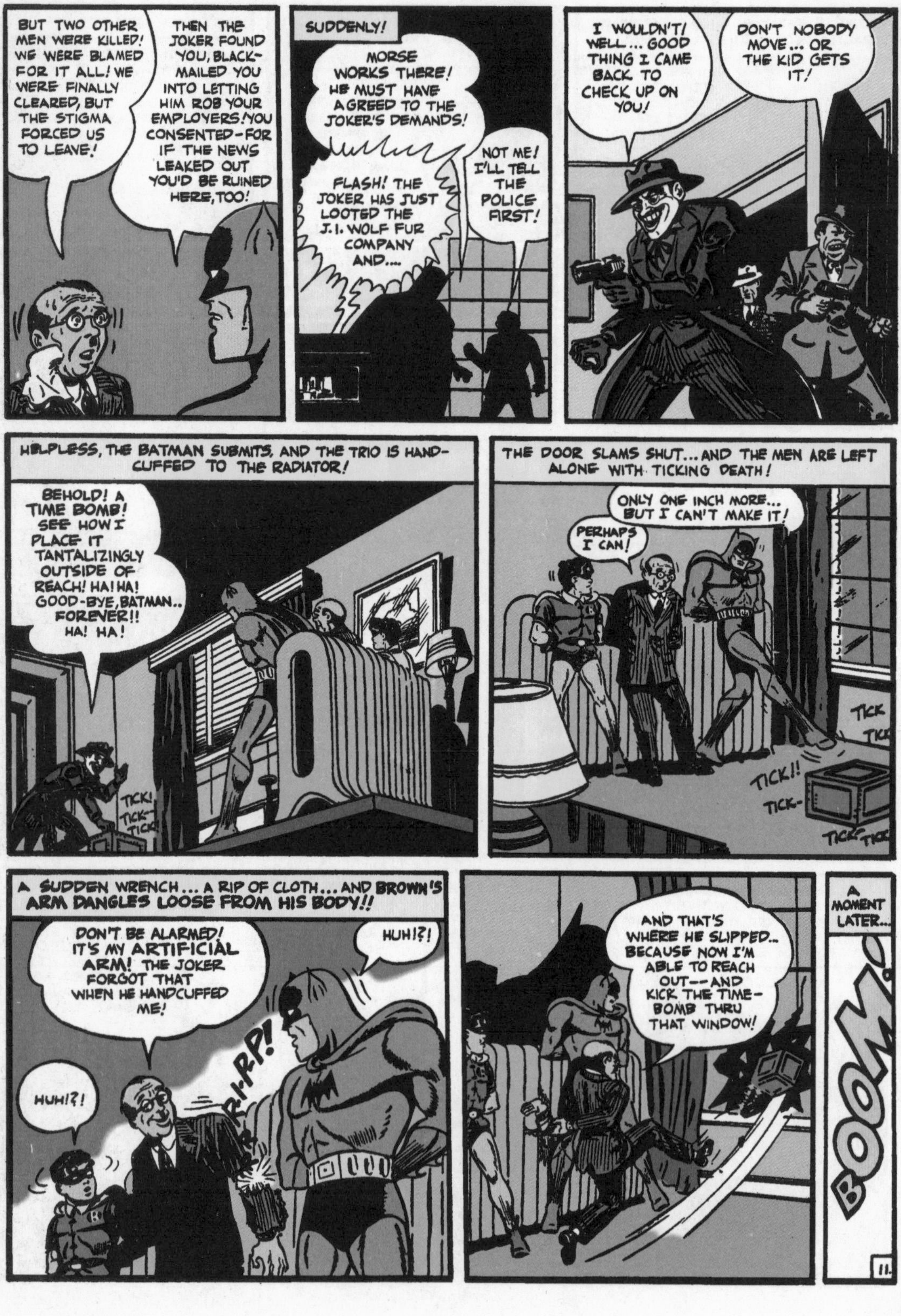
BUT TWO OTHER MEN WERE KILLED! WE WERE BLAMED FOR IT ALL! WE WERE FINALLY CLEARED, BUT THE STIGMA FORCED US TO LEAVE!
THEN THE JOKER FOUND YOU, BLACK-MAILED YOU INTO LETTING HIM ROB YOUR EMPLOYERS! YOU CONSENTED-FOR IF THE NEWS LEAKED OUT YOU'D BE RUINED HERE, TOO!
SUDDENLY!
MORSE WORKS THERE! HE MUST HAVE AGREED TO THE JOKER'S DEMANDS!
FLASH! THE JOKER HAS JUST LOOTED THE J. I. WOLF FUR COMPANY AND....
NOT ME! I'LL TELL THE POLICE FIRST!
I WOULDN'T! WELL... GOOD THING I CAME BACK TO CHECK UP ON YOU!
DON'T NOBODY MOVE... OR THE KID GETS IT!
HELPLESS, THE BATMAN SUBMITS, AND THE TRIO IS HAND-CUFFED TO THE RADIATOR!
BEHOLD! A TIME BOMB! SEE HOW I PLACE IT TANTALIZINGLY OUTSIDE OF REACH! HA! HA! GOOD-BYE, BATMAN.. FOREVER!! HA! HA!
TICK! TICK-TICK
THE DOOR SLAMS SHUT... AND THE MEN ARE LEFT ALONE WITH TICKING DEATH!
ONLY ONE INCH MORE... BUT I CAN'T MAKE IT!
PERHAPS I CAN!
TICK TICK
TICK!! TICK-
TICK TICK
A SUDDEN WRENCH... A RIP OF CLOTH... AND BROWN'S ARM DANGLES LOOSE FROM HIS BODY!!
DON'T BE ALARMED! IT'S MY ARTIFICIAL ARM! THE JOKER FORGOT THAT WHEN HE HANDCUFFED ME!
HUH!?!
HUH!?!
R-I-P-P!
AND THAT'S WHERE HE SLIPPED.. BECAUSE NOW I'M ABLE TO REACH OUT--AND KICK THE TIME-BOMB THRU THAT WINDOW!
A MOMENT LATER...
BOOM!
11.

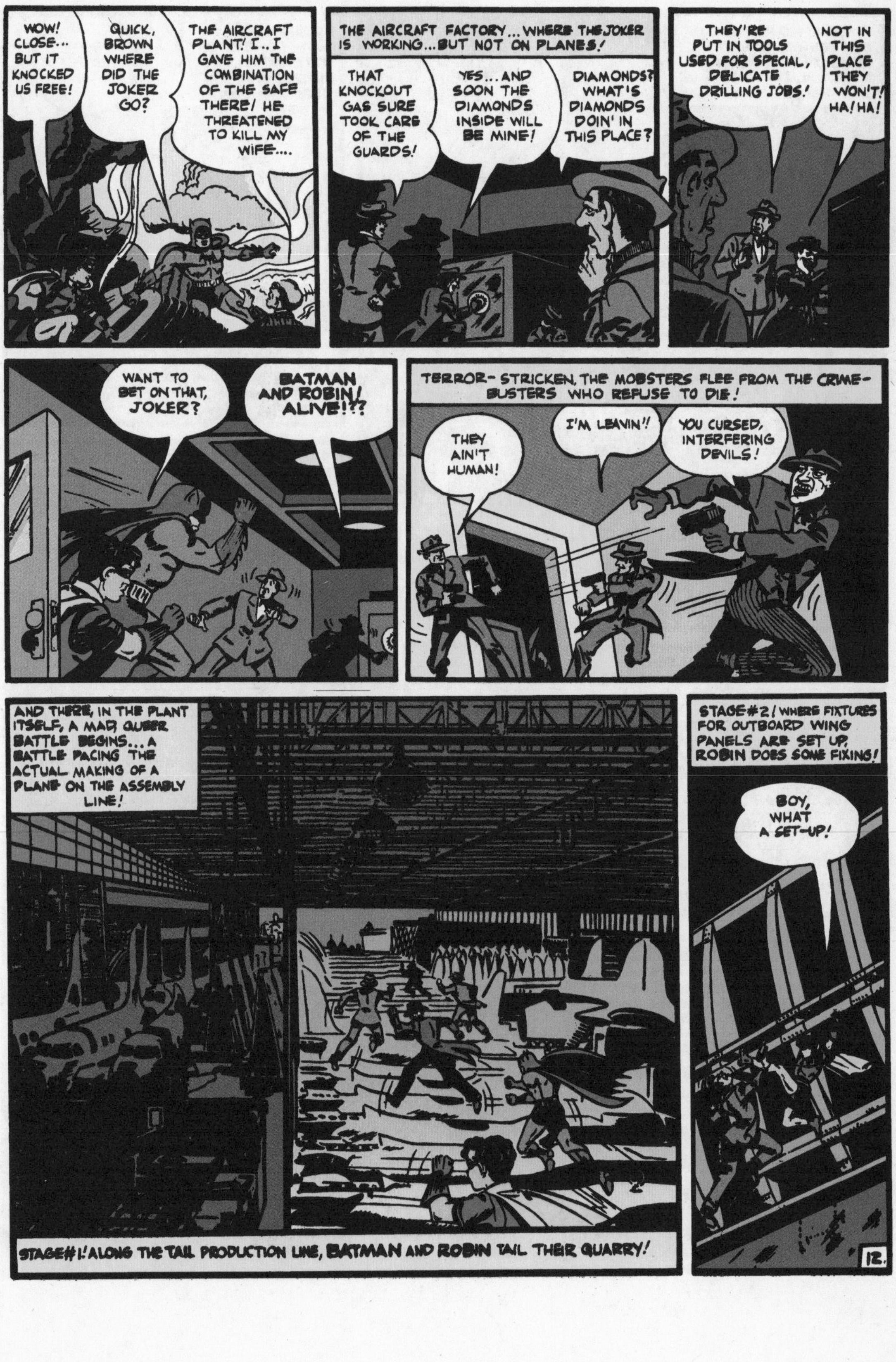
WOW! CLOSE... BUT IT KNOCKED US FREE!
QUICK, BROWN WHERE DID THE JOKER GO?
THE AIRCRAFT PLANT! I..I GAVE HIM THE COMBINATION OF THE SAFE THERE! HE THREATENED TO KILL MY WIFE....
THE AIRCRAFT FACTORY... WHERE THE JOKER IS WORKING... BUT NOT ON PLANES!
THAT KNOCKOUT GAS SURE TOOK CARE OF THE GUARDS!
YES... AND SOON THE DIAMONDS INSIDE WILL BE MINE!
DIAMONDS? WHAT'S DIAMONDS DOIN' IN THIS PLACE?
THEY'RE PUT IN TOOLS USED FOR SPECIAL, DELICATE DRILLING JOBS!
NOT IN THIS PLACE THEY WON'T! HA! HA!
WANT TO BET ON THAT, JOKER?
BATMAN AND ROBIN! ALIVE!??
TERROR-STRICKEN, THE MOBSTERS FLEE FROM THE CRIME-BUSTERS WHO REFUSE TO DIE!
THEY AIN'T HUMAN!
I'M LEAVIN'!
YOU CURSED, INTERFERING DEVILS!
AND THERE, IN THE PLANT ITSELF, A MAD QUEER BATTLE BEGINS... A BATTLE PACING THE ACTUAL MAKING OF A PLANE ON THE ASSEMBLY LINE!
STAGE #1! ALONG THE TAIL PRODUCTION LINE, BATMAN AND ROBIN TAIL THEIR QUARRY!
STAGE #2! WHERE FIXTURES FOR OUTBOARD WING PANELS ARE SET UP, ROBIN DOES SOME FIXING!
BOY, WHAT A SET-UP!
12.

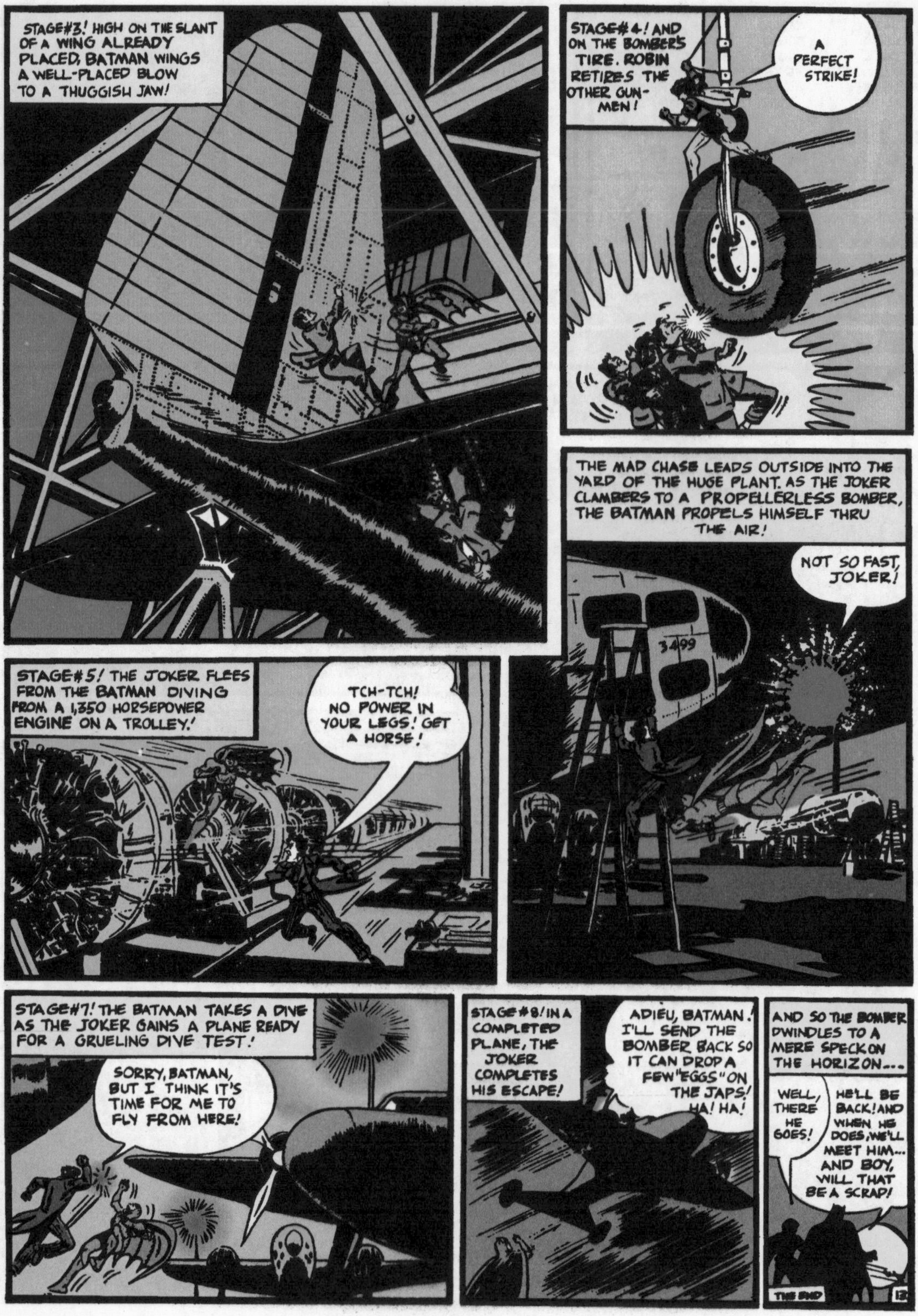

STAGE#3! HIGH ON THE SLANT OF A WING ALREADY PLACED, BATMAN WINGS A WELL-PLACED BLOW TO A THUGGISH JAW!
STAGE#4! AND ON THE BOMBER'S TIRE. ROBIN RETIRES THE OTHER GUN-MEN!
A PERFECT STRIKE!
STAGE#5! THE JOKER FLEES FROM THE BATMAN DIVING FROM A 1,350 HORSEPOWER ENGINE ON A TROLLEY!
TCH-TCH! NO POWER IN YOUR LEGS! GET A HORSE!
THE MAD CHASE LEADS OUTSIDE INTO THE YARD OF THE HUGE PLANT. AS THE JOKER CLAMBERS TO A PROPELLERLESS BOMBER, THE BATMAN PROPELS HIMSELF THRU THE AIR!
NOT SO FAST, JOKER!
3499
STAGE#7! THE BATMAN TAKES A DIVE AS THE JOKER GAINS A PLANE READY FOR A GRUELING DIVE TEST!
SORRY, BATMAN, BUT I THINK IT'S TIME FOR ME TO FLY FROM HERE!
STAGE#8! IN A COMPLETED PLANE, THE JOKER COMPLETES HIS ESCAPE!
ADIEU, BATMAN! I'LL SEND THE BOMBER BACK SO IT CAN DROP A FEW "EGGS" ON THE JAPS! HA! HA!
AND SO THE BOMBER DWINDLES TO A MERE SPECK ON THE HORIZON...
WELL, THERE HE GOES!
HE'LL BE BACK! AND WHEN HE DOES, WE'LL MEET HIM... AND BOY, WILL THAT BE A SCRAP!
THE END
13

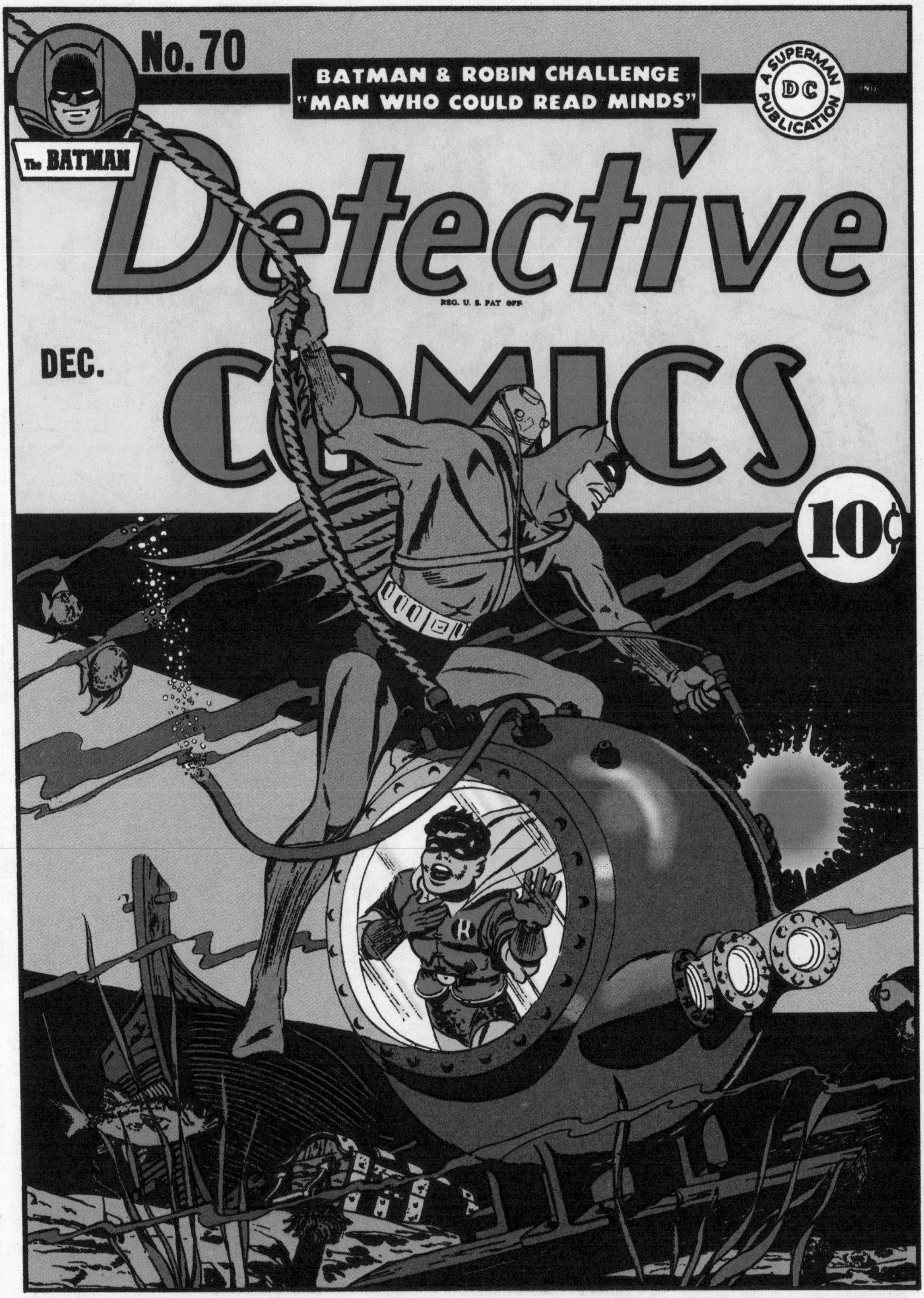
No. 70
BATMAN & ROBIN CHALLENGE
"MAN WHO COULD READ MINDS"
A SUPERMAN DC PUBLICATION
The BATMAN
Detective
REG. U. S. PAT. OFF.
DEC.
COMICS
10¢

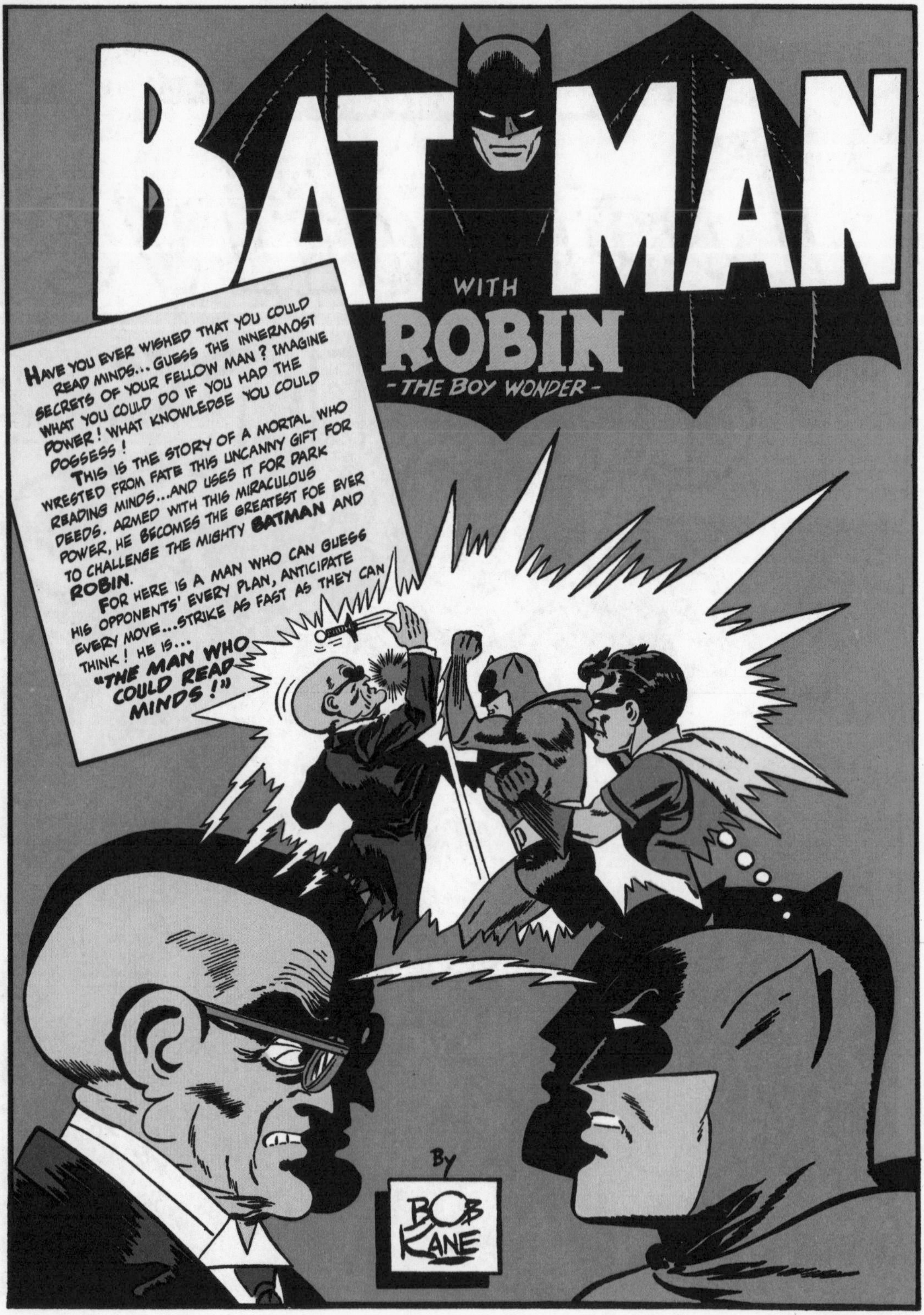
BATMAN
WITH
ROBIN
-THE BOY WONDER-
HAVE YOU EVER WISHED THAT YOU COULD READ MINDS... GUESS THE INNERMOST SECRETS OF YOUR FELLOW MAN? IMAGINE WHAT YOU COULD DO IF YOU HAD THE POWER! WHAT KNOWLEDGE YOU COULD POSSESS!
THIS IS THE STORY OF A MORTAL WHO WRESTED FROM FATE THIS UNCANNY GIFT FOR READING MINDS...AND USES IT FOR DARK DEEDS. ARMED WITH THIS MIRACULOUS POWER, HE BECOMES THE GREATEST FOE EVER TO CHALLENGE THE MIGHTY BATMAN AND ROBIN.
FOR HERE IS A MAN WHO CAN GUESS HIS OPPONENTS' EVERY PLAN, ANTICIPATE EVERY MOVE...STRIKE AS FAST AS THEY CAN THINK! HE IS...
"THE MAN WHO COULD READ MINDS!"
By
BOB KANE

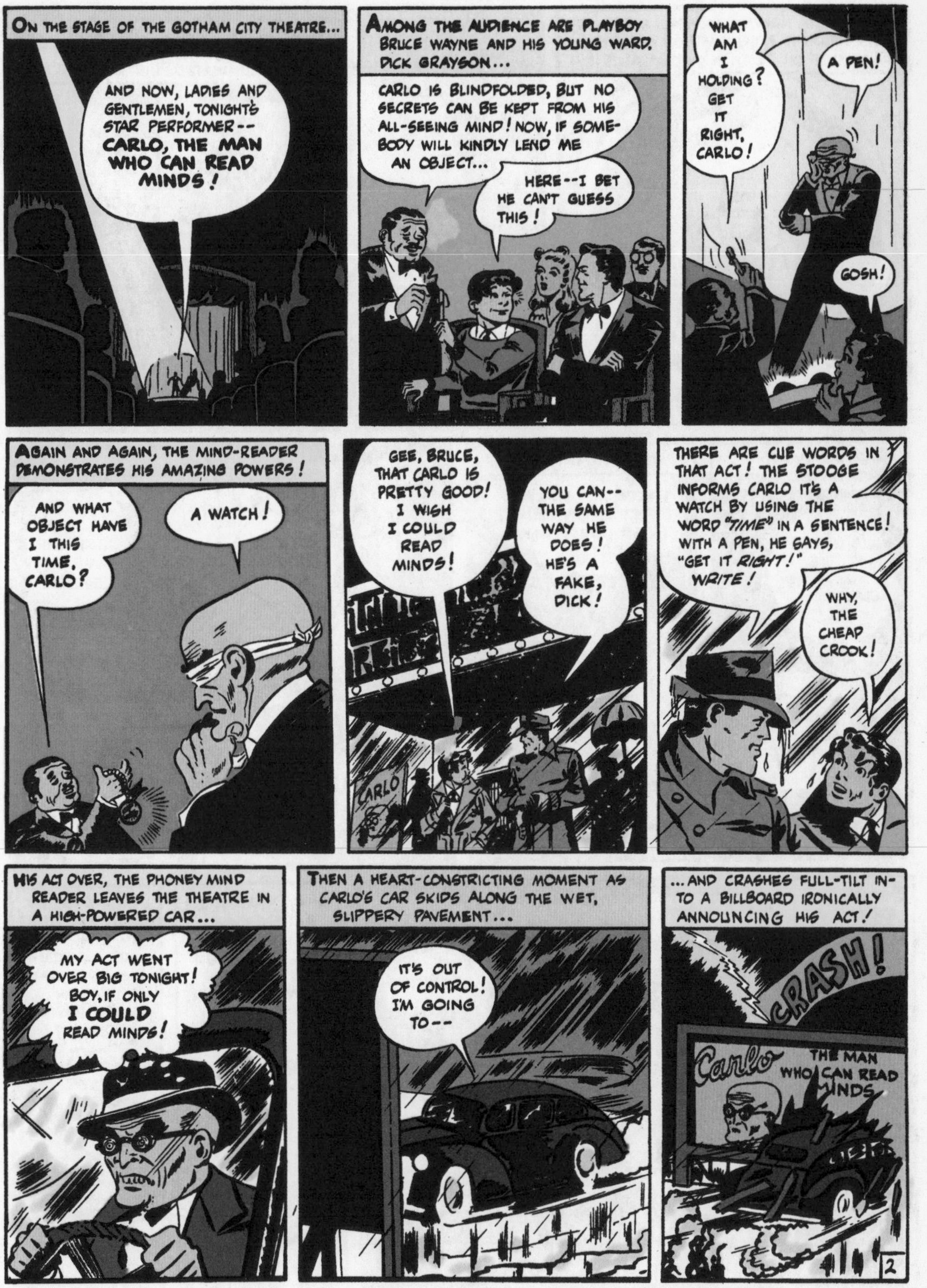
ON THE STAGE OF THE GOTHAM CITY THEATRE...
AND NOW, LADIES AND GENTLEMEN, TONIGHT'S STAR PERFORMER-- CARLO, THE MAN WHO CAN READ MINDS!
AMONG THE AUDIENCE ARE PLAYBOY BRUCE WAYNE AND HIS YOUNG WARD, DICK GRAYSON...
CARLO IS BLINDFOLDED, BUT NO SECRETS CAN BE KEPT FROM HIS ALL-SEEING MIND! NOW, IF SOMEBODY WILL KINDLY LEND ME AN OBJECT...
HERE--I BET HE CAN'T GUESS THIS!
WHAT AM I HOLDING? GET IT RIGHT, CARLO!
A PEN!
GOSH!
AGAIN AND AGAIN, THE MIND-READER DEMONSTRATES HIS AMAZING POWERS!
AND WHAT OBJECT HAVE I THIS TIME, CARLO?
A WATCH!
GEE, BRUCE, THAT CARLO IS PRETTY GOOD! I WISH I COULD READ MINDS!
YOU CAN-- THE SAME WAY HE DOES! HE'S A FAKE, DICK!
CARLO
THERE ARE CUE WORDS IN THAT ACT! THE STOOGE INFORMS CARLO IT'S A WATCH BY USING THE WORD "TIME" IN A SENTENCE! WITH A PEN, HE SAYS, "GET IT RIGHT!" WRITE!
WHY, THE CHEAP CROOK!
HIS ACT OVER, THE PHONEY MIND READER LEAVES THE THEATRE IN A HIGH-POWERED CAR...
MY ACT WENT OVER BIG TONIGHT! BOY, IF ONLY I COULD READ MINDS!
THEN A HEART-CONSTRICTING MOMENT AS CARLO'S CAR SKIDS ALONG THE WET, SLIPPERY PAVEMENT...
IT'S OUT OF CONTROL! I'M GOING TO--
...AND CRASHES FULL-TILT INTO A BILLBOARD IRONICALLY ANNOUNCING HIS ACT!
CRASH!
Carlo THE MAN WHO CAN READ MINDS
2

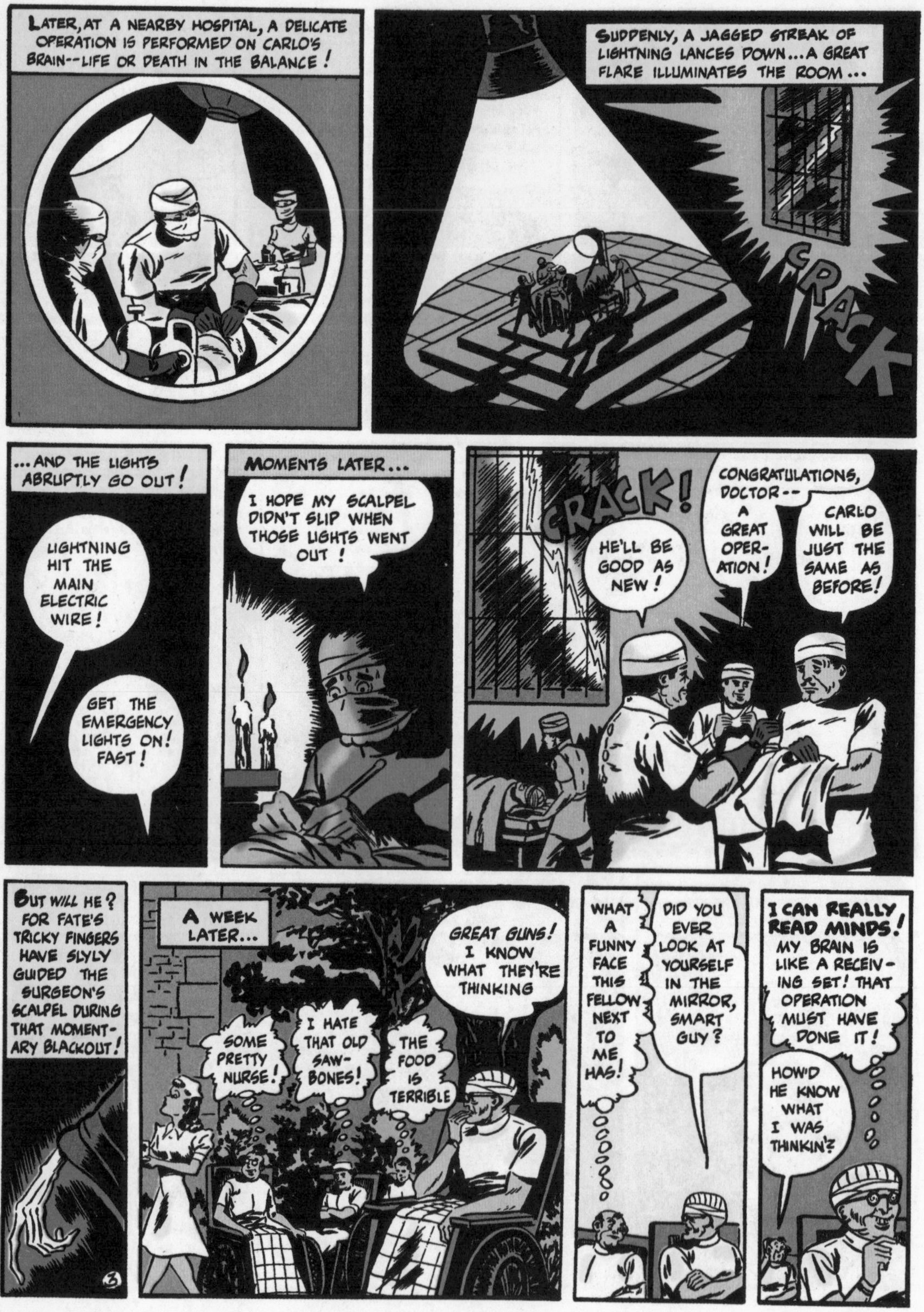
LATER, AT A NEARBY HOSPITAL, A DELICATE OPERATION IS PERFORMED ON CARLO'S BRAIN--LIFE OR DEATH IN THE BALANCE!
SUDDENLY, A JAGGED STREAK OF LIGHTNING LANCES DOWN... A GREAT FLARE ILLUMINATES THE ROOM...
CRACK
...AND THE LIGHTS ABRUPTLY GO OUT!
LIGHTNING HIT THE MAIN ELECTRIC WIRE!
GET THE EMERGENCY LIGHTS ON! FAST!
MOMENTS LATER...
I HOPE MY SCALPEL DIDN'T SLIP WHEN THOSE LIGHTS WENT OUT!
CRACK!
HE'LL BE GOOD AS NEW!
CONGRATULATIONS, DOCTOR-- A GREAT OPERATION!
CARLO WILL BE JUST THE SAME AS BEFORE!
BUT WILL HE? FOR FATE'S TRICKY FINGERS HAVE SLYLY GUIDED THE SURGEON'S SCALPEL DURING THAT MOMENTARY BLACKOUT!
3
A WEEK LATER...
SOME PRETTY NURSE!
I HATE THAT OLD SAW-BONES!
THE FOOD IS TERRIBLE
GREAT GUNS! I KNOW WHAT THEY'RE THINKING
WHAT A FUNNY FACE THIS FELLOW NEXT TO ME HAS!
DID YOU EVER LOOK AT YOURSELF IN THE MIRROR, SMART GUY?
I CAN REALLY READ MINDS! MY BRAIN IS LIKE A RECEIVING SET! THAT OPERATION MUST HAVE DONE IT!
HOW'D HE KNOW WHAT I WAS THINKIN'?

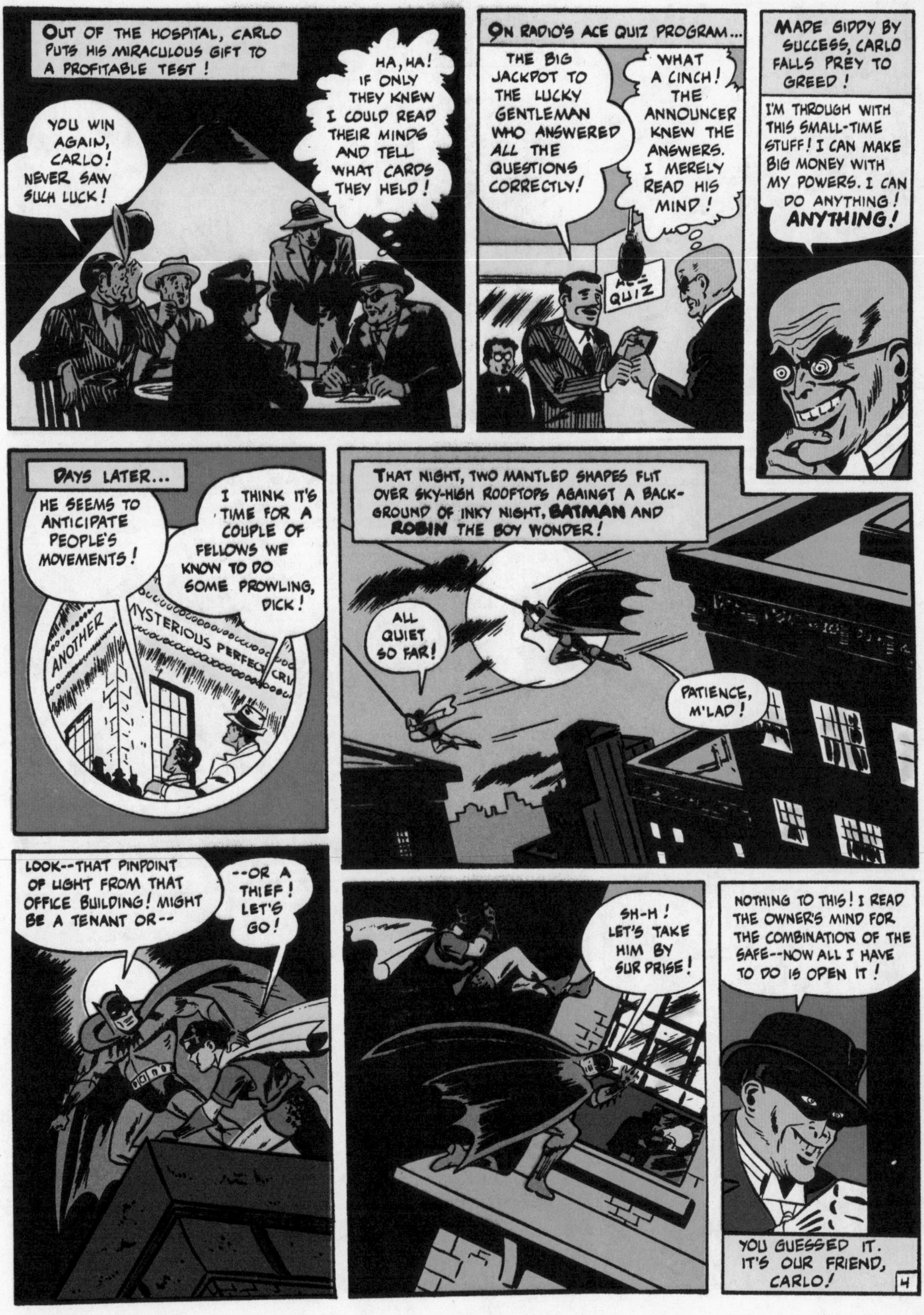

OUT OF THE HOSPITAL, CARLO PUTS HIS MIRACULOUS GIFT TO A PROFITABLE TEST!
YOU WIN AGAIN, CARLO! NEVER SAW SUCH LUCK!
HA, HA! IF ONLY THEY KNEW I COULD READ THEIR MINDS AND TELL WHAT CARDS THEY HELD!
ON RADIO'S ACE QUIZ PROGRAM...
THE BIG JACKPOT TO THE LUCKY GENTLEMAN WHO ANSWERED ALL THE QUESTIONS CORRECTLY!
WHAT A CINCH! THE ANNOUNCER KNEW THE ANSWERS. I MERELY READ HIS MIND!
QUIZ
MADE GIDDY BY SUCCESS, CARLO FALLS PREY TO GREED!
I'M THROUGH WITH THIS SMALL-TIME STUFF! I CAN MAKE BIG MONEY WITH MY POWERS. I CAN DO ANYTHING! ANYTHING!
DAYS LATER...
HE SEEMS TO ANTICIPATE PEOPLE'S MOVEMENTS!
I THINK IT'S TIME FOR A COUPLE OF FELLOWS WE KNOW TO DO SOME PROWLING, DICK!
ANOTHER MYSTERIOUS PERFECT CRI
THAT NIGHT, TWO MANTLED SHAPES FLIT OVER SKY-HIGH ROOFTOPS AGAINST A BACKGROUND OF INKY NIGHT, BATMAN AND ROBIN THE BOY WONDER!
ALL QUIET SO FAR!
PATIENCE, M'LAD!
LOOK--THAT PINPOINT OF LIGHT FROM THAT OFFICE BUILDING! MIGHT BE A TENANT OR--
--OR A THIEF! LET'S GO!
SH-H! LET'S TAKE HIM BY SURPRISE!
NOTHING TO THIS! I READ THE OWNER'S MIND FOR THE COMBINATION OF THE SAFE--NOW ALL I HAVE TO DO IS OPEN IT!
YOU GUESSED IT. IT'S OUR FRIEND, CARLO!
4

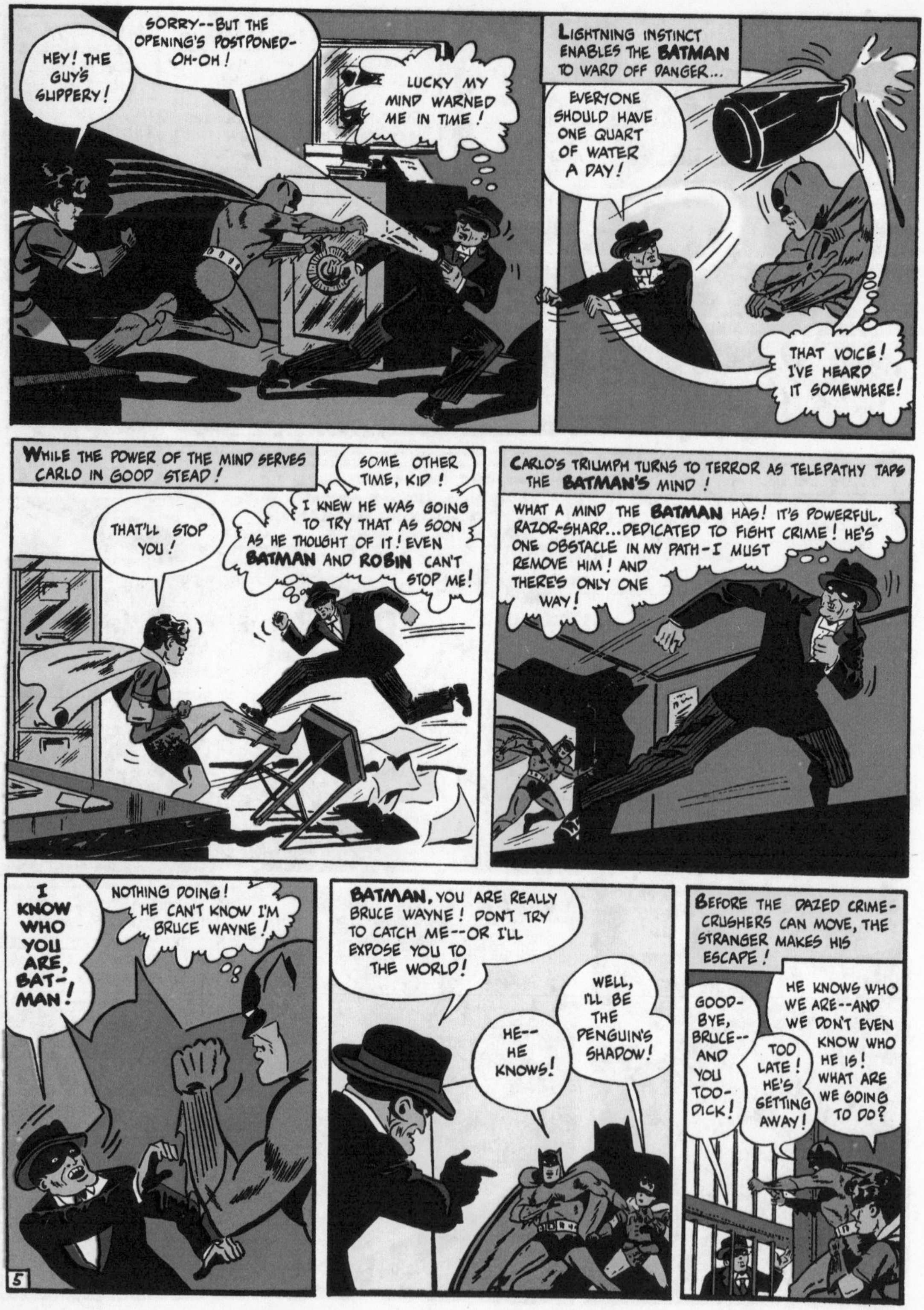
SORRY--BUT THE OPENING'S POSTPONED-OH-OH!
HEY! THE GUY'S SLIPPERY!
LUCKY MY MIND WARNED ME IN TIME!
LIGHTNING INSTINCT ENABLES THE BATMAN TO WARD OFF DANGER...
EVERYONE SHOULD HAVE ONE QUART OF WATER A DAY!
THAT VOICE! I'VE HEARD IT SOMEWHERE!
WHILE THE POWER OF THE MIND SERVES CARLO IN GOOD STEAD!
SOME OTHER TIME, KID!
THAT'LL STOP YOU!
I KNEW HE WAS GOING TO TRY THAT AS SOON AS HE THOUGHT OF IT! EVEN BATMAN AND ROBIN CAN'T STOP ME!
CARLO'S TRIUMPH TURNS TO TERROR AS TELEPATHY TAPS THE BATMAN'S MIND!
WHAT A MIND THE BATMAN HAS! IT'S POWERFUL, RAZOR-SHARP...DEDICATED TO FIGHT CRIME! HE'S ONE OBSTACLE IN MY PATH-I MUST REMOVE HIM! AND THERE'S ONLY ONE WAY!
I KNOW WHO YOU ARE, BAT-MAN!
NOTHING DOING! HE CAN'T KNOW I'M BRUCE WAYNE!
5
BATMAN, YOU ARE REALLY BRUCE WAYNE! DON'T TRY TO CATCH ME--OR I'LL EXPOSE YOU TO THE WORLD!
HE--HE KNOWS!
WELL, I'LL BE THE PENGUIN'S SHADOW!
BEFORE THE DAZED CRIME-CRUSHERS CAN MOVE, THE STRANGER MAKES HIS ESCAPE!
GOOD-BYE, BRUCE--AND YOU TOO-DICK!
TOO LATE! HE'S GETTING AWAY!
HE KNOWS WHO WE ARE--AND WE DON'T EVEN KNOW WHO HE IS! WHAT ARE WE GOING TO DO?

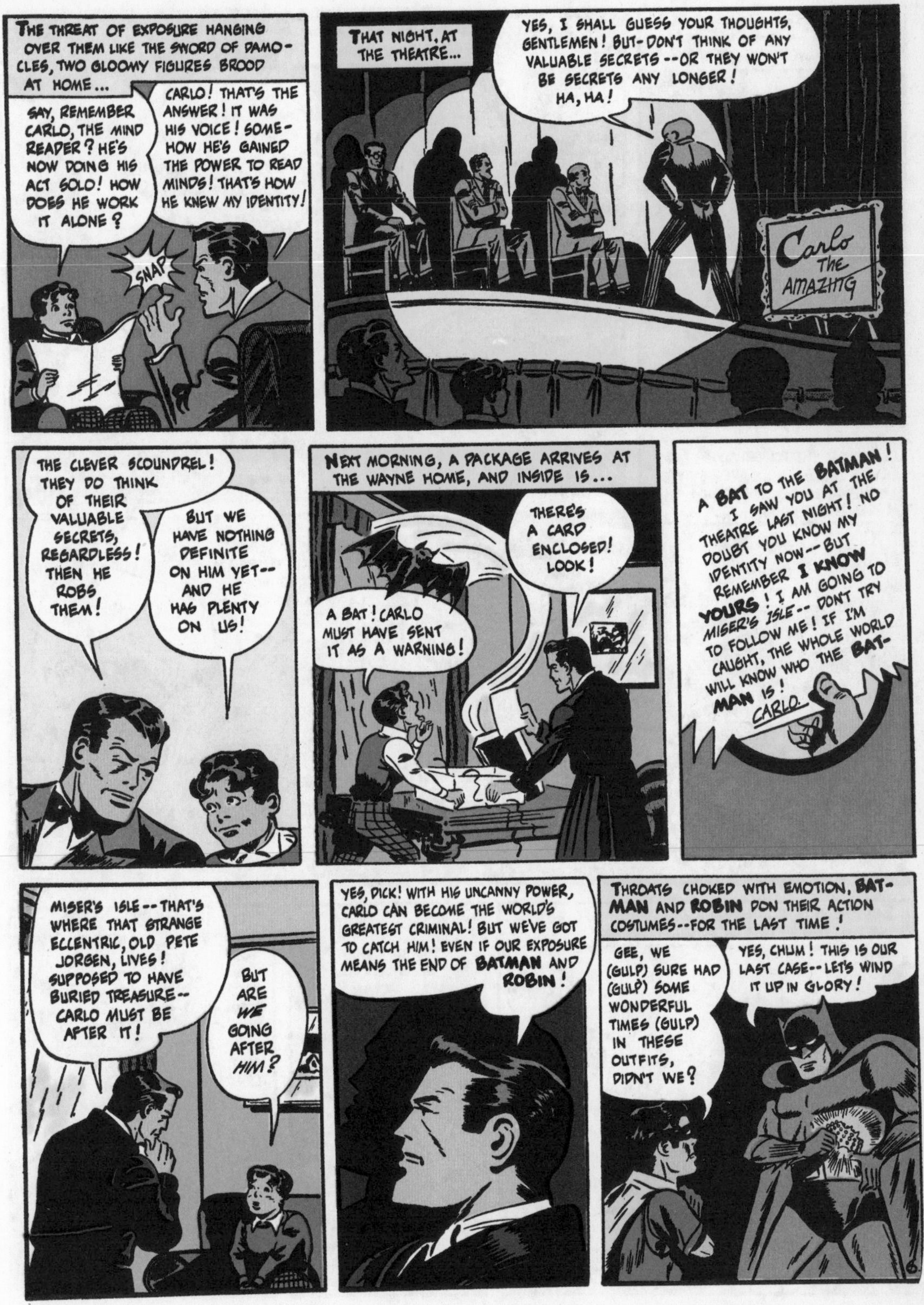
THE THREAT OF EXPOSURE HANGING OVER THEM LIKE THE SWORD OF DAMOCLES, TWO GLOOMY FIGURES BROOD AT HOME...
SAY, REMEMBER CARLO, THE MIND READER? HE'S NOW DOING HIS ACT SOLO! HOW DOES HE WORK IT ALONE?
SNAP
CARLO! THAT'S THE ANSWER! IT WAS HIS VOICE! SOMEHOW HE'S GAINED THE POWER TO READ MINDS! THAT'S HOW HE KNEW MY IDENTITY!
THAT NIGHT, AT THE THEATRE...
YES, I SHALL GUESS YOUR THOUGHTS, GENTLEMEN! BUT-DON'T THINK OF ANY VALUABLE SECRETS --OR THEY WON'T BE SECRETS ANY LONGER! HA, HA!
Carlo THE AMAZING
THE CLEVER SCOUNDREL! THEY DO THINK OF THEIR VALUABLE SECRETS, REGARDLESS! THEN HE ROBS THEM!
BUT WE HAVE NOTHING DEFINITE ON HIM YET-- AND HE HAS PLENTY ON US!
NEXT MORNING, A PACKAGE ARRIVES AT THE WAYNE HOME, AND INSIDE IS...
THERE'S A CARD ENCLOSED! LOOK!
A BAT! CARLO MUST HAVE SENT IT AS A WARNING!
A BAT TO THE BATMAN! I SAW YOU AT THE THEATRE LAST NIGHT! NO DOUBT YOU KNOW MY IDENTITY NOW--BUT REMEMBER I KNOW YOURS! I AM GOING TO MISER'S ISLE-- DON'T TRY TO FOLLOW ME! IF I'M CAUGHT, THE WHOLE WORLD WILL KNOW WHO THE BATMAN IS! CARLO
MISER'S ISLE--THAT'S WHERE THAT STRANGE ECCENTRIC, OLD PETE JORGEN, LIVES! SUPPOSED TO HAVE BURIED TREASURE-- CARLO MUST BE AFTER IT!
BUT ARE WE GOING AFTER HIM?
YES, DICK! WITH HIS UNCANNY POWER, CARLO CAN BECOME THE WORLD'S GREATEST CRIMINAL! BUT WE'VE GOT TO CATCH HIM! EVEN IF OUR EXPOSURE MEANS THE END OF BATMAN AND ROBIN!
THROATS CHOKED WITH EMOTION, BATMAN AND ROBIN DON THEIR ACTION COSTUMES--FOR THE LAST TIME!
GEE, WE (GULP) SURE HAD (GULP) SOME WONDERFUL TIMES (GULP) IN THESE OUTFITS, DIDN'T WE?
YES, CHUM! THIS IS OUR LAST CASE--LET'S WIND IT UP IN GLORY!
6

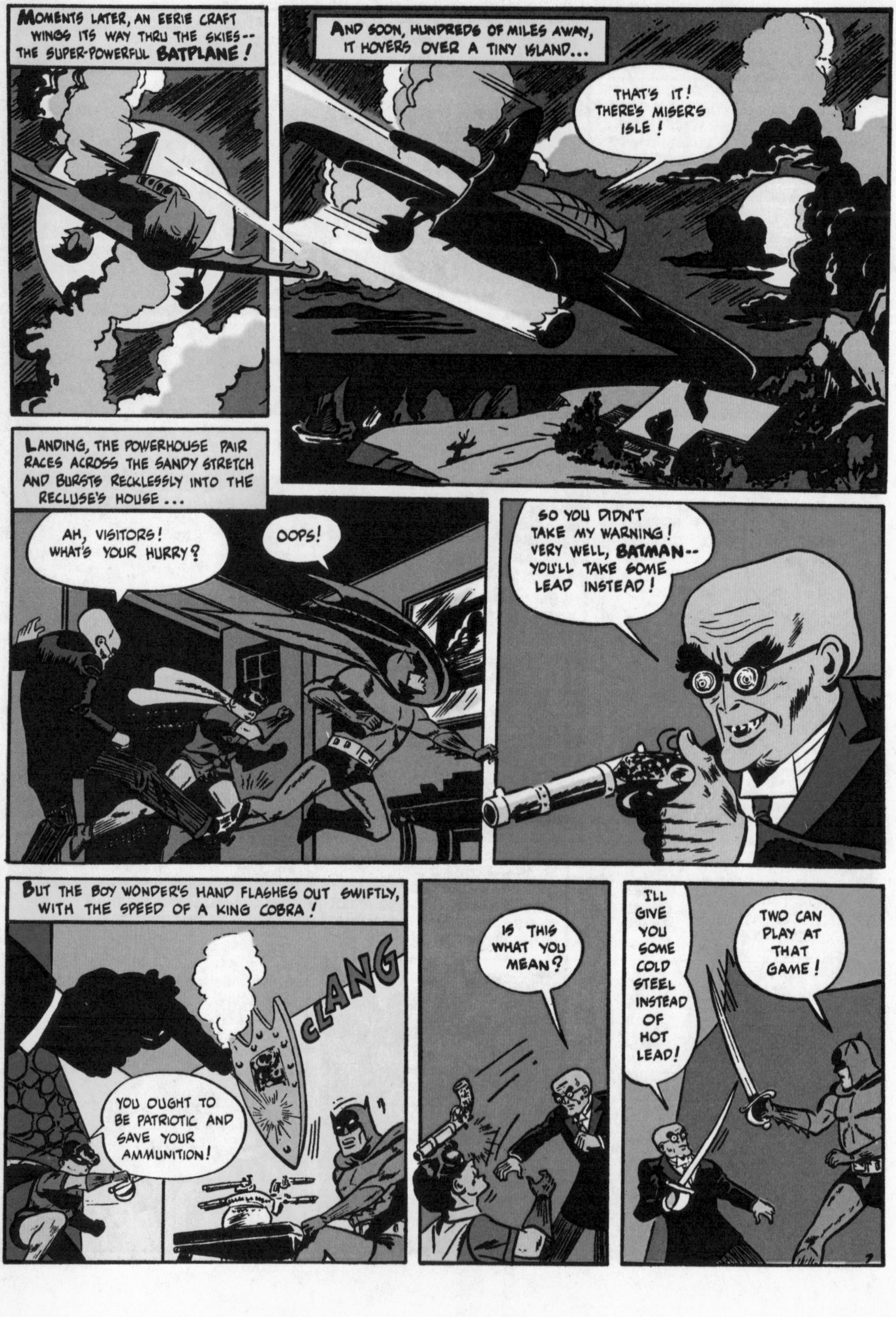
MOMENTS LATER, AN EERIE CRAFT WINGS ITS WAY THRU THE SKIES-- THE SUPER-POWERFUL BATPLANE!
AND SOON, HUNDREDS OF MILES AWAY, IT HOVERS OVER A TINY ISLAND...
THAT'S IT! THERE'S MISER'S ISLE!
LANDING, THE POWERHOUSE PAIR RACES ACROSS THE SANDY STRETCH AND BURSTS RECKLESSLY INTO THE RECLUSE'S HOUSE...
AH, VISITORS! WHAT'S YOUR HURRY?
OOPS!
SO YOU DIDN'T TAKE MY WARNING! VERY WELL, BATMAN-- YOU'LL TAKE SOME LEAD INSTEAD!
BUT THE BOY WONDER'S HAND FLASHES OUT SWIFTLY, WITH THE SPEED OF A KING COBRA!
CLANG
YOU OUGHT TO BE PATRIOTIC AND SAVE YOUR AMMUNITION!
IS THIS WHAT YOU MEAN?
I'LL GIVE YOU SOME COLD STEEL INSTEAD OF HOT LEAD!
TWO CAN PLAY AT THAT GAME!

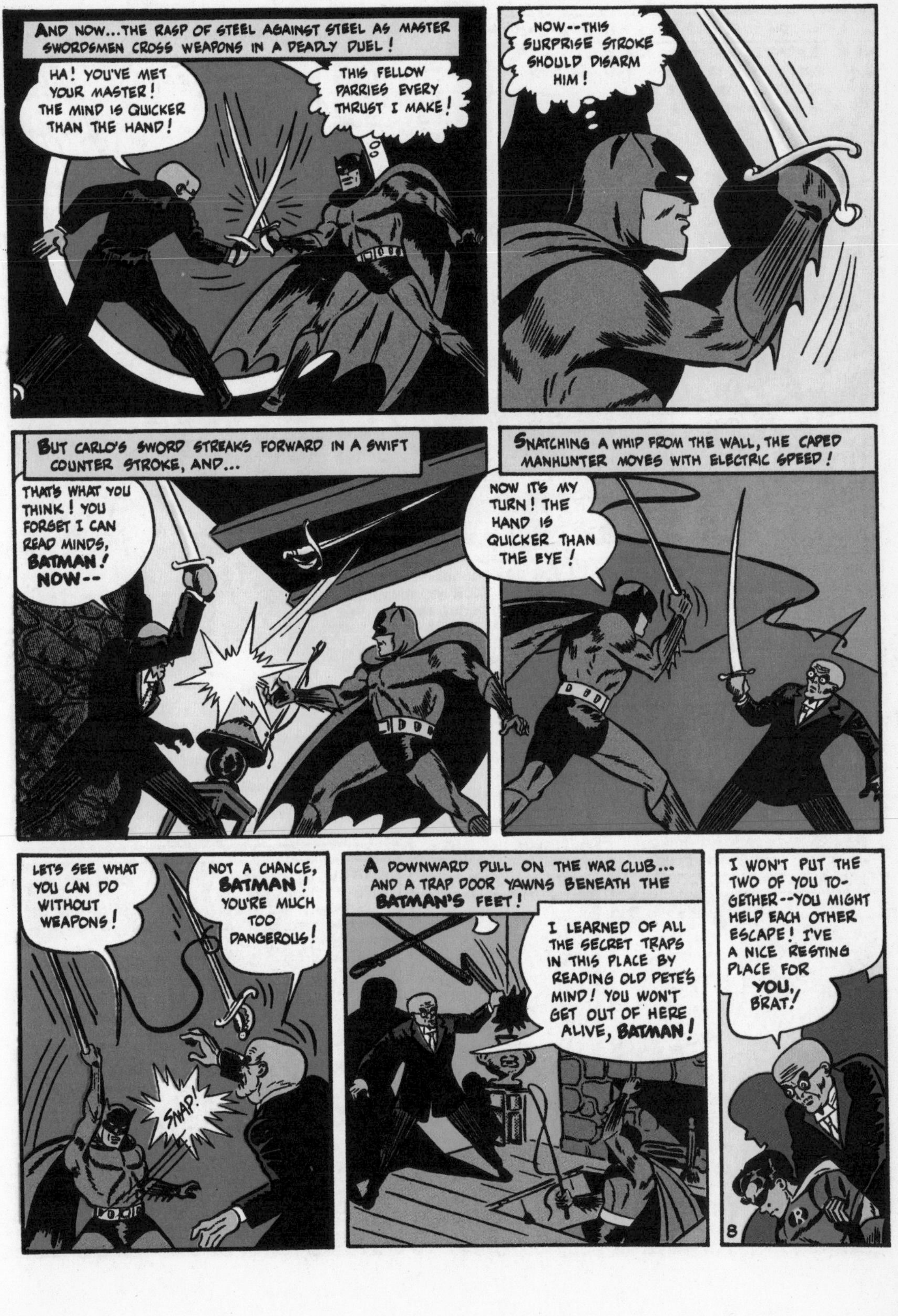

AND NOW...THE RASP OF STEEL AGAINST STEEL AS MASTER SWORDSMEN CROSS WEAPONS IN A DEADLY DUEL!
HA! YOU'VE MET YOUR MASTER! THE MIND IS QUICKER THAN THE HAND!
THIS FELLOW PARRIES EVERY THRUST I MAKE!
NOW--THIS SURPRISE STROKE SHOULD DISARM HIM!
BUT CARLO'S SWORD STREAKS FORWARD IN A SWIFT COUNTER STROKE, AND...
THAT'S WHAT YOU THINK! YOU FORGET I CAN READ MINDS, BATMAN! NOW--
SNATCHING A WHIP FROM THE WALL, THE CAPED MANHUNTER MOVES WITH ELECTRIC SPEED!
NOW IT'S MY TURN! THE HAND IS QUICKER THAN THE EYE!
LET'S SEE WHAT YOU CAN DO WITHOUT WEAPONS!
NOT A CHANCE, BATMAN! YOU'RE MUCH TOO DANGEROUS!
SNAP!
A DOWNWARD PULL ON THE WAR CLUB... AND A TRAP DOOR YAWNS BENEATH THE BATMAN'S FEET!
I LEARNED OF ALL THE SECRET TRAPS IN THIS PLACE BY READING OLD PETE'S MIND! YOU WON'T GET OUT OF HERE ALIVE, BATMAN!
I WON'T PUT THE TWO OF YOU TO-GETHER--YOU MIGHT HELP EACH OTHER ESCAPE! I'VE A NICE RESTING PLACE FOR YOU, BRAT!
8

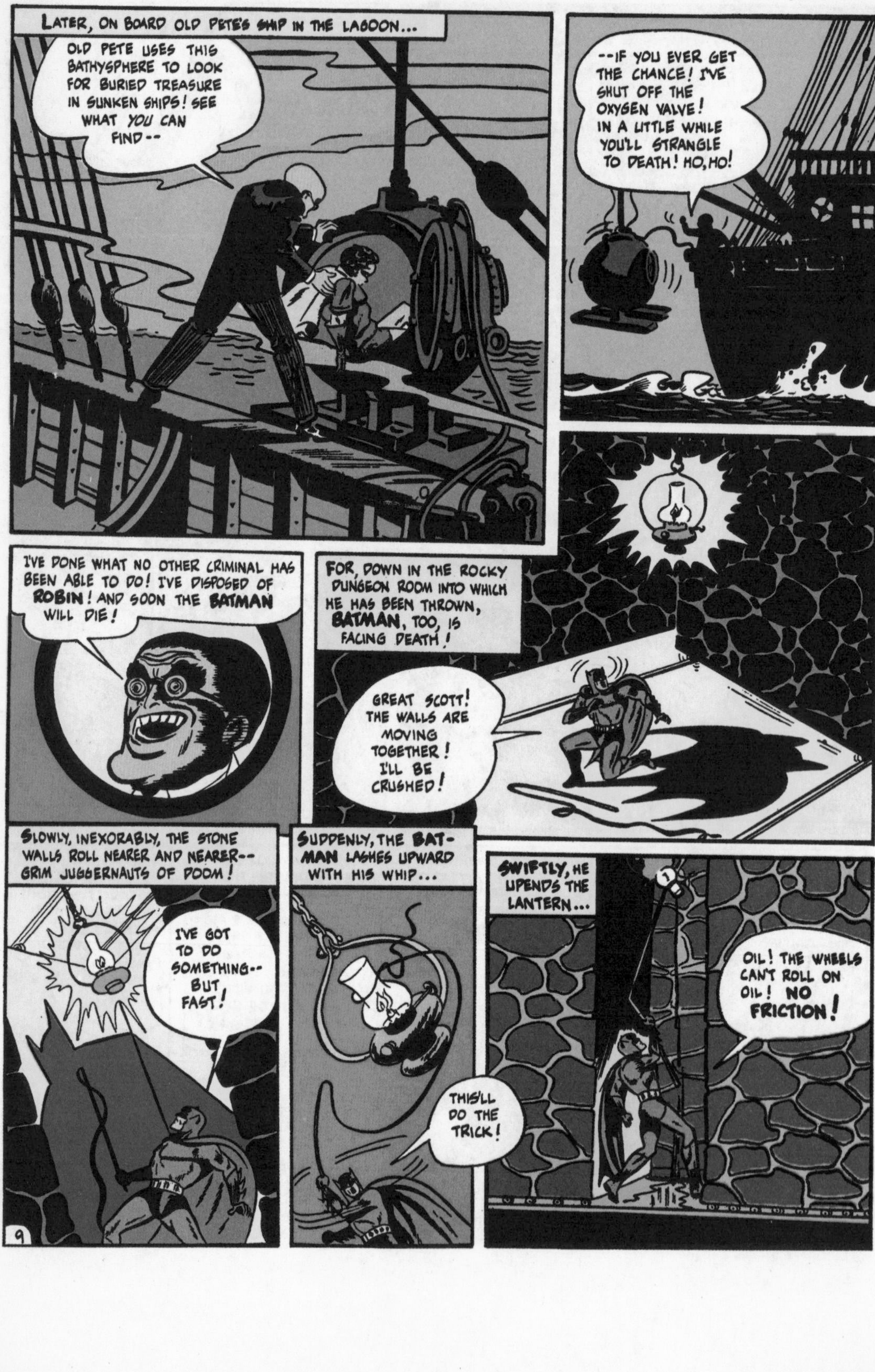

LATER, ON BOARD OLD PETE'S SHIP IN THE LAGOON...
OLD PETE USES THIS BATHYSPHERE TO LOOK FOR BURIED TREASURE IN SUNKEN SHIPS! SEE WHAT YOU CAN FIND--
--IF YOU EVER GET THE CHANCE! I'VE SHUT OFF THE OXYGEN VALVE! IN A LITTLE WHILE YOU'LL STRANGLE TO DEATH! HO, HO!
I'VE DONE WHAT NO OTHER CRIMINAL HAS BEEN ABLE TO DO! I'VE DISPOSED OF ROBIN! AND SOON THE BATMAN WILL DIE!
FOR, DOWN IN THE ROCKY DUNGEON ROOM INTO WHICH HE HAS BEEN THROWN, BATMAN, TOO, IS FACING DEATH!
GREAT SCOTT! THE WALLS ARE MOVING TOGETHER! I'LL BE CRUSHED!
SLOWLY, INEXORABLY, THE STONE WALLS ROLL NEARER AND NEARER-- GRIM JUGGERNAUTS OF DOOM!
I'VE GOT TO DO SOMETHING-- BUT FAST!
9
SUDDENLY, THE BAT-MAN LASHES UPWARD WITH HIS WHIP...
THIS'LL DO THE TRICK!
SWIFTLY, HE UPENDS THE LANTERN...
OIL! THE WHEELS CAN'T ROLL ON OIL! NO FRICTION!

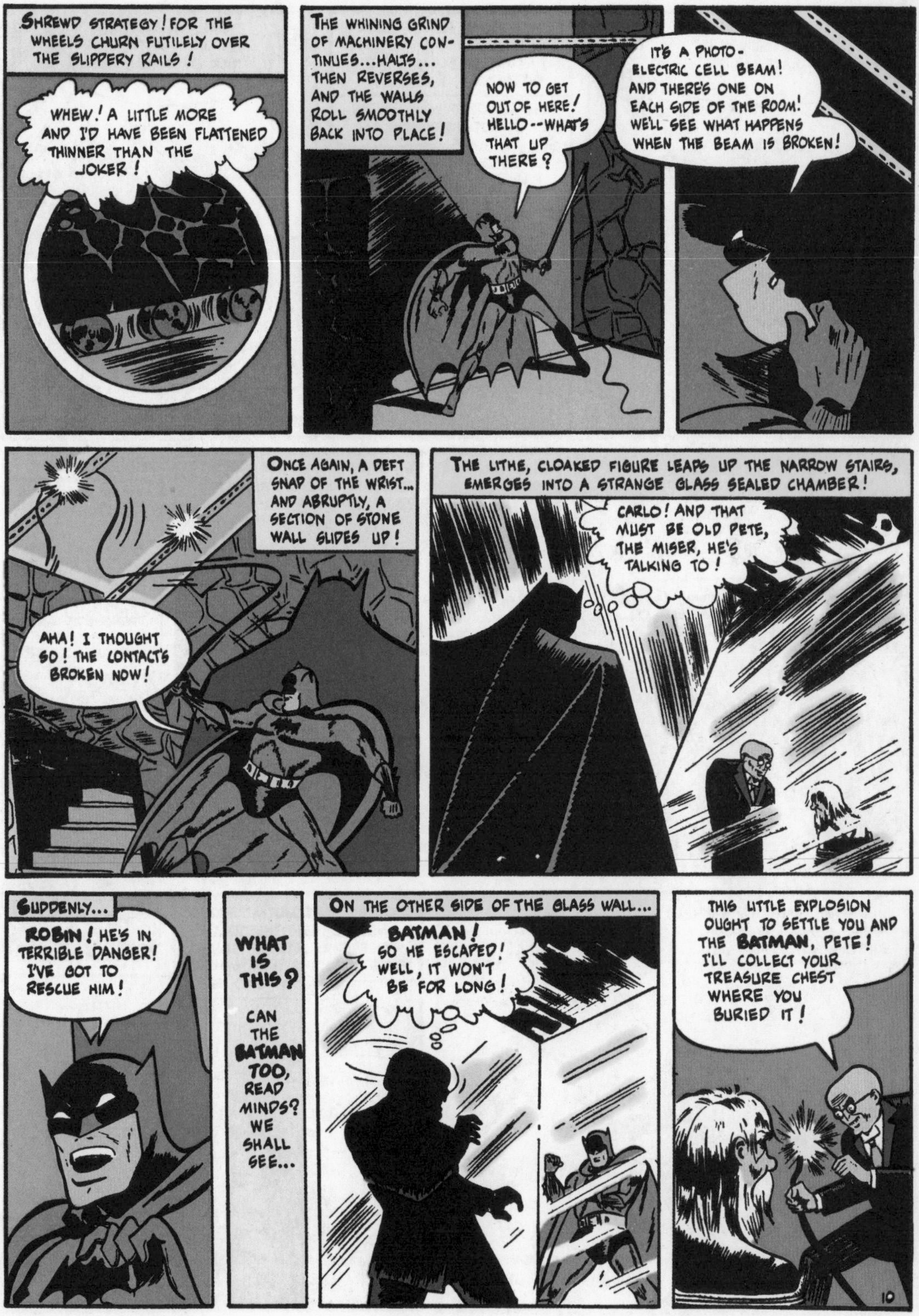
SHREWD STRATEGY! FOR THE WHEELS CHURN FUTILELY OVER THE SLIPPERY RAILS!
WHEW! A LITTLE MORE AND I'D HAVE BEEN FLATTENED THINNER THAN THE JOKER!
THE WHINING GRIND OF MACHINERY CONTINUES...HALTS... THEN REVERSES, AND THE WALLS ROLL SMOOTHLY BACK INTO PLACE!
NOW TO GET OUT OF HERE! HELLO--WHAT'S THAT UP THERE?
IT'S A PHOTO-ELECTRIC CELL BEAM! AND THERE'S ONE ON EACH SIDE OF THE ROOM! WE'LL SEE WHAT HAPPENS WHEN THE BEAM IS BROKEN!
ONCE AGAIN, A DEFT SNAP OF THE WRIST... AND ABRUPTLY, A SECTION OF STONE WALL SLIDES UP!
AHA! I THOUGHT SO! THE CONTACT'S BROKEN NOW!
THE LITHE, CLOAKED FIGURE LEAPS UP THE NARROW STAIRS, EMERGES INTO A STRANGE GLASS SEALED CHAMBER!
CARLO! AND THAT MUST BE OLD PETE, THE MISER, HE'S TALKING TO!
SUDDENLY...
ROBIN! HE'S IN TERRIBLE DANGER! I'VE GOT TO RESCUE HIM!
WHAT IS THIS? CAN THE BATMAN TOO, READ MINDS? WE SHALL SEE...
ON THE OTHER SIDE OF THE GLASS WALL...
BATMAN! SO HE ESCAPED! WELL, IT WON'T BE FOR LONG!
THIS LITTLE EXPLOSION OUGHT TO SETTLE YOU AND THE BATMAN, PETE! I'LL COLLECT YOUR TREASURE CHEST WHERE YOU BURIED IT!
10

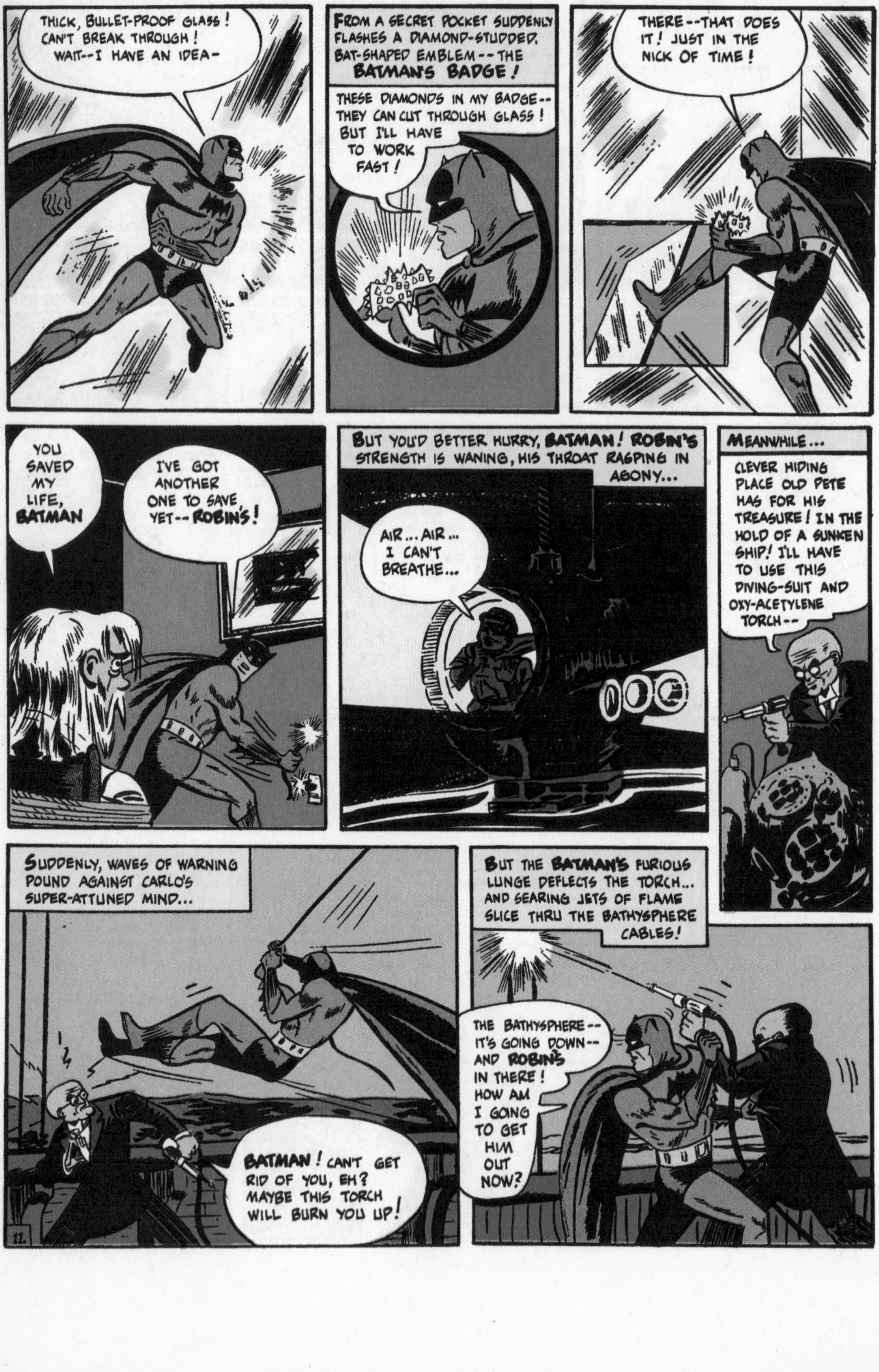
THICK, BULLET-PROOF GLASS! CAN'T BREAK THROUGH! WAIT--I HAVE AN IDEA-
FROM A SECRET POCKET SUDDENLY FLASHES A DIAMOND-STUDDED, BAT-SHAPED EMBLEM -- THE BATMAN'S BADGE!
THESE DIAMONDS IN MY BADGE-- THEY CAN CUT THROUGH GLASS! BUT I'LL HAVE TO WORK FAST!
THERE--THAT DOES IT! JUST IN THE NICK OF TIME!
YOU SAVED MY LIFE, BATMAN
I'VE GOT ANOTHER ONE TO SAVE YET-- ROBIN'S!
BUT YOU'D BETTER HURRY, BATMAN! ROBIN'S STRENGTH IS WANING, HIS THROAT RASPING IN AGONY...
AIR... AIR... I CAN'T BREATHE...
MEANWHILE...
CLEVER HIDING PLACE OLD PETE HAS FOR HIS TREASURE! IN THE HOLD OF A SUNKEN SHIP! I'LL HAVE TO USE THIS DIVING-SUIT AND OXY-ACETYLENE TORCH--
SUDDENLY, WAVES OF WARNING POUND AGAINST CARLO'S SUPER-ATTUNED MIND...
BATMAN! CAN'T GET RID OF YOU, EH? MAYBE THIS TORCH WILL BURN YOU UP!
11.
BUT THE BATMAN'S FURIOUS LUNGE DEFLECTS THE TORCH... AND SEARING JETS OF FLAME SLICE THRU THE BATHYSPHERE CABLES!
THE BATHYSPHERE-- IT'S GOING DOWN-- AND ROBIN'S IN THERE! HOW AM I GOING TO GET HIM OUT NOW?

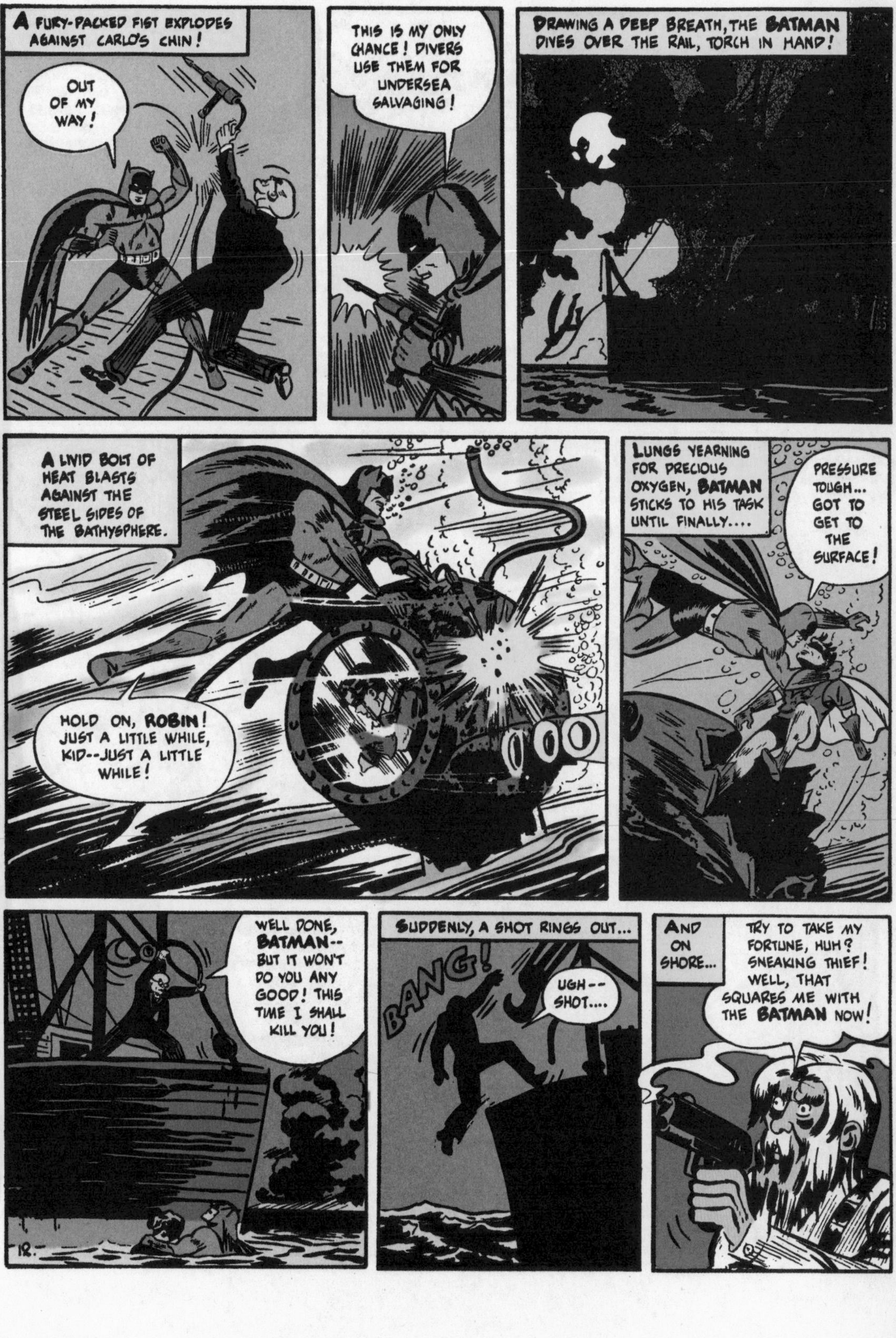
A FURY-PACKED FIST EXPLODES AGAINST CARLO'S CHIN!
OUT OF MY WAY!
THIS IS MY ONLY CHANCE! DIVERS USE THEM FOR UNDERSEA SALVAGING!
DRAWING A DEEP BREATH, THE BATMAN DIVES OVER THE RAIL, TORCH IN HAND!
A LIVID BOLT OF HEAT BLASTS AGAINST THE STEEL SIDES OF THE BATHYSPHERE.
HOLD ON, ROBIN! JUST A LITTLE WHILE, KID--JUST A LITTLE WHILE!
LUNGS YEARNING FOR PRECIOUS OXYGEN, BATMAN STICKS TO HIS TASK UNTIL FINALLY....
PRESSURE TOUGH... GOT TO GET TO THE SURFACE!
WELL DONE, BATMAN-- BUT IT WON'T DO YOU ANY GOOD! THIS TIME I SHALL KILL YOU!
18.
SUDDENLY, A SHOT RINGS OUT...
BANG!
UGH-- SHOT....
AND ON SHORE...
TRY TO TAKE MY FORTUNE, HUH? SNEAKING THIEF! WELL, THAT SQUARES ME WITH THE BATMAN NOW!

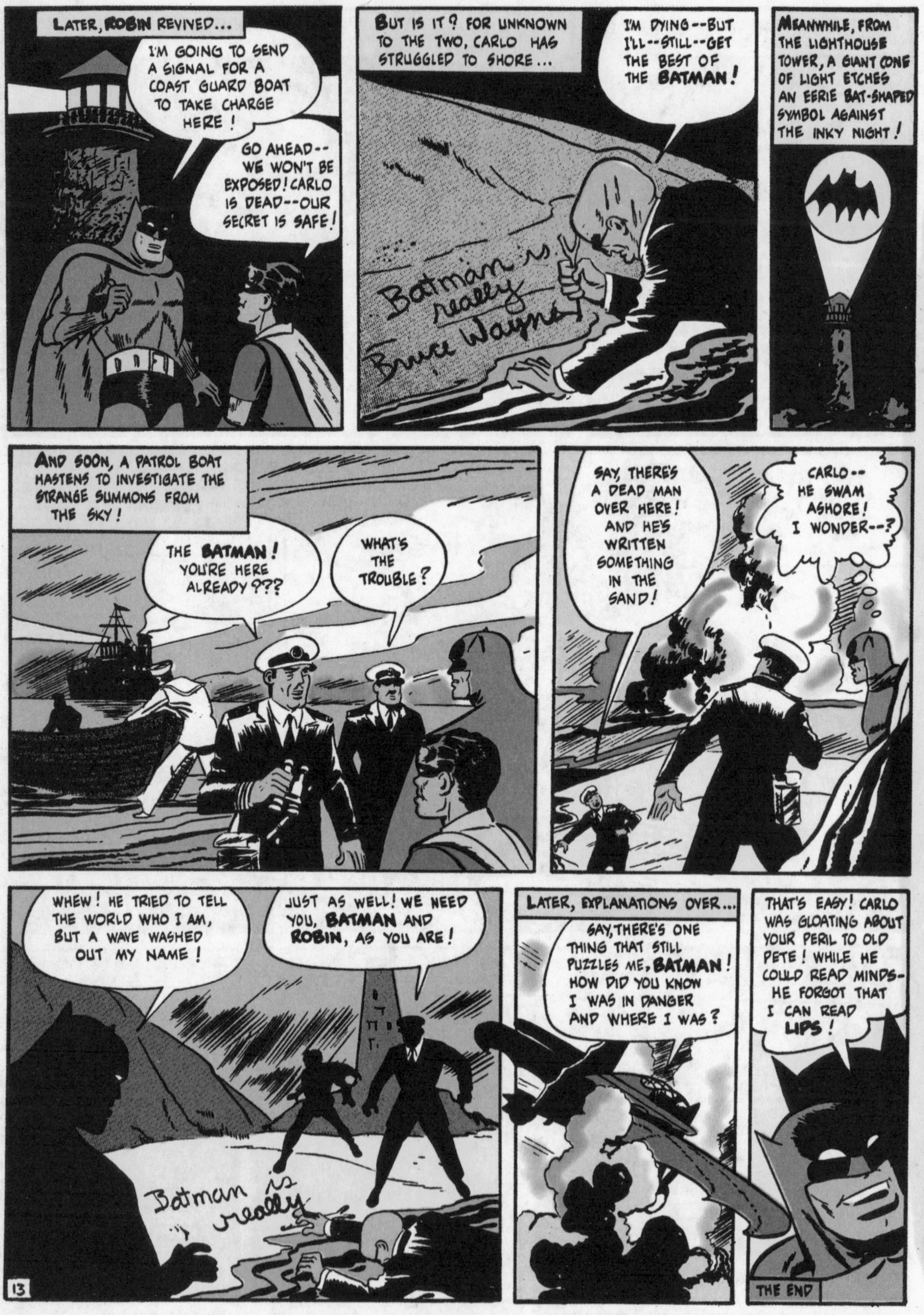
LATER, ROBIN REVIVED...
I'M GOING TO SEND A SIGNAL FOR A COAST GUARD BOAT TO TAKE CHARGE HERE!
GO AHEAD--WE WON'T BE EXPOSED! CARLO IS DEAD--OUR SECRET IS SAFE!
BUT IS IT? FOR UNKNOWN TO THE TWO, CARLO HAS STRUGGLED TO SHORE...
I'M DYING--BUT I'LL--STILL--GET THE BEST OF THE BATMAN!
Batman is really Bruce Wayne
MEANWHILE, FROM THE LIGHTHOUSE TOWER, A GIANT CONE OF LIGHT ETCHES AN EERIE BAT-SHAPED SYMBOL AGAINST THE INKY NIGHT!
AND SOON, A PATROL BOAT HASTENS TO INVESTIGATE THE STRANGE SUMMONS FROM THE SKY!
THE BATMAN! YOU'RE HERE ALREADY???
WHAT'S THE TROUBLE?
SAY, THERE'S A DEAD MAN OVER HERE! AND HE'S WRITTEN SOMETHING IN THE SAND!
CARLO--HE SWAM ASHORE! I WONDER--?
WHEW! HE TRIED TO TELL THE WORLD WHO I AM, BUT A WAVE WASHED OUT MY NAME!
JUST AS WELL! WE NEED YOU, BATMAN AND ROBIN, AS YOU ARE!
Batman is really
13
LATER, EXPLANATIONS OVER...
SAY, THERE'S ONE THING THAT STILL PUZZLES ME, BATMAN! HOW DID YOU KNOW I WAS IN DANGER AND WHERE I WAS?
THAT'S EASY! CARLO WAS GLOATING ABOUT YOUR PERIL TO OLD PETE! WHILE HE COULD READ MINDS-HE FORGOT THAT I CAN READ LIPS!
THE END